American Arbitration Association

Handbook on Arbitration Practice

Second Edition

American Arbitration Association
Dispute Resolution Services Worldwide

JURIS

Questions About This Publication

For assistance with shipments, billing or other customer service matters, please call our Customer Services Department at:

1-631-350-2100

To obtain a copy of this book, call our Sales Department:

1-631-351-5430
Fax: 1-631-673-9117

Toll Free Order Line:

1-800-887-4064 (United States & Canada)

See our web page about this book:
www.arbitrationlaw.com

Printed in the United States of America
ISBN 978-1-937518-80-6

JurisNet, LLC
71 New Street
Huntington, New York 11743
USA
www.arbitrationlaw.com

FOREWORD

It is with a great deal of pleasure that, five years after the publication of the last editions of the American Arbitration Association HANDBOOK series, I am writing these introductory comments for yet another edition as well as additional titles in this growing series. Their continued success attests both to their value as a resource and to the ongoing interest in arbitration and mediation as expeditious and economical alternatives to litigation.

As before, the primary source for many of the articles that appear in this and other Handbook volumes remains the AAA's well-respected *Dispute Resolution Journal*, with vital updates and new material added to ensure that readers enjoy the latest analysis and perspectives from top professionals and scholars across the spectrum of alternative dispute resolution, legal and business focus areas.

The bottom line is that alternative dispute resolution in a variety of forms has been used to resolve conflicts for thousands of years; it is here to stay. Resources such as the HANDBOOK series will remain a valuable adjunct to our efforts to improve access to justice on a global scale. So I look forward—five years from now, 10 years from now—to introducing Third, Fourth, Fifth and further editions of these excellent books to those who are familiar with what ADR has to offer, and to those who are just becoming acquainted with its benefits. Finally, I offer my thanks to our partners at Juris for their continued exceptional contributions to the AAA HANDBOOK Series.

India Johnson
President & CEO
American Arbitration Association

AAA HANDBOOK ON ARBITRATION PRACTICE

TABLE OF CONTENTS

PART I:

ISSUES IN ARBITRATION PRACTICE AND PROCEDURE

CHAPTER 1

WHERE SHOULD YOU LITIGATE YOUR BUSINESS DISPUTE? IN AN ARBITRATION OR THROUGH THE COURTS?

John H. Henn[*]

I. Introduction

Lawyers who advise business entities commonly confront the question of whether to resolve disputes by arbitration. This question usually arises at the time the parties are negotiating a transaction agreement, including the matter of how if at all to provide for the resolution of future disputes. Often the decision is made, not as a result of any systematic consideration of the merits of arbitration versus a judicial forum, but rather as a result of anecdotal information about good or bad experiences with each process. This chapter aims to provide the basis for a more systematic consideration of the arbitral versus judicial alternatives.

At least since the early 1990s, arbitration has become more popular with American business, which has been moving away from resolving commercial and business disputes through courtroom litigation and toward arbitration.[1] I use the term "courtroom litigation" to distinguish it from arbitration, which is also a form of litigation, because both processes are adversarial and are conducted before an independent, neutral decision maker. Courtroom litigation is always administered by

---

[*] John H. Henn is an arbitrator, and sometime ADR counsel to Foley Hoag LLP, in Boston, where he was a partner for over thirty years. He serves on the commercial, large complex case, international and national panels of the American Arbitration Association. He also serves as an arbitrator for CRP and FINRA. He has over forty-five years of experience in business and commercial litigation and experience as a sole arbitrator and panel chairman. He can be reached at 617-832-1130; via e-mail at *jhenn@foleyhoag.com*; or at http://johnhennarbitrator.com.

[1] DAVID B. LIPSKY & RONALD L. SEEBER, THE APPROPRIATE RESOLUTION OF CORPORATE DISPUTES: A REPORT ON THE GROWING USE OF ADR BY U.S. CORPORATIONS 5 (1998).

independent administrative staff, while arbitration is administered by a neutral administrative body only if the parties agree to it.[2] While an arbitral award can be voluntarily complied with by the losing party, often it must be entered in a court of law so that judicial mechanisms made possible by governmental power will allow for its enforcement against a noncomplying party. The era of judicial hostility to enforcing arbitration agreements, and enforcing arbitration awards, has been dead for several decades.[3]

Arbitration of commercial disputes always results from an agreement to arbitrate entered into either before or after a dispute arises. Whether to agree to arbitration turns on an understanding of the pros and cons of arbitration and courtroom litigation, in the context of considerations that matter to commercial entities. These will be discussed next.

II. Key Factors in Deciding Whether to Arbitrate

Most companies involved in a business-to-business (B2B) dispute consider minimizing out-of-pocket costs and the cost of tying up management to be of high importance. When compared with courtroom litigation, arbitration is normally the more economical alternative. The principal factors informing this view are lower discovery costs in arbitration, fewer pre-trial motions (*e.g.*, dispositive motions in arbitration can only be allowed in certain cases, and only in the arbitrator's discretion; they are not that common), and a more limited right to appeal. In addition, companies are increasingly concerned with keeping their dispute private, as many filing in court are now available on the Internet. Also, senior management time can more easily be accommodated, including in those cases where limited deposition discovery might be allowed. Finally, companies usually favor the more expedited nature of arbitration, as compared to judicial proceedings.

---

[2] Occasionally *ad hoc* arbitration is used. In this type of arbitration, the arbitrator administers the arbitration working with the parties.

[3] Moses H. Cone Mem'l Hosp. v. Mercury Constr. Corp., 460 U.S. 1 (1983) and Mitsubishi Motors Corp. v. Soler Chrysler-Plymouth, Inc. 473 U.S. 614 (1985). *See also* Steelworkers v. Warrior & Gulf Nav. Co., 363 U.S. 574, 582-83, 80 S. Ct. 1347, 4 L. Ed. 2d 1409 (1960) (arbitration should be ordered "unless it may be said with positive assurance that the arbitration clause is not susceptible of an interpretation that covers the asserted dispute").

A. Discovery

Discovery in arbitration almost always involves lower discovery costs than courtroom litigation. While document discovery is routinely authorized in arbitration under the rules of most ADR providers, arbitral supervision and control of wide-ranging document requests is routine.[4] Moreover, interrogatories are not authorized, even in large, complex commercial cases.[5] Depositions are also limited to such cases, and allowed only in "exceptional cases" and for "good cause shown."[6] And the arbitrator's discretion to authorize depositions may well not be exercised absent some likelihood that the deposition testimony can be used as evidence.[7] As a result, depositions are rarely taken in small cases, and they are limited in the large, complex case.

There is a good reason why depositions have been available for many decades in courtroom litigation. They are thought to be a particularly effective means of discovery. However, this general proposition should be evaluated in the context of the dispute for which an arbitration is being considered. For example, the need for depositions may be much reduced in a B2B dispute between contracting parties who already know each other and each other's personnel relating to the dispute (or can be expected to have this knowledge by the time a dispute arises), so that a "surprise" witness is unlikely to surface. Depositions also may be unnecessary when the parties know (or probably will know) much of the evidence that will be critical at a hearing on the merits. This evidence usually takes the form of the parties' written and electronic communications, and notes of meetings they attended relating to the dispute.

Since the taking and defending of depositions are usually the most costly aspect of courtroom litigation, the fact that they are used in a much more limited way in arbitration substantially reduces attorneys' fees and interference with management time. Indeed, the main savings in arbitration compared to litigation may well be the avoidance of depositions. These costs can seem particularly wasteful to a business executive whose B2B dispute is filed in court and then settles (as

---

[4] *E.g.,* Rule R-22 of the Commercial Arbitration Rules of the American Arbitration Association (AAA Comm'l Rules), effective October 15, 2013.

[5] *See* Procedures of Large, Complex Commercial Disputes, Rule L-3, of the AAA Comm'l Rules.

[6] *Id.*

[7] *See, e.g.,* the Mass. Uniform Arbitration Act (MUAA), Mass. Gen. Laws, ch. 251, § 7(b) (arbitrator may permit a deposition "for use as evidence"); Revised Uniform Arbitration Act 2000 (RUAA), § 17 (same). The Federal Arbitration Act is silent on depositions.

courtroom litigation usually does).[8] While federal courts have made it possible to reduce courtroom litigation costs by imposing some discovery limitations in the Federal Rules of Civil Procedure,[9] in general, these limitations are not followed.

There is one exception to the generally lower cost of discovery in arbitration. That is if the parties agree to conduct the arbitration under state or federal rules of judicial procedure. This is usually undesirable because most if not all of the benefits of arbitration will be lost.

B. Need for Third-Party Discovery

An issue related to discovery, but not a cost issue, is the possible need for discovery from third parties. This issue bears on the choice of arbitration versus courtroom litigation. There is a split in the federal circuit courts on the issue of whether arbitrators have the power to subpoena documents from non-parties.[10] Whether or not this power exists in the relevant jurisdiction, the Federal Arbitration Act grants arbitrators the power to summon witnesses to appear before them at the hearing and order those witnesses to bring documents with them. Thus, if documents or other information in the hands of a third party is likely to be critical to a resolution of a B2B dispute, then arbitration will be less attractive than courtroom litigation.

C. Evidence, Scheduling, and Finality as Cost Factors

Many pre-trial procedures associated with courtroom litigation are not used in arbitration, so the costs of these procedures will be saved in

---

[8] It may be argued that discovery in arbitration is inadequate because the arbitration demand is usually less informative than a notice-pleading complaint. However, arbitrators can and do see that they and the parties have an adequate statement setting forth the nature of the dispute. *See* AAA Comm'l Rules, Rule 21 and Rule P-2(a)(iii).

[9] *See* Fed. R. Civ. P. 16(a)(3), 26(b)(2), and, *e.g.*, D. Mass. Local Rule 26.1(C).

[10] *See* Life Receivable Trust v. Syndicate 102 at Lloyd's London, 539 F.3rd 210 (2nd Cir. 2008)(Section 7 of FAA does not authorize pre-hearing discovery from non-parties); Hay Group, Inc. v. E.B.S. Acquisition Corp., 360 F.3d 404 (3d Cir. 2004) (plain language of the FAA grants arbitrators the power to order subpoenas to witnesses to bring documents with them to a hearing, but nothing more), COMSAT Corp. v. Nat. Sci. Found., 190 F.3d at 269, 276 (4th Cir. 1999) (arbitrators cannot generally issue pre-hearing document subpoenas, but noting in dicta that arbitrators may be able to do so upon "a showing of special need or hardship"). *But see* In re Sec. Life Ins. Co. of Am., 228 F.3d 865, 870-871 (8th Cir. 2000)("implicit in an arbitration panel's power to subpoena relevant documents for production at a hearing is the power to order the production of relevant documents for review by a party prior to the hearing.").

the arbitral forum. For example, quite detailed and lengthy pre-trial memoranda (with multiple exhibits/attachments) are typically required in many federal courts. This expensive undertaking is designed to save time for a federal judge, whose services are paid by the taxpayers. Arbitration is usually conducted with considerably more informal and less expensive pre-hearing filings.

A courtroom trial is also likely to be more expensive than an arbitration hearing on the merits for several reasons.

First, evidence in arbitration can be introduced more quickly and with less dispute. In arbitration, fewer motions are filed challenging the admissibility of evidence because court rules of evidence do not apply. Thus, hearsay and other proof that might be excluded in a courtroom are usually admitted into evidence in arbitration but then reviewed quickly, and often given little or no weight by the arbitrator. As a result, the costs of reviewing the evidence may be less in arbitration.

Second, courtroom trials are often conducted only in the morning so that judges can deal with motions in the afternoon. Trials conducted this way last longer but usually are no cheaper than trials conducted on a full-day basis, as lawyers always find more work to do for every day "on trial." Arbitration hearings, in contrast, normally are conducted on a full day schedule, often continuing past 5 p.m. Thus, it is not uncommon for an arbitration to continue well after the time a trial court has suspended its activities for the day due to the need to accommodate the limited workday of court clerks and other court personnel.

Third, judges are frequently interrupted by emergency matters that will take precedence over a trial. This problem normally has no counterpart in arbitration.

Finally, in comparing bench trials to arbitration, the judge's decision may be delayed by the time it takes for the judge to be furnished with a hard copy of the transcript. In arbitration, however, transcripts can be provided by private reporting services, which usually generate hard copy transcripts faster than official court reporters.

Parties generally have much more control over the schedule in an arbitration than they have in a court proceeding. Arbitrators tend to set schedules that are convenient and not contrary to the wishes of the parties. They also tend to grant a modest number of extensions to the schedule. The convenience of a party's senior executive will likely be given much more consideration by an arbitrator than by a judge.

D. Finality as an Issue

An arbitration award is more likely to produce a final resolution of the dispute than is a trial court judgment, which can be appealed as of right on much broader grounds than those on which an award can be challenged in court. This will save both parties the cost of appellate legal fees and costs. To be sure, the loss of expanded appellate review may seem significant on the surface. But since the typical contract-based, B2B dispute is unlikely to present novel legal issues, even if tried in court, appellate interference with a jury verdict or bench trial judgment is not very likely.[11]

E. Controlling Arbitrators' Fees

In a lengthy arbitration, the arbitrator's compensation can become expensive. This is especially true if the parties are using a panel of three arbitrators. Parties can reduce arbitration costs by choosing a single arbitrator. If a panel is a must, the parties could select panelists from the same geographic location as the location of the hearing, since this should ease scheduling difficulties and lower travel expenses.[12] In addition, the parties can further reduce expenses by agreeing that all procedural and discovery disputes will be resolved by the chair of the panel.

In a consumer arbitration (*i.e.*, a consumer dispute with a business), depending on which ADR provider is selected, the filing fees in arbitration could be much higher than judicial filing fees. However, this is less true of the American Arbitration Association, which has adopted special procedures and very low fees for consumer-related disputes involving small amounts at issue.[13]

---

[11] Award confirmation is "usually routine or summary." Riccard v. Prudential Ins. Co., 307 F.3d 1277, 1288 (11th Cir. 2002). "Manifest disregard of the law" is probably no longer a valid ground for vacating or modifying an arbitral award in cases brought under the FAA. *See* Hall Street Assocs., LLC v. Mattel, Inc. 128 S. Ct. 1396 (2008). *See* Henn, "Judicial Involvement in Arbitrations and in the Review of Arbitration Awards," 94 Mass. L. Rev. 8, 15-16 (2011)(discussing Hall Street and its implications).

[12] Note that in considering relative cost, and absent the parties' contrary agreement, an arbitrator may be able to award punitive damages, even where they might be unavailable in court. Raytheon Co. v. Automated Bus. Sys., 882 F.2d 6, 9 (1st Cir. 1989).

[13] AAA Supplementary Procedures for Consumer Related Disputes, pp. 12-14, effective September 15, 2005. *See* Resnick, "Diffusing Disputes: The Public in the Private of Arbitration, the Private in the Courts, and the Erasure of Rights, 94 Yale L. Journal, 2804 (2015)(noting, *inter alia*, how rare are actual arbitration requests from consumers purchasers who agree to arbitrate in order to purchase; the article's concerns do not extend to arbitration between commercial entities).

F. Speed as a Factor

Arbitration proceedings are typically concluded more expeditiously than courtroom litigation (unless the court has a "rocket docket" or the case is susceptible to early resolution via summary judgment, which is easier to obtain in federal court[14]). The speed of arbitration is likely to be a favorable factor from a business standpoint, unless you're the defendant and have a weak case. Then you might prefer to postpone the day of financial judgment.

The principal reason that arbitration is usually faster, at least in the case of B2B litigation, is that depositions generally are not taken and disputes over document production are quickly resolved by the parties or the arbitrator.

But whatever the reason, expedition also supports reduction of costs, as every business client knows that the longer a litigation lasts, the more lawyers can think of work to be done.

G. The Danger of Juries for Business

Businesses may have good reasons to prefer an arbitrator to a jury. If the case involves a large "out-of-state" party, there is the specter of jury bias. There is also the possibility of jury cynicism toward business, which can make litigation unpredictable, regardless of the strength of a party's case. There are also certain "infamous" locations where businesses may prefer arbitration to litigation.[15]

There is considerable evidence (albeit of the polling variety) that the recent corporate scandals have increased juror skepticism.[16] A nationwide survey of 1,000 jury-eligible subjects revealed that American jurors' distrust was "on the rise" after the "dot com" and "tel com" bubble burst in

---

[14] The AAA Commercial Rules, which are in common use in business arbitrations, authorizes the arbitrator to hear and rule on a dispositive motion "only if" the arbitrator determines that the motion is "likely to succeed" and would "dispose of or narrow the issues in the case. *See* Rule 33. Given the wording of the rule, this determination should be made in advance, before the opposing party has to spend time and money on a response. Nonetheless, arbitrators will remain wary of the danger of vacatur under § 10(a)(3) of the FAA for "refusing to hear evidence pertinent and material to the controversy." In state law governed cases, Section 15 of the RUAA expressly provides for summary disposition of a claim or particular issue.

[15] *See* State v. Homeside Lending, 826 A.2d 997 (Vt. 2003) refusing to give full faith and credit to an Alabama judgment, which it characterized as a "'drive by' class action."

[16] *See* e.g., Sylvia Hsieh, *Post-Enron Juror Attitudes Are Hardening Against Corporate Defenders*, LAW. WKLY USA (Sept. 2, 2002).

the early 2000s, and warned "Corporate counsel [to] beware."[17] A study of 543 mock jurors conducted by Litigation Insights found that "our mock jurors have taken a decidedly cynical turn" about business corporations.[18] One writer noted that "[a] study of juror attitudes [shows that] companies across the board will be paying the price in the courtroom for the corporate misdeeds that have dominated this year's [2002] headlines . . . [J]urors in communities with a significant corporate presence, such as in . . . the Northeast, are actually the most hostile to corporations."[19]

The recent 2008-2009 "Great Recession" and the widespread publicity of unwise financial speculations on Wall Street, followed by highly-publicized Wall Street bonuses, will undoubtedly make jurors even more hostile to any evidence of arguable corporate misdeeds.

H. Control over the Process

Business entities do not like ceding control. In arbitration, the parties retain considerably more control over the process than they do in courtroom litigation. This often overlooked factor should be of considerable importance to those who decide whether to arbitrate or litigate disputes.

In arbitration, the parties have considerable control over the selection of the arbitrator, using whatever process they have agreed upon in their contract. The parties also can agree on the type of experience and expertise the arbitrator should have. They may wish to have an arbitrator with expertise in the subject matter if the transaction out of which the dispute arose is complicated (*e.g.*, sale and license agreements in the high tech industry, construction, or venture capital limited partnership matters), or if standard business practices or possibly even the course of performance (*e.g.*, parties to a particular trade association or treaty) are relevant to the dispute.

In contrast, parties to courtroom litigation have little control over which judge hears the case and cannot choose a judge with particular knowledge or experience. Thus, in courtroom litigation, the parties risk having a judge with no subject-matter expertise, nor even any business law experience, unless they can litigate in a specialty business court.[20]

---

[17] DecisionQuest/MCCA Juror Perception Survey (10/16/02), *available at* infor@decisionquest.com.

[18] Litigation Insights, June 20, 2002.

[19] Tamara Loomis, *Business Scandals Rock Jury Attitudes*, 228 N.Y.L.J. 1 (2002).

[20] *E.g.*, the Delaware Chancery Court, or the Massachusetts Superior Court Business Law Session.

Some lawyers believe that an arbitrator who lacks knowledge of the subject-matter may be more likely to "split the baby" than an arbitrator with such knowledge. However, there is no empirical support for this belief. Indeed, a survey of all AAA commercial awards in 2000 comparing the amount originally claimed to the amount awarded showed that awards were clearly in one party's favor 75% of the time. Only 9% of the time, did arbitrators award between 41-60% of the amount claimed.[21] Arbitrators who handle B2B litigation, such as those serving on the AAA commercial arbitration panel, simply want their awards to reflect good analytical and reasoning skills.

I. The Confidentiality Factor

One of the particularly salient reasons for choosing arbitration is its supposed provision for confidentiality -- and privacy. A dispute resolution out of sight of competitors, media, and government authorities, not to mention the avoidance of possible bad publicity – all provide an attractive benefit to arbitration.

It is not quite that simple, however. First, it is important to note that, properly speaking, confidentiality and privacy are not identical, though the terms are often used as though they were interchangeable. Privacy means that the hearings are private, and a party cannot invite the public or the press (or government authorities) in to observe.[22] Any judicial order to the contrary would be impermissible, at least where the arbitration agreement includes an incorporation of the rules of an arbitral forum, and those rules provide for privacy.[23]

Confidentiality is another matter, and simply signing up for arbitration does not guarantee the confidentiality that a party might

[21] Stephanie E. Keer & Richard W. Naimark, *Arbitrators Do Not "Split the Baby:" Empirical Evidence from International Business Arbitration*, 18 J. INT'L ARB., 573-578 (2001).

[22] The author has read of one exception: where the hearing took place in China during the Cultural Revolution in front of a mass meeting invited by one party, following which the revolutionary masses "applauded the decision and sang … 'Sailing the Seas Depends on the Helmsman'." Reported in "The Decision of the High Court of Australia in Esso/BHP v. Plowman," Arbitration International (Kluwer Law International 1995 vol. 11, issue 3), 231-234, citing Loeber, 4 East West Trade (1977), at 476.

[23] *See* AAA Commercial Arbitration Rule 25 (eff. October 1. 2013)("the arbitrator and the AAA shall maintain the privacy of the hearings unless the law provides to the contrary"). Like many arbitral forum rules, including those for the International Centre for Dispute Resolution, these commercial rules are available online at www.adr.org.

assume.[24] While the arbitrator(s) and the arbitral forum will keep their files confidential -- including motion or other papers, hearing evidence, briefs and other filings, and the award -- what the parties do to maintain confidentiality between or among them is a matter of their agreement (or possibly, court order). "Thus, whatever other confidentiality provisions the agreement of the parties may contain, further language may be required if the parties also wish to guard against unwelcome disclosures of matters relating to the arbitration or award by a party."[25] Any such agreement will, of course, be subject to whatever disclosures may be required by law.

How might the judicial system become involved? First, papers from an arbitration may be sought during discovery or at trial in a subsequent judicial proceeding (or arbitral proceeding, for that matter) involving one of the arbitration parties and a third party. Since arbitration does not enjoy the "settlement negotiations" privilege of mediation, it stands to reason that such papers can be obtained from a judge upon a proper showing of good cause, subject to whatever conditions of limited access the judge may impose.[26]

A more interesting, but surely more rare, situation arises when one or all arbitration parties wish to keep an award confidential, but one of the parties seeks to confirm, modify or vacate it. This may not be possible in certain FAA-governed cases, as awards are required to be part of the filings on a motion to confirm, modify or correct.[27] The FAA's vacatur provisions, however, do not contain that requirement. Assuming, as appears to be commonplace, that the award is attached to a motion seeking some judicial action on an award, a party seeking confidentiality of that award would have to move the court to impound it (and any papers referring to it), based on the court's standards for impoundment of judicial filings.

---

[24] In the international context, *see* Paulsson & Rawling, "The Trouble With Confidentiality," Arbitration International (Kluwer Law International, *supra* note 138), 303. *See also* Collins, "Privacy and Confidentiality in Arbitration Proceedings," 30 Tex. Int'l L. Journ. 121 (1995)(English law and international arbitrations).

[25] Hoellering, "How to Draft An AAA Arbitration Clause," 7 Foreign Investment L. Journ. 141, 152 (1992).

[26] The AAA Commercial Arbitration Rules actually consist of a set of Commercial "Arbitration Rules" and of separate "Mediation Procedures." Rule M-10 of the Mediation Procedures expressly provides for confidentiality, with privacy separately covered in Rule M-9. There is no comparable confidentiality provision in the Arbitration Rules.

[27] 9 U.S.C. § 13(b).

In some situations, the parties may wish to agree in advance for award confidentiality. For example, where each arbitration party does business in an environment of significant competitors, the confidentiality of the award itself might be a subject the parties would want to consider when negotiating a confidentiality agreement/stipulation, whether as part of a pre-dispute arbitration agreement, or as a stipulation made during the pendency of an arbitration. In such a case, the agreement would have to include a provision that the parties would agree to any request for impoundment in a post-arbitration judicial proceeding concerning the award.

As to a court's involvement, it seems reasonable to conclude that a trial court's inherent power to impound papers for good cause could upon a proper showing extend to an award. That said, courts might in some situations not uphold an agreement between arbitration parties to extend confidentiality to an award, particularly where the agreement was one of several unconscionable provision in a contract of adhesion that had been imposed in a pre-dispute arbitration clause.[28] In the international area, at least, there is also some case law indicating that a party to an arbitration should be able to use the award where necessary to establish facts in a subsequent proceeding again a non-party to the arbitration.[29]

III. Other Issues to Consider

A. Enforceability

Enforceability is not a major concern when comparing arbitration to litigation. Arbitration awards can be confirmed in court. First they are converted to court judgments, and then they are enforced in exactly the same manner as any other judgment.[30]

B. Consolidation

The possibility of consolidation of related arbitrations is also not a major concern. The parties can expressly agree to consolidation of

[28] *See* Davis v. O'Melveny & Myers, 485 F.3d 1066, 1078 (9th Cir. 2007)(large law firm's new employment contracts, provided to employees on a "take it or leave it" basis, were unconscionable, including the confidentiality clause which was held unconscionable because too broad).

[29] *See* Collins, "Privacy and Confidentiality in Arbitration Proceedings," 30 Tex. Int'l L. Journ. 121, at 130-132 (1995)(English law and international arbitrations).

[30] This legal judgment is authorized by statute: *e.g.*, FAA § 10; *see also* RUAA § 22.

specified arbitrations between named parties. This is not uncommon in multi-party transactions. The Revised Uniform Arbitration Act expressly provides in § 10 for consolidation where each agreement to arbitrate has one party in common. The FAA is silent on consolidation and thus may not allow it absent authorization in state law.[31] In the First Circuit at least, a designation of state law can supplement the FAA to allow consolidation,[32] if the arbitration agreements do not prohibit it, although this is probably a minority view.

IV. Conclusion: Going Forward in Arbitration

If the parties decide to use the arbitration process to resolve their future disputes, they also need to consider whether the arbitration arrangements to which they propose to agree will serve the ends they seek. A narrow arbitration clause might well lead to courtroom litigation about whether a particular dispute is arbitrable under the terms of the contract in question, while a broad clause might not.

---

[31] *See* Michael Hoellering, *Consolidated Arbitration: Will it Result in Increased Efficiency or an Affront to Party Autonomy?*, 52 DISP. RESOL. J. 41 (1997), and cases cited at ns. 25-30; MARTIN DOMKE *ET AL.*, DOMKE ON COMMERCIAL ARBITRATION, § 27.02.

[32] New England Energy v. Keystone Shipping Co., 855 F.2d 1 (1st Cir. 1988). An express choice-of-law clause designating Massachusetts law may enhance the likelihood of consolidation because the Massachusetts arbitration statute expressly permits it. *Cf.* Volt Info. Sci. v. Bd. of Tr. of Leland Stanford Jr. Univ., 489 U.S. 468 (1989) (state arbitration rules can be incorporated into parties' arbitration agreement).

CHAPTER 2

KEEPING ARBITRATION EASY, EFFICIENT, ECONOMICAL AND USER FRIENDLY

Louis L. C. Chang[*]

I. Introduction

Arbitration is used in a broad range of circumstances and it enjoys exceptionally strong support by American courts. A general goal of arbitration is to achieve fair and appropriate resolutions of disputes with efficiency and economy. Some of the most important characteristics of arbitration are:

- the decision maker is selected by the parties,
- the proceedings and award are private,
- the process is less formal than litigation,
- legal rules of procedure and evidence do not apply, and
- the process can be understood without formal legal training.

Arbitration is a consensual process that can be customized to suit specific circumstances and relationships. Whether governed by the Federal Arbitration Act, the 1955 version of the Uniform Arbitration Act, which has been adopted by most states, or the revised version (RUAA), which has been adopted by a handful of states (18 as of June, 2015), there are opportunities to shape the process to the parties' needs. Although one party

* Louis L.C. Chang is a mediator, arbitrator, and lawyer in Honolulu, Hawaii. Since 1973, he has worked primarily on commercial and contract matters, construction, insurance and labor and employment disputes. Reflecting the growth of ADR, his practice has increasingly involved increased service as a mediator, arbitrator, facilitator, umpire and discovery master. Mr. Chang serves on panels of a number of ADR provider organizations, including the American Arbitration Association, Dispute Prevention & Resolution, Inc., and the Federal Mediation & Conciliation Service. He also serves on the arbitration panel of the Hawaii Labor Relations Board and on the mediation panel of the federal and bankruptcy court in Hawaii. He can be reached by phone at (808) 384-2468 and by e-mail at louchang@hula.net. His website is http://louchang.com.

can take advantage of the other through process design, that is not advisable since it invites legislatures to act to impose constraints on certain types of arbitration, particularly those involving parties with little or no bargaining power, such as consumers and employees.

II. Achieving Efficient Arbitration

Thus, supporters of arbitration should promote the fairest possible process as well as one that is efficient, cost-effective and user-friendly. To do this the following elements must be present.

A. Establish an Overall Spirit of Cooperation for the Arbitration

Arbitrators can set the tone for the arbitration by stating that they expect civility and cooperation from the parties and their attorneys. They should emphasize the differences between litigation and arbitration and urge parties to avoid importing judicial procedures into the arbitration if they want a swift but fair process. Arbitration honors substance over form so that parties can obtain the process that they bargained for. If the arbitration is overly adversarial and legalistic, it will probably take longer to resolve. The goal should be to keep moving forward so that the arbitrator can resolve all arbitrable issues in a timely, user friendly and efficient manner.

B. Arbitrators Should Be Accessible

Arbitrators should be easily accessible to the parties. Telephone conference calls between the party representatives and the arbitrators should be promptly and easily scheduled. Working with the parties or their advocates, arbitrators can encourage parties to simplify administrative and scheduling matters. Parties can agree that direct telephone or email communication to the arbitrator's office can be made where it is limited to requesting and coordinating an immediate or prompt conference call including all parties or their representatives. In a case involving a panel of arbitrators, one arbitrator could be designated to address issues and motions concerning discovery. Another could be designated to issue subpoenas. The parties can agree that facsimile copies of the arbitrator's signed subpoenas can be used for all purposes to the same extent as the signature on an original signed subpoena.

C. Shape and Organize the Arbitration Process

Arbitrators must be flexible and willing to tailor the process to fit the parties' needs. As stated by Prof. Frank Sanders, the challenge is to work together to "fit the forum to the fuss." Invite discussions at preliminary conferences of ways to simplify and streamline the arbitration process and to keep the proceeding on schedule. Arbitrators should encourage counsel to bring up all procedural and substantive issues and their ideas to accelerate the process during preliminary conferences. This can foster a more efficient and economical arbitration process.

D. Focus on the Issues in the Case

It is essential to define the issues for resolution in arbitration as early as possible. During an early preliminary conference, the arbitrator should determine whether all claims, counterclaims and defenses have been communicated and are clear between the parties. If not, the arbitrator can set a schedule for the clarification or supplementation of claims, counterclaims and defenses. Frequently, a case will turn upon a few specific crucial issues. If the critical issues can be identified during pre-arbitration conferences, the parties can then focus their discovery needs and witness presentations based on those critical issues. Hearings can then be shorter, more focused and more efficient.

Before the hearing, review with the parties the facts and issues in contention so that they can identify evidence and witnesses who have information pertinent to resolving these matters. Facts and issues not in contention can be the subject of stipulation. Review with the parties the facts and issues in contention so that they can identify evidence and witnesses who have information pertinent to resolving these matters. Facts and issues not in contention can be the subject of stipulation.

Identifying facts not in dispute and those remaining in dispute will also help the parties to focus their preparation and presentation to the arbitrator upon what is legitimately at issue. Parties can be encouraged and asked to prepare and submit uncontested facts, by stipulation to the extent possible. An alternative is that parties can submit a statement of proposed uncontested facts that the other party can respond to. If no objection is noted to a proposed fact, the case can proceed with the understanding that the uncontested facts are accepted as established for the purposes of the case. The goal is to only spend valuable time and resources developing and presenting information pertinent to matters in dispute to the arbitrator. In this way, the hearing can again be limited and focused only upon the key matters and issues in dispute.

E. Identify and Arrange for Necessary Information

To minimize the need for subpoenas, encourage parties to voluntarily produce relevant documents and employee witnesses. In some cases, parties need records from persons who are not a party to the arbitration proceeding. The arbitrator has authority to issue document subpoenas to third parties for production at the hearing.[1] There is also case law authority confirming the arbitrator's authority to subpoena documents during the "discovery" phase of a case (i.e., prior to the hearing). Early production of documents can help the parties to more accurately assess their positions and lead them to resolve some or all issues prior to the hearing on the merits.

F. Establish Communication Protocols

Encourage the parties to agree to communicate using the most efficient technology. Ask whether counsel would be comfortable using e-mail communications in lieu of faxes, U.S. mail, or hand delivery. If so, clarify whether e-mail is to be limited to administrative and scheduling matters or be used only to transmit memoranda and motions. Encourage the parties to limit their communications to the arbitrator to those matters that relate to the arbitrator's role or seek responsive action from the arbitrator. All communications sent to the arbitrator must be simultaneously provided to the other parties. If e-mail is to be used in a limited way, encourage the parties and counsel to use faxes to transmit other documents.

G. Dispose of Preliminary and Dispositive Issues

The arbitrator should identify and address all preliminary and dispositive legal issues for early disposition at a pre-arbitration hearing, where appropriate. Resolving these gateway issues early can save the parties work and reduce the scope of (or necessity for) further proceedings.

H. Group and Bifurcate When Appropriate

The arbitrator can bifurcate issues for hearing in a logical or efficient manner. For example, in a construction defect case, the arbitrator could address causation and liability in the first phase, then the appropriate

---

[1] *See* under § 7 of the Federal Arbitration Act and § 17 of the RUAA.

remedy and damages in a second phase. It might also be appropriate to bifurcate issues by the parties or the contracts involved (*i.e.*, claims against design professionals or subcontractors might be more efficiently handled in separate hearings).

I. Consider Using a Neutral Fact Finder

Where there are lots of disputed and/or detailed facts, the arbitrator could ask the parties if they want to consider jointly retaining a neutral fact finder who will investigate and determine the facts. To make the fact finder's findings more credible, the person so appointed should be an appropriate expert. If a neutral fact-finder is to be used, the scope of his or her review should be clear. The fact-finder's report and conclusions should be provided to the parties in advance of any hearing. Using a neutral fact finder can remove factual issues that would be laborious and time-consuming to establish in an arbitration hearing (and usually involve questioning of multiple witnesses), thereby saving costs and reducing the number of issues to be decided at the hearing. It also avoids the need for each party to retain its own expert for purposes of factual review.

J. Promptly Exchange Exhibits and Evidence

The information exchange or discovery portion of arbitration has been discussed by many arbitrators. Like those arbitrators, I ask the parties to exchange lists of the document exhibits they intend to introduce at the hearing on the merits. Then, I like the parties to exchange numbered (or lettered in combination with numbers) exhibits in tabbed binders. I like internal pages of voluminous documents to be numbered for ease of reference. In a case with multiple issues, the parties can group the exhibits pertinent to each issue by assigning a different letter prefix (e.g., Documents A-1 through A-15, B-1 through B-6, and C-1 though C-3 pertain to issues A, B, and C respectively). This organization permits the addition of related exhibits so that all issue-related exhibits are together and will help the arbitrator find the pertinent evidence with relative ease.

I also ask parties to provide me with a binder containing joint exhibits to avoid duplication. This avoids duplicative work and helps to expedite things.

Make sure the parties understand that, except for impeachment and rebuttal purposes, all exhibits intended to be introduced at the hearing on the merits (either in support of a claim or defense) will be provided to the other party and the arbitrator prior to the commencement of hearing.

Dispense with the formality of litigation with respect to document exhibits. Propose that the parties accept the protocol that all document exhibits are deemed admitted unless a specific concern or objection is raised to a particular document. At the hearing the parties can focus their arguments upon the merits, applicability and reliability of any piece of evidence.

K. Decide on Witnesses and Means of Expediting the Introduction of Evidence

Try to minimize the necessity of subpoenas. Ask the parties to agree to produce the attendance of those witnesses within their employ or control without the necessity of subpoenas. If subpoenas will be needed to summon the attendance of witnesses at the hearing, make sure that the parties follow the rules of notice and service.

Arbitrators should obtain from the parties their anticipated order of witnesses prior to the date they are expected to testify. This permits the other party to prepare for cross-examination of the identified witnesses.

Expediting the introduction of evidence may entail persuading the parties' attorneys to use more informal means of providing witness testimony and to take advantage of new technology.

Consider witness conferencing where fact or expert witnesses can provide testimony on common topics or issues at the same time. There are advantages to this type of evidence presentation. Some people believe that witnesses are more likely to be truthful when giving evidence in the presence of other witnesses. Moreover, one witness may be able to fill in a gap left by another or supplement something that was said. The arbitrator can receive all evidence pertinent to a specific issue at the same time. Witnesses can explain and clarify their areas of agreement and disagreement.

Another means of expediting the introduction of evidence at the hearing is through written witness statements in lieu of direct testimony. Sometimes, parties are willing to have all direct testimony submitted through written witness statements. This can help to focus the direct testimony as well as shorten the hearing time. All written witness statements must be provided to the arbitrator and exchanged by the parties in advance of the hearing. If written witness statements are used, they should refer to the relevant portions of the key exhibits. This is quite helpful to the arbitrator. At the hearing, once everyone has had an opportunity to read the witness statement, the witness is made available in person for cross and redirect examination.

Direct testimony also could be introduced from a deposition in the case (this would be a vital witness, since depositions are not taken as liberally in arbitration as they are in a judicial proceeding) or trial testimony in another proceeding. Parties can consider providing written summaries, but only if it will result in saving time.

L. Use Graphics to Tell a Story

A chronology of key events and key documents can be extremely helpful to the parties in identifying the disputed facts and to the arbitrator in understanding the facts. I ask the parties to prepare this jointly.

An organization chart or list of the key individuals referenced in the documentary exhibits, with a brief description of their title, position and role in the dispute also can help the arbitrator more easily understand the case and the role and capacity of the involved players. Floor plans, diagrams and photos of the scene may also be useful in certain kinds of cases. Sometimes a picture is indeed worth a thousand words. A site visit can be invaluable in construction and other kinds of cases to acquaint the arbitrator with the pertinent settings and issues.

M. Use Expert Witness Panels

A recognized weakness of an adversary dispute resolution system is its high cost, some of which may be attributable to the battle of technical experts. If the parties can agree on one acceptable expert who had no involvement in the case, they can eliminate the cost of one expert. (If they can't agree on the expert, they can suggest names to the arbitrator, who will make the choice.) For example, in a partnership accounting dispute, the parties could agree to have a mutually trusted accountant make findings, conclusions or recommendations to the arbitrator. Where technical expertise is needed to persuade the arbitrator how to rule, the parties could consider jointly retaining one technical expert at their shared cost. Using a neutral expert also makes sense where there is a technical interpretation to be decided. The parties can thus avoid a costly "battle of experts" and cut their expert costs by at least half. Also, issues of credibility or bias of expert witnesses who are suspected of being paid advocate witnesses is then minimized.

Whether one or more experts will testify about a particular disputed issue or fact, establish ground rules for their qualifications. Also determine whether written reports will be produced and, if so, require the expert report to (1) contain the bases for the expert opinions stated in the report, (2) reflect the theories and opinions of the expert after all investigation and testing has been done, and (3) be disclosed to the adversary prior to the hearing. To avoid unfair surprise, clarify with the parties a mutual understanding that unless good cause is shown to the arbitrator, all expert opinions of the experts must be included in their report as their testimony will be limited only to the opinions contained and disclosed in their reports.

If expert reports are not going to be produced, suggest having both experts' direct testimony submitted in writing and exchanged in advance of the hearing. As in the case of ordinary witnesses, the experts will be available in person for cross-examination.

Pre-qualify experts by having the parties exchange the experts' resumes well before the hearing. If there are no objections, the parties can be asked to stipulate that their respective experts may testify as experts in the relevant field. If needed, the parties can utilize a formal voir dire process to examine their expert qualifications. This can be done by telephone conference in advance of the hearing. If done in person, it can involve considerable travel expense, especially when there are multiple experts involved. Resolving the expert qualifications issue before the hearing is necessary so that the hearing itself is used only to deal with the disputed issues in the case.

If multiple experts will be testifying on the same issue, consider having them all testify at the same time. This works as follows (assuming that prior to the hearing, their resumes were exchanged and provided to the arbitrator and the parties did not object to their testifying, and their written reports were also exchanged in advance of the hearing):

The expert witnesses are sworn in together. The arbitrator questions the experts first. This is more productive than having the attorneys question them first because the arbitrator will ask what he or she wants to know. This way the parties' advocates won't have to guess what the arbitrator is thinking or what issues are on the arbitrator's mind.

After the arbitrator finishes questioning all the experts, the parties' attorneys ask their questions, bringing out information they believe is desirable and necessary for the arbitrator to resolve the dispute. In addition, the experts can be invited to ask questions of each other and provide additional information they believe to be helpful or pertinent.

The principal advantage of the expert panel format is that the opinions of all of the experts can be expressed at one time, one issue at a time. Moreover, the experts have the opportunity to offer information, not only respond to questions.

Many times there is a consensus among the experts on significant areas. These can be identified and noted. The inquiry can then move on to areas or issues where the experts disagree. In the panel format, experts can respond immediately to each other's opinions. Opinions can be tested and clarified. The arbitrator gains the benefit of the expertise of all the experts as they clarify the issues.

Arbitrators should have a chart of questions and issues prepared beforehand on which to capture the experts' opinions and rationales, and identify the areas of contention. The panel questioning can be divided into phases based on the issues to be addressed: for example, causation, liability, damages.

The expert panel is a useful way of collecting the testimony of multiple witnesses on a single subject and learning about the critical differences that exist between them. It also reduces the study time the arbitrator needs to make sense of divergent technical testimony.

N. "Chess Clock" Arbitration

Sometimes, the parties may be willing to agree to present their case and cross-examine witnesses within a specified amount of time. Called the "chess clock" technique, this hearing management tool focuses the parties on what they need to accomplish at the hearing. However, this process should not be forced on the parties. Some experienced arbitrators caution that the chess clock technique should only be used by agreement of the parties and that agreement should be adequately documented and confirmed by the lawyers as well as the parties because it is a modification of their arbitration agreement.

Tallying the time used can be done by the arbitrator, a court reporter, or another person. I recommend that the arbitrator announce the time used and remaining at least twice a day, first at the beginning of the hearing day and second at the end of that day. This way, if there are any problems with timekeeping, they can be addressed promptly.

Some of the available time for each side should be allotted to cover unexpected events and delays. Some arbitrators recommend giving the arbitrator discretion to grant additional time if necessary for a party to fully and fairly present its case.

O. Use Technology to Enhance the Efficiency of the Process

Consider the use of available new technologies that can help to streamline and make the arbitration process a practical and efficient process. Excellent video conferencing tools are now readily available to allow the participation of parties and witnesses from remote sites. Computer, smartphone and internet technologies now make video-conferencing easy and efficient. Witnesses who may not be available to easily attend a hearing in person can participate by smartphone, I-Pad or computer based speaker and video camera. These technological tools make distant witnesses, expensive and busy doctors, expert witnesses and witnesses who for physical, economic or other reason more readily available to participate substantively and fully in arbitration proceedings. Arrangements can be made to have pertinent documents made available to the witness beforehand or by means of facsimile or digital pdf transmission.

Other technological tools can also be used. Consider the possible use of digitized exhibits and searchable database records in cases involving voluminous records.

III. Conclusion

Arbitration remains a very valuable, useful and flexible dispute resolution process. Thoughtful use and adaptation of the arbitration process can preserve and protect arbitration as an efficient, cost-effective and user-friendly private procedure for the fair and prompt resolution of a wide range of civil and commercial disputes.

CHAPTER 3

CREATING AN ECONOMICAL AND EFFICIENT ARBITRATION PROCESS IS EVERYONE'S BUSINESS

*Kent B. Scott and Adam T. Mow**

I. Introduction

Arbitration is thousands of years old. From Aristotle to the Elizabethan era, people have recognized that disputes are often best resolved outside of the courts. And until very recently, arbitration was the preferred dispute resolution method in the United States for the construction industry. Other industries also have chosen to arbitrate instead of using the courts to resolved disputes, and companies of all kinds have chosen to use it for employment disputes. Within the last few decades, however, arbitration has been criticized for evolving into a process that mirrors litigation. The causes most likely were advocates who were unfamiliar with arbitration and did not understand that it differed from litigation, as well as arbitrators who failed to exercise adequate control over the process. In fact, many arbitrators viewed themselves as powerless referees and so they routinely granted requests for postponements, allowed long drawn-out proceedings, and refused to hear dispositive motions that could bring the case to an early conclusion. On the other hand, arbitrators who would exercise authority had little ability to sanction a party for failure to comply with an arbitral order.

---

* Kent B. Scott is a shareholder in Babcock Scott & Babcock, a construction law firm in Salt Lake City, as well as an arbitrator and mediator. Adam T. Mow is an attorney with Jones Waldo Holbrook & McDonough in the Salt Lake City office, specializing in construction law. Mr. Mow also serves as an arbitrator and mediator. Both authors serve on the commercial panel of the American Arbitration Association and both are members of the Utah Bar Association's Dispute Resolution Section and Utah Dispute Resolution. In addition, Mr. Scott serves on the panel for the U.S. District Court (Utah) and is a member of the ABA's Dispute Resolution Section and its Forum on the Construction Industry. The authors wish to thank Carl Ingwalson for his invaluable contributions and refinements to this article.

The process clearly needed change. For decades, the American Arbitration Association (AAA) has been at the forefront of improving and streamlining the process through its rule revisions. In 1999, the AAA released significantly revised commercial arbitration rules that, among other things, encouraged the use of preliminary hearings, clarified the discretion and authority of the arbitrator, addressed the issue of arbitral interim relief, created Optional Rules for Emergency Measures of Protection (i.e., relief needed before the arbitrator is appointed), added Optional Procedures for Large Complex Cases, and amended the Expedited Procedures for small cases to make them more efficient.

The AAA Construction Industry Arbitration Rules and Mediation Procedures underwent a similarly significant revision in 2009. One major improvement was the creation of a three-track system for small, regular, and large construction cases. The rules also expanded the powers of the arbitrator in regular and large cases and provided a more efficient process keyed to the size and complexity of the dispute.

Meanwhile, the National Conference of Commissioners on Uniform State Laws (NCCUSL) formed a committee to draft a new Uniform Arbitration Act to replace the 1955 version (enacted in many states) and bring arbitration law in line with judicial arbitration decisions. In August of 2000, the NCCUSL and the American Bar Association approved the Revised Uniform Arbitration Act 2000 (RUAA) and the ABA agreed to promote it to the states for enactment. So far 18 states and the District of Columbia have done so. The RUAA contains vastly expanded arbitrator powers, including the power to issue provisional remedies, determine the appropriate amount of discovery, impose sanctions, issue and enforce third-party subpoenas, hear and decide dispositive motions, streamline the presentation of evidence, and award punitive damages and attorney fees in specified circumstances. In many other states the original UAA remains in effect, while a few states have unique arbitration statutes, including New York and California.

Notwithstanding these reforms, parties and lawyers remained concerned that arbitration is no longer efficient and economical. Some say it has become the mirror image of "scorched earth" litigation and some call it an "arbi-trial" or "arbrigation".

In 2009, many professional arbitrators turned their attention to the problem of the increasing time and cost of arbitration. This took place at a summit convened in the nation's capital by the College of Commercial

Arbitrators (CCA). The summit had the backing of major sponsors.[1] Participants included arbitrators, attorneys (both in-house and outside counsel) and representatives of ADR providers. The purpose of the summit was to gather data about the causes of the problem and develop solutions. In 2010, the CCA published its findings and recommendations in a report called "Protocols for Expeditious, Cost Effective Commercial Arbitration."[2]

The report contained four protocols, one for each stakeholder in the process. Each protocol contains valuable recommendations to control cost and time in arbitration. In combination, the protocols make it clear that the responsibility for designing an efficient and less costly arbitration process rests with all stakeholders. Parties, counsel, arbitrators, and providers all must recognize this responsibility. To carry it out, arbitration providers should offer the parties a wide variety of streamlined arbitration programs. When parties enter into new contracts or renegotiate old ones, they should customize the arbitration provisions to achieve their goals for efficiency and economy. After a dispute arises, when the arbitration provisions are implemented, the parties, their advocates and the arbitrator should cooperate with each other in order to reach an agreement on cost-effective and efficient procedures.

Having a wide choice of arbitration programs, and customizing the arbitration process so that it is appropriate for the size and type of anticipated disputes, along with cooperation are central to achieving fair, yet expeditious proceedings.

II. What Parties Can Do

Designing an efficient and cost-effective dispute resolution process should begin well before a dispute arises, preferably before a company intends to enter into a large contract. This will enable it to be ready to propose this process when that big contract negotiation approaches. Unfortunately, business too often give little or no thought to the dispute resolution provisions they put in their own contracts. These provisions are often considered to be mere boilerplate and, as a result, they are copied

[1] Sponsors: the AAA, the American Bar Association, the Chartered Institute of Arbitrators, the CPR Institute for Conflict Prevention and Resolution, JAMS, and the Straus Institute for Dispute Resolution at Pepperdine University.

[2] Protocols for Expeditious, Cost Effective Commercial Arbitration, College of Commercial Arbitrators (2010). A product of the National Summit on Business-to-Business Arbitration (October 2009), as reported by Thomas Stipanowich, Curtis von Kann & Deborah Rothman.

from one agreement and pasted at the end of another. And that copy-and-paste job could end up being a defective clause that has enforceability problems, or a "one size fits all clause" that, as described in the CCA Protocol for Business Users and In-House Counsel (User Protocol), "creates many opportunities for counsel to expand, often excessively, the dimensions and density of the arbitration." These opportunities can result in lawyers trying to turn arbitration into litigation.

The arbitration clause should be a part of a dispute resolution system that reflects the company's overall dispute resolution objectives. Such a system usually has a number of steps, beginning with less adversarial processes (e.g., direct discussions followed by mediation) and ending with binding arbitration if the earlier steps fail to resolve the dispute. The earlier steps are conditions precedent to arbitration.

At the time a contract is being negotiated, the arbitration step should be tailored to meet the company's objectives with respect to the likely future disputes that they anticipate could arise as a result of the transaction. Is it likely that future disputes will be large or small, complex or small? Will they involve multiple parties? Will they involve precedent-setting issues? Anticipating the nature, size and complexity of future disputes can help determine whether all or just some disputes should be arbitrated (i.e., the scope of arbitrability).

To avoid becoming enmeshed in a future "arbi-trial," the drafter of arbitration provisions should be wary of including procedures that mirror traditional rules of civil procedure or evidence, or providing for awards that contain detailed findings of fact and conclusions of law. Doing so will defeat the goal of having efficient, cost-effective arbitration proceedings. To achieve that goal, the arbitration provisions could state that the parties agree to:

- Use "fast-track" rules or "expedited procedures" for disputes below a certain size or of a certain type.
- Place a time limit on the arbitration (i.e., from filing to issuance of award), or on different phases of the arbitration (e.g., the evidentiary hearing).
- Consolidate related arbitrations that involve common facts and legal issues and join related parties to avoid multiple proceedings (very costly) and worse, inconsistent results.
- Limit the document and information exchanges to that which is relevant or even essential to the project or transaction.

- Use the International Centre for Dispute Resolution (ICDR) Guidelines for Arbitrators Concerning Exchanges of Information.
- Limit the number of depositions according to the size or type of disputes.
- Use interrogatories only for good reason.
- Require the arbitrator's consent to filing motions and/or briefs.
- Limit dispositive motions to those based on a statute of limitations or failure to satisfy all conditions precedent.
- Use a single arbitrator, except in cases above a certain size that require technical expertise.
- Use expeditious evidence presentation techniques.
- Require an award with a brief explanation of the outcome. This costs less and takes less time to prepare than an award with extensive reasoning.

III. Staying Out of Court

An obvious goal of having an arbitration clause is staying out of court. Therefore, it is essential to have an enforceable arbitration clause. Efficiency and cost effectiveness cannot be achieved if the parties must spend time and money litigating enforceability. Contract drafters who are unfamiliar with dispute resolution must become familiar with the requirements of an enforceable arbitration clause, which include all of the following:

(1) An unequivocal obligation to arbitrate.[3]

(2) A statement of the scope of disputes to be arbitrated (e.g., only contract claims or all disputes relating to the transaction including tort claims).

(3) Designation of:

  (a) An administering institution and the rules that will govern arbitration (e.g., the American Arbitration Association and the AAA Commercial Arbitration Rules),

  (b) The venue of the arbitration, and

  (c) The governing procedural and substantive law.

(4) A statement that judgment may be entered on the award in a court that has jurisdiction.

[3] This does not mean that there cannot be conditions precedent to arbitration.

Equally important, the drafter must make sure that the arbitration agreement would not be revocable under state contract law, such as on the ground of unconscionability.[4]

Care must also be taken not to make the terms of the arbitration provisions unrealistic, unnecessarily restrictive, or contradictory. If that happens, the parties could become involved in collateral litigation.

IV. Use Administered Arbitration Under Well-Tested Arbitration Rules

Agreeing to AAA administration and incorporating AAA rules into the arbitration agreement can advance the parties' efficiency goals because the AAA offers many different kinds of arbitration rules, including industry arbitration rules; fast-track construction rules; Expedited Procedures and Large, Complex Case Procedures, as well as regular rules for commercial cases. The AAA has Optional Rules for Interim Relief, and the ICDR has Guidelines for Arbitrators Concerning Exchanges of Information, both of which parties can elect to use regardless of the type of dispute.

In general, AAA rules are drafted by committees made up of individuals who have substantial knowledge of the field and experience with arbitration and mediation. In the case of industry arbitration rules, relevant trade associations are involved in the drafting process. In addition, the rules have enjoyed decades of use and are familiar to most attorneys, arbitrators and courts, which have interpreted them.[5] Another advantage of AAA administration is access to the AAA roster of neutrals. Other arbitration providers may offer similar types of options.

The benefit of having efficient arbitration procedures in the parties' agreement is that it puts all stakeholders, not just the parties, on notice of the desire for an efficient, less costly arbitration process. If a dispute later arises that requires different treatment, the parties, with input from the case manager, the arbitrator, and outside counsel, could agree to a different arrangement for that dispute.

---

[4] FAA § 3.

[5] All AAA rules can be downloaded from the AAA website at www.adr.org.

V. Suggestions from the CCA User Protocol

Next we turn to some suggestions from the User Protocol. An important suggestion is that companies first decide on their corporate dispute resolution objectives, and then make a case assessment whenever a claim arises. This is when a decision can be made about the importance of the case, the budget for resolution and the dispute resolution process believed to be most effective. These decisions should be communicated to outside counsel. Without knowing the client's dispute resolution objectives for the case, outside counsel cannot commit to carrying them out.

One suggestion regarding outside counsel is to retain an advocate who is a good negotiator and has substantial case management skills and experience using time-saving techniques in arbitration. It is also suggested that this advocate be committed to carrying out the client's goals for speed and economy. Advocates who meet these criteria are more likely to cooperate with opposing counsel and the arbitrator in designing an efficient case management plan.

The User Protocol also recommends continuing involvement of company representatives (from the legal and business side) in, and management of, arbitration proceedings. Presumably this includes having a senior in-house attorney participate in the preliminary management hearings. Practitioners who favor this idea believe that, with the client in the room, outside counsel are less likely to seek postponements for their convenience, or make proposals that would unnecessarily delay the arbitration (unless that happens to be the company's strategy).

VI. The CCA Protocol for Outside Counsel

Outside counsel have a great deal of influence over the cost and length of arbitration proceedings because they are involved in every aspect of the process, except that they do not decide the dispute and issue awards. That is the arbitrator's job.

Participants in the CCA summit were asked if outside counsel could do more to improve the economy, efficiency and fairness of the arbitration process. Eighty-nine percent of those responding said that attorneys could do more to help clients realize their expectations for arbitration.

But first, they need to know what the client's expectations are. If in-house counsel has not conveyed the company's expectations regarding the dispute to be arbitrated, outside counsel should ask the client to provide this information. Even if the client's goals have been communicated to outside counsel, it would be prudent for counsel to confirm them with in-house counsel prior to the initial preliminary management conference.

Second, in order to help realize the client's goals for arbitration, outside counsel must understand the difference between arbitration and litigation. The CCA Protocol for Outside Counsel (OC Protocol) recognizes the importance of understanding these differences when it says that outside counsel "exploit the differences between arbitration and litigation" when representing the client in arbitration.

Outside counsel must be able to work in harmony with everyone involved in the arbitration, including the case manager (if AAA arbitration is used), opposing counsel, the party representatives and the arbitrator. Cooperation is often essential in arbitration, particularly if the goal is an expeditious process. For example, cooperation among counsel is essential in order to efficiently appoint the arbitrator. This involves determining the arbitrator's qualifications, one of which should definitely be strong case management skills.[6]

In selecting the arbitrator, we recommend inquiring into the arbitrator's philosophy of case management to ensure that it is consistent with the client's goals for an expeditious process.

Cooperation among outside counsel and other stakeholders is also needed to develop an efficient case management plan that will set out the pre-hearing activities that must be completed, the dates for completing these activities, and the dates for the evidentiary hearing.

We would like to mention three suggestions from the OC Protocol that are especially noteworthy. They would have outside counsel agree to limit discovery consistent with client goals, discuss settlement opportunities with the client and, after the arbitration ends, make changes to the dispute resolution provisions based on lessons learned.

VII. What Arbitrators Can Do

Arbitrators should always manage the arbitration as economically, efficiently, and fairly as possible. To begin this process, the arbitrator must promptly set a date for the initial preliminary management hearing. Arbitrators should never lead this hearing without being thoroughly prepared. Thorough preparation includes becoming familiar with the

---

[6] The CCA Protocol for Business Users and In-House Counsel User Protocol stresses selecting an arbitrator with strong case management skills. However, it is usually the parties' outside counsel who decide on the arbitrator.

pleadings, the arbitration clause and other relevant provisions of the parties' contract (e.g., loss limitation provisions and statute of limitations). By the day of this hearing, the arbitrator should know the scope of arbitral jurisdiction, the venue of the proceeding, the governing procedural law (e.g., the Federal Arbitration Act or a state arbitration law), the applicable arbitration rules, and any limitations stated in the parties' agreement on the scope of arbitrability, arbitration procedures (e.g., discovery limits), or arbitral remedies. The arbitrator should prepare an agenda in advance of the preliminary hearing that includes any questions the arbitrator may have concerning these matters with and send it to the parties and their counsel with instructions to be ready to discuss all agenda items.

The initial preliminary management hearing is vitally important. The Arbitrator Protocol stresses the importance of conducting a meaningful hearing and then issuing a detailed case management order memorializing what occurred and what was decided.[7]

It is at the initial preliminary hearing that the arbitrator works with counsel and the party representatives to clarify the issues submitted to arbitration and establish the pre-hearing activities that need to be completed (e.g., the exchange of documents, other information and witness lists, and other types of discovery in an appropriate case), and the dates for completion of these activities (as well as the dates for the evidentiary hearings and related matters). If speed and economy are to be achieved, the arbitrator and counsel must work together to streamline the pre-hearing activities lest they drag on, leading to increased cost and time to conclusion of the dispute. The initial preliminary hearing is an opportune time to remind counsel and the party representatives that arbitration is not litigation in a private forum. It is supposed to be faster and more efficient than arbitration and, to make that happen, the cooperation of all parties and counsel is expected.

To create an efficient process, the arbitrator should address the following subjects and issues at the initial preliminary management hearing:

Confirmation Issues. It is important to confirm that there are no issues concerning the venue of the arbitration, the governing law, the applicable arbitration rules, nonparties who need to be joined in the arbitration, the arbitrator's jurisdiction to hear the matter, or the scope of arbitrable issues.

---

[7] The arbitrator should schedule subsequent preliminary hearings to make certain that the parties and counsel are doing what they agreed to do, that there is no slippage in the schedule, and be ready to deal with any other issues that arise.

Ground Rules. The arbitrator should advise the participants that the following ground rules must be followed.

- Incivility will not be tolerated. Everyone is expected to treat each other with respect. (The arbitrator could consider making compliance with applicable professional conduct rules and ethics codes or standards part of the case management order.)
- *Ex parte* communications are prohibited. All communications to the arbitrator should be sent to the case manager and all parties simultaneously.
- The arbitrator's consent must be obtained prior to submitting any motions or briefs.
- The parties are obligated to preserve all relevant documents and electronically stored information (ESI) and should be prepared to exchange such documents and information during the pre-hearing period. Spoliation of ESI is prohibited and may lead to sanctions.
- "Fishing expeditions" seeking broad discovery will not be permitted.

Stipulation of Facts. At the beginning of the initial preliminary hearing, the arbitrator should encourage the parties' counsel to work together to prepare, as part of the Arbitration Record: (1) a statement of facts and issues not in dispute and (2) a statement of issues that are in dispute. The latter statement will provide a road map that all arbitration participants can use throughout the proceeding. The stipulation of issues in dispute can also be used as a checklist to help the arbitrator make sure that the award covers all issues to be decided in the arbitration.

Preliminary and Dispositive Issues. The arbitrator should work with counsel to identify all preliminary and dispositive issues that need to be addressed at the initial preliminary hearing. These issues could include, for example, challenges to venue or arbitral jurisdiction (such as by reason of the expiration of the statute of limitations or the claimant's failure to satisfy all conditions precedent, or for other reasons), joinder or consolidation issues, or other matters that are troubling counsel.

The arbitrator should emphasize the ground rule that the filing of motions is not discretionary with the parties. Counsel must request permission from the arbitrator to submit a motion.

Briefs are generally not necessary when the parties have entered into a comprehensive stipulation of facts and there are no novel issues of law to be determined. Conversely, briefs may be helpful when there are disputed issues of both fact and law to be decided.

If the arbitrator consents to a request to file a brief, the arbitrator should work with counsel to identify the issues to be briefed and then set a reasonable length limitation on the briefs. The arbitrator may request that counsel use the form of a "letter brief" consistent with a more informal process.

If there are any issues still troubling counsel, the arbitrator should invite counsel to prepare a letter describing the issue and promptly e-mail it to the case manager.

Expedite Communications. In an AAA-administered proceeding, the arbitrator can allow the parties to use the AAA Accelerated Exchange Program. This program allows the parties to e-mail and fax each other (with a copy to the case manager) documents, motions and briefs. This provides more expedited communication than sending these materials to the case manager, who then distributes them to the parties.

Fact Discovery in General. The arbitrator should direct counsel to agree to a prompt exchange of relevant documents and other information, as agreed by the parties in their arbitration agreement, or if there is no agreement, in accordance with the applicable arbitration rules. Early production helps the parties assess the merits of their case. The arbitrator should also direct counsel to bring any disputes concerning this exchange to the arbitrator's attention in an e-mail addressed to the case manager.

ESI can present a problem because it is pervasive and expensive to gather and produce. The scope of ESI is generally determined on a case-by-case basis, unless the parties have reached an agreement concerning ESI in their arbitration agreement.

In order to address ESI, counsel for each party needs to learn about the client's ESI. This generally involves a consultation with the client's IT personnel to discuss what kind of ESI the client has, how and where it is stored, and how it can be retrieved. The parties' attorneys should then meet to establish a protocol for producing material, non-privileged ESI. The protocols agree upon by counsel, if reasonable and expeditious, should be incorporated into the arbitrator's case management order. If the protocol is not reasonable, the arbitrator may ask the requesting party to justify its expansive request. The allocation of costs involved in satisfying an expansive ESI request also may have to be discussed.

If the parties have not already agreed to use the ICDR Guidelines for Arbitrators Concerning Exchanges of Information, the arbitrator could suggest that they do so now to facilitate the exchange of ESI.

When it comes to written discovery, such as interrogatories and requests to admin, the arbitrator must be willing to exercise his or her managerial authority to discourage their use unless expressly authorized by the arbitration rules, or good cause can be shown and the information cannot be obtained through the information exchange or a deposition. If allowed, interrogatories should be severely limited in number, including subparts.

Depositions should be allowed only when authorized by the arbitration rules or the arbitrator concludes that they would be beneficial to the resolution of the case. Thus, counsel should be asked to explain why a proposed deposition is relevant, beneficial, and appropriate. If the arbitrator allows a deposition, its length should be limited.

In some cases counsel may seek an inspection, a site visit by the arbitrator, a specific test, or third-party discovery. In some construction defect cases, a site visit can be very helpful to the arbitrator in deciding the case or, depending on what the site visit shows, in moving the parties to decide on their own that it might be prudent to consider a settlement. It is up to the arbitrator to determine if allowing any of these kinds of discovery would be helpful to resolving the dispute.

Expert Discovery. Expert testimony can be the linchpin of a party's case, but it can also be expensive. Accordingly, the arbitrator should ask the attorneys if they each intend to engage an expert to testify and why. If they both say yes, and there are many technical issues to be decided, the arbitrator could suggest that the experts be asked to confer to narrow the issues and agree on those remaining in dispute. The arbitrator could also ask the parties to agree on the scope of the expert's anticipated testimony. Such agreements serve to control experts' fees because they limit the scope of the expert's work.

The arbitrator should not allow an expert who will testify at the hearing on the merits to be deposed if the expert provides a written expert report. There is no unfair surprise since the expert's opinions are in the report and the report is exchanged by the parties prior to the merits hearing.

Since legal privileges are respected by arbitrators, an arbitrator should not permit an expert who will neither testify nor provide a written report to be deposed, since the expert's communications with counsel would likely be considered attorney work product.

Witnesses. The arbitrator should require the parties' attorneys to agree to an early date for disclosing the names of "may call" witnesses. Early disclosure permits the arbitrator to determine if he or she has any possible conflicts of interest and, if so, promptly disclose them. It also enables the parties to better prepare for the evidentiary hearing. Disclosure of the names of "will call" witnesses – those who will definitely be called to present evidence – is usually made closer to the evidentiary hearing.

Delegating Authority to the Chair. If there is a panel of three arbitrators (although only one is needed unless the case is large and complex and requires special expertise), it is more efficient if one arbitrator (usually the chair of the panel) decides all procedural and non-dispositive matters (such as discovery disputes and requests for a third-party subpoena) without having to consult with the wing arbitrators. The parties should be asked to approve this arrangement.

Scheduling the Hearing. The arbitrator should work with the parties to identify consecutive dates for the evidentiary hearing. When the dates are not consecutive, the cost of arbitration goes up each time the arbitrator and counsel need to re-prepare. The number of days should be kept to a minimum. In accordance with Parkinson's law, attorneys will fill all the days scheduled for the hearing.

The arbitrator also should determine the duration of the hearing after asking the attorneys how much time they will need to present their case. It is a good idea to add one or two days extra at the end in the event of unexpected problems (e.g., a witness, counsel, or the arbitrator has a serious but transient illness).

Another decision that has to be made concerns the length of each hearing day. The arbitrator should not agree to banker's hours or even 10 a.m to four p.m. A too-leisurely proceeding conveys the message that time and cost are not important.

Detailing Claims and Defenses. The arbitrator should set a date for the parties to exchange and submit to the arbitrator detailed statements of their claims, counterclaims and defenses, along with the facts supporting each one, the remedy sought for each claim, and their method of calculating damages.

The arbitrator also should set cut-off dates for filing new or amended claims, defenses and motions related to discovery, joinder of additional parties, and/or consolidation with other proceedings, where permitted by the arbitrator.

It is also important to determine whether any party is seeking attorney fees and if so, the basis for this claim (e.g., a contract or a statute).

Exhibits. The subject of exhibits may be addressed at the initial preliminary hearing or at a later scheduled hearing. Some arbitrators require the parties' attorneys to combine their exhibits in a single exhibit binder or set of binders. This is a time-consuming procedure that generates counsel fees. As a result, it should not be used in regular cases. Arbitrators should be willing to work with more than one set of exhibit binders.

It can save time at the hearing if the exhibit binders are not crowded with documents that the attorneys have no plan to introduce at the hearing on the merits. So it is a good idea for the arbitrator to instruct counsel to use the binders only for exhibits that will actually be introduced in evidence. The arbitrator could also obtain counsel's agreement that all exhibits are deemed admitted into evidence absent a timely objection when the document is first offered or discussed during the merits hearing. The arbitrator could also require counsel to give the arbitrator a core set of exhibits to review prior to the evidentiary hearing.

VIII. Pre-Arbitration Hearing Matters

It is useful to spend time at the initial preliminary hearing (or a later one) discussing efficient methods of presenting evidence at the hearing. One method often used in international arbitration has witnesses testify on direct via a written affidavit as long as they will be available for live cross-examination. The written witness statement may not be a cost-effective or efficient way of presenting evidence for a key witness.

Another option is to present evidence on an issue-by-issue basis when doing so would make it easier for the arbitrator to understand the evidence. For example, in a construction case, it might make sense to present all of the evidence relating to the plumbing and electrical issues together. Similarly, in a construction case with many subcontractors, evidence could be grouped according to the parties and their subcontracts.

Another efficient way of presenting testimony is the "witness panel." This involves having the witnesses (percipient and expert) testify on a specific issue at the same time. Counsel can question the witnesses on the panel in any order. Suppose Witness 1 states, "When the pipe burst, Witness 2 and 3 were there with me." Counsel could then ask Witness 2, "Is this correct?" If he says yes, counsel could then ask Witness 3, "Is that correct?" If she says, "No, I got there a few minutes later," counsel could go back to witness 1 or 2, asking, "Was Witness 3 correct?" and so forth. Testimony obtained in this fashion can produce more accurate evidence. It may also be easier for the arbitrator to understand the evidence.

When both counsel agree to use an expert witness panel (also known as "tandem experts"), a party that was planning to hire a marginally qualified expert may decide to retain a more qualified person.

The arbitrator should alert counsel at the preliminary hearing that if any third-party witnesses will need to be subpoenaed to testify, counsel must request the subpoenas sufficiently in advance to avoid delaying the final hearing.

Another evidence presentation technique that the arbitrator can suggest is a chess clock to hold counsel to his or her time estimate for conducting direct and cross-examination. An alternative is to agree to use the chess clock only during direct examination.

An arbitrator should not automatically accept an estimate of how much time counsel says is needed. The arbitrator's experience and familiarity with the issues should be helpful in determining if either counsel has overstated the time needed.

The Case Management and Scheduling Order. At the end of the initial preliminary hearing, the arbitrator should prepare a case management and scheduling order that indicates all agreements of the parties, whether made by stipulation or otherwise, regarding pre-hearing matters (including the document and ESI exchanges, other types of discovery, the witness list exchange, the evidentiary hearings (including their location, length of hearing day, exhibit book requirements, and efficient evidence presentation techniques), along with the schedule for everything that has been agreed upon. (It may also contain other information that would be helpful to the parties.) The arbitrator's order also should state that the parties will be held to the schedule and that requests to change it will not be granted except for good cause as determined by the arbitrator. The arbitrator should also make this clear orally at the initial preliminary hearing.

IX. What Providers Can Do

Every dispute is important and deserves to be treated as such by everyone involved in the arbitration process. The integrity of the process demands nothing less.

There is no "one size fits all" arbitration process. Providers should offer choices to enable the design of economical and efficient dispute resolution processes, teach courses in mediation and arbitration advocacy, train their case managers, arbitrators and mediators in efficient case management, continually improve their arbitration and mediation rules, publish information on the value and effectiveness of their procedures, attract arbitrators with personal and case management skills, and provide other administrative services to meet the needs of users.

The CCA protocols urges providers to:

- Promote “stepped” dispute resolution processes.
- Limit discovery to essential information.
- Promote restrained but effective motion practice.
- Create rules to set presumptive deadlines for each phase of the arbitration.
- Develop a system of evaluation and feedback for users of arbitration.

Notwithstanding these suggestions, the protocol expresses concern that if providers tinker too much with the process, parties may “feel they did not have their day in court (arbitration).” This places more responsibility on parties and arbitrators to reach agreements that will result in an economical and cost-effective process.

In July of 2015, the AAA Construction Industry Arbitration Rules and Mediation Procedures were revised to incorporate many of the CCA protocols. Among others, these rules now include automatic referral to mediation for all cases with claims exceeding $100,000 (subject to opting out), a greater degree of arbitrator control over the exchange of information, including expensive electronic document production, new preliminary hearing procedures providing detailed guidance to parties and arbitrators, and the authority for arbitrators to sanction parties that refuse to comply with the rules or the arbitrator’s orders.

X. Conclusion

Parties, attorneys, arbitrators and providers can build a better way to resolve disputes if they work together to do so. Parties and their in-house attorneys should identify the company’s dispute resolution goals and objectives and communicate them to outside counsel. Attorneys who don’t yet have arbitration advocacy training should obtain it so that they can arbitrate cases without “turning over every stone” and bringing every conceivable motion. Arbitrators should wisely exercise their management authority and not be afraid to say no. They should also be teachers as they suggest techniques more appropriate for arbitration. Finally, arbitration providers must train arbitrators to better manage cases and create rules that will expedite the arbitration process.

CHAPTER 4

WHAT PARTIES MIGHT BE GIVING UP AND GAINING WHEN DECIDING NOT TO LITIGATE: A COMPARISON OF LITIGATION, ARBITRATION AND MEDIATION

Donald L. Carper and John B. LaRocco[*]

Deciding whether to litigate, arbitrate, or mediate requires an understanding of three dispute resolution processes. The authors begin with the major characteristics of litigation, and then discuss whether these characteristics are present in arbitration and mediation, and if not, how these processes differ.

I. Introduction

Why one might choose to use an alternative dispute resolution (ADR) process to resolve a legal problem is an interesting question, but it is not the focus of this article. Instead, it focuses on the fundamental attributes of litigation and explores whether these attributes are present in private arbitration and mediation. The purpose is to help people make an informed decision about the process they wish to use to resolve their dispute. This comparison also could help designers of ADR systems identify and preserve attributes desired by parties and jettison those that are not.

We grew up when litigation was the main avenue of dispute resolution. Arbitration was not then accepted by the courts. The attitude of the time toward righting wrongs was to litigate. The phrase "sue the bastard" was in common use.[1]

---

[*] The authors teach at the College of Business Administration, California State University, in Sacramento, where Donald L. Carper is a professor emeritus of legal studies in business and conflict management, and John B. LaRocco is a professor of law. Prof. Carper is also an arbitrator and mediator and Prof. LaRocco is a labor arbitrator, mediator and fact finder. He serves on the American Arbitration Association's labor panel.

[1] This was the caption on a comedic figurine sold in the 1960s that looked like (but wasn't) "Rumpole of the Bailey." These figurines, called "Creepy Creatures," were sold

The acceptance of the courthouse as the place to resolve disputes has improved the lot of millions of persons worldwide. However, as important a civilizing influence as this was, the courtroom is not, and should not be, the only means of dispute resolution in a civilized society. Abraham Lincoln predicted the importance of litigation alternatives when he wrote, "Discourage litigation. Persuade your neighbors to compromise whenever you can. Point out to them how the nominal winner is often the real loser—in fees, expenses, and waste of time."[2] He also suggested that lawyers should help the parties settle their disputes out of court and not worry that their income will suffer.[3] He recognized that even if the rule of law is the foundation of a civil society, litigation should be used only as a last resort.

In recent years we all have become more familiar with ADR processes. Even the courts have adopted their own ADR programs to better control their dockets and close cases faster. Thus, we now see ADR processes playing a role in maintaining social stability and order.

Yet the main reason for the growth in the use of ADR is not that these processes are inherently superior to litigation. Rather, it is dissatisfaction with the litigation model. Here are some often-quoted reasons for using ADR[4]:

- to lower court caseloads and expenses;
- to reduce the parties' expenses and the time it takes to resolve disputes;
- to encourage speedy settlements;
- to improve the public's satisfaction with the justice system;
- to encourage resolutions that are suited to the parties' needs;
- to increase voluntary compliance with resolutions;
- to restore the influence of neighborhood and community values and the cohesiveness of communities;
- to provide accessible forums to people with disputes;

---

in the late 1960s and early 1970s by Russ & Wallace Berrie & Co. Rumpole is a fictional character created by British barrister and author John Mortimer. The BBC series "Rumpole of the Bailey" aired on U.S. television on the Public Broadcasting System.

[2] Quoted in Frederick Trevor Hill, *Lincoln the Lawyer* 102-103 (Legal Classics Library, Gryphon ed. 1996) (facsimile of 1906 ed. by Century Co.).

[3] *Id.* ("As a peacemaker the lawyer has a superior opportunity of becoming a good man. There will always be enough business.")

[4] Stephen Goldberg *et al.*, *Dispute Resolution, Negotiation, Mediation and Other Processes* (Little, Brown 1992).

- to teach the public to try more effective processes for settling disputes;
- to permit parties to select the person(s) who will judge the dispute;
- to bring expertise to dispute resolutions; and
- to overcome flaws in jury decision-making.

It is no coincidence that the first three reasons involve the perception that litigation costs too much and takes too much time. The other reasons are clearly important, but it is doubtful that ADR would have achieved its current popularity without the perceived deficiencies of the courts. We suspect that if court reforms could reduce the time and expense of discovery as well as the time it takes to get to trial, the impact on ADR would be dramatic. But effective pre-trial reforms of the litigation process are not being made.

II. Essential Attributes of the American Judicial System

American court systems have the following features:

1. They are created and funded by government and are available in every U.S. jurisdiction.
2. Courts provide theoretical access to all upon application by those with a claim.
3. Decisions are made by a judge trained in the law, and a jury of one's peers (unless waived).
4. A variety of legal and equitable remedies are available depending on the facts and law.
5. Court proceedings take place in public.
6. Court proceedings are recorded.
7. Court litigation is adversarial in nature.
8. Litigants in court must adhere to strict rules of procedure and evidence.
9. Courts must apply the law.
10. Due process must be afforded in court.
11. A prevailing litigant can obtain assistance from the court to force compliance with a judgment or verdict.
12. Appeals are allowed for legal error.
13. Appellate decisions are usually published.

Next we examine each listed attribute and then determine whether arbitration and mediation are comparable, and if not, how they differ.

1. Courts are Created and Funded by Government and are Available in Every U.S. Jurisdiction

The federal and state court systems are created by state and federal constitutions. Government pays the costs of maintaining the judiciary through tax dollars or other revenue.

Courts exist in every state throughout the United States and in most counties. One generally does not need to travel far to find a court to hear a legal claim, although a conflict may arise over which court is the proper forum.

Courts are staffed with judges who are either elected or appointed to office, as well as with clerks, marshals, bailiffs and others who carry out their operations. These employees are provided at taxpayer expense. Litigants do not pay judges to hear their cases. Thus, from the point of view of the public, courts are convenient, easy to find, and not expensive. Court filing fees vary by jurisdiction and are usually not very high.

While the cost of access is low, the cost of prosecution and defense can be onerous because litigants must pay the costs of legal representation (unless the lawyer accepts a contingency fee arrangement). Under the American rule, the parties are responsible for paying the fees of their own counsel.[5] Because litigation is a lengthy process, counsel fees are the largest part of the cost of litigating in court. In addition, litigants must pay the fees and expenses for their own expert witnesses (and expert reports) as well as deposition costs (i.e., court reporter fees).

There are also non-monetary costs due to the disruptive nature of litigation as well as an emotional toll. For business people, the time spent on litigation can not only increase workload, but also reduce business revenue.

Arbitration: A key difference between litigation and arbitration is that arbitration involves additional fees that the parties must pay in addition to their counsel and witness fees.

Filing and other fees. Whether there is a filing fee depends on whether the arbitration is *ad hoc* or administered. In *ad hoc* arbitration, the parties and the arbitrator take care of all the details themselves,

---

[5] In some instances, however, a statute will allow a prevailing party to have its legal costs and expenses paid by the losing party. Also, in a contract, the parties may agree that the prevailing party can recover its attorney fees.

including negotiating the arbitrator's compensation. As a result, unless the arbitrator has a filing fee, no fee is necessary to initiate the arbitration process.

In administered arbitration, the parties contract with a neutral arbitration provider, like the American Arbitration Association (AAA), to help facilitate the dispute, provide the arbitration rules and a roster of neutrals from which the parties can select an arbitrator with the appropriate expertise. The provider assigns a case manager to help the parties' counsel. Providers charge filing and possibly other fees for their services.

Provider filing fees vary based on different factors. Under the AAA Commercial Arbitration Procedures, the claimant pays a filing fee based on the amount of the claim, while the respondent pays a filing fee if it asserts a counterclaim. The AAA also charges a case service fee, which applies only if the case does not settle before the first hearing. The fee is payable in advance of the first hearing date but it will be refunded if the case settles with no hearing held.[6]

The AAA has different fee schedules for different kinds of cases. In employment cases arbitrated under employer-sponsored ADR programs, the AAA Employment Arbitration Rules cap the amount of the filing fee that the employee must pay, placing most of the cost on the employer.[7]

In consumer cases, the AAA's filing fees are based on the actual damages claimed, and not on any additional damages, such as attorney fees or punitive damages. A special waiver rule applies to consumer cases in California.[8]

Hearing room fees. The parties may need a conference room in a neutral location to hold the hearing. The venue of the arbitration is often stated in the parties' agreement. In administered arbitration, the parties may be able to rent a conference room from the provider. This cost is borne by the parties. Alternatively, space might be provided free by one of the parties or counsel. The arbitrator may also provide space for a fee.

Arbitrator compensation and expenses. Unlike parties to a lawsuit, arbitrating parties have to pay the decision maker's (i.e., the arbitrator's) compensation. Arbitrator fees vary widely. Arbitrators usually bill by the hour but some bill by the day.

Arbitrator compensation includes "study time" and the time spent writing the award. If the parties request a brief written explanation of the

[6] The AAA arbitration rules can be accessed at www.adr.org.
[7] AAA Employment Rule R. 48.
[8] AAA Consumer-Related Supplementary Procedure C-8.

award, or more detailed findings of fact and law, the arbitrator's compensation will be more than if the arbitrator writes a one-line award stating the prevailing party on each of the claims and counterclaims and the amount awarded, if any. Arbitrator compensation will be still higher if the parties desire to use a panel of three arbitrators.

One arbitrator is usually appointed to hear small disputes. However, having to pay the compensation of even one arbitrator in a small dispute could be a disincentive to arbitrating. This impediment is eliminated in employment arbitration cases under employer-promulgated plans and in small consumer arbitrations administered by the AAA. The AAA places the burden of paying the arbitrator's compensation on the employer. The AAA also has a special rule applicable to consumer arbitrations. It caps the consumer's portion of the arbitrator's fee at $125 for claims under $10,000.[9]

The parties have to pay the arbitrator's expenses, including those for travel. If the arbitrators do not reside locally, travel expenses will be higher.

Counsel and witness fees. Arbitrating parties must pay their own counsel and witness fees. If a party prevails in arbitration, the arbitrator may award attorney fees only if provided for in the arbitration agreement or allowed by law.

Arbitration at its best is less rule-driven (discussed on page 56), and therefore more streamlined and efficient than litigation. For that reason and because there are limited grounds to appeal an arbitration award (discussed on page 58), arbitrating parties should incur significantly lower counsel fees than they would if they were litigating in court.

Mediation: In addition to counsel fees, the main cost of mediation to the parties is the mediator's compensation. Most mediators bill by the hour, but some very "in-demand" mediators charge by the day. The parties share the mediator's fee.

There is no "hearing" in mediation and witnesses are rarely needed. In technical cases, however, one or both parties may retain an expert to assist with some aspect of the case. The party who retains the expert must pay the expert's fees and expenses.

---

[9] *Id.* and AAA Employment Rule R-48.

Mediation can be arranged directly with a mediator or through an ADR provider, such as the AAA. The AAA does not charge a filing fee for mediation.[10]

Mediation can be held in any room. A mediation involving a large number of participants might require a conference room, which could involve a room rental fee.

Mediation is likely to be the least expensive private ADR process in terms of counsel fees. However, if the mediation does not succeed, the parties may later find themselves in arbitration or litigation. Statistics show that mediation has a high settlement rate, which offsets this risk for parties that seriously want to find a mutually satisfactory way to end their dispute.

2. *Courts Provide Theoretical Access to All Upon Application by Plaintiffs*

Access to court is provided by the U.S. and state Constitutions. Anyone can file a complaint in court, although some statutes or court rules require the complainant to verify the claim to screen frivolous lawsuits.[11]

Courts permit parties to appear without counsel (*pro se*), which theoretically increases access. Nevertheless, most parties do not wish to litigate without legal representation. The problem is that their claim may be too small to obtain a lawyer. This is a particular problem with employment and consumer disputes.

There are conditions to access particular courts. The plaintiff must ensure that the court has subject matter jurisdiction over the dispute and personal jurisdiction over the defendant. When the court has personal jurisdiction, the defendant must appear. A defendant that fails to appear can have a default judgment entered against it.

As discussed above, there is a relatively small fee to file a case in court, which is not usually an impediment to litigating.

Arbitration and Mediation: Private arbitration and mediation are not accessible in the way that courts are. Both ADR processes are contractual in nature. In other words, they require the parties to have

---

[10] A portion of the mediator's compensation is allocated for AAA's services. AAA Commercial Mediation Rule M-17.

[11] Some states require plaintiffs in a medical malpractice action to file a verified written medical expert opinion indicating that reasonable grounds exist to find that each named defendant was negligent. Fla. Stat. Ann. § 766.203.

entered into an agreement to arbitrate or mediate prior to or after the dispute arose (even after litigation has commenced). When the parties have signed a pre-dispute ADR agreement, each can take legal steps to compel the other to participate in the ADR process.

Sometimes a nonparty to an arbitration agreement tries to compel a signatory party to arbitrate and *vice versa.* There are some theories on which to compel arbitration in these circumstances.[12]

Thus, access to arbitration or mediation is conditioned on voluntary participation by the parties or a court compelling compliance with an arbitration or mediation agreement.

Ironically, parties who have not entered into an ADR agreement may be compelled to use an ADR process under a court-annexed ADR program. Usually this process is mediation. The prospect of ending up in a court-ordered mediation (or arbitration) should be compared to using private ADR. It may be that the private process has significant advantages, such as the ability to select the neutral.

Parties have the right to be represented by counsel in arbitration and mediation. But having counsel is not a requirement in these more informal processes.

Arbitration fees, discussed in the previous section can create an access problem in consumer and employment cases. However, some providers, including the AAA, have ameliorated this problem in their rules by limiting the amount that employees and consumers must pay.

An access problem can arise in consumer contracts where the vendor's arbitration agreement designates a far-away inconvenient forum for the arbitration. In a few cases involving small consumer claims and the contention that this was unconscionable, consumers were successful in having the forum changed to a more convenient one.[13]

3. Decisions in Court are Made by a Judge Trained in the Law or a Jury (Unless Waived)

The United States appears to make the most comprehensive use of juries in the modern world. The jury has virtually disappeared as means of resolving civil disputes in England where it was developed.[14] The waning use of juries was supposedly a response to the growing

---

[12] These involve theories of equitable estoppel, agency piercing the corporate veil, etc.

[13] *See*, e.g., B*rower v. Gateway 2000, Inc.*, 676 N.Y.S.2d 569 (App. Div. 1998) and *Patterson v. ITT Consumer Fin. Corp*., 18 Cal. Rptr. 2d 563 (Cal. Ct. App. 1993).

[14] Charles Joiner, *Civil Justice and the Jury* 59 (Prentice Hall 1962).

complexity of the civil law and the time and expense consumed by the jury process. A civil jury is now the exception in the United Kingdom.[15]

Views about the jury process vary. "Why should anyone think that 12 persons brought in from the street, selected in various ways, for their lack of general ability, should have any special capacity for deciding controversies between persons?"[16] Nevertheless, the jury is still held in high regard in America.

Court litigants cannot select the judge or jurors. However, they can exclude certain jurors "for cause." (Neutral decision makers are discussed on pages 57-58.) Most jurisdictions have rules to prevent judge shopping.

A judge assigned to the case or selected through a random process decides the applicable law if it is in controversy (which it often is), and the jury decides the facts based on the evidence submitted and applies the law (as instructed by the judge) to the facts. An exception is the bench trial, in which the litigants waive the right to a jury. In equity cases, the judge is also the finder of fact.

Judges and juries rarely have special knowledge about the field of the dispute. It is not unusual for a juror with special knowledge to be excused for cause from a jury by counsel for one of the parties.

Jurors are essentially unpaid (they may receive a nominal amount per day) and untrained, which can cause flawed verdicts.

Arbitration: Arbitration has an important advantage over litigation in that the parties can select the person who will decide their dispute. This advantage is due to the contractual nature of arbitration, which allows the parties to establish the process that they want.

The arbitrator finds the facts, applies the law, and is the sole decision maker on the issues submitted to arbitration. In effect, the arbitrator performs the same functions as a judge in a bench trial.

The parties can decide whether they want to use one arbitrator or a panel of three. (As noted above, three arbitrators cost more to use, so they are more often used in large cases where there is much at stake.) The parties can agree on the qualifications they want the arbitrator to have and even name the arbitrator.

---

[15] Woolf & Williams, "Juries, Justice for a Generation" 9 (Plenary Sessions ABA, The Senate of the Inns of Court and the Bar. The Law Society of England and Wales, 1985).

[16] Quote attributed to former Harvard Dean Erwin Griswold in Stephen J. Adler, *The Jury: Trial And Error in the American Courtroom* 119 (Times Books 1994).

Arbitrators who are selected by parties to decide cases are rarely, if ever, ordinary laypersons. Most disputants want an expert in the field of the dispute (e.g., a patent lawyer, a construction lawyer) to decide the dispute.[17] For the most part, arbitrators selected to hear cases are usually lawyers. This is probably because arbitrators are selected by lawyers (i.e., counsel for the parties and not the parties themselves) and lawyers are likely to feel more comfortable with an attorney-arbitrator. Another reason for selecting a lawyer as the arbitrator is that the parties' attorneys may be concerned that an arbitrator who lacks legal training might be less able or inclined to apply the law.

Non-lawyer arbitrators are more often chosen when a dispute involves highly technical or scientific matters, calls for a contract interpretation rather than an issue of law, and is highly fact-dependent. It can be advantageous to have a non-lawyer expert on a panel with one or two lawyer-arbitrators.

People expect arbitrators to come up with better decisions than ordinary jurors, especially in highly complex commercial cases. They also expect arbitrators to come up with less emotional decisions.

Mediation: Mediation is also a consensual process, which means the parties can select the mediator of their choice. People who want a facilitative mediation tend to choose a mediator who has excellent mediation skills. People who want a more evaluative mediator tend to select a lawyer-mediator who specializes in the field in dispute (e.g., a patent or construction lawyer). Mediation does not involve a decision by a third party. The mediator's goal is to help the parties reach a mutually acceptable settlement.

4. A Variety of Legal and Equitable Remedies are Available Depending on Facts and Law

Court litigants can seek any remedy in law or equity that is legally allowed for each stated cause of action. Courts may not order other remedies. For example, a court may not require a party to sell its interest in a partnership unless a contract required that party to do so.[18]

---

[17] The expert neutral must not stray from the record by using the neutral's own extensive experience (unknown by the parties) to decide the dispute. Going outside the record deprives the parties of due process.

[18] Donald Carper, "Remedies in Business Arbitration," 46(3) *Arb. J.* 49-58 (Sept. 1991).

In commercial transactions, the parties can agree to limit their legal remedies. However, courts are reluctant to enforce agreements to limit damages that they deem unfair.

Arbitration: Arbitrators have very broad remedial powers compared to a judge. They are not limited to awarding remedies that a court can award. They can order any remedy they consider just and proper in the circumstances. The only limitations on this are state law and the parties' agreement. The revised Uniform Arbitration Act (RUAA), which has been enacted in 13 jurisdictions, takes this approach.[19] It restricts an award of punitive or exemplary damages to situations in which such damages are allowed by law and allows awards of attorney fees only if permitted by law or the parties' agreement.[20]

Parties have great latitude in restricting the arbitrator's remedies. But this is not the case in consumer and employment arbitration. Limitations on arbitrator remedies in consumer and employment contracts are likely to be held unenforceable if they prevent the consumer or employee from obtaining a remedy available by statute (e.g., treble damages, attorney fees).

Mediation: Damages are not "awarded" in mediation because, as noted previously, there is no third-party decision maker awarding any remedy or relief. Mediation is an assisted negotiation and the parties must agree to the terms of settlement.

5. Court Proceedings Take Place in Public

Consistent with free speech and a free press, trials in American courts are public, with a few exceptions. Anyone can attend a criminal or civil trial, including journalists. Cases that make the front page of the newspaper are an exception because they generate so much interest. Thus, in those cases, court attendance is restricted and monitored.[21]

There is seldom any restriction on trial observers making public their observations about the trial. However, the court may place some constraints on what the parties and their counsel may say. Thus, in general, information about disputes is available to the community and the nation. Court TV and the Internet have provided new meaning to making

[19] These jurisdictions are Alaska, Colorado, District of Columbia, Hawaii, Nevada, New Jersey, New Mexico, North Carolina, North Dakota, Oklahoma, Oregon, Utah and Washington.

[20] RUAA (2000) § 1.

[21] Dominick Dunne provides an amusing discussion of jockeying for seats and placement at the O.J. Simpson trial in *Another City, Not My Own* 70-74 (Crown Pub 1997).

litigation public.[22] In many states, trials can be televised, substantially broadening the public's exposure to cases that otherwise might not attract much interest.

Not only are court proceedings public, so are pre-trial filings. Anyone interested in a case can go to the clerk's office to view the court's file. Also, private databases have copies of briefs and memoranda of law prepared by counsel. These, however, usually are available for a fee.

Trial court decisions are also published in the legal press. But the greatest exposure of court proceedings comes from the national press and journalists who routinely report on high profile cases and their outcomes.

The publicity that flows from court litigation may be unwanted, particularly by defendants and counterclaim-defendants who see the airing of claims against them as damaging to their reputations.

Arbitration and Mediation: While litigation is public, ADR processes are not. Arbitrations and mediations are held in private offices and conference rooms. This is a key reason that parties choose to use them.

While there is no law in the United States protecting the confidentiality of arbitration, institutional arbitration rules usually require the arbitrator to maintain the confidentiality of the proceedings. The parties can agree to keep the existence of their arbitration and the arbitration award private through a confidentiality agreement. Even when parties enter into a confidentiality agreement, one (or both) could decide it is in its best interest to make public that an arbitration exists or reveal what occurred there. Sometimes this gets reported in the press. When this happens, the cat is out of the bag. The only remedy may be a lawsuit for breach of contract.

Unlike court decisions, arbitrators' awards are seldom made public.[23] Even when they are published, sensitive information is redacted so that the awards contain limited useful information.

Mediation, on the other hand, has legal privacy protections. There is the privilege in the Federal Rules of Evidence for settlement discussions. In addition, most states have confidentiality laws in place to encourage mediation. The Uniform Mediation Act, which has been enacted in 10 jurisdictions, confers a nondisclosure privilege on private communications between the mediator and each participant in mediation.[24] This privilege,

---

[22] Although most web searches for filings provide incomplete information, they can now take place in many jurisdictions. For example, for Sacramento County see website www.saccourt.com/indexes.

[23] Some labor awards are published, especially when precedent takes on some importance.

[24] The District of Columbia, Illinois, Iowa, Nebraska, New Jersey, Ohio, South Dakota, Utah, Vermont, and Washington.

however, only protects mediation communications from disclosure in future legal or administrative proceedings.

Arbitrations and mediations involving a public sector entity may be subject to open meeting laws.

6. *Court Proceedings are Recorded*

Court reporters keep a record of court proceedings. This record is available to the litigants, the court and appellate courts if necessary. Having a record of proceedings is invaluable since it provides a way of determining whether the process was fair and whether any legal errors were committed.

Arbitration and Mediation: Arbitration proceedings (except labor cases) are rarely transcribed. If the parties want a record of the hearing, they must pay for it. Thus, there is rarely any record that a reviewing court can examine. Since the grounds to obtain judicial review of an arbitration award are limited, the need for a hearing transcript may be diminished and may not be worth the cost.

Mediation proceedings are rarely, if ever, recorded or transcribed, since doing so could jeopardize the confidentiality of mediation communications. Even in court-annexed mediation, the court generally may be told only whether the case settled or not.

7. *Court Proceedings are Adversarial in Nature*

A fundamental characteristic of the U.S. judicial process is its adversarial nature. The adversarial system places responsibility on each party to prove that it is right and the other side is wrong. As a consequence of the adversary system, each litigant has an absolute right to legal representation (at their own expense in civil trials).

The adversarial process is extremely competitive. It is the reason for our dependence on lawyers. The party with plentiful resources is in a better position because it can afford to pay counsel and thoroughly investigate and prepare its case. Attorney contingency fee arrangements somewhat neutralize this advantage. However, contingency fee arrangements are usually acceptable to attorneys only when they determine that the case involves substantial damages and has a strong likelihood of success. This means that many litigants with small claims may be unable to find legal representation, preventing them from participating in the adversarial process unless they appear *pro se*, which most people do not feel equipped to do.

The adversary system of litigation exacerbates, rather than reduces, conflict. Litigation may be civilized combat but it is very wearing, emotionally and financially, on the parties.

Arbitration and Mediation: Arbitration is an adversarial process in that each side is responsible for persuading the finder of fact that it is right. But unlike litigation, arbitration is less formal and highly flexible. The parties can decide to do certain things together, like prepare a book of joint exhibits or a time line that would help the arbitrator understand or decide the case. They would be unable to do this in litigation because of the authentication requirements.

As in the adversarial process, parties in arbitration have the right to legal representation but they must pay for it.[25]

Mediation is not an adversarial process, even though the parties are on the opposite side of the issues and are likely to be very angry at each other. It is a facilitated negotiation. The mediator will generally seek to reduce the tensions caused by the conflict. One mediator technique is to move the parties away from focusing on their "rights" to focusing on their "interests." Mediators also can diffuse emotions by allowing each side to vent their feelings in private caucuses. This helps the parties address their negative feelings and then move on to considering ways to put the dispute behind them. Mediation is often therapeutic for the disputants.

8. Litigants in Court Must Adhere to Strict Court Procedures

The courts provide a forum for the parties to present their evidence so the fact finder (usually the jury) can decide which evidence is credible and then apply the law (determined by the judge) to the facts.[26]

The parties' counsel must strictly follow the applicable codes of civil procedure and evidence. These procedures include, among other things, rules for making various kinds of pre- and post-trial motions, conducting discovery, authenticating evidence, objecting to evidence, and filing pleadings in proper form.

---

[25] This right cannot be waived in jurisdictions that have enacted the RUAA. *See* cmt. to RUAA § 16: "Section 4(b)(4) provides that a waiver of the right to be represented by an attorney under Section 16 prior to the initiation of an arbitration proceeding under Section 9 is ineffective, but an employer and a labor organization may waive the right to representation by an attorney in a labor arbitration."

[26] "A court's task thus divides into two parts: First, it finds the facts of the case—whether one man killed another, or drove eighty miles an hour, or paid his rent, or signed a certain paper. Second, it determines what legal rule covers those facts. The court's decision then results." Jerome Frank, *Courts on Trial, Myth and Reality in American Justice* 3 (1949).

Discovery. Most attorneys consider discovery essential. It often is the only way of obtaining information in the possession and control of the other party. For example, much corporate information is not available unless acquired through document discovery. Discovery also helps to somewhat level the playing field for parties who do not have the resources to conduct an investigation, such as consumers and employees.

Discovery in litigation is usually a long, drawn-out process. It tends to go to excess because the parties usually serve broadly worded document requests and lengthy interrogatories, and take numerous depositions of each other's employees. Sometimes this is designed to intimidate the other party. Discovery disputes are common. They often involve refusals to produce documents based on a legal privilege or an objection. Disputes may also arise out of a refusal to produce a party witness for a deposition, or to allow the witness to answer certain questions. These disputes delay the trial and increase counsel fees.

Motion practice/dispositive motions. Motion practice is also common in litigation. Parties often challenge the court's jurisdiction or venue, or remove the case to another court, or seek a dispositive ruling in the case, such as on a motion to dismiss for failure to state a claim or for untimeliness (statute of limitations defense), or for a summary judgment. Dispositive motions play an important part in litigation because they provide a means to stop litigations that clearly lack merit or are untimely. If a dispositive motion ends the litigation, it saves money.

Motions, especially dispositive ones, are expensive because they must be accompanied by a well written and well-reasoned memorandum of law supplemented by affidavits. Each side has a chance to respond to the other's motion with an opposing brief. Once all the parties have filed their responding papers, the court usually holds a hearing on the motion, which requires an appearance by all counsel. Then the court issues a decision on the motion, which could be appealed. All of this delays the progress of the litigation and raises the cost of litigating.

Arbitration: Arbitration is not as rule-driven as litigation. The arbitrator has great discretion to manage the process in an efficient way while applying the governing arbitration rules. Because arbitration is consensual, the arbitrator induces opposing counsel to reach an agreement on pre-hearing activities and their scheduling, as well as scheduling the hearing.

In arbitration, judicial rules of procedure and evidence do not apply "unless directed by the contract."[27] As a result, the parties can prepare joint exhibit books for the arbitrator. Authentication of evidence is not required.

Discovery. Discovery in arbitration is much more limited. This is supposed to speed up the resolution of the dispute and reduce cost and is said to be one of the reasons parties agree to arbitrate. We think the assumed benefits of more limited discovery are worthy of study in the next few years.

The AAA Commercial Arbitration Rules place authority to order document production in the hands of the arbitrator.[28] The RUAA requires the arbitrator to take the parties' needs into account in making this decision.[29]

The AAA rules call for all exhibits and witness lists to be exchanged by the parties before the hearing. There is no mention of depositions or other types of discovery. But this does not mean that the arbitrator cannot permit them. The RUAA expressly provides that the arbitrator may allow pre-hearing depositions if requested by a party, and doing so would make the proceedings fair, expeditious and cost-effective.[30] Depositions are just not an automatic feature of every arbitration.

The larger and more complex the dispute, the more discovery will be allowed in arbitration. The more discovery, the longer and more expensive the process.

Motion practice is very limited and infrequent in arbitration. In general, the arbitrator determines objections to his or her own jurisdiction (arbitrability issues), including challenges to the validity of the contract containing the arbitration clause. This is the case under both the AAA rules and the RUAA.[31] However, some courts are required to rule on certain arbitrability challenges. Going to court on an arbitrability issue can seriously delay and increase the cost of resolving the dispute.

Dispositive motions may be submitted and heard by arbitrators (these motions are discussed in more detail on page 62), but this is not the norm. Therefore, early dismissal of a meritless claim is less likely in arbitration than in litigation.

---

[27] Elkouri & Elkouri, *How Arbitration Works* 341 (6th ed. BNA 2003). See AAA Commercial Rule R-31.

[28] AAA Commercial Rule R-21.

[29] RUAA § 17(c)(c).

[30] RUAA § 17(b).

[31] AAA Commercial Rule R-7 and RUAA § 6(c).

Mediation: The mediator determines the procedures. Court procedures do not apply at all. There is no motion practice.

Some (but not full) discovery must have been undertaken for the parties to be able to negotiate and decide whether they want to settle. If no (or an insufficient amount of) discovery has taken place, the mediator may postpone the mediation session until the needed discovery is completed.

If a claim in mediation lacks legal merit, that should become apparent to the party making the claim in private caucus with the mediator, leading to an early end to the mediation.

The length of a mediation depends on the complexity of the dispute and the number of disputed issues. Small disputes can be mediated in a day or less.

9. Courts Must Apply the Law

The Internet has made access to the sources of U.S. and state law easier to access than at any time in history. Courts apply the sources of law—federal and state constitutions, statutes, administrative regulations, and judicial precedent (appellate decisions and decisions by the U.S. Supreme Court)—in individual cases. This enables courts to decide cases with similar facts in a similar way. The rule of *stare decisis* makes it possible to predict how a court might rule. But the outcome is far from certain because judges and juries often make unexpected (and wrong) decisions.

As we note later, because trial court decisions may be reviewed for errors of law, judges tend to be cautious in their application of the law.

Arbitration and Mediation: There is probably less outcome-predictability in arbitration because arbitration awards do not usually serve as legal precedent. More importantly, arbitrators are not required to follow the law unless the parties otherwise provide in their arbitration agreement. Thus, they can decide cases based on principles of fairness and equity. There is also the fact that some arbitrators are not lawyers and thus have no legal training, which could lead to less predictable outcomes. On the other hand, it is the job of the parties' advocates to make the arbitrator aware of the applicable law so that the arbitrator, whether a lawyer or not, can apply it to the material facts.

In arbitration of statutory disputes, arbitrators must apply the law. The Employment Due Process Protocol, promulgated by the AAA and other organizations, calls for arbitrators to be trained in the relevant statutes.[32] The AAA will not administer employment arbitrations under employer ADR programs that do not comply with this protocol.[33]

The law is also supposed to be applied in international arbitration. The AAA International Arbitration Rules provide that the arbitrator should follow the law designated by the parties, or if no law is designated, the law the arbitrator deems appropriate.[34]

The issue of outcome predictability does not arise in mediation because, once again, there is no outcome decided by a third party. The parties either agree on a settlement or they don't, in which case the mediation ends. However, a party's decision to settle is often based on the view that the applicable law is not in its favor. Conversely, a party may resist settlement when it believes the law supports its claims.

10. Due Process Must Be Afforded in Court

To protect litigants in court, the basic due process requirements are: fair notice and an opportunity to be heard. Other beacons of due process are a fair hearing, a neutral decision maker, and trial by jury.

Litigation procedures call for the defendant to receive adequate notice of the filing of a claim and its nature so the defendant has time to prepare a response to the claim. Litigants can vacate a default due to inadequate or defective notice.

Litigation rules also provide the parties with the opportunity to gather facts, respond to pretrial motions, and to have their side of the case heard at trial where they can present evidence and testimony, subject to the rules of evidence, and cross-examine adverse witnesses to test their credibility. To help parties present their case, courts can compel witnesses to appear. The court's subpoena power is critical when adverse witnesses are necessary.

Judges and juries are supposed to be unbiased. Parties can seek the recusal of a judge who has an interest in the matter. As to juries, the parties have a set number of juror challenges for cause when they think a juror may be partial to one side. However, true neutrality is never assured.

Arbitration: Arbitration is supposed to be a fair and expeditious process. When it is properly designed, it has due process protections for users, including notice, a neutral and independent decision maker, an

---

[32] The Due Process Protocol for Statutory Employment Disputes can be accessed on the AAA's website at www.adr.org/sp.asp?id=22019.

[33] *See* "AAA's Policy on Employment ADR" in the AAA employment rules.

[34] Art. 28(1).

opportunity to challenge the arbitrator for bias, and an opportunity to be heard.

Federal arbitration law provides that arbitrators can subpoena witnesses to attend the hearing and compel them to produce documents.[35]

As noted above, the AAA adheres to the Employment Due Process Protocol. The Association also was involved in promulgating, with other interested organizations, due process protocols for consumer and healthcare disputes.[36]

Courts are sensitive to the issue of due process in employment and consumer arbitration and they have closely examined arbitration agreements that are infected with procedural unfairness, and may refuse to enforce them. Federal and state arbitration laws also allow an arbitration award to be vacated on any ground for the revocation of a contract.[37] This includes unconscionability.

The classic arbitration process contemplates that each side will be able to present its case at a hearing that is somewhat less formal than in court. At the hearing, the parties can put on their direct witnesses and cross-examine each other's witnesses. Failure to allow a party to present any evidence or witnesses surely constitutes a procedural defect that would result in an award being vacated.[38] However, an arbitrator's refusal of a party's request to hear certain witnesses might not warrant this result if the testimony would be repetitive. The AAA rules instruct arbitrators to make sure to give each side the opportunity to present its case.[39]

---

[35] The RUAA permits arbitrators to subpoena witnesses for pre-hearing depositions. Some courts have found that the FAA does not allow witnesses to be subpoenaed except to the hearing.

[36] Available on the AAA website at www.adr.org.

[37] *E.g.* Federal Arbitration Act, 9 U.S.C. § 2 and Cal. Civ. Pro. Code, tit. 9 § 1281, both of which make a written agreement to arbitrate enforceable "save upon such grounds as exist for the revocation of any contract." Awards can be vacated on various grounds, some of which might involve a denial of due process. However, the losing party must allege the specific grounds stated in the applicable statute. See e.g., 9 Cal. Civ. Pro. Code § 1286.2(3).

[38] Refusing to postpone the hearing, upon sufficient cause shown, or in refusing to hear evidence pertinent and material to the controversy are grounds for vacating an award under FAA § 10. This could cover the refusal to allow presentation of witnesses and opportunity to cross-examine. See also RUAA § 23(3).

[39] AAA Commercial Rule R-30.

There is some case law allowing dispositive motions in arbitration and holding that the right to present one's case does not mean that the parties have a right to a plenary hearing on the merits.[40]

The AAA employment rules directly address dispositive motions. The rule requires the arbitrator's permission to file a dispositive motion. The arbitrator may allow the filing only if he or she determines that there is "substantial cause that the motion is likely to succeed and dispose of or narrow" the issues in dispute.[41] Other AAA rules do not preclude arbitrators from hearing dispositive motions and they impliedly authorize them.[42]

Allowing the parties adequate discovery can be a due process issue in arbitration if an arbitrator is considering a dispositive motion.[43]

Arbitrators are required to be neutral and have no interest in the case they are deciding. The rules for disclosure of conflicts of interest are fairly rigorous.[44]

The training and qualifications of neutrals in ADR proceedings are highly variable. Whether neutrals should be certified is a controversial issue.

Mediation: In commercial mediation between sophisticated parties, due process is not an issue because there is no imbalance in bargaining power and no decision by a third party. Since there is no "hearing" as such, witnesses are less important than in litigation.

Neutrality is also expected of mediators. However, it may be less important if the parties perceive a prior relationship with one of the parties as a benefit.

11. Successful Litigants Can Obtain Assistance from the Court to Force Compliance with a Judgment or Verdict

Court rules provide for post-judgment processes to assist successful litigants in securing compliance with a judgment or verdict. These processes leave much to be desired, but they do exist.

---

[40] *See Schlessinger v. Rosenfeld, Meyer & Susman*, 40 Cal. App. 4th 1096 (1995). See also Albert G, Ferris & W. Lee Biddle, "The Use of Dispositive Motions in Arbitration," 62(3) *Disp. Resol. J.* 16, 23-24 (Aug-Oct. 2007).

[41] AAA Employment Rule R-27.

[42] AAA Commercial Rule R-30(b).

[43] Ferris & Biddle, *supra* . 40, at 23-24.

[44] The Arbitrator Disclosure Sheet provided for arbitrations in California, if applied to judges would, in our opinion, significantly impact the ability of judges to sit on many court cases.

Arbitration and Mediation: In arbitration, parties who wish to enforce an arbitration agreement against an uncooperative signatory have remedies to enforce the agreement. Likewise, prevailing parties in arbitration have court remedies to enforce an arbitration award. The latter process involves transforming an award into a court judgment. Thereafter, judicially provided collection processes are available.

In mediation, one hopes there will be compliance with the mediation agreement. However, if a party to a mediation agreement refuses to mediate, the other party can seek to have the agreement enforced in court, albeit not under the Federal Arbitration Act in the view of the 11th Circuit, which recently held that a mediation agreement is not enforceable under the FAA.[45]

When a party breaches a settlement agreement reached in mediation, the agreement may be enforceable in court, unless it requires ADR to resolve the dispute.

12. Appeals are Allowed for Legal Error

The court system allows the losing party to appeal an error of law made by the judge in the case (for example, the denial of a motion, the refusal to allow certain evidence, or the giving of a wrong jury instruction). In order to be appealable, counsel for the losing party must have made an objection on the record in the trial. Appeals are routinely filed in litigation, crowding the dockets of the appellate courts.

On appeal, the reviewing court acts as a check on judicial fairness and ensures consistency in the application of the law in the court's jurisdiction.

Arbitration: A losing party in arbitration can appeal an award but only under limited circumstances set forth in federal or state arbitration law, or under accepted common law doctrine. Technically, this is not an appeal but review by a district court.

The statutory grounds for judicial review of an arbitration award are a denial of due process, arbitrator bias, fraud, or exceeding the scope of the arbitrator's authority.[46] A recognized common law ground is a violation of public policy, which applies mainly in the labor arbitration

[45] *Advanced Bodycare Solutions, LLC v. Thione Int'l,* No. 07-12309, 2008 WL 1775001 (11th Cir. April 21, 2008).

[46] FAA § 10.

area.[47] None of the statutory or common law grounds permit a party to appeal an error of law by the arbitrator.

The fact that there are limited grounds for judicial review of arbitration awards is considered by many lawyers and parties to be a key disadvantage of arbitration. But the limited scope of arbitration appeals is what makes arbitration less expensive and shorter than litigation.

Does the absence of appeals for legal correctness discourage arbitrators from taking their decision-making responsibilities as seriously as they should in order to produce a fully reasoned decision? It has been suggested that parties require arbitrators to produce a short written explanation of the award to make sure that the arbitrator has thought through the decision.

Mediation: In mediation, there is no decision and therefore no appeal. The result of mediation is a mutually acceptable agreement with which the parties should be satisfied. Unsuccessful mediations simply place the parties back where they were before the mediation; i.e., with an unresolved conflict.

13. Appellate Decisions Are Usually Made Public

Appellate court decisions are usually published, creating legal precedent. Commentators often scrutinize and then publish criticism of these decisions, which are sometimes further appealed to a higher court. In this way, obviously wrong trial court decisions are checked by appellate scholarship. The prospect of having their rulings appealed deters judges from making outrageous rulings.

Arbitration: Arbitration awards seldom are published (except for labor awards and international awards involving investor-state arbitration[48]). Even when they are, they are not legal precedent. However, this does not mean that an arbitrator will not follow another arbitrator's reasoning, if known. This happens all the time in the labor area. Labor arbitration has volumes of published decisions creating precedent, which is necessary due to the continuing relationship of labor and management.

---

[47] The public policies must be supported by specific legal precedents as opposed to speculative public interests. *United Paperworkers Int'l Union v. Misco, Inc.*, 484 U.S. 29 (1987); *W.R. Grace & Co. v. Local Union 795, Int'l Union Rubber Workers,* 461 U.S. 753 (1983).

[48] Decisions are supported by extensive written opinions and sometimes published in labor publications which creates precedent and instills some degree of predictability in labor-management relations.

Mediation: There are no appeals in mediation because there are no decisions by a third-party.

III. Conclusion

The litigation system has served America well. It has done so as a protector of freedom and an insurer of stability, infusing trust in the rule of law. Despite its strengths, the judicial system has weaknesses that have created a need for alternatives.

The most well-known of these alternatives are arbitration and mediation. Mediation can be more creative than arbitration or litigation in devising solutions to disputes, especially if the parties are educated and experienced with interest-based bargaining. But it is still relatively new to America. While corporate users seem to like the process, the amount of confidence parties have in the process is unknown.

Arbitration has been around a long time. The FAA dates back to 1925. When first proposed, arbitration was disparaged as an insult and invasion of the court's jurisdiction. It gained credence and converts over the years, including those disturbed by excesses of the judicial system. It overcame the disapproval of the courts and was endorsed by the U.S. Supreme Court. As a result, arbitration has been extended to many different areas, from anti-trust disputes to securities disputes. But no process or idea is without shortcomings and when academics and commentators become aware of them, they can make a career of publicizing them.

We believe that the long-term acceptance, promise, and viability of arbitration and mediation are tied to their appropriate use. One way of assuring appropriate use is to understand how they differ from litigation and from each other. Hopefully this discussion assists that determination.

Using arbitration and mediation has proven in many instances to make good business sense. This is evident from the decision to incorporate arbitration into the collective bargaining grievance process. Long ago, labor and management understood the enormous advantages of having an alternative dispute resolution mechanism in their contract. As a result, they have come to rely heavily on the predictability, consistency, integrity, and high quality of labor arbitration decisions.

With appropriate protocols in place, the same advantages apply to a wide range of business disputes.

We see litigation facing many long-term problems, the effect of which is likely to curtail public access to the courts. Now is the time to establish ADR processes that are infused with due process and demand the highest quality decision-making. Eventually, if done correctly, ADR could become the forum of choice for civil dispute resolution.

CHAPTER 5

MAJOR ARBITRATION ISSUES RECENTLY ADDRESSED BY COURTS

PRACTICAL TIPS FOR THE ARBITRATOR, PRACTITIONER AND CONTRACT DRAFTER

*Scott D. Marrs and Sean P. Milligan**

I. Introduction

Arbitration is a creature of contract, making it prone to change. The touchstone for a successful arbitration is careful drafting of the arbitration clause, according to authors Scott Marrs and Sean Milligan. They pose 10 critical questions that will help drafters of arbitration agreements, parties counsel and arbitrators understand recent developments in arbitration.

Parties increasingly turn to arbitration for the resolution of business disputes—with positive results, including less adversarial relationships, faster decisions and lower dispute resolution costs. But because arbitration is a creature of contract, the process the disputants get, and their satisfaction with it, turn largely on the arbitration clause itself. Whether their pursuit of an efficient and cost-effective arbitration is successful will depend in part on how carefully the arbitration agreement is negotiated and drafted, and on the arbitration experience and managerial abilities of the arbitrator the parties select to decide their case. Using a "form" arbitration clause borrowed from another contract may not be as safe as you thought. The appropriate arbitration language will often depend on the circumstances and how the courts have recently interpreted and applied arbitration provisions, laws and rules. This article summarizes recent court decisions on 10 important arbitration issues, including:

---

* Scott D. Marrs is a partner at Beirne, Maynard & Parsons, L.L.P., in Houston, Texas. He represents clients in commercial disputes in court, and arbitration throughout the country and serves as arbitrator on the American Arbitration Association's Commercial panel. Sean P. Milligan is Senior Counsel at Claim Legal Travelers in Houston, Texas. The authors' e-mail addresses are smarrs@bmpllp.com and SPMILLIG@travelers.com.

(1) Whether parties can expand the grounds to appeal an award;
(2) Whether parties can restrict the statutory grounds to appeal an award;
(3) Whether arbitrators can award attorney fees when a court cannot;
(4) Whether parties can waive their right to attorney fees;
(5) When a party waives its right to arbitrate;
(6) The effect an unconscionable provision has on an arbitration clause;
(7) Whether arbitrators can compel discovery from a non- signatory to an arbitration agreement;
(8) Whether parties who are unaware of the arbitration agreement can be required to arbitrate;
(9) Whether an arbitration agreement signed by only one party is enforceable; and
(10) Whether heirs and beneficiaries of a decedent will be bound by the decedent's arbitration agreement?

The cases discussed here will help contract negotiators and drafters devise a better arbitration agreement, help practitioners better advise their clients, and update arbitrators on what courts are thinking and doing.

II. Can Parties to an Arbitration Agreement Expand the Grounds to Appeal an Award?

The advent of modern arbitration arose largely to offer an alternative to the time-consuming and costly nature of traditional litigation. Two characteristics of arbitration that distinguishes it from litigation are finality and a limited right to appeal. Allowing broad judicial review is generally at odds with the primary goal of obtaining a relatively swift, cost effective and final resolution of disputes, since such review opens the door to expensive litigation, including judicial proceedings to test the validity of an award.

The Federal Arbitration Act (FAA), which governs arbitration agreements that involve or affect interstate commerce,[1] provides in

[1] The Federal Arbitration Act (FAA) applies to diverse parties and any "maritime transaction or ... contract evidencing a transaction involving commerce." 9 U.S.C. § 2. The term "commerce" is defined in Section 1 to mean "commerce among the several States or with foreign nations...." The reach of the FAA has been broadly construed to coincide with the reach of the "Commerce Clause." *Allied Bruce Terminix v. Dobson*, 513 U.S. 265 (1995), quoting *Perry v. Thomas*, 482 U.S. 483 (1987)." The FAA ensures the validity and enforcement of arbitration agreements and furthers the national policy

Section 10 that a court may vacate an award in extremely limited circumstances. These circumstances are when the evidence shows:

(1) corruption, fraud, or undue means in the procurement of the award;
(2) the arbitrator was partial or corrupt;
(3) the arbitrator refused to postpone the hearing despite a showing of sufficient cause, or refused to hear pertinent and material evidence, or otherwise denied a party due process and prejudiced its rights; or
(4) the arbitrator exceeded his or her powers, or failed to issue a mutual, final, and definite award.

The grounds to vacate an award are the grounds on which judicial review may be sought. Judicial review of the award by a district or trial court is the first level of appeal. If the court vacates or confirms the award, the court's decision may be appealed. In FAA cases, Section 16 of the FAA establishes the court's jurisdiction to hear such appeals.

Since the FAA severely limits the right of a party to seek judicial review of an arbitrator's award, the question of whether the parties can agree to expand the right to obtain judicial review has been a subject of disagreement in the federal courts. The U.S. Supreme Court finally addressed this issue in 2008 in *Hall Street Associates, Inc. v. Mattel, Inc.*,[2] a case governed by the FAA. *Hall Street* involved an arbitration clause providing for judicial review of arbitrator errors of fact and law. The Supreme Court ruled that parties do not have the right to expand the grounds for judicial review because the FAA's grounds to vacate or modify an award "are exclusive." It also stated that manifest disregard of the law is no longer a recognized ground for review of an award.[3] The

---

favoring binding arbitration. The FAA preempts state laws that conflict with the FAA. Since there is no congressional intent to occupy the field, state arbitration statutes may govern arbitration agreements that involve interstate commerce, to the extent that they are not in conflict with the FAA. See *Volt Info. Sciences v. Board of Trustees of Leland Stanford Univ.*, 489 U.S. 468, 477 (1989).

[2] 128 S. Ct. 1396 (2008).

[3] The phrase "manifest disregard" was used by the Supreme Court in *dicta* in *Wilco v. Swan*, 346 U.S. 427 (1953), overruled on other grounds by *Rodriguez de Quijas v. Shearson/Am. Express*, 490 U.S. 477, 485 (1989). The *Wilco* Court stated:

"While it may be true that a failure of the arbitrators to decide in accordance with the provisions of the Securities Act would 'constitute grounds for vacating the award pursuant to section 10 of the Federal Arbitration Act,' that failure would need to be made clearly to appear. In unrestricted submissions, such as the present margin agreements envisage, the interpretations of the law by the arbitrators in contrast to

Court observed that the national policy favoring arbitration with limited review furthers the goal of resolving disputes in a timely manner. Thus, an alleged misinterpretation or misapplication of the law will never be a sufficient ground on which to vacate an arbitration award under the FAA.

Hall Street appeared to resolve the split in the circuits on the ability of the parties to expand judicial review. However, it soon became clear that this was not the case. The reason is that *Hall Street* specifically left open the possibility that authority outside the FAA, including "state statutory or common law," might provide a basis for expanding judicial review.

The Supreme Court of California took advantage of this opening. Six months after the *Hall Street* decision, it decided *Cable Connection, Inc. v. DIRECTV, Inc.*[4] The arbitration agreement provided that "[t]he arbitrators shall not have the power to commit errors of law or legal reasoning, and the award may be vacated or corrected on appeal to a court of competent jurisdiction for any such error." California's highest court held that parties to arbitration agreements have the contractual right to expand judicial review of arbitration awards governed by the California Arbitration Act. The court explained that although this statute sets out certain grounds on which a court may vacate an award, it does not limit the parties' right to expand review by contract. Moreover, the court held that the above-quoted language was enforceable. In so holding, it stressed that freedom of contract is fundamental to arbitration.

To date, California is the only state to address whether one can expand the ground for judicial review by contract. California often dances to a different drummer, so it is possible that other states will not permit judicial review to be expanded beyond the provisions in state arbitration statutes.

Several federal and state courts have not followed *Hall Street's* statement that manifest disregard of the law is no longer a viable ground to vacate an award. These courts have concluded that the statement was not definitive because the Supreme Court in *Hall Street* listed several

manifest disregard are not subject, in the federal courts, to judicial review for error in interpretation." (Emphasis added).

The Supreme Court in *Hall Street* rejected the argument that the existence of the manifest disregard review standard supported the expansion of judicial review. It indicated that manifest disregard may refer to the Section 10 grounds "collectively, rather than adding to them." Moreover, it said that manifest disregard may just be a shorthand for the grounds identified in Sections 10(a)(3) and 10(a)(4), the "subsections authorizing vacatur when the arbitrators were 'guilty of misconduct' or 'exceeded their powers.'"

[4] 190 P.3d 586 (Cal. 2008).

possible readings of the doctrine, including the view that manifest disregard could be shorthand for an existing ground in FAA Section 10.[5]

TIP: Consider the law governing arbitration before trying to expand judicial review to cover errors of fact and law. If California law governs, *Cable Connections* will allow you to do it. If the FAA governs, you will have to find state law authority for expanding judicial review by contract.

In the 2nd and 9th Circuits, you could expressly provide in the arbitration agreement that awards are reviewable on the ground of manifest disregard of the law. However, other circuits may follow the statement in *Hall Street* that manifest disregard is dead.

TIP: There is a way to avoid judicial scrutiny of contract provisions that alter the grounds for judicial review, while also protecting parties against anomalous awards: provide for review of errors of law by an "appellate" arbitration panel.[6] To prevent a cycle of appeals, the provision should state that the appellate panel's decision is final and binding, and that no further appeal is allowed. The American Arbitration Association (AAA)[7] recently suggested language to effectuate this private—and final—appellate process:

> Within 30 days of receipt of any award (which shall not be binding if an appeal is taken), any party may notify the AAA of an intention to appeal to a second arbitral tribunal, constituted in the same manner as the initial tribunal. The appeal tribunal shall be entitled to adopt the initial award, modify the initial award or substitute its own award for the initial award. The appeal tribunal has no authority to modify or replace any part of the award that does not relate to the manifest disregard of the law claim. The

---

[5] *Comedy Club, Inc. v. Imrpov W.* Assoc., 553 F.3d 1277, 1290 (9th Cir. 2009) (on remand from the U.S. Supreme Court); *Stolt-Nielsen SA v. AnimalFeeds Int'l Corp.*, 548 F.3d 85, 94-95 (2d Cir. 2008), cert granted, __ U.S. __ (2009). See also *Citigroup Global Markets v. Bacon*, 562 F.3d 349 (5th Cir. 2009).

[6] *See* Paul Bennett Marrow, "A Practical Approach to Affording Review of Commercial Arbitration Awards: Using an Appellate Arbitrator," 60(3) *Disp. Resol. J.* 10 (Aug.-Oct. 2005).

[7] The American Arbitration Association rules neither authorize nor prohibit appeals to an appellate panel of arbitrators. Indeed, they give parties the freedom to contract for procedures that work best in their situation. AAA Commercial Arbitration Rule 101(a) ("The parties, by written agreement, may vary the procedures set forth in these Rules.").

award of the appeal tribunal shall be final and binding, and judgment may be entered by a court having jurisdiction thereof.[8]

This solution would afford meaningful appellate review for manifest disregard of the law, since there is ample case law to guide appellate arbitrators on this standard. This approach also would give appropriate deference to the arbitrator's award.

Having broader appeal rights may be extremely important to parties involved in large cases that involve significant sums of money or extremely onerous consequences. The manifest disregard standard, while not perfect, is better than a total inability to appeal an error of law.

The time and cost involved in an appeal to a second panel of arbitrators could be ameliorated by providing for a "short fuse" appeal (meaning one with very limited or no briefing and a short hearing). If briefs are to be allowed, the parties should agree to limit their number (for example: only initial briefs from each party), and their length (for example, a maximum of 50 double-spaced pages, using 13-point type for text and 10 point type for footnotes, and one-inch margins all around). Providing that an appeal can lie only for manifest disregard of the law prevents abuse of the appellate review process. Requiring the appellate arbitrator or panel to be specialists in appeals in federal or state appellate courts should give the parties confidence in the process.

TIP: In order to make the appeal provision meaningful, the parties should provide for a transcript or recording of the arbitration hearing.

III. Can Parties Restrict Judicial Review?

Many lawyers criticize arbitration because appeal rights are severely limited. So of course, no one would advocate that the ability to appeal should be even more restricted than the narrow grounds set forth in the FAA—right? Wrong. Existing case law on this issue indicates a split, with the 2nd Circuit holding that parties to cases governed by the FAA may not undermine the FAA's specifically enumerated grounds for review, and the 10th Circuit allowing parties to narrow the grounds for review.[9]

---

[8] In Drafting Dispute Resolution Clauses: A Practical Guide, effective Sept. 1, 2007, available at www.adr.org/si.asp?id=4125.

[9] Teresa Snider, "Enforceability of Agreements to Expand or Restrict the Scope of Judicial Review of Arbitration Awards," *Corp. Counsel Mag.* A6, A7 (Jan. 2006), citing *Hoeft v. MLV Group*. 343 F.3d 57 (2d Cir. 2003), and *Bowen v. Amoco Pipeline*, 254 F.3d 925 (10th Cir. 2001).

TIP: Parties should consider the pros and cons of restricting the grounds for judicial review in the location where they intend to arbitrate, as well as the locales where they might decide to enforce the award.[10] They should also consider what could happen if the court were to sever the contracted judicial review provision and enforce the award.[11]

IV. Can Arbitrators Award Attorney Fees When a Court Cannot?

Under the American Rule, prevailing parties do not recover their attorney fees unless authorized by contract or statute. Many statutes for the protection of the public authorize recovery of attorney fees by the winning party (for example, antitrust, civil rights and consumer protection laws). In addition, state legislatures have also made attorney fee relief available by statute for certain types of contract and declaratory judgment claims.

Neither the FAA nor the original Uniform Arbitration Act (1955), which has been enacted in many states, addresses the issue of attorney fees in arbitration. Therefore, in arbitration cases subject to the FAA or UAA, arbitrators generally may award any form of relief they believe is appropriate if not in conflict with the arbitration agreement. If the parties are arbitrating under the AAA Commercial Arbitration Rules, Rule 43(a) provides that an "arbitrator may grant any remedy or relief that the arbitrator deems just and equitable and within the scope of the agreement of the parties...."

The Revised 2000 Uniform Arbitration Act (RUAA)[12] specifically addresses attorney fees in Section 21(b). This provision authorizes arbitrators to award reasonable attorney fees and costs in their discretion in two situations. The first is if the law authorizes such an award in a civil action involving the same claim. The second situation is if the arbitration agreement authorizes such fees and costs. (The commentary notes that Section 21(b) does not require the arbitrator to apply any particular legal or evidentiary standard when addressing a claim for attorney fees under a statute.) However, RUAA Section 4(a) allows the parties to an arbitration agreement to waive the right to recover attorney

[10] Cf. Peter Michaelson, "In International Arbitration Disclosure Rules at the Place of Enforcement Matter Too, 62(4) *Disp. Resol. J.* 82 (Nov. 2007-Jan. 2008).

[11] Snider, *supra* n. 9.

[12] Available at www.nccusl.org (final acts and legislation).

fees "to the extent permitted by law." These provisions apply in Alaska, Colorado, District of Columbia, Hawaii, Nevada, New Jersey, New Mexico, North Carolina, North Dakota, Oklahoma, Oregon, Utah, and Washington, all of which have enacted the RUAA.[13]

Some states that have not enacted the UAA or the RUAA have arbitration statutes that provide for the recovery of attorney fees in arbitration when the law or the parties' agreement would allow them to be recovered.[14]

Thus, the availability of attorney fees depends on the contract or the law in the relevant jurisdiction.

What if the contract does not specifically authorize attorney fee awards but incorporates arbitration rules into the agreement that give arbitrators authority to grant any relief they believe to be just and equitable? The court addressed this in *Providian Bancorp Services v. Thomas*, where an employee initiated arbitration against his employer for assault and battery.[15] The agreement to arbitrate called for the Texas Arbitration Mediation Services (TAMS) rules to apply and to supersede any conflicting rules in the employee's employment agreement. A TAMS rule states that arbitrators may grant any relief deemed just and equitable. The arbitrator awarded the employee $1 in compensatory damages and $24,500 in attorney fees. Providian challenged the attorney fee award on the ground that it was not authorized by law or contract. The court ruled against Providian and confirmed the award.

On appeal, the Texas Court of Appeals upheld the award. It concluded that the award fell within "just and equitable" relief allowed by the TAMS rule. The court noted that other jurisdictions, such as New York and Illinois, have also held that "just and equitable" relief can include attorney fees.

V. Can Parties Waive the Right to Recover Attorney Fees?

Drafters of arbitration agreements in employment and other contracts sometimes put a clause in the arbitration agreement prohibiting arbitrators from making attorney fee awards to a prevailing party. For example, in

---

[13] www.nccusl.org/Update/uniformact_factsheets/uniformacts-fs-aa.asp.

[14] 12 Vt. Stat., ch 191, § 5665; Tex. Civ. Prac. & Rem. Code, ch. 171 § 048(c).

[15] No. 04-07-00540-CV, 2008 WL 2038826 (Tex. Ct. App. May 14, 2008). The employee sued in court, but the employer won a motion to compel arbitration. The parties entered into an arbitration agreement after the employer won this motion.

Security Service Federal Credit Union v. Sanders,[16] the contract limited the consumer's right to recover attorney fees and costs and dictated that the consumer was responsible for the other party's attorney fees, contrary to the Texas Deceptive Trade Practices Act (DTPA). The court held that this provision was unconscionable and unenforceable.[17]

TIP: If you seek to limit recovery of attorney fees permitted by the substantive law of the state governing the dispute, this intent should be expressly stated in the arbitration agreement.

VI. What Circumstances Constitute a Waiver of the Right to Arbitrate?

A party may unwittingly waive its right to enforce an arbitration clause. Generally, a waiver occurs when the party substantially invokes the judicial process and the other party can show that it suffered prejudice as a result. A waiver can also occur by making statements or taking actions that are inconsistent with the right to seek arbitration. However, courts strongly favor arbitration and waiver is difficult to establish.

A recent case out of Texas gives a good summary of the circumstances in which a waiver could be found. In *Perry Homes v. Cull*,[18] the plaintiffs sued the builder of their home in court, rather than invoking the arbitration clause in the purchase agreement. The home builder cried foul when the plaintiffs took depositions, opposed the builder's request for arbitration, then attempted to invoke arbitration themselves late in the case. The Supreme Court of Texas stressed the strong presumption in favor of arbitration and against waiver (noting it had never found such a waiver). It concluded that the following actions alone were insufficient to constitute a waiver of the arbitration clause: filing a lawsuit; moving to dismiss a claim for lack of standing; moving to set aside a default judgment and requesting a new trial; opposing a trial and seeking to move the litigation to federal court; moving to strike an intervention and opposing discovery; serving written discovery; noticing (but not taking) a single deposition, and agreeing to a trial

---

[16] No. 04-07-00540-CV, 2008 WL 2038826 (Tex. Ct. App. May 14, 2008).

[17] *See* also, In *re Poly-America, L.P.*, 262 S.W.3d 337 (Tex. 2008) (holding that a remedy-limiting clause in an arbitration agreement was unenforceable); *Chalk v. T-Mobile U.S.A.*, 560 F.3d 1087 (9th Cir. Mar. 27, 2009) (noting that a class action waiver and a waiver of attorney fees in an arbitration provision are unconscionable).

[18] 258 S.W.3d 580 (Tex. 2008).

resetting; or taking four depositions, and moving for dismissal based on standing.

The court used the "totality of circumstances" test to decide whether a waiver occurred, considering the following factors:

- which party invoked arbitration (the plaintiff who chose to initially file in court, or the defendant who merely responded);
- the length of time the moving party delayed before seeking arbitration;
- whether that party was previously aware of the arbitration clause;
- the amount of pre-trial activity that took place relating to the merits, rather than arbitrability or jurisdiction;
- the amount of time and expense incurred in litigation;
- whether the moving party opposed arbitration earlier in the case;
- whether that party filed affirmative claims or dispositive motions;
- whether important discovery would be unavailable in arbitration;
- the extent to which activity in court would be duplicated in arbitration; and
- when the case was to be tried.

Like 10 federal circuit courts, the Supreme Court of Texas adopted the rule requiring the party arguing that there has been a waiver to show that the moving party's delay in seeking arbitration caused *prejudice*. It defined that term to mean inherent unfairness (for example, a party's attempt to have it both ways by switching between litigation and arbitration to its own advantage).

Next, the court, after examining the circumstances, concluded that the plaintiffs substantially invoked the litigation process by taking 10 depositions, filing a 79-page document stating objections to the defendant's request for arbitration, filing five motions to compel document production, serving numerous deposition notices, and waiting late in the trial process to invoke arbitration. The court also found that the plaintiffs' actions in initially objecting to arbitration and later insisting on it after the defendant acquiesced to the litigation unfairly prejudiced the defendant.

TIP: The question of waiver is fact intensive, and not all cases are as cut and dried as *Perry Homes*. Because of the risk of waiver, parties to the agreement should not ignore the arbitration clause.

VII. What Effect Does an Unconscionable Contract Have on an Arbitration Clause?

Drafters should avoid drafting an unconscionable contract. The risk is that the arbitration clause will survive but the contract will not. In *Security Service Federal Credit Union*,[19] the court found unconscionable a limitation on the consumer's statutory right to recover its attorney fees and costs, and the requirement that the consumer pay the other party's attorney fees. However, it also found that the parties intended illegal or unenforceable provisions to be severed from the contract, leaving the remainder enforceable. This intent was evidenced by the arbitration clause, which expressly provided for severability. Therefore, the court severed the unconscionable provisions from the rest of the agreement and held that the arbitration clause was enforceable.

Would the decision be the same if the agreement did not have a severability clause? A court would look at the facts and circumstances to determine whether the parties intended unconscionable or unenforceable provisions to be severed.

TIP: To avoid any problem, drafters should always include a severability clause in the contract.

VIII. Can Arbitrators Compel Discovery from Non-Parties?

There is a split in the federal circuit courts on this issue.[20] Most recently, the 2nd Circuit held in *Life Receivables Trust v. Syndicate 102*

[19] *See* n. 16 *supra.*

[20] Allowing pre-hearing document discovery from third parties: *Security Life Ins. Co. of Am. v. Duncanson & Holt*, 228 F.3d 865 (8th Cir. 2000) (holding that "implicit in an arbitration panel's power to subpoena relevant documents for production at a hearing is the power to order the production of relevant documents for review by a party prior to the hearing"). See also *Comsat Corp. v. National Sci. Found.*, 190 F.3d 269 (4th Cir. 1999) (stating in *dicta* that the FAA may give arbitrators authority to issue pre-hearing document subpoenas to non-parties, but only if there is a special need for such documents). Not allowing such discovery: *Life Receivables Trust v. Syndicate 102 at Lloyds' of London*, 549 F.3d 210 (2d Cir. 2008); *Matria Healthcare, LLC v. Duthie*, 2008 WL 4500173 (N.D. Ill. Oct. 6, 2008) (an arbitrator's subpoena power over non-parties under Section 7 of the FAA is limited to compelling them to testify or produce documents at the hearing). In *Stolt-Nielsen SA v. Celanese AG*, 430 F.3d 567 (2d Cir. 2005), the 2nd Circuit declined to decide this issue because the subpoenas sought to compel testimony of non-parties and document production at the hearing.

at Lloyds' of London[21] that arbitrators have no authority under Section 7 of the FAA to order third parties to produce documents for discovery purposes (i.e., before the hearing). Accordingly, the court refused to give effect to an arbitration panel's order compelling discovery of documents from a third party.

To date, the Supreme Court has not weighed in on the extent to which an arbitrator may compel pre-hearing testimony and documents from a non-party. However, buckle up, because this split of authority will likely culminate in the Supreme Court considering the issue sooner, rather than later. It should be noted that the 3rd Circuit opinion[22] on which the 2nd Circuit relied was written by the Hon. Samuel A. Alito Jr. before his appointment as Associate Justice on the Supreme Court.

As the 2nd Circuit noted in *Life Receivables Trust*, arbitrators are not powerless to order the production of documents from non-parties; they can order non-parties to bring documents with them to the hearing when they are called to testify.

TIP: If the non-party resides outside the jurisdiction of the district court in which the hearing is located, the arbitrator could, it has been suggested, move the hearing to the state where the witness lives.[23]

IX. Can You Require a Party Who Is Unaware of the Arbitration Clause to Arbitrate?

In *Connectu, Inc. v. Quinn Emanuel Urquhart Oliver & Hedges, LLP*,[24] a law firm client signed an engagement letter containing an arbitration clause. During a subsequent dispute, the client contended it was unaware of the clause and challenged the arbitrability of the dispute. The court enforced the agreement, holding that arbitration clauses will be enforced absent a showing that the clause was obtained without consent, or as a result of fraud, misrepresentation, or duress. This is consistent

---

[21] Cited *supra n. 20.*

[22] *Hay Group v. E.B.S. Acquisition Corp.*, 360 F.3d 404, 407 (3d Cir. 2004).

[23] Leslie Trager, 'The Use of Subpoenas in Arbitration," 62(4) *Disp. Resol. J.* 14 (Nov. 2007-Jan. 2008). Lowell Pearson, "The Case for Non-Party Discovery Under the Federal Arbitration Act," 60(3) *Disp. Resol. J.* 46 (Aug.-Oct. 2004). See also Timothy V. Krusl, "The Limits on Enforcement of Arbitral Third-Party Subpoenas: Should They Be Loosened?" 59(4) *Disp. Resol. J.* 30 (Nov. 2002-Jan. 2003) (discussing territorial limitation).

[24] 873 N.Y.S.2d 510 (N.Y. Sup. Ct. 2008).

with common law, which applies the rule that failing to read a contract provision is no defense to its enforcement.

But what about circumstances where an agent, rather than the principal, signed the agreement? Will the principal be bound? The answer is obviously yes. Courts apply a variety of common law doctrines (e.g., assumption of the agreement, piercing the corporate veil, equitable estoppel and incorporation by reference) to prevent a non-signatory from avoiding the consequences of an arbitration agreement. *Southern Illinois Beverage, Inc. v. Hansen Beverage Co.*[25] is an example of an unusual application of the estoppel doctrine. In this case Hansen, a beverage manufacturer, had a contract containing an arbitration clause with a distributor. The subdistributor sued Hanson, who responded with a motion to compel arbitration even though the subdistributor was a non-signatory. The trial court held that under the estoppel doctrine, the subdistributor must arbitrate because it sued a party to the contract and made claims premised on the contract in order to enforce subdistribution rights that arose from that contract. The court said the subdistributor's claims were "fundamentally rooted in and dependent on rights and conditions defined in the agreement between Hansen and its distributor."

When an arbitration agreement is subject to the FAA, state substantive law is still likely to apply in determining whether a non-signatory may be required to arbitrate. One court recently addressing the issue held, "Pending an answer from the United States Supreme Court, we have determined to apply state substantive law and endeavor to keep it consistent with federal law."[26]

X. Is an Arbitration Agreement Enforceable If Only One Party Signs It?

In general, under federal and state arbitration statutes, an arbitration agreement must be in writing to be enforceable. There is no requirement that it be signed. However, the parties may provide that the signatures of both parties are required to make the agreement effective. If such a provision is included in the parties' agreement, courts will enforce it, as happened in a recent case decided by a Maryland appeals court.[27]

---

[25] No. 07-CV-391, 2007 WL 3046273 (S.D. Ill. Oct. 15, 2007).

[26] *In Re Labatt Food Servs.*, 2009 WL 353524 (Tex. Feb. 13, 2009).

[27] *All State Home Mortgage v. Daniel*, No. 579, 2009 WL 1617092 (Md. Ct. App. June 9, 2009).

XI. Will Heirs and Beneficiaries Be Bound by a Decedent's Agreement to Arbitrate

Most states addressing this issue, including Texas, Mississippi, Alabama and Michigan, have resolved it based on whether the wrongful death action is an independent or derivative cause of action under state law. If the beneficiaries' right to sue is based solely on the decedent's right to sue for negligence, the claim is derivative of the decedent's rights. In that situation, the beneficiaries will be bound by the decedent's agreement to arbitrate. The Supreme Court of Texas so held in *In Re Labatt Food Service*[28] because the Texas Wrongful Death Act expressly conditions the beneficiaries' wrongful death claims on the decedent's right to sue for the injuries if he had lived.

Other states, such as Utah and Missouri, have held to the contrary. In *Bybee v. Abdulla*,[29] the court held that beneficiaries were not bound to arbitrate because wrongful death is an independent cause of action under Utah law. In *Lawrence v. Manor*,[30] the court also held that beneficiaries were not required to arbitrate because under Missouri law, the wrongful death act creates a new cause of action belonging to beneficiaries.

TIP: Practitioners representing beneficiaries of a decedent who was a party to an arbitration agreement should become familiar with the wrongful death law of the state in which the decedent resided, because how that law treats wrongful death actions will determine whether the beneficiaries will have to arbitrate those claims.

XII. Conclusion

The cases discussed here show that arbitration is a continually evolving process. Drafters of dispute resolution clauses should keep abreast of the latest court decisions affecting arbitration. This will help them craft arbitration provisions that benefit their clients when a dispute arises. It will also help arbitrators and practitioners do their job better.

---

[28] Cited in n. 26 *supra.*
[29] 189 P.3d 40, 43 (Utah 2008).
[30] No. SC89291, 2009 WL 77897 (Mo. Jan. 13, 2009).

PART II:

KEY INGREDIENTS FOR A BETTER ARBITRATION

CHAPTER 6

YOU CONTROL THE PROCESS V. THE PROCESS CONTROLS YOU

John Arrastia, Jr.[*]

I. Introduction

What trial lawyer would not want to be able to select the judge hearing the case? Arbitration allows the parties to determine the arbitrator's background. Unlike litigation, it gives them choices and flexibility to design a process to fit their needs.

The advantages of a properly structured and well-managed arbitration are especially valuable today. With clients insisting on more manageable litigation budgets and the courts clogged with the fallout from a struggling economy, efficiency and reduced overall costs are becoming the polestars of healthy client relations.

Arbitration is intended to be quicker, less expensive, and more efficient than litigation. But many litigators complain that the process has become cumbersome and expensive. This happens when trial attorneys treat the arbitration process as they would federal or state court litigation. Why? One explanation is that they are taught to litigate using the court's rules of procedure and evidence, and when faced with the less structured and less familiar arbitration process, they naturally turn to what they know and thus, try to incorporate the rules and procedures of court into the arbitration process. This transforms arbitration into a mirror image of court litigation, with the attendant expense and delay.

Trial attorneys can satisfy their clients' desires to economize on dispute resolution by understanding the differences between arbitration

---

[*] John Arrastia, Jr., a Miami, Florida-based attorney, practices mainly in the areas of domestic and international commercial litigation and arbitration. He has represented quasi-governmental entities as well as commercial enterprises of every size, both public and private. He serves on the AAA panel of arbitrators. He holds an LL.M. in international arbitration and litigation from Cambridge University. He may be reached at www.arrastia-law.com.

and litigation, for it is these differences that provide the benefits of arbitration. Only then can counsel maximize those benefits and use the inherent flexibility of arbitration to tailor the process to the needs of the client and the circumstances of the dispute.

Part I of this article discusses the core concept of arbitration and the ways that arbitration differs from litigation. Part II, which will be published in a subsequent issue of this *Journal*, will discuss techniques trial counsel can use to achieve an efficient and cost-effective arbitration.

II. Core Concept of Arbitration

The core concept of arbitration is its flexibility. This means that it is not governed by rigid, detailed rules. The parties have a significant amount of freedom of choice when it comes to designing the process. The concepts of choice and flexibility are recurring themes in this article.

A. Flexible Rules

Institutional arbitration rules are purposely very general and give the arbitrator great discretion in the management of the process. This allows the parties and the arbitrator to consider the most efficient ways to proceed. Thus, the American Arbitration Association's (AAA) Commercial Arbitration Rules provide that the parties may vary the procedures stated in the rules.[1] In addition, nearly all the AAA rules state that they apply "unless the parties otherwise agree." This is a far cry from litigation, which is highly regulated by detailed, step-by-step rules of procedure, supplemented by case law, and subject to the preferences of the presiding judge.

B. Choice

The flexibility of arbitration provides choices on many levels. First, there is choice relating to the selection of the arbitrator. What trial lawyer would not want to be able to select the judge hearing the case? The ability to choose the decision maker in arbitration is one of the primary benefits of the process. There is also choice in matching the speed of the process and the amount of discovery that is allowed to the size of the dispute. Thus, one can fast-track a small case and agree to little or no

[1] R-R3 "Enforcement Powers of the Arbitrator," and R-32 "Conduct of Proceedings" AAA Commercial Arbitration Rules, available online at www.adr.org.

discovery, and in a large case employ large, complex case procedures and agree to more discovery. In addition, the parties can agree on the form of the award. They can also agree to limit the extent to which the final decision is disclosed to third parties.

Suppose that an existing client comes to you with two new matters that it wants to arbitrate, arising out of the same standard form contract, each raising the same complex issues, but one claim involves $100,000, while the other involves $8 million. Would you approach each dispute the same way? Probably not, and it is fairly certain your client would prefer the resolution of the smaller matter to be resolved faster and cost substantially less. But court rules of procedure generally do not distinguish between cases based on the amount in controversy (except for jurisdictional purposes and except for claims that qualify for small claims court). Most institutional arbitration rules automatically provide for different procedures for small, mid-size and large disputes tailoring the time, extent of discovery allowed, and costs accordingly.

The best time to decide arbitration details is before a dispute arises in the arbitration clause of the parties' contract.[2] However, if the arbitration does not contain such details, the remaining points can be decided at a preliminary conference with the arbitrator.

C. Fair Results

Most decisions rendered by arbitrators will be made after a great deal of thought and time has been given to reviewing the presentation of evidence and they will be based on an underlying knowledge of the subject matter of the dispute and commercial reasonableness where applicable. Unlike jurors, arbitrators are trained in how to give appropriate weight to evidence, how to manage the process to maintain a level playing field, and provide a decision that is just and fair.

D. Self-Determination to a Point

The flexibility of arbitration decreases as the final hearing approaches. For example, once the arbitrator has issued a pre-hearing scheduling order establishing the framework for the arbitration procedures and deadlines, unless the parties agree, it may be as difficult to persuade the arbitrator as

[2] For a complete discussion of the options available to parties when drafting alternative dispute resolution clauses, see "Drafting Dispute Resolution Clauses: A Practical Guide," available online at www.ADR.org/AAA/ShowPDF?doc=ADRSTG_002540

it would be to persuade a judge to make any changes to the order. More importantly, after the final award is entered there is little flexibility since the arbitrator will have no authority to change the decision on the merits under the doctrine of *functus officio*. Final arbitration awards are binding, enforceable and almost impossible to challenge in court, since the grounds to appeal such awards are very limited and courts afford them great deference.[3] The lesson is that a party should focus on establishing a procedure early in the process.

III. Differences Between Arbitration and Litigation

Applying the core concepts of flexibility and party choice, arbitration can differ from litigation in almost every way.

A. Decision Maker

We have already pointed out that arbitration differs from litigation in that the parties can participate in the selection of their decision maker. At most, in litigation, trial attorneys can decide whether to file the case in state or federal court and whether to seek a jury or a bench trial. In any event, a judge will likely be assigned to the case by a blind draw of the clerk of the court.

Arbitration does not offer the option of a jury. What it does offer is the ability to have a decision maker with far more expertise than a judge or jury would have in the specific issues presented by the case. Not only that, the parties can decide how many decision makers there will be.

i. Size of Tribunal. The parties can agree on a single arbitrator or a panel of three. Some parties believe that the "collective wisdom" of three decision makers may encourage more accurate results. Though panels raise the cost of arbitration, they make the most sense in large, complex matters.

The parties can state how many arbitrators there should be in their arbitration clause. Or they can agree to follow the rules of an arbitration institution. If they opt to use the AAA Commercial Arbitration Rules, there will be a panel of three if the dispute qualifies for the Large,

---

[3] *See Hall Street Assoc. v. Mattel, Inc.*, 128 S. Ct. 1396 (2008) (holding that the grounds stated in Section 10 of the FAA are the exclusive grounds on which a party may seek to vacate an award under the FAA). Nevertheless, parties may agree to a private appellate arbitration process if an appeal right is important to the clients.

Complex Case Procedures and the parties have not agreed otherwise.[4] When parties agree to use three arbitrators, they can also decide if all three will be neutral, or if two will be partial to the party that appointed them. The trend is toward a panel of all neutral arbitrators. AAA commercial rule R-12 provides that party-appointed panel members must be impartial unless the parties have specifically agreed otherwise.[5]

Arbitrations involving three arbitrators may take longer because of scheduling difficulties and the need for the panelists to find time to confer, deliberate and write an award. Even if an arbitration clause calls for three arbitrators, the parties can agree to use one arbitrator if they are concerned about reducing the cost of resolving the dispute.

ii. Qualifications of the Arbitrator. Arbitrators are usually chosen for their ability to efficiently manage an arbitration proceeding and/or their knowledge of a particular field or issue. For example, the parties to a construction dispute may want the arbitrator to be a construction lawyer, a general contractor, an architect, or an engineer, or some combination of these professions. Each skill set brings a different perspective to the arbitration. Having expertise in the subject matter is considered an advantage because the arbitrator should understand the facts and issues more quickly than judges or jurors who are likely unfamiliar with construction. The same is true whether the dispute involves real estate, biotech, telecommunications, international trade, or some other area of specialization.

Parties should want an arbitrator who is a good manager, who will be proactive in keeping the arbitration moving forward. Some want an arbitrator who asks questions at the final hearing while others prefer minimal or no questioning by the arbitrator.

Then there are practical considerations, such as the arbitrator's availability to serve. If you need the final hearing in October but the arbitrator is scheduled for a three-month trial in the fall, then that arbitrator is not the one for you. To avoid delays, parties with particular scheduling needs should ask the administering institutional case manager

---

[4] *See*, e.g., R-1 (c) and AAA Large, Complex Case Procedures, L-2, which provides that in disputes over $1,000,000, "three arbitrator(s) shall hear and determine the case" if the parties are unable to agree on the number of arbitrators.

[5] *See* also Canons IX and X of the AAA-ABA Code of Ethics for Arbitrators in Commercial Disputes, available at www.adr.org and www.abanet.org/dispute/commercial_disputes.pdf. They provide that party-appointed arbitrators shall be presumed neutral. If they are not neutral, they must inform the parties and other arbitrators.

to screen prospective arbitrators in advance of their appointment concerning their availability.

The parties may also have other requirements that in their mind will result in a more fair hearing. For example, in an employment case, the employee might want a more ethnically diverse panel. In AAA arbitrations, the case manager provides a list of arbitrator candidates that match the criteria requested by the parties.

B. Rules

As indicated above, a key difference between the two processes is that litigation is governed by procedural and evidentiary rules that the parties cannot change, while arbitration proceedings are governed by rules selected by the parties, which can be changed if they both agree. Arbitrators are charged with following the rules unless the parties agree otherwise. In addition, an arbitration proceeding may be subject to the Federal Arbitration Act (FAA),[6] a state arbitration act, or an international convention if the dispute is international in nature. These laws and treaties generally do not take away the flexibility of arbitration. Rather, they focus on the enforcement of and challenge to arbitration agreements and awards.

C. Confidentiality

An important benefit of arbitration that is not available in litigation is that it is more private than litigation. Litigation is public and often newsworthy. The Internet has made news of litigation more widely available. Also, anyone has the right to review the court file and attend the court proceedings, absent an order sealing the case or closing the proceedings. Sealing any part of a court record is exceptionally difficult, and typically includes notice to the press so that it may object to any such proposed order.

The public cannot attend arbitration proceedings between private parties. Under AAA commercial rule R-23, only a party with a direct interest in the proceedings is entitled to attend, unless the arbitrator directs otherwise. The privacy of arbitration derives from its contractual nature, not a statute. There is no federal or state law making arbitration confidential. Thus, in order to obtain confidentiality, parties often enter into a confidentiality agreement concerning the arbitration itself.

---

[6] 9 U.S.C. § 1, *et seq.*

Sometimes a party may also enter into a separate confidentiality agreement with an expert witness. However, a confidentiality agreement is effective only to the extent that the signatories adhere to it. In addition, a confidentiality agreement will not prevent a party from revealing the arbitration if disclosures are required by law or government regulation (such as a security law filing). It should also be noted that arbitration providers may have a legal obligation to disclose information about their cases. For example, administering institutions that do business in California are required by state law to provide detailed information about their national consumer case load. "Consumer" is broadly defined.

D. Consequences of a Failure to Appear

In court, a failure to appear or file a written response to pleadings can result in a default judgment. The concept of a default judgment is not recognized in arbitration. In arbitration, if the respondent does not appear, the claimant must still sustain its burden of proof and submit evidence sufficient to sustain the award.[7]

E. Court Scheduling Conference v. Preliminary Conference

The court scheduling conference is usually held to schedule the discovery in the case, rather than to set the trial. Indeed the trial date will not be set until much later (often years later in large cases) and they are often postponed several times if the court has a backlog of cases. The discovery dates will be set in accordance with rigid court rules. Following the scheduling conference, the judge often orders the parties to participate in a settlement conference.

The preliminary conference in arbitration is far more collaborative and broader in scope. Its main purpose is to identify and organize the steps necessary to prepare for the final hearing (i.e., the pre-hearing procedures), establish the dates for completing these procedures, and set a date certain for the final hearing on the merits.

At the first preliminary conference (there can be more than one), the arbitrator and counsel for the parties (and sometimes party representatives) will discuss a variety of matters. The first conference usually takes place on the telephone 30-45 days after the arbitrator is appointed. The matters discussed include, for example, the parties' needs

[7] For example, Rule R-31 of the AAA Commercial Arbitration Rules states that "[a]n award shall not be made solely on the default of a party."

for discovery, whether the parties expect to retain experts, and the use of cost-saving measures that can be used to control the time and cost of the proceeding. As a result of these discussions, the parties and the arbitrator will agree on the pre-hearing procedures and deadlines, and set the date for the final hearing.

Some arbitrators will ask the attorneys if they have raised the subject of mediation with their clients. However, in arbitration the parties will not be forced to mediate or to participate in a settlement conference as a condition to a final hearing.

F. Paperwork

i. Pleadings. From a work standpoint, arbitration requires less paperwork than litigation. The pleadings are simpler than in court and not highly regulated. The first pleading is the demand, the purpose of which is to give the adversary notice of the intention to arbitrate. The AAA commercial rules require the demand (as well as a counterclaim) to contain a statement of the nature of the dispute, the names and addresses of all parties, any claims and counterclaims, the amount involved, if any, the remedy sought and the hearing locale requested.[8]

The adversary is not required to file an answering statement but has the option of doing so. The rules also encourage the parties to describe their claims "in sufficient detail to make the circumstances of the dispute clear to the arbitrator." Often, the parties are given an opportunity to better define their positions after the first preliminary conference.

ii. Motions Generally. Arbitration contemplates fewer motions than litigation. The only motions specifically contemplated by the AAA rules are those seeking interim relief, resolution of a discovery dispute, or challenging the arbitrator's jurisdiction or the arbitrability of a claim.

There are no formal requirements in the AAA rules for motions or applications (except for emergency interim relief prior to the appointment of the arbitrator). Therefore, in an arbitration of any agreement or order of the arbitrator, a party may file a motion or application in the form of a letter or an e-mail. There are no briefing requirements in the rules, and no need to prepare proposed orders. The arbitrator normally informs the parties what kind of supporting materials should be submitted with their letter or e-mail. The arbitrator will also set a date for the other side to submit its written comments.

---

[8] *See* R-4.

iii. Dispositive Motions. Motions that decide all or part of a case in arbitration are called dispositive motions; in litigation they are summary judgment (SJ) motions. SJ motions are standard practice in litigation. This is not the case in arbitration where parties have a strong expectation of being able to present their case at the final hearing. Nevertheless, dispositive motions are sometimes very carefully used in arbitration.[9] This is possible because arbitrators are required to manage the arbitration proceedings with an eye toward efficiently resolving the case and this includes focusing the parties on dispositive issues. At the same time, they have the duty to treat the parties equally and give each a fair opportunity to be heard.[10] The efficient management obligation can include the authority to hear and decide a dispositive motion in an appropriate situation, as long as all parties have been given a fair opportunity to be heard. The case law on this issue is not extensive, but several cases that exist have upheld arbitral rulings granting such motions.[11] For example, the opportunity to be heard does not necessarily mean an oral hearing on the merits.[12]

However, the authority to grant a dispositive motion should not be used cavalierly or misused because the award may be subject to challenge under Section 10 of the FAA on the ground that the arbitrators exceeded their authority or refused to hear evidence, or both.[13] To protect the award and afford appropriate process rights of the parties, many arbitrators believe it is prudent to obtain the agreement of the parties to the dispositive motion procedure before agreeing to hear and decide a dispositive motion.

The arbitrator can ask the parties at the first preliminary conference if anyone has a dispositive issue (such as one based on the statute of limitations, or an alleged waiver of consequential damages) that could be resolved by a summary judgment motion. If the answer is yes and the opposing parties agree to allow the arbitrator to rule on the issue in order

---

[9] R-33 of the AAA Commercial Arbitration Rules provides the circumstances under which a dispositive motion may be presented.

[10] *See* R-32 "Conduct of Proceedings".

[11] *Sherrock Bros. Inc. v. DaimlerChrysler Motors Co., LLC*, No. 06-4767, 2008 WL 63300 (3rd Cir. Jan. 7, 2008) (confirming award granting summary judgment motion under AAA commercial rules); see also *Schlessinger v. Rosenfeld, Meyer & Susman*, 47 Cal. Rptr. 2d 650 (Cal. Ct. App. 1995); *Intercarbon Bermuda, Ltd. v. Caltex Trading & Transport Corp.*, 146 F.R.D. 64 (S.D.N.Y. 1993); *Stifler v. Seymour Weiner*, 488 A.2d 192 (Md. Ct. App. 1985); *Campbell v. American Family Life Assurance Co. of Columbus, Inc.*, 613 F. Supp. 2d 1114 (D. Minn. 2009).

[12] *See* the *Sherrock Bros.* and *Intercarbon* cases, *supra,* n. 10.; see also R-32 (c).

[13] *See Campbell, supra,* n. 10.

to narrow issues or dispose of the case altogether without the necessity of a full hearing, the parties can agree on the procedure to be followed. Such flexible procedures can save time and money while giving the parties a full opportunity to have the pertinent issues heard.

G. Discovery

In litigation, discovery can generate the largest single expense. Depositions are standard in court cases. Each deposition requires counsel to spend time to prepare the witness to testify (or to question the witness), review relevant documents and attend the deposition itself. This is followed by summarizing the deposition and paying for a copy of the transcript.

There is almost no restriction on the amount of documents that may be requested from the adversary or third parties, all of which need to be reviewed and analyzed after they are produced. These often result in objections.

Interrogatories and requests for admission are standard in litigation. They invariably generate written objections and few substantive responses. As a result, discovery disputes often arise. They require the parties to file with the court motions and supporting memoranda of law seeking a protective order or to compel a witness to answer particular questions at a deposition or to compel a party to produce withheld documents or to answer certain interrogatories. The court may require oral argument on the motion. This means that before appearing in court, the attorneys will have to spend time preparing an argument and anticipating the other side's arguments and the judge's questions.

In arbitration, discovery is not so broad. Indeed, the amount of discovery used in litigation was never contemplated to be a part of arbitration. The AAA rules provide for the exchange of information (i.e., documents) and don't refer to discovery or depositions (except for the Large, Complex Case Procedures). The rules leave it to the parties and the arbitrator to fashion the amount of discovery appropriate for the dispute.

Thus, arbitrators expect the parties to agree to very limited discovery and where they disagree, the arbitrator can and should streamline the process. This is necessary to curtail costs.

When discovery disputes arise in arbitration, and they do, they are handled more informally than in litigation, so resolving the dispute costs much less. They are usually resolved in telephone conference with the arbitrator or by a written order from the panel chair.

i. Absence of Third-Party Discovery. An important distinction between litigation and arbitration concerns discovery of information in the hands of third parties. Article 7 of the FAA authorizes arbitrators to issue subpoenas for witnesses to appear at the final hearing, and bring documents along with them.[14] Some jurisdictions have interpreted this provision to permit third-party discovery.[15] However, some federal appeals courts have not authorized pre-hearing document discovery from third parties.[16] They have interpreted Article 7 to mean that the witness can only be required to bring documents when he or she testifies as a witness before the arbitrators.[17] This area is constantly evolving, so arbitration advocates should determine the law on third party discovery in the locale where arbitration is contemplated or pending.

H. Final Hearing

We have alluded to the expertise of the arbitrators (as opposed to jurors and some judges) and the confidentiality of the hearing versus the public nature of a trial. We have discussed the fact that rules of civil procedure do not apply in arbitration, making arbitration a process of choice and more informal. There are, however, other differences between a trial and an arbitration hearing.

i. Venue. In litigation, venue is determined by the facts and rules of procedure. When it is contested, the resolution of the dispute can be tied up in controversy, including appeals, for years at a time.

Venue is determined differently in arbitration. The parties to the arbitration can agree on venue in their arbitration agreement or during the arbitration at an early preliminary conference. If not predetermined in the contract, venue normally will be based on the convenience of the parties. In an arbitration under the AAA Commercial Arbitration Rules, if the parties cannot agree on the locale of the hearing, the AAA will make

---

[14] Article 7 of the FAA provides that the arbitrator "may summon in writing any person to attend before them or any of them as a witness in the proper case to bring with him or them any book, record, document, or paper which may be deemed material as evidence in the case."; see also R-34 and R-35, addressing evidence.

[15] Third-party discovery in arbitration has been upheld in *Security Life Ins. Co,* 228 F. 3d 865 (8th Cir. 2000); *Illinois, in Amgen, Inc. v. Kidney Ctr. of Del. County, Ltd.*, 879 F. Supp. 878 (N.D. Ill. 1995); *Meadows Indemnity Co. v. Nutmeg Ins. Co.*, 157 F.R.D. 42 (M.D. Tenn. 1993); *Stanton v. Paine Webber Jackson & Curtis, Inc.,* 685 F. Supp. 1241 (S.D. Fla. 1988). But see *Kennedy v. American Express Travel Related Serv. Co., Inc.*, No. 09-61157, 2009 WL 2488298 (S.D. Fla. Aug. 12, 2009).

[16] *See*, e.g., *Hay Group, Inc. v. E.B.S., Acquisition Corp.*, 360 F.3d 404 (3d Cir. 2004).

[17] *Life Receivables Trust v. Syndicate 102 at Lloyd's of London,* 549 F. 3d 210 (2d Cir. 2008) (barring document discovery from entities that are not parties to the arbitration proceeding).

that decision.[18] In a construction dispute, under Rule R-12 of the recently amended AAA Construction Industry Arbitration Rules, if the parties cannot agree on venue, the hearing will be held in the city nearest the project in dispute, subject to the arbitrator's approval.

As for the location of the hearing, it usually takes place in a conference room, the arbitrator's office, or a hearing room specifically provided by the service provider, almost never a courtroom.

ii. Presentation of Evidence in Arbitration. Since arbitrators are not bound by specific rules of evidence, the parties have greater flexibility with regard to the presentation of evidence. This means that hearsay can be introduced, as well as copies of business records. In addition, efficiency techniques can be used to introduce evidence, techniques that would not be permitted in a courtroom but which are very effective.

Most arbitrators are open to new ideas to make the arbitration process more efficient. And AAA arbitrators are trained to give affidavit evidence the weight it deserves in light of the adversary's objections.[19]

IV. Conclusion

There has always been a need to have disputes addressed fairly but in a faster, less costly way than the court system allows. That need is even greater in the current economic downturn as companies seek to make the dollars allocated to dispute resolution more productive. Counsel can achieve client goals by using arbitration. To make good use of arbitration, counsel must understand the core concepts that distinguish it from litigation.

Arbitration is flexible. It allows the parties to determine most procedural aspects of the process, including the scope of discovery. Litigation does not. Arbitration allows the parties to select an experienced decision maker or panel and to enter into a private agreement to keep the arbitration and its outcome confidential. Litigation does not. In addition, arbitration allows the parties to set a hearing date that is months (not years) away and to agree on steps that should make the process more efficient. These are just a few advantages that arbitration has over litigation. How to make the most of these advantages to make arbitration more efficient and cost effective is the subject of Part II of this article.

---

[18] Rule R-11.

[19] R-32, R-34, R-35 of the AAA Commercial Arbitration Rules.

CHAPTER 7

TELLING THE STORY: INTEGRATING WITNESSES, EXPERTS, AND DOCUMENTS INTO A COHESIVE NARRATIVE IN ARBITRATION

Evan Slavitt[*]

I. Introduction

At the heart of every dispute are at least two competing narratives. By the end of the hearing, the factfinder—whether jury, judge, or arbitrator—must decide which is more convincing. Many counsel, however, seem to think that just because they are presenting a case to an arbitration panel rather than a jury, they can dispense with the task of shaping the case into a coherent story. As a result, the arbitrators are left with lengthy testimony and notebooks full of exhibits that have to be pieced together. Instead of evaluating the conflicting stories, the arbitrators *become* the storytellers to the detriment of the process and the parties.

This problem is particularly acute in business cases for which credibility is at issue. Each side presents well-spoken witnesses who are prepared, coherent, and reasonably convincing on their own. Nonetheless, the witnesses profoundly disagree on critical events—conversations, meetings, etc.—in a way that cannot be reconciled as mere defects in recollection or narration. The panel must decide whom to believe, but, without the context of a coherent narrative, the panel has no touchstone to differentiate truth from fiction.

This article will describe some techniques for counsel to create a narrative that not only flows from the witnesses, experts and documents, but integrates them into a persuasive whole.[1]

---

[*] Evan Slavitt is the General Counsel of a publicly traded corporation and is an AAA arbitrator.

[1] The theoretical relationship between law and literature has been explored in various articles. *See, e.g.,* Wendy Nicole Duong, Law Is Law and Art Is Art and Shall the Two Ever Meet? Law and Literature: The Comparative Creative Processes, 15 S. CAL. Interdisc. L.J. 1, 2 (2005). It has also been addressed, to some degree, in terms of

II. What Is a Good Narrative?

A narrative is a spoken or written account of connected events. It is critical to understand that the narrative is ***not*** the sequence events themselves (that is, the mere chronology itself)—it is the ***way*** the story is told—the "account." The critical aspects of good narrative are the choices of which events are emphasized (or diminished) and the explanation of the connection between them. Pooh-Bah describes "corroborative detail, intended to give artistic verisimilitude to an otherwise bald and unconvincing narrative."[2] It is in that detail that good story-telling resides.

In this respect, a narrative is more than just a theme or a case theory, although it contains elements of both.[3] It is, instead, an integration of theme, theory, and facts in a way that conveys both logical force and a self-reinforcing structure. That means it is more than a mere accumulation of facts hooked onto a legal argument—instead it convinces the listener through its very nature.

As an example, there are any number of histories of World War I. In large measure, they all start with the same corpus of evidence. And yet the narratives range from "World War I was an accident that was no one nation's fault" to "World War I was created by the capitalist/colonialist structure of the nations involved" to "It was Germany's fault." What each historian does is marshal the facts and emphasize the connections in a way that carries the reader to accept his or her viewpoint. This requires much more than simply listing facts and presenting documents.

Accordingly, histories advocating the first theory emphasize the general instability of 1914 Europe, the logistical implications of military mobilization, and the continuing diplomatic conflict; they de-emphasize the expansionist nature of Germany and its less-than-stable Kaiser. This creates a general sense of inevitability that reinforces the impact of any particular fact or contemporaneous memoir. In contrast, histories advocating the second theory are less interested in the particular persons involved and emphasize big-picture societal, structural issues. Proponents of the third theory present the inverse of the first theory, telling a story that

---

application. *See, e.g.*, Michael Burt, The Importance Of Storytelling At All Stages Of A Capital Case, 77 UMKC Law. Rev. 877 (2008). This article, however, assays a more practical, pragmatic approach of use to practitioners.

[2] W.S. Gilbert, The Mikado or The Town of Titipu (1885).

[3] *See, e.g.*, Jay E. Grenig and Rocco M. Scanza, Developing A Case Theory and a Case Theme (68 Dispute Resolution Journal 51 (2014) ("The case theory is the strategic plan for achieving your goals in arbitration.").

focuses on the internal dynamics of Germany and its relationship to the other great nations. Each must mold its approach to convince the reader if it is to be persuasive.

Taking a common arbitration scenario, a claimant asserts that his investment advisor failed to take into account the claimant's real investment objectives and did respond to questions or phone calls to explain various investments. The legal theory of the claimant is clear—the advisor failed to meet her fiduciary obligations. The mere fact that there is a valid legal theory does not, however, itself make the claimant's case persuasive because, on her part, the respondent advisor asserts that each of the risks was explained and that the portfolio was consistent with such objectives. This legal theory absolves the respondent of liability. Each side has, therefore, established both theme and theory.

If the facts are so plain that they speak for themselves, the matter is unlikely to progress to a full hearing. On the other hand, if the matter has not resolved before the hearing, then neither side has a case that is so obvious and so powerful that the outcome is a foregone conclusion. That means that counsel must do more than present unshaped testimony and a stack of emails, prospectuses, trade confirmations and the like. They must create a narrative that integrates theory, facts and testimony into a persuasive whole. To do that, counsel must decide which interactions and which documents or parts of documents are important.

III. Key Narrative Tools

What v. Why—Lawyers tend to think that presenting a case means setting forth ***what*** happened. The fallback question is often some variation of "what happened next?". This is the beginning of a narrative but it is not the narrative itself. What makes a narrative convincing is that it answers the question "why?". It is essential for counsel to explain—or at least posit—an explanation of why the events occurred as they did.

In the arbitration example, the claimant must often overcome some initial skepticism from the panel based on their assumption that professional investment advisors, in general, would have no reason not to respond to the inquiries of an investor. After all, that is part of their job. Without an answer to "why?", the claimant's credibility is at risk. If, on the other hand, the claimant explains that the advisor was dealing with personal problems, or was overloaded with work from other, bigger clients, then the lack of response becomes more plausible.

This requires that counsel go beyond stringing events together. Instead, counsel must decide what events must be placed in the foreground and how to connect them in a comprehensible way. That does not mean that a chronological structure to the narrative is inherently improper; quite often that structure is appropriate. There is, however, a huge difference between a narrative that is chronological and a mere recounting of events one after another.

Narrative Focus—there are neither dwarves nor billy goats gruff in the story of Goldilocks and the Three Bears. They have no place in the story and would be terribly distracting. Instead, the story gets its power from the simplicity of the story and its easily understandable message.

So too, counsel presenting an arbitration case must make the hard decisions on what competing narratives to exclude. One story explaining a course of events is strong; two are occasionally possible; three suggest that there is no real explanation. Thus, a child explaining a broken lamp with "It didn't happen, I wasn't there, and it was an accident" is unlikely to convince a parent.

Creating narrative focus can be emotionally and strategically difficult. Most lawyers are risk-averse and are reluctant to give up anything. Clients often are wedded to multiple explanations and may criticize when one is cut. To these responses, the advocate must internally acknowledge that elimination of all but the best story actually increases the chances of prevailing and then convince the client of this truth.

Narrative focus also requires recognizing when enough is enough. It takes only three pigs to make the point that only a substantial structure can withstand the wolf's huffing/puffing. Additional pigs constructing houses of gelatin, cardboard, and the like would not really advance the story or make the point any better. In arbitration, there always comes a point even in the most complex dispute when additional examples lose explanatory power and become counterproductive. Again, this requires that lawyers and their counsel find the fortitude to make the necessary cuts. If they do, however, they will be well-rewarded.

Having discussed narrative in the abstract, it is time to turn to some concrete ways counsel can improve their arbitration cases.

IV. Testimony: Time as Investment, Time as Structure

The principal way counsel signals importance in a hearing is by investing time. Much as movie directors signal significance by screen time—sometimes even using "slow motion" to artificially add to the time of experience—so too must counsel take control of the time at the hearing. In the arbitration example above, assume there were four meetings over the course of six months between claimant and respondent. The claimant could just describe the four meetings and then say "they occurred over six months." This course, however, does not focus the panel on the passage of time. Instead, it plays into the hands of the respondent who also wants to create the impression of continual communications.

Instead, claimant's counsel should intentionally frame an integrated narrative that tells the story of defective communication. Thus, counsel can ask the claimant to discuss the contacts month by month. When the meetings come up, the focus is not on the substance of the meetings but on their brevity. The same approach applies when cross-examining the respondent. Instead of:

Q. "Did you communicate in November or December?"

Counsel could instead ask this line:

Q. "You got an email from claimant toward the end of October?
Q. "Did you respond the next day?"
Q. "Did you respond by Friday?"
Q. "Not an email? Not a call?"
Q. "Did you respond even in a week?" "In fact, you didn't even respond in the first part of November, correct?"
Q. "Nothing between the email and Thanksgiving?"
Q. "Nothing in the first part of December?"
Q. "Did you even send a Christmas card?"

Now the assertion of inadequate contact by the claimant is reinforced by emphasis on the passage of time in the testimony of both claimant and respondent. The story becomes self-reinforcing, each aspect lending credibility to the others.

Another way to use time as an investment is to consider submission of some testimony in writing. In complex arbitrations, there is no reason that the panel must take in less important testimony at the same rate as critical testimony. This self-editing allows the most important events to be in the foreground, allowing the relationship between those links to become clearer.

In fact, given that arbitrations are not subject to the same rigid rules as trials, counsel can seek permission to submit testimony summaries as well as the testimony itself. These summaries allow counsel to connect events in ways that detailed affidavits or pre-filed testimony cannot. These summaries could be in various forms—bullet point lists, PowerPoint presentations, and integration with document excerpts.

A second use of time arises in the structure of the testimony. For example, one common temporal tool used in literature and movies is foreshadowing. By pre-figuring key events, they are imbued with importance when they then arise in the narrative. Thus, witnesses in arbitration can begin:

> Q: "Before we start at the beginning, can you tell me why you are here?"
>
> A: "All the time the broker was trying to convince me to invest, she was always available to me but once she had my money, and as time went by, she never returned my calls."

Now, when the narration gets to the fall events, the panel already knows to listen harder because those events have been emphasized by being taken out of sequence.

A similar technique is to start the story when the critical events begin and then fill in the background. Thus, an investor might begin his testimony with the first meeting with the advisor. Only when his experience becomes relevant would his prior investment history be brought in. This allows the panel to put this information in context rather than wading through it as part of general background.

Attention to sequence applies not just to the order of testimony of a witness, but to the order of the witnesses. Inherent in the order of presentation is the importance of the facts related by the witness and the importance of the witness himself or herself. Sometimes that means that the claimant is neither the first nor the last witness. On occasion, the best strategy is to lead with an expert, as discussed below.

V. Integrating Documents into the Story

On the first day of most complex arbitration hearings the panel is greeted by stacks of black binders presented by all parties. Most likely, by the end of the arbitration, only a fraction of those documents will even be mentioned. Of those, many will be multi-page documents and the panel will only be asked to look at a few of the pages. As a result, the impact of the documents is minimal at best.

There is no reason that the panel must be burdened with complete copies of every document. Although evidentiary rules generally require complete documents, no such obligation obtains in arbitrations. Accordingly, the ritual presentation of multiple binders—or the more modern CD equivalent—should be a thing of the past.

At the very minimum, important passages in documents should be highlighted. On the one hand, this does allow the panel to find the important text more easily. It also minimizes the possibility of dispute with other parties; if they believe other passages should be highlighted as well, that can be easily accomplished. On the other, it often still requires paging through many pages of extraneous material.

Even better, therefore, is to present the documents in excerpted form.[4] Proper and focused excerpts can efficiently weave the documents into the narrative. As each excerpt becomes relevant during the hearings, the panel can seamlessly review the text or it can be projected onto a screen. Similarly, accounting or other numerical documents can be summarized and integrated into convenient formats.[5] Such summaries should not just be in the form of numerical tables. Instead, to the extent possible, they should also be translated into easily understood graphs or charts. This approach does require more preparation and more planning than the traditional approach. It pays off in increased effectiveness and persuasion.

Using documents this way has several benefits. First, the panel is much more likely to look at documentation if it has a reason to do so. Second, it is much more likely to pay attention to documents when the relevance is readily apparent. Third, the documents become an integrated part of the narrative, strengthening the case.

VI. Experts as Storytellers

The standard approach to expert testimony was developed to meet the foundational requirements of formal rules of evidence. First, the expert sets forth his or her qualifications to demonstrate expertise. Next, the expert recounts in detail what he or she did to investigate the problem at hand to demonstrate that the opinion being offered has an appropriate

---

[4] In the interests of caution, counsel should always have available a set of complete documents in case of dispute.

[5] Of course, such summarization must be done fairly and accurately to maintain credibility.

factual foundation. Only then is the opinion itself offered. This requires that the factfinder listen to a vast amount of material without knowing what, if anything, will turn out to be important. Further, it is inherently expert-focused rather than focused on the case as a whole.

In an arbitration, however, there is no reason to mimic this formalistic presentation. First, the rules of evidence do not apply. Second, by the time of the hearing, the panel will, most likely, have resolved any qualification and foundation issues. Indeed, in many arbitrations, the expert will have issued a detailed report.

That allows experts to be used in a very different way, to weave together various pieces of factual testimony and documents. Rather than shining the spotlight on the expert, the expert can assist the panel by reinforcing the narrative.

In the investor example, the expert could start by describing the appropriate interaction between advisor and client. He or she could then walk the panel through the initiation of the relationship and describe the points of failure contrasting the facts with the standard. In particular, he or she can identify when communications would be expected, highlighting lacunae in the communications records.

This use of experts also tends to ameliorate the perception of the expert as "hired gun." As the spotlight shifts away from the expert as such, the expert instead is perceived as assisting the panel rather than simply proffering paid-for testimony. As the panel comes to accept the story, they inherently will give credit to the expert, thereby reinforcing the narrative.

VII. Pictures—Show, Don't Tell

It sometimes seems that as soon as counsel hear the word arbitration, they forget everything they ever learned about using graphics as an advocacy tool. Instead of looking for opportunities to persuade with diagrams, graphs, or simple illustrations, they seem to be under the impression that arbitrators will not benefit from or, indeed, will think less of them for using such devices. Nothing could be further from the truth.

Take a case involving the evolution of a portfolio that gets increasingly weighted with risky investments over time. It is, of course, the case that most arbitrators can wade through an Excel spreadsheet and work out the allocation of assets from year to year. Even the most sophisticated arbitrator, however, will then be using a substantial part of their time and attention holding various numbers in mind and making internal calculations. A series of pie charts, or even a line graph of portfolio components over time, however, releases much of that time and attention to focus on the message and its implications. Even better, using red for high risk, yellow for moderate risk, and green for low risk resonates with cultural norms thereby reinforcing the narrative itself and allows the advocate to ***show*** that risk increased over time rather than just telling the arbitrators.

The same can be said for devices such as timelines, organization charts, relationship charts, and the like. These may seem simple-minded to the advocate that has been living with a dispute for many years and is intimately familiar with even the minutest details of the case. To an arbitrator who may have read pre-arbitration briefs just the day before the arbitration starts and is still struggling with the basic shape of the case, such tools can be a godsend.

Good graphics can also help tie the case together. A chart used in the opening, adopted by fact witnesses, explained by experts, and then reproduced in closing briefs anchors the abstract narrative into a concrete image. It makes it easier for the panel not only to remember pieces of testimony, it helps them understand their relationship.

VIII. The Freedom of No Appeal

In most arbitrations, there is no appeal. Even in those that permit such appeal, it is very limited in scope.[6] Many litigators, if put under truth serum, would admit to being terrified by this lack of recourse. Instead, they should be liberated.

One of the most pervasive impediments in any trial is the need to "preserve the record." It so often seems the case that just when some testimony is reaching an emotional crescendo, it is interrupted by one side or the other taking time to preserve some issue on appeal. Similarly, documents are introduced not because they have any real importance, but because counsel are concerned that failure to introduce them will later be considered a waiver of some appellate argument or other.

When there is no appeal, there is no need to preserve issues. Counsel can, instead, focus exclusively on the progress of the narrative as it unfolds before the panel. For example, suppose an advocate seeking to offer the testimony of a witness on a particular point is told that the arbitrator (or panel) does not find such point particularly relevant. In a trial, counsel would feel compelled to interrupt the proceedings, approach the bench,

---

6 *See* AAA/ICDR Optional Appellate Arbitration Rules (2013).

and make a proffer. The judge is distracted—he or she has already determined that the subject of the proffer is not important—and the jury winds up doodling or staring at the ceiling. Nonetheless, to preserve the record, counsel feel obliged to go through this procedure. In an arbitration, however, except in the most unusual situation counsel can simply move on, keeping the attention on the narrative as a whole without losing the thread of the story or the attention of the panel.

In short, any time counsel in an arbitration feels prompted to "make a record," counsel should suppress that impulse. Instead, he or she should focus attention on how the point relates to the overall narrative story and determine how best to reinforce the narrative or make the point in another way. It will frequently turn out that the point is not critical and that the narrative does not suffer. Thus liberated from the obligations imposed by any appellate process, counsel can focus on what is important to win the arbitration.

IX. Conclusion

William Zinsser, the author of On Writing Well, once said "One of underestimated tasks in nonfiction writing is to impose narrative shape on an unwieldy mass of material." This task, however, is no less essential when presenting an arbitration case than in writing. A well-shaped, thoughtfully edited presentation that pulls together witnesses, exhibits, and advocacy into a coherent whole is much more likely to persuade and to win. Counsel should grasp the opportunity to make the format of arbitration work in the client's favor rather than allowing the absence of formal rules and process to drain urgency and interest.

CHAPTER 8

DEVELOPING A CASE THEORY AND A CASE THEME*

*Jay E. Grenig and Rocco M. Scanza***

I. Generally

Developing a theory of the case is one of the most important tasks you perform in preparing for an arbitration hearing. The case theory is the strategic plan for achieving your goals in arbitration. Development of a case theory begins after you learn the initial facts through interviews and informal investigations.[1] Throughout the preparation and presentation of the arbitration case, the theory of the case will be revised and updated as more information becomes available.

The theory of the case provides a tactical structure serving as your organizing principle for the arbitration hearing. A properly developed theory of the case will provide guidance for every action—from

---

* This article was originally published in JAY E. GRENIG AND ROCCO M. SCANZA, CASE PREPARATION AND PRESENTATION: A GUIDE FOR ARBITRATION ADVOCATES AND ARBITRATORS (JurisNet LLC 2013).

** Rocco M. Scanza and Jay E. Grenig both serve on the American Arbitration Association's labor panel.

Mr. Scanza is an Attorney, Arbitrator and Mediator of labor and employment disputes. He is also the Executive Director of Cornell University's Scheinman Institute on Conflict Resolution, where he teaches courses in workplace alternative dispute resolution. Mr. Scanza was formerly a National Vice President at the American Arbitration Association. He graduated from Queens College in New York City and Loyola Law School of Los Angeles. He lives and works in Ithaca, N.Y.

Mr. Grenig is a Professor of Law at Marquette University Law School. He has served as an Arbitrator or Mediator in over 2,000 labor and employment disputes. A member of the National Academy of Arbitrators, the American Law Institute, and the Order of the Coif, Professor Grenig is also a fellow of the College of Labor and Employment Lawyers. He formerly chaired the Labor and Employment Law Section of the Association of American Law Schools and served as a consultant to the National Commission on Employment Policy. He has written or co-written numerous books and articles.

[1] Bocchino & Solomon, *What Juries Want to Hear: Methods for Developing Persuasive Case Theory*, 67 TENN. L. REV. 543, 543 (2000).

investigating, interviewing, selecting witnesses, preparing an opening statement, selecting exhibits, examining witnesses, and preparing closing arguments.

In developing a theory of the case, you must understand both the development of the legal theories and the factual theories of your case and your opponent's case. The legal theories and factual theories are interrelated, and linked through law, information, and the client's objectives.[2] The legal theory is the legal framework developed from review of applicable rules and standards, including statutes, regulations, contract provisions, and case law. The factual theory is the party's story, justifying relief under the legal theory and based on the information and inferences from that information.[3]

Your theory of the case must maximize your opportunity to win.[4] You should try to turn the difficult facts to your advantage. You do not want the opposing party to set the agenda. In developing your theory of the case, however, you must always keep in mind the goals and objectives of the client.

II. The Legal Theory

The legal theory shows why, as a matter of law, the party you represent should prevail.[5] In determining your legal theories, you must consider legal principles, contract provisions, and other authority applicable to the dispute. The legal theory must take into account the legal requirements for the claim or defense, and identify the evidence required to establish each element.[6] Development of the legal theory may require you to research judicial decisions, administrative rulings, prior arbitration awards, and contract language.

In order to develop the legal theory, you must learn as much information about the case as you can. You must take into account available witnesses and evidentiary support for your case. It is important to keep an open mind and not ignore the significance of factual and legal

[2] *See* Berger et al., TRIAL ADVOCACY: PLANNING, ANALYSIS, & STRATEGY 16 (Aspen Law and Business 1989).

[3] *See* Berger et al., TRIAL ADVOCACY: PLANNING, ANALYSIS, & STRATEGY 17 (Aspen Law and Business 1989).

[4] Perrin et al., THE ART & SCIENCE OF TRIAL ADVOCACY 36 (Anderson Publishing Co. 2003).

[5] Bocchino & Solomon, *What Juries Want to Hear: Methods for Developing Persuasive Case Theory*, 67 TENN. L. REV. 543, 544 (2000).

[6] Perrin et al., THE ART & SCIENCE OF TRIAL ADVOCACY 34 (Anderson Publishing Co. 2003).

information that may suggest different, more promising case theories. Development of the legal theory varies according to whether the party you represent is a claimant or respondent (or is a grievant or an employer in labor-management arbitration).

You may decide to use more than one legal theory in some cases. One must be cautious in using conflicting legal theories that undermine your case. You may decide to pursue several tentative theories during the investigation. After information is received and reviewed, you may then narrow the legal theories you intend to use.

There may be strategic reasons for using multiple or alternative legal theories. For example, in a discharge case under a collective bargaining agreement's just cause clause, the union may decide to use as its legal theory that the discharged employee was not insubordinate. It may also desire to use the alternative theory that, even if the employee was insubordinate, the disciplinary penalty imposed on the employee was too harsh.

III. Complainant's Legal Theory

For the claimant (or grievant in a labor-management case), the legal theory will correspond to the claim for relief in civil litigation.[7] In the case of labor-management disputes, the legal theory may also correspond to "common law" labor arbitration principles.[8]

After considering all the case law, prior arbitration decisions, treatises, statutes, and regulations, there may be numerous legal theories from which the complainant may choose. In choosing which theory or theories to use, it is necessary to assess the strengths and weaknesses of each potential legal theory, considering:

- Whether the theories are so novel or creative as to invite likely legal attack or rejection. For example, the employee's theft should be excused because the employee was worried about the behavior of the employee's teen-age daughter.
- The practical advantages and disadvantages of each potential legal theory, including the difficulty of establishing a legal

[7] For examples of the elements of civil claims, see O'Malley, Grenig & Lee, FEDERAL JURY PRACTICE AND INSTRUCTIONS (Thomson Reuters 6th ed. 2012).

[8] *See, e.g.,* THE COMMON LAW OF THE WORKPLACE: THE VIEWS OF ARBITRATORS (St. Antoine ed. BNA Books 2d ed. 2005); DISCIPLINE AND DISCHARGE IN ARBITRATION (Brand & Biren eds. BNA Books 2d ed. 2008).

theory. For example, there may be problems satisfying a legal theory requiring proof of intent or culpable state of mind.
- The availability of evidence to support a legal theory must be considered. For example, the investigation may disclose that certain legal theories cannot be established in the arbitration hearing because of lack of witnesses or documentary evidence.[9]

IV. Respondent's Legal Theory

A responding party has a somewhat easier task than the complainant. With respect to legal theories, a respondent can attempt to show the following:

- There is no such legal theory as that urged by the complainant. The claimant may have established all the elements of the claimant's claim, but the respondent may assert that, as a matter of law, the claimant's theory should not be recognized as one for which the arbitrator should provide a remedy.
- The complainant is unable to or has not proven the facts required by the elements of the claim. A factual sufficiency attack takes the position that, even if the legal theory exists, the claimant's allegations are insufficient to permit the arbitrator to find one of the essential elements of that legal theory has been proven.
- The arbitrator should not be persuaded because of the applicable quantum of proof. Under this theory, the respondent seeks to show that the claimant has failed to carry its burden of persuasion as to one or more of the elements of the claim.
- The claimant is barred because of some procedural insufficiency such as an untimely appeal to arbitration. Under this legal theory, the respondent may show that the demand for arbitration was not properly filed or that other time limits have not been satisfied. Procedural requirements may be found in the contract, statutes, and administrative regulations.[10]

---

[9] *See* Berger et al., TRIAL ADVOCACY: PLANNING, ANALYSIS, & STRATEGY 17 (Aspen Law and Business 1989).

[10] *See* Berger et al., TRIAL ADVOCACY: PLANNING, ANALYSIS, & STRATEGY 18-20 (Aspen Law and Business 1989).

A respondent must also consider affirmative defenses.[11] Affirmative defenses include fraud, self-defense, and waiver. The responding party must consider the elements of any defenses. A respondent's affirmative defenses are composed of elements just as the complainant's legal theories contain elements, too.[12]

V. The Factual Theory

Once tentative legal theories are determined, the facts should be examined, unrestricted or unlimited by any artificial limit imposed by strict compliance with a legal theory.[13] The factual theory defines what the facts of the case actually are.[14] The factual theory takes the information accumulated and organizes it into a coherent and logical story supporting your legal theory.

You must review what you presently know about the uncontested and contested facts. You must organize the facts and legal theory into a believable story. A good factual theory avoids evidence that appears to be inconsistent with the weight of other evidence, that is unimportant or immaterial, or that may be confusing to the arbitrator.[15] The factual theory should also avoid evidence that is inadmissible.[16]

Your factual theory should explain what happened and why. You must

- take into account the established facts in the case,
- avoid contradicting any disputed fact the arbitrator will likely find to be true,
- select a theory maximizing your likelihood of prevailing, and
- reject any inconsistent claims or defenses.[17]

---

[11] An "affirmative defense" can be defined as a new fact or set of facts operating to defeat a claim even if the facts supporting that claim are true.

[12] *See* O'Malley, Grenig & Lee, FEDERAL JURY PRACTICE AND INSTRUCTIONS (Thomson Reuters 6th ed. 2012) for examples of elements of defenses.

[13] *See* Bocchino & Solomon, *What Juries Want to Hear: Methods for Developing Persuasive Case Theory*, 67 TENN. L. REV. 543, 548 (2000) ("In addition, to limit the factual development of a case to whether a particular fact fits a particular legal theory misses entirely the point of having each legal matter decided on its own factual and legal merits.").

[14] Bocchino & Solomon, *What Juries Want to Hear: Methods for Developing Persuasive Case Theory*, 67 TENN. L. REV. 543, 545 (2000).

[15] Tanford, THE TRIAL PROCESS: LAW, TACTICS, AND ETHICS 52 (LexisNexis 4th ed. 2009).

[16] Tanford, THE TRIAL PROCESS: LAW, TACTICS, AND ETHICS 52 (LexisNexis 4th ed. 2009).

[17] Perrin et al., THE ART & SCIENCE OF TRIAL ADVOCACY 35 (Anderson Publishing Co. 2003).

You must anticipate what the arbitrator may do in resolving factual conflicts, including which facts the arbitrator is likely to believe and which facts the arbitrator is not likely to believe.[18] You must ensure that your theories take into account all the facts that may be established at the hearing and do not contradict facts the arbitrator will most likely find to be true.

You should recognize, acknowledge, and be able to explain weaknesses in your case. A weakness means inherent problems in your case that arise regardless of what you do.[19] A weakness may be a gap, inconsistency, improbability, or flaw in your factual theory. Weaknesses arise when key facts cannot be proved, are uncorroborated, come from witness with credibility problems, or are remembered inconsistently by your witnesses.[20]

As you gather evidence, the view of what is provable, what is not provable, and what really happened and why, probably changes.[21] Accordingly, it is usually unwise to decide upon a final factual theory to the exclusion of all other theories until all the evidence is gathered.

VI. Claimant's Factual Theory

The claimant's factual theory shows what happened using a structure providing clarity and coherence.[22] The claimant's factual theory must provide organization for the "plot" and tell a logical and a credible story.

The claimant's factual theory must be developed to withstand three types of a respondent's legal theories:

- **Attacks on Factual Sufficiency.** An attack on factual sufficiency can be withstood by being careful to set forth sufficient information to fulfill every element of the claimant's legal theory.
- **Attacks on Persuasive Sufficiency.** To withstand this type of attack, the claimant's story must be sufficiently persuasive to

---

[18] Perrin, et al., THE ART & SCIENCE OF TRIAL ADVOCACY 35 (Anderson Publishing Co. 2003).

[19] Tanford, THE TRIAL PROCESS: LAW, TACTICS, AND ETHICS 53 (LexisNexis 4th ed. 2009).

[20] Tanford, THE TRIAL PROCESS: LAW, TACTICS, AND ETHICS 53 (LexisNexis 4th ed. 2009).

[21] Bocchino & Solomon, *What Juries Want to Hear: Methods for Developing Persuasive Case Theory*, 67 TENN. L. REV. 543, 545 (2000).

[22] *See* Berger et al., TRIAL ADVOCACY: PLANNING, ANALYSIS, & STRATEGY 22 (Aspen Law and Business 1989).

convince the arbitrator that the complainant has established every element of the claimant's legal theory under the required burden of proof.

- **Attacks Based on Affirmative Defenses.** The complainant's factual theory must anticipate and neutralize the respondent's affirmative defenses.[23]

VII. Respondent's Factual Theory

In developing its factual theory, the respondent must anticipate the claimant's factual theory. A review of the demand for arbitration or, in the case of a labor-management dispute, the grievance, provides some indication of the factual theories of the claimant.

The respondent must determine whether, based on the evidence, which facts the claimant is likely to be able to prove and which facts the claimant is not likely to prove. In addition, the respondent should determine which affirmative defenses it can prove.

The respondent's defenses should be consistent with each other. The danger in asserting multiple-choice defensive theories is that this may imperil the respondent's credibility before the arbitrator. Inconsistent arguments raise the possibility that the respondent is not concerned about the truth, and that the respondent lacks confidence in the respondent's case.[24] The respondent, however, generally should challenge both liability and, if liability should be shown, the damages claimed.[25] To focus solely on liability, a respondent risks the imposition of unreasonably high damages should the complainant prevail in the arbitration.

VIII. Identifying Opposing Theories and Evidence

It is essential to analyze the opposing party's case to determine where disputes or differences may arise as well as the opposing party's

---

[23] *See* Berger et al., TRIAL ADVOCACY: PLANNING, ANALYSIS, & STRATEGY 22-23 (Aspen Law and Business 1989).

[24] Perrin et al., THE ART & SCIENCE OF TRIAL ADVOCACY 38-39 (Anderson Publishing Co. 2003).

[25] Perrin et al., THE ART & SCIENCE OF TRIAL ADVOCACY 40 (Anderson Publishing Co. 2003).

strengths and weaknesses.[26] This information will assist you in deciding where to challenge the other side. It will also help you determine the strengths and weaknesses of your own theories. You want to emphasize your strengths and attack the other party's weaknesses.

IX. Using Case Theory in Preparing and Presenting Your Case

Your case theory provides a basis for preparing for the arbitration hearing and presenting the case in arbitration. A properly developed case theory directs you to the central issues in dispute. Evidence supporting every element of the legal theory must be persuasively presented.

In most cases there are critical areas on which the outcome of the case turns—these are the central issues in dispute.[27] For example, in an insubordination case, the case may turn on whether the supervisor had the authority to give the order, or it may turn on whether the supervisor warned the employee of the consequences of disobeying the order.

The case theory guides the investigation and preparation of the case. Interviews seek to obtain information developing, supporting, modifying, or discarding plausible case theories.[28] The case theory will assist you in preparing the demand for arbitration or the response to the demand. It will also provide assistance in developing the opening statement, selecting witnesses and exhibits, and preparing the closing argument.

X. Developing a Case Theme

In developing a case theme,[29] you must synthesize the facts into the core truths of the case—its essence.[30] Good advocates recognize the

---

[26] Bocchino & Solomon, *What Juries Want to Hear: Methods for Developing Persuasive Case Theory*, 67 TENN. L. REV. 543, 549 (2000); Tanford, THE TRIAL PROCESS: LAW, TACTICS, AND ETHICS 54 (LexisNexis 4th ed. 2009).

[27] *See* Berger et al., TRIAL ADVOCACY: PLANNING, ANALYSIS, & STRATEGY 26 (Aspen Law and Business 1989).

[28] *See* Berger et al., TRIAL ADVOCACY: PLANNING, ANALYSIS, & STRATEGY 26-27 (Aspen Law and Business 1989).

[29] Sometimes referred to as "persuasive theory." *See* Bocchino & Solomon, *What Juries Want to Hear: Methods for Developing Persuasive Case Theory*, 67 TENN. L. REV. 543, 546 (2000).

[30] Perrin et al., THE ART & SCIENCE OF TRIAL ADVOCACY 41 (Anderson Publishing Co. 2003).

importance of the need for a theme—a central idea harnessing the power of the work and focusing its message.[31] The case theme may be conceptualized as a storyline.[32]

The theme should present an idea or image that will resonate with the arbitrator, causing the arbitrator to fully and deeply understand what the case is about. The theme must be coherent and should appeal to logic and common sense. An effective case theme will resonate with the concepts of fairness, redressing a wrong, doing the right thing, and the necessity for punishment.[33]

---

[31] Perrin et al., THE ART & SCIENCE OF TRIAL ADVOCACY 41 (Anderson Publishing Co. 2003).

[32] Miller, *Teaching Case Theory*, 9 CLINICAL L. REV. 293, 297 (2002).

[33] Bocchino & Solomon, *What Juries Want to Hear: Methods for Developing Persuasive Case Theory*, 67 TENN. L. REV. 543, 546 (2000).

CHAPTER 9

THE TOP 20 MISTAKES ATTORNEYS MAKE IN ARBITRATION AND HOW TO AVOID THEM: HOW TO AVOID COMMON MISTAKES AND REPLACE THEM WITH TOOLS FOR PERSUASIVE ADVOCACY

Judith B. Ittig and Harold Coleman, Jr.[*]

I. Introduction

Arbitration has three distinct phases: the pre-hearing stage; the evidentiary hearing and the post-hearing period, which begins at the conclusion of the hearings until the arbitrator issues the award. As arbitrators who have heard hundreds of commercial and construction cases, we have come across numerous mistakes attorneys make – in cases large and small – mistakes that can negatively affect the time the arbitration takes, the cost of the process, and even more significant from the clients' point of view, the outcome.

---

[*] Judith Ittig serves on the AAA's commercial arbitrator panel, the ICDR's commercial arbitrator panel, and the AAA's Construction Mega Project Panel. Mrs. Ittig, an attorney at Ittig & Ittig, P.C. based in Washington, DC, is a Fellow of the American College of Construction Lawyers, a Chartered Arbitrator/Fellow of the Chartered Institute of Arbitrators (London), and a Fellow of the College of Commercial Arbitrators. Harold Coleman, Jr., Esq., is senior vice president for mediation at the American Arbitration Association (AAA) and executive director/mediator for MEDIATION.org, a division of the AAA. Coleman also trains new AAA arbitrators and aspiring mediators in basic/advanced arbitration case management techniques and basic/advanced mediation skills. A former multi-disciplinary project manager and complex litigation attorney, Coleman has mediated and arbitrated multiplied hundreds of litigated and non-litigated disputes during a 28-year legal and ADR career. He is a Fellow and director of the College of Commercial Arbitrators (CCA) and board member of the International Mediation Institute (IMI). Coleman serves from the Association's Los Angeles and New York offices. The authors can be reached by e-mail, Mrs. Ittig at jbi@ittig-ittig.com and Mr. Coleman at ColemanH@mediation.org.

To help attorneys recognize the mistakes they are making when representing the parties in arbitration, we compiled a list of the ones we see most often and suggest ways to handle the particular issue or tasks in a manner that will be helpful to the arbitrator. These strategies could help attorneys improve the quality of their arbitration advocacy and obtain for their clients the benefits that arbitration was designed to produce.

II. Five Pre-Hearing Mistakes and How to Avoid Them

1. Postponing Itemization of Damages and Grounds for Recovery

Attorneys often file demands for arbitration and answering statements that do not specify the full nature of, and dollar amounts involved in, the clients' claims and counterclaims. Vague arbitral pleadings can be made because the arbitration rules of the American Arbitration Association (AAA) do not require much specificity at this point. General demands and answers are understandable if the claimant wants to get the arbitration underway as soon as possible; the claims and damages are not completely known; or the respondent is still considering its counterclaims and offsets, which it does not want to present until the claimant's claims are fully fleshed out. But when attorneys choose to do only what is minimally required by the AAA rules, even when the legal theories and damage calculations are known, they are missing an early opportunity to highlight their cases for the arbitrator.

Recommended Solutions

The statement of claims does not need to follow the format of a complaint in a lawsuit, but it should set forth the factual grounds and legal theories for recovery, and all types of damages or other relief sought, both legal and equitable, as well as the amounts claimed.

The answering statement should do the same with respect to the defenses, counterclaims and offsets. In a recent arbitration involving allegations of malpractice by a real estate broker, after five days of evidentiary hearings, the arbitrator denied the claimant's request for damages because the demand asserted only a claim for breach of contract, even though a negligence claim could have been asserted as well. Possibly counsel assumed, wrongly, it turns out, that the arbitrator would award damages for negligence if the claimant proved that the broker's conduct fell below the requisite standard of care. However, the arbitrator determined that he was limited by the scope of the disputes presented for arbitration.

Indicating all the theories of recovery and relief sought, including the calculation of monetary damages, makes it possible for the arbitrator to determine whether the case will be complex or simple, and if it will be dominated by factual or legal issues. It will also help the arbitrator understand the case and recognize which pre-hearing procedures need to be scheduled.

2. *Fear of Committing to a Schedule*

Poor or delayed scheduling of the arbitration comes about because the parties' attorneys do not realize why they are required to participate in the preliminary hearing (called a "preliminary management hearing" in the AAA Construction Industry Arbitration Rules); therefore, they do not adequately prepare for it. They often regard this hearing as the responsibility of the arbitrator. They expect that the arbitrator will set the schedule for pre-hearing events, such as exchanges of witness lists and exhibits. As a consequence, the attorneys often end up requesting postponements after the schedule is established, and then accuse each other of delaying tactics.

Recommended Solutions

Attorneys should be prepared to answer the arbitrator's questions, or initiate discussion, about their needs for discovery, a site visit, and experts. There are a number of steps attorneys should take to prepare for the preliminary hearing.

Since scheduling the proceeding is an important goal of the preliminary hearing, the attorneys should find out the dates on which their clients and witnesses (both fact and expert, if any) will be available. Before the preliminary hearing, the attorneys should meet and confer to discuss:

- The scope of document discovery.
- The dates for exchanging documents, exhibit lists and witness lists.
- The dates for exchanging their experts' reports.
- Whether either party plans to file any pre-hearing motions and if so, the dates for filing and replying to them.
- Whether a site visit is needed.

- How much time each side will need for direct and cross-examination (and perhaps rebuttal) at the evidentiary hearing. It is prudent to plan for rebuttal, even if the time allotted is not used.
- Available dates for the evidentiary hearing.

As a result of the meet and confer, the attorneys should have a jointly outlined schedule of all pre-hearing activities as well as possible dates for the hearing that accommodate both clients and their witnesses. The dates and amount of time reserved for the hearing on the merits should be realistic because arbitrators take seriously their duty to manage the arbitration efficiently and they are bound by law to postpone hearings only for good cause shown. Moreover, they are not required to grant a postponement request that lacks good cause, even if all other counsel were to agree to the request, unless the underlying arbitration agreement provides otherwise, which is not usually the case.

Unfortunately, litigators are notoriously inexpert at estimating how much time they need to present their case. The attorneys could suggest that the arbitrator set aside a day or two of additional hearing time in case it is needed. Blocking out more hearing time makes more sense than scheduling an inadequate amount of time and then trying to arrange additional days for the hearing at the last minute.

Because the schedule and hearing dates agreed to at the preliminary hearing will be incorporated into a case management order by the arbitrator and be considered final, the attorneys should notify their clients and fact and expert witnesses of the hearing dates as soon as possible after the preliminary hearing. They also should alert the arbitrator and opposing counsel as early as possible if any scheduling problems arise and propose a remedy that does not alter the overall schedule. Potential remedies include extending the hearing day, reducing the break and lunch periods, taking witnesses out of order, and supplanting in-person testimony with telephone testimony or with transcripts of the witness's deposition. In proper situations, the witness's affidavit can be an effective substitute.

Finally, we suggest that attorneys consider allowing their clients to participate in the preliminary hearing. It is good for clients to learn about how the arbitration will be conducted. Clients who learn this tend to have a more positive attitude toward, and respect for, the ultimate award.

3. *Buried Exhibits and Not Having a "Red Book" of Core Documents*

Too often, documents that will be used as exhibits in the evidentiary hearing are haphazardly assembled and too little thought is given to organizing them in a way that is useful to the arbitrator. It is a mistake to prepare exhibits without consulting with opposing counsel to avoid duplication.

Recommended Solutions

The arbitrator has to juggle books of exhibits submitted by both parties. It takes a surprisingly long time for the arbitrator to locate the portions of exhibits referred to during the evidentiary hearing, especially when the exhibit is a multi-page document. Each exhibit should be numbered. In addition, the documents that make up each exhibit should have a unique consecutive identifying number (or combination of letter and number) on every page. Exhibits that are not pre-marked and introduced at the hearing should be labeled for easy insertion with the pre-marked exhibits (e.g., Exhibit 10A). You don't want the arbitrator to have a mass of loose pages that can be misplaced or put aside.

To make it easier for the arbitrator to work with the parties' exhibit books, the attorneys should remove from each party's separate binders uncontested "core exhibits" (e.g., in a construction dispute, the construction contracts, plans and specifications, change orders, etc.) that will be referred to frequently and place them in a joint exhibit binder sometimes called a "Red Book." In addition, they should remove documents of the same type (e.g., invoices, time sheets and payroll records) that will rarely be referred to individually ("bulk documents") and place them in a separate bulk document binder.

Eliminating duplicate exhibits reduces the risk that the arbitrator's notes from the hearing will be scattered on different copies of the same exhibit. The attorneys should not want important notes to be overlooked when the arbitrator reviews the exhibits during deliberations. Keep bulk documents separate so that they do not interfere with the exhibit books on which most of the testimony will be based.

4. Not Disclosing Demonstrative or Summary Exhibits

Attorneys expect arbitrators to welcome demonstrative or summary exhibits and often fail to anticipate that the adversary might object to the use of such an exhibit. They may think, rightly or wrongly, that the source documents and testimony for a summary exhibit (such as a timeline or chart) have already been admitted into evidence, so there is no basis for any objection. For these reasons, attorneys often fail to disclose their intention to use such exhibits prior to the attempted introduction at the evidentiary hearing. Sometimes summary exhibits are not prepared until just before the hearing closes. Sometimes they are purposefully not disclosed in order to catch the other party off guard.

Recommended Solutions

Counsel should pre-qualify summary and demonstrative exhibits in advance of their use. Doing so will save time during the hearing and avoid the objection that they are "surprise" exhibits. In one case, a scale model of a dam, made at great expense out of Plexiglas with working parts, was excluded from evidence because it would have been too time-consuming for the other party to check the model for accuracy and completeness.

In another case, a sample window and frame were not admitted into evidence because of objections as to whether the sample conformed to the window that was installed. The purpose for which the sample was offered might have been clarified in a pre-hearing setting and any objections could have been overcome. At the hearing, it was too late.

Summary exhibits should only summarize and not add new information. The attorney risks losing the opportunity to use a helpful exhibit if it contains facts or opinion that were not elicited in testimony. If admissibility is not addressed prior to the hearing or at least prior to the attempted introduction, and the adversary voices a strenuous objection, the arbitrator may get the impression that there is something incomplete or misleading about the exhibit, or that it contains information that was not properly placed in evidence. Even if the arbitrator allows it to be used, the exhibit may not be given the attention it should be if its admission was surrounded by so much controversy. Worse yet, the arbitrator may feel compelled to postpone the hearings until the other party has reviewed the exhibit, thereby delaying the proceeding.

5. Not Requesting the Form of the Award

Attorneys err when they fail to tell the arbitrator the format of the award they want. This could result, on the one hand, in an award that does not address every claim and counterclaim submitted to arbitration, or it could be missing specific language that is useful, even necessary, for a party to initiate further proceedings. On the other hand, it could result in a more extensive, detailed and costly award than the parties think is required or wise.

For years, lump-sum awards starting which party prevailed, with no explanation of the result, were standard. Arbitrators may continue this practice under the AAA Commercial Arbitration Rules. Rule R-42 of these rules provides that arbitrators are not required to issue a reasoned award unless one is requested before their appointment. However, the arbitrator has discretion to grant a request for a reasoned award at a later time.

The default award under R-44 of the AAA construction rules calls for "a concise written financial breakdown of any monetary awards and, if there are non-monetary components of the claims or counterclaims, the arbitrator shall include a line item disposition of each non-monetary claim or counterclaim." A recent amendment of that rule provides that the parties may request "a specific form of award, including a reasoned opinion, an abbreviated opinion, findings of fact or conclusions of law." There is a timing restriction on this request: it must be made before the conclusion of the first preliminary hearing. After the conclusion of that hearing, the parties may not change the form of the award without the arbitrator's express consent.

Recommended Solution

The attorneys should find out if their clients would prefer to know the reasons behind the arbitrator's decision, and advise them that a reasoned award will cost considerably more than the standard commercial or construction award. The reason is that the arbitrator charges for "study time" and the time it takes to draft and finalize the award. It will also take longer to obtain. If both parties decide a reasoned award is worth the extra cost and time involved, the attorneys should advise the arbitrator as early as possible so that he or she knows to take notes of the proceedings in sufficient detail.

III. Ten Evidentiary Hearing Mistakes and How to Avoid Them

1. Failing to Provide a Road Map of the Case

It is a mistake to limit the opening statement to a recitation of the events that led to the dispute. Attorneys should connect the fact with the claims and the supporting evidence to be presented, and cast doubt on the other party's position.

Recommended Solution

The attorneys should present a road map in their opening statements that guides the arbitrator to the issues and the supporting evidence. Opening statements should do more than explain the "story" behind the dispute. They are more effective when they give the arbitrator a perspective from which to view the evidence. This is a good time for the attorneys to use graphics or other visual material, for example, summary charts, tables, graphs, photographs, blowups of contract language, or other items that will be introduced as exhibits. As noted in Mistake Four, all such exhibits should be disclosed prior to use.

2. Not Correlating the Elements of Proof and the Order of Witnesses

There is great risk in thinking that disorder in the testimony can be cured by a closing statement that ties everything together. It is vital for counsel to plan the sequence of testimony. Without planning, the order in which the evidence is presented could simply confuse the arbitrator and lead to an adverse award.

Recommended Solution

Each attorney's case should be made in a logical sequence, which does not always mean chronological. There are two distinct basic concepts to keep in mind: elements of proof and order of proof. For many cases, a chronological approach makes the most sense. But a different method might also work well: for example, a topical approach that deals with each item of claim in sequence. Or, with a construction case, for example, claims of specialty subcontractors could be dealt with separately.

The guiding principle should be to present the evidence in a manner that would be most helpful to the arbitrator. (See Rules R-30, R-31 and R-32 of the AAA commercial rules and Rules R-32, R-33 and R-34 of the AAA construction rules.) Counsel is allowed to ask the arbitrator at different points during the hearing if he or she is following the evidence presentation, or whether a different approach would work better. Most arbitrators will respond to such inquiries. In our opinion, many attorneys fail to take this opportunity to ask the arbitrator if the case makes sense.

3. Repeating the Direct Examination on Cross

Two objectives of the cross-examiner are: (1) to catch the witness in a lie or mistake that challenges his or her credibility, and/or (2) to show that the witness has made an honest mistake or omission when the correction of that mistake helps your case. Without luck, these objectives could be achieved only if the cross-examiner thoroughly prepared the questions in advance. At a minimum, counsel should prepare for cross by outlining the main headings for the cross-examination, concentrating on the elements of proof that are at issue.

Attorneys who ask questions on cross-examination that are similar to those asked during the direct examination appear to be unprepared. Perhaps they hope the witness will give a different answer the second time around, or will elaborate in the second answer, revealing an inconsistency or giving new ground to probe. It often just allows the witness to repeat testimony that is harmful to the questioner's case.

Recommended Solution

The attorney who conducts a cross-examination is the real witness. Cross should be used to confirm the views of the cross-examiner. Repeating questions asked on direct and getting the same answers usually only reinforces the testimony in favor of the other side. The goal of the cross-examiner should be to delve into those areas where the witness must agree with your point of view, or be tied to a statement that can be contradicted.

It is helpful to the arbitrator if the questions on cross do not wander. One approach is to break the witness's testimony into topics so the arbitrator can understand how the witness's answers correlate to the disputed issues. Consider announcing each new topic to the witness before beginning the examination. For example, counsel could say: "Now, let's turn to the discussion you had with the lender on the day you received the notice of foreclosure." Both the arbitrator and the witness will benefit from this approach.

Lastly, it is vital to be respectful of witnesses during cross-examination. Arbitrators value civility and respect. It is distracting to the arbitrator to have to manage an attorney who behaves badly to a witness under cross-examination. Moreover, the witness's bad reactions could negatively affect the arbitrator's view of the cross-examiner's case.

4. Surprise Exhibits

We previously alluded to the problem of surprise exhibits submitted for the first time at the hearing on the merits, suggesting the importance of exchanging all exhibits before the evidentiary hearing. We raise it again here because this is where the consequences of the error will be felt. The arbitrator's pre-hearing order commonly sets a date for the exchange of all exhibits that will be used at the hearing, with the normal exception of exhibits used in cross-examination or rebuttal.

Unless there is a very good reason why a new exhibit should be admitted, and objection to that evidence by opposing counsel is likely to be sustained. Even if the new exhibit is admitted, the arbitrator may postpone the hearing to allow the opposing party time to examine it and prepare a response. Arbitrators want to be fair to both parties. They are more likely to admit an exhibit under questionable circumstances if they know that any prejudice to the other party can be minimized or overcome.

The arbiter may also assess costs and fees associated with responding to a new exhibit. Introducing a surprise exhibit can hurt the credibility of the attorney who introduced it. There are, of course, allowable surprises, for example, for newly discovered evidence. But that is rare. It is not often that pertinent evidence not available earlier is discovered.

Recommended Solution

A good faith "meet and confer" with opposing counsel often works well to resolve any issues with late exhibits. Even if opposing counsel does not agree, the attempt to resolve the issue outside of the hearing could persuade the arbitrator to admit the exhibit if the basis for the adversary's objection seems thin. Arbitrators appreciate when the attorneys have first tried to work things out themselves and they sometimes give credit for that effort when the objection can be minimized.

5. Not providing a Clear, Concise Calculation of Damages

This mistake is probably the most common, and the most dangerous for the client. The attorneys who make this mistake probably fail to include sufficient information about damages in the demand or answering statement (see Mistake One) and do not file an amended damages calculation. These attorneys place all the emphasis on why the client is entitled to recover (the "story" of the case) and give little or no attention to quantum (i.e., the amount of damages being sought).

Recommended Solutions

Counsel should always calculate the damages claimed before the hearing commences, and create an exhibit that will show the arbitrator each item of claim and the related damages account. This exhibit helps keep all claims and damages in plain sight of the arbitrator and helps prevent any of them from being inadvertently overlooked. An attorney's failure to make a claim or defense understandable may cause the arbitrator to conclude that the claimant or respondent failed to meet its burden of proof. Even where liability for one or more claims has been established, the arbitrator may decide not to award damages if they are not understood.

A question could arise whether a charge only in the amount of a claim should be considered a new claim. Rule R-6 of the AAA commercial rules provides that new or different claims may not be added after the appointment of the arbitrator without his or her consent. However, Rule R-6 of the AAA construction rules provides that increases or decreases in the amount of a claim do not give rise to a new or different claim. This rule allows changes in the amount of a claim at any time before the hearings are closed unless the arbitrator establishes a different date.

Possibly changes in the amount of a claim are acceptable under the commercial rules. But that cannot be assured. Counsel should avoid the possibility that the commercial rules might be interpreted differently by making clear damages claims at the outset. If the damages increase for any claim, counsel should formally amend the demand or answer accordingly. If damages decrease, however, it is not as important to amend the claim because counsel can offer to enter into a stipulation.

6. *Not Specifying All Related Relief Requested*

This is another mistake of omission. It usually happens when the attorney assumes that the relief is authorized by the parties' contract. Making assumptions can get attorneys into trouble. For example, assuming that it is not necessary to request certain types of relief (for example, declaratory relief, specific performance, interest on the award) is a serious error. Arbitrators have been known to omit relief not specifically requested, even when they have contractual authority to award such relief. There have even been constructional cases in which a party forgot to demand contract retention because the amount was undisputed.

Requests for attorney fees can be tricky because Rule R-43(d)(ii) of the commercial rules and Rule R-45(d)(ii) of the construction rules permit such an award only under three conditions: the parties' arbitration agreement provides for the recovery of attorney fees, such fees are authorized by law (i.e., there is a statutory basis for the recovery of attorney fees), or the parties have agreed that attorney fees may be awarded. Attorneys have been known to put an attorney fee request in their demand for arbitration for the purpose of luring the opposing party into answering with its own request for fees. This is an important practice point because some arbitrators consider a reciprocal request for attorney fees to be a fee-shifting agreement.

Recommended Solutions

If there is no attorney fee clause in the parties' contract, counsel should think about whether it is prudent to request attorney fees for the prevailing party. It is the responsibility of the attorneys to make certain there is no misunderstanding about the requested relief and how it is calculated. It is helpful to reference the basis for claims for attorney fees and various types of interest. For example, a claim for interest on the award could be based on the contract clause stating the interest rate, while a claim for pre-judgment interest could be supported by a statue.

Attorneys should present interest calculations as a *per diem* amount so the arbitrator can easily calculate the total up to the date of the award. It is also appropriate to request interest on the award itself until paid. The date on which interest starts to run could vary. It could be the date of the invoice, or the date of completion, or the date of a lien filing, to name just a few of the options. Counsel should be clear about the date the arbitrator should use and explain why it is appropriate.

7. Not Listening or Reacting to the Arbitrator's Questions

Attorneys can become so focused on their own questioning, the pace of the arbitration, and the smoothness of their presentation, that they do not listen closely to the questions asked by the arbitrator.

Recommended Solution

Attorneys must be active listeners, especially when the arbitrator asks a question of either counsel or a party's witness. An active listener evaluates what the arbitrator is asking and analyzes why the question is being asked. Has the arbitrator missed an important point or misunderstood the testimony or document? Or, is the arbitrator opening a new line of inquiry or argument that counsel needs to address?

Attorneys should clearly answer any question asked by the arbitrator. A question by the arbitrator gives the attorney an opening to ask that question of the current witness or another witness, if the answer would be to the client's advantage. Counsel should never admonish the arbitrator for pursuing a topic or line of questioning. An arbitrator who believes that the answer to a question is necessary to a complete understanding of the dispute will resent any attempt by counsel to terminate that questioning. If the arbitrator is truly on the wrong path, then counsel should set him or her straight, but in a diplomatic way.

If the arbitrator's question was helpful, the attorney should remember it when preparing the closing argument. Referring to an arbitrator's question and emphasizing the correct answer can enhance the impact of that argument.

8. Failing to Notice that the Arbitrator Does Not Understand the Testimony

This error is a corollary to the last mistake. However, the cues lie not in the arbitrator's questions, but in his or her facial expressions. Attorneys miss them when they are not watching the arbitrator.

Recommended Solution

An attorney should always be aware of the arbitrator's reactions during the evidentiary hearing. A colleague could be asked to assist counsel in making these observations. An arbitrator who appears to be confused or uneasy, or whispers to a colleague on the panel, might need a clearer explanation of some point made in the testimony.

It is not out of line for an attorney to ask the arbitrator if she or he would like to hear more testimony about a particular subject, or discuss previously given testimony that could reveal whether the arbitrator understood it. Finding out whether the arbitrator understands a claim is acceptable practice.

The informality of arbitration makes it possible to converse with the arbitrator at the hearing. That is a key advantage of arbitration. During a trial one cannot ask the jurors, or a judge in a bench trial, whether they have heard enough and understand the presentation. But that can be done in arbitration. Most arbitrators are receptive to counsel engaging them in a dialogue about the claims so long as he or she is not searching for the arbitrator's point of view and conclusions.

9. Using Rebuttal to Repeat Earlier Testimony

This is a mistake similar to Mistake Eight. Recalling a witness to rebut testimony given on cross is fine, but having that witness repeat earlier testimony is not. The arbitrator could exclude repetitive or cumulative testimony based on an objection or on his or her own initiative. Rule R-31 of the AAA commercial rules permits the exclusion of evidence deemed by the arbitrator to be "cumulative or irrelevant," and Rule R-33 of the construction rules authorizes the arbitrator to exclude the testimony that he or she deems to be "cumulative, unreliable, unnecessary, or of slight value compared to the time and expense involved."

Recommended Solution

Rebuttal testimony should be fresh. It often requires the use of a new witness. Attorneys should present in rebuttal only evidence that qualifies, contradicts or nullifies the adverse party's evidence. Repetition may merely serve to dilute the strength of earlier testimony.

10. Making a Closing Statement that Does Not Match the Opening or Fails to Highlight the Most Important Exhibits or Testimony

We have heard attorneys saying in closing that now they finally understand their case and are fully convinced of its simplicity and merit. When this happens, the closing statement is probably very different in content and tone from the opening statement. It is helpful to write both statements before the evidentiary hearing begins. This will give the author a better understanding of the case and avoid the disconnect between opening and closing statements.

As the hearing progresses, new questions may arise, requiring additional analysis or revision. Therefore, it will be necessary to change the closing statement. Thus, a closing statement prepared before the hearing is a work in progress until all witnesses have completed their testimony. Nevertheless, it can serve as a checklist to make sure that the revised statement addresses all the elements of proof required to prevail.

Before presenting the closing statement, counsel could prepare for the arbitrator a bullet-point outline (or give the arbitrator a binder with the key exhibits and arguments that support each claim). This outline will focus the arbitrator's attention on the closing and may provide enough information so that the arbitrator will not need to take notes at the same time. We guarantee that the arbitrator will refer to the closing outline during deliberations and in writing the award.

Arbitrators often ask questions during closing argument. Counsel must be prepared to respond. Many arbitrators, the authors included, often schedule closing argument to follow the receipt of post-hearing briefs so that they can clarify any points they did not fully understand.

IV. Five Post-Hearing Mistakes and How to Avoid Them

1. Adding New Claims for Relief

It is usually less costly and more efficient to include all claims arising out of a particular project or transection in one arbitration, rather than commence separate arbitrations for multiple claims. Attorneys who do not identify all claims in the demand or answer sometimes find themselves adding new ones later on. Adding new claims in the post-hearing phase condemns them to being disallowed and makes the attorney who made this mistake look unprepared or perhaps sly.

A note of caution: If the amount of damages sought for any claims have changed, explain to the arbitrator in the closing statement or post-hearing brief why the claim is not new or different and provide the reasons why it should be considered. New claims that attorneys can add in the post-hearing phase are claims for arbitration costs and arbitrator fees caused by the adversary's delay tactics or obstreperous behavior.

2. Including New Arguments in Post-Hearing Briefs

It is just as disconcerting for an arbitrator to find legal arguments in a post-hearing brief, as it is to find new claims. If a different legal analysis is needed to rebut contentions made by the opposing party during the hearing, counsel should explain that fully to the arbitrator in the brief.

It is best to avoid causing the arbitrator to reopen the hearing. Under Rule R-36 of the AAA commercial rules and Rule R-38 of the construction rules, the arbitrator may reopen the hearing if there is a need for further information. Post-hearing briefs that direct the arbitrator to the evidence needed to decide the dispute should preclude reopening of the hearing. A practice point: Attach judicial opinions or statutory law to the post-hearing brief. Arbitrators appreciate having at hand the law upon which the parties are relying.

3. Not Highlighting the Most Important Exhibits or Testimony in the Post-Hearing Brief

We have said that the closing statement should match the opening. But that doesn't mean that the post-hearing briefs should match the earlier briefs. Post-hearing briefs should do more than just restate the pre-hearing brief. If they don't, they are likely to be disregarded. The post-hearing brief should address issues and evidence of particular concern to the arbitrator. It is wise to ask the arbitrator at the close of the evidence if he or she has any concerns that should be addressed in the post-hearing brief. The answer can be very revealing. This procedure is more common in arbitration than in court.

Post-hearing briefs should:

- Use sub-sections to delineate the elements of proof.
- Refer to significant testimony, particularly unrebutted testimony. Quote from the hearing transcript, if there is one.
- Emphasize the failings in the other party's proof.
- List the damages sought and how they were calculated.
- Attach key exhibits to the post-hearing brief.

4. Not Providing the Arbitrator with a Proposed Award

Even if the attorneys did not make Mistake Five (failing to ask for a particular type of award), they may make the mistake of not offering the arbitrator a proposed award at the conclusion of the evidentiary hearing. If post-hearing briefs are to be filed, the attorneys should attach a copy of their proposed award to their briefs.

The proposed award should address each item of relief sought for each claim and break down the damages into subcategories. A lump-sum award is often unsatisfactory, as it does not tell the client anything about the components of the award. Counsel for the respondent should be especially careful to include any offsets in the respondent's proposed award.

Itemizing the recovery of damages in the proposed award may be necessary if, for example, further legal or arbitral proceedings are contemplated (i.e., the client intends to follow this arbitration with another proceeding against insurers or other contracting parties). Without a breakdown of the amount awarded, it may be impossible for a party to determine if it prevailed on claims covered by insurance. An itemized award may also be needed to pursue other parties, for example, suppliers or subcontractors.

Further proceedings may require that the award contain particular language. Recovery under consumer protection laws, for example, may depend upon certain findings having been explicitly stated. Counsel for the party who intends to file further proceedings should include such language in the proposed award, along with a statement explaining why this language is important.

If the parties want a "reasoned award," they should discuss with the arbitrator and opposing counsel what is meant by "reasoned," since that term's meaning varies among arbitrators and counsel. For example, the word could mean detailed findings of fact and conclusions of law, or a legal opinion in the style typically issued by many courts and boards of contract appeals, or a brief explanation of the reasons for the decision on each claim.

5. Leaving the Hearings Without a Closing Date

Many times attorneys rely on the arbitrator to decide when to declare the hearing closed. It can be a mistake to do so. Although Rule R-35 of the AAA commercial rules and Rule R-37 of the construction rules address the timing of the closing of the hearing, there is enough latitude for an arbitrator to extend the closing of the hearing beyond the end of the evidentiary hearing.

The AAA rules call for the hearing to be closed when the arbitrator is satisfied that the record is complete and the parties have no further proof or witnesses to put on (usually upon the conclusion of the last hearing day). But if post-hearing documents are to be submitted, the arbitrator is to close the hearing as of the due date for those documents.

The attorneys should not assume that an arbitrator would accept post-hearing briefs or other documents. A request to submit such materials should be made at the hearing before the arbitrator declares it closed. This way the arbitrator can decide whether to accept post-hearing materials, what they may contain, and whether to permit a reply. Once the hearing is closed, it is too late.

Post-hearing briefs are not always desirable. For one thing, they delay the issuance of the award and increase the cost of the proceeding. If the hearing is not long, the issues in dispute are few and not complex, or the pre-hearing statements and other written submissions are adequate, there is no need for a post-hearing brief. The attorneys should have a frank discussion with the arbitrator about whether briefing after the hearing is closed would be helpful and whether budgetary considerations make it sufficiently valuable.

Rule R-41 of the commercial rules and Rule R-43 of the construction rules provide that the time for issuance of the award runs from the date of closing of the hearing. The attorneys should ask the arbitrator to confirm the date of closing of the hearing before they leave in order to determine when the award will be due. In some instances, it may be impractical or impossible for the arbitrator to finalize the award in the time allowed under the AAA rules. If the parties agree, the time for issuance of the award may be extended.

V. Conclusion

A unique aspect of arbitration, when contrasted with a judicial proceeding, is the extent of the interaction between the arbitrator and counsel. Because arbitration is a creature of contract, initiated by agreement of the parties, the opportunity exists to tailor the process to the individual case. Indeed, the AAA rules specifically provide that the parties may vary its rules by agreement.

Avoiding the mistakes described in this article requires that attorneys collaborate with each other and the arbitrator in order to obtain an efficient arbitration, with clearly presented and easily understood evidence that will allow the arbitrator to carry out his or her decision-making responsibilities.

CHAPTER 10

A PRELIMINARY HEARING IS NOT ENOUGH: TIPS FOR A WELL-MANAGED ARBITRATION

Michael Chambers[*]

I. Introduction

A preliminary hearing is a required first step in most arbitrations to ensure that the process is orderly and efficient. This hearing, however, is not enough to ensure a timely arbitration that will meet the goal of holding the final hearing within one year of the filing of the demand. This article provides insights and tips on critical issues that help meet this goal: hands-on management by the arbitrator, a comprehensive scheduling order, and a pre-hearing conference one week before the final hearing to resolve any remaining problems. Although this article is written for arbitrators, it should hold as much interest for attorneys and parties in the process.

II. Issue a Comprehensive Scheduling Order

The arbitrator must issue a scheduling order setting deadlines for the completion of all the critical steps in the pre-hearing phase of the arbitration. There are several issues in this phase that affect the hearing on the merits. These include the identification of claims, defenses and counterclaims; the calculation of damages; arbitrability and jurisdiction of the arbitrator; the exchange of relevant documents; the deposition of

---

[*] Michael Chambers is a member of the AAA commercial, large complex case, employment and international panels. He has often served as a trainer at AAA training programs and previously co-chaired several national panels of arbitrators created in class action settlements. Licensed to practice law in New York, Washington, D.C., and Alabama, he is of counsel to the Alabama-based firm of Cabaniss, Johnston, Gardner, Dumas & O'Neal LLP. He holds a J.D. degree from the University of Alabama and a doctorate from the University of Geneva in Switzerland. He has been certified as a Civil Trial Advocate by the National Board of Trial Advocacy.

key witnesses, if allowed or agreed; and the retention of experts, the taking of their depositions, if needed and permitted by the arbitrator, and the exchange of expert reports. If any one of these issues is not handled in a timely way because of missed deadlines, the entire schedule can fall apart because most of these issues are linked. Once there is even one missed deadline, the agreed date for the final hearing may not work. Then, the arbitrator has not helped deliver on the promise that arbitration will be faster and less expensive than litigation.

Reasonable deadlines in the scheduling order are not enough. Success in keeping to the schedule requires getting into more detail at the first preliminary hearing so that a detailed scheduling order can be prepared. You must make sure that counsel and the parties meet them. No arbitrator wants to be accused of turning a preliminary hearing into a federal pre-trial conference. But, no arbitrator wants to receive a request for a continuance weeks before the evidentiary hearing because deadlines for document production did not occur, which in turn delayed the depositions, which then side-tracked the timing and choice of experts. You know the problem.

III. Nail Down the Claims, Damages, Counterclaims and Defenses

Here are a few suggestions for the preliminary hearing to help address some of these potential problems. For example, start by asking each side if the claims, counterclaims, defenses and damages have been sufficiently outlined in the Demand and Answer. If not, give each side a short period of time to confirm the claims or counterclaims and then answer consistent with the applicable rule governing responses. A short period of time could be 10 days or even less, depending on the complexity of the case. The goal is to make sure everyone has notice of the issues before the document exchange, the depositions, the selection of experts and the hearing on the merits. For these reasons, you want the attorneys and their clients to decide early what the case is about and stick to it, unless some new claims legitimately arise from new information.

IV. Establish Reasonable Limits on Discovery

Most parties agree to some level of discovery even if, as in the current American Arbitration Association Commercial Arbitration Rules, none is specifically permitted, apart from the document exchange. But, even if the attorneys agree on how much discovery, the arbitrator has the responsibility to ensure that it does not get out of control. As a result, the arbitrator should specifically ask how much discovery is really needed and on what topics. You must establish reasonable limits. If the parties want to serve document requests to facilitate the document exchange, then ask about the type of information and the scope of the requests. For example, you can determine whether electronically stored information can be produced in electronic format, or whether a hard copy of everything must be produced. You can ask at this point if there are any anticipated areas in which a discovery dispute is expected. If there are, you may be able to decide these issues or give the parties guidance before valuable time is lost. Establish firm dates for submitting document requests and responses. Then, in your order, direct the parties to immediately contact the arbitration provider's case manager to set up a conference call with you in the event of a dispute.

V. Identify Depositions and Calendar Them

Next, if the rules permit depositions, or if the parties agree to take them, during the preliminary hearing, ask each side how many they need, the names of the persons to be deposed, how long each deposition should take, where the depositions will be taken and in what order. Asking all these questions may be overkill in simple cases where the attorneys appear to work well together, but it is absolutely necessary in hard fought and acrimonious cases. Once these points are discussed, you are in a position to set reasonable limits on discovery in the scheduling order. This can head off any fights before they start. Then, calendar the deposition dates. These dates will naturally follow deadlines for filing production requests and responding to them.

In the scheduling order, direct the parties to contact the case manager or you immediately in the event that any deadline is not met. If the parties comply, you will have the ability to resolve the problem and keep everyone on track.

VI. Plan for Experts Even If the Parties Say They Don't Need Them

During the preliminary hearing, ask if there will be experts. Even if the attorneys say that experts are not anticipated, plan for them anyway. Set a date for identifying experts, since an expert disclosed late in the process can wreak havoc. No attorney or client likes to be ambushed by a new opinion. Also, set the date for the filing of an expert report by each one. The dates should be well in advance of the final hearing. Make sure the scheduling order requires the report to state the expert's background, the specific opinions to be offered at the hearing and the facts upon which those opinions are based.

VII. Schedule the Completion of Key Activities Well Before the Hearing on the Merits

There are still a few things to plan for in the scheduling order that left undone can torpedo the final hearing. Do not ask counsel how much time is needed to hear the case. If you do, they will tell you how much time it should take. Instead, ask each attorney how much time he or she needs to present the client's case and cross-examine the other side's witnesses. When you total each side's response you may have a better idea of the truth. Hold the attorneys to that number and put their conclusions in the scheduling order. But just in case, add an additional day. There are two good reasons to do this. First, you do not want to run out of time and have to schedule more hearing days in the future. It could be another four months before everyone is available again. Second, if you have a three-person panel, the additional day can be used for deliberations and to write a preliminary draft of the final award.

Here are my recommended due dates for some other critical items, including subpoenas and exhibit exchanges. Setting the dates sufficiently in advance of the hearing on the merits allows for a more orderly hearing. For sending subpoenas to the arbitrator for signature, I recommend 30 calendar days before the final hearing; for the physical exchange of exhibits, exhibit lists, and witness lists in the anticipated order of call, I suggest 21 calendar days before the hearing; and for written objections to exhibits and service of subpoenas, I recommend 14 calendar days before the hearing. The early completion of these activities should be routine. If any one of them is not completed before the hearing, you will hear about it at the beginning of the final hearing and have to spend the first couple of hours trying to resolve the problem. Using hearing time to resolve pre-hearing matters could make you run out of time before both sides have completed their presentations.

VIII. Schedule a Final Pre-Hearing Conference Before the Hearing on the Merits

During the preliminary hearing, schedule a final pre-hearing conference call. I find it works best to schedule this conference roughly one week before the commencement of the final hearing. Include this conference in the initial scheduling order, along with the purpose of the call, which will address, and hopefully resolve, any remaining issue concerning exhibits, witnesses or subpoenas.

In my opinion there is no better way to invest your time after you have issued the scheduling order than in the final pre-hearing conference call. It is similar to the pre-trial conference held in federal court, but without all the homework.

When the final pre-hearing conference call is held, all of the items to be exchanged or served will be completed if the parties adhered to the due dates in the scheduling order. But if there is a problem, you have one week to resolve it. Then, one week later when the final hearing starts, you can immediately begin to hear opening statements or the first witness, not a litany of complaints.

IX. Conclusion

A well-managed, orderly process is critical to ensure that arbitration is faster and less expensive than litigation. This can be accomplished with a thorough preliminary hearing conference that includes hands-on management by the arbitrator, a comprehensive scheduling order, and a pre-hearing conference one week before the final hearing to resolve any remaining problems. Many steps in the pre-hearing phase of arbitration are interdependent. If one is delayed, the others can be as well. This can delay the final hearing. By using these recommendations, the final hearing should take place as scheduled and be completed in an orderly manner within the allotted time.

CHAPTER 11

THIRTY STEPS TO A BETTER ARBITRATION

Judith B. Ittig and Michael J. Bayard[*]

I. Introduction

Our skills as arbitrators improve with every arbitration we hear. Each case brings unique situations, unusual requests for relief, scheduling problems, different approaches to the presentation of evidence, and new award-writing challenges. We learn from the process, from the parties in each case, and from our fellow arbitrators. What follows are our top thirty tips, which you cannot find in any arbitration rules, since they are gleaned from actual cases we have heard and those our colleagues have told us about. We thought other arbitrators might find them worth adopting, or adapting, in future arbitrations.

II. Before the First Preliminary Conference

Tip 1: One reading of the pleadings is not enough

Reread the demand, answering statements and counter-demand. Then diagram them, including the names of the parties and their counsel, and the parties' claims and defenses. When you have finished the diagram, ask yourself: "Can I describe in my own words (in less than one minute)

---

[*] Michael J. Bayard is a full-time construction arbitrator, mediator and project neutral. He chairs the AAA's Construction Advisory Subcommittee for the Los Angeles Region and teaches a graduate course in construction management at the University of Southern California, where he is an adjunct professor. He was recently named to the AAA's National Construction Master Arbitrator Roster. Mr. Bayard may be reached toll free at (800) 652-2927 or at michaeljbayard@yahoo.com.

Judith Ittig serves on the AAA's commercial arbitrator panel, the ICDR's commercial arbitrator panel, and is on the AAA's National Construction Master Arbitrator Roster. Mrs. Ittig, an attorney at Ittig & Ittig, P.C. based in Washington, DC, is also a Fellow of the American College of Construction Lawyers and a Chartered Arbitrator/Fellow of the Chartered Institute of Arbitrators (London). She can be reached by e-mail at jbi@ittig-ittig.com.

who the parties are and the relief they are seeking?" We remember a case where an arbitrator continually mistook the subcontractor for the supplier and another where the arbitrator consistently referred to the subcontractor as the contractor. These mistakes undermined the authority of the arbitrator with all of the attorneys. It is worth taking the time at the outset to acquaint yourself with the parties, their counsel, and their claims so that you do not appear confused.

Tip 2: Keep up with your disclosure obligations

Review the disclosure statement you prepared for the parties before you were selected to serve as the arbitrator. Update your "conflicts check" to address any additional parties, new counsel, fact witnesses and experts, and, if necessary, update your disclosure statement. Our rule of thumb on conflict disclosure is "when in doubt, send it out."

Tip 3: Make sure you have the key documents at hand

Make a list of the documents you think will be central to the case and then check to see if they have been provided. If not, bring that issue up at the first preliminary conference so that you may avoid potential serious problems. Case in point: the arbitrators' early review of the three separate contracts at issue revealed an arbitrability question. A stipulation from the parties dispensed with the problem and waived a significant jurisdictional issue that could have invalidated part of the arbitration had it been discovered post-award.

Tip 4: Confer with your fellow arbitrators

If you are serving on a panel, convene an "arbitrators only" conference call to:

- Introduce each other.
- Discuss the role of the chair and the arbitral procedures. For example, will the chair resolve any discovery disputes that arise? During the hearing, will the chair speak for the panel in questioning counsel or witnesses? Will the chair make sure to call a break when other members of the panel have questions or comments?
- Identify the issues to be discussed in the preliminary conference.
- Explore ways to expedite the arbitration process.

A common complaint in arbitration is that "the hearings took too long." While addressing scheduling and timing concerns at this juncture, you can explore methods for expediting the hearings. Parties are less likely to have reason to complain about the length of the hearings if the arbitrators implemented the timesaving techniques that the parties agreed to at the beginning of the arbitration.

Tip 5: Prepare agendas

For high-dollar cases and complicated matters involving multiple parties and issues, there is likely to be more than one preliminary conference. It is helpful to prepare an agenda listing the points to be covered during each preliminary conference and send it to the parties approximately two weeks before the scheduled date. Then the parties have time to add any additional issues. In the cover memorandum for the first preliminary hearing, thank the parties and their counsel for the opportunity to work with them in the arbitration. Good public relations from the outset of the case can establish a rapport that may be needed when tough decisions arise.

III. At the First Preliminary Conference

Tip 6: Use proven checklists

Use the AAA's pre-hearing checklist for large, complex cases (found in Rule L-3 of the Large Complex Case Procedures in the Commercial Arbitration Rules) or the more elaborate preliminary hearing checklist available from your AAA case manager to make sure you cover all the basics during the conference. Confirm the names (with correct spelling and pronunciation) of the parties' counsel and their key representatives. Ask the parties' counsel if any additional parties will be named or if any additional claims will be forthcoming. Sometimes the first preliminary conference can be intense, leaving important issues forgotten in the moment. By using a proven checklist you greatly decrease the chance you will overlook an important item.

Tip 7: Suggest using informal procedures when appropriate

Using informal procedures can, in certain situations, expedite the process without a loss of fairness. For example, allow the parties to arrange a conference call with the panel chair so long as all parties are on the line; permit correspondence and briefs to be sent directly to the arbitrators so long as opposing counsel is copied; and agree to use e-mail or fax for prompt notice.

Tip 8: Set the date for the next preliminary conference

Be sure to schedule the next preliminary conference before bringing the present conference to an end. Even in small cases, it is often helpful to have a status conference about a month after the first preliminary conference to make sure everyone is keeping to the schedule. The second preliminary hearing provides a perfect opportunity to resolve any discovery disputes or other outstanding pre-hearing issues. Also, setting the date well in advance shows the parties that you are conducting the arbitration in a business-like manner and that you will be checking on their progress on a date certain (*i.e.*, the date of the next preliminary conference). This calendar marker prompts the parties to complete interim tasks in preparation for the arbitration.

Tip 9: Require early identification of claims and specification of damages

Establish the date for the identification of the parties' claims and the specification of damages. Make it clear to all that no new claims will be allowed after that date without demonstrating good cause or unless all parties agree. Consider asking the attorneys to provide separate notebooks that detail the damages requested for every element of their claims, with citations to the supporting documents the parties plan to use. Claims of "surprise" can result in postponed hearings. By setting these dates and following up, you can better ensure that the hearings will commence as scheduled.

Tip 10: Time-lines add context and understanding to the case

Create a time-line identifying all of the major events for the project or transaction, or ask the parties to prepare one as a joint exhibit, if possible. A time-line is particularly helpful in fact-intensive construction disputes. A joint time-line will highlight any differences between the parties that could be important to the case.

IV. Between the First and Last Preliminary Conferences

Tip 11: Keep your fellow arbitrators informed

As the panel chair, you should keep the other arbitrators on the panel and the case manager informed about changes in the status of the case. You should copy all communications to the parties to your co-arbitrators and the case manager. They need to know what is happening so they can make informed decisions and add to your thinking when necessary. Also, you need to make sure your colleagues know every aspect of how the arbitration has progressed so that at the end the panel produces the best possible decision. Not only is it rude to ignore your fellow arbitrators and the case manager, it is also a disservice to the parties and yourself not to have the full attention and participation of the entire panel.

Tip 12: Use the Meet-and-Confer process to resolve disputes

Direct the parties to "meet and confer" on disputed issues, such as depositions, document production, assertions of privilege, or other pre-hearing matters before allowing them to bring any of these issues before the panel for a decision. This sends the parties the message that they have a high degree of control over the arbitration process. This strategy can substantially reduce the number of times the panel has to rule on pre-hearing disputes.

Tip 13: Be serious about deadlines

Set a tone of urgency to keep the hearings on track. Respond to requests or formal motions immediately or as quickly as possible. Set short, but fair, time limits for the parties to act or respond to directives from the arbitrators. By so doing, you communicate to the parties that the arbitration will continue to proceed as planned. This message not only keeps the parties working hard on preparing for the hearings, it encourages them to work on settling the dispute because they know it is unlikely there will be a continuance of the hearings.

Tip 14: Encourage streamlining whenever possible

Encourage the parties to enter into agreements, such as stipulations of fact and law, and to file any motions that could expedite the hearings or narrow the issues to be arbitrated. These strategies can greatly decrease the time needed for the live hearings. Also, stipulations relating to facts and documents can avoid having the initial evidentiary hearings conducted more like depositions than arbitration hearings.

Tip 15: Involve the parties in developing case-presentation methods for hearings

Suggest to the parties that they consider methods of presenting testimony that could expedite the proceedings, such as written witness statements and the use of damages notebooks. Encourage them to suggest methods for streamlining or altering the arbitration procedures to make the case presentation more efficient and effective. One of the trends in arbitration efficiency is conducting the evidentiary hearings with time limits imposed on the parties' presentations. This is done only with the parties' agreement.

Tip 16: Pictures can be worth a thousand words to arbitrators too

Photographs and videos can serve as excellent visual aids to understanding the dispute. If they are going to be used, ask the parties to put a date and locale description on each picture and video. Preview these visual aids to eliminate irrelevant or repetitious photos or sections of video so as not to unduly delay the proceedings. The use of visual evidence should be encouraged because even the most experienced arbitrators find that pictures or charts are valuable aids.

Tip 17: Be proactive

Stay on top of the parties' progress. Ask to be copied on the parties' key correspondence so that you receive "early warning signals" of problems that might be brewing. Your goal is to have the parties prepared to arbitrate on the date set to begin the arbitration. If you sense they are falling behind schedule, set up another preliminary conference. You cannot expect that the parties themselves will make sure that the case is "on track."

V. At the Final Preliminary Conference

Tip 18: Plan to stave off most evidentiary objections

Tell the parties how evidentiary objections will be handled at the hearing. Tell them that the panel will use its expertise to weigh the value of the evidence. The usual rule is: "If it is relevant and material, it is going to come in." However, settlement discussions and privileged communications are usually going to be excluded.

Tip 19: Manage the admission of exhibits

Tell the parties how exhibits will be admitted at the hearing. One approach is to admit all exhibits; another is to ask the parties to stipulate that any exhibit or document referred to in the hearings will be deemed admitted in the absence of objection when introduced.

Tip 20: Take only copies if possible

Make sure the parties provide copies, not originals of their exhibits. Anything that must be returned to a party at the conclusion of the arbitration should be clearly marked "Return to _____."

Tip 21: Verify adherence to the pre-hearing schedule

Review the schedule for submitting pre-hearing briefs, motions in limine, or other motions, witness lists and exhibits prior to the hearings on the merits, and make sure they have all been submitted (or will be).

Tip 22: Scan the horizon for late developments

Give the parties a chance to raise any last minute issues. This is the point when arbitrators need to heighten their sensitivity to possible interference or disruptions to the hearings. Witnesses with last-minute scheduling conflicts, or who become unavailable due to an emergency can be rescheduled, and the sequence of testimony rearranged, if necessary. Both of us remember arbitrations where elective surgeries were planned at the last minute and we were able to adjust the order of witnesses to accommodate the unplanned absences.

VI. At the Evidentiary Hearings

Tip 23: Keep a detailed record of each hearing day

Take attendance every day and keep account of the start and finish times for each hearing day. It also is helpful to note the time when each witness begins and ends his or her testimony. Indicate the amount of time devoted to direct examination, cross-examination, redirect, and the arbitrators' questions. We recommend doing this even when a court reporter is transcribing the proceedings because these notes help recreate the hearings and recall the testimony more clearly during deliberations on the award.

Tip 24: Keep a separate record of rulings and stipulations

Maintain a daily hearing summary of any agreements or stipulations and note important rulings from the panel.

Tip 25: Perform a daily schedule review

If the parties have not agreed to time limitations on their examinations, monitor their progress by having open discussions with them at the end of each day.

Tip 26: Flexible scheduling can solve many problems

Be flexible if bona fide scheduling problems arise. Feel free to adopt irregular hearing hours with the parties' consent. In one of our cases where there were multiple parties and residents of different time zones, the hearings were scheduled from 7 a.m. to 1 p.m. every day without a lunch break. That schedule gave the parties time to conduct other business and still devote significant time to the arbitration. The six hours of arbitration, with minimal break time, afforded the equivalent of a normal hearing day.

Tip 27: Tread firmly and softly

Keep a balance between moving the arbitration forward and not disrupting or interfering with the presentation of each side's case. Arbitrators who ask lots of questions are often perceived to be arrogant and possibly biased. Some arbitrators prefer to actively question witnesses during their testimony and many, but not all, attorneys welcome those interruptions. Try to get a handle on the attorneys' preferences by discussing the subject with them before the hearings get underway.

Tip 28: Winding up the hearings

At the end of the last evidentiary hearing day, write an order setting the briefing schedule for post-hearing briefs, if any, and the date for closing arguments, if they are to be held later. For purposes of later deliberations, it can be helpful to obtain from the parties a list of their most important exhibits. You can ask them to provide that list in their post-hearing briefs. If the case has multiple issues, ask the parties for a proposed form of award to make sure that no items of claim are omitted and find out the parties' preferences for how the damages should be broken out. Our preference is to hear closing arguments after the post-hearing briefs. It helps put the briefs in context and gives the arbitrators the opportunity to ask questions they might have after reading the briefs. Any questions asked should not reveal the arbitrator's leanings on the issues to be decided. At the end of the hearings on the merits, the parties and their counsel should have no idea how the arbitrators are going to rule on the case. The arbitrators' questions and unspoken, non-verbal behavior should always be non-partisan and unquestionably fair.

VII. Deliberations and Award

Tip 29: Prepare a road map for your deliberations

One member of the panel should volunteer or be assigned to outline the issues that need to be decided. Before deliberating together, circulate the outline among the panel so each arbitrator can review it and add issues or make revisions. This road map of the issues and sub-issues, sometimes with the dollar demands for each item, can focus the deliberations and speed resolution.

Tip 30: When your deliberations bog down

If a panel is hearing the case, the arbitrators' deliberations should be a free and open exchange of ideas and conclusions. If all members of the panel do not agree on every important point, the majority should ask the dissenting arbitrator to present his or her views (orally or in writing or both) and the majority should commit to listening to (or reading) those views with an open mind.

If you are the sole arbitrator and you are having great difficulty reconciling the parties' views on a point, don't hesitate to ask them for further factual explanation or additional legal references, even if you have to reopen the proceedings and conduct another evidentiary hearing to obtain this information. Just be sure you leave yourself enough time to make your decision and submit the award to the AAA before the award is due.

VIII. Conclusion

We have the most confidence in our awards when the testimony clearly addressed the real issues in the case, we were able to listen and absorb the information presented and without distractions, and our deliberations followed a road map for analyzing the issues. These tips have helped us achieve these objectives and manage the arbitration process so that the time spent with the parties and their witnesses is valuable and we have learned the case from them so we can make a sound award.

PART III:

ARBITRATOR SELECTION AND CONDUCT

CHAPTER 12

DUE DILIGENCE IN ARBITRATOR SELECTION: USING INTERVIEWS AND WRITTEN "VOIR DIRE"

Jeffrey P. Aiken[*]

I. Introduction

Trial lawyers have helped create a cottage industry of jury consultants who, for considerable fees, assist them in identifying jurors who have either an inherent bias[1] against certain matters or a leaning in favor of others. "Voir dire" is the name of the process of questioning prospective jurors to determine if they should be disqualified either for bias or for another reason using one of counsel's peremptory challenges.[2] The objective of voir dire is to select jurors who are most inclined to find in favor of one's client and eliminate those who are predisposed to finding against the client.

If lawyers could engage in this process to select the judge hearing the case, they would. The good news is that they can engage in a kind of voir dire before selecting the arbitrators and they should. Judge Richard Posner has observed that judges sometimes make decisions based not on legalistic methods, but on other factors:

---

[*] Jeffrey Aiken is semi-retired, having practiced with the law firm of Whyte Hirschboeck Dudek, S.C. where he was involved in arbitration practice as a neutral and party representative for nearly 40 years in addition to serving as a commercial litigator and transactional attorney. He continues to serve on the AAA's Large and Complex Claim panels for construction and other commercial disputes. His full biography is available at http://aikenadr.weebly.com.

[1] The term "bias" has a negative connotation (equivalent to prejudice) although it has also been defined as "an inclination of temperament or outlook." *Webster's 7th New Collegiate Dictionary* (1965).

[2] The French term *voir dire* is defined as "a preliminary examination of prospective jurors or witnesses under oath to determine their competence or suitability." *American Heritage Dictionary of the English Language,* (4th ed. Houghton Mifflin).

> Legal uncertainty… creates *the open area* in which the orthodox (the legalist) methods of analysis yield unsatisfactory and sometimes no conclusions, thereby allowing or even dictating that emotion, personality, policy intuitions, ideology, politics, background and experience will determine the judge's decision.[3] (Emphasis added)

If law were logical, "good judgment" would not be an admired quality in judges.[4] But good judgment *is* an admired quality in a judge. It entails, in the words of Judge Posner, "a compound of empathy, modesty, maturity, a sense of proportion, balance, a recognition of human limitations, sanity, prudence, a national sense of reality and common sense."[5]

Parties also want good judgment in an arbitrator. It may even be more important due to the arbitrator's role as finder of fact and law, the finality of arbitration award, and the limited grounds for an appeal.[6] The arbitrator biographies made available by most established arbitration provider organizations generally are insufficient to make one of the most important decisions in the arbitration process – arbitrator selection. Consequently, it is essential to conduct a due diligence investigation to try to learn the predilections of the candidates for the position of the arbitrator. Indeed, it is difficult to imagine why one would not research each potential arbitrator under consideration.

The American Arbitration Association (AAA) and other arbitration organizations have tried to raise the level of training of arbitrators. Nevertheless, there is a wide range of opinion on arbitrator abilities. In addition, arbitrators hold a wide range of views on matters that could have an impact on counsel's arbitration strategy and case presentation. For example, some believe in limiting witnesses to only those disclosed in a pre-hearing witness list, while others are more flexible, recognizing that arbitration presents a more fluid process where it is not always known what opposing witnesses will say – especially when depositions are permitted or held to a minimum.

---

[3] Richard A. Posner, *How Judges Think* 11 (Harvard University Press 2008).

[4] *Id.* At 117.

[5] *Id.*

[6] Section 10 of the Federal Arbitration Act sets forth the grounds to vacate or modify an award. See Katherine Helm, "The Expanding Scope of Judicial Review of Arbitration Awards: Where Does the Buck Stop?," 61(3) *Disp. Resol. J.* 16 (Nov. 2006/Jan. 2007); David A. Senter & Andrew L. Chapin, "Statutory Grounds for Challenging Arbitration Awards," 19 *Construction L.* 30-36 (October 1999).

Arbitrators also have equitable powers not available to judges.[7] That is because in the United States, unless restricted by arbitration rules or the agreement of the parties, an arbitrator may consider or base a decision on equitable principles.[8]

What may not be as well known is that arbitration has had its foundation in equity going back to ancient times. The fundamental distinction between arbitration and litigation has been stated in various ways but all essentially the same. In 320 B.C., Aristotle wrote, "The arbitrator looks to what is equitable, the judge to what is law; and it was for this purpose that arbitration was introduced, namely, that equity might prevail."[9]

Commenting on Aristotle, Martin Domke is quoted as saying, "Equity is justice in that it goes beyond the written law. And it is equitable to prefer arbitration to the law court, for the arbitrator keeps equity in view, whereas the judge looks only to the law, and the reason why arbitrators were appointed was that equity might prevail."[10]

Even in the early 20th century arbitration was recognized in the United States as part of a dispute resolution system. *Ballentine's Law Dictionary* (1916) defined "arbitrium" to mean "an arbitration award." Both this dictionary and *The Cyclopedic Dictionary of Law* (1901) defined the phrase *arbitrium est judicium boni viri, secundum aequum et bonum* to mean: "an award is the judgment of a good man according to equity and goodness."

The concept of equity in arbitration remains today. For example, the AAA's Commercial Arbitration Rules and Construction Industry Arbitration Rules both indicate that arbitrators may grant any remedy or relief that they deem "just and equitable," so long as it is within the scope of the parties' agreement.[11] Most experienced arbitrators are aware, while they are not entitled to disregard the law in developing an award (unless a case involves a statutory violation), they are not necessarily bound to follow it.

---

[7] Courts of equity and courts of law have been merged in this country for centuries and it is usually the rule that one cannot access the equitable powers of the court if there is a legal remedy, even though more restrictive.

[8] "Fundamentals of the Arbitration Process" in *Training Manual for Construction Industry Arbitrators* 9 (American Arbitration Ass'n 1996).

[9] Aristotle's *Rhetoric*, bk. 1, ch. 13.

[10] Quoted in the front matter of *The Arbitrator's Manual* (Securities Industry Conference on Arbitration, August 2007).

[11] These rules are available on the AAA Web site at www.adr.org.

When it comes to case administration, arbitrators also have considerable discretion in managing the procedures in a manner consistent with the expedited nature of arbitration and in interpreting the applicable rules. For example, R-22(d) of the AAA construction rules provides: "There shall be no other discovery, except as indicated herein or as ordered by the arbitrator in extraordinary cases where the demands of justice require it." How one defines an extraordinary case is subject to a wide range of interpretation.

Thus, a party who desires to take a few pre-hearing depositions or to seek discovery of electronically stored information in a large, complex case should try to determine what an arbitrator candidate's inclinations are on these matters before making the appointment.

Consequently, the inclinations of prospective arbitrators on case management and substantive issues are extremely important in gauging the extent to which a candidate may be inclined to look past legal technicalities and apply equitable concepts of fairness. This overlay of equity on top of strict legal concepts creates, in the words of Judge Posner, a "gap" between inherent tendencies and strict legalistic analysis. This makes it wise, in most cases, to explore whatever avenues are available to discern those tendencies before choosing who should serve as a neutral. This in essence is "why" voir dire should be pursued in one form or another.

II. Conducting Proper Due Diligence

The more difficult question is how to engage in an effective due diligence investigation of prospective arbitrators. It requires planning and follow through. On the planning side, immediately after submitting the client's pleading in the arbitration, decide what you want in an arbitrator in terms of style, personality, management skills, activism at the hearing, and views on specific issues. Make a list of these qualities and use them to develop two lists of questions, one to ask practitioners who have experienced arbitration before your arbitrator candidates, and one to ask the candidates themselves.

After receiving the list of arbitrator candidates from the arbitration administration and narrowing the candidates down to three, rank the candidates. Ask them for a list of half a dozen lawyers who have argued before them and to include both winners and losers. Then arrange to interview these attorneys. Next, give the arbitrator candidates a list of written questions to answer. This is, essentially, a written voir dire.

III. Interviewing Practitioners

When seeking to interview lawyers who have arbitrated before one or more of the arbitrator candidates, be sure to contact a few who prevailed and some who lost so as to obtain a balanced perspective. Keep in mind that some lawyers prefer not to comment on arbitrators they have appeared before on the ground that it would violate their obligation to keep prior proceedings confidential. No disclosure violation should result from sharing personal observations about the arbitrator, as long as there is no disclosure of information about the parties or the award..

In order to obtain useful information from these interviews, your list of questions should be tailored to discover what the lawyer knows or senses about the arbitrator's views and preferences, without delving into facts that should not be disclosed. The questions should focus on issues that arise in every arbitration, such as the arbitrator's temperament, style, and approach to the hearing and decision making. For example, with regard to style, you could ask whether the arbitrator asked questions of witnesses or counsel and whether he or she required strict adherence to witness and exhibit lists (requiring advance identification of impeachment documents previously disclosed). In addition, you could ask if written witness statements or other evidence presentation techniques were used in order to make the hearing more efficient. If the answer is no, you could ask whether these techniques were ever discussed in a pre-hearing conference.

If your case will require pre-hearing interim relief, you could ask whether that issue was involved in the practitioner's case and if so, whether such relief was granted or denied. If your arbitration will require discovery, you could ask whether the arbitrator limited discovery or was flexible in allowing anything the parties agreed to. What procedure did the arbitrator follow when a party had a problem with discovery? Did the arbitrator ask for letters instead of motions and decide discovery disputes over the phone?

You could ask about the arbitrator's familiarity with the applicable arbitration rules. You could also ask which rules applied without violating any non-disclosure obligations. In addition, you could ask whether the award was issued within the time frame required by the rules. This leads to questions about the efficiency of the proceeding and the cost. You could ask whether the lawyer's client was satisfied with both.

In addition, you could ask counsel whether the arbitrator was familiar with the type of subject matter involved in the prior dispute and whether that seemed to help or hinder the prompt resolution of the case.

The answers to these questions could help you determine whether an arbitrator candidate is likely to follow the literal provisions of the law or a contract or focus on overall fairness.

It is also worthwhile inquiring into whether counsel believed that the arbitrator candidate made a tough decision by ruling in favor of one party or reach a divided decision, ruling partly in favor of one party and partly in favor of the other.

The reliability and value of the information acquired from lawyer interviews will depend on how much the lawyer recalls and the quality of his or her insights and observations. For this reason, it may be useful to make inquiries into the qualifications of the lawyers you plan to interview.

IV. Using the *Voir Dire* Questionnaire

The questionnaire for the arbitrator candidate could provide the answers you need to decide whether to select or eliminate a candidate. But it also may not. People are not always completely candid or accurate when answering questions about themselves since memory is fallible and people interpret events in different ways. The questions you can ask a prospective arbitrator are much more limited than those you can ask in the *voir dire* of prospective jurors. For example, personal questions are out. For example, you cannot ask arbitrator candidates about the bumper stickers on their cars or the schools that their children attend. But there are a host of worthwhile questions that you can include in the questionnaire.

A recent questionnaire sought information about he number of arbitrations the candidate was or had been involved with where the claims arose out of the same field as that in the present dispute. In addition, it sought to find out how many of these cases:

- involved claims over a specified sum,
- used written witness statements,
- involved writing a reasonable award,
- involved awards of interest on a liquidated sum,
- awards were not unanimous, and
- did the candidate disagree with the award.

If some technical knowledge would be helpful, the questionnaire could ask the candidate to state whether he or she has that knowledge and where it was acquired – for example, at school, a training program or through experience.

To determine familiarity with the industry out of which the dispute arose, the questionnaire could ask the candidate to state the amount of time previously spend in providing services to or writing articles for, entities or trade associations that operate in the businesses of the parties to the dispute. It should also ask whether the prospective arbitrator has ever been a party representative in an arbitration involving issues similar to your case.

The questionnaire could ask if the candidate ever had an award challenged in a judicial enforcement action and the result of those challenges. The sidebar on this page contains a number of "yes" or "no" questions that could also be asked of arbitrator candidates. A final catch-all question that is always important to ask is whether there are other considerations or factors of which the candidate is aware that would be relevant to the parties regarding his or her potential service on an arbitration panel (other than as listed in the candidate's resume), and if the answer is "yes," to explain them.

If references for an arbitrator candidate cannot be obtained from colleagues, ask the candidate for the names of several parties and counsel on the questionnaire, making sure to ask for arbitration winners and losers. This investigative process is likely to generate both positive and negative information about each candidate. Make up a grid to compare the views of the arbitrator candidates. With this positive and negative information, it should be possible to decide who would be the most suitable candidate to serve as the arbitrator.

CHAPTER 13

SELECTING THE IDEAL ARBITRATOR

Charles J. Moxley, Jr.[*]

I. Introduction

The quality of an arbitration obviously depends on the fair-mindedness, experience and ability of the arbitrator or panel selected to hear the dispute. But is it sufficient for counsel to select arbitrators having such qualities? If the question were asked in the context of jury selection, the answer would clearly be "no." Litigators go to famous lengths to select jurors who seem likely to view their case favorably. Why shouldn't those who select arbitrators do the same?

Yet many attorneys seem to believe that, in arbitration, it is sufficient to select well-qualified arbitrators without regard to their potential responsiveness to the client's case. I believe that following such an approach misses a crucial step in the process. In over 30 years as a commercial arbitrator I have seen many cases in which intelligent and fair-minded arbitrators hearing the same evidence have reached significantly different conclusions as to the appropriate award.

Identifying arbitrator candidates who are likely to be responsive to one's case is a daunting task. However, with the Internet and ever-expanding databases, information from which to make such a judgment is greater than ever before.

---

[*] Charles J. Moxley, Jr., the principal in MoxleyADR LLC, has been an arbitrator on panels of the American Arbitration Association (AAA) for over 35 years, presiding over more than 250 cases, many of them large and complex involving multiple parties, substantial issues and high stakes. He trains arbitrators for the Dispute Resolution (DR) Section of the New York State Bar Association (NYSBA), teaches arbitration law at Fordham Law School, and serves as Distinguished ADR Practitioner in Residence at the Benjamin N. Cardozo School of law. He was recently selected by the AAA to provide training in effective arbitration practices in AAA training programs This article is adapted from a presentation he made at the American Arbitration Association in New York in June 2005 on the process of selecting an arbitrator. Mr. Moxley welcomes comments from readers about their experiences with arbitrator selection. He may be reached at cmoxley@moxleyadr.com.

II. The Need for Early Evaluation of One's Case

Asked to identify the differences between arbitration and litigation, most lawyers and experienced business people would mention arbitration's relative informality and substantial limitations on discovery and the right to appeal, which generates savings in both time and cost. Many would also mention the ability to participate in the selection of a decision maker (whether a sole arbitrator or a panel of three) who has knowledge and expertise in the subject area of the dispute.

But a further major difference between the two processes is the fact that in arbitration the attorneys need to have much greater knowledge of their case when they are launching or preparing to defend it than is generally necessary at the early stage of a lawsuit. In litigation, by the time the attorneys select the jury, they have generally lived with the case for years.

In arbitration, the arbitrator selection process starts at the administrative conference held shortly after the case is filed. At that conference, counsel for both parties have the opportunity to tell the case manager what types of persons they want to see on the list of potential arbitrators. In order to do this well, both counsel must know their clients' case inside and out, and have determined their arbitrator preferences—for example, whether the arbitrator should be male or female; young or old; experienced or inexperienced; employed (full time or part time) or retired; a lawyer or non-lawyer; if a non-lawyer, an accountant, business person, or technical expert; an "in-demand" arbitrator with a busy calendar or an arbitrator who can deal with the case right now; an entrepreneurial or "establishment" type of person; a naturally bright high achiever or a serious hard worker; or a proactive or laid back individual.

To select sympathetic and qualified arbitrators, the attorneys need to understand the strengths and weaknesses of their clients' case and have a sense of the personalities involved. The ideal arbitrator always depends on the particular case. At the deepest level, both counsel need to figure out the chain of logic whereby the client has the potential to win—whether based on the facts, the law, the equities, or sleight of hand. Then they must determine what types of potential arbitrators would be likely to respond in a favorable manner to such a case.

A. "Broad-Picture" People versus Sticklers

Perhaps the broadest distinguishing characteristic of arbitrators, cutting across such categories as age, gender, education, experience, profession and substantive knowledge, is a psychological one—the distinction between the conceptual, open-minded, equity-oriented person at one extreme, and the rule-oriented, no-nonsense, by-the-numbers strict constructionist at the other. These two types of individuals have very different ways of looking at the world and may generally be expected to view many fact patterns in very different ways.

It seems to me that the relatively few cases that go to trial do so largely because they involve a gray area of fact or law that causes each side to believe its position is correct. In such circumstances, there is often no strong objective basis for either side to convince the other it is wrong. One side often urges strict construction of the contract and related documents, while the other argues the parties' intent and the equities of the case. Daunting as the task may be, counsel for both sides need to anticipate the likely mindset of potential arbitrators in making their selections.

B. Importance of the Chair

The interpersonal dynamics on a panel, particularly between the arbitrator selected to chair the panel and the two co-arbitrators, can have a substantial impact on the outcome of a case.

In my experience, the chairperson usually has a strong leadership voice with one co-arbitrator and often with both. This multiplies the importance of the arbitrator who is likely to be designated to chair the panel.

In arbitration proceedings administered by the AAA, the AAA will designate the chair based on experience as an arbitrator, knowledge of ADR, the amount of AAA training the arbitrator has taken (for example, training for the large, complex case panel, and training as a chair), and good feedback from users of AAA services. There is no rule of which I am aware calling for a lawyer to be appointed to serve as the chair, although it appears to me that lawyers are often selected for this role. However, a non-lawyer who has more experience with, knowledge of and training in arbitration, who is positively reviewed by AAA clients, could be appointed to chair the panel.

III. Investigative Steps

Experienced counsel take steps to check out the people whose names are on the list of arbitrator candidates prepared by the ADR provider. The first step is to review the list of candidates and the accompanying biographical information and circulate them to the attorneys at the firm and to other trusted colleagues at other firms, seeking feedback about candidates of potential interest. Some law firms active in the field of arbitration collect information about arbitrators and potential arbitrators in a computer database. In addition, it is important to send the arbitrator candidate list to the client, who may have access to independent information about persons on the list.

It is very useful to search for information about the potential arbitrators on the Internet using search engines such as Google and Yahoo, and legal and news-oriented databases (for example, the Lexis/Nexis and Westlaw databases are available only to subscribers). These searches can yield valuable information about arbitrator candidates, which could include titles of articles and books they have written. Counsel should always read whatever the potential arbitrator has written in order to learn how this person thinks and perhaps his or her views on issues involved in the case. Sometime briefs can be found on the Internet that were written by candidates who are (or were) litigators, as well as information about litigation in which candidates (or entities or persons with whom they are closely identified) have been involved. As to potential arbitrators of any prominence, it may be possible to find leads to people they have dealt with in other cases. Calling these people for information can mean avoiding a big mistake.

It can be helpful to interview potential arbitrators. However, arbitrator interviews should only be conducted on a joint basis with the adversary to avoid risking disqualification of the candidate or undermining the award.

A. AAA's Enhanced Neutral Selection Process

The AAA recently introduced the Enhanced Neutral Selection Process to facilitate counsel's selection of arbitrators in certain large, complex cases. This process has the potential to greatly facilitate the process of identification and selection of desirable arbitrators.

As part of the new process, the AAA will provide the parties with an early, initial sample of arbitrator resumes selected on the basis of qualifications identified by the parties. This should enable the parties' attorneys to determine whether the Association is on the right track in offering arbitrator candidates. If necessary, the AAA can redirect its efforts in preparing the list.

The AAA also will send out so-called "block lists" of arbitrators, categorizing potential panel members by professional expertise—such as attorney, retired judge, industry expert, accountant, or other categories of experience requested by the attorneys.

The new program specifically contemplates joint interviews of potential arbitrators by both sides, either by telephone or written questions. In the interview, both counsel will have the opportunity to ask prospective arbitrators a reasonable number of general questions agreed upon by the parties and the arbitrator (but not questions specific to the fact pattern involved), in order to get a sense of the prospective arbitrator and his or her view of the world. Given the importance of arbitrator selection, the opportunity to interview the candidates in large, complex cases is always worth taking.

The new process also contemplates that counsel may request references for prospective arbitrators. References would be of great value in evaluating candidates.

The AAA Enhanced Neutral Selection Process is only available if both sides agree and the case is administered pursuant to the AAA's Procedures for Large, Complex Disputes. Otherwise, the case will be administered according to the regular arbitrator selection process in the AAA Commercial Arbitration Rules.

IV. Types of Arbitrators

A. Lawyers versus Industry Experts

How important is it to select arbitrators with industry expertise? Again, it depends on the case. Many experienced business people and attorneys provide arbitration clauses in their contracts precisely because arbitration offers the opportunity to have potential disputes resolved by decision makers who know the practices of the industry the parties are involved in and are likely to decide any dispute that arises in accordance with such practices. Being judged by one's peers is believed to lead to decisions that better reflect industry expectations. "Architects judging architects" should produce decisions that make sense in the context of architectural practice. Decision making by arbitrators with industry expertise also fosters efficiency, since less time needs to be spent educating them about technical matters. Arbitrators with such expertise can "cut through" the issues.

Yet once disputes arise, the law comes into play. The arbitrators, whatever their technical expertise, will need to have "process" expertise. By that I mean experience conducting arbitration proceedings effectively and expeditiously. Litigators who come to an arbitration with expectations derived largely from their litigation experience (i.e., those who do not have a great deal of experience in arbitration) may not understand this.

In cases involving substantial legal or procedural issues, each side will typically want at least one lawyer. In cases involving substantial technical issues, each side will typically want at least one technical expert. Yet such predilections should not be followed on a knee-jerk basis. Attorneys need to exercise judgment based on the specific case. If their client seems more likely to win based on application of the law, perhaps an effort should be made to select an all-lawyer panel. If the client seems more likely to win based on industry practice or other non-legal considerations, perhaps a panel made up solely of industry experts should be sought.

The issue is most acutely posed in a case to be heard by a single arbitrator where significant legal and technical issues are presented. In such a case, the attorneys for each side have to make the hard choice and seek to select the type of arbitrator believed to be most likely to respond favorably to their client's case.

I do not mean to suggest that there is always a disconnect between decisions based on application of law and those based on industry practice or other non-legal considerations. Having participated in many deliberations on panels with lawyers and industry experts, it seems to me that industry practice is generally substantially consistent with the law and provides a fair result. Yet there are cases where law and practice conflict and where strict application of law conflicts with considerations of fairness and equity. One of the distinctive advantages of arbitration is that it offers the potential for decision-making based on industry practice and equitable considerations in such circumstances. Such decision making, however, does not come automatically. Attorneys must seek to select arbitrators who are potentially amenable (or not amenable) to decision making on a particular basis.

One potential problem with basing the selection of an arbitrator largely on industry expertise is that the arbitrator candidate may have gained the expertise working on one side or the other of the relevant issue. This could make the person desirable to one party and undesirable to the other.

B. Retired Judges

Do retired judges make better arbitrators than lawyers? This depends on the judge and the case. Perhaps the central questions for parties who are seeking to obtain (or avoid) decision making based largely on industry expertise and equitable considerations are: (1) is the retired judge open to such decision making? (2) does the former judge have the arbitration mindset of expedition and economy? and (3) will he or she be open to spending substantial study time in a particular case if necessary and desired by counsel?

If a case fits into a familiar legal paradigm, the party whose case fits that paradigm may fare better with a retired judge. Correspondingly, the party who needs to overcome that paradigm may fare better with an arbitrator who is not a judge, perhaps a lawyer who specializes in an area of law other than the one involved in the case, or a non-lawyer. Such a person may be more inclined to take a fresh look at the matter.

Some retired judges are more sympathetic to requests for extensive discovery (particularly depositions) than arbitrators imbued with the arbitral mindset of speed and expedition. So retired judges may appeal to parties who think there is something to be gained (but not a speedy proceeding) from more discovery.

An important consideration in deciding whether to select a retired judge is the attitude of the client toward arbitration. If a client is nervous about the prospect of arbitrating, having a prominent former judge as the arbitrator might increase the client's comfort level and acceptance of the result, even if it is adverse.

V. Additional Considerations

A. Single Arbitrator or Panel of Three

Should there be a single arbitrator or a panel of three? Often this question is answered in the parties' arbitration agreement. Of course, the parties can always reach a new agreement on that point when the dispute arises. So the issue is always, in a sense, open. The question is an important one in a case where expense or a speedy decision is of major concern. Having three arbitrators increases the arbitrator fees. It also makes scheduling more difficult and can cause delays.

On the other hand, having a panel brings more perspective to the decision-making process. I never cease to be amazed at the range of recollections and perceptions of the evidence that members of panels bring to deliberations. Lawyers who do jury trial often say that the jury sees everything. In my experience, the same can be said of a panel of arbitrators.

A key factor in deciding whether to have a sole arbitrator or a panel is the attorney's level of confidence in the potential sole arbitrator. After all, in federal and state courts throughout the land attorneys regularly appear before a single trial judge, even in the largest of cases. However, at the appellate level there are at least three judges and sometimes more. Given the limited scope of appeal in arbitration, arbitrators in a sense act as both trial and appellate judges.

B. Reasoned versus Conclusory Awards

Should you ask for a reasoned decision? This question is closely related to the type of arbitrator and, in a broader sense, the type of process, desired for a given case. Requiring a reasoned decision requires the selection of at least one arbitrator who is capable of writing the decision. It also raises the likelihood that the arbitrators will view the case in a legalistic fashion, focusing on the fine points of counsels' arguments rather than an overall sense of the equities of the case. It also will increase the cost of the process. Clients, however, are often better able to come to terms with an arbitral award, particularly an adverse one, when they are given the reason for the award.

C. Use of Consultants

Understanding a case does not necessarily imbue counsel with the wisdom to fathom which arbitrator candidates are likely to be favorably disposed to the client's side. Many litigators who do jury trials use consultants to help with jury selection. It seems that jury consultants are used little if at all in arbitrator selection, although the same expertise is involved. Based on a recent informal survey conducted by a law student at my request, jury consultants regard themselves as qualified to provide arbitrator selection services and would be interested in such assignments.

D. An Arbitrator Who Has Time

An arbitrator may be superb but must have time for the case. The most experienced and capable arbitrators may be overbooked in the short run. However, in my experience, most complex commercial cases need at least three to five months from the preliminary hearing for document production and preparation of expert reports, pre-hearing memoranda, and exhibits and witness lists. When additional discovery is sought or substantive motions are made, more time—over a longer period of time—is needed to deal with the case. This reality generally allows for the selection of very sought-after arbitrators (as long as they commit to be available for discovery and pre-hearing issues in the interim).

VI. Conclusion

Arbitrator selection is one of the most important steps in the arbitration process. Counsel for both parties must have a solid grasp of their case before they go into the administrative conference so they can tell the case manager what kind of arbitrator or panel they want. Then, using available investigative methods and information provided to the parties about the arbitrator candidates, counsel should strive to find arbitrators who are most likely to be responsive to the client's case.

CHAPTER 14

AN ARBITRATOR'S WISH LIST

Stanley Weinstein[*]

I. Introduction

What can the attorneys and the parties to arbitration do to help the arbitrator decide their case? Put more accurately, what can they do that will make it easier for the arbitrator to gather all the key facts and render an appropriate decision?

The question is often asked by those who have never participated in arbitration as well as those who have, but have never before dealt with the arbitrator who is selected to hear the dispute. The question embodies an important principle—that the attorneys for the parties should help the arbitrator as much as possible. This article discusses the ways in which they can carry out this principle.

II. The Wish List

A. Treat the Arbitrator with Respect

The parties, with their attorneys, have selected an arbitrator with integrity, sound judgment, and specialized knowledge, rather than an anonymous jury or generalist judge to decide their case. They have done so presumably in order to benefit from the arbitrator's experience arbitrating cases and his knowledge in the field involving the dispute. Accordingly, the attorneys should not underestimate the intelligence or abilities of the arbitrator. It is a "no-no" to talk down to the arbitrator or to belittle his or her experience or knowledge in any way. As the decision maker in the case, the arbitrator is entitled to the utmost respect. If in doubt as to whether the arbitrator understands a particular point, ask the

[*]Stanley Weinstein, a non-practicing attorney and CPA, is an arbitrator specializing in commercial and real estate disputes. He has been on the American Arbitration Association roster since 1994 and can be reached at stanwein@aol.com.

arbitrator directly if further documentation, testimony or explanation would be helpful to him. The arbitrator should appreciate the question and the care the attorney is making to present the client's case.

Treating the arbitrator with respect also means that everyone should be on time for pre-hearing conferences and for the hearing. The arbitrator will not appreciate having to spin wheels waiting for a latecomer. The parties should also be civil to one another and neither engage in direct conversation or accusations nor make provocative facial expressions during the hearing It is unacceptable to threaten anyone.

B. Joint Homework Assignments

There are certain aspects of the arbitration that are more helpful to the arbitrator when counsel for both sides do them together. Even though they are opposing parties, working together can expedite the case, make the arbitrator's life easier to understand what the issues are, and save the parties time and money.

1. Joint exhibits

Usually, the parties each give the arbitrator an exhibit binder, both containing many of the same documents but with different exhibit numbers. This makes reviewing the exhibits more cumbersome. Arbitrators routinely make notes on the exhibits that have been introduced and it is much easier if they are all in one book and not duplicated in two books without a valid reason. In my experience, it helps greatly if both parties agree on the exhibits and present them to the arbitrator in a single three-ringed binder. The joint exhibits should also be indexed and categorized in a logical order.

If there is a question about the authenticity or relevance of a particular document and the challenger has a version he or she believes is authentic or why another document is not appropriate, both versions of the document or explanation should be included in the binder of joint exhibits and given consecutive exhibit numbers. Remember, arbitrators generally will let in all evidence and give it the weight it deserves. By agreeing to the documents to be submitted, there is no need to go through witness testimony to introduce each document.

It is helpful to give the joint exhibits binder to the arbitrator prior to the hearing for him to review and should be referenced in any briefs. If there are particular documents you want the arbitrator to review prior to the hearing so he can have a basic understanding when you present your case, you should make the arbitrator specifically aware of those documents and exhibit numbers. All documents used at the hearing should have been previously disclosed to the adversary, in compliance with the arbitrator's scheduling order. Arbitrators dislike surprises and want full and timely disclosure by all involved.

2. Joint statements

Most of the time, each side prepares for the arbitrator its own statement of facts. However, I find it much more helpful to have the parties prepare certain items jointly, which are given to the arbitrator a few days before the hearing to provide an opportunity to review and become familiar with the dispute and help him focus on the right issues during the hearing.

The items that are on my arbitrator wish list are: a joint statement of agreed facts, a joint statement of disputed facts, and a joint list of items to be decided.

The **joint statement of agreed facts** is extremely helpful to the arbitrator. Done properly, it helps streamline the case, leading to a shorter, less costly arbitration, which benefits the parties. The more detailed the joint statement, the better, because the more facts that can be agreed upon, the fewer facts are left to dispute. The items in the joint statement are essentially stipulated facts. Those items need not be re-established at the hearing. During the hearing the attorneys can refer the arbitrator to the joint statement of facts when it is necessary to their presentations.

I encourage both counsel to prepare a **detailed joint statement of disputed facts**, focusing on the facts that they believe are key to resolving the dispute. By this, I do not mean allegations. The attorneys should state the specific facts that would support their allegations. Don't write, "Respondent breached the contract;" instead, state the specific acts or omissions that constituted the alleged breach. The joint statement of disputed facts can be prepared on a two-column sheet, one column for each party. This should be brief (one to two sentences for each disputed fact). First one party fills out its column, and then the other party responds with its facts and vice versa. With a single document containing both parties' views of the facts in dispute, the arbitrator can focus more directly on the differences in the parties' positions on precise issues. Preparing the joint statement of agreed facts and the joint statement of disputed facts helps narrow the issues for the arbitrator to decide and saves time and money.

Finally, I urge the parties to prepare for the arbitrator a detailed **joint list of items to be decided**. This helps counsel and the arbitrator focus on the evidence needed to decide each issue. As the case moves on, counsel often find that the items on the list change and they need to update it.

Preparing any kind of joint statement necessitates cooperation between the parties. If the adversary won't participate, it is worth trying to find a way to obtain a positive response. Take the laboring oar and draft proposed agreed-upon facts, disputed facts and issues to be decided by the arbitrator, and invite the adversary to review and comment on them within a reasonable amount of time. Keep communications with the adversary open and discuss the issues that are blocking its participation. If the adversary still will not respond, counsel can ask the case administrator to arrange a pre-hearing conference by telephone with the arbitrator to help resolve the matter. If this action is taken, the proposed lists and copies of any written communications with the adversary should be shared with the arbitrator (while copying the opposing party) before the preliminary conference call.

Counsel should complete the jointly prepared documents early enough so that they can send them to the arbitrator a few days prior to the hearing in compliance with the arbitrator's pre-hearing order.

C. Discovery

Discovery is a cost factor in arbitration as it is in litigation. The more discovery, the more time the proceeding will take and the higher the attorneys' and the arbitrator's fees. Parties should make reasonable document requests for relevant evidence. To facilitate the arbitration, the parties should not hide information, but rather respond liberally and in a timely manner. Arbitrators do not enjoy being called because a party has not complied with the scheduling order. If there is a problem complying with the discovery schedule, the parties should try to work out the problems themselves, and then advise the case administrator, or the arbitrator directly depending which is permitted in your case. But if they can't agree to a modification of the schedule, they should advise the case administrator, who can arrange a telephone conference call with the arbitrator. Although it is hard to enforce an order to produce documents, the arbitrator can, as with any matter, draw an inference from a party's failure to produce relevant evidence. Arbitrators do not like to get a request for extension of time on the eve of a deadline. The request should come early enough so if it is refused, the party can still be in compliance.

Counsel should not try to turn arbitration into litigation by seeking to use other discovery devices commonly used in litigation. To do so eliminates two key advantages of arbitration, which are speed and cost savings. The limits of discovery will be determined by the arbitrator. It is his job to streamline the process. Counsel should curb their enthusiasm to take depositions, which are a privilege and not a right in arbitration. Remember arbitration is intended to be speedy and less costly than litigation while at the same time have the parties be able to properly present all their evidence. Depositions are appropriate only in certain arbitrations (usually large, complex cases). If depositions are to be taken, the parties should agree on a limited number and tell the arbitrator why they are necessary; the arbitrator will make the decision for them.

D. Witnesses

In the preliminary and final list of witnesses, the parties should specifically describe what each witness intends to testify about. The more detail, the better. Counsel also should not put the arbitrator in the position of having to exclude repetitive or irrelevant evidence. Thus, counsel should not put on multiple witnesses who will give the same testimony or witnesses who will ramble on about issues that are not germane. Arbitration is supposed to be a quicker alternative to litigation.

Before witnesses testify, counsel should properly prepare their witness making sure they know what facts they need to testify about and that they shouldn't ramble. Before each witness speaks, counsel can help the arbitrator by making a detailed proffer (written or oral) of each item the witness will establish. Proffers are not testimony and will not sway the arbitrator. Rather they help the arbitrator focus on the disputed facts and how the party who is offering the witness intends to establish its version of those facts.

Because the arbitrator has the authority to question witnesses, counsel should ask whether the arbitrator has any questions to ask the witness on this particular topic before moving on to a new line of questioning. It is always better to answer the arbitrator's questions before moving on. Otherwise the question will linger in the arbitrator's mind while others are testifying. Knowing the arbitrator's question helps the attorney know what the arbitrator's concerns are and what the arbitrator believes should be explored in greater detail. Obtaining the answer may correct misinformation or a misunderstanding of the evidence. However, based upon the arbitrator's questions, no inference should be taken by the parties as to how the arbitrator is leaning on this matter. The arbitrator doesn't make his decision until all the witnesses have been heard and all the evidence introduced.

Because in most arbitration proceedings witnesses can be asked leading questions and testify as to hearsay evidence (Rules of Evidence are generally not followed in arbitration), opposing counsel shouldn't interrupt with objections. Arbitrators are trained to give hearsay the weight it deserves. Moreover, opposing counsel will have the opportunity to ask leading questions and have the witness testify to hearsay as well.

The claimant's first witness should be able to clearly and concisely outline the whole case. Although an arbitrator's perception of the case can change as it moves along, the claimant has only one chance at making a first impression.

E. Evidence

The parties should avoid introducing previously undisclosed evidence late but if they can't avoid doing so, they should have a convincing reason for it. An arbitrator generally will allow late evidence for good cause if it is material and the other side is not prejudiced by this, because the failure to hear relevant evidence is grounds for overturning an arbitrator's award. However if this material was known substantially before its late introduction, the arbitrator will not look favorably upon the late introduction.

Introducing late evidence can prolong the proceedings because the arbitrator will generally give the other side sufficient time for further discovery so that the late production does not prejudice that party. As previously noted, arbitrators do not like surprises and want fair and complete disclosure to all involved in a timely manner.

III. Conclusion

Following these pointers will help the parties because making the arbitrator's job easier benefits everyone involved.

CHAPTER 15

WHY NOT PROVIDE FOR NEUTRAL PARTY-APPOINTED ARBITRATORS?

Robert D. Taichert[*]

I. Introduction

The common procedure to constitute an arbitral panel is for each party to appoint its own arbitrator. The party appointed arbitrators then select the third arbitrator, who serves as the chair. The parties naturally select as their arbitrator a person who is most likely to favor their side of the case. This can lead to party appointed arbitrators becoming advocates for the side which appointed them. There are situations in which the parties to a contract want to be sure of the complete objectivity of arbitral proceedings and to achieve that, provide for neutral arbitrators with no connection to the party which appointed them. This article suggests that the way to provide for neutral three member panel arbitration is to specify in the arbitration section of the agreement that party appointed arbitrators will not know which side appointed them. This only works in an administered arbitration with a neutral service provider serving as intermediary. The parties agree that the case administrator will notify the party appointed arbitrators of their selection and inform them that they are not to know which side appointed them.

II. Planning for Neutrality

Because arbitration is a creature of contract, the parties can provide in their arbitration agreement (or submission) for neutrality of all the

---

[*] The late Robert D. Taichert (d. 2013) was a prominent Albuquerque attorney of counsel to Hinkle, Hensley, Shanor & Martin, LLP. He served on the roster of the American Arbitration Association for commercial, construction and large, complex cases. Mr. Taichert had written and lectured on a variety of ADR subjects. He chaired the Revised Uniform Arbitration Act subcommittee of the AAA's New Mexico Advisory Committee.

arbitrators by specifying that the party appointed arbitrators will not learn who selected them. This will prevent any sense of allegiance from forming between the party appointed arbitrator and the appointing side.

A few years ago, I had the good fortune to be a party appointed arbitrator in a case where the anonymity of the appointing party was preserved by agreement of counsel for the parties. The case arose out of ongoing litigation of some duration between two large corporations. involving complex technical and scientific issues. Considerable money had been spent on the case and there was no end in sight. The parties and their lawyers agreed to submit the case to arbitration, rather than continue to endure the financial hemorrhaging and uncertainty that characterizes complex litigation.

Because of the nature of the issues, the parties wanted to appoint arbitrators with subject matter expertise. Both sides wanted a decision reflecting the best independent judgment of a panel of three arbitrators, whose collective judgment would be assuredly impartial. The lawyers crafted a submission to arbitration agreement that specified that the party appointed arbitrators would never know which side appointed them. The arbitration was administered by the American Arbitration Association under its Commercial Arbitration Rules. The case administrator was the key to the process.

The case administrator told me and the other party appointed arbitrator that we had each been selected by one of the parties, but would not be informed of the identity of the party that appointed us. This eliminated any possible baggage that can follow knowing who appointed you.

After we selected the third arbitrator, the three of us proceeded to hear and decide the case as a panel of three neutrals. To sit as a party appointed arbitrator without any possibility of extraneous influence was refreshing. I recommend this approach for arbitration proceedings in which the parties want to assure the neutrality of the entire panel of three arbitrators. Below is a sample arbitration clause to achieve a neutral panel with party appointed arbitrators:

"The parties agree that any controversy or claim arising out of or relating to this contract or the breach thereof shall be determined by arbitration in the City of [ ], administered by the American Arbitration Association (AAA) under its Commercial Arbitration Rules, by a panel of three neutral arbitrators appointed in the manner specified in the following paragraph, and judgment on the award may be entered in any court of competent jurisdiction.

Each party shall inform the case administrator of their choice of arbitrator. The case administrator will follow the AAA procedure for the qualification of arbitrators, and will inform the party appointed arbitrators that they will not be told which side appointed them. The party appointed arbitrators will name the third arbitrator, who shall serve as chair of the panel. The parties agree that the party appointed arbitrators shall never be informed by the parties, the attorneys, or the case administrator, of the identity of the party appointing them."

III. Conclusion

While not a new concept, providing for neutral party appointed arbitrators in the arbitration agreement is a useful tool in situations where the parties want to be sure of the complete impartiality of the panel. The anonymity of the appointing party assures the parties to a dispute of the impartiality of the party appointed arbitrators and, in such cases, improves the quality of the arbitration process and of awards. Transactional lawyers and principals in contract negotiations should focus on the possibility of conflict during the course of the contractual relationship and consider this approach when they wish to obtain the best impartial judgment of a panel of three neutral arbitrators.

CHAPTER 16

THE STOIC ARBITRATOR V. THE ACTIVIST ARBITRATOR—A SOLUTION

Jeffrey Aiken[*]

I. Introduction

A hearing on the merits is where the evidentiary record and the parties' legal theories regarding the issues submitted to commercial arbitration are presented to the arbitrator. It is here where the arbitrator can decide the extent to which she will question witnesses and/or counsel for the parties.[1] At one end of the spectrum is the essentially passive arbitrator who receives the evidence and arguments as presented (the "stoic arbitrator") while at the other, is the arbitrator who actively questions witnesses and engages in discussions with counsel regarding factual and legal positions that the arbitrator either does not understand or does not agree with (the "activist arbitrator"). Thus, the activist arbitrator affords the parties' counsel an opportunity to address the arbitrator's concerns while the stoic one does not. In addition, an arbitrator may decide that one approach is not necessarily suitable for all disputes.

An arbitrator's view of her role as the ultimate decision maker of the issues submitted to arbitration is likely to determine whether she will be

---

[*] Jeffrey Aiken is semi-retired, having practiced with the law firm of Whyte Hirschboeck Dudek,S.C. where he was involved in arbitration practice as a neutral and party representative for nearly 40 years in addition to serving as a commercial litigator and transactional attorney. He continues to serve on the AAA's Large and Complex Claim panels for construction and other commercial disputes. His full biography is available at http://aikenadr.weebly.com.

[1] While it is permissible for non-lawyers to represent parties in arbitration under certain circumstances, it will be assumed for simplicity purposes that lawyers are the party representatives. Non-lawyer representatives are generally permissible when serving as an employee of a party. Representation of an unrelated third party may constitute the unauthorized practice of law by a non-lawyer or even an unlicensed lawyer in that jurisdiction. See, *Arbitration and the Unauthorized Practice of Law*, Paul M. Lurie and Carl F. Ingwalson, The Construction Lawyer, Winter 2007, p. 14 et. seq.

a stoic or activist arbitrator during the hearing.[2] This article is intended to make arbitrators and counsel aware that this decision can influence the outcome of the proceeding. In the next sections, the rules that govern an arbitrator's conduct at the hearing will be explored.

II. Arbitral Discretion vs. Arbitral Obligations

The American Arbitration Association Arbitration (AAA) rules give arbitrators in commercial cases authority to grant any relief that they deem "just and equitable." By using the phrase "may grant",[3] the rules make clear that the arbitrator has the discretion to exercise this power and is not obligated to do so (although arbitrators may have been obligated to use their equitable powers at one time).[4]

Some arbitrators may believe, notwithstanding the above-stated discretionary power to award equitable remedies, that arbitral decisions should be fair and equitable and that they have an obligation to exercise their equitable powers. There are undoubtedly other arbitrators who believe that their role is to decide a dispute according to the strict confines of the law, or the unambiguous terms of the parties' contract.[5] In addition, there may be stoic arbitrators who believe that in some circumstances there is room to consider basic principles of equity. Finally, there may be stoic arbitrators who believe that awards should be fair but they will not consider principles of equity despite flaws in the way evidence was adduced at the hearing or in the legal arguments presented by counsel. It is difficult to see, however, that stoicism in such circumstances can serve the objective of issuing fair awards.

---

[2] It is probably a good idea to acknowledge that personality traits could influence this as well. For example, highly outgoing arbitrators are unlikely to be completely passive at a hearing, while very shy and introverted arbitrators are unlikely to be very active questioners at the hearing.

[3] Rule R-43 of the Commercial Rules and Rule R-45 of the Construction Rules of the American Arbitration Association each provide: "The arbitrator may grant any remedy or relief that the arbitrator deems just and equitable and within the scope of the agreement of the parties…".

[4] In 320 B.C., Aristotle said, "The arbitrator looks to what is equitable, the judge to what is law; and it was for this purpose that arbitration was introduced, namely, that equity might prevail." Rhetoric, bk. 1, ch. 13. Goldmann Trust v. Goldmann, 26 Wis. 2d 141, 153, 131 N.W.2d 902, 909 (1965) (dissenting opinion).

[5] These arbitrators most likely include retired judges and many lawyer arbitrators.

III. The Effect on the Conduct of the Hearing

There is often a connection between the arbitrator's view of her obligations as an impartial decision maker and the manner in which she conducts the hearing on the merits. An arbitrator who believes she is to simply apply the law to the facts presented by the parties tends to take a stoic approach. That approach is not necessarily unfair. The arbitrator will rule on counsel's objections, if any, and control the hearing so that the parties have a fair opportunity to present their case. But if one party fails to submit evidence that would be helpful to its cause (either due to an oversight or a strategic decision of its counsel), the stoic arbitrator will accept that omission or oversight as one of the hazards of an adjudication process. One cannot unduly criticize this approach which essentially mimics a trial in court where judges routinely remain stoic.

An arbitrator who believes her obligation is to see that justice is done is not likely to ignore the bungling of counsel. This arbitrator is likely to take an activist approach, questioning witnesses and counsel during the hearing.

The limited nature of judicial review of arbitration awards does not require the activist arbitrator or the stoic arbitrator to change her approach. But they both bear a greater burden than trial judges to "get it right" the first time because most errors in the arbitrator's decision making, whether factual or legal, are not subject to appeal.[6] By contrast, equivalent errors of law and fact in a judicial proceeding are subject to appeal.

IV. Arbitrator's Right to Direct Evidentiary Presentations

The AAA and other provider rules emphasize the arbitrator's managerial authority at the hearing in order to provide the parties with a faster and more economical process. The rules discourage arbitrators from being passive participants in the process and allowing the hearing to go on at length. Rule R-31(b) of the AAA Construction Arbitration Rules and Rule R-30(b) of the AAA Commercial Arbitration Rules both state that:

> An arbitrator, exercising his or her discretion, shall conduct the proceedings with a view to expediting the resolution of the

[6] *See*, 9 U.S.C. § 10, itemizing the limited grounds for vacating an arbitration award in a proceeding subject to the Federal Arbitration Act.

> dispute and may . . . direct the parties to focus their presentations on issues the decision of which could dispose of all or part of the case.

Rule L-4 (a) in both the AAA rules for large, complex commercial disputes and large, complex construction claims mention "just" results. This rule provides: "Arbitrator(s) shall take such steps as they may deem necessary or desirable…to achieve a just, speedy and cost-effective resolution of Large, Complex Construction Cases."

Unlike the discretionary "just and equitable" remedies provisions in the AAA's regular rules, rule L-4(a) is mandatory. It requires an arbitrator to exercise discretion to do what is necessary—which could include questioning witnesses and having discussions with counsel about their arguments—in order to achieve a just resolution. It appears that an arbitrator who takes a purely stoic stance throughout the hearing in a large, complex case would not be in compliance with this rule. This analysis leads to two questions:

1. Should the regular rules be interpreted not to require a just result because the ability to apply equitable remedies is discretionary?
2. What should an arbitrator do during the presentation of evidence and legal theories at the hearing when it is apparent that one or both attorneys are not appropriately developing their client's cases so that a "just resolution" can be achieved?

Rule R-30 of the AAA Commercial Arbitration Rules and Rule R-32 of the Construction Industry Arbitration Rules both provide: "Witnesses for each party shall…submit to questions from the arbitrator…." These rules clearly authorize, but do not seem to require, an arbitrator to participate in witness examinations. At several past training sessions, AAA arbitrators were instructed that they may question witnesses if some evidence or testimony does not seem right in her professional experience, but that they should "rarely ask questions about some point not raised by the parties." So when a party fails to raise a point which the arbitrator deems pertinent to deciding an issue in the case, the arbitrator who undertook this training will be more likely to refrain from asking any questions.

However, the cannon of ethics for commercial arbitrators prepared by the AAA and American Bar Association does not deter arbitrator questioning of witnesses. Canon IV(G) states: "When an arbitrator determines that more information than has been presented by the parties is required to decide the case, it is not improper for the arbitrator to ask questions ...."[7] Consequently, an arbitrator has a right to question witnesses when she feels a party's presentation is inadequate to decide a dispute. Whether the arbitrator exercises this right, however, will be governed by the arbitrator's view of his role in the arbitral process.

V. An Obvious Solution to This Dilemma

If an arbitrator asks questions of witnesses at the hearing, as she is empowered to do,[8] she should take care to avoid "tipping her hand" concerning her decision in the case. It can be very difficult to draw a line between gathering information to "decide the case" under the theories presented by counsel and deciding the case on other theories (such as on purely equitable considerations as authorized under the AAA's rules). Canon VI(C) of Ethics for Commercial Arbitrators states, "It is not proper at any time for an arbitrator to inform anyone of the decision in advance of the time it is given to all parties."[9] It is unclear whether this would prohibit an arbitrator from informing the parties early of the arbitrator's likely decision based on the evidence presented to that point (i.e. in advance of the final award). It seems logical that the prohibition applies only to the communication of a decision to any one person without all parties being present. Otherwise, an arbitrator could not ask a question of a witness necessary to flush out factual evidence that communicates to one or both the parties that the evidence elicited to that point is insufficient for a decision for or against a party.

There is a solution to this problem that is expressly permitted by Canon VI(C), of the Code of Ethics. That solution is for parties to address in their arbitration or submission agreement, or in a stipulation at an early preliminary hearing, the scope of the arbitrator's participation in development of the factual evidence and associated legal theories, in support and in opposition to the various claims. This express authorization would provide an exception to the prohibition against certain conduct of the arbitrators. The ethical restrictions "may be governed by agreements of the parties" and the ethics code "does not take the place of or supersede such agreements." Simply put, the parties can resolve the arbitrator's

---

[7] Canon IV(G).

[8] Even questions that go beyond the scope of the testimony elicited by counsel.

[9] Canon VI(C).

dilemma by entering an agreement describing the scope of the arbitrator's participation in development of the factual evidence and associated legal theories in support and in opposition to the various claims. Unfortunately, most counsel handling arbitration matters are so accustomed to the court room process where stoicism reigns supreme, that they do not appreciate the flexibility afforded by the arbitration process. It may be because of the inherent self-serving bias of counsel whose evaluation of a case, of necessity, includes a self-assessment of their ability to control the outcome.[10] In any event, an attorney experienced in the arbitration process should relish the opportunity to obtain input from the trier of fact and law (i.e. the arbitrator) while the evidence is being developed, presented and argued in order that the client's best position is put forth. Yet, it is not a common practice in the arbitration arena for opposing counsel to capitalize upon this potentially beneficial feature of the arbitration process.

It is certainly an arbitrator's prerogative to explain or refrain from offering an activist role to opposing parties. If offered, however, it is advisable that this be done in writing and any concurrence by counsel also be in writing. One method of accomplishing this is to include provisions to this effect in a hearing protocol order requiring all parties to consent in writing to active involvement.[11] This should also address two

---

[10] *See*, "Insightful or Wishful: Lawyers' Ability to Predict Case Outcomes," by Loftus, Granhag, Hartwig and Goodman-Delahunty, Psychology, Public Policy, and Law, 2010, Vol. 16, No. 2, 133-157; and, "Psychological Impediments to Mediation Success: Theory and Practice," Russell B. Korobkin, UCLA School of Law, Law & Economics Research Paper Series, Research Paper No. 05-09, http://ssrn.com/abstract=689261.

[11] For example, an order on hearing protocols (such as describing dress code, etc.) might include a provision such as the following: Rule 30 of the Commercial Rules and Rule 32 of the Construction Rules both provide: "Witnesses for each party shall…submit to questions from the arbitrator…" and "[t]he arbitrator, exercising his or her discretion, shall conduct the proceedings with a view to expediting the resolution of the dispute. The cannon of ethics of the AAA and American Bar Association (the "Ethics Code") acknowledge that "[w]hen an arbitrator determines that more information than has been presented by the parties is required to decide the case, it is not improper for the arbitrator to ask questions…" [Canon IV(G)]; yet, "[i]t is not proper at any time for an arbitrator to inform anyone of the decision in advance of the time it is given to all parties" [Canon VI(C)] although conduct of the arbitrators "may be governed by agreements of the parties" and the Ethics Code "does not take the place of or supersede such agreements." As a result, an arbitrator may, in his or her discretion: (a) act in a predominantly passive manner, deciding the dispute solely upon the information submitted by each party without questioning witnesses or providing feedback on the evidence as it is being presented ("Passive Involvement"); or (b) questioning witnesses on points raised by the parties or as the arbitrator determines is required to decide the case but without disclosing a forthcoming decision on the merits ("Limited Involvement"). If counsel believes any

critical points: first, that a prompt failure to object to an arbitrator's question is a waiver of such an objection; and, second, entry of the agreement on active involvement constitutes a waiver of any later assertion as part of an attempt to overturn the eventual award. In short, such activist involvement in developing the factual evidence and appropriate legal theories governing the proceeding will not be deemed evidence of the arbitrator having been biased or prejudiced against a party's position.

VI. *Sua Sponte* in Arbitration

While the scope of an arbitrator's involvement does not necessarily dictate whether she will conduct an independent analysis of potentially applicable legal theories, it is far more likely with a more activist arbitrator. Judges have the inherent authority to consider matters bearing on a case *sua sponte*—i.e. on their own motion. As one Wisconsin court held fairly recently:

> There are two apparently inconsistent theories of the proper role of the trial (or appellate) court. One theory is that the litigants control the course of the lawsuit and determine the nature of the questions presented to the courts. The other theory is that the courts have the responsibility to decide cases in accordance with the law and this responsibility is not altered or diminished because counsel fail to identify an issue. That the parties, not the courts, should determine the nature of the questions presented is a natural

---

question by the Arbitrator posed to a witness or counsel is improper for any reason, an immediate objection shall be made specifying the ground for such objection; otherwise such objection shall be deemed waived. The Arbitrator in this proceeding will engage in Passive or Limited Involvement unless the parties stipulate in writing that he may engage in "Active Involvement" and that by doing so the parties agree that such Active Involvement will not later be asserted as a basis for a claim of arbitrator bias, lack of independence or other inappropriate conduct (such as raising an issue not raised by one of the parties or providing an indication of a forthcoming decision) which might serve as a ground for challenging the final award. "Active Involvement" is defined to include active questioning of witnesses and communications with respective counsel (in the presence of each other) by the Arbitrator during the hearing regarding questions he has concerning (or difficulty he has in understanding or accepting) the viability, validity, veracity or sufficiency of evidence or a party's legal position being taken, in an effort to assist each counsel in presenting their best case from a factual and legal point of view as comprehended by the arbitrator at that point in the proceeding.

> outgrowth of the adversary system and the heavy workload of most courts. The litigants are most familiar with the case, and courts, especially trial courts, do not have the time or staff to do original research in every case to discover issues not raised by the parties. That a court should raise issues *sua sponte* is the natural outgrowth of the court's function to do justice between the parties. Although theory and practice militate against a court's *sua sponte* raising legal issues, it is well recognized that courts may *sua sponte* consider legal issues not raised by the parties.[12]

Again, the authority of a judge clearly exists although it is not mandatory that the burdens of independent analysis be undertaken regarding issues not raised by the parties. Similarly, it would seem, an arbitrator has the same authority and likewise is not derelict in her role as an arbitrator by refraining from taking on the burdens of such analysis. Just as courts have the power to visit issues *sua sponte*, without being required to provide added opportunity to the parties to brief those new issues,[13] it is highly recommended that such an opportunity be afforded. So too, an arbitrator should tend to provide additional briefing opportunities to counsel when an issue is raised *sua sponte* although the decision to do so would seem to rest in the discretion of the arbitrator.

The position of an arbitrator may legitimately be viewed as closely analogous to that of a civil law justice who has direct responsibility for assembly of all relevant evidence and then applying the correct legal principles to arrive at a just result.

VII. The Lawyer's Lesson

If one realizes the potential impact that an arbitrator's overall philosophy toward her role may have on how a dispute is handled, there are several lessons to be learned. First, when it comes to drafting an arbitration provision for a contract, it is advisable to consider incorporating a provision calling for a written *voir dire* of prospective arbitrator candidates in an effort to gain as much insight as reasonably

---

[12] State v. Holmes, 106 Wis. 2nd 31 (Wis. 1982).

[13] *See, for example*, Bartus v. DHSS, 176 Wis. 2d 1063, 1073 (1993)(court discussed a judges right to consider overlooked issues sua sponte and "decline[d] to adopt a per se rule requiring courts to permit the submission of additional briefs whenever an issue is raised sua sponte").

available into the overall approach such a candidate may take towards resolving a dispute.[14] A broad brush approach in this manner would allow for a party to then drill down to determine the fundamental attitude a candidate has on questioning witnesses, the use of *sua sponte* as a means of arriving at a "just and equitable" result and the inclination to providing an opportunity for the parties to brief issues raised on a *sua sponte* basis. Considering that most law firms and in-house legal departments are structured in a way that those handling resolution of disputes are often not involved in transactional drafting, it is certainly wise for the litigators to communicate these intricacies of the arbitration process with their transactional counterparts to make sure they are considering, from a practical perspective, fundamental issues concerning the arbitration provisions they are drafting.

[14] *See*, Jeffrey Aiken, *Due Diligence in Arbitrator Selection: Using Interviews and Written Voir Dire*, American Arbitration Association's Dispute Resolution Journal, May-July 2009.

CHAPTER 17

CHAIRING AN ARBITRATION

*Judith B. Ittig and Michael J. Bayard**

I. Introduction

We have each chaired many arbitration panels, and in one very large, multi-party case, one of us (Judith) was an arbitrator on a tribunal that the other (Mike) chaired. Mike is located in Los Angeles and Judith lives and works in Washington, D.C. Working together at a long distance from each other required special attention to case management among the three arbitrators. That experience, along with our separate work as chairs of other panels, led us to offer our perspectives on the unique role of a panel chair. This article contains our shared thinking about how to manage the responsibilities of chairing an arbitration.

The panel chair is the leader and the voice of the panel. However, the chair has no more authority than the other arbitrators do to decide the dispute. To be effective, the chair must treat the co-arbitrators with a high level of respect. The chair's job is to manage, not usurp, the authority of the other arbitrators. What follows is our vision of how a panel chair should act from the time of appointment through the signing and delivery of the award.

---

* Michael J. Bayard is a full-time construction arbitrator, mediator and project neutral. He chairs the AAA's Construction Advisory Subcommittee for the Los Angeles Region and teaches a graduate course in construction management at the University of Southern California, where he is an adjunct professor. He was recently named to the AAA's National Construction Master Arbitrator Roster. Mr. Bayard may be reached toll free at (800) 652-2927 or at michaeljbayard@yahoo.com.

Judith Ittig serves on the AAA's commercial arbitrator panel, the ICDR's commercial arbitrator panel, and the AAA's Construction Mega Project Panel. Mrs. Ittig, an attorney at Ittig & Ittig, P.C. based in Washington, DC, is a Fellow of the American College of Construction Lawyers, a Chartered Arbitrator/Fellow of the Chartered Institute of Arbitrators (London), and a Fellow of the College of Commercial Arbitrators. She can be reached by email at jbi@ittig-ittig.com.

II. Working Effectively as a Panel

A. Style of Arbitrating

Each arbitrator on a panel has his or her own professional style for managing the hearings. For a panel to work effectively together, there should be a congruence of styles, with agreement on how the arbitration will be conducted. For example, should the arbitrators agree to hold their questions of witnesses until after the attorneys have completed their questioning? Should they discuss the case as the hearings progress? Should the panel meet informally on a daily basis to review how the arbitration is progressing? These matters should be raised by the chair at the outset so the panel can work comfortably as a team.

B. Lines of Communication

If the three panel members have not arbitrated together before, and especially if they do not know each other well or at all, the chair should convene a meeting before the hearings commence, and even earlier if important pre-trial matters must be considered. One of the great benefits of serving on a panel is the trust and cooperation that develops among arbitrators. The chair should not hesitate to take the lead in making these early connections. When distance makes it unfeasible to meet in person, we contact our co-arbitrators by phone or e-mail to introduce ourselves if we haven't met before. The chair who reaches out to co-panelists sets a pattern of conduct that is much appreciated and aids the development of good-working relationships.

C. Agenda

The preliminary hearing is the first time that the panel and the parties discuss the case together. An agenda is advisable for all preliminary hearings and the chair, as the leader of the panel, is usually the preparer. The chair should circulate the agenda to the co-arbitrators when important or complicated matters will be addressed. We like to talk to our co-arbitrators on the telephone about the agenda to see if they have any additions or suggested revisions. These discussions can reveal differences in the arbitrators' approaches that can then be addressed in advance of the hearings.

D. Conferencing

Today, most pre-hearing conferences are conducted by telephone. When there are more than two people on the line, it can be difficult to determine who is speaking. The most practical approach is to have the chair speak for the panel as a whole. Yet the chair has the responsibility to ensure that the views of the co-arbitrators are heard. The chair should arrange for the arbitrators to break away during the conference for private discussions, if necessary. The chair should elicit the co-arbitrators' comments and suggestions and find out if there are commitments that need to be accommodated when scheduling the hearings. By drawing the co-arbitrators into the discussion, the chair demonstrates that their thoughts and opinions are valued. That approach should produce active and cooperative participation throughout the arbitration.

E. Act in Unison

The chair should make every effort to engage the co-arbitrators in the case so that they are fully committed to it and act cooperatively and respectfully. The chair should be sensitive to the behavior of co-arbitrators that might signal a problem. Is one arbitrator always late for the start of each day? If so, why? Are the co-arbitrators focusing on the testimony or does their attention lapse at times? Is anyone fidgeting or distracted by messages on a PDA? If so, the panel may need more short breaks in the hearing day. By observing the conduct of fellow arbitrators, the chair can make accommodations so that the parties receive the arbitrators' complete attention.

F. Circulate Drafts

Whenever the chair is preparing a decision or ruling for the panel, it is vital to circulate drafts for comment by the co-arbitrators. Not only does this approach bring the co-arbitrators into the decision-making, it also results in clearer, more logical decisions and rulings. Recently, one of us was called on to make an important ruling on arbitrability. The co-arbitrators' comments and revisions to the draft ruling immeasurably improved the quality and clarity of the ultimate decision. This approach allowed the panel to rule with the full confidence that it was of one view.

G. Develop Camaraderie

It is possible to sense when people are pulling together and working toward the same goal. If it appears that the three arbitrators are not satisfied with the way the arbitration is proceeding, it is the chair's responsibility to uncover the problem and lead the panel to a mutually agreeable solution. To make sure this happens, the chair should often take the "temperature" of the panel to see if things are going well.

Share duties. One way to maintain the co-arbitrators' commitment and interest in the proceedings is to share responsibilities. Often, the chair takes on the responsibility of managing discovery, but the co-arbitrators can be assigned other duties, such as circulating the first draft of a pre-hearing order, keeping track of additional exhibits, keeping notes of all stipulations, or memorializing important rulings during the hearings. The chair is the designated leader, but the chair doesn't always have to take on all of the administrative work.

H. Maintain Contact

When the arbitrators reside far from each other, the chair should keep the lines of communication open with e-mail updates and stay in frequent contact even when the panel is not in hearings, especially during lengthy breaks between hearings. Just a brief message that reports any recent developments in the case, or even that all is quiet in the interim and the case is proceeding as planned, helps cement the panel's working relationship. Moreover, the three arbitrators will be "on the same page" when the hearings begin if they are kept aware of each other's thinking about pre-hearing developments.

When counsel and the chair are communicating directly, which often occurs when the co-arbitrators and counsel have delegated discovery matters to the chair, copies of all communications should be sent to the co-arbitrators. A major part of the chair's job is to keep them "in the know."

I. Exercise Control

What might the chair do when a co-arbitrator acts inappropriately? For example, a co-arbitrator can be deterred from "taking over" and interrupting testimony if the panel has agreed in advance on ground rules for posing arbitrator questions. The chair must be sensitive to maintaining the integrity of the arbitration and never "reprimand" a co-arbitrator in front of the parties or counsel. If attention flags, the chair can intervene. We've all felt ourselves drift mentally at one time or another. If the chair calls for a break, the co-arbitrators will get the message without the chair needing to "say" anything.

III. Ensuring Efficiency of the Arbitral Process

A. Time Saving

Keeping the cost of arbitration reasonable is part of a chair's responsibility. The chair should be on the lookout for time-saving measures that will reduce costs. For example, the chair can initiate discussions with the co-arbitrators about streamlining the arbitration where feasible and appropriate. One fertile area of streamlining is the presentation of evidence.

There are many different ways to present evidence in arbitration. For example, many arbitrators and counsel are using witness panels as a way to adduce the testimony of several witnesses at once. Written witness statements are also being used in place of a large part, or all, of direct testimony because it makes efficient use of the time of arbitrators, witnesses and counsel.

The chair can also explore different scheduling options for the order of witnesses so that their contributions to the proceedings are most effective and efficient. Flexibility in scheduling is a part of the arbitration process that benefits from the arbitrators' creativity and willingness to implement non-traditional techniques of case presentation. The chair should lead the co-arbitrators and the other participants in the arbitration in the direction of adjusting the process to the demands of the individual case. These approaches can produce valuable benefits, not least among them being cost savings.

B. Equipment Scheduling

The chair should ask the parties if they intend to use audio-visual or other presentation equipment. If the parties are not planning to provide all the equipment they need, the chair should put them in contact with the AAA office if the hearings will be held there. It will be necessary to follow up to be sure all arrangements are satisfactory. Part of the chair's job is making sure that there are no avoidable delays in the hearings.

C. Handling Exhibits

If the arbitration involves a large quantity of exhibits, the chair should consult with the co-arbitrators about devising easy ways to handle them, such as asking the parties to produce joint exhibits. One of the biggest time wasters is "notebook overload," a condition where there are shelves of notebooks that the arbitrators must refer to for each exhibit mentioned in testimony. The chair can involve the co-arbitrators in fashioning solutions that will help them manage the evidence, such as separate notebooks for each witness. The chair should not presume to know how other arbitrators like to take notes or review exhibits.

D. Case Manager Involvement

The chair should ensure that the case manager receives a copy of everything that is sent to the parties. With so much communication now being done by e-mail, the chair should make it a policy to copy the case manager and the other arbitrators on all e-mail correspondence and ask them to do the same. It is helpful to make the case manager the fourth member of the team.

IV. Conducting the Hearings

A. Ruling on Evidence

As in the case of discovery rulings, most panels delegate to the chair the responsibility for making evidentiary rulings. This approach is the only practical way to proceed if the panel is to speak with one voice. But because evidentiary rulings could likely form the basis for a challenge to the award, the chair should not rule alone. It is essential to make sure the co-arbitrators are in agreement with the ruling. If they want to discuss the situation before the ruling is made, the chair can call a recess so that the arbitrators can have a private discussion.

B. Confer with Colleagues

The co-arbitrators may at times be less engaged in the arbitration than the chair, especially when the chair is ruling on evidentiary objections. Thus, the chair must be attentive to the level of the co-arbitrators' participation and their understanding of the proceedings. If the chair senses a "disconnect," she should confer with the co-arbitrators about how the hearings are progressing and consider ways to increase each arbitrator's involvement. These considerations may be especially important when the three arbitrators have different experience and professions.

C. Keep to the Schedule

The chair must insist on adhering to the schedule. We check with counsel frequently, even as often as the close of every hearing day, to find out if the schedule is being maintained and whether there are ways to make the presentations more efficient. On the other hand, the chair needs to be flexible when circumstances warrant. Illness and family emergencies are examples of unplanned but sincere schedule impacts. When these problems arise, the chair should consult with the panel, as all arbitrators are affected by schedule changes and any ruling should come from the panel as a whole.

D. Respect Everyone's Time

The chair's own behavior should demonstrate respect for everyone's time. The chair should never be late for the start of a hearing. Similarly, we advise calling a recess at or close to the time that breaks have been scheduled. We also end each hearing day when planned. If someone has a legitimate need to alter the schedule, the chair should make every effort to accommodate this person while taking into account possible inconveniences to others. The chair should alleviate as many burdens as possible. The chair is the "front person" for the AAA and the panel and must keep in mind that they are providing a service. While the most important product is a quality decision, everyone will remember how the panel conducted themselves.

E. Breaks

The chair should establish times for breaks and lunch and adhere to them. Counsel often plan on those breaks to schedule witnesses, consult with co-counsel, and perform a myriad of other tasks. We have found that because court reporters concentrate on one task throughout the hearing, they need a break about every one-and-a-half-hours. So we schedule morning and afternoon breaks at those intervals. A couple of shorter five-minute breaks may be needed for the convenience of all. Sometimes, an unscheduled "stretch" break is appreciated, with everyone remaining in the room.

F. Disclosures

The chair should be vigilant about arbitrator disclosures. We advise putting them on the record and informing the parties that if they have objections or need more information (or both), they should contact the AAA case manager.

In a recent arbitration, one of us was chair of a panel with two arbitrators from out of town. When the chair learned that on some evenings there were plans for them to have dinner with friends who were attorneys in town, those dinner plans were disclosed in advance to the parties. The concern was that one of the local attorneys might have had some involvement in the case, perhaps as the mediator. The chair also learned that morning jogs might possibly take the arbitrators by the building site that was the subject of the arbitration. Since the co-arbitrators didn't know the location, the chair inquired as to whether anyone objected to the arbitrators seeing the building. As it turned out, both parties urged all three arbitrators to drive or jog by the site. The parties and their counsel appreciated the fair-mindedness of the arbitrators.

G. Daily Hearing Reports

At the end of each hearing day, the chair should prepare a report summarizing the day's events. This report should include the names of witnesses, the examinations that were conducted, descriptions of new exhibits that are not in the exhibit notebooks, stipulations and other agreements made by the parties, as well as key rulings of the panel. If feasible, copies of the report should be given to the co-arbitrators and counsel for the parties on the next hearing day. This daily hearing summary is a helpful shorthand record of the hearings that can aid the chair in managing the arbitration. Providing it to counsel gives the parties a sense that the hearings are well organized. Moreover, the panel will find it useful during deliberations.

V. Conducting Deliberations

A. Summarize the Case

We like the "tell the story" approach to deliberations as a way to gain understanding and consensus. During the arbitration each party presented its version of the story of the case. We begin our panel deliberations by asking each arbitrator to relate the story of the dispute as he or she sees it. This approach is a great vehicle for uncovering areas of agreement and disagreement that the chair can raise for discussion before tackling the dollars at issue.

B. Disagreements

When panel members have a fundamental disagreement during deliberations, the chair can convene a "mini-hearing" of the panel at which the arbitrator holding the minority point of view will argue the facts and law in support of that position to the other members of the panel. Open-minded listening may result in reconciling once disparate views.

C. Completing the Arbitration

The chair is responsible for coordinating the deliberations and the process of award writing and signing. Illness, vacation, business commitments, the arbitrators' distance from one another, and the complexity of the case are factors that make it more difficult for the chair to meet these obligations. Arranging time for three arbitrators to deliberate, draft and review an award and then make sure it is signed and delivered to the case manager in the allotted time (usually 30 days after the hearings are closed) is usually a challenge. Although it is often necessary to review notes and contemplate the legal issues, too much time between the end of the hearings and deliberations and award writing allows memories to fade and clear points to become muddled. We suggest the first and most comprehensive deliberations should take place immediately (or very soon after) the conclusion of all the testimony. Usually the case can be decided at that meeting and the three arbitrators can then work out the details of award writing without having to meet again.

VI. Arbitrator Compensation

A. Notice to the AAA

Although each arbitrator projects the fees and expenses he or she expects to incur and communicates this information to the case manager, the chair who conducts some oversight earns the appreciation of the co-arbitrators. In carrying out this role, the chair should keep the case manager informed about the number of planned hearing days, additional hearing time that is later scheduled, how much "study time" the arbitrators anticipate, and whether large disparities of time charged should be expected among the panel members. For example, the chair might expect to devote more time than the co-arbitrators do to managing discovery or drafting the award. If a co-arbitrator is taking on additional case-management responsibilities, the chair should assist in calculating how much additional time will be allocated to those tasks and be sure the case manager is notified so that sufficient arbitrator compensation is collected.

B. Periodic Billings

In lengthy cases, arbitrators should bill for fees and expenses on a monthly basis. In AAA arbitration, the chair should encourage the co-arbitrators to submit their bills to the AAA in a timely manner. Regular billing is particularly helpful where the chair is spending a much greater amount of time than the other arbitrators are. The chair should consider having the case manager forward the bills to the parties on a monthly basis so they are kept current on the cost of the arbitration.

VII. Being the Only Neutral

A. Special Considerations

There are special considerations when the co-arbitrators are non-neutral, meaning that they may be advocates for the parties who appointed them. Knowing that they will be in contact with the parties during the arbitration places the chair in a hotter seat than the chair occupies with an entirely neutral panel.

B. Social Contacts

The neutral chair should limit social contacts with the other arbitrators and avoid meeting with one arbitrator alone, even for seemingly innocuous meals or travel.

C. Keep Your Own Counsel

Because of the relationship between non-neutral arbitrators and the appointing parties, the chair should be circumspect about revealing his or her developing opinions of the testimony and other evidence to the non-neutral co-arbitrators. The prudent chair keeps his or her own counsel until decision time arises for interim or final rulings.

D. Show Equal Respect

The chair should, of course, give equal consideration to the views of the co-arbitrators, even if they are not neutral. But the chair should also remain cognizant that his or her behavior is under more scrutiny from the parties, counsel and the witnesses when the panel includes non-neutral arbitrators.

E. Limited Sharing

Sharing arbitral duties, as we suggested when the entire tribunal is neutral, shouldn't work the same way when two of the tribunal members are non-neutral. If the chair decides to assign some duties to another arbitrator, they should be strictly administrative.

F. Recognizing Advocacy

The chair should consider with caution the suggestions, ideas and concerns expressed by non-neutral arbitrators, and should presume that the non-neutrals are disposed in favor of their party. Thus, their views should be placed in that context.

G. Differing Expertise

There may be an imbalance on the panel because of the different expertise of the two non-neutrals. For example, if one non-neutral has greater knowledge of the subject matter of the dispute because of education and experience, that arbitrator's view should not be allowed to over-influence the chair's thinking. The chair must decide the dispute based on his or her own understanding of the evidence, and if it is confusing or inadequate, the chair should request clarification from the parties.

H. Issue List

Prior to deliberations, the chair should ask each non-neutral arbitrator to submit a list of the issues framed in a "neutral manner." This approach helps avoid partisanship and steers the deliberations to the issues rather than to advocacy.

I. Listen to the Non-Neutrals

The chair must keep an open mind throughout the arbitration hearings and not judge the case without first hearing from the non-neutral arbitrators. The chair who appears to have decided the case without hearing the views of both sides is likely to lose credibility with the co-arbitrators, the parties and their counsel. As a result, the parties and their counsel may not trust the chair enough to select or recommend him for future appointments.

VIII. Conclusion

It is a privilege and responsibility to chair a panel. With planning and thoughtfulness for others, the chair can make this experience fulfilling and enjoyable for everyone on the panel. The goal is not universal agreement or a unanimous award. It is to allow all panel members to be part of an arbitration that is fair, orderly and affords the greatest opportunity for full contemplation of the facts and issues.

CHAPTER 18

MUSCULAR ARBITRATION AND ARBITRATORS SELF-MANAGEMENT CAN MAKE ARBITRATION FASTER AND MORE ECONOMICAL

Mitchell Marinello and Robert Matlin[*]

I. Introduction

The importance of making arbitration more efficient and less costly has such a high profile that the *Dispute Resolution Journal* devoted the last issue to this theme. The challenge of protecting the time and cost advantages of arbitration will continue until parties and arbitration counsel learn to think of arbitration as a process that is distinct from litigation and arbitrators learn to be more "muscular" and disciplined managers of the process and themselves.

The American Arbitration Association (AAA) is committed to improving the arbitration process and regularly asks users of AAA services and their counsel about their arbitration experience and how it could be better. More often than not, parties and counsel say they want arbitrators to exercise greater control over the arbitration process to prevent delay and the escalating cost of the process. In a keynote address at the 2010 AAA Neutrals Conference, William Slate II, the past president and CEO of the AAA, emphasized that an important part of arbitration's mission is to avoid the undue expense and delay that characterizes litigation. He urged arbitrators to "take a cold, hard look" at every arbitration case to see what they can do to deliver a more economical and efficient process.

The term "muscular arbitration" describes a disciplined arbitration in which the arbitrator actively manages the pre-hearing and hearing phases of the case so that there are no delays and the issues submitted to arbitration are decided on the merits in an efficient and timely manner. An important part of muscular arbitration is arbitrator self-discipline,

[*] Mitchell Marinello is a Partner with the law firm of Novack and Macey. Robert Matlin is Senior Vice President with the American Arbitration Association.

which requires the arbitrators to manage not only the process, but also to manage themselves. This article explores these ideas.

It is now clear to the arbitration community that importing litigation procedures into arbitration is one of the main causes of the increased cost and time involved in arbitration. In that regard, the AAA's Commercial Arbitration Rules specifically caution that "care must be taken to avoid importing procedures from court systems as such procedures may not be appropriate to the conduct of arbitrations." Litigation activities, such as broad discovery and frequent motion practice, require additional work by counsel and the arbitrators, and delay the evidentiary hearing and award. However, broad discovery requests and motion practice are usually unnecessary and often generate additional disagreements. Therefore they are at odds with main reasons parties choose arbitration in the first place—to obtain a fair, but faster and less costly resolution of their disputes.

II. Arbitrators Must Be Efficient and Disciplined

AAA arbitration rules and the *Standards and Responsibilities for Members of the AAA Roster of Neutrals* make neutrals responsible for managing arbitration in a way that prevents delay and controls costs. The *Standards and Responsibilities for Members of the AAA Roster* requires that arbitrators have "an understanding that the arbitration process is an expedient, more efficient and less formal alternative to litigation" as well as "a commitment to speed, economy and a just resolution for controversies brought before them."

However, arbitration is a group enterprise and the arbitrator cannot achieve these ends without the cooperation of the parties and their counsel. To obtain that cooperation, the arbitrator must immediately convey the expectation that the arbitration will be conducted efficiently and that delays and procedural wrangling will not be permitted. Yet, counsel and the parties will not be able to take these expectations seriously if the arbitrator does not back them up with up with good organizational skills. The first opportunity the arbitrator has to demonstrate these skills is before the initial preliminary hearing. This is when the arbitrator should prepare an agenda for the hearing and send it to the parties with instructions to be prepared to discuss all the listed items and agree on a discovery plan and schedule for the entire case. The arbitrator also needs to demonstrate to counsel and the parties that they are serious about deadlines by advising counsel and the parties that the schedule that is agreed upon will be lean and firm. In other words, it will not be subject to change except in extraordinary circumstances. Conveying the importance of efficiency at the very inception of the arbitration is vitally important because it will set the tone for the entire proceeding and let the parties and their counsel know that they will be expected to behave differently than if they were involved in litigation.

The arbitrator also has to act efficiently in the hope that his or her efficient behavior will be contagious. This means that every issue that arises must be promptly and decisively addressed by the arbitrator. There are many issues that can challenge an arbitrator's case management skills. Here are some common examples:

- The demand for arbitration is hopelessly vague and the respondent persuasively argues that it fails to state a claim.
- The respondent asks to submit a dispositive motion that the arbitrator knows is unlikely to be granted. Instead of objecting, the claimant requests 30 days to file a response.
- In a case that does not seem all that complicated, one party proposes to take 12 depositions and the other party, which plans to take only one or two depositions, raises no objection.
- The parties' attorneys have agreed to take 10 depositions each, several of which involve non-party out-of-state deponents.
- A case reasonably requires about six to eight months to prepare for the evidentiary hearing, but the attorney for one party claims that her calendar won't allow her to participate in the hearing unless it is scheduled at least twelve or fourteen months down the road.
- One or both parties continue to present repetitive and cumulative evidence at the evidentiary hearing.
- Both parties want to submit post-hearing briefs (limited to 150 pages in length). They are asking for a briefing schedule of three months, assuming no requests for an extension of time.

All of these issues require muscular arbitration to be employed. If it is not, counsel and the parties will get the impression that time is not of the essence and that the process in which they are participating is just like litigation, as opposed to arbitration. In addition, the more time the arbitrator grants to the advocates, the more time they will spend on the case. Consequently, arbitrators must exercise self-discipline and resist the desire to please counsel by giving them whatever they ask for, particularly if this decision would be a disservice to an efficient process.

One of the difficulties that arbitration providers occasionally encounter in encouraging arbitrators to be more muscular and firm in managing arbitration is an apparent concern by at least some arbitrators that doing so might upset counsel and jeopardize their chance of being selected by parties for future cases. Needless to say, arbitrators must not consider their perceived self-interest against providing the parties with the efficient process they contracted for. In any event, it should comfort arbitrators to know that a significant number of users of AAA services report that the more forceful arbitrators who take greater control over the process are precisely what they do want.

III. Demands and Answers

An arbitration demand that is so vague or unclear might be considered deficient by some arbitrators. But instead of permitting the respondent to move to dismiss it, the arbitrator could consider asking the claimant to amend the demand to make the claims clearer or more specific. This may be much more efficient and less costly than having a motion to dismiss briefed, granting it, and *then* allowing the claimant to amend its claims.

Ideally, arbitration claims should be explanatory and specific, so the issues presented can be understood and a sensible plan developed for preparing the case for hearing. Answers usually have a less important role. An arbitrator should consider encouraging the respondent *not* to answer each allegation. Such answers, which take time and money to prepare, rarely serve any practical purpose, because respondents typically do not admit anything that matters. Instead, an arbitrator should consider encouraging the respondent to file a general denial to all the material allegations of the arbitration demand. To avoid unfair surprise and help identify the matters on which discovery may be needed, the arbitrator should require the respondent to file affirmative defenses that are truly informative and that set forth the specific facts on which each affirmative defense is based.

IV. Dispositive Motions

It is very rare that an arbitrator can properly grant a dispositive motion with prejudice. Most cases involve genuine issues of fact, and refusing to hear evidence is one of the grounds stated in under the Federal Arbitration Act for vacating an award. In terms of speed and cost, having an award vacated is one of the worst possible outcomes. It means the parties have wasted their time and resources presenting the case and that the whole process must begin anew. That does not suit the interests of either party, it defeats arbitration's purpose, and it is a black mark against the arbitrator. Parties, with attorneys used to litigation, sometimes file dispositive motions, particularly motions to dismiss, reflexively. They usually do not accomplish very much.

When a party wants to file a dispositive motion, the arbitrator should explain the reasons why dispositive motions usually do not succeed and ask the moving party to spell out why its motion would call for a different outcome and, even if it did, whether deciding the case on a motion truly would be in the moving party's best interests. The arbitrator should also explore what would be involved in presenting such a motion as compared to having an evidentiary hearing. For example, holding an evidentiary hearing might not require much more time than briefing and arguing a motion for summary judgment and the decision rendered would be much less likely to be overturned. The arbitrator should also remind the parties that motion practice, albeit usually unproductive, still requires the arbitrator to bill the parties for the time spent on the motion. Through such discussion, a party sometimes will be persuaded not to file its motion.

If, despite the arbitrator's best efforts, a party insists on filing a dispositive motion, all is not lost. The arbitrator should promptly evaluate the motion and determine whether it deserves briefing by the other side. Sometimes, the correct action is simply to defer the motion until the evidentiary hearing and to invite both parties to address the issues it presents in their pre-hearing memoranda. This takes away the sting of flatly denying the motion or refusing to require the other side to brief it, while at the same time saving expense and avoiding the delay that full briefing and a hearing on the motion would create.

There is, however, at least one important exception to this approach. Sometimes there is a disputed legal issue that can have a large impact on discovery and the amount and type of evidence that will need to be presented at the hearing. If that issue is one that the arbitrator can decide at an early stage of the proceedings, it can provide the parties with invaluable guidance and sometimes it can save them a lot of time and expense or make settlement more likely.

V. Discovery

Excessive discovery requests also present the arbitrator with an opportunity to exercise leadership. For example, contention interrogatories and requests to admit generally should not be permitted; their value often is minimal, so they are usually not cost-justified. In contrast, interrogatories can be useful for identifying witnesses, obtaining the bases for damage calculations, and disclosing the opinions of experts, and they generally should be limited to these functions.

Whether and how many depositions should be permitted presents a more difficult question. If each side wants to take a couple depositions and the case involves enough money to justify that expense, then no difficulty is presented. Problems arise when both sides want to take more depositions than the case seems to justify economically or when one party wants to take an inordinate number of depositions and for some reason the other party does not object.

Here it is essential for the arbitrator to manage the process. The arbitrator should discuss the substance of the case with the parties to find out why so many depositions are being requested and to flush out arguments for and against the requested discovery. Does one side hold all the information? If so, is there a better way to get the information that is needed without relying entirely on depositions? In cases that are based on oral agreements or statements, the parties may believe that the case turns on the credibility of the witnesses and they may want to depose each witness so that the chance of surprise at the hearing is reduced. The arbitrator might remind the parties of the cost in taking so many depositions and the fact that cross-examination can be more effective when the witness is not deposed (and lines of cross-examination revealed) ahead of time. If such comments are not convincing, the arbitrator should strongly consider limiting the number of depositions that each side may take, leaving open the possibility that additional depositions may be possible but only if good cause is shown. If the parties are forced to be more strategic in the depositions they chose to take, they may eventually come around to the idea that they do not need so many of them.

When faced with excessive discovery requests by *both* sides, some arbitrators believe that they "lack the authority" to rein the parties in. However, that is not necessarily the case. For example, the AAA's Commercial Arbitration Rules provide that arbitrators have the authority to "manage any necessary exchange of information among the parties with a view of achieving an efficient and economical resolution of the dispute..." With regard to depositions, the AAA's Procedures for Large Complex Commercial Disputes provide that they may be allowed "In exceptional cases, at the discretion of the arbitrator, upon good cause shown" where the potential testimony is "determined by the arbitrator to be relevant and material to the outcome of the case." So, even if both sides to a dispute maintain that they need more discovery than the case seems to justify, an arbitrator can step in and manage the process.

VI. The Evidentiary Hearing

An arbitrator should allow the parties sufficient time to prepare their case and be considerate of counsel's legitimate scheduling issues, but must remember that one of arbitration's major objectives is to give the parties a prompt evidentiary hearing on the merits of their claims. The parties should not be permitted to push the hearing date far into the future. A prompt hearing date is an important disciplinary tool for all concerned; it requires the parties to focus on the case and either to settle it or get it prepared for presentation. Courts with "rocket dockets" have demonstrated that even high stakes, complex lawsuits can be readied for trial in a short time period. Similarly, complex multi-million dollar disputes filed with the AAA are often decided within nine months of the case being filed. Although arbitrators should not impose a schedule on the parties that is harsh or needlessly inconvenient, they should insist on diligence, schedule as early a hearing date as is reasonable and not postpone the hearing date except for good reason. This last point has some qualifications. The AAA rules state than an arbitrator may grant a postponement of the hearing if both sides request it. Moreover, the FAA provides that an award may be overturned if the arbitrator did not grant a postponement for which there was sufficient justification. Thus, arbitrators must always be reasonable when faced with requests for a postponement. Even so, they have plenty of discretion and can and should move their cases along in a timely manner.

Frustrating circumstances sometimes arise with scheduling the evidentiary hearing. For example, sometimes even though the hearing date is six or eight months in the future and allows plenty of time to get the case ready, one side claims it is too busy to schedule the evidentiary hearing at that time and will not be available for several weeks or even months thereafter.

There are several things an arbitrator can do in this situation. For example, if one party is tied up in months six and seven, an arbitrator can suggest the hearing be held in month five and that the time for preparing the case for hearing be truncated a bit. Another approach is to find out what specific event is causing the scheduling problem and to require the party with that problem to keep the arbitrator apprised of any changes in that event. Trials have a way of being postponed and cases of settling. Sometimes it makes sense to schedule the arbitration hearing for a definite date but also tentatively to schedule it for an earlier date in case the matter that is tying up one party's schedule is postponed or settled. In the end, however, the arbitrator cannot lose sight of the ultimate goal: giving both sides a fair hearing on the merits. If the case must be delayed a few weeks so that everyone's schedule can be accommodated, that is not the end of the world. It is lengthy or repeated extensions of time that pose a greater problem.

VII. Repetitive and Cumulative Evidence

Lawyers sometimes get carried away with the evidence that supports their case. Everything seems important, even the small details. Major themes get repeated over and over again and the same testimony is elicited from witness after witness. The fact that the arbitrator is a captive audience who wants to maintain a pleasant relationship with both sides can contribute to this problem. However, such circumstances offer the arbitrator an opportunity to remind the advocates that the arbitrator is being paid by the hour and that it costs their clients money to unnecessarily prolong the proceedings.

There are also steps an arbitrator can take to prevent the hearing from being dragged out. When faced with repetitive testimony, the arbitrator can simply state that he or she understands the position being asserted and does not need to hear more evidence on that point. It usually helps to summarize the repetitive testimony and restate the position being asserted so that the party presenting it has confidence that its position has been heard. If that does not work, the arbitrator can be a bit more critical, stating that the testimony is becoming repetitive and asking if there are any new points the witness has to add. If, despite such entreaties, a party persists in presenting repetitive testimony, the arbitrator can forbid further questions on that topic or place a time limit on any more testimony from a particular witness. And, if there are too many witnesses and their testimony is repetitive and unhelpful, the arbitrator should consider asking for an offer of proof before each witness takes the stand and limiting, in advance, what each witness may testify about or the time that the witness may be on the stand.

During this process, it is important for the arbitrator to be diplomatic and not to create the impression of favoring one side over the other. It often is helpful to explain why the testimony is being limited—it is not because the party's position or the particular testimony is unimportant but because the arbitrator understands the points being made and does not believe that further evidence on those points will aid the arbitrator's decision-making process. Sometimes the opposing side can be helpful, because the points being made in the repetitive testimony are not really in dispute. In those situations, the arbitrator can ask the other side, "Is this point disputed?" If the answer is no, then that should help the situation.

VIII. Post-Hearing Briefs

Whether to permit post-hearing briefs and on what schedule is sometimes a difficult question. After an evidentiary hearing, the evidence is fresh in the arbitrator's mind and that may be the best time for the case to be decided. If the pre-hearing briefs have done their job and covered the central legal and factual issues, there may be no reason to add the cost and delay of post-hearing briefs.

Of course, there are occasions when post-hearing briefs are appropriate, such as in complicated cases and when a lot is at stake and both sides have a strong desire to submit post-hearing briefs. In such circumstances, the prudent arbitrator probably should allow them. This is especially true if the hearing was transcribed and the arbitrator can refer to the transcript to refresh his or her recollection of the evidence. Of course, page limitations should be established and enforced, and deadlines should be set so that the briefing schedule does not get out of hand.

IX. Type of Award

Generally, there are three types of arbitration awards: (1) standard; (2) reasoned; and (3) findings of fact and conclusions of law. Standard awards are the simplest; they involve stating the result and little more. Reasoned awards, which are probably the most popular for significant commercial disputes, require the arbitrator to explain the rationale or basis for the award. Findings of fact and conclusions of law are the most involved and require just what they suggest: detailed findings of fact and conclusions of law, usually in numbered paragraphs, just as one typically would see in the opinion of a federal trial court.

Standard awards, because of their simplicity, present no issue of cost or delay, and it is rare for the parties to require the arbitrator to prepare detailed findings of fact and conclusions of law. Reasoned awards are efficiency's battle ground. How "reasoned" must an award be? How complete? How polished? Stated differently, when is an arbitrator writing more than is necessary or appropriate given the parties' needs and arbitration's goal of being faster and less expensive than litigation?

Legally speaking, a reasoned award does not need to be lengthy or all that explanatory. The Eleventh Circuit recently held that a short, simple explanation is all that is needed to make an award a "reasoned" award instead of a standard one. *Cat Charter LLC vs. Schurternberger*, 646 F.3d 836, (11th Cir. 2011). It should be recognized, however, that preparing a reasoned award of sufficient quality is important for the parties' understanding, the arbitrator's reputation, and the reputation of arbitration itself. When an award is issued, there generally is a winner and a loser, and the loser is unlikely to be happy about the result. An award that provides a reasonable explanation for the decision may not remove the disappointment felt by the losing party, but it may gain that party's respect and prevent it from becoming a critic of the arbitrator or arbitration itself.

That said, an arbitrator should be careful to write a decision for the parties and not for him- or herself. After all, the point is not to write an academic piece or an opinion that will be cited by other arbitrators. Arbitration is private, and awards are not useful as precedent. The point of writing a reasoned award is to show the parties that the arbitrator's decision is the result of a reasoned process in which each side's arguments were given due respect and consideration. Discretion is involved in deciding just when enough has been said in an award to reach this point. An arbitrator needs to apply self-discipline so that preparing the award does not give rise to unnecessary expense.

Although it is rare for the parties to ask the arbitrator to prepare findings of fact and conclusions of law, it occasionally happens. When it does, the arbitrator should discuss the parties' reasons for wanting an award in that form and, if they do not have a good reason for it, try to dissuade them. Even when the parties themselves prepare competing findings of fact and conclusions of law for the arbitrator to select from, the process of putting together a final award that accurately reflects the record and the arbitrators' view of it takes a lot of time and ultimately costs the parties a significant sum. Unless an award in such a detailed format is needed for a practical purpose, it is an unnecessary expense that should be avoided.

X. Don't Over-Manage

Notwithstanding efforts to control the cost of the arbitration, arbitrators must be careful not to over-manage a case. One reason parties choose arbitration is to have more control over the process. Too much case management can be a problem—not only because it can deprive the parties of control but also because, from a cost perspective, it can be self-defeating. An arbitrator who schedules unnecessary conference calls, sends unnecessary e-mails, or excessively reviews the file—all in the name of managing the case—also increases the cost of the arbitration.

As an organization, the AAA charges only an administrative fee and takes no percentage of the fees arbitrators charge on matters. The AAA has every incentive to ensure that its cases are resolved as cost-effectively as possible. In this regard, the AAA has been aggressively training its panel members on the ways they can maximize efficiency and economy in arbitrations. In 2011, the AAA created two comprehensive training courses on managing the arbitration process for efficiency and economy for its panel members. To date, over 1500 AAA neutrals have taken these courses. In addition, in 2012, the AAA hosted its annual neutrals conference with the entire program being focused on maximizing efficiency in arbitration.

XI. Arbitrator Compensation Issues

Canon VII of the Code of Ethics for Arbitrators in Commercial Disputes states that when making arrangements for compensation and reimbursement of expenses, arbitrators should "adhere to standards of integrity and fairness." Among practices the Code identifies as tending to preserve integrity and fairness is establishing the basis for compensation before accepting appointment to a case.

The AAA's Billing Guidelines for neutrals reminds arbitrators that "one of the major objectives of arbitration is to reduce the costs of dispute resolution". The Guidelines also acknowledge that arbitrators "deserve to be fairly compensated for their time and services." Arbitrators who are paid on a time-based system should demonstrate their awareness of costs by considering whether the time they actually spend on each phase of a matter is fair and reasonable.

Requiring a lawyer's fee to be reasonable is an accepted practice, according to the ABA Model Rules for Professional Responsibility. Rule 1(a) of the Model Rules provide: "A lawyer shall not make an agreement for, charge, or collect an unreasonable fee or an unreasonable amount for expenses." Among the factors lawyers must consider in determining the reasonableness of a fee include "the time and labor required, the novelty and difficulty of the questions involved, and the skill requisite to perform the legal service properly." Even though arbitrators are not acting as lawyers representing clients in arbitration, there is no reason that they should not also apply a "rule of reasonableness" in terms of evaluating their bills and the time spent on a particular aspect of a case. For example, this would enable them to consider whether an issue was novel or routine and therefore reasonably required more or less times spent. If an arbitrator determined that the time spent was more that might be considered reasonable under the circumstances, they should adjust their bill accordingly.

Given that an arbitrator is considered to be a quasi-judicial figure, one might argue that an arbitrator has an even higher duty than an attorney to self-police his or her fees. This is so because the parties may find it awkward to question fees charged by the person deciding their case, even if such question is raised through an intermediary such as the AAA. The AAA often reviews bills submitted by arbitrators and it reserves the right to refuse to forward bills that do not comply with its billing guidelines. So arbitrators should be-"mindful of the cost of the arbitration process," as set forth in the *Standards and Responsibilities* document AAA neutrals are required to sign and take care that their bills are consistent with that responsibility.

Because arbitrators are paid by the hour, they must avoid any perception that they are prolonging a case for their own financial benefit. The arbitrator must also look for ways to reduce costs. In this regard, it may be useful for the arbitrator to discuss with the parties a budget for the arbitration. At the very least, this will give the parties a chance to discuss their cost expectations and let the arbitrator know how important costs are to the parties. Arbitrators should also estimate the amount of time they anticipate having to spend on a matter so that such information can be provided to the parties early on. The AAA typically requires parties to advance funds for payment of arbitrator compensation deposits based on the arbitrator's calculation of his or her anticipated time and costs. When making such estimates arbitrators need to be realistic. However, if an arbitrator submits an inflated estimate, there's a good chance that the actual amount of time spent on the matter by all participants will increase sufficiently to equal the estimate. Parkinson's law suggests that a more accurate and efficient estimate will encourage more efficient behavior from all concerned.

XII. Conclusion

Arbitrators should actively manage their cases and themselves. Arbitrators must lead by example and never lose sight of their commitment to "speed, economy and a just resolution" for controversies brought before them. They should strive to achieve arbitration's goals of being faster and less expensive than litigation. To meet that challenge, arbitrators need to look for opportunities to streamline the arbitration process and must dissuade the parties from importing litigation practices into the arbitration. Arbitrators also need to be self-disciplined and to recognize that they have a duty to be economic in their own actions and in the fees they impose on the parties for their compensation.

Sidebar

Muscular Arbitration in Action—Arbitrator Tips

In muscular arbitration, arbitrators must take steps to rein in efforts to transform arbitration into a private litigation.

- When you prepare the scheduling order you do not need to anticipate every possible event that may occur. If you do, you will end up with an unnecessarily long schedule, which could encourage the parties to engage in activities that they otherwise would not engage in. Instead, set a schedule that is more Spartan and that includes a short period of time for completing pleadings and discovery and sets the date of the evidentiary hearing.
- Limit document production to exchanges of demonstrably relevant and material evidence. Also, limit each side to a certain number of depositions.

- If a party indicates at the preliminary management conference that it plans to file a motion to dismiss, or has already sent its motion to you and the other party via the case manager, do not automatically or routinely issue a briefing schedule. Parties should be advised that the permission of the arbitrator is needed to file any kind of motion. So you should ask the moving party to explain the basis for the motion (and if it has already been prepared, read and evaluate it). If the motion is unlikely to win *and to* advance the progress of the case, then deny or defer it. If on the other hand, the motion would clearly narrow the issues in the case, or even dispose of the entire matter (such as a decision on the running of the statute of limitations), then the motion should be heard.
- Do not avoid deciding legal issues that can narrow the scope of the case and guide the parties' subsequent efforts in the case. For example, if before your appointment, one party added a dubious antitrust claim to what would otherwise be a straightforward breach of contract case, granting a motion to dismiss the antitrust claim, if appropriate, could save the parties considerable time and effort in discovery and in preparing the case for hearing. (The permission of the arbitrator is required to add a claim after the arbitrator is appointed under AAA rules. A muscular arbitrator would not grant permission to add a dubious claim to the case.)
- Always encourage the attorneys to resolve discovery issues without your intervention. Remind them that they know the case better than you do and should be able to resolve their discovery disagreements more efficiently than you could. Also remind them that you are being paid for your time and that requiring you to decide discovery conflicts adds to their clients' bill. If, however, the disagreement is so serious that counsel cannot promptly resolve it, you must take charge and decide it. If you don't, you run the risk that the discovery disagreements will multiply. In contrast, if you resolve the dispute, your ruling will provide the parties with some guidance and help them resolve future discovery disputes without your involvement.
- Let the parties know from the beginning that you intend to enforce deadlines and especially the scheduled date for the evidentiary hearing. Stand by that statement. If you believe an extension of time is necessary in a given instance, then do

your best to make it as short as possible and let the parties know that you do not expect to receive a request for any additional time.

- Do not permit motions for summary judgment unless they concern extremely narrow issues, such as a statute of limitations or a release. Most of the time, it is faster, less expensive and more prudent to decide the case at an evidentiary hearing rather than to try to resolve it on a motion for summary judgment. And there usually is little or no advantage to resolving only part of a case on a summary judgment motion.

CHAPTER 19

CALLING ALL ARBITRATORS: RECLAIM CONTROL OF THE ARBITRATION PROCESS—THE COURTS LET YOU

David E. Robbins[*]

I. Introduction

Arbitration has been billed as the cost-effective, expeditious alternative to commercial litigation. It has, however, to a large extent, become a costly, dilatory and unpredictable melding of litigation and arbitration, primarily due to the parties' representatives who are responsible for grafting the implements of litigation onto the much simpler system of arbitration. The forum of equity has become the forum of law.

Regrettably, arbitrators are often their "aiders and abettors" when they permit attorneys to wrest control of the process. Such arbitrators are fearful that the courts, when reviewing their conduct, will vacate their awards. That fear is unfounded and this chapter will show you why that is so. The consequence of arbitrators relinquishing responsibility for managing the arbitration process is twofold: first, it will lead constituents of arbitration—i.e., businesses and attorneys—to lose respect for the process. Second, it will cause those arbitrators to suffer a loss of income (not surprisingly), since users of the process want an efficient arbitration and will no longer select them. The purpose of this chapter is to provide

---

[*] David E. Robbins has been an AAA arbitrator for 30 years and is a partner in Kaufmann, Gildin & Robbins LLP, in New York City, where he specializes in commercial arbitration, mediation and disciplinary proceedings before regulatory authorities. Previously, he served as Special Deputy Attorney General of New York State and was Director of the Compliance, Arbitration and Disciplinary Hearings Departments of the American Stock Exchange. The author of the Securities Arbitration Procedure Manual (5th ed., 2015, Matthew Bender/Lexis/Nexis), he also writes the annual "Practice Commentary" in Article 23-A of the New York General Business Law for McKinney's Consolidated Laws of New York. In addition, he chairs the New York State Bar Association program on securities arbitration and mediation.

a backbone transplant to my fellow arbitrators, to endow them with the courage to reclaim control of the process while still affording all parties a fair opportunity to present their case.

The places to look to resolve this problem are court decisions on motions to vacate awards. Hindsight is 20/20 and we can learn from it. The disappointed parties who filed these motions hoped for an arbitration afterlife, but what they more often found was a second loss in the courts.

Despite the occasional headline declaring the overturning of an arbitration award, courts have overwhelmingly held that they will not second-guess arbitrators since the parties voluntarily agreed to arbitrate their dispute and since arbitration is a forum of equity. Doubts as to the correctness of arbitrator conduct are outweighed by the agreement of the parties to forgo certain judicial procedures in exchange for a hearing by an experienced arbitrator of their choosing who is mandated by ethical principles to "cut to the chase." Since arbitration is intended to be a final and binding process, courts steadfastly resist efforts by parties to get a "second bite of the apple"—i.e., another arbitration hearing between the same parties.

This chapter explains the grounds for vacating arbitration awards primarily based on arbitrator conduct and rulings. Arbitrators are given wide latitude in managing cases, but when they go seriously "off course"—such as in failing to make required disclosures, or deciding issues not in the pleadings, or taking part in *ex parte* communications, or refusing to grant a reasonable adjournment request or admit pertinent and material evidence, or denying parties the basics of due process—courts will vacate their awards. But not often.

II. What the Law Demands of Arbitrators

Generally speaking, arbitration requires an impartial decision maker, fair procedures, an adequate opportunity for the parties to present their case and an award based on the evidence and not on an arbitrator's surmise of "what really happened." Thus, if an impartial arbitrator provides the parties with an opportunity to make their arguments and offer evidence to enable the arbitrator to make an informed decision, the benchmark of fundamental fairness is met.[1] However, since arbitration is intended to be

[1] *Sunshine Mining Co. v. United Steelworkers of Amer.* 823 F.2d 1289 (9th Cir. 1987); *Hoteles Condado Beach, La Concha & Convention Ctr. v. Union de Tronquistas Local 901*,

an efficient and less costly process than litigation, arbitrators have authority (accorded by well-established arbitration rules) to manage the process efficiently, provided they give the parties a fair hearing.[2]

Hearing from every witness imaginable, however duplicative the testimony, and admitting into evidence documents that may cause the hearing to take a path to nowhere, are unnecessary and counterintuitive to the process. Just as party representatives must have the courage to simplify their cases, experienced arbitrators, as "active listeners," know that most cases involve very few issues in controversy. This chapter, updated in 2015 from its previous publication, will enable arbitrators to achieve the goal of fairness without prolonging the process.

III. Grounds to Vacate an Award

The circumstances in which a party may seek to vacate an award are limited by statute and common law (court decisions). In the spring of 2008, the United States Supreme Court, in *Hall St. Assocs. v. Mattel, Inc.*[3], held that §§ 10 and 11 of the Federal Arbitration Act provided the exclusive grounds for vacatur and modification of arbitration awards, seeing manifest disregard of the law (to be discussed below) as a ground related to those statutory grounds. The Court did not reject that ground, but stated that it should be considered within the sphere of those statutory grounds. The grounds in Section 10 of the Federal Arbitration Act (FAA)[4] apply to agreements "involving commerce." These grounds are:

- when the award was procured by corruption, fraud or undue means—§ 10(a)(1);

763 F.2d 34 (1st Cir. 1985); *Matter of Sprinzen,* 46 N.Y.2d 623, 415 N.Y.S.2d 974 (N.Y.1979).; *Matter of Silverman,* 61 N.Y.2d 299, 308 473 N.Y.S.2d 774 (1984).

[2] *See, e.g.*, American Arbitration Association (AAA) Commercial Arbitration Procedures, Rule R-30(b):

> The arbitrator, exercising his or her discretion, shall conduct the proceedings with a view to expediting the resolution of the dispute and may direct the order of proof, bifurcate proceedings and direct the parties to focus their presentations on issues the decision of which could dispose of all or part of the case.

AAA Rule R-31(b) makes it the arbitrator's province to "determine the admissibility, relevance, and materiality of the evidence offered and exclude evidence deemed by the arbitrator to be cumulative or irrelevant."

[3] 128 S.Ct. 1396, 170 L. Ed. 2d 254 (2008).

[4] 9 U.S.C. § 10. State statutes usually mirror these grounds.

- when there was evident arbitrator partiality or corruption—§ 10(a)(2);
- when the arbitrator refused to postpone the hearing, or to hear evidence pertinent and material to the case, or engaged in any other misbehavior that prejudiced the rights of a party—§ 10(a)(3); or
- when the arbitrator exceeded his or her powers, or so imperfectly executed them that a mutual, final and definite award was not made—§ 10(a)(4).

The 1955 Uniform Arbitration Act (adopted in whole or in part in most states) and the 2000 Uniform Arbitration Act (to date enacted in 49 states)[5] contain similar grounds. In addition, the courts have created grounds for vacatur that, with one exception, allow a losing party to challenge the award based on its content, rather than on arbitrator conduct. The judicially-crafted "common law" grounds are:

- an award in manifest disregard of the law (although the Supreme Court folded this into the statutory ground of exceeding authority);
- an award contrary to public policy;
- an award lacking a factual basis (i.e., irrational, arbitrary or capricious); or
- due process was not afforded to one or more parties.

However, these grounds are not recognized in all states. For example, Tennessee and Colorado do not recognize manifest disregard as a possible ground for vacatur.[6] And, since the Supreme Court's decision

---

[5] Available at http://www.nccusl.org/Update/ActSearchResults.aspx?ActId=2

[6] *Coors Brewing Co. v. Cabo*, No. 03CA2452, 2004 WL 2903515 (Colo. Ct. App. Dec. 16, 2004) (use of manifest disregard of the law standard "would weaken the effectiveness and legitimacy of arbitration"); *Arnold v. Morgan Keegan & Co.*, 914 S.W.2d 445, 450 (Tenn. 1996). In the latter case, the investor claimed the broker misrepresented a material fact and admitted making a negligent misrepresentation about the riskiness of an investment, which the Tennessee Securities Act mandated recovery for losses. The AAA arbitrators, in a seven-page opinion, dismissed the claim on the ground that there was no material misrepresentation. The Tennessee trial court vacated the award finding it irrational. However, Supreme Court of Tennessee reversed and reinstated the award. It stated that under the Tennessee UAA, judges are limited to the statutory grounds for vacatur of arbitration awards. The court went on to say:

> We do not find that the award was irrational; that is, that the panel failed to follow the law. Even if it were irrational, an arbitration award may be vacated only for

in *Hall St. Assocs. v. Mattel, Inc.*[7], courts which had previously adopted it have rejected it (see discussion below).

This chapter will look at each ground primarily in the context of claims that the arbitrator (as opposed to the party representative) did something wrong. Motions to vacate based on arbitrator rulings on jurisdiction or the merits of a case make up a separate category of cases; this type of challenge generally does not involve an arbitrator's hearing management skills. However, cases of this type will be briefly discussed because they make up most of the case law based on judicially created grounds for vacatur.

Inexperienced parties in arbitration believe that if they lose, they have an automatic right of appeal as they do in litigation. The post-arbitration process is not even called *appeal* and, of course, there is no automatic right to do so. In order to challenge an arbitration award in a petition to vacate, the aggrieved party must allege a recognized ground for vacatur. Invariably, the moving party will assert multiple grounds based on the same conduct. The next section looks at each ground for vacatur as interpreted by the courts.

IV. Specific Grounds

A. Corruption, Fraud, Undue Means

1. Standard

Federal courts rarely have found that arbitrators engaged in corruption, fraud or undue means within the meaning of Section 10(a)(1) of the FAA. The reason is that courts impose a very high burden of proof on the party seeking vacatur on this ground.[8] That burden is one of clear and convincing evidence, not a preponderance of the evidence.[9]

If the moving party can meet this exacting burden of proof, it must also establish that due diligence could not have resulted in discovery of

the reasons set forth in the statute. Tennessee Code. Ann. § 29-5-313(a) simply does not provide for the vacation of an award because it is irrational.

[7] 128 S.Ct. 1396, 170 L. Ed. 2d 254 (2008).

[8] *La Farge Conseils et Etudes, S.A. v. Kaiser Cement & Gypsum Corp.*, 791 F.2d 1334, 1339 (9th Cir. 1986).

[9] *Foster v. Turley*, 808 F.2d 38, 42 (10th Cir. 1986); In *re Doreen Goldbronn*, 263 B.R. 347 (Bankr. M.D. Fla. 2001). Federal courts do not apply a preponderance of the evidence standard in this situation.

the fraud prior to or during the arbitration.[10] If not earlier discoverable by the exercise of due diligence, the moving party must demonstrate that the malfeasance was materially related to an issue in the arbitration.[11] That is, the moving party must demonstrate that the undisclosed and undiscoverable misconduct influenced the outcome of the arbitration.[12]

What constitutes corruption, fraud or other undue means? In *Rosenthal-Collins Group v. Reiff*,[13] an Illinois appeals court stated that "*ex parte* contact [between the arbitrator and a party to the dispute] involving disputed issues raises a presumption that an arbitration award was procured by fraud, corruption or other undue means."[14] This presumption, however, can be rebutted by sufficient evidence showing that the presumption is unwarranted. If such evidence can be shown, the Illinois court said, "no reliance should be placed on the fact presumed."[15]

2. Examples (Award Vacated)

Direct Communication — In *Rosenthal-Collins Group*, the plaintiff moved to vacate the arbitrator's award based on the claim that, after the hearing but before the award was issued, the defendant sent two letters to an arbitrator on the panel for the purpose of rebutting the plaintiff's claim at the hearing that the defendant was a convicted drug dealer. The letters were received by the arbitrator's law firm, but possibly not by the arbitrator, who was said to be out of the country. The defendant argued that the panel had already decided the case before he sent the letters to the arbitrator. The trial court vacated the award after granting limited discovery on the matter. It reasoned that it was impossible to really know when the letters were sent and there was contradictory evidence in the record about the timing. Applying *de novo* review (because the trial court's decision was based solely on a review of documentary evidence), the Illinois Court of Appeals affirmed the decision to vacate the award.[16] It held that the receipt of letters by the arbitrator's law firm was enough to

---

[10] *Karppinen v. Karl Kiefer Mach. Co.*, 187 F.2d 32, 35 (2d Cir. 1951).

[11] *Harre v. A.H. Robins*, 750 F.2d 1501, 1503 (11th Cir. 1985); *Rozier v. Ford Motor Co.*, 573 F.2d 1332, 1339 (5th Cir. 1978); *Newark Stereotypers Union No. 18 v. Newark Morning Ledger Co.*, 397 F.2d 594, 599 (3d Cir.), cert. denied, 393 U.S. 954 (1968).

[12] *Remmey v. Paine Webber*, Fed. Sec. L. Rep. (CCH) ¶ 98,366, at 90,504 (4th Cir. Aug. 19, 1994).

[13] 748 N.E.2d 229 (Ill. Ct. App. 2001).

[14] In this case the *ex parte* contact was initiated by a party to the case.

[15] *See Hahn v. A.G. Becker Parabas, Inc.*, 518 N.E.2d 218 (Ill. App. Ct. 1987).

[16] *Rosenthal-Collins*, *supra* n. 13 (manifest weight of evidence standard applies if court heard courtroom testimony).

create a presumption that the arbitration was tainted by an *ex parte* contact. In making this ruling, the court found it significant that the award was subject to change when the letters were received by the law firm. Possibly of greater importance was the fact that there were no sworn statements in the record by the arbitrator to whom the letters were sent, or any of his law firm's employees, to establish that he was out of town during the relevant period and was never informed of the contents of the letters.

Thus, arbitrators must be vigilant to prevent *ex parte* contacts and if such contacts are initiated by a party but not completed, arbitrators should create a strong record to show that the *ex parte* contact never took place.

Excluding Witness — An award was vacated when arbitrators disqualified an investor's expert witness and then did not permit the customer an adjournment to procure a replacement.[17] "When a party is required to arbitrate before an industry-controlled arbitration panel in accordance with rules promulgated by the industry, it is incumbent upon the arbitrators to provide a fair forum and to respect fundamental due process rights." The vacated award had dismissed all of the customer's claims. "The refusal of the arbitrators to allow plaintiff a reasonable period of time to present expert testimony," added the court, "rises to the level of misconduct where the accused brokers were permitted to serve as their own experts and plaintiff was seriously prejudiced by preclusion of her expert."

Arbitrator Misstatements of Background[18] — A Federal District Court vacated an award because a FINRA replacement arbitrator was untruthful in an updated Arbitrator Disclosure Statement when he disclosed that he had been served with a complaint for the unauthorized practice of law. He explained to FINRA that all he had done was help a friend in a small matter, mistakenly failed to file a *pro hac vice* motion and that he was resolving the matter. After his disclosure was made, none of the parties, nor FINRA, objected to his continued service. However, "In reality," said the court, "his unauthorized practice of law was not limited to the one isolated incident. Instead, he actually opened an office in [that state and] actively practiced out of that office for nearly one year, if not longer. [He] was indicted by a Grand Jury and" engaged in other misconduct in that state and in another one. In vacating the award, the

[17] *Wilde v. O'Leary, Gurien & Zachary Jackson Securities, LP*, 866 A.2d 205 (N.J. Super. Ct. App. Div. 2005).

[18] *Goldman, Sachs & Co. v. Athena Venture Partners, L.P.;* 2013 U.S. Dist. LEXIS 107966 (E.D. Pa. Aug. 2013).

court was especially harsh on FINRA, finding it hard to understand why it took the arbitrator's word and did not probe him further. FINRA has since strengthened its verification process.

3. Example (No Vacatur)

Broad Scope of Arbitrator Authority[19] — A FINRA panel awarded a former broker $600,000 in back pay based on a claim that he was unlawfully terminated from his job by Raymond James because he is an alcoholic. A federal District Court vacated the award, concluding that the arbitrators lacked authority to grant that remedy because the broker brought no claims under the state law the arbitrators applied. He sought reinstatement of the award, arguing that the District Court failed to give due deference to the arbitrators' ruling. The Court of Appeals reversed the District Court's judgment, ruling that although the award may have been incorrect as a matter of law, it was not beyond the scope of the panel's authority. The panel's award of damages based on Florida law, despite its denial of the broker's request to amend his Statement of Claim to include a claim under the Florida Civil Rights Act troubled the District Court. "We understand its discomfort," said the Court of Appeals. "Yet we cannot conclude, in the particular circumstances of this case, that the arbitrators' decision to impose liability on RJFS under Florida law 'willfully flouted the governing law' or otherwise exceeded the bounds of the arbitrators' authority to resolve the parties' dispute."[20] "Briefly stated, the arbitrators were empowered to resolve claims of employment discrimination against [Raymond James] under Florida law, and that is what they did."[21]

B. Evident Partiality or Corruption

1. Standard

As arbitrators, we have no greater duty than to be neutral and unbiased, deciding each case on the evidence presented to us and on that

---

[19] *Raymond James Financial Services, Inc. v. Robert Michael Fenyk*, 2015 U.S. App. LEXIS 3803 (1st Cir. March 11, 2015).

[20] *Stolt-Nielsen*, 559 U.S. at 672 n.3.

[21] Cf. *Kashner Davidson*, 531 F.3d at 77 (citing *George Watts & Son, Inc. v. Tiffany and Co.*, 248 F.3d 577 (7th Cir. 2001), parenthetically noting the court's hypothesis that an arbitration award based on state law different from the state law specified in an arbitration agreement "could be deemed a 'manifest disregard of the law' or, alternatively, as exceeding the arbitrator's powers").

evidence alone. Motions to vacate for evident partiality or bias are frequently based on the arbitrator's failure to disclose conflicts of interest and other information that could give the appearance of bias. To prevail on a claim of bias, the moving party must be able to demonstrate that the arbitrator had an interest in the subject matter of the arbitration or a preexisting business or social relationship with one of the parties or counsel, which would color the arbitrator's judgment.[22] According to the 2004 American Arbitration Association (AAA)–American Bar Association Code of Ethics for Arbitrators in Commercial Disputes ("Ethics Code"), arbitrators have a duty to disclose such information prior to and even after selection, since there is a continuing obligation to disclose.[23] Under Canon II A(2), this duty applies to personal, financial, or other relationships with a party, its lawyer, any co-arbitrator, or any individual whom the arbitrator has been told will be a witness. Information that is pertinent is the kind that could lead a reasonable person to believe that the arbitrator might be biased toward or against a party.[24] State laws may have their own disclosure requirements, so arbitrators should become familiar with the requirements of the states in which they work.

Supreme Court Justice Byron White suggested in *Commonwealth Coatings Corp. v. Continental Casualty Co.* that a "disclosable" business interest is one that involves "more than trivial business with a party."[25] Thus, the nature and character of the arbitrator's undisclosed relationship or interest is critical to a court's determination of whether there was evident partiality.

The arbitrator's duty to disclose raises the issue of whether there is also an obligation to investigate potential conflicts of interest by the arbitrator's current and former employers. Canon II.B of the Ethics Code says that arbitrators should make a reasonable effort to inform themselves of the kinds of interests or relationships they are required to disclose.[26]

---

[22] *Nagler v. Hartman Group*, 2003 WL 21750992 (Cal. Ct. App. 2003). *See also Luster v. Collins*, 15 Cal. App. 4th 1338 (Ct. App. 1993).

[23] *See* the AAA-ABA Code of Ethics for Arbitrators in Commercial Disputes (Ethics Code), Canon II C, effective March 1, 2004, available at www.adr.org.

[24] Canon II A(2) discusses the types of interests to be disclosed. *See also International Alliance of Theatrical Stage Employees & Moving Picture Mach. Operators, Local 16 v. Laughon*, 14 Cal. Rptr. 3d 341 (Ct. App. 2004).

[25] 393 U.S. 145 (1968) (concurring opinion), *reh'g denied*, 393 U.S. 1112 (1969).

[26] *See also Betz v. Pankow*, No. 902532 (Cal. Super. Ct. Jan. 25, 1994) (duty to investigate prior employer); *Schmitz v. Zivetti*, 20 F.3d 1043 (9th Cir. 1994) (duty to investigate current employer).

What constitutes bias? Examples include nondisclosure of prior employment by a party or prior representation by a firm (or its predecessor-in-interest) with which the arbitrator is or was associated. An Illinois court has stated that a rebuttable presumption of bias is created by negotiating in another matter with the same parties to the current proceeding.[27]

2. Examples (Nondisclosure/Awards Vacated)

Similar Cases — The Arizona Court of Appeals vacated an award for evident partiality when the arbitrator failed to disclose that he had represented investors with similar claims in other arbitrations against the predecessor-in-interest to the brokerage firm respondent. Another problem the court cited was that the arbitrator had precluded the brokerage firm from presenting evidence or defenses at the hearing as a sanction for providing an untimely Answer and not responding to document requests, which the rules of the National Association of Securities Dealers (NASD) and the New York Stock Exchange (NYSE) [now, collectively, the Financial Industry Regulatory Authority — FINRA] permit and which all arbitration forums should authorize.[28]

Prior Service — The California Court of Appeal vacated a labor award in the union's favor when the arbitrator failed to disclose service in an earlier case involving the union's attorney.[29]

Prior Business — A trial court found a perception of possible bias based on the arbitrator's failure to disclose a prior business relationship between his former firm and a party, even though the arbitrator was unaware of the relationship.[30] The court said that a finding of actual bias was unimportant since a "reasonable impression of possible bias" is sufficient legal cause for vacating an award under Section 1286.2 of California's Code of Civil Procedure. This case indicates that in California, arbitrators have a duty to investigate potential conflicts arising out of business conducted by the arbitrator's former firm.

Prior Dealings — A New York trial court held that the failure of an arbitrator in an uninsured/underinsured motorist insurance coverage case to disclose that 25 years before he had been employed as counsel to the

---

[27] *Driniane v. State Farm Mutual Auto. Ins. Co.*, 606 N.E.2d 1181 (Ill. 1992).

[28] *Wages v. Smith Barney Harris Upham & Co.*, 17 937 P.2d 715 (Ariz. Ct. App. 1997).

[29] *International Alliance, supra* n. 20.

[30] *Betz, supra* n. 22.

insurance company was a ground to vacate an award.[31] And in a case decided nine years earlier, an intermediate appeals court in New York vacated an award based on the arbitrator's failure to disclose that he had received an *ex parte* communication from the representative of a third party to the arbitration (which had received the arbitrator's name from the law firm representing a party to the arbitration), stating that it was considering an arbitrator for another matter.[32] "Significantly," said the court, "the [arbitrator] did not disclose this communication to the parties at any time prior to the issuance of the panel's determination. . . ." The court found that the communication raised a question of possible bias, compromising the integrity of the arbitration process.

Prior Representation — The U.S. Court of Appeals for the Ninth Circuit held that the arbitrator's failure to disclose that his law firm had frequently represented an affiliate of a party gave rise to an "objectively reasonable perception of possible bias."[33] The court said that evidence that the arbitrator was unaware of the representation only indicated that he was not actually biased, but that did not, in the court's opinion, dispel the "perception of potential bias." This case indicates that, in the Ninth Circuit, arbitrators have a duty to investigate potential conflicts arising out of business conducted by the arbitrator's current employer.

Failure to Disclose Family Connection (however tenuous)[34] — While a number of courts hold that the *appearance* of partiality is insufficient to vacate an award, others, such as a California statecourt, hold that it should do so. When the non-disclosure by the arbitrator is material, said the California Supreme Court, the failure to disclose creates the impression of partiality. After a customer won a $5 million FINRA award, the brokerage firm sought it vacatur because of an arbitrator's alleged evident partiality. The court found that the arbitrator was not forthcoming in his disclosures generally or in his responses to the FINRA *Arbitrator Disclosure Report*. Questions 8 and 17 of the Report ask whether any person in the arbitrator's immediate family has maintained an account with or worked for a brokerage firm party. The arbitrator failed to disclose that his daughter had worked for and currently maintained an account with the brokerage firm Respondent in the arbitration. "The mere failure to disclose" in a matter such as this

---

[31] *Seligman v. Allstate*, 756 N.Y.S.2d 403 (N.Y. Sup. Ct. 2003).

[32] *Kern v. 303 E. 57th St. Corp.*, 611 N.Y.S.2d 547 (N.Y. App. Div. 1994).

[33] *Schmitz, supra* n. 22.

[34] *Vitale v. Morgan Stanley Smith Barney, LLC* , No. 37-2012-00099813 (Calif. Super. Ct., Sept. 17, 2012).

"creates the impression of partiality," the court ruled. "Under FINRA rules, the duty lies with the arbitrator to disclose—there is no duty on the part of the participants to Google matters or otherwise." FINRA's arbitration rules require its arbitrators to make reasonable inquiry, which was not done here.

Divided Loyalties[35] — Five years into an arbitration, after closing arguments were presented but before the award was issued, the Chair's law firm was retained in two matters from one of the parties. The Sixth Circuit Court of Appeals, in affirming the lower court's vacatur of the award, noted, "Nearly five years and 50 hearing days into an arbitration already checkered by irregularities, its adversary in the arbitration and its adversary's appointed arbitrator, in the space of about eight weeks, had both retained the neutral's law firm for engagements that any litigator would have regarded as lucrative." To establish evident partiality, the challenging party must show that a reasonable person would have to conclude that an arbitrator was partial to one party to the arbitration. "The arbitration itself was a model of how not to conduct one," said the Court. "The least of its blemishes was that it dragged on for years. Here, Kinkade established a convergence of undisputed facts that, considered together, show a motive for [the Chair] to favor the Whites and multiple, concrete actions in which he appeared actually to favor them. To begin with the motive: nearly five years into this arbitration, and in the space of eight weeks, the purportedly neutral arbitrator's law firm—of all the law firms that practice commercial litigation in Michigan—was hired by one party's arbitrator-advocate and then again by that same party for engagements that by all appearances would be substantial. It is no answer to assert that [the Chair] fully disclosed these arrangements to the parties. Five years into an arbitration, those disclosures were little better than no disclosure at all."

3. Examples (Nondisclosure/Awards Upheld)

There are innumerable cases holding that various types of nondisclosures do not create a perception of bias requiring vacatur of an award. Here are a few examples.

Unrelated Prior Matter — A federal District Court in the District of Columbia held that an arbitrator had no duty to disclose business relationships between his former law firm and a party in unrelated

---

[35] *Thomas Kinkade Co. v. White*, 711 F.3d 719 (6th Cir. 2013).

matters.[36] This case involved a "med-arb" (an arbitration following an unsuccessful mediation) in which Kenneth R. Feinberg (who later went on to be the person in charge of the September 11th reparation fund) served as both mediator and arbitrator. The prevailing party moved to vacate Mr. Feinberg's $1.1 million award on the ground that Mr. Feinberg's former law firm had represented the respondent on matters unrelated to the dispute. Since Mr. Feinberg did not know of that representation at the time of the arbitration, the "[a]ppellant's argument, therefore, depends on the proposition that Feinberg had a duty to make inquiry as to whether or not his former law firm had ever had any connection with any of the parties to the arbitration and thereafter make disclosure of the results." The court ultimately concluded, "We can find no source for any such generalized duty."

Similar Matters — A federal District Court in California held that an arbitrator's failure to disclose government investigations of an affiliate of his employer regarding matters similar to those at issue in the NASD securities arbitration (*i.e.*, stock analyst fraud) did not warrant granting the investor's motion to vacate in the absence of a disqualifying relationship between the arbitrator or his firm and a party.[37] The court found "no evidence of any social, business or financial relationships" between the arbitrator or the brokerage firm under investigation and the respondent brokerage firm "that would be affected by the outcome of the arbitration." The court concluded that the investor failed to raise a "reasonable probability" of partiality.

Prior Representation — The U.S. Court of Appeals for the Seventh Circuit held that a party-appointed arbitrator's failure to disclose his role over four years earlier as counsel to a subsidiary of the appointing party in an unrelated matter did not warrant vacatur for evident partiality. The court reasoned that the award should be upheld because the arbitrator met the statutory impartiality standards for a judge. The court also emphasized the understanding that party-appointed arbitrators (prior to the 2004 revision of the Ethics Code[38]) are understood to be advocates for the appointing party.[39]

Financial Relationship — The Ninth Circuit held that being a limited partner in the same limited partnership in which a party's expert invested

---

[36] *Al-Harbi v. Citibank*, 85 F.3d 680 (D.D.C. 1996).

[37] *Arbitration between Lemoine Skinner III v. Donaldson, Lufkin & Jenrette Sec. Corp.*, No. C 03-2625 VRW, 2003 WL 23174478 (N.D. Cal. Dec. 29, 2003).

[38] *See* text at n. 19, *supra*.

[39] *Sphere Drake Ins. v. All Amer. Life Ins. Co.*, 2002 WL 31255618 (7th Cir. 2002).

as a limited partner does not gives rise to an objectively reasonable impression of bias. That was the holding in *Apusento Garden (Guam) v. Superior Court of Guam*,[40] where the party seeking vacatur of the award argued that such relief should be granted due to the arbitrator's failure to disclose this financial relationship. The court disagreed, noting that limited partners are passive investors and that the arbitrator and the expert had no knowledge of their financial relationship.

What Bias Can Entail — In a case addressing the evident partiality ground, a Texas federal District Court noted that this can entail the arbitrator's failure to disclose relevant facts about himself or his display of bias during the proceeding, the former dealing with the integrity of the process by which arbitrators are chosen and the latter with the integrity of the arbitrator's decision (i.e., nondisclosure or actual bias).[41] In their argument of actual bias during the hearing in this case, the customers asserted that the arbitrators committed misconduct in refusing to grant their motion to amend their Statement of Claim to add as parties stock brokers employed by the brokerage firm and the financial advisors on whom the brokerage firm relied. They maintained that the Panel abused its discretion and engaged in evident partiality and misconduct. In denying the customers' motion to vacate, the court reasoned that when the customers filed their motion to amend, the case had twice been set for final hearing and was almost two years old. They attempted to add six additional respondents and the arbitrators could reasonably have concluded that none of the six was a necessary party for them to obtain complete relief.

Permitting Arbitrator to Stay — The U.S. District Court for the District of Connecticut denied a motion to vacate an award that was challenged due to one of the arbitrators' alleged bias.[42] All of the arbitrators were required to keep current biographical information on file with the NYSE (administering the arbitration at the time) with respect to any personal conflicts of interest or circumstances which could affect or give the appearance of affecting impartiality. On the first day of the hearings, just after the arbitrators were sworn in, the following disclosure was made on the record:

---

[40] *Apusento Garden (Guam) v. Superior Court of Guam*, 94 F.3d 1346 (9th Cir. 1996).

[41] *Weber v. Merrill Lynch* 455 F. Supp. 2d 545 (N.D. Tex. 2006).

[42] *Alfred Vigorito v. UBS PaineWebber, Inc.*, 477 F. Supp. 2d 481; 2007 U.S. Dist. LEXIS 17360.

NYSE Director of Arbitration: I think those are the only procedural things I have with the exception of a quick disclosure on behalf of Mr. Miller. Why don't you go ahead?

Arbitrator: Sure. Since this has started, within the past two months or so my youngest son, who lives out in California as a full-time student, has become employed, part time, by UBS, as a data entry clerk. I don't see any conflict of interest from my standpoint. I wanted you to be aware of it. If anybody has questions for me on it, I will take it.

Defense Counsel: He is not a member of your household?

Arbitrator: No.

Claimant's Counsel: I guess we are the ones that if anybody had a concern it would be us. I want to make sure you wouldn't have any compunction rendering an award against PaineWebber, the firm where your son is now employed.

Arbitrator: Correct.

Claimant's Counsel: As long as you are comfortable with that—

Arbitrator: I have no problem.

Claimant's Counsel: Then we don't have any problems.[43]

On the final day, the Chair asked plaintiffs: "And you feel Mr. Vigorito and Linda and Mark, do you feel you had a good opportunity to present your side of the case?" According to the court's decision, the attorneys nodded affirmatively. But the investors' attorney did not so affirm orally on the record. The award was challenged but the court affirmed it. While both counsel agreed that the arbitrator improperly failed to timely disclose his son's employment at UBS as required by the NYSE Rules, particularly before taking the oath at the arbitration hearing, the issue was whether the investors demonstrated that the nature of the arbitrator's disclosure was *materially erroneous* such that the

[43] Jan. 13, 2004 Hrg. Tr. at 9-10.

investors' attorney would have objected on that first day had she known the true facts, thus constituting an exception to the waiver rule. The court found that there was no such exception to the waiver rule, based on the following:

> 1. While plaintiffs offer no evidence showing when Miller knew about his son's employment at UBS, it is clear that he knew about it before taking the oath at the PaineWebber arbitration, yet failed to make the disclosure beforehand. At the very least, Miller informed Kupersmith that he had something "quick" to disclose. The fact that she took no steps to remove him or to further investigate his disclosure before administering his oath and losing her removal authority does not permit determination of whether she was advised of the substance of the disclosure, or that she was so advised but deemed it inconsequential.
>
> 2. Plaintiff's counsel was a seasoned arbitrator and attorney in the securities field, and waived objection to Miller as arbitrator when she responded to his disclosure. No grounds have been presented for an exception to the waiver rule in this case.

The case was before the court again two years later.[44] In *Vigorito v. UBS PaineWebber, Inc.*, a federal District Court judge in Connecticut explained the standard for waiving an objection to an arbitrator on the ground of alleged evident partiality. In the underlying arbitration, a family of customers filed a claim at the NYSE against UBS PaineWebber, Inc. to recover $1.5 million in alleged compensatory damages but were only awarded approximately $33,000 in costs and fees. It their motion to vacate on evident partiality grounds, the customers asserted that the disclosure by one of the arbitrators (that his son was a part-time clerk for UBS) was an untimely disclosure and that the arbitrator's relationship with the brokerage firm was substantial. The court denied the motion to vacate but granted a motion to reconsider because of the Second Circuit's earlier ruling on the issue of partiality[45] and because it was learned that

---

[44] 2009 U.S. Dist. LEXIS 51132 (June 17, 2009).

[45] *See Applied Indus. Materials Corp. v. Ovalar Makine Ticaret Ve Sanayi, A.S.*, 492 F.3d 132 (2d Cir. 2007).

the son had a more substantial professional relationship with the brokerage firm. However, in this decision, the court again denied the motion to vacate, concluding that even assuming, *arguendo*, that "evident partiality could be found" from the arbitrator's omissions, the motion to vacate should be denied because the customers waived any objection to the conflict.

How Far Back to Disclose?[46] *Question:* Is an arbitrator required to disclose an event that took place 20 years before the arbitration and which was unrelated to the arbitration? *Answer:* No. The California Civil Procedure Code, § 1281.9, subdivision (a), imposes on arbitrators a duty to "disclose all matters that could cause a person aware of the facts to reasonably entertain a doubt that the proposed neutral arbitrator would be able to impartial." The losing party in a FINRA arbitration asserted that the Chairman of the Panel violated this rule by failing to disclose that he acted as counsel in a case against CitiCorp/Citibank, now known as Citigroup, one of the defendants in the underlying dispute. *San Franciscans for Reasonable Growth,* a 1982 case, involved a challenge to the City of San Francisco's certification of Environmental Impact Reports for two projects sponsored by CitiCorp/Citibank and the Chairman of the Panel was of counsel for plaintiff (which he did not disclose). [In this case], *San Franciscans for Responsible Growth* occurred more than 20 years ago. The subject matter was completely unrelated. The instant arbitration involved the provision of flawed investment advice. The one link was the existence of the same party - Citigroup. A corporation the size of Citigroup, however, is likely to appear in a broad swath of litigation involving any number of subject matters. Award confirmed.

New York Federal Court Standard[47] — A broker who lost a FINRA arbitration claimed the arbitrators exhibited partiality by: allowing certain defenses to be heard; refusing to admit some of his evidence while admitting certain evidence from his former employer; and, disproportionately assessing costs. Motion denied/ Award confirmed. "Evident partiality under 9 U.S.C. § 10(a)(2)," said a New York District Court, "means more than a mere appearance of bias.[48] '[E]vident partiality' ... will be found where a reasonable person would

---

[46] *Farhang Oshidary v. Grace Purpura-Andriola*, 2012 U.S. Dist. LEXIS 81367 (N.D. Cal. June 12, 2012).

[47] *Nicholas A. Owoyemi v. JPMorgan Chase & Co.,* 2014 U.S. Dist. LEXIS 105768 (E.D.N.Y. July 2014).

[48] *Florasynth, Inc. v. Pickholz,* 750 F. 2d 171, 173 (2d Cir. 1984).

have to conclude that an arbitrator was partial to one party to the arbitration.[49] Courts do not examine an arbitrator's evidentiary decisions unless the arbitration proceedings were fundamentally unfair.[50] Plaintiff has not shown that he was denied a fundamentally fair hearing."

Disclosure Required[51] — In a promissory note FINRA arbitration, after the broker lost, he repeated his claim of bias on the part of the Chair, even though the Chair had disclosed his wife's customer-broker relationship with the brokerage firm Respondent (Merrill Lynch). The Chair disclosed that his wife maintained an investment account at Merrill Lynch, but stated that it would not affect his ability to arbitrate the parties' claims fairly and impartially. The former broker objected to the Chair's continued service on the panel, but the Chair declined to recuse himself and FINRA also denied Petitioner's request to replace the Chair. Not surprisingly for a promissory note case, the panel issued an award in Respondent's favor, directing Petitioner to pay $180,337.55 in compensatory damages, interest at the rate of 5.25% per annum and $75,000 in attorney's fees. Evident partiality may be found only "where a reasonable person would have to conclude that an arbitrator was partial to one party to the arbitration."[52] Proof of actual bias is not required.[53] However, a showing of evident partiality "may not be based simply on speculation."[54] Evident partiality can be inferred "from objective facts

---

[49] *Morelite Constr. Corp. v. New York City Dist. Council Carpenters Benefit Funds*, 748 F. 2d 79, 84 (2d Cir. 1984) (finding evident partiality when there was a father-son relationship between an arbitrator and one of the parties); *see also Sanford Home for Adults v. Local 6, IFHP*, 665 F. Supp. 312, 319-23 (S.D.N.Y. 1987) (finding no bias when arbitrator had a former attorney-client relationship with one of the parties).

[50] *See M. Slavin & Sons, Ltd. v. Cirillo*, 1990 WL 299933, at *3 (E.D.N.Y. May 18, 1990) (denying petitioner's motion to vacate when petitioner alleged that the arbitrator improperly considered certain evidence, but did not show that arbitrator denied petitioner a full opportunity to present its case).

[51] *Robert Chester v. Merrill Lynch, Pierce, Fenner & Smith, Inc.*, 2014 WL 2111690 (S.D.N.Y. May13, 2014).

[52] *Applied Indus. Materials Corp. v. Ovalar Makine Ticaret Ve Sanayi, A.S.*, 492 F.3d 132, 137 (2d Cir.2007) (quoting *Morelite Constr. Corp. v. N.Y.C Dist. Council Carpenters Benefits Funds,* 748 F.2d 79, 84 (2d Cir.1984)).

[53] *Scandinavian Reins. Co. v. Saint Paul Fire & Marine Ins. Co.*, 668 F.3d 60, 72 (2d Cir.2012).

[54] *Id.* at 72 (quoting *United States v. Int'l Bhd. of Teamsters,* 170 F.3d 136, 147 (2d Cir.1999)).

inconsistent with impartiality."[55] The Chair did not fail to disclose his potential conflict or attempt to hide a potential bias.[56]

4. Examples (Arbitrator Statement and Rulings/Awards Upheld)

Can a successful motion to vacate be made on the ground that something the arbitrator said or did during the arbitration constituted bias? The courts generally have not vacated awards for bias based on the arbitrator's management of the process or statements made during the hearings.

Hearing Comments — The U.S. Court of Appeals for the Fourth Circuit held that bias was not established by an arbitrator's comments during a securities arbitration.[57] The investor in *Remmey v. Paine Webber* complained that the Chair of the panel was especially solicitous to the respondent brokerage firm and made several comments indicating empathy for that party. "A review of the record," the court said:

> …indicates that [the 88-year-old chair's] style, although colloquial, was consistent throughout the proceeding. It was no more a sign of bias for [the arbitrator] to tell [a witness] to "enjoy the wedding" than it was for him to tell [the] appellant's step-daughter she was "with friends." His humor—or attempts at humor—were even directed at himself.

The court found that since the arbitrator was simply attempting to create a relaxed, informal atmosphere, the conduct complained of did not indicate bias. "It is well established that a mere appearance of bias is insufficient to demonstrate evident partiality," the court said.

Negotiating with Same Parties — The Illinois Supreme Court found evidence sufficient to rebut the presumption of bias created by the arbitrator's negotiating in another matter with the same parties to the

---

[55] *Id.* at 72 (quoting *Pitta v. Hotel Ass'n of N.Y.C, Inc.,* 806 F.2d 419, 423 n. 2 (2d Cir.1986)).

[56] *Compare Lucent Techs. Inc. v. Tatung Co.,* 379 F.3d 24, 28 (2d Cir.2004) (failure to disclose a material relationship with one of the parties can constitute evident partiality); *see also STMicroelectronics, N.V. v. Credit Suisse Sec. (USA) LLC,* 648 F.3d 68, 74 (2d Cir.2011) (stating that the overwhelming majority of decisions applying the evident partiality standard in Section 10(a)(2) have only addressed the "non-disclosure[ ] of facts bearing on partiality—namely, a relationship with a party, lawyer, or another arbitrator").

[57] *Remmey, supra* n. 10; *Peoples Sec. Life Ins. Co. v. Monumental Life Ins. Co.*, 991 F.2d 141 (4th Cir. 1993); *Health Servs. Mgmt. Corp. v. Hughes*, 975 F.2d 1253 (7th Cir. 1992).

arbitration. The evidence consisted of sworn affidavits and deposition testimony from the arbitrator, the defendant and its law firm, indicating that disputed issues in the arbitration were not discussed.[58]

Expressions of Personal Hostility — The federal District Court in the District of Columbia recognized that making legitimate efforts to expedite the arbitration proceedings might involve some abrasive conduct by the arbitrator. The court ruled that showing personal hostility toward a party's attorney and interrupting the proceedings did not establish evident partiality. It said, "An arbitrator's legitimate efforts to move the proceedings along expeditiously may be viewed as abrasive or disruptive to a disappointed party. Nevertheless, such displeasure does not constitute grounds for vacating an arbitration award." The court explained, "Absent some sort of overt misconduct, a disappointed party's perception of rudeness on the part of an arbitrator is not the sort of 'evident partiality' contemplated by the Act as grounds to vacate an award."[59]

Denial of Continuance — In a federal case in Pennsylvania, a District Court said that evident partiality was not established where the Chair of the arbitration panel denied the respondent a continuance to secure the testimony of a missing witness. On the last hearing day, the respondent asked for a postponement, stating for the first time that he had a rebuttal witness who was not available to testify that day. The court denied the request to vacate, stating:

> Although the applicable rules of arbitration procedure did not require [the respondent] to identify [the rebuttal witness] as a witness because he was being called in rebuttal, [the respondent's] counsel should have informed the arbitration panel before the last day of the hearing that she was planning to call [that individual] because she knew that [he] would not be available. The arbitrators had set the schedule in this case based on the availability of themselves and the parties. It simply was poor judgment on the part of [respondent's] counsel to wait until the last day of the hearing to inform the arbitrators that it planned to call a witness who simply was not available that day.[60]

---

[58] *Supra* n. 23.

[59] *Fairchild & Co. v. Richmond, Fredericksburg & Potomac R.R. Co.*, 516 F. Supp. 1305 (D.D.C. 1981).

[60] *Maiocco v. Greenway Capital Corp.*, 1998 U.S. Dist. LEXIS 836 (E.D. Pa. Feb. 2, 1998).

Procedural Errors — A federal district court in Virginia ruled that evident partiality was not shown through allegations of procedural or evidentiary errors, or by legitimate efforts to move the case along, or by the failure of the arbitrators to follow the rules of evidence.[61]

Expressed Opinion of a Witness — A federal court in Wisconsin upheld an award and rejected the respondent brokerage firm's claim of evident partiality based on this statement by the arbitrator at the hearing: "It seems that you have demonstrated that [a witness] was not exactly a paragon of virtue with his conduct in his affairs and what he did wrong with respect to numerous other accounts has questionable relevance as far as this hearing is concerned." In the court's view, this statement showed that the arbitrator's assessment of the witness was drawn from the evidence presented to the panel and did not show that the arbitrator was partial to one side or the other. "An arbitrator," said the court, "may develop an opinion during the course of the hearing and even express it."[62]

C. Misconduct by the Arbitrator

1. Standard

The test for arbitrator misconduct under Section 10(a)(3) of the Federal Arbitration Act is whether the arbitrator's determination prejudiced a party's right to a fair hearing.[63] This ground for vacatur has been raised when awards were issued on a motion for summary judgment or for dismissal of all claims. Vacatur has also been sought when the arbitrator, during the hearing, refused to grant a postponement or allow discovery or hear evidence.

New York courts have held that an aggrieved party must immediately object to an arbitrator's misconduct or else the claim will be deemed waived.[64]

In evaluating an arbitrator's decisions as a process manager, such as the decision to deny a postponement request, courts consider whether there was a reasonable basis for the decision and whether the denial created a fundamentally unfair proceeding. It is critical for arbitrators to

---

[61] *Sisti v. Merrill Lynch, Pierce, Fenner & Smith*, 1991 U.S. Dist. LEXIS 15817 (E.D. Va. Apr. 22, 1991).

[62] *Hayne, Miller & Farni, Inc. v. Flume*, 888 F. Supp. 949 (E.D. Wis. 1995).

[63] *Tempo Shain Corp. v. Bertek*, 120 F.3d 16 (2d Cir. 1997). *See also DaSilva v. First Union Sec. Inc.*, 249 F. Supp. 2d 286, 290 (S.D.N.Y. 2003).

[64] *See*, e.g., *Matter of Kaminsky v. Segura*, 2004 WL 1945007 (N.Y. Sup. Ct. July 6, 2004).

appreciate that if there is a reasonable basis for the arbitrators' decision, courts will rarely interfere with the award.[65]

Nowhere is this deference to arbitrators more pronounced than with respect to their hearing conduct. Whether evidence proffered by a party is relevant is a decision within the discretion of the arbitrators.[66] An arbitrator's determination of what is pertinent and material will be set aside only if that determination severely prejudiced the rights of a party so as to deny that party a fundamentally fair hearing.[67] Thus, the federal court for the Southern District of New York has said that where the hearing is fair overall, even improperly excluded evidence will not be a ground for vacatur. According to this court, "The arbitrators must not only have been in error when they chose to exclude evidence but that error must have been so severe as to have damaged the rights of the party to the extent that he was deprived of a fair hearing."[68]

2. Examples (No Misconduct/Awards Upheld)

Excluded Evidence — When excluded evidence is cumulative, the decision to exclude it does not constitute misconduct. For example, in a dispute over a terminated arbitrageur's entitlement to a bonus, a New York intermediate appeals court found that the challenged award was proper, despite the arbitrators' refusal to hear testimony of a proposed witness who would have presented a different version of events than the one provided by the respondent. The court ruled that the refusal to hear evidence was not fundamentally unfair since the panel had been apprised of the contents of the proposed witness's testimony during the hearing and his testimony would have been cumulative.[69]

Refusal to Admit Evidence — The Eleventh Circuit Court of Appeals refused to vacate an NASD arbitration award in favor of a broker[70] who had brought the arbitration to recover damages allegedly resulting from his termination. The other party to the case was the broker's former

---

[65] *See, e.g.*, *Bisnoff, v. King*, 154 F. Supp. 2d 630, 637 (S.D.N.Y. 2001).

[66] *Dean v. Paine Webber, Inc.*, Fed. Sec. L. Rep. (CCH) ¶ 97,034, at 94,546 (S.D.N.Y. Oct. 13, 1992).

[67] *Sebbag v. Shearson Lehman*, Fed. Sec. L. Rep. (CCH) ¶ 95,775, at 98,729 (S.D.N.Y. Jan. 8, 1991).

[68] *Matter of Kubarcych (Siegal)* (N.Y. Sup. Ct.) *reported in* 209 N.Y.L.J. 33, p. 31, col. 2., on Feb. 22, 1993.

[69] *Credit Suisse First Boston Corp. v. Crisanti*, 734 N.Y.S. 2d 150 (N.Y. App. Div. 2001). *See also*, *Areca v. Oppenheimer & Co.*, 960 F. Supp. 52 (S.D.N.Y. 1997).

[70] *Rosensweig v. Morgan Stanley & Co., Inc.*, 494 F.3d 1328 (11th Cir. 2007).

employer, which claimed, in its motion to vacate, that the arbitrators committed misconduct by refusing to hear evidence about certain computer disks that contained the client data. The appeals court noted the broad authority arbitrators have in determining what evidence to admit and concluded that they had several reasons, all reasonable, to limit the evidence in the underlying arbitration.

Excluding Rebuttal Evidence — Similarly, where the arbitrator excluded proposed rebuttal testimony covering issues discussed at length in the case-in-chief of the party putting on the witness, an appeals court in New York held that the arbitrator's decision did not constitute misconduct sufficient to vacate the award, since the rebuttal testimony was improper for rebuttal.[71]

In a case brought before the U.S. District Court for the Western District of Pennsylvania,[72] an NASD award was challenged on ground that the arbitrators improperly refused to permit a party to submit rebuttal evidence in the form of an expert. In denying the motion, the court held that an award may be vacated if the arbitrator refuses to hear evidence pertinent and material to the controversy. The court also recognized that the NASD Code of Arbitration gives the arbitrators wide discretion to determine which evidence is pertinent or material (citing then Section 10323 of the NASD Arbitration Code, which stated that, "The arbitrators shall determine the materiality and relevance of any evidence proffered and shall not be bound by rules governing the admissibility of evidence.")

Dismissal without Hearing — In a construction case, a Washington appeals court did not consider the arbitrator's dismissal of both parties' claims without conducting a hearing on the merits to be misconduct warranting vacatur of the award where the arbitrator concluded that neither party was entitled to damages because neither had complied with the claims procedures in their agreement.[73]

Refusal to Require More Evidence — An arbitrator's refusal to require production of additional evidence, even if a clearly erroneous

---

[71] *Republic of Croatia v. Trustee of the Marquess of Northhampton 1987 Settlement*, 203 A.D. 2d 167, 169 (N.Y. App. Div. 1994).

[72] *The Edward Mellon Trust v. UBS PaineWebber, Inc.*, 2006 U.S. Dist. LEXIS 80922 (W.D. PA. Nov. 6, 2006).

[73] *Pegasus Constr. Corp. v. Turner Constr. Co.*, 929 P.2d 1200 (Wash. Ct. App. 1997) (AAA Construction Industry rules "vest discretion in the arbitrator to vary the procedures by which a matter is to be heard, subject to the duty of ensuring that both sides have the opportunity to present material and relevant evidence," which was done in this case, despite the fact that a full hearing did not occur).

decision, did not warrant vacatur of the award unless the refusal was so egregious as to clearly deprive a party of a fundamentally fair hearing.[74]

Incorrect Award — Will a party be able to successfully attack an award if it was, allegedly, a "grossly incorrect award?" In a dispute over a charter party, the defendant argued that the award, which was the product of a majority decision, should be vacated by the court on the ground, *inter alia*, of misconduct under Section 10(a)(3) of the FAA. The court said that vacatur was not warranted since there was no evidence of a lack of fundamental fairness. The court stated, "[E]xcept where fundamental fairness is violated, arbitration determinations will not be opened up for evidentiary review." Moreover, the aggrieved party failed to cite any precedent to establish its claim for vacatur under Section 10(a)(3).[75]

Gift to Arbitrators — Soliciting and accepting a gift from a party certainly sounds like misconduct. But when the party who gave the gift ultimately seeks to vacate the award, the court may balk at allowing that party to benefit from its own misconduct. That's what happened in *Matter of Kubarcych*.[76] The losing party in the arbitration had, during the course of the case, secretly furnished New York Knicks basketball tickets to the arbitrator at the arbitrator's request. When the basketball game and arbitration were over, the losing party moved to vacate the award, claiming arbitrator misconduct, despite the fact that he knew his conduct was improper (having been admonished by the AAA administrator against such conduct). The prevailing party had no knowledge of this *ex parte* conduct. The court ruled that the loser in this case waived its claim, since an alleged aggrieved party must immediately object to an arbitrator's misconduct. "It is therefore simply a case of his being 'hoist with his own petard' (Shakespeare, Hamlet, Act III, Scene 4)," said the court. "[T]he sheer effrontery of his contentions (often termed chutzpah) would in and of itself be a sufficient reason for its denial."

Scheduling Hearings — In an unpublished decision in *Alexander Julian, Inc. v. Mimco Inc.*, the U.S. Court of Appeals for the Second Circuit rejected the claim that the arbitrator engaged in misconduct by setting the hearing on a day when the defendant's attorney was scheduled to be in federal court. The court acknowledged the "tremendous amount of discretion" vested in arbitrators but found no evidence of fundamental

---

[74] *Coppola v. Charles Schwab & Co.*, Fed. Sec. L. Rep. (CCH) ¶ 96,216, at 91,133 (S.D.N.Y. Sept. 4, 1991).

[75] No. 03 Civ 2038, 2004 WL 2721072 (S.D.N.Y. Nov. 30, 2004), (quoting the Second Circuit in *Tempo Shain*, *supra* n. 38, 120 F.3d at 20).

[76] *Supra* n. 51.

unfairness, even though the defendant did not attend the hearing. The defendant had ample notice of the hearing date and it would have been unfair to the parties to set that date too far in the future. Moreover, said the federal appeals court, the defendant could have sent another lawyer from its counsel's office to attend the hearing or it could have obtained substitute counsel.[77]

During prehearing conferences, arbitrators (encouraged by the Canons to provide the parties an expeditious alternative to litigation) are often confronted by attorneys who insist that they cannot take part in substantive hearings until sometime in the distant future. Rightly so, the opposing party (usually the claimant) implores the arbitrators for much sooner hearing dates. Based on these court decisions, arbitrators should feel confident in telling the "busy" advocate that he or she should get someone else at the law firm to appear at the hearings and then schedule the dates.

Settlement Evidence — The Fourth Circuit held that the panel's consideration of settlement evidence as potentially mitigating evidence in a franchise dispute did not render the arbitration proceeding fundamentally unfair. The panel believed the settlement evidence was relevant to the mitigation defense. It also believed that the use of such evidence for this purpose did not violate the rule against using settlement communications to establish liability. The court did not decide whether the panel was right or wrong on this point, only that its use was not fundamentally unfair.[78]

Settlement Figures — Similarly, a federal district court in New York held that the panel's review of settlement figures was not prejudicial misconduct. "It appears that the arbitrators had concluded that the settlement was not relevant to the resolution of the arbitration issues. The viewing of the settlement agreement by the arbitrators was a routine and fair in camera inspection."[79]

Adjournment Denied — An arbitrator's refusal to grant an adjournment was not considered an abuse of the arbitrator's discretion by a New York appellate court, where the request was founded on the requesting party's personal choice not to attend due to another commitment. The court stated: "Appellant risked the possibility that he would be unavailable to testify by leaving the jurisdiction for a

---

[77] *Alexander Julian v. Mimco*, No. 01-7621, 2002 WL 243306 (2d Cir. Feb. 19, 2002).

[78] *Gallus Inv. LP v. Pudgie's Famous Chicken Ltd.*, 134 F.3d 231 (4th Cir. 1998).

[79] *Perahia v. Viceroy Int'l Sec. Corp.*, No. 92 Civ. 1228, 1992 WL 162825, 1992 U.S. Dist. LEXIS 8874 (S.D.N.Y. June 23, 1992).

prolonged period of time when he knew or should have known that his case would be called for a hearing."[80]

Similarly, in *Bisnoff v. King*, the federal court for the Southern District of New York held that the denial of a stockbroker's request for a postponement on health grounds did not warrant vacatur of an award on misconduct grounds.[81] While the arbitrators denied the postponement request, they said that the broker, who had suffered a heart attack a few months earlier and claimed to suffer from recurring symptoms, could appear for a videotaped deposition and present telephone testimony at the hearing. When the broker sought reconsideration of the panel's decision, the arbitrators asked for a written prognosis of his medical condition. They also asked how many hours he was then working. The broker's credibility was apparently more strained than his heart, for the arbitrators learned from the broker's responses that, despite his illness, he was then working about 30 hours a week as a stock broker. Noting that this is a stressful occupation (an understatement at best), the panel again denied his postponement request.

The broker advised the panel in a letter that he had no intention of testifying under any circumstances and neither he nor his attorney appeared at the hearing. The panel conducted the hearing in their absence and ultimately issued an award in favor of the investor. In a very wise move, one of the arbitrators wrote a letter informing the broker that their decision to proceed with the hearings was partially based on the fact that he had been working so many hours per week. The court upheld that award, finding that the panel's decision to deny the adjournment was "reasonable." The broker contended that the panel's denial of a postponement caused substantial and irreparable prejudice by foreclosing him from presenting material and pertinent evidence at the hearing. The court rejected this argument since the broker was offered the opportunity to present evidence by alternative means. Moreover, the court observed that the panel gave a clear and reasonable explanation for its conclusion that the petitioner was fit to participate in a hearing by videotaped deposition and/or telephone testimony.

The court said it was not authorized to second-guess the panel's "uncomplimentary assessment" of the broker's credibility. It found ample "circumstantial evidence" supporting the panel's determination that the broker's stated reason for seeking the adjournment was not credible and

---

[80] *State Farm Mut. Auto. Ins. Co. v. Bermudez*, 111 A.D.2d 858 (N.Y. App. Div. 1985).
[81] *Bisnoff, supra* n. 48.

that his real purpose was to delay. This evidence was the broker's participation in the preliminary conference only one month after his heart attack, his failure to mention the heart attack or potential medical problems during the preliminary hearing, his waiting two-and-a-half weeks before the hearing to bring up his medical problems, and his working thirty hours a week in a stressful job. The court also held that the decision to deny the postponement was fundamentally fair since the broker received an opportunity to proffer evidence through less stressful alternatives. The fact that he did not participate at the hearing was his decision.

A federal District Court in the District of Columbia similarly held that the arbitrators' refusal to postpone the hearing, despite the hospitalization of the losing party's daughter for a broken arm, was not misconduct that would warrant vacatur of the award. The court observed that the daughter's injury was never presented as a life-threatening situation and there were no medical complications arising out of the injury.[82]

A federal District Court in California found that the arbitrators acted within the scope of their discretion in declining to postpone the hearing and conducting it in the claimant's absence. Here the claimant investor received more than two months' notice of the hearing date, yet he neglected to hire an attorney or prepare for the hearing. The court also noted that he waited until the very week of the hearing to request an extension of time.[83]

In affirming an NASD award, a federal District Court in New York found that the arbitrators denied an adjournment request because petitioners failed to show that there was sufficient reason to postpone the hearing.[84] The arbitrators had listened to the petitioner's arguments for an adjournment and decided that the absence of certain documents did not merit postponement. The arbitrators sought to proceed with the hearing and told petitioners that they could renew their motion to adjourn after the panel had heard the testimony of the available witnesses, if petitioners so desired. The arbitrators' denial of petitioners' request for an adjournment was not found by the court to be unreasonable or unjustified.

The U.S. District Court for the Eastern District of Virginia, Norfolk Division, was presented with an award challenge by a party claiming it was denied a fundamentally fair hearing due to the panel's refusal to

---

[82] *Berlacher v. Paine Webber, Inc.*, 759 F. Supp. 21 (D.D.C. 1991).

[83] *PaineWebber v. Barca*, 2000 WL 1071836, 2000 U.S. Dist. LEXIS 10873 (N.D. Cal. July 28, 2000).

[84] *Kober v. Kelly* 2006 U.S. Dist. LEXIS 48275 (S.D.N.Y.)

grant an adjournment request and by permitting a witness to testify by phone and without a prior written statement, deviating from its own earlier order. The court denied the motion to vacate,[85] holding that a court may vacate an award when a request for postponement is arbitrarily denied or when the denial leads to the inability of the party to present pertinent and material evidence. An arbitral panel should be granted a degree of discretion, said the court, as long as it had a reasonable basis for refusing to postpone.

Discovery Denied — In a federal case in New York, the court found that the party seeking vacatur failed to make a clear showing that the arbitrators abused their discretion in refusing to grant discovery and in excluding evidence that the complaining party deemed relevant. The court observed that whether proffered evidence is relevant is a decision that is within the discretion of the arbitrators.[86]

Excluding Evidence — Even when the arbitrators excluded a portion of an expert's testimony, a court still upheld the award, stating that arbitrators are not obliged to observe the same "niceties" required by the Federal Rules of Civil Procedure, and that they must only grant a fundamentally fair hearing. If the hearing was fair overall, said the court, even improperly excluded evidence will not be a sufficient ground for vacatur.[87]

Refusal to Hear Madoff Related Evidence Post-Hearing[88] — An investor in a Bernard Madoff "feeder fund" (Ascot Partners, L.P., which was managed by J. Ezra Merkin) who lost his arbitration sought its vacatur, arguing that after the hearing the Panel refused to hear "pertinent and material evidence" in the form of certain deposition testimony by a non-party. The motion was denied by a New York state court. "Unless an arbitrator's determination is rendered totally irrational, his refusal or failure to pass upon an arguably relevant issue or item of evidence is a matter of arbitral judgment that is not judicially reviewable. The refusal of the arbitrators to hear the particular testimony which the record shows was attempted to be submitted after the hearing proceedings were closed is not reviewable by this court."

---

[85] *Al-Haddad Commodities Corporation v. Toepfer International Asia Pte., LTD.* 485 F. Supp. 2d 677; 2007 U.S. Dist. LEXIS 29405.

[86] *Dean, supra* n. 49.

[87] *Pompano Windy City Partners v. Bear Stearns*, 794 F. Supp. 1265 (S.D.N.Y. 1992).

[88] *J. Ezra Merkin v. Joshua M. Berman,* 2014 N.Y. Misc. LEXIS 3043 (Sup. Ct. July 7, 2014).

California Courts and Requests to Adjourn[89] — FINRA Rule 13601(a)(2) permits adjournments if "good cause" is shown. In this California case, a motion for continuance that was filed the day before the arbitration hearing based on an Respondent's incomplete and inconclusive investigation of Claimant's conduct - that had nothing to do with the claim - did not meet FINRA's good cause requirement for granting the postponement. In this industry compensation arbitration, the brokerage firm that the former employee was suing sought to "briefly" postpone the hearing to continue its ongoing investigation of the broker. The Panel denied the request and after it awarded the employee $3.5 million, the firm moved to vacate based on the adjournment denial, which the California appeals court rejected, reasoning as follows: In order to conclude an arbitration panel abused its discretion, a court must determine whether the denial of a request for a postponement exceeded the bounds of reason. "When two or more inferences can reasonably be deduced from the facts, we have no authority to substitute our decision for that of the arbitrators. Wedbush failed to make an adequate showing at the time its motion for a postponement was made that the investigation was relevant to Kelleher's claim of compensation."

3. Examples (Misconduct/Awards Vacated)

Adjournment Denied — The U.S. Court of Appeals for the First Circuit has held that the refusal to grant an adjournment constituted a denial of fundamental fairness where the party requesting the adjournment argued that he could not proceed because his wife had cancer.[90]

Inadequate Notice — Inadequate notice can also lead to vacatur. In *Wedbush Morgan Securities v. Brandman*, the NYSE's arbitration department sent a notice of the hearing and the rescheduled hearing to the respondent's former counsel, even though the department had been advised by the respondent that he was no longer represented by an attorney. When the respondent found out about the scheduled hearing, he notified the NYSE and said that he was still seeking counsel. However, the hearing proceeded in his absence and resulted in an award against him. When he moved to vacate the award, a New York trial court granted the motion, finding that his rights were prejudiced because he was not

---

[89] *Wedbush Securities, Inc. v. Kelleher,* 2013 Cal. App. Unpub. LEXIS 2520 (Ct. App. CA, 1st App. Dist, Div. 4, April 9, 2013).

[90] *Hoteles Candado Beach, supra* n. 1; *see also Roche v. Local 32B-32J Serv. Employees Int'l Union,* 755 F. Supp. 622 (S.D.N.Y. 1991).

properly apprised of the hearing and afforded an opportunity to obtain counsel.[91]

Questioning Denied — Other instances of vacatur on misconduct grounds have resulted when, for example, there was a refusal to permit a party to cross-examine the other party's expert witness[92] and when a party was not given the opportunity to completely present his proof on the merits of his grievance.[93] In the former case, a federal District Court in Pennsylvania granted a broker's motion to vacate an NYSE arbitration award when the arbitrators failed to allow his counsel to participate in colloquy concerning the basis for cross-claims against the broker and for failing to allow counsel to cross-examine the customer's expert.

D. Exceeding Powers

1. Standard

The standard for granting a motion to vacate under Section 10(a)(3) of the FAA is whether a party's rights were prejudiced by an arbitrator who, in making the award, exceeded his or her powers or so imperfectly executed them that a final and definite award on the subject matter submitted was not made.[94]

2. Examples (Powers Not Exceeded/Awards Upheld)

Ruling on Dispositive Motions — In *Schlessinger v. Rosenfeld Meyer & Susman*,[95] the California Court of Appeal ruled that since the California Arbitration Act does not preclude dispositive motions, arbitrators may (but are not required to) hear such motions under the Act. The court explained, "In a case where a legal issue or defense

---

[91] *Wedbush Morgan Sec. Inc. v. Brandman*, 597 N.Y.S.2d 39 (N.Y. App. Div. 1993); *Leblon Consultants Ltd. v. Jackson China Inc.*, 459 N.Y.S.2d 93 (N.Y. App. Div. 1983) (abuse of discretion in denial of adjournment request where unavailable witness was the only employee of respondent with knowledge of underlying dispute); *Lehman Millet Inc. v. Parish*, 109 Misc. 2d 288, 440 N.Y.S.2d 164 (N.Y. Sup. Ct. 1981) (adjournment denial not unreasonable where problem regarding defendant's presence at the hearing should have been discovered long before the hearing date was scheduled).

[92] *Pacilli v. Philips Appel & Walden, Inc.*, 1991 WL 193507 (E.D. Pa. Sept. 1991).

[93] *Teamsters, Chauffeurs, Warehousemen & Helpers, Local 506 v. E.D. Clapp Corp.*, 551 F. Supp. 570 (N.D.N.Y. 1982).

[94] *Blumenthal v. Merrill Lynch, Pierce, Fenner & Smith*, 910 F.2d 1049 (2d Cir. 1990).

[95] 47 Cal. Rptr. 2d 650 (Cal. Ct. App. 1995). *See also Inter Carbon Bermuda Ltd. v. Caldex Trading Corp.*, 146 F.R.D. 64 (S.D.N.Y. 1993) (upholding a summary award without holding live hearings).

could possibly be resolved on undisputed facts, the purpose of the arbitration process would be defeated by precluding a summary judgment or summary adjudication motion and instead requiring a lengthy trial." Having established that arbitrators may rule on dispositive motions, the court held that the arbitrator in this case did not exceed his authority under the Act by granting summary judgment based on written submissions and telephonic conferences with the attorneys, and he did not refuse to hear evidence material to the controversy. The court also held that while the arbitrator is required to "hear evidence" and a party is entitled to cross-examine witnesses if they appear at a hearing, parties do not have an absolute right to present oral testimony in every case.

Authority to Assess Costs — The federal District Court in the District of Columbia held that arbitrators do not exceed their powers in an NASD wrongful termination case by dismissing the Statement of Claim and assessing the claimant half of the costs of an adjournment requested by both parties, filing and forum fees and administrative costs. The court held that the arbitration panel acted within the scope of its authority since the NASD Code of Arbitration Procedure gave its arbitrators the authority to assess forum and adjournment fees and costs for pre-hearing proceedings, as well as the authority to decide who pays those fees. In addition, said the court, the arbitrators did not exceed their powers by refusing to stay the arbitration based on claimant's court challenge to the assessment of fees.[96]

Granting Motion to Dismiss — A federal court in Kentucky held that an NASD arbitrator did not exceed his authority by granting a motion to dismiss the plaintiff's claims against one defendant prior to discovery and a hearing on the merits. The claimant argued that this was a refusal to hear evidence that warranted vacatur of the award, but the court found that the claimant failed to show that the excluded evidence was material to the panel's determination, or that it was so prejudicial as to deny the parties fundamental fairness. Significantly, the court also emphasized that the claimant had the opportunity to respond to the motion to dismiss and, therefore, was not denied an opportunity to present her case. Furthermore, the court added that the claimant was not entitled to full-blown discovery and that the case could be decided on a pre-hearing motion.[97]

---

[96] *Brown v. Wheat First Sec.*, 101 F. Supp. 2d 1(D.D.C., Jun 13, 2000).

[97] *Warren v. Tacher*, 114 F. Supp. 2d 600 (W.D. Ky 2000).

These cases make clear that arbitrators do not exceed their power by ruling on dispositive motions in an appropriate case, as long as each side has an opportunity to present its case, usually at the hearing on the dispositive motion.

Permitting Late Counterclaims — In a Texas state case, the intermediate appeals court held that an arbitrator did not exceed his powers in permitting the respondent to file a counterclaim after the deadline provided in the AAA rules. The court found that the arbitrator had discretion under these rules to extend the deadline for filing a response and counterclaim.[98]

Claims Decided — Claims that the arbitrators exceeded their powers have also been made based on allegations that the arbitrator decided a claim not subject to arbitration or not set forth in the claim.[99] Similarly, vacatur motions have been made based on the arbitrators' failure to decide all of the claims submitted to them, which generally might be characterized as the arbitrators having imperfectly exercised their powers. However, these types of challenges are not directed at arbitrator management issues per se, so they will not be discussed further. Arbitrators should take care in making their jurisdictional rulings and deciding only the claims submitted that are subject to the parties' agreement to arbitrate.

Late Awards — In an interesting recent case dealing with the timing of an award under Section 10(a)(3), the Seventh Circuit held that issuing a late award in violation of the applicable arbitration rules is not a ground for vacatur, unless the parties provide in their agreement that "time is of the essence," which was not the case here.[100]

Telephonic Hearings are Sufficient[101] — The Ninth Circuit Court of Appeals upheld the decision of a FINRA arbitration panel to dismiss the claims of a former employee based on statute of limitations, decided after two pre-hearing teleconferences, without an in person substantive hearing. When the losing party charged the panel with exceeding their authority in rendering such an award without a full

---

[98] *General Cinemas v. CEI Roofing*, No. 05-99-00357-CV, 2000 WL 898861 (Tex. Ct. App. July 7, 2000).

[99] For example in *Ferrarini v. Fenner Fin. Inc.*, 641 So. 2d 82 (Fla. Dist. Ct. App. 1994), a $50,000 NASD award against a brokerage firm was vacated because the arbitrators based the award "on issues not submitted."

[100] *Hasbro Inc. v. Catalyst USA*, 367 F.3d 689 (7th Cir 2004).

[101] *Robert J. Knight v. Merrill Lynch, Pierce, Fenner & Smith*, 350 Fed. Appx. 119, 2009 U.S. App. LEXIS 23091 (9th Cir. 2009).

hearing, the federal appeals court stated that the Code of Arbitration Procedure gave them that authority. While no witnesses were sworn; no witnesses were cross-examined; no documents were formally received into evidence; and, only counsel for the parties, but not the parties themselves, took part in the teleconferences, the Court held that neither the Code of Arbitration nor the parties' arbitration agreement defines the requirements of a hearing and that the panel reasonably decided to conduct the hearings telephonically without live witness testimony and cross-examination.

Awarding More Than Sought[102] — In this oilfield-related arbitration, a single arbitrator awarded the Claimant more than the contract provided, yet the Supreme Court of Louisiana affirmed the award. In reviewing arbitral awards challenged under Louisiana's arbitration statute,[103] said the court, it is not the judiciary's role to correct errors of fact or law. While the calculation of damages was beyond the court's review,[104] the court was nevertheless able to examine whether the arbitrator had the contractual authority to issue that particular award.

3. Examples (Powers Exceeded/Awards Vacated)

Full Panel Required — When one arbitrator was disqualified at the hearing and the other two arbitrators continued the hearing over the objection of the respondent brokerage firm, the U.S. Court of Appeals for the Eleventh Circuit found that the arbitrators exceeded their powers because the arbitration agreement required three arbitrators to decide the dispute. The court held, "Because the arbitrators violated the provisions of the arbitration agreement requiring arbitration before at least three arbitrators, they exceeded their authority under the arbitration agreement."[105]

Terms of Agreement — The Ninth Circuit Court of Appeals held that when an investor altered the standard-form option agreement to require the arbitrators to issue findings of fact and conclusions of law and the

---

[102] *Mack Energy Co. v. Expert Oil and Gas, L.L.C.*, 2015 La. LEXIS 14 (Sup. Ct. La. Jan. 28, 2015).

[103] La. R.S. 9:4210(D):"Where the arbitrators exceeded their powers or so imperfectly executed them that a mutual, final, and definite award upon the subject matter submitted was not made."

[104] *See National Tea Co.*, 548 So.2d at 932; *Louisiana Physician Corp. v. Larrison Family Health Center, L.L.C.*, 03-1721, pp. 2-4 (La. App. 3 Cir. 4/7/04), 870 So.2d 575, 577-78.

[105] *Szuts v. Dean Witter*, 931 F.2d 830 (11th Cir. 1991).

arbitrators thereafter failed to do so, they exceeded their powers.[106] Arbitrators should render their award in the form required by the agreement.

Failed to Follow the Law —Judge Posner, writing for the Seventh Circuit Court of Appeals, vacated an award that failed to follow the law.[107] There was a provision in the arbitration agreement requiring the arbitrators to follow the law. As such, the court held that the arbitrator's failure to strictly apply Wisconsin law in deciding the dispute exceeded their contractual powers, necessitating the award's vacatur and remand to permit the arbitrators to make a certain determination of that law's applicability. "The question in our case is ... whether the arbitrator can be directed to apply specific substantive norms and [to be] held to the application. The Supreme Court held in the *Volt* case that parties to a contract may include in the contract's arbitration clause a choice of law provision defining, by reference to a state's arbitration law (provided it does not undermine the federal arbitration law), the rules under which that arbitration will be conducted... Precisely because arbitration is a creature of contract, the arbitrator cannot disregard the lawful directions the parties have given them. If they tell him to apply Wisconsin law, he cannot apply New York law."

Failure to Give Reasons[108] — A Florida U.S. District Court vacated an AAA award when the arbitrators failed to provide reasons for dismissing certain of the underlying claims, despite being requested by the parties to issue a Reasoned Award on all the claims. The arbitrators determined that two of the claims were proven by "the greater weight of the evidence" but summarized that the remaining claims of both parties were denied without offering reasons. The Court found the Panel exceeded its authority by not providing a Reasoned Award. "Because the Panel was authorized only to provide a Reasoned Award, but instead merely announced the winners and losers, the Panel exceeded its powers, and the Award must be vacated."

---

[106] *Western Employers, Inc. v. Jeffries & Co.*, 958 F.2d 285 (9th Cir. 1992), *See also Graniteville Co. v. First Nat'l Trading Co.*, 578 N.Y.S.2d 183 (N.Y. App. Div. 1992) (where panel's interpretation completely ignored the contract, effectively imposing a new contract on the parties, the panel exceeded its powers.

[107] *Edstrom Industries, Inc. v. Companion Life Insurance Company*, 516 F.3d 546 (7th Cir. 2008).

[108] *Cat Charter L.L.C. v. Schurtenberger,* 691 F. Supp. 2d 1339, 2010 WL 662171 (S.D.Fla).

E. Manifest Disregard of the Law, Irrational Awards, Lack of Due Process

1. Standards

The non-statutory grounds for vacatur provide a means to second-guess arbitrator decisions. However, since courts, by and large, do not criticize arbitration awards, parties that challenge awards on these grounds have a more difficult time of succeeding than when they seek vacatur on one of the statutory grounds. And, given the Supreme Court's decision on one of those judicially-created grounds, the burden is even greater. Thus, arbitrators have even less to be concerned about if a party raises these grounds during the course of a case (in memoranda of law or arguments during a hearing).

Manifest disregard of the law has been interpreted in different ways, even by the same court. Most require more than an error or misunderstanding of the law. Some courts now hold that it is no longer a recognized ground for vacatur. For those that recognize the ground, they require the existence of a governing legal principle, which must be well-defined, explicit and clearly applicable. Second, the law must have been obvious and capable of being readily and instantly perceived by an average person qualified to serve as an arbitrator.[109] Then, once those two predicates have been met, the moving party must convince the court that the arbitrators intentionally disregarded that law in rendering their award.

In *Prestige Ford v. Ford Dealer Computer Services*, the U.S. Court of Appeals for the Fifth Circuit said:

> To adopt a less strict standard of judicial review would be to undermine our well-established deference to arbitration as a favored method of settling disputes when agreed to by the parties. Judicial inquiry under the manifest disregard standard is

[109] *Merrill Lynch, Pierce, Fenner & Smith v. Bobker*, 808 F.2d 930 (2d Cir. 1986); *Banco de Seguros del Estado v. Mutual Marine Office*, 344 F.3d 255, 263 (2d Cir. 2003); *Goldman v. Architectural Iron Co.*, 306 F.3d 1214, 1216 (2d Cir. 2002); *DiRussa v. Dean Witter Reynolds*, 121 F.3d 818, 821 (2d Cir. 1997), *cert denied*, 522 U.S. 2049 (1998); *Gov't of India v. Cargill Inc.*, 867 F.2d 130, 133 (2d Cir. 1989); *Hoeft v. MCL Group*, 343 F.3d 57 (2d Cir. 2003); *N.Y. Tel. Co. v. Commc'ns Workers of Amer. Local 1100*, 256 F.3d 89 (2d Cir. 2001); *Hardy v. Walsh Manning Sec., L.L.C.*, 341 F.3d 126 (2d Cir. 2003). The 7th Circuit departed from this standard in *George Watts & Sons v. Tiffany & Co.*, 2001 WL 37622 (7th Cir. 2001), where it held that manifest disregard of the law occurs when the arbitrator's award requires a party to violate the law or doesn't adhere to the legal principles specified in the contract.

therefore extremely limited. The governing law alleged to have been ignored by the arbitrators must be well defined, explicit and clearly applicable.[110]

In *Wallace v. Buttar*, the Second Circuit added the further caution that the doctrine of manifest disregard of the law should be used sparingly. In this important case, the court stated:

> In sum, the Second Circuit does not recognize manifest disregard of the evidence as proper ground for vacating an arbitrator's award. We recognize only the doctrine of manifest disregard of the law, which doctrine holds that an arbitral panel's legal conclusions will be confirmed in all but those instances where there is no colorable justification for a conclusion.[111]

U.S. Supreme Court and Manifest Disregard of Law — In the spring of 2008, the United States Supreme Court, in *Hall St. Assocs. v. Mattel, Inc.*, held that Sections 10 and 11 of the FAA provide the exclusive grounds for vacatur and modification of awards, seeing manifest disregard of the law as a ground *related* to those statutory grounds. The Court did not reject that ground, but stated that it should be considered within the sphere of those statutory grounds.

The parties in *Hall Street* bargained for an arbitration provision requiring a reviewing court to modify, vacate or correct an award if the arbitrators' conclusions of law were erroneous. The Supreme Court rejected Hall Street's arguments and reinforced the statutory scope of judicial review of awards but did not cut off review for manifest disregard of the law. It rejected the idea that manifest disregard embodies a separate, non-statutory ground for judicial review under the FAA. Courts that have followed *Hall Street* have viewed manifest disregard as a judicial *interpretation* of the §10 requirement, rather than as a *separate* standard of review.

The Second Circuit Court of Appeals decided a post-*Hall Street* manifest disregard of the law case in *Stolt-Nielsen SA v. AnimalFeeds International Corp.*[112] In the decision – construing an arbitration clause in an international maritime agreement to permit class arbitration when the

---

[110] *Prestige Ford v. Ford Dealer Computer Servs.*, 324 F.3d 391 (5th Cir. 2003). *See also* cases cited *supra* n. 85.

[111] 378 F.3d 182 (2d Cir. 2004).

[112] 548 F.3d 85, 2008 U.S. App. LEXIS 22838.

clause was silent on that issue – the appeals court ruled that the arbitrators had not manifestly disregarded the law and that while such a judicially-created ground was no longer a *per se* ground to vacate, it was akin to one of the statutory grounds (i.e., where the arbitrators exceeded their powers, or so imperfectly executed them that a mutual, final, and definite award upon the subject matter submitted was not made.§ 10(a)(4).) The Court's three part manifest disregard standard is as follows:

1. Was the law that was allegedly ignored clear and in fact explicitly applicable to the matter before the arbitrators?
2. Was such a clear and plainly applicable law improperly applied, leading to an erroneous outcome?
3. Did the arbitrator know of the law's existence and its applicability to the problem before him?

Since *Hall*, some courts have concluded or suggested that the doctrine simply does not survive.[113] Others think that manifest disregard, re-conceptualized as a judicial gloss on the specific grounds for vacatur enumerated in Section 10 of the FAA, remains a valid ground for vacating arbitration awards.[114] The Second Circuit agrees with those courts that take the latter approach and holds that *Hall* did not abrogate the manifest disregard doctrine altogether.

In *Vaughn v. Leeds, Morelli & Brown, P.C.*,[115] the Second Circuit reviewed the limited statutory grounds for vacatur, starting with the fact that the FAA provides four statutory grounds. "In addition, the Second Circuit recognizes one non-statutory ground: a court may review an arbitral decision for 'manifest disregard of the law,' which we explained, in light of the Supreme Court's recent decision in *Hall Street Associates, L.L.C. v. Mattel, Inc.* is 'severely limited, highly deferential, and confined to those exceedingly rare instances of egregious impropriety.'"[116] "We

---

[113] *See Ramos-Santiago v. United Parcel Service*, 524 F.3d 120, 124 n.3 (1st Cir. 2008) (dicta); *Robert Lewis Rosen Assocs., Ltd. v. Webb*, 566 F.Supp.2d 228, 233 (S.D.N.Y. 2008); *Prime Therapeutics LLC v. Omnicare, Inc.*, 555 F. Supp. 2d 993, 999 (D. Minn. 2008); *Hereford v. D.R. Horton, Inc.*, No. 1070396, 2008 WL 4097594, *5, 2008 Ala. LEXIS 186, *12-*13 (Ala. Sept. 5, 2008).

[114] *See MasTec N. Am., Inc. v. MSE Power Sys.*, No. 1:08-cv-168, 2008 WL 2704912, at *3, 581 F. Supp. 2d 321, 2008 U.S. Dist. LEXIS 52205, at *8-9 (N.D.N.Y. July 8, 2008); *Chase Bank USA, N.A. v. Hale*, 19 Misc. 3d 975, 859 N.Y.S.2d 342, 349 (Sup. Ct. N.Y. County 2008).

[115] 315 Fed. Appx. 327, 2009 U.S. App. LEXIS 5441(2nd Cir. 2009).

[116] *Stolt-Nielsen SA v. AnimalFeeds Intern. Corp.*, 548 F.3d 85, 91, 95 (2d Cir. 2008).

have not recognized any other non-statutory bases for vacatur, and we have specifically rejected a challenge to the rationality of an award."[117]

In deciding whether there has been manifest disregard of the law, a court may not review the weight the arbitrators accorded conflicting evidence; nor may it question their credibility findings.[118]

The difficulty in prevailing on this judicially-created ground for vacatur is well-known among practitioners. Indeed, the Second Circuit stated in a 2003 decision that, since 1960, it had vacated awards in whole or in part for manifest disregard of the law in just four cases out of a total of 48.[119] Thus, over a 40year period, that court had vacated only 8% of arbitration awards on this ground.

Courts that do not recognize the doctrine of manifest disregard of the law often use the "irrational" award or "arbitrary and capricious" standard.[120] It has been said that "a scintilla of evidence"[121] or a "barely colorable" or "rational justification" or a "proper basis" is all that is needed to deny a petition to vacate alleging that an irrational award was rendered. It has also been said that a labor award will be held to be irrational only "if... no judge or group of judges could conceivably have made such a ruling" or if the award was "actually and indisputably without foundation in reason or fact."[122] Similarly, an award could be vacated if based on "reasoning so palpably faulty that no judge ever could conceivably have made such ruling; or, mistakenly based on a crucial assumption that is concededly not fact."[123]

---

[117] *See Porzig v. Dresdner, Kleinwort, Benson, North Am. LLC*, 497 F.3d 133, 139 (2d Cir. 2007).

[118] *Tripi v. Prudential Sec.*, 303 F. Supp. 2d 349 (S.D.N.Y. 2003).

[119] *Hardy*, *supra* n. 85 (*citing Duferco International Steel Trading v. T. Klaveness Shipping A/S*, 333 F.3d 383, 389 (2d Cir. 2003)).

[120] *Raiford v. Merrill Lynch, Pierce, Fenner & Smith*, 903 F.2d 1410 (11th Cir. 1990). In *Brown v. Rauscher Pierce Refsnes*, 994 F.2d 775, 779 (11th Cir. 1993), the court applied the "arbitrary and capricious'' standard in affirming an award that was challenged for failure to apply the formula for damages in the Florida statute for failing to register as a stockbroker. The arbitrators did not apply this law even though the broker was unregistered because, in their opinion, the violation was an administrative oversight and not a willful violation. The Eleventh Circuit upheld the award because at the time of the arbitrators' decision, there was no definitive interpretation of the statute. Accordingly, the award "was not wholly unfounded, arbitrary or capricious."

[121] *Peckerman v. D & D Assocs.*, 567 N.Y.S.2d 416 (N.Y. App. Div. 1991).

[122] *Loveless v. E. Airlines*, 681 F.2d 1272, 1276 (11th Cir. 1982).

[123] *Local 1445, United Food & Commercial Workers v. Stop & Shop Cos.*, 776 F.2d 19 (1st Cir. 1985).

In *In re Goldbrunn*,[124] the arbitration award was challenged in bankruptcy court on the ground that it had no factual basis. Quoting the Eleventh Circuit, the court noted that for an award to be vacated on this ground, there must be "more than an error of law or interpretation. Rather, there must be no ground for the Panel's decision."

In one case where the arbitrators did not provide a rationale for the amount of the award, the court remanded for further explanation, noting that an "incomprehensible" award would clearly be set aside if it were a jury verdict.[125] Few arbitration rules require reasoned awards, although it is my belief that parties in all cases deserve a relatively brief, fact-based decision.

One court has said that an award should not be considered irrational merely because the amount awarded may have involved an element of speculation.[126]

2. Examples (No Manifest Disregard/Awards Upheld)

In *Hoeft v. MCL Group*, the Second Circuit held that the moving party failed to prove that an arbitrator manifestly disregarded the law by refusing to apply generally-accepted accounting procedures, or that GAAP was a sufficiently well-defined standard to constitute the law applicable to the case. The court found that the arbitrator decided the issue he was asked to decide.[127]

In *Goldman v. Architectural Iron Co.*, the Second Circuit also held that manifest disregard of the law had not taken place when the arbitrator decided that a homeowner was acting as a general contractor for the project and not as a consumer. The court found that the question before the arbitrator required application of "an unclear rule of law to a complex factual situation."[128]

The Sixth Circuit, in *Dawahare v. Spencer*, confirmed a $50,000 award in favor of an investor (who sought $600,000 in damages for churning and unsuitable investments) over the investor's claim that the arbitrators disregarded the law of damages in rendering an insufficient award. The court ruled, "This is not a case where one of the parties clearly stated the law and the arbitrators expressly chose not to follow

---

[124] *In re Goldbronn, supra* n. 9.

[125] *Tripi, supra* n. 94.

[126] *Sec. Monitoring Servs. v. Koh*, (Sup. Ct. 1A Part 2, Queens Cty.) *reported in* 205 N.Y.L.J. 56, Mar. 25, 1991.

[127] *Supra* n. 85.

[128] *Supra* n. 85.

it." The court noted that in the arbitration hearing, the investor's attorney had offered several damage theories and told the arbitrators that he would leave it to their wisdom. The court essentially held that the failure to cite any law in support of the investor's damages claim was fatal to arguing that the arbitrators disregarded that law.[129]

In *Josephthal & Co. v Cruttenden Roth Inc.*, the Southern District of New York upheld an award of damages against a claim that the panel, in calculating the award, manifestly disregarded the law. The case involved a dispute between two brokerage firms over the compensation to be earned from a public offering. The arbitrators ruled that the firm holding the shares could sell them as long as the proceeds of sale were placed in an unencumbered, separate escrow account. One of the firms contended that the panel acted in manifest disregard of the law by not measuring the other party's damages at a particular time. In order to establish manifest disregard of the law, the court said that the arbitrators had to have "intentionally ignored what they knew to be obviously applicable and clearly governing law and, further, expressly did so on the record." The court said that it is not at liberty to set aside an award because of an "arguable difference regarding the meaning or applicability of laws urged upon it . . ." Moreover, the court said, "an error in applying the 'wrong' theory of damages is not a manifest disregard of the law." Nor is a miscalculation of damages.[130]

Two Part Test[131] — In this raiding case, Wachovia alleged that four of its former financial advisors employees misappropriated confidential and proprietary information and solicited current Wachovia customers and employees to join their new firm. Both sides sought attorney's fees, although Wachovia thereafter argued that under the South Carolina Arbitration Act, neither party was entitled to such fees. The Panel issued an award in which it denied all of Wachovia's claims and awarded the former employees $15,080.67 in treble damages on their Wage Act claims and $1,111,553.85 for attorneys' fees under the South Carolina Frivolous Civil Proceedings Act. Wachovia argued that such an award was in manifest disregard of the law. In confirming the Award, the court

---

[129] 201 F.3d 666 (6th Cir. 2000), *cert denied* (Oct. 2, 2000).

[130] 177 F. Supp. 2d 232 (S.D.N.Y. 2001). *See also Deiulemar Compania di Navigazione v. Transocean Coal Co.*, 2004 WL 2721072 (S.D.N.Y. Nov. 30, 2004) (arbitrators did not manifestly disregard the law by failing to deduct amounts earned in mitigation of damages); *Cole Publ'g Co. v. Wiley & Sons*, 1994 U.S. Dist. LEXIS 13786 (S.D.N.Y. 1994).

[131] *Wachovia Securities, LLC v. Frank J. Brand, II*, 671 F.3d 472 (4th Cir. 2012).

held: "In *Long John Silver's*,[132] we adopted a two-part test that a party must meet in order for a reviewing court to vacate for manifest disregard: (1) the applicable legal principle is clearly defined and not subject to reasonable debate; and (2) the arbitrator refused to heed that legal principle. We see no reason to depart from our two-part test which has for decades guaranteed that review for manifest disregard not grow into the kind of probing merits review that would undermine the efficiency of arbitration. In this case, we find that whether the Panel erred by not applying the FCPA's procedural requirements is a question that was itself not clearly defined and was certainly subject to debate. Accordingly, we cannot hold that the arbitrators manifestly disregarded the law when they awarded Appellees $1.1 million in attorneys' fees and costs under the FCPA."

Second Circuit Requirements[133] — The New York Southern District Court had vacated an award on the ground that the arbitrators had acted in "manifest disregard of the law" by improperly applying Conn. Gen. Stat. § 20-325a(b), which requires real estate brokers to meet certain statutory prerequisites before commencing an action to recover a commission.[134] The Second Circuit Court of Appeals reversed the decision and upheld the award, stating that it is necessary to impose the following three requirements for an Award to be in manifest disregard of the law: First – "We must consider whether the law that was allegedly ignored was clear," as "[a]n arbitrator obviously cannot be said to disregard a law that is unclear or not clearly applicable. Second – We must find that the arbitrators did in fact err in their application of the law and that the outcome reached was erroneous. "Even where explanation for an award is... non-existent, we will confirm it if a justifiable ground for the decision can be inferred from the facts of the case. Third – We must find that the arbitrators knew of the law's existence and its applicability to the problem before them."

3. Examples (Manifest Disregard/Awards Vacated)

In an employment discrimination case, a court held that the arbitrators manifestly disregarded the law by failing to grant attorney's

[132] 514 F.3d at 349.

[133] *Sotheby's Int'l Realty, Inc. v. Relocation Group, LLC*, 2015 U.S. App. LEXIS 81 (2d Cir. Jan. 2015).

[134] *See Sotheby's Int'l Realty, Inc. v. Relocation Grp., LLC*, 987 F. Supp. 2d 157, 168-69 (D. Conn. 2013).

fees to the prevailing party in a dispute under the Age Discrimination in Employment Act.[135]

In *Hardy v. Walsh Manning*, in which I represented the victorious Mr. Hardy in a "market manipulation" arbitration, the Second Circuit held that the standard for vacating an award based on manifest disregard of the law gives extreme deference to arbitrators. In this case, however, the court found the standard for demonstrating manifest disregard was shown, "at least to the extent of requiring a remand" on the issue of the panel's ruling on derivative liability against an individual respondent.[136] And when ordered by the appellate court to reconsider their earlier reasoned award, the arbitrators' more articulate explanation in a re-written award was later confirmed by a federal district court.

In this NASD case, Mr. Hardy, a British resident, alleged that the brokerage firm and Skelly, its president, had engaged in stock manipulation with respect to Hardy's account. The arbitration panel found that the brokerage firm and its president were jointly and severally liable "based upon the principle of *respondeat superior* liability." The Second Circuit held that it is "certainly possible to find that the panel disregarded the principles of *respondeat superior*, the very principles that it purported to apply." The panel was made aware during the hearing that an individual could not be held derivatively liable for the acts of another employee. The appeals court found no reading of the facts by which Skelly could be held liable on *respondeat superior* grounds. Since the award stated no other basis for liability, the court felt compelled to order a remand so that the arbitrators could state whether there had been enough evidence to hold Skelly liable, but not on *respondeat superior* grounds. On remand, the award was confirmed and, thereafter, a federal jury convicted Skelly of securities fraud involving the same securities in the *Hardy* arbitration.

The *Hardy* court distinguished the case before it from *Westerbeke Corp. v. Diahatsu Motor Co.*,[137] where it held that an award could not be vacated because the panel did not come up with the "optimal construction" of the contract. The court said it was enough that the facts,

---

[135] In a discrimination case, the claimant's employment agreement excised attorneys' fees and punitive damages as remedies, although they were requested in arbitration. The court found that since the claimant received an award on the Title VII gender and race discrimination claims, he was also entitled to attorney's fees as a prevailing party. *DeGaetano v. Smith Barney*, 983 F. Supp. 459 (S.D.N.Y. 1997).

[136] *Supra* n. 85.

[137] 304 F.3d 200 (2d Cir. 2002).

as determined by the arbitrators, supported their interpretation. Here, by contrast, there were no facts set forth in the award to support the conclusion that Skelly was liable under *respondeat superior*.

The *Hardy* court also distinguished *GMS Group v. Benderson*,[138] where the parties asserted various theories of recovery but the arbitrators issued no written opinion in making the award. In that situation, the Second Circuit said that if a ground for the award can be inferred from the facts, the award should be upheld. Thus, if one of the theories that were argued would support the award or could have formed the basis for the award, it did not matter that other theories might not be a basis for liability. In the *Hardy* case, the appeals court declined to infer an alternate theory of liability where the panel had already supplied one. Even though the award contained no legal reasoning, it stated a legal conclusion; one that the court found contained "a fundamental mistake of law." Since the court was reluctant to invalidate the award, it exercised its authority to remand the case to the arbitration panel to seek a clarification of the panel's intent in making the award.

In another NASD case, an intermediate appeals court in New York vacated an award when it found that the arbitrator refused to consider the law when she said on the record that she would not read relevant cases or statutory authority and placed, in the court's phrase, a "bizarre limitation" on the number of decisions the parties could cite in their post-hearing briefs, without giving any explanation. The court found this conduct outrageous. "The arbitration panel, at a minimum, must have at least considered the law which it erroneously applied. The panel not only acted irrationally, but also exhibited a manifest disregard for well-established public policy."[139]

In yet another NASD arbitration, a New York appeals court held that a $25 million punitive damages award was excessive, irrational and in manifest disregard of the rule of proportionality, of which the arbitrators were specifically advised. The court vacated the award and remanded the case to the arbitrators for reconsideration of the law of proportionality. On remand, the arbitrators again awarded $25 million in punitive damages because the firm and its president "demonstrated reprehensible conduct . . . [and] conducted a horrible campaign of deception, defamation and

---

[138] 326 F.3d 75 (2d Cir. 2003).

[139] In re *Arbitration Between UBS Warburg LLC and Auerbach, Pollack & Richardson*, 744 N.Y.S.2d 364 (N.Y. App. Div. 2002).

persecution of claimant. . . ." Thereafter, a New York trial court vacated that award and remanded it before a brand new panel.[140]

What we learn from this exercise in frustration is this: if a court orders arbitrators to reconsider their award and presents them with a standard by which to render their award, arbitrators should adhere to that standard.

Some parties have argued, unsuccessfully, that awards should be vacated because they were in manifest disregard of statutes of limitations. For example, certain former "licensed individuals" of a defunct brokerage firm sought to nullify an award against them based, in part, on the ground that the investor's claims were time barred under the Securities Exchange Act of 1934 and New York law. The movants argued that the arbitrators acted in manifest disregard of the law in hearing the case. Concluding that the movants had failed to meet "the high standard" of proof for invalidating an award based on manifest disregard of the law, the Southern District of New York gave the arbitrators the benefit of the doubt (which courts generally do). It stated, "The Panel heard [the licensed individuals'] motion to dismiss the claim on the basis of the statute of limitations, and denied such claim, which indicates to this Court that the claim was fully and fairly considered."[141]

In another case, the Third Circuit held that a $6 million cash bond award was irrational in light of the maximum $1.5 million liability under the agreement between the parties. "An award may not stand if it does not meet the test of fundamental rationality," the court said.[142]

In a New York case, the arbitrators absolved the primary wrongdoer—the securities trader—but found his employer liable. The intermediate appeals court found that this award was "inherently inconsistent," since the "gravamen of [the investor's] claim against [the employer] was predicated upon [the trader's] conduct." The court said that where there is "no independent basis for finding [the employer brokerage firm] solely liable for over a million dollars in damages . . . the award must be set aside as irrational."[143]

Arbitrators walk a fine line in explaining the basis for their awards. The cases discussed here certainly indicate that great care should be taken when imposing liability on a derivative basis, so be sure that there is a legal basis for the award. However, since it is my belief that parties

---

[140] *Sawtelle v. Waddell & Reed*, 754 N.Y.S.2d 264 (N.Y. App. Div. 2003).
[141] *Decicco v. Columbo*, 234 F. Supp. 2d 320 (S.D.N.Y. 2002).
[142] *Swift Indus. v. Botany Indus.*, 466 F.2d 1125, 1131 (3d Cir. 1972).
[143] *Spear Leeds & Kellogg v. Bullseye Sec.*, 738 N.Y.S.2d 27 (N.Y. App. Div. 2002).

have a right to know how arbitrators came to their decisions, I encourage my colleagues to have the courage of their convictions and write so-called Reasoned Awards (referred to by FINRA as Explained Awards) as long as they are sensitive to the possible misinterpretation of their words.

Applying the Wrong State's Statute[144] — After brokerage firm Raymond James terminated its relationship with Mr. Fenyk, a FINRA Panel awarded the broker $600,000 in back pay and $36,042 in attorney's fees and costs; the firm filed a motion to vacate. When the firm (based in Florida) discovered that the broker (based in Vermont) was abusing alcohol, it concluded it could not adequately supervise him and therefore terminated him, prompting the broker to file an arbitration alleging that the firm retaliated against him because of his sexual orientation and his disability as an alcoholic in violation of the Vermont Fair Employment Practices Act. Applying a choice of law clause in the contract the parties signed, the arbitrators determined that Florida law governed the proceeding, stating that it considered the pleadings, evidence and testimony in issuing its award, but, as is usually the case, it provided no reasoning. The arbitrators concluded that Florida law governed the case and under Florida law, the contract claim was barred by that state's one-year statute of limitation. *Why Vacatur?* "The arbitrators ignored that statute and somehow construed Florida law to find a violation of a Vermont statute—a statute which, given the governing law, was wholly inapplicable to the case. Awarding damages to a plaintiff who has pled no claims under the applicable law plainly transgressed the limits of the arbitrators' power. For this reason, the award must be vacated."

Settlement Disregarded by Arbitrator[145] — In this rare instance of an award vacatur on the ground of manifest disregard, a lower New York state court and an appeals court did so because the arbitrators had been provided with a settlement by the parties and nevertheless granted an award in Claimant's favor. The arbitrators manifestly disregarded the law by failing to enforce the settlement that respondent and petitioner entered into. Petitioners provided the relevant law regarding the enforcement of settlement agreements in their motions to enforce the agreement, but the arbitrators ignored the law and denied the motions without explanation.

---

[144] *Raymond James Financial Services, Inc. v. Robert Michael Fenyk*, 2014 U.S. Dist. LEXIS 15219 (D. Mass. Feb. 6, 2014).

[145] *Matter of Citigroup Global Mkts., Inc. v Fiorilla,* 2015 NY Slip Op 03056 (App. Div., 1st Dept. April 9, 2015).

F. Public Policy

1. Standard

Courts may be asked to determine whether an award is contrary to a well-defined and dominant public policy. When they do, courts hold that the policy must be ascertainable by reference to positive law. General notions of public policy or considerations of supposed public interest are not sufficient and the violation of public policy must be clearly shown.[146]

One question a court will ask is this: Would enforcement of the award clearly violate a public policy?[147] Like manifest disregard of the law, it is another way of challenging an award a party does not like. For example, public policy has been used to challenge labor awards that reinstate employees in safety sensitive positions when they were discharged for using drugs or drinking in the workplace.[148] Because cases on this subject do not address arbitrator management issues, this chapter does not review specific cases. However, these cases teach us that arbitrators should at least consider public policy arguments in rendering their awards.

G. Lack of Due Process

1. Standard

This ground for vacatur is similar to misconduct that adversely affects the parties' rights to a fair hearing. To afford due process, arbitration hearings have to provide: (1) adequate or reasonable notice; (2) a hearing before an impartial decision maker; (3) the opportunity to present evidence

---

[146] *United Paperworks Int'l Union v. Misco*, 484 U.S. 29 (1987); *W.R. Grace & Co. v. Local Union 759*, 461 U.S. 757 (1983); *PaineWebber v. Agron*, 49 F.3d 347 (8th Cir, 1995); *Exxon Shipping Co. v. Exxon Seamen's Union*, 11 F.3d 1189 (3d Cir. 1993); *Maul v. Aznavoorian*, 1997 U.S. Dist. LEXIS 153, at *7 (N.D. Cal. Jan. 9, 1997).

[147] *Valentino v. Smith*, Fed. Sec. L. Rep. (CCH) ¶ 97,256, at 95,150 (W.D. Okla. Sept. 30, 1992). For cases involving public policy, see *Sea Dragon, Inc. v. Gebr. Van Weelde Scheepvaartkantoor B.V.*, 574 F. Supp. 369 (S.D.N.Y. 1983) (award violated public policy inherent in comity between courts); *Manhattan & Bronx Surface Transit v. Transport Workers Union*, 582 N.Y.S.2d 227 (N.Y. App. Div. 1992), *app. denied*, 588 N.Y.S.2d 823 (1992) (award violated public policy in broad statutory mandate to run a safe and efficient transit system).

[148] *Delta Air Lines v. Airline Pilots Ass'n*, 861 F.2d 665 (11th Cir. 1988), *cert. denied*, 493 U.S. 871 (1989) (award reinstating a pilot who had flown while drunk violated public policy); *Coast Indus. Workers Union v. Exxon Co., USA*, 991 F.2d 244 (5th Cir. 1993) (award reinstating employee to a safety-sensitive position violated public policy where employee repeatedly violated the company's drug abuse policy).

and witnesses who will testify under oath (*i.e.*, a full and fair opportunity to be heard); and, (4) judicial review. In addition, "due process" requires the parties to have representation, whether it is by an attorney or other representative. Because the due process standard is a minimal one, courts rarely find that a "lack of due process" took place in arbitration.

In one NASD case, the award was upheld despite the fact that an NASD representative was not present at the hearing and a recording of the hearing was not made, as required (with regard to the latter point) by the NASD Code of Arbitration Procedure. The parties agreed that at the hearing they had been able to present all witnesses and introduce all exhibits they deemed appropriate and relevant. They had not requested a continuance to secure the presence of a court reporter or recording equipment. Still, the losing party argued that it had been denied due process because no recording was made of the hearing. However, because that party acquiesced to the lack of a court reporter or recording equipment and proceeded with the hearing, the court ruled that he waived his right to object to this procedural defect.[149]

2. Examples (Due Process/Awards Upheld)

The New York Court of Appeals upheld an award in an NASD arbitration against a broker who never received actual notice of the arbitration proceeding because the notice was sent by certified mail to the broker's former brokerage firm, which he had recently left. The hearing was conducted in the broker's absence and resulted in a substantial award in favor of the customer. New York's highest court held that there was no due process violation. It stated:

> [D]ue process does not require actual receipt of notice before a person's liberty or property interests may be adjudicated. It is sufficient that the means selected for providing notice was reasonably calculated, under all the circumstances, to apprise interested parties of the pendency of the action and afford them an opportunity to present their objections. The notice procedure chosen need not eliminate all risk that notice might not actually reach the affected party. Mailed notice may suffice.[150]

---

[149] *Valentino, supra* n. 117.

[150] *Beckman v. Greentree Sec.*, 663 N.E.2d 886 (N.Y. 1996).

In another case, a judge in the Southern District of New York held that the broker's failure to amend his Form U-4 [Uniform Employment Application] to provide for a change of permanent address was not a defense to his claim of insufficient notice of the ongoing arbitration, which was held in his absence. He had provided a relative's address, but that relative, apparently, did not forward his mail or advise him of the hearings.[151]

3. Examples (Due Process/Awards Vacated)

Only a small number of cases have so offended the courts that they vacated awards on this ground. A New York trial court vacated a net $2.1 million award against Anchor Construction based on a due process challenge that the arbitrator precluded Anchor from active participation in two days of hearings after it was unable to pay its half of the arbitrators' fees. In all, 12 witnesses testified during seven days of hearings, and 137 exhibits were presented. Both parties attended the first five days of hearings, but Anchor did not attend the subsequent ones because the arbitrators severely restricted its participation for the balance of the case. For example, it was not permitted to cross-examine the other party's witnesses or present a case of its own. Anchor's attorney quit and no company representative appeared on the remaining hearing days. New York statutory law states that parties in arbitration are entitled to be heard, present evidence and cross-examine witnesses. Thus, the court had no problem concluding that Anchor had been denied its statutory right to participate, as well as its right to counsel. As a result, the court vacated the award.[152]

Due Process Denied — FINRA Arbitration Rule 10303(a) provides that "Any dispute, claim or controversy ... shall require a hearing unless all parties waive such hearing in writing and request that the matter be resolved solely upon the pleadings and documentary evidence." A Louisiana appellate court vacated an award because, following a pre-hearing telephonic conference and without an evidentiary hearing (now required under the new arbitration Code), the arbitrators dismissed the customer's claims on statute of limitations grounds.[153] The court concluded that due process had not been served. "Although arbitration proceedings are not held to the same strict rules as are the courts,

[151] *Marsillo v. Geniton*, 2004 WL 1207925 (S.D.N.Y. June 2004).
[152] *Coty, Inc. v. Anchor Constr.*, 776 N.Y.S.2d 795 (N.Y. App. Div. 2004).
[153] *Pennington v. CUNA Brokerage Securities, Inc.*, 2008 La. App. Unpub. LEXIS 483.

nonetheless, an arbitrator must be vigilant in affording basic due process requirements. The first and foremost requirement is the opportunity to present evidence and to be heard."

V. Conclusion

Arbitrators should be emboldened by the knowledge that since a losing party's challenge to their award will usually fail, they should promptly establish and thereafter maintain control of the case to its conclusion.

As long as arbitrators (1) provide a fundamentally fair hearing to all parties, (2) do not engage in *ex parte* communications with a party or party representative, (3) do not refuse to permit a party to cross-examine witnesses, (4) give each party an opportunity to complete his or her presentation of proof (even if only at a hearing on a dispositive motion to dismiss), (5) decide only the issues set forth in the pleadings, (6) decide all of the issues submitted, (7) disclose information about themselves that satisfy their obligation to be impartial, (8) have a reasonable basis for the denial of a request to adjourn or the refusal to admit certain evidence; and, (9) as long as the award is (a) not completely irrational, (b) contrary to a well-defined and dominant public policy or (c) lacking a factual basis, there is little to fear from the courts that the award will be vacated.

So, go ahead, take control of the process. The parties will appreciate the fact that, with a firm hand, you are expeditiously and fairly hearing their dispute and rendering your award.

CHAPTER 20

ATTORNEY ARBITRATORS SHOULD RESEARCH LAW: PERMISSION OF THE PARTIES TO DO SO IS NOT REQUIRED

*M. Ross Shulmister**

I. Introduction

An article recently published in the New York State Bar Association Journal (NYSBAJ), May 2013, is titled, "Can an Arbitrator Conduct Independent Legal Research? If Not, Why Not?" The author says "no" and explains why he believes he is correct.

The NYSBAJ article may not have been vetted, because the grounds for the article's conclusions are not supported by the authorities quoted. Indeed, in most cases, arbitrators (at least those who are attorneys) are not only permitted to conduct independent research of the law, but are actually under at least a moral obligation to do so, even if the parties argue their positions on what the law is.

As a preliminary caveat, it is clear in both judicial and non-judicial fora that the decision maker is not permitted to independently research facts. As discussed below, that prohibition generally extends to specialized knowledge that might have been provided by an expert witness.

II. Understanding Opinions in Appellate Cases

This discussion will analyze appellate case opinions, so it may be helpful to non-attorney arbitrators to understand how case decisions are properly cited, analyzed, and interpreted by lawyers and judges.

* M. Ross Shulmister is a retired USAF officer, who has been a Florida attorney for more than 40 years, also serving as an AAA arbitrator for more than 30 years. He serves on AAA's Commercial, Construction, and Consumer panels. He is also certified as a state court arbitrator by the Fla. Supreme Court, serving in the 17th Circuit (Ft. Lauderdale area).

First, cases are referred to by the names of the principal parties, the first name being the name of the first appellant (party appealing), and the second name is the name of the first appellee (party defending the appeal). Those references are called "the style" of the case, and it is normally italicized (*i.e.*, *Smith v. Jones*). That is followed by "the citation", which is the name of the court reporter (the book containing opinions), with two numbers: the volume and the starting page, followed in parentheses by the name of the court and the year of publication. You can normally search the Internet for a case using just the style, or using the citation (*i.e.*, 123 F.2d 456—volume 123 of the Federal Reporter, 2nd series, beginning at page 456). If you see a second page number, that number refers to the page in the opinion where you can find a specific reference. Armed with that skill, you should be able to find a case and read it for yourself.

In discussions about a case, it is normal to provide full information about a style and citation. Subsequent references to that case usually use the name or portion of the name of the appellant (*i.e.*, *Smith*). "*Ibid*" or "*Id.*" refers to the most recent previous reference or citation.

In order to understand what legal propositions are contained in an opinion, it is sometimes necessary to understand the context in which the decision is rendered, and that is normally explained in the decisions.

Appellate decisions are normally analyzed based on (i) the legal issues decided in the opinion, (ii) the HOLDING (which is the crux of the decision), and (iii) the rationale. It's also important to understand that sometimes a judge who writes a decision can go off on a tangent and discuss matters which are not essential to the Court's decisions. Those discussions are called "*obiter dicta*" or "*dicta*" for short. HOLDINGS and the rationale for holdings has precedential value—that is, courts try to follow established law so that a later panel of judges, and often other courts, try to make decisions consistent with existing HOLDINGS and the rationale for these HOLDINGS.

Dicta, on the other hand, may persuade a court to agree with the *dicta*, but *dicta* is not considered to be binding, and is often disregarded.

One must be careful when reading analyses of cases, because some writers will say a court "*HELD*" something, when in fact the writers are referring to *dicta*.

III. Arbitrators Are Expected to Follow the Law

That's a plain and simple statement, often stated in appellate decisions on arbitration.

One court made a slightly different statement, in *Montes v. Shearson Lehman Brothers*, 128 F.3d 1456, 1461 (11th Cir. 1997). That Court said, "Arbitrators are expected to follow the law in the absence of a valid and legal agreement not to do so." That seems to suggest that the parties can agree that the law doesn't apply.

Or can they? "When parties decide to arbitrate a statutory claim, they do not give up substantive rights—they merely decide to resolve issues 'in an arbitral, rather than a judicial, forum.'" *Gilber v. Interstate/Johnson Lane Corp.*, 500 U.S. 20, 26, 111 S.Ct. 1647, 1652, 114 L.Ed.2d 26 (1991).

In the *Montes* case, there was no agreement to not follow the law. That statement was therefore partially a HOLDING and partially *dicta*. You would properly say that the court HELD that "Arbitrators are expected to follow the law", and since there was no issue about an agreement to not follow the law, the implication that parties could agree not to follow the law was *dicta*.

Steelworkers v. Warrior & Gulf Navigation Co., 363 U.S. 574 (1960), a US Supreme Court case more than a half century old, was a case in which the issue was whether or not a labor union could compel management to arbitrate a grievance. Note that legal research done by an arbitrator was never an issue. Following the law was an issue.

The Court stated that "The labor arbitrator's source of law is not confined to the express provisions of the contract, as the industrial common law—the practices of the industry and the shop—is equally part of the collective bargaining agreement, although not expressed in it."[1]

It is common in arbitration agreements for the parties to identify what law applies, and normally that is the law of a particular state or other forum.

It appears there is no case involving an arbitration agreement that contained a provision that a law, otherwise applicable, shall not apply. So there is no legal precedent for how to deal with a situation where the parties agree the law shall not apply.

In the absence of legal precedent, and since arbitration is a creature of contract, it would seem that an arbitrator faced with such an

[1] *Steelworkers v. Warrior & Gulf Navigation Co.*, 363 U.S. 574, 581-82 (1960).

agreement would defer to the wishes of the parties, at least until some appellate court opines otherwise.

IV. Parties Are Expected to Brief Non-Lawyer Arbitrators on the Law

Wallace v. Buttar, 378 F.3d 182 (2d Cir. 2004) was a securities case, involving more than a million dollars in damages. Dr. Buttar was talked into making substantial investments in two companies and a bridge loan to another.

The investment company (Montrose Capital Management) filed for bankruptcy, blocking any suit against the company, but the automatic bankruptcy stay did not apply to cases involving individuals (including Wallace) who worked for Montrose. Wallace and other parties to the arbitration were alleged to be "control parties" under North Carolina law, and, under North Carolina law, potentially liable for damages.

An agreement, signed by the Buttars, provided for arbitration of disputes by the National Association of Securities Dealers (NASD), under their rules. The dispute was assigned by the NASD to a panel of three business executives as arbitrators, none of whom were attorneys.

In the arbitration, the claimants (the Buttars) presented evidence that the appellants were "control persons" under North Carolina law, and briefed their position. Respondents presented little evidence, and (according to the 2d Cir. *Wallace* Opinion) Respondents' closing brief was mostly invectives which did not address state law.

The arbitration panel found in favor of the Buttars, awarding $1,064,543 in compensatory damages, $127,629 in prejudgment interest, and $604,805 in punitive damages because of fraud. The procedural history is set forth in the opinion, and is irrelevant to this analysis, but in essence the "control persons" asked the Federal District Court in New York to vacate the arbitration award, because the arbitrators hadn't followed North Carolina law.

The Federal District Court (SDNY) "*HELD* that the Panel manifestly disregarded the law and the evidence" noting (erroneously) that "the Second Circuit recognizes [statutory grounds plus] two additional bases for vacating arbitration awards: manifest disregard of the law and manifest disregard of the facts."[2] Those two "manifest disregard"

---

[2] *Id.* at 188.

grounds are important to understand. The Federal District Court vacated the arbitral award, and an appeal was taken.

Appeals from New York federal district courts go to the Second Circuit Court of Appeals. The Second Circuit reviewed the lower tribunal (the District Court's decision) *de novo* (as if the circuit court had not made its decision). The 2nd Circuit said that a challenge to an arbitral award is not an occasion for a district court to conduct its own *de novo* review of that arbitral award (by reviewing the arbitration record), but that the challenger "bears the heavy burden of showing that the award falls within a very narrow set of circumstances delineated by statute and case law."[3] The Second Circuit rejected the "manifest disregard of the facts" ground, and listed the elements of Manifest Disregard (of the law):

1. The arbitrators knew of a governing legal principle yet refused to apply it or ignored it altogether; and
2. The law ignored by the arbitrators was well defined, explicit, and clearly applicable to the case.

The Second Circuit stated: "In sum, a court reviewing an arbitral award cannot presume that the arbitrator is capable of understanding and applying legal principles with the sophistication of a highly skilled attorney. Indeed, this is so far from being the case that an arbitrator 'under the test of manifest disregard is **ordinarily** assumed to be a blank slate unless educated in the law by the parties.'"[4] The opinion went on to state, "counsel forego their obligation to educate arbitral panels as to governing legal principles at their great peril."[5]

In a footnote, the court stated, "until such time as all arbitrators are required to be attorneys, an arbitrator does not have 'a duty [under the FAA] to ascertain the legal principles that govern a particular claim through … independent legal research.'"[6]

So what does that all mean? That opinion seems to select attorneys for special treatment. Attorneys are, after all, educated in the law. The *Wallace* decision merely excuses **non-lawyers** from a **duty** to research the law, but not a duty to follow the law (at least to the extent they know or understand what the law is).

---

[3] *Id.* at 189.
[4] *Id.* at 190 (emphasis added).
[5] *Id.*
[6] *Id.*

The most important point for attorneys representing parties in an arbitration is that they are expected to explain the law (from their perspective) to non-lawyer arbitrators, and are probably well advised to also argue their view of the law to attorney arbitrators.

V. Manifest Disregard of the Law

Over the past half century, courts have developed a respect for the way arbitrators do their jobs. This is the result of the evolution of judicial attitudes toward the arbitration process. Today, arbitral awards are given great deference by courts. *See Steelworkers*, *supra*, from over 50 years ago, when the US Supreme Court considered labor arbitration as protected while contract arbitration was viewed with suspicion.

Congress enacted four statutory grounds for vacating arbitral awards under the Federal Arbitration Act, and those basically involve fraud and misconduct.

Some courts feel that there should be at least some review of arbitral awards where the arbitrator's award is, legally speaking, off the wall. So they created a new ground, Manifest Disregard of the Law. It's a judicially-created ground for vacating an arbitration award—a ground, although currently controversial, that has been rejected in only two federal circuits (the 5th and the 11th). *Montes v. Shearson Lehman Bros., Inc.*, 128 F.3d 1456, 1460 (11th Cir.1997).

The elements required to prove Manifest Disregard of the Law are (1) there was clear legal authority explicitly applicable to the matter before the arbitrator(s); (2) if that legal authority had been properly applied, the outcome would have been different; and (3) the arbitrator(s) had actual knowledge of the law and intentionally did not apply it.

But how do arbitrators get that actual knowledge? No decision involving Manifest Disregard addresses the source of the arbitrators' knowledge of the law. Until it does, you should assume the source doesn't matter. For the courts, an arbitrator has knowledge of the law when the parties call it to the arbitrator's attention (such as in a legal brief), or the arbitrator mentions it in his decision (or an order or other writing).

VI. Researching Facts

For the most part, it is universally understood that arbitrators are prohibited from independently researching facts bearing on a particular case. The same is true of judges.

But what about researching knowledge? Judges are allowed to take "judicial notice" of some kinds of facts. Federal Rule of Evidence 201 allows judges to take judicial notice of facts that are not subject to reasonable dispute, because it is either (1) generally known within the territorial jurisdiction of the trial court, or (2) capable of accurate and ready determination by resort to sources whose accuracy cannot reasonably be questioned. They are "universally known". Like what? Examples of facts susceptible to judicial notice are such things as "Atlanta is the capitol seat of Fulton County, Georgia", "September 13, 2013 occurred on a Friday", and "common table salt consists of sodium and chlorine".

Whether a particular address is located within a particular city, however, may or may not be susceptible of judicial notice. In *People v. Strook*, 347 Ill. 460, 179 N.E. 821 (1932), Illinois Supreme Court said that the trial court could not take judicial notice that a crime committed at 7956 South Chicago Avenue was committed in Cook County (Chicago is in Cook County). But some 32 years later the Illinois Supreme Court took judicial notice that it was a local practice not to mention the city when referring to local addresses, and since the witness was in Chicago, his testimony that the crime occurred at 8900 South Anthony Avenue was sufficient for the trial court to take judicial notice that the crime was committed in Cook County. *People v. Pride*, 16 Ill.2d 82, 156 N.E.2d 551 (1951).

A disputed fact normally cannot be resolved by judicial notice. The parties must present evidence to support the existence or non-existence of a fact.

A Florida court recently vacated an arbitral award because the arbitrator researched facts on the Internet. In *Quesada v. City of Tampa*, 96 So.3d 924 (Fla. 2d DCA 2012), there was a claim that an employee had tested positive for Nandrolone or a related steroid, and the defense presented testimony that the employee had consumed 17-HD and it produced the same test results as Nandrolone. The arbitrator checked the website of the company that produced and marketed 17-HD, and found that the company stated 17-HD was just a number of herbs and would not have produced any drug test results. The arbitrator found the defense was not based on fact, and ruled in favor of the City.

Florida's Second District Court of Appeals vacated the award, stating that "arbitration panels should not, in the course of their deliberations, go outside the evidence presented to them."[7] It's difficult to characterize the kind of research done by that arbitrator taking judicial notice. This was really just a case where the City's expert failed to do his homework.

Taking judicial notice is discretionary, whether or not a party requests it, but is mandatory if a party requests judicial notice and supplies the judge with the necessary information.

As for arbitrators, Rules of Evidence are an effort to afford due process. Arbitrators are not required to strictly adhere to rules of evidence, and generally accept whatever evidence is presented. Does that mean that arbitrators are allowed or prohibited from taking judicial notice? This author found no federal case addressing the point.

The question of arbitrators taking judicial notice of facts is open, pending an appellate decision on the subject. It may nevertheless be wise for arbitrators to be very cautious about doing so, under penalty of having a court treat it as a prohibited independent research of facts—unless, of course, those "facts" are "so universally known that they are not susceptible to dispute."

VII. Judicial Notice of Law

The same Federal Rule of Evidence (201) allows judges to take judicial notice of law, including decisional law and statutory law. There is NO FEDERAL CASE which prohibits an arbitrator from accepting decisional or statutory law as existing and pertinent to his/her case.

Is that judicial notice? In Federal Courts, every court is bound by decisions of superior courts in their jurisdictional chain, under the well established principle of *stare decisis*. A district court is bound by the decisions of its circuit court of appeals, and all courts are bound by decisions of the US Supreme Court. Thus there is no need for a federal court to take judicial notice of a decision from a superior court.

While the same principle is generally true throughout the United States, many states, such as Florida, have laws which require their courts to take judicial notice of superior court decisions, and of federal decisions which bind that state. *E.g.*, §90.201, FLORIDA STATUTES.

---

[7] *Id.* at 926.

The safest course for arbitrators is to follow the law of their respective jurisdictions (or of the jurisdiction which governs the case they are hearing). In the absence of controlling law, the law of another jurisdiction may be interesting, and may be treated as *dicta*—nice to know with no obligation to follow it or ignore it. The law of California does not control the law of South Carolina.

VIII. Does Silence in the Arbitration Agreement (on Arbitrators' Authority to Conduct Legal Research) Prohibit Legal Research?

The NYSBAJ article (referred to in the beginning of this article) claims that silence about an arbitrator's authority to conduct independent research means there is no such authority. For this proposition, that article cites *First Options of Chicago, Inc. v. Kaplan*, 514 U.S. 938 (1995).

In order to understand whether or not that proposition is accurate, one must analyze the case upon which it relies.

First Options involved a firm which cleared stock trades, and three investors: Kaplan, his wife, and his solely-owned investment company. As a result of the 1987 stock market crash, the three investors lost substantial sums. First Options began to liquidate pledged assets, and demanded that the Kaplans personally pay deficiencies. There were four workout agreements, but only one (the one with the investment company) contained an arbitration provision. The arbitrators ruled they also had jurisdiction over the individuals, and issued an award which was confirmed by the Federal District Court.

The Third Circuit Court of Appeals reversed, and the US Supreme Court took *certiorari*[8] jurisdiction to decide (1) whether courts or arbitrators should decide whether arbitrators have jurisdiction of **merits** of any particular dispute (*i.e.*, arbitrability), and (2) if courts can review arbitrators' decision on jurisdiction, does an appeals court review that decision *de novo*, or apply an abuse of discretion standard.[9] The US Supreme Court decided the two issues separately, and explained its decisions (HOLDINGS) separately.

Based on *First Options*, the NYSBAJ article claims that in cases involving arbitrability, when silence comes into play, a two-step analysis

[8] The nature of jurisdiction (*certiorari*) is largely significant to judges and lawyers—it has little meaning for non-lawyers.

[9] *Steelworkers*, 363 U.S. 574, 940-41.

is required before a power can be implied: (1) is the power reserved by law for the courts; and (2) there must be clear and convincing evidence that the parties intended that an arbitrator have a power.

Well, that's not exactly what *First Options* says. It really says that when it comes to the question of who rules on arbitrability, if there is silence or ambiguity the courts "should not assume that the parties agreed to arbitrate unless there is clear and unmistakable evidence that they did so."[10] Simply, without clear and unmistakable evidence of an agreement to arbitrate, an arbitrator has no power to arbitrate.

But the NYSBAJ article tries to extend that analysis to all arbitrator authority. Contrary to the NYSBAJ article's premise, the US Supreme Court went on to say, "... the law treats silence or ambiguity about the question 'who (primarily) should decide arbitrability' differently from the way it treats silence or ambiguity about the question 'whether a particular merits-related dispute is arbitrable because it is within the scope of a valid arbitration agreement'—for in respect to this latter question the law reverses the presumption."[11]

Perhaps that is better explained as meaning that while arbitrators have the first word on whether or not a party is obligated to arbitrate, if there is ambiguity (in the agreement to arbitrate) the courts will not find there is an agreement to arbitrate unless there is clear and unmistakable evidence that they did so. But once the authority to arbitrate is found, there is a presumption that the arbitrators have all other powers associated with that arbitration.

Note that *First Options* has absolutely nothing to do with what law an arbitrator is supposed to apply, nor the right or obligation of an arbitrator to conduct independent legal research, nor any other authority of an arbitrator, other than as it relates to arbitrability.[12]

Thus, the proposition in the NYSBAJ article (that silence about an arbitrator's authority to conduct independent research means there is no such authority) is simply wrong.

---

[10] *Id.* at 944.

[11] *Id.* at 944-45.

[12] For the curious, the *First Options* court ruled that when a district court has reviewed the arbitrability issue, circuit courts review such decisions by accepting those facts found by the lower tribunal that are not clearly erroneous, but deciding issues of law *de novo*. *Id.* at 947-48.

IX. Is an Arbitrator Bound by What the Parties Think the Law Is?

The NYSBAJ article quotes *Steelworkers v. Warrior & Gulf Navigation Co.*, 363 U.S. 574 (1960) where it says that an arbitrator "has no general charter to administer justice for a community which transcends the parties" but rather "is a part of a system of self-government created by and confined to the parties." From this small portion of that decision the article concludes that an arbitrator is bound by the wishes of the parties, even if the arbitrator thinks that the law as stated by both parties is wrong.

If one is allowed to cherry-pick language of a judicial opinion that, in isolation, supports a premise, almost any premise can find support. That quotation from *Steelworks* does not, however, support the article's premise.

First, keep in mind that this decision was written more than 50 years ago, at a time when courts had hostility toward arbitration, and commercial arbitration in particular.[13] Then consider the context of the case. *Steelworkers* was a case in which the issue was whether or not a labor union could compel management to arbitrate a grievance. The issue was arbitrability. Legal research by an arbitrator was never an issue. Thus, at best, the *Steelworkers* language quoted in the article is *dicta*, but more importantly irrelevant to the proposition that arbitrators cannot research the law absent consent of the parties.

Even more significant, that *dicta* has no bearing on commercial arbitration—obvious from the Court's statement that, "Since arbitration of labor disputes has quite different functions from arbitration under an ordinary commercial agreement, the hostility evinced by courts toward arbitration of commercial agreements has no place here."[14]

The decision went on to explain that a collective bargaining agreement is an effort to erect a system of industrial self-government.

Even if one could stretch the application of the *dicta* discussed above, the Court stated that "The labor arbitrator's source of law is not confined to the express provisions of the contract, as the industrial common law—the practices of the industry and the shop—is equally part of the collective bargaining agreement, although not expressed in it."[15] Thus, *Steelworkers* not only does NOT support the article's premise, it

[13] *Id.* at 578.
[14] *Id.*
[15] *Id.* at 581-82.

actually stands for the proposition that the law is a part of arbitration agreements, even if that is not expressly stated in the agreements.

X. Does the Principle of Manifest Disregard of the Law Prohibit "Unauthorized" Legal Research?

The NYSBAJ article uses the "Manifest Disregard" ground (for vacating arbitral awards) to conclude that arbitrators may not conduct independent (*i.e.*, on their own) research to help decide a case, unless granted authority by the parties. The case cited for that proposition, *Wallace v. Buttar*, 378 F.3d 182 (2d Cir. 2004), is discussed above.

The article states that "no court has found that an arbitrator has a duty to independently investigate issues of law and apply what was discovered." That statement is technically accurate, but as a basis for claiming the lack of duty to research the law equates to a prohibition of research without authority from the parties is a logical *non sequitur*. Lack of duty does not equate to prohibition. You have no duty to wash your hands before eating, but you are not prohibited from doing so without permission from someone.

The NYSBAJ article also argues that the *Wallace* court's rejection of a comment by Norman Posner [sic] supports the argument that an arbitrator does not have a duty to conduct "unauthorized" independent legal research, and is therefore prohibited from doing so. Norman Poser is a Brooklyn Law School Professor who (as set forth in the article) believes the Manifest Disregard principle should be broadened, because it encourages arbitrators to not find out what the law is. The Second Circuit disagreed, "because it seems to imply that arbitrators will not approach their task in a professional manner."[16]

In that same footnote, the Second Circuit said, "It may be true that '[a]rbitrators should not be potted palms. As decision-makers, they have an obligation to ascertain what the law is and to apply it correctly.'"[17] The footnote continued to reject any contention that as long as arbitrators are not required to be attorneys, there could be no duty imposed upon them to conduct independent legal research.

A simple reading of footnote 3 in *Wallace* discloses that the 2d DCA merely rejected Poser's argument that Manifest Disregard should be replaced by a broader standard, but acknowledged arbitrators' obligation

[16] *Id. fn.* 3.
[17] *Id.*

to follow the law. The court decided not to discuss arbitration disputes between parties that are unequal in wealth and sophistication, because that wasn't an issue before the court[18] (and that discussion would have been *dicta*).

Wallace not only fails to support the NYSBAJ article's conclusions, but also supports the contrary principle that arbitrators should ascertain and follow the law.

XI. Final Thoughts

The NYSBAJ article concludes by setting up what is a highly unlikely scenario: "As an arbitrator, you receive a call from the case manager, informing you your award has been vacated," and the implication is that you violated the institution's policy concerning independent legal research.

Yet the article seems to acknowledge:

- The International Institute for Conflict Prevention and Resolution (CPR) requires only that the arbitrator apply the law designated by the parties, if any (and that appears to be pretty much a standard for all arbitration tribunals), but has no policy regarding independent legal research;
- The American Arbitration Association (AAA) has no such policy;
- Judicial Arbitration and Mediation Services (JAMS) requires that some law be applied, but has no policy regarding independent legal research;

Article 35 of the United Nations Commission on International Trade Law (UNCITRAL) Arbitration Rules requires arbitrators to follow the law designated by the parties, if any. The article suggests that if one party submits a legal brief and the other does not, independent legal research is not authorized. This seems to ignore the rule that if the law is not designated by the parties (plural), the arbitrator may determine what the law is. The article seems to suggest that independent legal research, in such a case, is unfair to the party which did submit a legal brief, but there is no basis in the UNCITRAL articles for that suggestion.

Article 21 of the International Chamber of Commerce (ICC) Arbitration Rules allows the parties (plural) to agree upon the rules of

[18] *Id.*

law to be applied. The article seems to suggest that independent legal research, in such a case, is unfair to the party which did submit a legal brief, but there is no basis in the ICC Rules for that suggestion.

The London Court of International Arbitration (LCIA) has no such policy.

The Code of Professional Responsibility for Arbitrators of Labor Management Disputes says that reliance on independent legal research is dependent on the policies of the parties (plural) expressed in the contract, another agreement, or at the hearing.

Thus, there is no institutional policy against independent legal research by an arbitrator, except where the parties (plural) agree on what the law is. Even that doesn't block independent legal research where it is reasonably necessary. For example, the parties may cite a statute or statutes which control the outcome of the case, but it may be appropriate to research case law interpreting that statute or statutes.

That closing scenario is highly unlikely, and could occur only where the parties all agree (and that's also a rarity) on what the law is … and maybe not even then.

XII. The Bottom Line

The bottom line is that arbitrators, especially those who are attorneys, should do their best to determine what law applies to their arbitration, and apply that law to the facts. For attorney arbitrators, that may include independent legal research, if the arbitrator is to do his job according to law and the rules of the various tribunals. For non-attorney arbitrators, you are not required nor prohibited from independent legal research, but understand how to do it, and do it yourself.

If the law as you find it differs from the law as presented by the parties, it would be wise (although not required) that you advise the parties and allow them to respond to your findings (you may be mistaken, and it is always possible there are later decisions which reject your legal conclusions).

PART IV:

ARBITRATION PROCEDURE

CHAPTER 21

THE ENFORCEABILITY OF CLASS ACTION WAIVERS IN ARBITRATION CLAUSES

*Thomas W. H. Barlow**

I. Introduction

Employers are increasingly including in their arbitration agreements a provision waiving the right to bring class action claims in arbitration. The case law regarding the enforceability of class action waivers in the employment context is relatively sparse, but has grown over the last few years. There is more case law on this issue in the consumer arena. This article addresses the issues surrounding class action waivers as well as proposed legislation that would make this issue moot by making arbitration agreements in the employment setting unenforceable.

With the enforceability of arbitration agreements established in the labor and employment arena, even with respect to statutory discrimination claims, employers are fighting efforts by employees to bring collective claims in arbitration. The main tool employers are using is a provision waiving the right to bring a class or collective arbitration. Should courts enforce such waivers? Some proponents of class arbitration waivers argue that employees ought to be able to waive a procedural right in exchange for the benefits of arbitration; others argue that class arbitration waivers make it impossible to bring low-value claims to the arbitral forum because arbitration costs (if the employer is not required to pay them) and the employee's attorney fees could exceed the potential recovery, thereby depriving the employee of his or her substantive rights. On the other hand, if the whole point of a collective action is to help people bring meritorious

---

* Thomas W. H. Barlow is a partner in the Troy office of Giarmarco, Mullins & Horton, P.C. A labor and employment lawyer, he has more than 40 years of experience representing management in the negotiation and administration of collective bargaining agreements and in defending management in discrimination, harassment, wrongful dismissal, Sarbanes-Oxley, whistle-blowing, and retaliation cases. Nickolas Guttman, a summer associate, helped prepare this article.

claims despite financial barriers, does affordable access to arbitration accomplish this goal, making class proceedings unnecessary?

The presumption in the Federal Arbitration Act (FAA) is that arbitration agreements will be "valid, irrevocable, and enforceable" unless a generally applicable, state law contract defense would apply. Thus, to be enforceable, the contract—including any class arbitration waiver—must not violate state contract law.

What are generally applicable state law contract defenses? Examples include unconscionable provisions or provisions that violate public policy, such as one that protects a party from being held liable for violating the law. However, in *AT&T Mobility LLC v. Concepcion*[1] the U.S. Supreme Court limited the applicability of the doctrine of substantive unconscionability to invalidate class action waivers in the consumer context. While the U.S. Supreme Court took its stance on substantive unconscionability, it left the door open for courts to use procedural unconscionability to invalidate class action waivers.

Similarly, the California Supreme Court recently held that the FAA preempts any state-law rule that disfavors arbitration in practice, even in the employment context, in light of the *Concepcion* ruling.[2] These cases are discussed more fully below. In the meantime, Congress is currently considering a bill that would make mandatory arbitration provisions in employment agreements and consumer contracts unenforceable altogether.[3]

II. Waiver of Class Arbitration as the Default Rule

In 2010, the U.S. Supreme Court decided *Stolt-Nielsen S.A. v. AnimalFeeds International Corp.*,[4] which held that a party cannot be compelled to class arbitration where the arbitration agreement is silent on the issue. Petitioners were shipping companies that charged customers wishing to ship liquids in small quantities. AnimalFeeds International Corp. was one of the customers. The parties' arbitration agreement provided for compulsory arbitration, however, in lower proceedings both

---

[1] *AT&T Mobility LLC v. Concepcion*, 131 S. Ct. 1740, 179 L. Ed. 2d 742 (2011).

[2] *Iskanian v. CLS Transp. Los Angeles, LLC*, 59 Cal. 4th 348, 372, 327 P.3d 129, 141 (2014).

[3] The Arbitration Fairness Act of 2015 (H.R. 12087/S. 1133) was introduced in the House by Rep. Hank Johnson (D-Ga.) on Apr. 29, 2015, and in the Senate by Sen. Alan Franken (D-Minn..) on April 29, 2015.

[4] *Stolt-Nielsen S.A. v. AnimalFeeds Int'l Corp.*, 559 U.S. 662, 130 S. Ct. 1758, 176 L. Ed. 2d 605 (2010).

parties stipulated that the arbitration clause was silent on the issue of class arbitration.

The Court reasoned that since arbitration agreements are of a consensual nature, parties cannot be compelled to class arbitration of disputes when the agreement is silent on the issue. The Court noted that class-arbitration transforms the nature of arbitration into something to which parties cannot be assumed to have consented. Then *Stolt-Nielsen* disambiguated any notion that consent is not required to impose class arbitration. The case served as a big victory for corporations seeking to avoid risk of classwide proceedings under arbitration agreements.

III. Concepcion Makes Waves

In 2011, the Supreme Court issued a seminal decision on waivers of collective action in arbitration. *AT&T Mobility LLC v. Concepcion*[5] began as a class action lawsuit against AT&T where AT&T charged the Concepcions sales tax on the retail price of a cell phone that was advertised as free. The California Federal District Court ruled that the arbitration agreement was unconscionable because it disallowed classwide proceedings and thus denied AT&T's motion to compel arbitration under California's *Discover Bank*[6] rule. California's *Discover Bank* rule makes unconscionable all class action waivers entered into where the party with superior bargaining power organizes a scheme to cheat a large number of consumers out of relatively small sums of money.[7]

The Ninth Circuit agreed with the District Court and held that although the FAA preempts most state law involving arbitration, the saving clause excluded the doctrine of unconscionability because it was a state contract law of general applicability.

The U.S. Supreme Court held that the FAA preempts the *Discover Bank* rule because the rule stands as an obstacle to the achievement of the goals of the FAA. The Court relied on three conclusions in arriving at their holding. First, class arbitration is too expensive, inefficient and slow to have been intended by the FAA. Second, in order for absent class members to be bound by the arbitration, the arbitrator must ensure the protections of members' procedural due process rights. The Court reasoned that Congress could not have intended this issue to be left to an

[5] *See* n. 1 *supra.*

[6] *Discover Bank v. Superior Court*, 36 Cal.4th 148, 30 Cal.Rptr.3d 76, 113 P.3d 1100.

[7] *Id.*

arbitrator. Third, class arbitration increases the risk to the defendant of incurring a significant adverse judgment, protection from which was one of the foremost reasons companies choose binding arbitration.

The preemption of the *Discover Bank* rule leaves California with less room to demonstrate its hostility toward class action waivers; however the Supreme Court recently granted certiorari[8] in a case where the California Court of Appeals invalidated a class action waiver because the DirecTV agreement contained a choice of law provision electing the laws of California. The Court of Appeals reasoned the provision exempted the agreement from the FAA and chose state law instead. The Court further suggested that there are other states that are much more lenient to class action waivers and DirecTV should not have chosen California's if it did not want to subject to its laws.

IV. California's Post-*Concepcion* Cases

After the *Concepcion* decision, California courts were forced to develop new theories in their continuing efforts to find class action waivers in arbitration agreements unenforceable. In *Iskanian v. CLS Transp. Los Angeles, LLC*, the California Supreme Court held that *Concepcion* preempted the *Discover Bank* rule, but did not preempt the unenforceability of waivers in actions brought by employees under the Private Attorneys General Act (the "PAGA").[9] The PAGA allows employees to step into the shoes of a governmental agency in order to sue an employer for violations of the Labor Code. The employee would bring the action on behalf of himself as well as those similarly situated. Since the representative action is a substitute for a government action, it binds all those similarly situated, whether or not they actually participated. Seventy-five percent of the recovery goes to the Labor and Workforce Developmental Agency and twenty-five percent goes to aggrieved employees.

V. Cases Outside California

Few cases outside of California have addressed the enforceability of class arbitration waivers in employment contracts. Some of the courts that

---

[8] *Imburgia v. DIRECTV*, Inc., 225 Cal. App. 4th 338, 340, 170 Cal. Rptr. 3d 190, 192 (2014).

[9] *See* n. 2 *supra*.

have addressed the issue have ruled these waivers unenforceable on unconscionability grounds. An example is *Skirchak v. Dynamics Research Corp.*[10] In this case, plaintiffs sued their employer for overtime violations and sought recovery (including treble damages) under the Fair Labor Standards Act (FLSA) and the Massachusetts fair wage law. The 1st Circuit struck down the class arbitration waiver. It held that "the combination of a series of events ... [led] to a conclusion of unconscionability" under Massachusetts law. These events included adding confusing new terms that the employer disseminated via e-mail immediately before a holiday weekend; the e-mail did not notify employees that the new provision would modify their employment contracts and did not require employees to do anything to accept the modification.

The court specifically avoided "the policy debate about whether class action waivers essentially act as exculpatory clauses, allowing for violations of laws where individual cases involve low dollar amounts and so will not adequately address or prevent illegality."

In *Labor Ready Northwest Inc. v. Crawford*,[11] a federal court in Oregon upheld the arbitrator's decision to strike a class action waiver based solely on substantive unconscionability. The court based this conclusion on the fact that the putative class members were temporary workers who were unlikely to bring individual claims for a small sum of money. In upholding the arbitrator's ruling, the court noted that Oregon law only requires a finding of substantive unconscionability to invalidate an agreement.

VI. Class Action Waivers and the FAA's Purpose

Since the enforceability of a class action waiver depends on state contract law, and some state laws are more relaxed than others, such waivers may be enforced. Thus, in Georgia, the standard for unconscionability is quite high: to find unconscionability, the court must find that "no sane man not acting under a delusion" would make that agreement and no honest man would take advantage of it. The 11th Circuit, applying Georgia law in *Caley v. Gulfstream Aerospace Corp.*,[12] upheld a trial court decision to enforce a class action waiver in a case

[10] 508 F.3d 49 (1st Cir. 2007).

[11] *Labor Ready Northwest v. Crawford*, 2008 U.S. Dist. LEXIS 33259 (D. Or. Apr. 21, 2008).

[12] 428 F.3d 1359 (11th Cir. 2005).

involving claims under the FLSA and federal anti-discrimination statutes. Quoting the Supreme Court in *Gilmer v. Interstate/Johnson Lane Corp*,[13] the 11th Circuit said, "[T]he fact that certain litigation devices may not be available in an arbitration is part and parcel of arbitration's ability to offer 'simplicity, informality and expedition,' characteristics that generally make arbitration an attractive vehicle for the resolution of low-value claims."

A federal court in Florida upheld a class waiver, finding it neither procedurally nor substantively unconscionable. In *La Torre v. BFS Retail & Commercial Operations*,[14] the plaintiff, a mechanic, asserted class-wide claims for unpaid overtime wages under the FLSA. He alleged that the class action waiver was procedurally unconscionable due to the unequal bargaining power of the parties, and other factors. Ruling in favor of the employer, the trial court said that in Florida, a contracting party is not permitted "to avoid the consequences of a contract freely entered into simply because he or she elected not to read and understand its terms before executing it or because in retrospect, the bargain turns out to be disadvantageous." It also cited the *Caley* case, which similarly made acceptance of the arbitration agreement a condition of employment. The court said that class action bans and discovery limitations are consistent with the FAA's goals of "simplicity, informality, and expedition" touted by the Supreme Court in *Gilmer*."

VII. Class Arbitration Procedures

In 2008, the 4th Circuit, in *Long John Silver's Restaurants Inc. v. Cole*,[15] affirmed an order confirming a partial final award certifying an "opt-out" class under the American Arbitration Association (AAA) Supplementary Rules for Class Arbitrations. In so doing, it rejected the claim that the arbitrator manifestly disregarded the "opt-in" provision in the FLSA. It also rejected the argument that the arbitrator exceeded the scope of authority in the arbitration agreement, which provided that the arbitrator "shall apply the substantive law (and the law and remedies, if applicable), in the state in which the claim arose, or federal law, or both, depending upon the claims asserted."

[13] 500 U.S. 20 (1991).
[14] No. 08-22046, 2008 WL 5156301 (S.D. Fla. Dec. 8, 2008).
[15] 514 F.3d 435 (4th Cir. 2008).

Justice Robert B. King's opinion stated that the standard of review of an arbitration award is "extremely limited" so that "a reviewing court is entitled to 'determine only whether the arbitrator did his job—not whether he did it well, correctly, or reasonably, but simply whether he did it.'" Applying this standard, the court agreed with the district court that the arbitrator did his job. He decided the conflict between the FLSA's opt-in provision and the AAA's opt-out provision after hearing the arguments of both sides and found no evidence that Congress intended the opt-in provision to be nonwaivable. The district court concluded that the arbitrator was not bound by any clear principle of law and that the partial final award was based on a reasonable interpretation of the FLSA. The 4th Circuit held that the arbitrator did not ignore the law because there was a debatable contention that the FLSA opt-in provision did not explicitly overrule the opt-in provision in the parties' agreement. The 4th Circuit also agreed that the arbitrator did not exceed his authority. He did what he was supposed to do—he analyzed two conflicting interpretations of the arbitration agreement and made a reasoned decision.

The Supreme Court in *Oxford Health Plans LLC v. Sutter*[16] affirmed this line of reasoning holding that it is not for the Court to decide whether the arbitrator was right or wrong, but only that he actually interpreted the contract, "however good, bad, or ugly."

VIII. Class Action Waivers in Contracts Other than Employment

In addition to *Concepcion,* the U.S. Supreme Court decided another major case involving a class action waiver outside of the employment context.

In Re American Express Merchants' Litigation, Italian Colors Restaurant,[17] decided in June of 2013, the U.S. Supreme Court reversed the 2nd Circuit decision and upheld a class arbitration waiver in an antitrust case filed by merchants against a credit card company. Plaintiff argued that the costs associated with bringing individual antitrust claims against Defendant would make it prohibitively expensive and for that reason the class action waiver should be struck down on public policy grounds. The Court said that *Concepcion* all but resolved this case

---

[16] *Oxford Health Plans LLC v. Sutter*, 133 S. Ct. 2064, 186 L. Ed. 2d 113 (2013).

[17] *Am. Exp. Co. v. Italian Colors Rest.*, 133 S. Ct. 2304, 186 L. Ed. 2d 417 (2013)

concluding that even if it would be prohibitively expensive for plaintiffs to bring individual antitrust "tying arrangement" claims against American Express, failing to enforce the agreement would interfere with the fundamental attributes of arbitration. Under the Court of Appeals framework, before determining whether a waiver could be enforced the courts would have to undergo the costly task of evaluating all of the evidence to determine whether the claim would be prohibitively expensive, thus defeating the very purpose of the arbitration agreement. The Court further concluded that "the FAA does not sanction such a judicially created superstructure."

This year in *Sanchez v. Valencia Holding Co., LLC*,[18] the California Supreme Court reversed the California Court of Appeal and upheld a class action waiver in an arbitration agreement contained within an automobile sales contract. The agreement limited appeals to arbitral awards of $0 or greater than $100,000 or if the arbitrator grants, but not denies, requests for injunctive relief. Also, the appealing party had to pay the costs of the appeal up front and waive the right to class action litigation or arbitration. The trial court denied Valencia's motion to compel arbitration and found the entire arbitration agreement unenforceable. The California Supreme Court on appeal found that although the agreement was procedurally unconscionable, "a finding of procedural unconscionability does not mean that a contract will not be enforced. Instead, it forces the court to apply a higher degree of scrutiny to the substantive terms of the contract to determine if they are unfair or one-sided. After applying this analysis, the Court found that the agreement was not substantively unconscionable and that the agreement must be enforced as written in light of the *Concepcion* ruling.

The increasing trend toward enforcing class action waiver agreements in both employment and consumer contexts are getting stronger, even in California. Courts can use their judicial review powers as a sword or a shield when they review class arbitration waivers. If they continue to allow collective arbitration of employment claims, how those proceedings unfold is likely to be carefully scrutinized, given the limited right to appeal an arbitration award.[19]

---

[18] *Sanchez v. Valencia Holding Co., LLC*, No. S199119, 2015 WL 4605381 (Cal. Aug. 3, 2015)

[19] Nina Yadava, Note, "Can You Hear Me Now? The Courts Send a Stronger Signal Regarding Arbitration Class Action Waivers in Consumer Telecommunications Contracts," 41 *Colum. J.L. & Soc. Probs.* 547, 571 (2008).

IX. Conclusion

While courts are struggling with waivers of classwide arbitration in consumer and employment cases, legislators have been asked to contemplate imposing an absolute ban on pre-dispute mandatory arbitration clauses in these same contexts.[20] If the bill were to become law, it would make the case law on class action waivers moot.

As the 11th Circuit pointed out in *Caley*, "the fact that certain litigation devices may not be available in an arbitration is part and parcel of arbitration's ability to offer 'simplicity, informality and expedition....'" The plaintiffs' bar, which argues that employees lose the ability to assert their rights when class action waivers are enforced, rarely mention that class members in court typically do not collect much money. Most of the recovery goes to the attorneys representing the class. So long as courts continue to scrutinize class arbitration waivers on a case-by-case basis to determine if the contract is fair, an all-out ban on these waivers seems unnecessary and likely would do more harm than good.

---

[20] *See* n. 3 *supra*. If passed, this bill would amend the FAA to bar mandatory pre-dispute agreements to arbitrate employment, consumer rights, franchise or civil rights claims. The House and Senate versions are identical. A similar bill was introduced in 2009 but faced a certain veto by former President George W. Bush. It is unclear how the Arbitration Fairness Act of 2015 will fare in the current Congress.

CHAPTER 22

AN UPDATE ON MULTIJURISDICTIONAL PRACTICE AND ADR

Bruce E. Meyerson[*]

I. Introduction

As more and more national and international businesses expand their use of mediation and arbitration, attorneys representing these entities find themselves traveling from state to state representing clients in ADR proceedings.

In the past, state regulation of the practice of law had not kept up with this rapidly changing expansion in the use of ADR proceedings by companies doing business throughout the United States. Most states were slow to make their own legal ethics rules more flexible in permitting out-of-state attorneys to appear intermittently on behalf of clients in mediation and arbitration without becoming licensed in those jurisdictions.[1] To remedy this situation, the American Bar Association

[*] Bruce E. Meyerson, a mediator and arbitrator in Phoenix, Arizona, serves on the American Arbitration Association's roster of neutrals and is a member of the Association's Board of Directors. He formerly served as a Judge on the Arizona Court of Appeals and was General Counsel of Arizona State University. He is a past chair of the American Bar Association Section of Dispute Resolution. He can be reached at brucemeyerson@msn.com. The author acknowledges the assistance of John A. Holtaway of the American Bar Association, who kindly offered useful suggestions and reviewed this article.

[1] *See generally* RESTATEMENT (THIRD) OF THE LAW GOVERNING LAWYERS § 3 (1998); Kristen M. Blankley, Emily E. Root & John Minter, *Multijurisdictional ADR Practice: Lessons for Litigators*, 11 CARDOZO J. CONFLICT RESOL. 29 (Fall 2009); Rachel B. Cash & Meghan P. Stephens, *The Other Fifty Shades of Gray: Multijurisdictional Practice in Private Arbitrations*, 37 AM. J. TRIAL ADVOC. 1 (Summer 2013); Sarah Rudolph Cole, *Unauthorized Practice of Law Charges: A Risk for Lawyers Representing Clients in Mediation and Arbitration in a Multijurisdictional Practice Environment*, 13 DISP. RESOL. MAG 26 (Fall 2006); Arthur F. Greenbaum, *Multijurisdictional Practice and the Influence of Model Rule of Professional Conduct 5.5 – an Interim Assessment*, 43 AKRON. L. REV. 729 (2010); G. Hammond, *Multijurisdictional Practice: An Analysis of the ABA's proposed Changes to Rule 5.5 of the Rules of Professional Conduct*, 26 SETON

("ABA") made important additions to its Model Rules of Professional Conduct ("Model Rules") for states to consider concerning the multijurisdictional practice of law. This article concerns only one aspect of the multijurisdictional practice of law—the rules that apply when a lawyer admitted to practice in one state, occasionally appears in another state to represent a party in a private arbitration (as distinguished from a court-annexed arbitration).

II. Model Rule 5.5(c)(3)

The highest court in a jurisdiction regulates the practice of law in that jurisdiction. *Pro hac vice* rules permit lawyers to temporarily practice before courts in states where they are not admitted but with few exceptions noted later in this article, these rules do not apply to attorneys representing parties in private arbitration. Thus, courts have granted *pro hac vice* admission to lawyers in individual court cases for some time, but no comparable procedure typically exists in private arbitration.

Disturbing to many was the reaction by some courts to attorneys who travel out of their home jurisdiction to represent clients in arbitration in other states. For example, in 2003, the Florida Supreme Court, in *Florida Bar v. Rapoport*,[2] enjoined Mr. Rapoport, a lawyer licensed to practice in the District of Columbia, from representing parties in securities arbitrations in Florida. Not surprisingly, relying upon an earlier decision,[3] the court found that giving legal advice and performing the traditional tasks of lawyers in arbitration proceedings was "the practice of law." Rapoport's situation, however, was not particularly sympathetic as he actually operated a law practice in Florida and advertised in at least one Florida newspaper.

The Florida decision followed by five years the ruling of the California Supreme Court in *Birbrower, Montalbano, Condon & Frank, P.C. v. Superior Court*.[4] That decision involved a fee dispute in which an out-of-state law firm, in defending against a claim it had committed legal

---

HALL LEG. J. 533 (2002); Harriet Miers, *Recommended Reading: Issues for the Multijurisdictional Lawyer Where Pro Hac Vice Admission Does Not Apply*, ARK. L. NOTES 131 (2001); D. Ryan Nayar, *Unauthorized Practice of Law in Private Arbitral Proceedings: A Jurisdictional Survey*, 6 J. AM. ARB. 1 (2007).

[2] 845 So. 2d 874 (Fla. 2003).

[3] *Florida Bar re Advisory Opinion on Nonlawyer Representation in Sec. Arbitration*, 696 So. 2d 1178 (Fla. 1997).

[4] 949 P.2d 1 (Cal. 1998).

malpractice in California, sought to recover its attorneys' fees. Birbrower, an attorney at the firm, came to California to file a demand for arbitration with the San Francisco office of the American Arbitration Association, and to interview arbitrators; he subsequently returned to California to pursue a settlement of the dispute.

The California Business and Professions Code provided at the time that "[n]o person shall practice law in California unless the person is an active member of the State Bar." Because Birbrower, a New York lawyer, was not admitted in California, the court found he was engaged in the unauthorized practice of law, and therefore could not recover his attorney's fees.[5]

Recognizing the practice of law has taken on a truly national (and indeed, international) dimension, and in response to decisions such as the foregoing, the ABA proposed a solution to the increasing multijurisdictional nature of the practice of law and the periodic need of attorneys to be able to represent their clients outside of their home jurisdiction. The ABA established the Commission on Multijurisdictional Practice to look broadly at this issue and to determine whether special rules should apply to lawyers who travel on occasion to states where they are not licensed to practice law. The Commission determined that such rules were necessary. In its report, the Commission recognized that "lawyers commonly engage in cross-border legal practice," and that "such practice is on the increase." With respect to alternative dispute resolution, the Commission found:

> In ADR proceedings as well, it is common for lawyers to render services outside particular states in which they are licensed. Sometimes, the parties choose to conduct the ADR proceeding in

---

[5] It is commonly held by courts that representation of a party in an arbitration constitutes the practice of law. *E.g., Matter of* Creasy, 12 P.3d 214 (Ariz. 2002); *Nisha, LLC v. Tribuilt Constr.Group, LLC*, 388 S.W.3d 444 (Ark. 2012); *Doctor's Assocs. Inc. v. Jamieson*, 2006 WL 2348849 (Conn. Super. Ct. July 19, 2006); *Disciplinary Counsel v.Alexicole, Inc.*, 822 N.E.2d 348 (Ohio Sup. Ct. 2004); *contra Prudential Equity Group, LLC v. Ajamie,* 538 F.Supp.2d 605 (S.D.N.Y. 2008) and cases cited in note 49 *infra*. Labor arbitration, however, is viewed differently by the courts. The prevailing rule is that a nonlawyer can represent a party in an arbitration arising from a dispute involving a collective bargaining agreement. *E.g., In re Town of Little Compton*, 37 A.3d 85 (R.I. 2012); CAL. CIV. PRO. CODE § 1282.4 (2015) ("[A}any party to an arbitration arising under collective bargaining agreements in industries and provisions subject to either state or federal law may be represented in the course of . . . those proceedings by any person, regardless of whether that person is licensed to practice law in this state.").

a state that has no relation to the parties or the dispute, because they prefer a neutral site.

As part of its report, the Commission recommended the adoption of a new rule of professional conduct that would speak to the modern practice of law.

The Commission proposed, and in August 2002, the ABA House of Delegates approved, important amendments to Rule 5.5 of the Model Rules. The amendments addressed the entire subject of multijurisdictional practice, and specifically ADR.[6] The amended rule permits lawyers, on a temporary basis, to represent clients in arbitrations (and mediations and other ADR proceedings) in states where they are not licensed to practice law. The portion of Model Rule 5.5 addressing ADR is in subparagraph (c)(3). It states:

> (c) A lawyer admitted in another United States jurisdiction, and not disbarred or suspended from practice in any jurisdiction, may provide legal services on a temporary basis in this jurisdiction that
>
> . . . (3) are in or reasonably related to a pending or potential arbitration, mediation, or other alternative dispute resolution proceeding in this or another jurisdiction, if the services arise out of or are reasonably related to the lawyer's practice in a jurisdiction in which the lawyer is admitted to practice and are not services for which the forum requires *pro hac vice* admission. . . .

Model Rule 5.5(c)(3) became a part of the broader revisions to the Model Rules, completed by the ABA's Ethics 2000 Commission in February 2002. Thus, under Model Rule 5.5(c)(3), a lawyer would not run afoul of rules prohibiting the unauthorized practice of law in a jurisdiction if the lawyer is admitted to practice in another jurisdiction and (1) on a temporary basis, (2) represents a party in an arbitration, mediation or other ADR proceeding, (3) that is reasonably related to the lawyer's

[6] The ABA Center for Professional Responsibility maintains a website that contains a variety of resources on multijurisdictional practice including a chart which tracks each state's implementation of the ABA's multijurisdictional policies: www.americanbar.org/content/dam/aba/administrative/professional_responsibility/recommendations.authcheckdam.pdf; *see also* www.barreciprocity.com/mjp/.

practice in the jurisdiction where the lawyer is admitted to practice, and (4) the forum's rules do not require *pro hac vice* admission.

III. State Responses to Model Rule 5.5(c)(3)

Since the release of the ABA's Ethics 2000 Commission report, virtually all of the states have reviewed their own ethics rules for lawyers. Indeed, most states now have addressed multijurisdictional ADR practice issues and Model Rule 5.5(c)(3) has been widely adopted.

This section discusses each state's response to Model Rule 5.5(c)(3). It is important to keep in mind, however, some states that have adopted Model Rule 5.5(c)(3) impose other requirements that must be met by out-of-state attorneys appearing in private arbitrations.

Alabama

The Alabama Supreme Court, effective September 19, 2006, adopted a rule similar to Model Rule 5.5(c)(3), except it eliminates the requirement that the legal services "arise out of or are reasonably related to the lawyer's practice in a jurisdiction in which the lawyer is admitted to practice."[7]

Alaska

Effective April 15, 2009, the Alaska Supreme Court adopted new rules of professional conduct which include an identical version of Model Rule 5.5(c)(3).[8]

Arizona

In May 2002, a member of the Arizona State Bar Committee on the Rules of Professional Conduct issued an informal opinion[9] concluding that, because the representation of a party in arbitration is the practice of law, a member of the Arizona bar who serves as an arbitrator would be assisting another in the unauthorized practice law if counsel is not admitted as an attorney in Arizona.[10] This informal opinion was short

[7] www.judicial.alabama.gov/library/rules_bar_conduct.cfm.

[8] www.courts.alaska.gov/rules/prof.htm#5.5.

[9] Informal Op. Request No. 2191.

[10] Four years later, the State Bar Unauthorized Practice of Law Committee, citing Rule 31(a)(2), Rules of the Arizona Supreme Court, found that an out-of-state attorney

lived, as the Arizona Supreme Court subsequently adopted Model Rule 5.5(c)(3).[11] In addition, the Arizona rule requires lawyers engaged in multijurisdictional practice to advise their clients they are not admitted to law in Arizona and must obtain their client's informed consent to the representation.

Arkansas

Effective May, 1, 2005, the Arkansas Supreme Court adopted a rule identical to Model Rule 5.5(c)(3).[12]

California

Attorneys not admitted to practice in California may represent parties in arbitration proceedings if they prepare an "Out-of State Attorney Arbitration Counsel Certificate" containing information prescribed by statute, obtain the approval of the arbitrator, and file the certificate with the State Bar of California and provide a copy to all parties and counsel in the arbitration.[13]

Colorado

Effective January 1, 2003, the Colorado Supreme Court permitted out-of-state attorneys to practice law in Colorado. Rule 220 of the Colorado Rules of Civil Procedure permits an attorney licensed in another jurisdiction to practice law temporarily in Colorado so long as that attorney has not established domicile in Colorado and the attorney has not established a place for the regular practice of law in Colorado from which the attorney practices "Colorado law" or "accepts Colorado

---

representing a party in a securities arbitration was engaged in the practice of law. By then the Arizona Supreme Court adopted Model Rule 5.5(c)(3), and so the Committee concluded the attorney was not engaged in the unauthorized practice of law. UPL 06-04 (April 2006). www.azbar.org/media/75265/uplaa0604.pdf.

[11] www.azbar.org/Ethics/RulesofProfessionalConduct/ViewRule?id=51. Without considering the applicability of Model Rule 5.5(c)(3), the Arizona Court of Appeals held an arbitration award should not be vacated because one of the attorneys participating was not licensed in Arizona. *Nolan v. Kenner*, 230 P.3d 236 (Ariz. Ct. App. 2011).

[12] www.courts.arkansas.gov/rules-and-administrative-orders/%5Bcurrent%5D-arkansas-rules-of-professional-conduct. *Nisha, LLC v. Tribuilt Constr.Group, LLC, supra* note 5 (a nonlawyer's representation of a party in an arbitration constitutes the unauthorized practice of law).

[13] *See generally* CAL. CIV. PROC. CODE §§ 1282-1284.3; *see also* Rule 9.43, California Rules of Court. www.courts.ca.gov/cms/rules/index.cfm?title=nine&linkid=rule9_43.

clients."[14] If these conditions are satisfied an out-of-state attorney can periodically represent parties in arbitrations in Colorado.

Connecticut

Effective January 1, 2008, Rule 5.5 of the Connecticut Rules of Professional Conduct was amended to provide that a lawyer who is not admitted to practice in Connecticut, but who is admitted in another jurisdiction that accords similar privileges to Connecticut lawyers, may provide the legal services set forth in Model Rule 5.5(c)(3) on a temporary basis in Connecticut. This representation is permitted if the lawyer gives notice to the Statewide Bar Counsel prior to and at the conclusion of each representation and pays the fee prescribed by the Judicial Branch.[15] The Comments to the Rule state that the legal services in the arbitration must be "with respect to a matter that is substantially related to, or arises out of, a jurisdiction in which the lawyer is admitted. A variety of factors may evidence such a relationship. However, the matter, although involving other jurisdictions, must have a significant connection with the jurisdiction in which the lawyer is admitted to practice. A significant aspect of the lawyer's work might be conducted in that jurisdiction or a significant aspect of the matter may involve the law of that jurisdiction. The necessary relationship might arise when the client's activities and the resulting legal issues involve multiple jurisdictions."

Delaware

When the Delaware Supreme Court adopted a comprehensive new set of rules of professional conduct effective July 1, 2003, it included in those rules Model Rule 5.5(c)(3).[16] The rule was amended in 2007 to provide that in order to practice law on a temporary basis in Delaware a lawyer must not be disbarred or suspended from practice in any jurisdiction.

District of Columbia

Rule 49(12) of the Rules of the District Columbia Court of Appeals permits attorneys not admitted to practice in the District to engage in the

---

[14] www.coloradosupremecourt.com/pdfs/Registration/Rule%20220%20Out-of-State%20Attorney% 20--%20Conditions%20of%20Practice.pdf.

[15] www.jud.ct.gcv/Publications/PracticeBook/PB.pdf#page=8.

[16] www.depic.delaware.gov/sections/lobbying/related/dlrpc.pdf.

temporary representation of parties in "no more than five (5) ADR proceedings in the District of Columbia per calendar year."[17]

Florida

Under Rule 4-5.5, a "non-Florida lawyer" may appear in an arbitration in Florida for a client who resides in or has an office in the lawyer's home state or where the appearance arises out of or is reasonably related to the lawyer's practice in a jurisdiction in which the lawyer is admitted to practice. In all arbitration proceedings, except international arbitrations, prior to practicing pursuant to this rule, the non-Florida lawyer must file a verified statement with The Florida Bar and serve a copy of the verified statement on opposing counsel, if known. The verified statement must include certain information such as listing all jurisdictions where the lawyer is admitted to practice, a list of all arbitrations in which the lawyer has appeared in Florida during the preceding five years (confidential information may be excluded), and certain other information specific to the pending arbitration. A $250 fee must also be paid to The Florida Bar.[18]

Georgia

On April 5, 2003, the Board of Governors of the Georgia Bar approved the Final Report of the State Committee on Multijurisdictional Practice. The Report recommended adoption of the revised Model Rules in their entirety, including Model Rule 5.5(c)(3). That rule was adopted by the Georgia Supreme Court on June 8, 2004. Although the rule distinguishes between "domestic" and "foreign" lawyers, both are allowed to engage in the temporary practice of law.[19]

Hawaii

On June 25, 2013, the Hawaii Supreme Court entered an Order adopting amendments to the Hawaii Rules of Professional Conduct, effective January 1, 2014. The Court did not adopt Model Rule 5.5.[20] Hawaii's unauthorized practice of law statute makes it unlawful to engage in the practice of law in Hawaii "except and to the extent that the person . .

---

[17] www.dccourts.gov/internet/documents/rule49.pdf.

[18] www.floridabar.org/divexe/rrtfb.nsf/FV/AE4F324F9F246B2085257A2C00628278; *see generally In re Amendments to the Rules Regulating the Florida Bar and the Rules of Judicial Administration-Multijurisdictional Practice of Law*, 991 So. 2d 842 (Fla. 2008).

[19] www.gabar.org/barrules/handbookdetail.cfm?what=rule&id=129.

[20] www.courts.state.hi.us/docs/court_rules/rules/hrpcond.htm

. is licensed or authorized so to do by an appropriate court, agency, or office or by a statute of the State or of the United States."[21] The procedure for obtaining temporary permission to practice law in Hawaii is found in Hawaii Supreme Court Rule 1.9.[22] It is unclear whether the procedure in this rule applies to the representation of a party in a private arbitration.[23] However, in one decision the Hawaii Supreme Court held that, among other things, preparation of a statement in anticipation of mediation was the practice of law,[24] and in another case, the court held representation of a party before a state agency was the practice of law.[25]

Idaho

Rule 5.5 of the Idaho Rules of Professional Conduct contains language similar to Model Rule 5.5(c)(3). It provides that an out-of-state lawyer may temporarily practice in Idaho if the lawyer associates with an Idaho lawyer or if the representation "arises out of or is otherwise reasonably related to the lawyer's representation of a client in a jurisdiction in which the lawyer is admitted to practice."[26]

Illinois

When the Illinois Supreme Court amended its Rules of Professional Conduct effective January 1, 2010, the amendments included the adoption of Model Rule 5.5(c)(3).[27]

---

[21] HAW. REV. STAT. 605-14.

[22] www.hsba.org/images/hsba/HSBA/Forms/2015/Pro%20Hac%20Vice%20Instruction%202015.pdf.

[23] "Hawai'i court rules prohibit out-of-state attorneys who are not licensed to practice here from representing parties in any court proceedings related to arbitrations, such as pre-arbitration proceedings to compel or stay arbitration or post-award proceedings to confirm or vacate awards, unless the attorney is granted *pro hac vice* status and has local co-counsel who accepts the responsibilities of lead counsel. So the possibility of judicial proceedings related to the arbitration generally makes it appropriate and advisable to at least have local co-counsel for out of state attorneys who represent parties in arbitration here. However, I did have an arbitration case a couple of years ago in which an out-of-state attorney represented one of the parties. He had local co-counsel but conducted the arbitration himself. The opposing party did not object and, as indicated, Hawai'i arbitration law doesn't specifically prohibit it. No issue was raised about it in the arbitration." E-mail from Charles Crumpton, Crumpton Collaborative Solutions (July 25, 2015) (on file with author).

[24] *Fought & Co., Inc. v. Steel Eng'g & Erection, Inc.*, 951 P.2d 487 (Haw. 1998).

[25] *Office of Disciplinary Counsel v. Lau*, 941 P.2d 295 (Haw. 1997).

[26] www.isb.idaho.gov/pdf/rules/irpc.pdf.

[27] www.llinoiscourts.gov/SupremeCourt/Rules/Art_VIII/ArtVIII_NEW.htm#5.5. In *Colmar, Ltd. v. Freemantlemedia North America, Inc.*, 801 N.E.2d 1017 (Ill. Ct. App.

Indiana

Since 2005, the Indiana Rules of Professional Conduct have included the identical version of Model Rule 5.5(c)(3).[28]

Iowa

Rule 32:5.5 of the Iowa Rules of Professional Conduct is identical to Model Rule 5.5(c)(3).[29]

Kansas

On January 29, 2014, the Kansas Supreme Court adopted amendments to the Kansas Rules of Professional Conduct, effective March 1, 2014. These amendments include a rule identical to Model Rule 5.5(c)(3).[30]

Kentucky

Rule SCR 3.130 (5.5)[31] of the Kentucky Rules of Professional Conduct, effective July 15, 2009, permits a nonresident attorney to provide temporary legal services if the attorney complies with Kentucky Supreme Court Rule 3.030(2).[32] That rule requires the attorney to be subject to the jurisdiction of the Kentucky Supreme Court, pay a one-time fee to the Kentucky Bar Association and associate a member of the Kentucky Bar Association as co-counsel.

2003), the court held that representation of a party in an arbitration by an out-of-state lawyer was not a basis to vacate an arbitration award. "Though the ABA Model Rule 5.5 has not been adopted by the Illinois Supreme Court at the time that we decide this case, we find it persuasive in that it reflects the modern trend in the law of multijurisdictional practice and is also in keeping with well-reasoned decisions from other jurisdictions that have found that an out-of-state attorney's representation of a client during arbitration does not violate the rules prohibiting the unauthorized practice of law." *Id.* at 1026.

[28] www.in.gov/judiciary/rules/prof_conduct/index.html#_Toc418253547.

[29] www.legis.iowa.gov/docs/ACO/CourtRulesChapter/05-29-2015.32.pdf.

[30] www.kscourts.org/rules/Rule-Info.asp?r1=Rules+Relating+to+Discipline+of+Attorneys&r2=17. In *Pemberton v. Citigroup Global Markets, Inc.*, 2012 WL 223928 (Kan. Ct. App. Jan. 20, 2012), the court, citing Kansas Supreme Court Rule 116, refused to vacate an arbitration award because counsel for the prevailing party was not admitted to practice in Kansas and had not applied for *pro hac vice* admission. The court explained that *pro hac vice* admission did not apply in private arbitrations.

[31] www.kybar.org/resource/resmgr/SCR3/SCR_3.130_(5.5).pdf.

[32] www.govt.westlaw.com/kyrules/Document/ND42824B0A91C11DA8F5EE32367A250AE?viewType=FullText&originationContext=documenttoc&transitionType=CategoryPageItem&contextData=(sc.Default).

Louisiana

Effective April 1, 2005, the Louisiana Supreme Court amended its rules regarding multijurisdictional practice to include a provision identical to Model Rule 5.5(c)(3).[33]

Maine

The Maine Supreme Judicial Court amended the Maine Rules of Professional Conduct, effective August 1, 2009. These rules incorporate Model Rule 5.5(c)(3) with the caveat that the nonresident attorney's representation be on behalf of an "existing" client.[34]

Maryland

The Maryland Lawyers' Rules of Professional Conduct contain a rule identical to Model Rule 5.5(c)(3).[35] However, under Rule 14 of the Rules Governing Admission to the Bar of Maryland, special rules apply in cases involving "the application of Maryland law."[36] A Maryland attorney must move in writing that the nonresident attorney be associated as co-counsel. The motion must be filed in the circuit court where the arbitration is pending. The out-of-state attorney must be accompanied by the Maryland attorney unless the presence of the Maryland attorney is waived by the arbitrator.

Massachusetts

The Massachusetts Supreme Judicial Court adopted the identical version of Model Rule 5.5(c)(3) effective January 1, 2007, as part of the Massachusetts Rules of Professional Conduct.[37]

---

[33] www.ladb.org/Material/Publication/ROPC/ROPC.pdf; *see also* Louisiana Supreme Court Rule XVII(13)(B), (C).

[34] www.mebaroverseers.org/attorney_regulation/bar_rules.html?id=88251.

[35] www.courts.state.md.us/attygrievance/rules.html.

[36] www.courts.state.md.us/ble/pdfs/baradmissionrules.pdf.

[37] www. mass.gov/obcbbo/rpc5.htm#Rule 5.5. Prior to its adoption of ABA Model Rule 5.5(c)(3), the Massachusetts Supreme Judicial Court held that an appearance by an attorney not admitted to practice in Massachusetts was not a ground on which to vacate an arbitration award. *Superadio Ltd. P'ship v. Winstar Radio Productions, LLC*, 844 N.E.2d 246 (Mass. 2006).

Michigan

Effective January 1, 2011, the Michigan Supreme Court adopted Model Rule 5.5(c)(3).[38] However, under Michigan Court Rule 8.126, an out-of-state attorney who wishes to appear in a "specific arbitration" must associate with a lawyer licensed to practice in Michigan who files a motion for temporary admission of the out-of-state attorney with the arbitrator.[39] A copy of the motion with attachments must be filed with Attorney Grievance Commission which will then notify the arbitrator whether the out-of-state attorney has appeared temporarily in Michigan during the past 365 days. An out-of-state attorney may not appear temporarily in Michigan more than five times during each 365-day period. A fee also must be paid to the State Bar of Michigan.

Minnesota

On June 17, 2005, the Minnesota Supreme Court adopted amendments to its Rules of Professional Conduct incorporating Model Rule 5.5(c)(3).[40]

Mississippi

The Mississippi Rules of Professional Conduct have not been amended to include Model Rule 5.5(c)(3) although in 2014 the Mississippi Bar submitted a petition to the Supreme Court to adopt Model Rule 5.5 and also adopt a comprehensive definition of the practice of law. As of July 2015 no action had been taken on the petition.

The Mississippi Supreme Court has suggested in *dicta* that by participating in a private arbitration in Mississippi, an out-of-state attorney would be making an "appearance" within the meaning of Rule 46(b) of the Mississippi Rules of Appellate Procedure.[41] The court stated:

> A foreign attorney may further make an appearance in a Mississippi court by physically appearing at . . . an arbitration or

[38] www.mi.gov/Courts/MichiganSupremeCourt/rules/Documents/Michigan%20Rules%20of%20Professional%20Conduct.pdf.

[39] www.courts.mi.gov/Courts/MichiganSupremeCourt/rules/Documents/subchapters/Subchapter%208.100%20General%20Administrative%20Orders.pdf.

[40] www.lprb.mncourts.gov/rules/Documents/MN%20Rules%20of%20Professional%20Conduct.pdf.

[41] A nonresident attorney must be admitted *pro hac vice* in accordance with Rule 46(b) when making an "appearance" in a "proceeding in which testimony is given." www.courts.ms.gov/rules/msrulesofcourt/rules_of_appellate_procedure.pdf.

mediation proceeding. . . . These actions require that the foreign attorney be admitted pro hac vice.[42]

In a recent article, the former chair of the Mississippi Bar's Unauthorized Practice of Law Committee wrote that the "current status of the law in Mississippi regarding whether representation in a private arbitral proceeding is the unauthorized practice of law is unclear due to the lack of case law and the fact that the Mississippi Rules of Professional Conduct have not been revised to address this situation."[43]

Missouri

Effective January 1, 2006, the Missouri Supreme Court adopted a rule identical to Model Rule 5.5(c)(3).[44]

Montana

The Montana Supreme Court has not adopted Model Rule 5.5(c)(3). Rule IV of the Rules for Admission to the Bar of Montana provide that an attorney who is admitted in another jurisdiction may appear "pro hac vice in any action or proceeding, if an attorney admitted to practice in the courts of Montana is associated as attorney of record."[45] Although the rule does not specifically speak to private arbitrations, knowledgeable attorneys in Montana state that best practices in Montana would be for out-of state attorneys in private arbitrations to follow this rule. The rule requires that an application for *pro hac vice* admission be filed with the State Bar of Montana. Rule IV(C) provides that except "upon a showing of good cause, no attorney or firm may appear pro hac vice in more than

---

[42] *In re Williamson*, 838 So. 2d 226, 235 (Miss. 2002).

[43] Jim Warren & Scott Murray, *Is Representation in an Arbitration Considered the Unauthorized Practice of Law in Mississippi?*, 79 MISS. L.J. MISSING SOURCES 44 (2009). "It remains unsettled as to whether an out of state attorney can participate in a Mississippi arbitration. When The Mississippi Bar receives inquiries about it, we suggest the attorney contact the court administrator for that particular court and ask if the judge requires *pro hac vice* admission (Rule 46 of the Mississippi Rules of Appellate Procedure) for arbitration or not. Our feedback thus far is that it is determined on a court by court basis based upon that particular judge's interpretation of what types of cases require admission to practice." E-mail from Adam Kilgore, General Counsel, The Mississippi Bar (June 29, 2015) (on file with author).

[44] www.courts.mo.gov/courts/ClerkHandbooksP2RulesOnly.nsf/c0c6ffa99df4993f86256ba50057dcb8/84187ab9f9f1995486256ca600521226?OpenDocument

[45] www.http://montanabar.site-ym.com/?page=ProHacVice&hhSearchTerms=%22pro+and+hac+and+vice%22#Rules

two actions or proceedings in any state court or administrative agency in Montana." Because this limitation applies to "actions or proceedings in any state court or administrative agency," it is unclear whether this restriction would apply to private arbitrations.

Nebraska

Section 3-505.5 of the Nebraska Rules of Professional Conduct contains a provision identical to Model Rule 5.5(c)(3).[46]

Nevada

Effective May 1, 2006, the Nevada Supreme Court amended its Rules of Professional Conduct addressing multijurisdictional practice without adopting the language of Model Rule 5.5(c)(3). However, Nevada Rule 5.5 permits lawyers licensed in other jurisdictions to practice in Nevada so long as the "lawyer is acting with respect to a matter that is incident to work being performed in a jurisdiction in which the lawyer is admitted, provided that the lawyer is acting in [Nevada] on an occasional basis and not as a regular or repetitive course of business in" Nevada.[47] This rule appears to cover representation in arbitration. The Nevada Supreme Court also adopted a special rule for ADR proceedings that "are court-annexed or court ordered, or that are mandated by statute or administrative rule."[48] Under Nevada Supreme Court Rule 42, an out-of-state lawyer must file a written application to appear as counsel in ADR proceedings (similar to a *pro hac vice* application), and may do so only upon approval by the "court, arbitrator, mediator or . . . hearing officer." The out-of-state lawyer also must associate as counsel with a Nevada lawyer.

New Hampshire

Effective January 1, 2008, the New Hampshire Rules of Professional Conduct incorporated a rule identical to Model Rule 5.5(c)(3).[49]

---

[46] www.supremecourt.nebraska.gov/supreme-court-rules/1869/%C2%A7-3-5055-unauthorized-practice-law-multijurisdictional-practice-law.
[47] www.leg.state.nv.us/CourtRules/RPC.html.
[48] www.leg.state.nv.us/courtrules/SCR.html#SCRRule42.
[49] www.courts.state.nh.us/rules/pcon/pcon-5_5.htm.

New Jersey

The New Jersey Rules of Professional Conduct contain a provision substantially similar to Model Rule 5.5(c)(3) although nonresident attorneys are subject to the New Jersey Rules of Professional Conduct and the disciplinary authority of the New Jersey Supreme Court.[50]

New Mexico

Rule 16-505 of the New Mexico Rules of Professional Conduct incorporates Model Rule 5.5(c)(3).[51]

New York

Although the New York State Bar Association has recommended adoption of Model Rule 5.5(c)(3) (or equivalent language) three separate times in recent years (2003, 2008, and 2012), the New York Court of Appeals has not accepted the proposals.[52] Thus, when New York adopted a version of the Model Rules in 2009, the Court of Appeals did not adopt ABA Model Rule 5.5(c)(3), but instead essentially re-numbered former DR 3-101 as Rule 5.5 (which is based on the ABA's former Model Rule 5.5) without any significant changes. The Association of the Bar of the City of New York has adopted the report of its Arbitration Committee which has opined that the representation of a party in a New York arbitration by a lawyer admitted to practice in another jurisdiction is not the practice of law.[53] This conclusion is supported by a series of New York federal court decisions.[54] Thus, out-of-state attorneys may ethically

[50] www.judiciary.state.nj.us/rules/apprpc.htm#P745_78667.

[51] www.nmbar.org/NmbarDocs/forMembers/PHV/16-505_11-1-2013.pdf.

[52] The most recent proposal, which was sent to the New York Court of Appeals in 2012, sought to transform the language of ABA Model Rule 5.5 into a set of Court of Appeals Rules, but the Court of Appeals never circulated these proposals and never acted on them.

[53] Committee on Arbitration, Association of the Bar of the City of New York, *Unauthorized Practice of Law and the Representation of Parties in New York by Lawyers Not Licensed to Practice in New York*, 63 THE RECORD 700 (2008).

[54] *See generally Prudential Equity Group, LLC v. Ajamie*, 538 F. Supp. 2d 605 (S.D.N.Y. 2008) (participation by a non-New York attorney in a New York arbitration is not the unauthorized practice of law); *Seigel v. Bridas Sociedad Anomina Petrolera Indus. Y Commercial*, No. 90 Civ. 6108 (RJW) 1991 U.S. Dist. LEXIS 11455 (S.D.N.Y. Aug. 19, 1991) (representation of a party in a New York arbitration proceeding by a lawyer admitted to practice in another jurisdiction is not the unauthorized practice of law); *Williamson, P.A. v. John D. Quinn Const. Corp.*, 537 F. Supp. 613 (S.D.N.Y. 1982) (an unlicensed attorney could recover fees for representing a party in an arbitration because arbitration is not the unauthorized practice of law).

represent parties in private arbitrations in New York without violating the restrictions against the unauthorized practice of law.

North Carolina

The North Carolina Supreme Court approved amendments to the North Carolina Rules of Professional Conduct, effective March 1, 2003, substantially adopting Model Rule 5.5(c)(3).[55]

North Dakota

A nonresident lawyer may represent a party in an arbitration in North Dakota so long as the lawyer complies with Rule 3 of the Admission to Practice Rules. This Rule requires the lawyer to file an affidavit with the State Board of Law Examiners setting forth the information prescribed in the Rule.[56] The state's multijurisdictional practice rule permits an out-of-state lawyer to represent a party in an arbitration in North Dakota so long as the lawyer complies with Rule 3.[57]

Ohio

The Ohio Supreme Court has adopted a multijurisdictional practice rule similar to Model Rule 5.5(c)(3); the rule requires the nonresident attorney to "regularly practice law" in the home jurisdiction.[58]

Oklahoma

Effective January 1, 2008, the Oklahoma Rules of Professional Conduct incorporated Model Rule 5.5(c)(3).[59]

Oregon

The Oregon Rules of Professional Conduct have a provision identical to Model Rule 5.5(c)(3).[60] In addition, under Rule 5.5(e), out-of-state attorneys must submit a "Certificate of Representation" to the Oregon State Bar (with a copy to the arbitrator and other parties) and certify the lawyer is in good standing in every jurisdiction where the lawyer is

---

55 www.ncbar.gov/rules/rules.asp.

56 www.ndcourts.gov/court/rules/Admission/rule3.htm.

57 www.ndcourts.gov/rules/Conduct/frameset.htm.

58 www.supremecourt.ohio.gov/LegalResources/Rules/ProfConduct/profConductRules.pdf.

59 www.oscn.net/applications/oscn/DeliverDocument.asp?CiteID=448989.

60 www.osbar.org/_docs/rulesregs/orpc.pdf.

admitted to practice, maintains professional liability insurance equivalent to that required by Oregon lawyers (or informs the client the lawyer has no liability insurance), and pays a fee to the Oregon State Bar in the amount of $200.

Pennsylvania

The Pennsylvania Rules of Professional Conduct contain a rule identical to Model Rule 5.5(c)(3).[61]

Rhode Island

The Rhode Island Rules of Professional Conduct contain a rule identical to Model Rule 5.5(c)(3).[62]

South Carolina

The South Carolina Rules of Professional Conduct contain a provision identical to ABA Rule 5.5(c)(3).[63] However, under Rule 404(l) of the South Carolina Rules Governing the Practice of Law:

> For each matter in which a lawyer seeks to provide legal services pursuant to Rule 5.5(c)(3), the lawyer shall file a verified statement with the South Carolina Supreme Court Office of Bar Admissions stating that the lawyer has not filed more than three statements pursuant to this rule in a 365-day period. The statement shall be accompanied by a $250 fee . . . .[64]

If an out-of-state lawyer provides legal services pursuant to Rule 5.5(c)(3) more than three times during a calendar year it is "presumed" the lawyer is providing services on a regular and not temporary basis.[65]

---

[61] www.padisciplinaryboard.org/documents/rules-of-professional-conduct-with-toc.pdf.

[62] www.courts.ri.gov/PublicResources/disciplinaryboard/PDF/Article5.pdf

[63] www.judicial.state.sc.us/courtReg/displayRule.cfm?ruleID=407.0&subRuleID=RULE%205%2E5&ruleType=APP.

[64] www.judicial.state.sc.us/courtReg/displayRule.cfm?ruleID=404.0&subRuleID=&ruleType=APP.

[65] *Id.*

South Dakota

The multijurisdictional provision of the South Dakota Rules of Professional Conduct with respect to ADR proceedings is identical to Model Rule 5.5(c)(3), with the addition that any out-of-state attorney "obtains a South Dakota sales tax license and tenders the applicable taxes."[66]

Tennessee

Effective January 1, 2010, the Tennessee Rules of Professional Conduct include a provision corresponding to Model Rule 5.5(c)(3).[67]

Texas

The Supreme Court of Texas has not adopted Model Rule 5.5(c)(3). Although Texas has a broad definition of the practice of law, currently no Texas court decision or rule speaks directly to the question of whether an out-of-state attorney may temporarily represent a party in a private arbitration in Texas. Historically, the Supreme Court of Texas Unauthorized Practice of Law Committee, which is charged with preventing the unauthorized practice of law in Texas, has not challenged as the unauthorized practice of law, the representation of a party in a private arbitration in Texas by an attorney licensed to practice in another jurisdiction.[68]

Utah

The Utah Rules of Professional Conduct include Model Rule 5.5(c)(3).[69]

Vermont

The Vermont Rules of Professional Conduct include Model Rule 5.5(c)(3).[70]

---

[66] www.sdbar.org/Rules/rules.shtm.

[67] www.tncourts.gov/rules/supreme-court/8.

[68] Telephone interview with Leland C. de la Garza, Chair, Supreme Court of Texas Unauthorized Practice of Law Committee (Dec. 1, 2009).

[69] www.utcourts.gov/resources/rules/ucja/ch13/5_5.htm.

[70] www.vermontjudiciary.org/LC/Shared%20Documents/VermontRulesofProfessional Conduct_withamendmentsthroughJune2011.pdf.

Virginia

Rule 5.5 of the Virginia's Rules of Professional Conduct is substantially similar to Model Rule 5.5(c)(3) although the "foreign lawyer" must inform the client and interested third parties in writing that the lawyer is not admitted to practice in Virginia, the jurisdictions where the lawyer is admitted to practice, and the lawyers' address in the foreign jurisdiction.[71]

Washington

Since 2006 the Washington State Supreme Court Rules of Professional Conduct have included Model Rule 5.5(c)(3).[72]

West Virginia

On September 29, 2014, the Supreme Court of Appeals of West Virginia revised the West Virginia Rules of Professional Conduct, effective January 1, 2015, to include adoption of Model Rule 5.5(c)(3).[73]

Wisconsin

Effective July 1, 2007, the Wisconsin Supreme Court Rules of Professional Conduct for Attorneys, have included a provision, SCR 20:5.5, substantially similar to Model Rule 5.5(c)(3).[74]

Wyoming

The Wyoming Rules of Professional Conduct for Attorneys at Law include Model Rule 5.5(c)(3).[75]

IV. Conclusion

The area of multijurisdictional practice is rapidly changing to adapt to the greater fluidity in economic life. Keeping up with these changes is essential for attorneys whose practice calls upon them to travel to different

---

[71] www.vsb.org/pro-guidelines/index.php//main/print_view.

[72] www.courts.wa.gov/court_rules/?fa=court_rules.display&group=ga&set=RPC&ruleid=garpc5.05.

[73] www.courtswv.gov/legal-community/court-rules/professional-conduct/rule5.html#rule5.5.

[74] www.wicourts.gov/sc/scrule/DisplayDocument.pdf?content=pdf&seqNo=132538.

[75] www.courts.state.wy.us/WSC/CourtRule?RuleNumber=62.

states to participate in private arbitrations. With very few exceptions, the states have adopted Model Rule 5.5(c)(3) or substantial versions of it. This response to the ABA Commission on Multijurisdictional Practice has helped expand the use of ADR, and arbitration in particular, by allowing attorneys to meet client needs where representation is called for in a jurisdiction where the attorney is not licensed to practice law.

CHAPTER 23

THE USE OF DISPOSITIVE MOTIONS IN ARBITRATION

Alfred G. Ferris and W. Lee Biddle[*]

I. Introduction

This article addresses a basic arbitration practice question: what role do dispositive motions have in arbitration? For purposes of this article, dispositive motions are motions that would be considered dispositive by a court, such as a motion for summary judgment, a motion to dismiss for failure to state a claim, a motion for judgment on the pleadings, and a motion to strike particular claims or defenses. In arbitration, these motions are considered under the general rubric of "summary dispositions" or "partial summary dispositions."

Dispositive motions in litigation frequently provide the most efficient means of limiting the scope of the litigation or even ending it, saving the client's and the court's resources and reducing or eliminating the risk of an adverse judgment. The same considerations could apply in arbitration. The reason is that not every claim or defense brought in arbitration is sufficient to require a hearing on the merits. A claim made in arbitration could be just as ripe for disposition without a full evidentiary hearing as a claim brought in civil court. Thus, in some situations, it could be appropriate for a party to make, and the arbitrator to hear, a dispositive motion. Under these circumstances, hearing such a motion may facilitate the arbitrator's discharge of the duty that he or she "shall conduct the proceedings with a view to expediting the resolution of the dispute[.]"[1]

---

[*] Alfred G. Ferris is a full-time neutral and a commercial, construction and employment arbitrator and mediator. He serves on the American Arbitration Association's Large, Complex Case Panel. He is of counsel with the San Diego law firm of Ferris & Britton APC, of which he was a founding partner.

W. Lee Biddle is an associate with the firm, practicing in the area of business litigation.

[1] AAA Commercial Arbitration Rules, Rule R. 32(b).

There is little reason, however, to bring a dispositive motion in arbitration if resources saved by avoiding a hearing on the merits will have to be used before a court to defend an arbitral ruling granting the motion. So this article first discusses the legal framework surrounding dispositive motions, including how courts view such motions and what the law and institutional arbitration rules say about them. Next, the article discusses how the differences between civil courts and arbitration could have an impact on the decision to bring a dispositive motion and what kind of motion might be appropriate.

II. Statutory Authority

Two issues are central to a party contemplating a dispositive motion: first, whether the arbitrator has authority to grant such a motion and second, how a court would assess the motion on judicial review. Let's look at each in turn.

The Federal Arbitration Act (FAA), which was enacted in 1925, is silent on the issue of dispositive motions, as it is on all issues of arbitration management. So is the 1955 Uniform Arbitration Act (UAA), which was enacted in 49 states. The UAA seemed to require the arbitrator to determine all claims in an evidentiary hearing. Article 5 states that "the arbitrators shall appoint a time and place for the hearing" and that "[t]he parties are entitled to be heard, to present evidence material to the controversy and to cross-examine witnesses appearing at the hearing." What was meant by a "hearing" and the method of presentation of "evidence" left a vast area for arbitral discretion, subject to limited judicial review.

The language in the UAA led some commentators to believe that dispositive motions were not permitted in arbitration.[2] But as a few courts had occasion to review the propriety of a dispositive motion while considering a petition to vacate an award, it became increasingly clear that arbitrators had such authority. It also became obvious that it might be appropriate for arbitration law to make a more explicit statement about the power of the arbitrator to manage this aspect of the arbitration process.

This issue was addressed in 2000, when the National Conference of Commissioners on Uniform State Laws released the Revised Uniform

---

[2] *See* Schlessinger v. Rosenfeld, Meyer & Susman, 40 Cal. App. 4th 1096, 1108 (Cal. Ct. App. 1995), citing comments in a law review article and in the Rutter California Practice Guide stating that motion practice might not be available in arbitration. The *Schlessinger* court rejected this authority and determined that such motions were permitted.

Arbitration Act (RUAA).[3] One of the most significant changes in this extensive revision was the addition of a provision making it clear that an arbitrator has broad powers to manage the arbitration proceedings and the specific power to summarily dispose of claims. RUAA Section 15 reads in relevant part:

> (a) An arbitrator may conduct an arbitration in such manner as the arbitrator considers appropriate for a fair and expeditious disposition of the proceeding. . . .
> (b) An arbitrator may decide a request for summary disposition of a claim or particular issue:
> (1) if all interested parties agree; or
> (2) upon request of one party to the arbitration proceeding if that party gives notice to all other parties to the proceeding, and the other parties have a reasonable opportunity to respond.

Subsection (b)(2) calls for minimum due process by requiring "notice" and a "reasonable opportunity" to be heard.

At this point in time, the RUAA has been enacted (in some states with modifications) in 19 states. Some version of the 1955 UAA still governs in 30 states. One of these states, California, now has a unique arbitration statute. Although originally based on the 1955 UAA, it has been altered over the years by a legislature that has taken an active role in managing the arbitration process.[4] The California Arbitration Act (CAA) governs arbitrations that take place in the state where the parties have not otherwise agreed to the applicable arbitration rules.

Because California is such an influential jurisdiction, it is worth looking at the provisions of the CAA. Not surprisingly, since it was founded on the UAA, it is silent on the issue of dispositive motions, neither authorizing nor forbidding them. However, several newer sections addressing the management of the arbitration hearing could be perceived by imaginative counsel as supporting an argument limiting the arbitrator's ability to dispose of claims short of full hearing on the merits.[5] But this is only a potential argument. As discussed below,

---

[3] The RUAA can be viewed at www.uniformlawcommission.com (search for Uniform Arbitration Act).

[4] *See generally,* Roger Alford, *Report to Law Revision Commission Regarding Recommendations for Changes to California Arbitration Law*, 4 PEPP. DISP. RESOL. L.J. 1 (2003).

[5] *See* Cal. Code Civ. Proc. § 1282.2.

California case law makes clear that arbitrators have broad discretion in managing the arbitration process and that this includes the authority to grant a dispositive motion in appropriate cases.[6]

Nevertheless, the small uncertainty caused by the silence of the CAA on the issue has led some commentators to recommend that the California legislature adopt RUAA Section 15, since it closely tracks California judicial decisions on the powers of arbitrators.[7] To date, however, this has not been done, leaving at least the potential for an argument that the CAA does not permit dispositive motions.

III. Institutional Arbitration Rules

Since almost all commercial arbitration agreements contractually mandate the use of arbitration rules crafted by institutional providers, such as the American Arbitration Association (AAA) and others, it is appropriate to look specifically at such rules.

A. American Arbitration Association Rules

In 1996, Michael Hoellering, then-general counsel at the AAA, the largest not-for-profit arbitration provider in the United States, wrote in an article about dispositive motions that, although the AAA rules did not then address the arbitrator's authority to hear and decide dispositive motions, the rules did not prohibit them and "in actual practice," arbitrators have been exercising this authority.[8] Since that time, the AAA has amended its arbitration rules and some specifically address dispositive motions. For example, the most recent amendments to the AAA Commercial Arbitration added Rule 33 stating:

> The arbitrator may allow the filing of and make rulings upon a dispositive motion only if the arbitrator determines that the moving party has shown that the motion is likely to succeed and dispose of or narrow the issues in the case.

This language is identical to the current Rule 27 of the AAA Employment Arbitration Rules, which first came into effect on July 1,

---

[6] Schlessinger, *supra* n. 2.

[7] *See* Alford, *supra* n. 4.

[8] Michael Hoellering, *Dispositive Motions in Arbitration*, 1 ADR CURRENTS 1, 8 (1996).

2006 and was modified to its current form in 2009, making it clear that the arbitrator does have discretion to hear and grant dispositive motions.

The AAA's Construction Industry Arbitration Rules also address the issue of dispositive motions. Rule 34 provides:

> Upon prior written application, the arbitrator may permit motions that dispose of all or part of a claim, or narrow the issues in a case.

In all three cases, the rule places the onus on the arbitrator to determine if filing such a motion is appropriate in the first place. Thus, the Rules do not seem to allow a party the unilateral right to file such a motion as exists in most courts. However, all three Rules also appear to encourage the arbitrator to allow dispositive motions where such motions would expedite the proceeding. For example, Construction Industry Rule 33(b) provides:

> The arbitrator, exercising his or her discretion, shall conduct the proceedings with a view toward expediting the resolution of the dispute and may direct the order of proof, bifurcate proceedings, and direct the parties to focus their presentations on issues the decision of which could dispose of all or part of the case.

Similar language appears in Employment Rule 28 and Commercial Rule 32(b). Rule 21(b) of the Commercial Rules also supports the arbitrator's authority to hear and rule on dispositive motions because it encourages the parties to raise any potentially dispositive issues early in the proceeding. This rule provides: "At the preliminary hearing, the parties and the arbitrator should be prepared to discuss and establish a procedure for the conduct of the arbitration that is appropriate to achieve a fair, efficient, and economical resolution of the dispute."

In sum, these rules allow and encourage dispositive motions, but only when the arbitrator determines they will further the goal of efficiently resolving an action.

> On the other hand, the AAA/ICDR (International Centre for Dispute Resolution) International Rules do not address dispositive motions directly. Rather Article 20 seems to authorize them indirectly, giving the arbitrators broad authority to manage the arbitration. For example, subsection (1) provides that "the tribunal may conduct the arbitration in whatever manner it considers appropriate, provided that the parties are treated with equality and that each party has the right to be heard and is given a fair

opportunity to present its case." Subsection (2) says that "[t]he tribunal, exercising its discretion, shall conduct the proceedings with a view to expediting the resolution of the dispute." Subsection (3) further provides that the tribunal may in its discretion "direct the parties to focus their presentations on issues the decision of which could dispose of all or part of the case."

B. CPR Institute Rules

The CPR Institute's Rules for Non-Administered Arbitration are, at best, ambiguous on the issue of dispositive motions. There is no specific Rule on dispositive motions, but Rule 9 does direct that proceedings "shall be conducted in a expeditious manner." However, the commentary to Rule 9 suggests that arbitrators have authority to decide pure legal issues prior to the hearing on issues that involve undisputed issues of fact. The commentary states: "Some controversies hinge on one or two key issues of law which in litigation may be decided early by motion for partial summary judgment. At the pre-hearing conference, the desirability of the Tribunal's ruling on such issues before the hearings commence can be considered."

C. JAMS Rules

Similar to AAA Rules, JAMS Comprehensive Arbitration Rules give the arbitrator discretion to hear and decide dispositive motions. Rule 18 of these rules provides: The Arbitrator may permit any Party to file a Motion for Summary Disposition of a particular claim or issue, either by agreement of all interested Parties or at the request of one Party, provided other interested Parties have reasonable notice to respond to the request."

JAMS's International Rules are like the ICDR international rules quoted above. They do not directly authorize dispositive motions. But Rule 20.1 does so indirectly by giving arbitrators authority to "conduct the arbitration in whatever manner it considers appropriate, provided that the parties are treated with equality and that each party has the right to be heard and is given a reasonable opportunity to present its case." This rule also provides that the tribunal, "exercising its discretion, will conduct the proceedings with a view to expediting the resolution of the dispute." Similar to the ICDR international rules, Rule 20.3 of the JAMS international rules authorizes arbitrators to "direct the parties to focus their presentations on issues the decision of which could dispose of all or part of the case."

IV. Standard of Judicial Review

Statutory and case law in most jurisdictions make clear that arbitration decisions can be challenged only on very narrow grounds. The grounds on which an award may be challenged are contained in Article 10 of the FAA or in similar state arbitration laws. Two grounds are potentially relevant to the subject of dispositive motions. One is that the arbitrator refused to hear material evidence, prejudicing the rights of the parties. The other is that the arbitrator exceeded his powers.[9]

It is widely recognized that arbitral awards are entitled to great deference and that parties who have agreed to arbitrate are not entitled to a second bite of the apple in court. For example, in *Moncharsh v. Heily & Blase*, the California Supreme Court made it clear that a reviewing court is "not free to review the merits of the controversy, the arbitrators' reasoning, or the sufficiency of the evidence on which the award is based."[10] Indeed, a reviewing court cannot "examine the arbitration award for errors of fact or law" and "an error of law apparent on the face of the award that causes substantial injustice does not provide grounds for judicial review."[11] Other courts have noted that the "standard of review of arbitral awards is among the narrowest known to law."[12]

V. Judicial Review

This raises the issue of how courts have reviewed arbitral awards that make a summary disposition of the case. The fact is that case law dealing

---

[9] *See* FAA § 10(3) and (4), allowing an award to be vacated "where the arbitrators were guilty of misconduct … in refusing to hear evidence pertinent and material to the controversy" and "where the arbitrators exceeded their powers." *See also* Section 1286.2(a)(3) and (5) of the California Code of Civil Procedure, allowing an award to be vacated if "the rights of the party were substantially prejudiced by misconduct of a neutral arbitrator" or there was a "refusal of the arbitrators to hear evidence material to the controversy. . . ." The common law "manifest disregard of the law" doctrine also could be asserted, since it is in some ways similar to the argument that the arbitrator exceeded his powers.

[10] Moncharsh v. Heily & Blase 3 Cal. 4th 1, 11 (Cal. 1992).

[11] *Id.* at 33.

[12] Brown v. Coleman Co., 220 F.3d 1180, 1182 (10th Cir. 2000).

with dispositive motions is not extensive. What the case law teaches is that courts have not been receptive to arguments that granting a dispositive motion, by itself, constitutes an arbitrator error that would warrant a judicial decision to vacate an arbitration award for refusing to hear material evidence or exceeding arbitral powers.

These cases also show that, when the rules adopted by the parties fail to expressly provide for dispositive motions, the argument could be made that the arbitrator exceeded his or her powers in granting such a motion. Although this is an argument based largely on an unwarranted assumption, the lack of clarity in the rules may lead arbitrators to hesitate to hear and grant such motions. It could also lead parties to hesitate to bring them, even where warranted by the lack of any disputed material issue of fact. Fortunately, as rules are being altered or amended, the clear trend is to add language making explicit the arbitrator's power to hear dispositive motions.

The cases make clear that in the appropriate circumstances an arbitrator does not need to hear live testimony in a full evidentiary hearing and that the parties do not have an automatic right to cross-examine witnesses. What matters is that the arbitrator gives each side an opportunity to address the relevant issues before ruling on a dispositive motion. The Tenth Circuit has said that "a fundamentally fair [arbitration] hearing requires only notice, opportunity to be heard and to present relevant and material evidence and argument before the decision makers."[13] Evidence that is relevant and material need not be presented live. It could be offered through a declaration, affidavit or deposition transcript.

The leading case addressing the issues involved in dispositive motions is *Schlessinger v. Rosenfeld, Meyer & Susman*, decided in 1995 by the California Court of Appeal.[14] In *Schlessinger*, the court found that the arbitrator acted properly in rendering a final award without any hearings "on the merits," although dispositive motions were not specifically authorized by the parties' arbitration agreement, the AAA Commercial Arbitration Rules, or the CAA.

The *Schlessinger* arbitration was brought by a departing law partner who challenged a partnership agreement provision that limited his payout if he competed with the former firm. The arbitrator apparently viewed this claim as presenting a straightforward question of law: Was this contract clause lawful? The arbitrator entered a final award for the

[13] Bowles Fin. Group v. Stifel, Nicolaus & Co., 22 F.3d 1010, 1013 (10th Cir. 1994).
[14] *Supra* n. 2.

respondent law firm after deciding two summary adjudication motions. First, he ruled that the anti-competition clause was lawful, if reasonably limited in time, scope and location; second, he concluded that the specific limit on the partner's payout was reasonable.

Before the court ruled on the summary adjudication motions, extensive document discovery and depositions took place because the parties' agreement provided that California Code of Civil Procedure § 1283.05 applied. This section authorizes depositions and discovery regarding the subject matter of the arbitration. It also gives the parties the same rights, remedies and procedures, and the same duties, liabilities and obligations in arbitration that they would have if the case were pending in court.

With the aid of depositions and discovery, both sides obtained written evidence, which they submitted along with their motions. The arbitrator conducted motion hearings by telephone; however, there was no in-person hearing with live witness testimony.

Schlessinger challenged the final ruling, citing Civil Procedure Code § 1286.2(a)(5), which provides that an arbitration award must be vacated if the rights of a party were substantially prejudiced by the arbitrator's "refusal . . . to hear evidence material to the controversy." Schlessinger contended that the arbitrator did not "hear" any evidence because he disposed of the principle issues by way of summary adjudication motions instead of receiving live testimony and other evidence in a formal hearing on the merits. Schlessinger further argued that the lack of a hearing on the merits prevented him from exercising his fundamental right to cross-examine witnesses.

The court ruled that the absence of explicit authorization of dispositive motions in California law or the chosen arbitration rules did not mean the arbitrator lacked power to dispose of a claim without an evidentiary hearing on the merits. The court said that the nature of the arbitration process and the arbitrator's inherent power to determine the issues material to a controversy empowered the arbitrator to rule by dispositive motion:

> We decline to read section 1286.2(e) as requiring that an arbitrator always resolve disputes through the oral presentation of evidence or the taking of live testimony. To do otherwise would lead to anomalous results. The purpose of arbitration, as reflected in the [California Arbitration] Act, is to provide a "speedy and relatively inexpensive means of dispute resolution." Having chosen arbitration over civil litigation, a party should

"reap the advantages that flow from the use of that nontechnical, summary procedure."

The court went on to explain the philosophy behind dispositive motions:

> Schlessinger's position would require full-blown trials even where, as here, one of the parties believes that no material facts are in dispute. In a case where a legal issue or defense could possibly be resolved on undisputed facts, the purpose of the arbitration process would be defeated by precluding a summary judgment or summary adjudication motion and instead requiring a lengthy trial.

The holding in *Schlessinger* is echoed in several cases outside California.[15] These courts have also upheld dispositive decisions by arbitrators. Yet, as noted by some commentators, they have expressed the view that such motions are appropriate only when the opposing party is given a full opportunity to address the issues relevant to the motion.[16]

Only limited cases have been found in which a court vacated an award granting a dispositive motion.

The California Supreme Court has vacated an arbitration award granted by the arbitrator on summary judgment in *Pearson Dental Supplies, Inc. v. Superior Court.*[17] The Court found that the arbitrator made a clear error of law by misapplying a tolling provision to find that the statute of limitations barred the plaintiff's claims. The Court stated that "an arbitrator whose legal error has barred an employee subject to a mandatory arbitration agreement from obtaining a hearing on the merits

[15] *See* Intercarbon Bermuda, Ltd. v. Caltex Trading & Transp. Corp., 146 F.R.D. 64 (S.D.N.Y. 1993) (confirming a summary adjudication by an arbitrator based on documentary evidence but expressing reservations about deciding arbitration cases without an evidentiary hearing); Stifler v. Seymour Weiner, 488 A.2d 192 (Md. 1985) (dispositive motion is appropriate on issue of statute of limitations); Pegasus Constr. Corp. v. Turner Constr. Co., 929 P.2d 1200 (Wash. Ct. App. 1997) (hearing of all evidence regarding merits of a claim is unnecessary where a decision can be made on basis of motion to dismiss); Atreus Communities Grp. of Arizona v. Stardust Dev., Inc., 229 Ariz. 503, 508-09 (AZ Ct. App. 2012) (holding that summary judgment may be granted in arbitration "when the parties do not expressly prohibit summary judgment in their agreement, provided the parties receive a fair opportunity to present their case.")

[16] Timothy J. Heinz, *Revised Uniform Arbitration Act, An Overview*, 56 DISP. RESOL. J. 28 (2001).

[17] 48 Cal. 4th 665 (2010)

of a claim based on such right has exceeded his or her powers."[18] While this could be interpreted to mandate a "hearing" on all claims, there was no suggestion by the Court that it was overruling *Schlessinger* or otherwise barring summary judgment on employment claims in an arbitration. After all, such claims are routinely disposed of on summary judgment in court. The Court's sole concern appears to be that the arbitrator's error of law prevented the claimant from having any opportunity to proceed on his claims.

In *Prudential Securities v. Dalton*, a federal district court in Oklahoma vacated the award granting a motion to dismiss because the panel, prior to granting the motion, did not hear a broker's motion to compel the production of documents he contended were necessary to prove the claim. The court felt that the broker was not given the opportunity to present "factual evidence at a hearing relative to the factual issues presented by his claim."[19]

It is not clear whether the *Prudential* case stands for anything other than as a caution to arbitrators to be sure, when considering a dispositive motion, that the responding party has the maximum opportunity to provide the arbitrator with both legal points and authorities and relevant facts, either by affidavit, declaration under penalty of perjury, or signed deposition transcript. Also, since *Prudential* dealt with a motion to dismiss for failure to state a claim rather than a summary judgment motion, the panel should have assumed for purposes of the motion that all allegations of the claim were true. It is not clear if the panel did so. The case law suggests that courts will not disturb an award that grants a dispositive motion without a live hearing on the merits where the arbitrator took steps to ensure that the due process rights of the parties were protected through adequate notice and an opportunity to address the dispositive issues.

VI. Types of Dispositive Motions

Dispositive motions in civil actions may have different names in different courts and in different states. Generally, they fall into two broad categories.

The first type includes motions that attack the pleadings—for example, a motion to dismiss, to strike a claim or defense, or for a judgment on the

[18] *Id.* at 680.

[19] 929 F. Supp. 1411, 1418 (N.D. Okla. 1996).

pleadings. These motions generally do not require counsel to discover and analyze evidence because they focus on what the pleadings say to determine if the elements of a valid claim have been stated.

The second type of dispositive motion seeks a summary adjudication of the dispute. These motions cannot be made unless there is undisputed evidence showing that there is no genuine issue of material fact and that the moving party is entitled to a judgment as a matter of law."[20]

Each type of motion will be discussed in the context of arbitration.

A. Motions Attacking the Pleadings

These motions are common in civil court, particularly in "code pleading" states such as California. There, a pleading is ripe for attack if it fails to identify facts supporting each element of each cause of action.[21] However, motions attacking the pleadings would seem to have limited utility in arbitration proceedings. The primary reason is that the pleading requirements in arbitration are extremely relaxed.[22]

For example, to start an employment arbitration under the AAA rules, the claimant need only file "a brief statement of the nature of the dispute; the amount in controversy, if any; the remedy sought; and the requested hearing location."[23] Compare this to the notice pleading requirements for actions in federal court, which require "a short and plain statement of the claim showing that the pleader is entitled to relief."[24] However, this does not mean that an arbitrator should not agree to hear and decide a motion on a pleading in an appropriate case. How should an arbitrator go about deciding such a motion?

When a trial court decides a motion on the pleadings, it assumes the facts stated in the pleading are true and then determines if the facts alleged state a valid claim.[25] An arbitrator who hears a dispositive motion attacking a pleading should do the same: assume the facts stated in the

---

[20] Fed. R. Civ. P. 56. *See also* Calif. Code Civ. Proc. § 437(c): "Any party may move for summary judgment in any action or proceeding if it is contended that the action has no merit or that there is no defense to the action or proceeding."

[21] Calif. Code Civ. Proc. §425.10 states that complaints must include "a statement of the facts constituting the cause of action."

[22] However, under most institutional arbitration rules, the arbitrator has extensive power to require the parties to provide more detailed claims and defenses.

[23] AAA Employment Arbitration Rules, R. 4.

[24] Fed. R. Civ. P. 10.

[25] *See* Calif. Code Civ. Proc. § 430.10(e), noting the grounds for demurring to a claim are that "the pleading does not state facts sufficient to constitute a cause of action."

challenged pleading are true. If the arbitrator ruled in favor of the moving party without doing so, the award would be vulnerable to being overturned on the ground that the author of the challenged pleading did not have an opportunity to present relevant evidence. This is apparently what happened in the *Prudential* case. The court stated in that case:

> Before an arbitration panel should be able to dismiss a claim for failure to state a claim upon which relief can be granted, the claim should be facially deficient. Such is not the case here for if the allegations of the claimant's complaint are taken to be true, he would be entitled to some form of relief. . . . Thus, to assure fundamental fairness, claimant is entitled to offer evidence relevant to his claim.[26]

It is clear from this statement that the court assumed an arbitrator could grant a motion on the pleadings, provided that in deciding the issue the arbitrator assumed the facts pled to be true and found that they were insufficient to state a valid claim or defense.

We also need to consider one more factor. Civil courts typically allow plaintiffs leave to amend a deficient complaint at least once.[27] Thus, if a defendant moved to dismiss a complaint for failure to state a claim, the court probably would dismiss without prejudice and grant leave to replead with greater particularity.

An arbitrator should follow this practice. The arbitrator should not conclude an arbitration by granting a motion on a pleading without leave to amend except when the pleading in question has a flaw that cannot be remedied. An example of a non-remediable flaw is a pleading clearly filed beyond the applicable statute of limitations or one with an obvious jurisdictional defect. Even then, to avoid a possible later attack on the award, it might be advisable for both the party attacking a pleading and the arbitrator to allow the author of the pleading in question to produce extrinsic evidence by declaration or deposition that might be relevant to the issues raised by the motion.

---

[26] Prudential Securities, *supra* n. 17, at 1417-18.

[27] "It is an abuse of discretion for the court to deny leave to amend where there is any reasonable possibility that plaintiff can state a good cause of action." Goodman v. Kennedy 18 Cal. 3d 335, 349 (1976).

B. Motions for Summary Adjudication

As previously noted, motions for summary adjudication (also known as summary judgment) are appropriate only when no disputed material fact is at issue and the only question is one of law. Summary judgment motions filed in court usually must comply with the applicable rules of civil procedure.[28] That is not the case in arbitration because arbitrators are not bound by court rules of procedure or evidence unless the parties so agree.[29]

As the institutional arbitration rules quoted above show, arbitrators are generally required to manage the proceedings with a view to efficiently resolving the case. Where the arbitration rules expressly or implicitly allow for dispositive motions that would include hearing a motion for summary disposition. To reduce the risk of later challenge, it might be prudent for the arbitrator to encourage both parties to expressly buy into the procedural approach that the arbitrator intends to take to the dispositive motion, including notice and other procedural requirements.

Although arbitration is more flexible than litigation and not as formal, the procedures used must be fair. In other words they must satisfy arbitral due process. In the case of a dispositive summary judgment motion, this means that the party opposing the motion must have an opportunity to present, not only legal arguments, but relevant evidence to establish that there are material issues of fact in dispute, despite the moving party's claims to the contrary.[30] How and in what form that evidence is presented and received appears to be within the arbitrator's discretion.

VII. Discovery and Dispositive Motions

A key issue the arbitrator will have to decide is how much and what type of discovery to allow before hearing a summary adjudication motion. Absent an agreement by the parties, discovery in arbitration is

---

[28] *See, e.g.*, Calif. Code Civil Proc. §437(c), requiring 75 days' notice for such hearings, and Calif. Ct. R. 3.1350, describing the format of the papers for summary judgment or adjudication motions.

[29] *See* Schlessinger, *supra* n. 2, at 1108: "For instance, as stated, Code of Civil Procedure section 437c, the summary adjudication statute, did not apply to the arbitration here."

[30] Bowles Fin. Group, *supra* n. 13, at 1013.

usually quite limited compared to civil litigation. Arbitrators normally have discretion to determine how much discovery will be allowed, since most arbitral rules do not prescribe a specific type or amount. A party opposing a summary adjudication motion is likely to believe that extensive discovery is needed in order to develop supporting evidence.

The case law does not provide much guidance on how much discovery should be allowed. However, denying all discovery on an issue relevant to the judgment may be viewed as fundamentally unfair. In the *Schlessinger* case, the arbitrator allowed extensive discovery by agreement of the parties. Thus, the reviewing court easily found that Schlessinger, who challenged the summary judgment procedure, had an adequate opportunity to gather and present evidence.

If there is no agreement among the parties on discovery relating to a summary adjudication motion, should the arbitrator condition hearing the motion on the moving party agreeing to an appropriate amount of discovery? How much discovery is appropriate? Should the arbitrator allow the same amount of discovery that a court would have allowed if the action had been brought there? Should the arbitrator limit discovery to the issues he or she considers material to the motion? These are questions of judgment. The answers will depend on the nature of the case, the specific issues raised by the motion, and the costs associated with the motion and discovery. They also will depend on the arbitrator's view of his or her inherent power to manage the proceedings, including how much discovery is permitted by the rules or the parties' agreement.

VIII. Conclusion

Dispositive motions have the potential to play an important role in resolving disputes in arbitration more quickly and efficiently. They may benefit both parties by avoiding an unduly prolonged arbitration and they may assist the arbitrator in expeditiously resolving the dispute.

The relaxed procedural rules of arbitration proceedings allow the parties and the arbitrator to be more flexible in designing the procedures that will apply to dispositive motions. Whatever procedures are adopted, the party opposing the motion must be given adequate notice and a meaningful opportunity to respond.[31] Moreover, in the case of a

---

[31] *Id.*

summary adjudication motion, the arbitrator must give serious consideration to whether fairness requires granting the parties the opportunity to conduct discovery. If so, the arbitrator would then have to determine how much discovery would be reasonable. If the arbitrator believes that discovery could significantly raise the cost of the motion above what it might cost to proceed to a hearing on the merits, the arbitrator has sufficient discretion to deny the dispositive motion.

CHAPTER 24

IMPROVING ARBITRATION THROUGH TECHNOLOGY: A QUEST FOR BASIC PRINCIPLES

Thomas D. Halket[*]

I. Introduction

Arbitration's advantages over court litigation historically have focused on its potential speed and cost savings. Yet, these benefits can, and often do, disappear as cases have become larger and more complex and involve more parties. Nevertheless, this does not mean that nothing can be done to increase the efficiency of the arbitral process, even for the larger, more complex disputes. Some improvements—for example, encouraging arbitrators to exert more control over the process—are controversial;[1] others—such as the exercise by the parties of reasonable discretion in any discovery mechanisms they employ in the arbitration—much less so. The

---

[*] Thomas D. Halket is a partner in Halket Weitz LLP in New York and an adjunct professor at the Fordham University School of Law where he teaches courses on International Arbitration, IP Transactions Law and Entrepreneurship Law. An experienced arbitrator and mediator, he has chaired the American Arbitration Association's Technology Advisory Committee and is a member of the AAA's commercial, large complex, technology and IP and international panels. He also serves on the panels of the Chartered Institute of Arbitrators, the CPR Institute for Dispute Resolution and the World Intellectual Property Organization, among others. He is a Fellow of the Chartered Institute and Chartered Arbitrator, a Fellow of the College of Commercial Arbitrators, a Member of the London Court of International Arbitration and a Freeman of the Worshipful Company of Arbitrators. This article has been adapted from the author's previously published article, "The Use of Technology in Arbitration: Ensuring the Future Is Available to Both Parties," 81 St. Johns L. Rev. 269 (2007).

[1] *See, e.g.,* "International Colloquium Discusses Proactive Management of Arbitration Process and Other Key Issues," 55(1) *Disp. Resol. J. 5* (Feb. 2000) (discussing the possible proactive measures available to arbitrators); Deborah Masucci, "Taking Responsibility: Parties, Counsel Share Duty with Arbitrators to Ensure Integrity of Arbitration Process," *Disp. Resol. Mag. 22 (*ABA Fall 1998) (noting the need for professionalism on the part of parties).

approach to increasing arbitral efficiency discussed in this article—the use of technology (or technological aids—these terms will be used interchangeably in this article to mean information and communication technologies, such as email, the Internet, computerized document processing, video conferencing, and the like)—falls somewhere in between.

The use of technology can decrease the cost and increase the speed of and otherwise aid in the arbitral process. But its use is not without issue; it must be done in a way that is fair to both parties, while maintaining their expectations about the process. Fairness in the availability of a technical aid to both parties, however, is not a given. Of course, because the parties have almost unlimited ability to agree on the procedures to be used in their arbitration, they can agree on the use of various technological aids to facilitate their process.[2] The more complicated situation, and the topic of this article, is where at least one party objects to the use of the aid. When all parties do not agree to the use of an aid, fairness concerns arise because access to the aid could be an issue. For example, a party may not have high-speed access to the Internet available to it where it is located, Internet access may be restricted by its government, or the size of emails may be limited.

These fairness issues raise an important question for arbitrators: do arbitrators have the power—indeed, can they be required—to permit the use of a technical aid that is not equally available to both parties? In other words, to what extent in any of these situations should arbitrators be charged with responsibility for leveling the technological playing field?

First, however, we need to consider the nature of the task we have assigned to ourselves. That is, we need to consider whether it will be possible to develop a test for arbitrators to employ that would help them decide whether the use of a technical aid should be permitted or even mandated. An easy-to-administer black-and-white test for all cases would be desirable; but such a test is not feasible given the wide variety of possible technologies and circumstances in which the test would have to be applied. There is also the inevitable trade-off between the duration of a principle's applicability and its specificity. In other words, the more

---

[2] Standards for the implementation of technical aids whose use is desired by both parties have been dealt with extensively in a study by the International Chamber of Commerce (ICC). "Using Technology to Resolve Business Disputes," *ICC Int'l Court of Arbitration Bull.* (Supp. 2004). The ICC Task Force on IT in Arbitration, of which the author was a member, composed a report that considers issues pertinent to the question of whether to use technology in arbitration, although it focuses more on how to use it. The report is currently being updated.

specific the principle, the more likely it will become obsolete more quickly. In addition, in what may be more of a corollary to the first observation, rules that deal with methods of implementation—that is, rules that provide for or require certain means to accomplish the desired ends—are more likely to become obsolete sooner than rules which are general in nature as to the means of accomplishment. We are thus forced to conclude that any meaningful basic principles will need both to be relatively general in nature as well as to avoid the requirement, or even the context, of the use of specific technologies.

What then are the questions a tribunal should ask itself when it is confronted with a request to use, or need to use, a technical aid? Specifically, must the tribunal ensure in all cases that both parties have equal access to the technical aid in question? If not, does the tribunal have the power to regulate the use of that technical aid and what is the scope of that power? If so, to what issues should a tribunal look to guide it in doing so? Let's take each one in turn.

II. Due Process and Equality of Treatment

With respect to the question of equal access, a blanket general rule of equality of access would make no sense and be inconsistent with other aspects of the arbitral process. For example, there is no requirement that the parties be afforded equality of legal representation. Nor need the hearings be located at an equally convenient location. On the other hand, while a tribunal may not be required to level the playing field in all cases, procedural due process or other "fair access" or "equality of treatment" concepts may require a tribunal to do so in some circumstances. It should be noted that there is no provision in the statutes of the United States[3] or the fundamental international treaty[4] applicable to the enforcement of arbitral

---

[3] The grounds for vacating an award under the Federal Arbitration Act (FAA) are contained in 9 U.S.C. § 10. The ones arguably relevant are as follows: if the award was procured by undue means; where there was evident partiality in the arbitrators; where the arbitrators were guilty of misconduct in refusing to hear evidence pertinent and material to the controversy; if there was any misbehavior by which the rights of any party have been prejudiced; or if the arbitrators exceeded their powers.

[4] The only arguably pertinent grounds to refuse to recognize or deny enforcement to a foreign award are provided by the United Nations Convention on the Recognition and Enforcement of Foreign Arbitral Awards, art. 5. The enforcement of a foreign arbitral award may be refused when there is proof that: the party against whom the award is invoked was unable to present his case (art. 5.1.b), the arbitral procedure was not in accordance with the

awards that would require an arbitral tribunal in all cases to refuse to allow a party the ability to take advantage of a superior case preparation or presentation opportunity. It is true that some U.S. courts have found various non-statutory bases to vacate an award, namely manifest disregard of the law or capricious or irrational decision. These bases are not universally accepted by U.S. courts, and none of them has been extended to require a tribunal to level the playing field as a matter of general applicability. Accordingly, it is safe to conclude that none of these bases, either statutory or judge-made, rise to the level of requiring absolute equality of treatment. Nevertheless, the United States,[5] like most other countries,[6] as well as most arbitral bodies,[7] do have minimum procedural standards which vary somewhat from country to country, and body to body, and which, if not followed, are grounds for vacation of an arbitral award.

Generally speaking, these procedural due process standards tend to require minimum procedures to ensure that each party has a full and fair opportunity to present its case[8] and, as such, would certainly impact a tribunal's decision on whether to permit or require the use of a particular technical aid. Clearly, a tribunal could not do so if the use of the technical aid would deprive a party of fundamental procedural fairness. But it should be noted that the generally accepted procedural fairness grounds for vacating an award do not speak specifically in terms of the use of particular technical aids and are rather directed to the underlying effects of that use (for example, failure of notice, failure to allow cross examination, and so on). There also is no one-to-one correspondence between cause (the use of the technical aid) and effect (the alleged procedural defect). Thus, the use of email for party-tribunal communications may cause a failure of notice if a tribunal's email is not received by a party, or the failure of an opportunity to be heard if a party's email is not received by the tribunal, or the use of email may raise no procedural problem at all. Likewise, the use

---

agreement of the parties "or failing such agreement, was not in accordance with the law of the country where the arbitration took place" (art. 5.1.d), or the recognition or enforcement of the award would be contrary to the public policy of that country (art. 5.2.b).

[5] *See* FAA § 10(c); Gary B. Born, *International Commercial Arbitration in the United States* 545 (Kluwer 1994) (describing minimum levels of regulation in arbitration to create "procedural regularity and fairness").

[6] United Nations Commission on International Trade Law (UNCITRAL) Model Law on International Arbitration (UNCITRAL Model Law) art. 36(1)(a)(ii). *See generally* Nigel Blackaby, Constantine Partasides, Alan Redfern & Martin Hunter, *Redfern and Hunter on International Commercial Arbitration* 600-606 (5th ed. Sweet & Maxwell 2009).

[7] AAA, Commercial Arbitration Rules, R. 17(a)(i); ICC Rules of Arbitration, art. 15(2).

[8] *See* Redfern & Hunter, *supra* n. 6, at 600 -601.

of video testimony may deprive a party of the right to cross examine the witness in question, or it may deprive a party of the right to put on rebuttal witnesses, or similarly, it may raise no procedural problem.

Because the applicable procedural test is accordingly dependent not only on the identity of the jurisdiction whose law is to be applied but also on the procedural infirmity claimed (and even when the jurisdiction and procedural infirmity have been identified, the law on the issue may not be free from doubt and the outcome of the analysis may well be heavily driven by the facts of the situation), there are no easy rules to use to determine when procedural fairness precludes a tribunal from permitting or requiring the use of a particular technical aid. About the best that can be said is that a tribunal is free to do so unless its use deprives a party of the minimal procedural fairness required by the jurisdiction whose laws are applicable to the conduct of the arbitration.

Unfortunately, this does not end the analysis necessary to answer the first question. There is an additional "procedural" requirement that must be considered, namely a requirement in, for example, the UNCITRAL Model Law, that "the parties shall be treated with equality."[9] A number of countries have similar requirements,[10] as do many arbitral rules.[11] In an arbitration governed by these laws or rules, a tribunal could not approve or require the use of a technical aid if to do so would result in the tribunal treating the parties unequally, but what does that mean? At the extreme, it could require a tribunal to ensure equality in fact. In other words, under this interpretation a tribunal would be required to ensure a level playing field in fact and the inability of one party to use a technical aid would prevent the other party from using it as well. Or, it could

---

[9] UNCITRAL Model Law, art. 18.

[10] *See, e.g.*, Bundesgesetz uber das Internationale Privatrecht [IPRG], Swiss Private International Law Act, Systematische Sammlung [Federal Law] Dec. 18, 1987, SR 291, art. 182(3). Arguably, a provision like FAA § 10, which requires that the tribunal treat the parties impartially, could be read in a similar way.

[11] *See* AAA International Arbitration Rules, art. 16(1); UNCITRAL Arbitration Rules, art. 15(1). The latter is typical. It provides: "Subject to these Rules, the arbitral tribunal may conduct the arbitration in such manner as it considers appropriate, provided that the parties are treated with equality and that at any stage of the proceedings each party is given a full opportunity of presenting his case."

Not all arbitration rules have an equal-treatment requirement. Article 15(2) of the ICC Rules of Arbitration, for example, provide: "In all cases, the Arbitral Tribunal shall act fairly and impartially and ensure that each party has a reasonable opportunity to present its case." This rule has not been interpreted to require that the tribunal "treat the parties in exactly the same fashion." Michael W. Buhler & Thomas H. Webster, *Handbook of ICC Arbitration* 199 (Sweet & Maxwell 2005).

require that a tribunal afford each party an equal opportunity, whether or not they both have equal ability to exploit the opportunity. Under this interpretation, a party's ability to use a technical aid would not affect the analysis so long as it was afforded the opportunity to do so. Or, it may simply require that the parties must be treated impartially.

Guidance on the answers to these questions is mixed. A prior edition of a leading book on international arbitration by Alan Redfern and Martin Hunter has characterized the general effect of the requirement of equal treatment as "clear," summarizing it as:

> The arbitration tribunal should give the parties equal rights. It should not hear one party in the absence of the other; it should not communicate with one party without informing the other; it should not accord to one party privileges which it is not prepared to accord to the other. In a phrase, it should not demonstrate any favouritism; and this is so whether or not a positive obligation of "equal treatment" is imposed by the relevant rules of arbitration or of the *lex arbitri*.[12]

A closer examination of actual arbitration practice indicates a less clear practice in fact than that indicated by Redfern and Hunter. For example, the rule that a tribunal should be impartial has not always been extended to individual tribunal members. Until a little over ten years ago, a not uncommon practice in domestic U.S. arbitration, as opposed to international arbitral practice, included a presumption that party-appointed arbitrators were not impartial. Although this presumption of neutrality was reversed in the U.S., it is still possible to have non-neutral arbitrators.[13] This U.S. practice even extended to party-arbitrator communications. While there is a general prohibition under the AAA Rules against *ex parte* communications, it did not, and still does not in appropriate situations, extend to party-appointed arbitrators.[14] Other

---

[12] Redfern & Hunter, *The Law and Practice of International Commercial Arbitration*, 357 (2nd ed. Sweet & Maxwell 1991).

[13] A presumption of impartiality for party-appointed arbitrators (unless the parties agree that the party-appointed arbitrators may be partial) was incorporated into Rule 12(b) of the AAA Commercial Arbitration Rules on July 1, 2003 (subsequently amended in September 2005). Previously there was no such presumption in the commercial rules and party-chosen tribunal members were allowed to be partial; indeed in such cases they were expected to have extensive *ex parte* communications with that party.

[14] *See, e.g.*, AAA, Commercial Arbitration Rules, R. 18(a). This rule prohibits either party or anyone acting on their behalf from communicating *ex parte* with an arbitrator or a

examples where tribunals clearly need not treat parties equally include legal representation at the hearings, the location of the hearings, and most procedural rulings made prior to the hearings.

Where does this lead? Certainly, there is no rational basis to interpret the equal-treatment requirement to mean that arbitrators must level the technology playing field. On the other hand, it is clear that the requirement of equal treatment would prevent a tribunal from permitting one party to use a technical aid if it denies that use to the other. The thrust of the requirement is somewhere between these extremes but it may vary from jurisdiction to jurisdiction. Thus, it is reasonable to conclude that, like the question of minimum procedural fairness, the test of equal treatment is dependent not only on the identity of the jurisdiction whose law is to be applied but also on the claimed inequality and the facts presented. If so, there are no easy rules to use to determine when an unequal-treatment rule would preclude a tribunal from permitting or requiring the use of a particular technical aid. Again, the best that can be said is that a tribunal should be able to do so unless the use of the technical aid deprives a party of equal treatment as required by laws applicable to the conduct of the arbitration.

III. The Tribunal's Powers

Turning to the question of arbitral authority, if a tribunal is not obligated to provide technological equality, does the tribunal have any power to impose any restrictions on a party's use of technology in an arbitration? From the foregoing discussion, the answer to that question is definitely yes if the failure to do so would result in a party being deprived of fundamental procedural fairness or equality of treatment required by the arbitral rules or law of the applicable jurisdiction. But, what are a tribunal's powers to regulate the use of technical aids in the more common situation where the use of the aid does not affect either party's fundamental rights?

---

candidate for arbitrator concerning the arbitration. However, *ex parte* communications are allowed with a candidate for direct appointment by a party, but only regarding the general nature of the controversy and the anticipated proceedings, and to discuss the candidate's qualifications, availability, or independence, or the suitability of candidates for selection as a third arbitrator where the parties or party-designated arbitrators are to participate in that selection. While this rule does not apply to arbitrators directly appointed by the parties who the parties have agreed in writing are non-neutral, it does express a preference that the parties agree when the rule applies, at least prospectively, even in that circumstance.

A tribunal's powers arise from, and are constrained by, three sources: the agreement of the parties, applicable law, and the arbitral rules of the administering body, if there is one. The foundation of any arbitration is the parties' agreement to resolve their dispute through private rather than governmental means. Unless it is in conflict with applicable law or arbitral rules, the parties may agree on any procedure to be used in the arbitration and that agreement is binding on the tribunal.[15] Whether a technical aid may be used in an arbitral proceeding, and, if so, under what conditions, are procedural issues and, accordingly, may be agreed upon by the parties absent a conflict with applicable law or arbitral rule. But what if the parties do not agree or have not agreed? What powers does an arbitral tribunal have to permit or require the use of a technical aid over the objection of one of the parties? Needless to say, there are no provisions in the FAA or any of the more commonly used arbitral rules which speak either specifically to the use of a particular technical aid or more generally to the use of technology in the arbitral process. Applicable law and arbitral rules[16] do typically give arbitrators wide latitude to manage the proceedings. Many rules allow a tribunal to develop its own procedures for the arbitration so long as those procedures do not conflict with applicable law, the rules themselves, or the agreement of the parties. And, as noted above, most countries require that arbitral tribunals ensure that the proceedings be conducted according to some minimum standards of fair play. Indeed, the obligation of equal treatment would seem at the very least to require that a tribunal ensure a technical aid be available to both parties, even if they do not have equal ability to use it. Accordingly, absent an agreement of the parties, one party's use of a technical aid in developing or presenting its case should, or probably must, be subject to the control of the tribunal just like any other matters regarding the development and presentation of an arbitration.

IV. Factors a Tribunal Should Consider

The next and last question the tribunal needs to consider is really at the heart of the issue: to what factors should the tribunal look to

[15] *See, e.g.*, AAA, Commercial Arbitration Rules, R. 1(a), which provides: "The parties, by written agreement, may vary the procedures set forth in these rules."

[16] *See* UNCITRAL Arbitration Rules, art. 15(1); AAA International Arbitration Rules, art. 16(1); ICC Rules of Arbitration, art. 15(1).

determine whether it should permit or require the use of a technical aid? In other words, what standards are applicable to the use of technical aids in the arbitral process? The answer is not dictated purely by legal concerns, although the legal issues previously discussed bear heavily on it. Technical issues and efficiency of the arbitral proceedings must also be considered.

Certainly then at least the following factors, as may be and if appropriate, will enter into a tribunal's determination on whether to permit or require the use of any technical aid:

- The reason for the use of the technical aid.
- Whether the use of the technical aid advances the purposes of the arbitral process.
- Whether the use of the technical aid affects only one party's development or presentation of its case or whether both parties' cases are impacted.
- Whether the technical aid will be used by or available to the tribunal.
- The cost of the technical aid and who will bear it.
- Each respective party's ability to effectively use the technical aid.
- Whether there are any technical issues presented by the use of the technical aid.
- Whether the use of the technical aid is permitted by and complies with applicable law.
- Whether the use of the technical aid may deprive a party of the minimal procedural fairness or equality of treatment required by any law applicable to the arbitration.

The first two questions, the reason for the use of the aid and whether it advances the purposes of the arbitral process, are really part of the same issue. Inherent in any determination a tribunal may undertake to decide whether or not to permit or require the use of a technical aid is a balancing process which must weigh the reasons for using the aid against the problems engendered by that use. A finding that an aid advances the arbitral process—for example, by reducing the cost or increasing the speed of the proceedings—or generally promotes efficiency in the process would certainly weigh in favor of permitting its use. This should be the case in most circumstances. On the other hand, there is probably little reason to allow the use of any technology aid in the rare situation where its implementation cost substantially outweighs the benefits it produces in the administration of the arbitration, unless, of course, both parties desire to use it.

While the first two questions are two aspects of the same issue, the next question—whether the use of the technical aid affects only one party's development or presentation of its case or whether both parties' cases are impacted—raises two distinct issues. An aid can be used in the development of a party's case, in the presentation of that case, or in both. Alternatively, the use of an aid may affect only one party or it may affect both. Presumably, a party should be free, without the need to request tribunal permission, to use any aid (such as sophisticated document management software to process and categorize produced documents) in case development that does not materially deprive the other party of its ability to prepare or present its own case. On the other hand, the use of an aid (such as technology used to present evidence) by one party which affects the presentation of both parties' cases should typically require the permission of the tribunal.

Whether the technical aid is to be made available to the tribunal is a critical question. It is hard to envision a situation in which a tribunal should have access to a technology aid that is not equally accessible to both parties. Accordingly, it is probably a safe general rule that any technical aid made available to the tribunal by one party must be made available to the other party, at least for the purposes of dealing with the evidence presented by the first party. A much more difficult question is presented if the party who is not proposing to use the technical aid requests permission to use the aid for its own case. For example, consider the example of real-time video used to present witness testimony. It is one thing for the tribunal to ensure that the other party has a full and fair opportunity to cross-examine the witness; it is quite another to require that the party proposing to use real-time video make it available to the other party for the presentation of its witnesses.

Cost, the next factor on the list, may be *de minimus*. Some technical aids, such as email and use of the Internet, are virtually free provided each party has the minimal technology needed to use them. But others, such as video testimony, can involve significant costs. Clearly, an arbitrator should be reluctant to authorize the use of an aid if its cost is disproportionate to either the amount in controversy or the value to be gained by its use. Less clear is the situation where the cost, though justifiable, is more than one party is willing to, or can, bear.

Cost actually is just one factor that can affect a party's ability to use a given technology. Access, willingness, technical sophistication, existing technical resources, language and location (of the hearings and each party) are some other factors that may also do so. Is the fact that one party is unable to use the technology in question a decisive factor in the decision whether to permit its use by the other party? The answer is that while it is a factor to consider, it may not be a decisive factor. And, in fact, the reasons for a party's inability to use an aid could mitigate against cost being considered as a factor at all. Thus, a party should not be precluded from using a readily available, widely used, relatively inexpensive technical aid solely because the other side refuses to use it.

Among the technical issues presented by the use of a technical aid are security, privacy, reliability and compatibility. Some technical issues are decisive. Absent highly extraordinary circumstances, it is hard to envision a valid reason for approving the use of a technical aid that is either not sufficiently secure or does not have appropriate privacy controls. Although the lack of security may be decisive, that issue, and by extension privacy, are not absolute tests. No system is absolutely secure. The applicable test should be whether the security is reasonably sufficient under the circumstances.

Reliability is also important. An aid that is not reliable, either because it works inconsistently or unpredictably, or because it does not produce reliable data, should not be used. Finally, issues such as compatibility usually go to the parties' relative ability to use or exploit the technology in question and should be judged accordingly.

That the technical aid must be legal at first glance seems to be obvious. The tribunal clearly should not authorize the use of any procedure, technical or not, that would be illegal. But the concept is not so simple in practice. First, it involves two distinct issues. One is whether the use of the aid is permitted by the arbitral rules and national laws applicable to the arbitration. The other is whether the parties, and the tribunal, if appropriate, have the right to use the aid in question. The second question is mostly a matter of contract.

With respect to the first question, the tribunal must consider the rules of the appropriate administering body, if any, as well as the law of the applicable jurisdiction. While the identity of that body is usually fairly obvious, the identity of the country whose laws apply to the arbitration, or, more to the point, to the issue of the use of the technical aid in question, may not be so simple to discern. Many arbitrations, particularly in the international context, involve multiple jurisdictions. Each party and the arbitrators on the tribunal may be from a different country, the hearings may be in yet another country, and the administrating body may reside in a fourth, etc. Possible choice-of-law analyses can be complex. It is easy to conclude that the tribunal should not authorize any aid at the hearings the use of which would be illegal at the site of the hearings. But what about an aid that is illegal at the site of the hearings, but would be used only by one of the parties in its home country where such use is legal? Or, one that is legal at the hearing site, but illegal at the location of a witness who is scheduled to testify from a remote location? Clearly, in practice, the general rule may be less than absolute.

The second issue pertaining to the legality of the use of an aid arises from the fact that many, if not most, technical aids involve the use of computer software, databases, or other materials generally provided by suppliers under a license. Does the tribunal have the obligation to investigate whether the parties have the right to use the technical aids they propose to use? Perhaps more to the point, do the parties have the right to give the aid to the tribunal to use? That a party may regard a tribunal's inquiry into the rights that party has to use its own software as, to say the least, well beyond the tribunal's authority, at least for those instances where there is no prior indication of a cause for concern, is understandable. Whatever may be the tribunal's inclination to do so for aids which only the parties use, prudence dictates that it take whatever steps it deems necessary to satisfy itself that it has the right to use any aid given to it. Generally speaking, under the law of most nations, all knowing users of infringing software may be held liable for infringement.

The last consideration is whether the use of the technical aid deprives a party of the minimal procedural fairness or a requirement of equal treatment that applies under the arbitral rules in question and in the country whose law is applicable to the arbitration. In all events, the technical aid must pass whatever test is used. A tribunal should never allow one party to use any procedure the result of which would deprive the other party of the minimal procedural fairness or equal treatment required by applicable law or arbitral rule.

V. Some Proposed General Principles

What can we learn from this discussion? More to the point, can it be summarized in a meaningful way? No complete set of rules can be set forth, but there are some general basic principles:

1. The tribunal has inherent power to regulate the use of any technical aid proposed for use in an arbitration.
2. No technology should be permitted if (i) its use involves an unreasonable security risk, (ii) applicable privacy protocols cannot be, or are not, implemented, (iii) it is unreliable, (iv) its use deprives the other party of the minimal procedural fairness or equal treatment required by the law of any jurisdiction applicable in the circumstances, (v) its use is illegal under the applicable law, or (vi) its use is prohibited by the rules of the applicable arbitration administering body, if any.
3. Subject to principle 2, the tribunal should permit a party to use a technical aid if the advantages of its use in the arbitral process outweigh the disadvantages of such use, but the tribunal may impose conditions it deems necessary and reasonable.
4. Subject to principle 2, the tribunal should be allowed, on its own motion, to require the use of a technical aid if its advantages outweigh the disadvantages and the costs of implementation are not unreasonable in the circumstances.
5. Among the factors a tribunal should consider in applying the balancing test set forth in principles 3 and 4 are: (i) whether the aid advances a purpose of the arbitral process, (ii) the aid's cost, (iii) the effect of the aid on the other party's ability to prepare or present its case, (iv) the ability of the other party to use the aid in question, (v) any technical issues arising from its use, and (vi) any rules of the applicable arbitration administering body bearing on the issue in question.
6. Subject to principle 2, a party should be allowed, with or without advance permission of the tribunal, to use any technology it desires in the preparation of its case.

VI. Conclusion

Appropriate use of technology can significantly aid in the arbitral process and should be encouraged. It can increase the speed of an arbitration, decrease its cost and generally improve its efficiency. For example, software can analyze large amounts of documentary evidence in ways that would not be possible by hand; video technology is an alternative to traditional in-person, hearing- based procedures when those procedures prove to be overly costly or just plain impossible to implement; email can be a reliable, secure, and fast means of party-tribunal communications and online filing sites can provide safe, authoritative, and convenient repositories for all documents pertinent to an arbitration.

Many technical aids are easily available at low or no cost and in a very real sense they can be a win-win for the arbitral process. Low cost and equal availability, accessibility and usability, however, are not universal "givens" for all technical aids in all situations. Tribunals will be increasingly called upon to make decisions to permit the use of technology in arbitrations in situations where the arguments favoring its use may not be so clear. Those determinations need to be made in a way that is fair to both sides and that takes into account the purposes of the arbitral process.

PART V:

DISCOVERY AND EVIDENCE IN ARBITRATION

CHAPTER 25

ORGANIZING DOCUMENTS FOR ARBITRATION

Leslie Trager[*]

I. Introduction

Generally, we arbitrators tend to rely on the parties to determine how to organize and present their documents. So, unless the parties' advocates are skilled in arbitration and know techniques to make the process of presenting evidence more efficient, at the arbitration hearing each side could end up with ten boxes of documents nicely collected in three-inch binders. The problem for the arbitrator is that some of the documents are duplicative and many others may never be mentioned during the hearing. The more documents there are, the longer it takes to find the one that is the subject of discussion.

Even more time is usually necessary to locate specific language, or particular paragraphs or subparagraphs, in a large document, such as a contract. I have seen these logistical problems firsthand while serving as an advocate in arbitration and as an arbitrator. I think the arbitration could be made easier for the arbitrator if these problems were avoided or minimized. This can be accomplished if the arbitrator tells the parties in advance of the hearing—a good time would be the preliminary conference—how he or she would like documentary evidence to be organized. Here is my list of preferences concerning pre-hearing document organization.

II. Tips for Organizing Documents

A. Avoid Duplication on Proposed Exhibit Lists

The arbitrator should direct the parties and counsel to avoid duplication of exhibits, since that only creates the possibility for confusion.

---

[*]Leslie Trager is a practicing attorney in New York City. He also serves on the American Arbitration Association's panel of commercial arbitrators.

The scope and scheduling of document exchanges are usually discussed at an early preliminary conference. The standard procedure for document exchanges under the Commercial Arbitration Rules of the American Arbitration Association (AAA) first calls for both sides to prepare a list of all exhibits that they intend to introduce in evidence and then to exchange those lists. Second, the procedure calls for the parties to exchange the actual documents before the hearing on the merits.

I suggest that the parties, when preparing their exhibit lists, assign numbers to the proposed exhibits. The claimant takes the first group of numbers and the respondent takes the next group. The respondent should leave a small gap in numbering so that claimant can add a few exhibits in response to the respondent's list before or at the hearing itself, if that becomes necessary. Thus, for example, the claimant would use the numbers 1-90 for its proposed exhibits and the respondent would use the numbers 101-198.

I suggest that the standard document list exchange procedure be modified as follows. First, the claimant sends the respondent a list of proposed exhibits. This should be sent no later than 20 days prior to the first hearing day. I prefer 20 days over five days (the time specified for the list exchange in Rule 21(b) of the AAA Commercial Rules) because, in my opinion, five days before the hearing is too close for document control. Each proposed exhibit should be assigned a number (as discussed earlier) and sufficiently described in a neutral way so that it can be readily identified (e.g., contract between the parties). So that there will be no misunderstanding between the parties, I suggest that the claimant actually attach most if not all of the actual documents to its list of proposed exhibits.

Next, within ten days following receipt of the claimant's proposed exhibit list (with documents attached), the respondent should prepare and then deliver to the claimant its list of proposed exhibits, which should be similarly described and numbered. For the reason previously stated, the respondent should make an effort not to include the same documents as the claimant on its list. Many arbitrators suggest that the parties put together a book of joint exhibits for common documents that they both intend to use. I do not advocate this approach. In my view it just imposes more work on the parties. Each side always has the right to introduce a document included in the other side's book of exhibits. So, if the claimant doesn't include a document in its exhibit book, the respondent could include the document in its book. Either party can refer to the other's documents once they have been introduced. And if the claimant decides against introducing a document included in its exhibit book, the respondent can still introduce it by referring to the number given in the claimant's book of exhibits.

B. Produce Only the Most Relevant Documents

Attorneys preparing for a hearing tend to overproduce documents. Arbitrators often receive numerous bound volumes of documents from each side containing many documents that are never used at the hearing. This only makes for more work for the parties and the arbitrator. In arbitration, the parties should exchange and use as exhibits only the most relevant documents. Thus, the parties should carefully cull their lists of proposed exhibits after thinking about what each one is intended to prove and whether it is really necessary. If counsel does not intend to use particular documents, no purpose would be served by including them in their exhibit books.

Sometimes a party's attorney wants to include some documents on the list because there is a slight possibility that they will be needed at the hearing. I recommend grouping all questionable documents together in a separate list (and producing them later in a separate exhibit book) so that they are available but do not interfere with access to the important documents. The fewer documents in active use at the hearing, the faster the hearing will go.

C. Number All Exhibit Pages

I ask the parties' counsel to consecutively number all the pages of the exhibits that they intend to introduce at the hearing so that they can refer to relevant pages by numbers. Most attorneys follow the commendable practice of stamping a number on every page produced at the time of actual document production. Having numbered pages makes it much easier for the arbitrator to find internal pages in a document to which counsel is referring.

D. Put the Documents on a CD-ROM

If the total number of documents that the parties intend to refer to at the hearing requires more than three bound volumes, I ask the parties to put the documents on a CD-ROM (in addition to producing actual copies at the hearing) so I can use the computer to find the documents later on. There should be a table of contents on the CD with each document listed by exhibit number.

Today, creating a CD-ROM is no more expensive than making paper copies. A CD-ROM is a searchable, convenient electronic format that the arbitrator can use to review evidence during the course of the hearings or later on when deliberating or drafting the award (if a reasoned award is requested). This definitely beats looking through boxes of three-ringed binders.

E. There's No Substitute for Paper Documents

Using a computer as the exclusive method of finding documents or portions of documents at the hearing, however, is a practice I do not advocate. As noted above in the discussion of the CD-ROM, while computerized document searches can be quick and easy, it is likely that they will not provide the arbitrator with all the information he or she needs to be able to see at a particular time. For example, if a witness is testifying about a document and refers to several sections on different pages, the arbitrator may have difficulty seeing all the material referred to during the testimony. The arbitrator would probably be better off with the paper copy of the document. Thus, I believe that computerized documents should supplement and not substitute for paper copies of the documents.

III. Conclusion

By giving the parties some guidance on how to organize their documents, the arbitrator can reduce the time required to present the facts in the case and make it easier to learn the facts.

CHAPTER 26

E-DISCOVERY ISSUES: WHAT PARTIES AND THEIR COUNSEL NEED TO KNOW IN ANTICIPATION OF AND DURING ARBITRATION

*Steven C. Bennett**

I. Introduction

E-discovery has become a fixture in modern civil litigation. Almost inevitably, e-discovery will also increasingly affect arbitration. Because of the unique goals and processes of arbitration, rules for e-discovery must be adapted to meet the needs of parties in arbitration. The AAA and other arbitration-sponsoring organizations have begun to develop e-discovery processes appropriate for arbitration. This article discusses them and suggests drafting techniques and litigation strategies that could control the use of e-discovery in arbitration.

This article discusses the growing focus on the use, management, and discoverability of electronically stored information (ESI[1]) in litigation, and its potential use as evidence in arbitration. Court cases involving e-discovery frequently arise. There is also a mountain of literature on the subject.[2] These developments are due to such factors as:

- the explosive growth in computer power and storage capacity;

---

* Steven C. Bennett is a partner at Park Jensen Bennett LLP in New York City. He co-teaches a course on e-discovery at Rutgers Law School. The views expressed are solely those of the author and should not be attributed to the author's firm or its clients.

[1] ESI includes much more than the word processing files and e-mails that are on the hard drives of individual computer users. It may include all types of computer files (e.g., pdf, spreadsheet, power point, and photo files, backup tapes, digital information on portable drives, databases and metadata).

[2] Recent books on the developing law of e-discovery include Adam Cohen & David Lender, *Electronic Discovery: Law and Practice* (2003 and Supp. 2008 Aspen); Brent Kidwell *et al., Electronic Discovery* (2008 Law Journal Seminars Press); Ralph C. Losey, *E-Discovery: Current Trends and Cases* (2008 ABA).

- the widespread use of computers to prepare documents of all kinds;
- the increasing replacement of "snail mail" and faxes with e-mail and attachments;
- the use of digital voice mail, instant messaging and texting; and
- the ability to distribute e-mail widely to multiple computer users.

These developments have also made it inevitable that ESI would play a role in arbitration, particularly when the case is large and complex. Recognizing these developments, some arbitration organizations have developed guidance to help parties, counsel, and arbitrators deal with requests for ESI prior to the hearing – i.e., during "discovery." This article discusses available guidance from arbitration sponsoring organizations and suggests some key considerations with an eye on ESI, along with strategies for dealing with ESI after arbitration begins. We start with the duty to preserve ESI for potential use in arbitration.

II. The Duty to Preserve ESI

The Federal Rules of Civil Procedure, as amended in 2006, make clear that ESI is discoverable in federal civil litigation, even though the rules probably already applied to ESI.[3] Litigants have the duty to produce relevant, unprivileged ESI in response to a discovery request. Some courts have also ordered the production of a tiny form of ESI called metadata when the document to which it relates cannot be understood or used without it.[4]

The duty to produce ESI include an attendant duty to preserve it. This duty may be triggered when a party receives a letter from another party threatening to bring a legal action. This is called a "litigation hold" letter. Such a letter gives the recipient notice of threatened litigation and the need to "hold" (i.e., preserve) information and physical evidence relevant to the dispute in anticipation of litigation.

Efforts to find, preserve and produce ESI can be burdensome. The Federal Rules allow an application to a court to limit discovery of ESI

---

[3] FRCP 34 has long included a reference in the Advisory Committee Notes to "data compilations." This reference has been held to include a great deal of ESI.

[4] *See e.g.*, W. Lawrence Westcott II, "The Increasing Importance of Metadata in Electronic Discovery," 14 *Rich. J.L. & Tech.* 10 (2008) (noting cases).

upon a showing that it is not reasonably accessible because of undue burden or cost.[5] A litigant could argue in the motion that inaccessible forms of ESI, such as backup tapes, are not discoverable because production would require costly computer resources and overtime by IT [information technology] personnel.[6] In some cases, courts have shifted the cost of retrieving in inaccessible ESI from the producing party to the requesting party.

A party that fails to produce ESI without an excuse could be sanctioned. The range of possible sanctions includes imposing costs, precluding that party from introducing evidence, and even entry of a default judgment.[7]

III. Management of ESI

Many companies do not know what ESI they have or where to find it. One reason could be that most ESI is in "unstructured" data sources. To find out what ESI they have and ensure that it is not destroyed, companies should develop effective records management and preservation programs.[8] One part of such a program involves creating a "data map" showing the types and locations of ESI the company maintains. Typically, the map will be prepared by IT and records personnel. A data map can be invaluable in case of litigation.

Another part of a records management and preservation program involves establishing a policy to inform corporate personnel of their obligation to preserve ESI once a realistic threat of legal action appears. This is often referred to as a "litigation hold" policy.

The final piece of the program involves taking steps to prevent the destruction of relevant computerized documents and other forms of ESI

---

[5] FRCP 26(b). *See* Adam I. Cohen & G. Edward Kalbaugh, *ESI Handbook: Sources, Technology and Process* (2008).

[6] *See* Steven C. Bennett, "Backup Tapes in E-Discovery: Implications of New Technologies," 8(11) *BNA Digital Discovery & E-Evidence* 382 (2008).

[7] These cases present courts with the challenge of how to "fit the punishment to the crime." Steven C. Bennett, "Oops! E-Discovery Meets Spoliation," *N.Y.L.J.*, Aug. 21, 2006.

[8] *See* Steven C. Bennett, "Records Management: The Next Frontier in E-Discovery?," 7(08) *Prac. Litigator* 31 (2008) (nothing that effective records management is essential for litigation preparedness, especially as large portions of ESI arise from "unstructured" data sources). For guidance on development of records management policies, see generally Steven C. Bennett *et al.*, "Getting Started: Procedures For Developing a Document Retention System," 3(1) *BNA Acct. Pol'y & Prac. Spec. Rep.* 1 (2007).

under automated document destruction programs. This could involve reprogramming computer systems that delete obsolete ESI. It is also vital for the company to develop reasonable search and production techniques for ESI. For example, if the company has created indices of records for business purposes, it should be prepared to use them for purposes of discovery. The company may also wish to develop search routines and acquire search software, both of which can help demonstrate, in the event of litigation, that the company has taken reasonable steps to retrieve and produce responsive materials.

IV. ESI and Arbitration

Unlike the court system, arbitration is a creature of contract. Parties generally choose arbitration to reach a fair result more quickly and at less cost than through conventional civil litigation. Arbitration may achieve such results, in part, because judicial rules of procedure (which allow broad discovery[9] and assorted motions and evidence) do not apply to arbitration.[10]

Parties entering into arbitration agreements have the right to adopt arbitration rules that best suit their needs. Yet, they rarely craft all their own rules (though they could do so because arbitration is a contractual process). Instead, parties generally agree at the time of contracting to apply the arbitration rules of an established arbitration organization.[11] Such rules outline the arbitrator's power to manage the process and power the proceeding will unfold. For example, the American Arbitration Association (AAA) Commercial Arbitration Rules provides that arbitrators have broad power to manage the arbitration, while also

---

[9] FRCP 26(b)(1) allows discovery of "any nonprivileged matter that is relevant to any party's claim or defense." Discovery materials need not be admissible in evidence so long as the request is reasonably calculated to lead to the discovery of admissible evidence.

[10] In spite of this loosening of rules of evidence, arbitrators generally respect legal privileges. *See* AAA Commercial Rule R-31(c): "The arbitrator shall take into account applicable principles of legal privilege, such as those involving the confidentiality of communications between a lawyer and client." Although this rule appears in the section relating to evidence, arbitrators general do not require parties to exchange information protected by the attorney-client privilege. See AAA Large, Complex Case Rule L-4, which states that arbitrators should respect applicable rules of legal privilege and professional ethics.

[11] The parties, by written agreement, may vary the procedures set forth in the AAA rules. AAA Commercial Arbitration Rule R-1. After appointment of the arbitrator, such modifications may be made only with the consent of the arbitrator.

preserving arbitration's key goals of fairness and efficiency.[12] This does not mean that the parties have no say in the process; indeed, party autonomy is a recognized principle in arbitration. In AAA arbitration, for example, counsel are usually asked to be prepared to discuss how much discovery they need in an early preliminary conference with the arbitrator.[13] While the rules indicate that discovery is a matter to be agreed between the parties, they make clear that arbitrators have the final say, giving them authority to determine what is an "appropriate" amount of discovery for the case. They also give arbitrators authority to resolve any matters on which the parties cannot agree, provided their decisions are "consistent with the expedited nature of arbitration."

V. AAA Guidelines on ESI

Recognizing that most parties wish to control the costs of arbitration, which can escalate as the amount of pre-hearing discovery increases, the AAA's international division (the International Centre for Dispute Resolution, or ICDR) developed "Guidelines on the Exchange of Information in International Cases." Published in 2008, this document emphasizes that arbitrators have the authority, the responsibility and, in certain jurisdictions, the mandatory duty to manage arbitration proceedings to provide "a simpler, less expensive, and more expeditious process." The Guidelines repeat this efficiency theme several times. For example, Guideline 1(a) requires arbitrators to manage pre-hearing discovery "with a view to maintaining efficiency and economy."

Guideline 4 focuses specifically on ESI and the means of reducing ESI requests in discovery. For instance, it directs parties to keep their requests for ESI "narrowly focused and structured to make searching for them as economical as possible." It allows the arbitrators to "direct

[12] AAA Commercial Rule R-30(b) states: "The arbitrator, exercising his or her discretion, shall conduct the proceedings with a view to expediting the resolution of the dispute…."

[13] AAA Commercial Rule R-20(b) provides that, during the preliminary hearing, the parties and the arbitrator should discuss "the future conduct of the case, including clarification of the issues and claims, a schedule for the hearings and any other preliminary matters." R-21(a) discusses "exchanges of information." It states: "At the request of any party or at the discretion of the arbitrator, consistent with the expedited nature of arbitration, the arbitrator may direct … (i) the production of documents and other information…." Subsection (c) authorizes the arbitrator to resolve disputes concerning the exchange of information.

testing or other means of focusing and limiting any search." Importantly, it provides that ESI may be produced in the most economical form: "When documents to be exchanged are maintained in electronic form, the party in possession of such documents may make them available in the form (which may be paper copies) *most convenient and economical* for it…." (Emphasis added) Although Guideline 4 allows the party seeking discovery of ESI to apply to the arbitrators for an order requiring ESI production in a more accessible form, arbitrators may grant such an application only for good cause shown.

Guideline 6 permits arbitrators to order the inspection of "premises or objects," but it too limits this to when good cause is shown. A party could rely on this provision to request an inspection of an adversary's computers and servers. (Such requests sometimes occur in litigation.) In ruling on such a request, arbitrators should bear in mind that these inspections can be burdensome and disruptive of company operations.

Guideline 8 addresses the costs of e-discovery. It indicates that arbitrators have authority to condition receipt of ESI on the receiving party's payment of costs, in whole or in part.

Although the ICDR Guidelines were issued for international cases, they state that parties in other types of cases administered by the AAA may adopt them by agreement.

VI. Other Guidance on Discovery of ESI

The AAA/ICDR is not the only arbitral institution that has taken steps to address the issue of ESI. In 2008, the Chartered Institute of Arbitrators (CIA), a London-based provider of international arbitration services, published a "Protocol for E-Disclosure in Arbitration." The CIA Protocol provides guidelines for cases in which "potentially disclosable documents are in electronic form," and where "time and cost" may be an issue. For example, it calls for the tribunal and the parties to discuss e-discovery matters, including ESI preservation, privilege protection, and techniques to reduce e-discovery burdens and costs, "at the earliest opportunity." One technique it suggests to achieve these goals is an agreement of the parties on ESI search terms. The CIA Protocol also calls for the tribunal to consider issues of "reasonableness and proportionality" when ruling on requests for e-discovery. Like the ICDR Guidelines, it notes that the "primary source" of disclosure should be "reasonably accessible" data, and that documents should normally be produced "in the format in which the information is ordinarily maintained or in a reasonably useable form."

The CIA Protocol specifically addresses discovery of metadata, suggesting that the proper procedure should be for the requesting party to demonstrate both "relevance and materiality," since these factors outweigh the costs and burdens of producing metadata.

Finally, the CIA Protocol allows the tribunal to allocate the costs of e-discovery and fees for "technical guidance" on e-discovery issues to the requesting party, and tax these costs as part of the costs of the arbitration in the final award.

Another source of e-discovery guidance is the International Institute for Conflict Prevention and Resolution's "CPR Protocol on Disclosure of Documents and Presentation of Witnesses in Commercial Arbitration." The CPR Protocol was issued early in 2009.[14] It divides arbitration cases into four types based on the amount of discovery: Type A: no pre-hearing discovery, except for the exchange of exhibits to be used by each party at the hearing; Type B: discovery only where "substantial need" is shown; Type C: discovery only from party witnesses; and Type D: relatively full-scale discovery, including ESI. Type D discovery is subject only to limits of reasonableness, avoidance of duplication and undue burden.

The CPR Protocol gives parties the right to agree on the mode of disclosure, while bearing in mind that arbitration is not meant to be a "no stone unturned" exercise. Rather, it indicates that "disclosure should be granted only as to those items that are relevant and material, and for which a party has a substantial, demonstrable need in order to present its position."[15]

VII. Controlling E-Discovery Through Drafting

The ICDR Guidelines and the CPR Protocol provide food for thought for parties and lawyers who draft dispute resolution agreements. They set forth concrete principles that can be incorporated into

[14] The CPR Protocol on Disclosure of Documents and Presentations of Witnesses in Commercial Arbitration is available at www.cpradr.org. See C.R. Ragan & Robert F. Copple, "E-Discovery Enters the World of Arbitration," *Legal Times,* April 23, 2008.

[15] In 1999, the International Bar Association introduced its Rules on the Taking of Evidence in International Commercial Arbitration. These rule contemplate discovery of electronic information, but provide no guidance as to its use. They provide that a "document" includes writings of any kind, "whether recorded on paper, electronic means, audio or visual recording or any other mechanical or electronic means of storing or recording information." See John M. Barkett, "E-Discovery for Arbitrators," 1(2) *Disp. Resol. Int'l* 129 (2007) (suggesting potential revisions to IBA Rules, to address e-discovery issues).

arbitration agreements in whole or in part to prevent e-discovery from becoming a problem later on when a dispute arises. But adoption of such rules is not the only approach that parties can take to control e-discovery in arbitration.

Non-Binding ADR. One obvious approach to avoid expensive dispute resolution is first to use a dispute resolution process that typically involves little or no discovery. Examples include non-binding ADR processes, like negotiations between designated party representatives (or counsel, or both) and mediation. During these processes, the parties may voluntarily exchange a limited amount of information to foster settlement or aid mediation (such as by helping them understand key issues in dispute and decide whether settlement serves their interests). If negotiation or mediation succeeds in resolving a dispute, there would be no need to arbitrate and thus no disputes over ESI. But if arbitration becomes necessary, the traditional process is not the only option.

Scaled-Down Arbitration. For less complex disputes, there are at least two alternatives. One is non-binding (or advisory) arbitration, with discovery of essential documents only.[16] Typically in non-binding arbitration, a party dissatisfied with the award has the right to reject it and seek a trial within the time specified in the arbitration agreement. If a trial is not timely requested, the award becomes binding.

Another alternative is binding fast-track or expedited arbitration, with no discovery except in extraordinary circumstances. Such scaled-down arbitration processes are not likely to involve any exchange of ESI, even in its most accessible forms.[17] However, these processes may not be considered suitable for large, complex cases. For these disputes, traditional arbitration is usually preferred.

VIII. AAA Arbitration of Large, Complex Disputes

In large or complex cases, the parties often seek more extensive discovery, which could include ESI. For this reason, parties may wish to control the discovery of ESI in their arbitration agreement. One option they can use in an AAA case is to incorporate by reference into their

[16] Steven C. Bennett, "Non-Binding Arbitration: An Introduction," 61(2) *Disp. Resol. J.* 22 (2006). This type of arbitration appears, for example, in some state-sponsored arbitration programs for attorney-client fee disputes and similar programs created for the protection of consumers.

[17] The AAA offers shortened arbitration processes for certain cases.

arbitration agreement the ICDR Guidelines on the Exchange of Information in International Cases. If they prefer the CPR Protocol on e-discovery, they could write those rules into their agreement. However, they probably should not incorporate the CPR Protocol by reference since the AAA may not apply incorporated rules of another arbitration organization.

Alternatively, parties could draft their own limitations on e-discovery. For example, they could provide that, to fulfill the goal of efficiency, neither party would have any obligation to produce metadata, unless it is highly relevant. They could also provide that backup tapes need not be produced unless prior versions of the document are highly relevant and not available in hard copy form.

Placing limits on discovery, and e-discovery in particular, may not benefit claimants when the lion's share of relevant information is in the possession of the respondent. Thus, whether one party is more likely to be a claimant in a future arbitration could be relevant to deciding whether to limit ESI discovery. Employees and consumers are usually claimants and employers and manufacturer/sellers are typically respondents. Small vendors and contractors frequently tend to be claimants in disputes with certain large corporations with which they do business. However, some parties and their counsel may not find it easy to predict their position in a future arbitration.

On the other hand, limiting discovery may benefit parties in need of a more efficient resolution of their dispute, such as a contractor with serious financial issues. However, it may be difficult to predict at the time of contracting whether financial issues would make controlling the costs of dispute resolution a high priority. Also, financial status can change, as we have seen in the current economic crisis. Because some parties may be unable to predict with the accuracy their future position in a dispute and their financial needs, it may not be easy for them to craft the "best" arbitration clause.

However, some neutral principles almost always apply. For example, limiting the use of ESI in arbitration in a large, complex case could minimize the risk of inadvertent production of privileged information. This has often been a problem with ESI. Inadvertent production may result when the producing party does not have enough time to review all ESI for privilege before producing it to the adversary.[18] At other times inadvertent

[18] Rule 502 of the Federal Rules of Evidence has been adopted to deal with the issue of inadvertent production of privileged information. See Alvin F. Lindsay, "New Rule 502 to Protect Against Privilege Waiver," *Nat'l L.J.*, Sept. 2, 2008, available at www.law.com.

production has occurred because the producing party could not tell from hard copy review that metadata contained privileged information.[19]

IX. International Disputes

For international disputes, other considerations bear on discovery and ESI. Primarily among them is the legal tradition followed by the country where the arbitration is held (the "seat" of the arbitration). If the seat is in a common law jurisdiction, the arbitrators are likely to allow relatively broad discovery; but if the seat is in a civil jurisdiction, the arbitrators may disfavor discovery or allow only a minimal amount. For this reason, choosing a civil law jurisdiction, such as France or Germany, as the arbitral seat could minimize the use of ESI in arbitration.[20]

X. E-Discovery and Arbitrator Selection

Arbitrator selection is one of the most important decisions to be made in an arbitration proceeding. The choice of arbitrator could have a major impact on the amount of discovery. Some arbitrators are less concerned with managing the amount of discovery, while others are serious about controlling the process. Arbitrator attitudes toward discovery will almost certainly be colored by their experiences in prior arbitration proceedings. Those who have seen arbitrations go on and on due to extensive discovery may be keen to curb discovery as much as possible.[21] Thus, it is important to research the backgrounds of the arbitrator candidates and talk to parties who have used them to gain insight into their experiences.

---

[19] *See* Kenton Hutcherson, "The Art of Redacting Privileged Data," *Law Tech. News*, Jan. 28, 2008, available at www.law.com (attorneys may accidentally produce privileged information by redacting only the imaged document, leaving intact metadata and other file information).

[20] *See* Anke Meier, "The Production of Electronically Stored Information in International Commercial Arbitration," 6(4) *SchiedsVZ [German Arbitration J.]* 179, 188 (July/Aug. 2008) ("In international commercial arbitration, production of electronically stored documents appears to be particularly challenging, because frequently arbitrators, parties and counsel come from different legal systems which may have a different understand of discovery in general and e-discovery in particular.") See generally *Electronic Disclosure in International Arbitration* (David J. Howell, ed., Juris Publ. 2008).

[21] *See* Robert B. Davidson & Margaret L. Shaw, "Arbitrators Hold Significant Power Over Discovery," *N.L.J.*, Nov. 27, 2006, available at www.nlj.com.

When a dispute arises (even before an arbitration demand issues), counsel should consider talking to the adversary about the possible need for e-discovery. The purpose of the discussion is to negotiate an agreement if possible. Such efforts are generally appreciated by arbitrators. Even if they prove unsuccessful, they will (at the very least) create a record (for example, correspondence, contemporaneous notes of telephone calls, and/or e-mails) showing counsel's good faith efforts to negotiate the scope, form and procedures for e-discovery, which counsel can present to the tribunal at a preliminary conference that has pre-hearing discovery on the agenda. Counsel should also provide the arbitrators with a list of issues that remain unresolved. When raising e-discovery issues with the tribunal, counsel should give the arbitrators the impression of having made reasonable proposals to the adversary, and that it is the adversary in seeking the sun, the moon, and the stars. They also should be prepared to both advocate the client's position on e-discovery and explain why its position on e-discovery is more reasonable, and how the resolution sought from the tribunal would address the balance between the need for, and burden from, e-discovery. Counsel should be prepared to accept any reasonable compromise the tribunal proposes.

If the size of the matter and the complexity of the issues warrant the expensive, counsel should bring an IT professional to the preliminary conference on discovery to answer questions from the tribunal. Counsel should avoid putting the tribunal in the position of having to make a "seat of the pants" decision, since it could be difficult to modify once made.

XI. Moving to Compel Production

As arbitration progresses, one of the attorneys may decide to seek the aid of the tribunal in obtaining production of one or more items of ESI from the adversary. If the adverse party has been particularly obstreperous, counsel could couple the request to compel production of ESI with a request that the tribunal preclude the adversary from offering contrary proof, and draw an adverse inference if the adversary continues to refuse to produce the ESI. These remedies are essentially self-executing; if the tribunal grants them, the award could be adverse to the resisting party.[22]

---

[22] Thus, the tribunal may, as remedy: (1) preclude the recalcitrant party from offering evidence on the point for which discovery is requested, and/or (2) apply an inference, in reaching its decision, that the information withheld would have bene harmful to the

Counsel should keep such requests to a minimum and only seek what is highly relevant and necessary. Before approaching the tribunal, counsel should first try to negotiate with the adversary and explain why the client needs the ESI. Here, too, it is important to make a record of the steps taken to resolve the matter amicably before approaching the tribunal for assistance.

XII. Dealing with E-Discovery Issues at the Hearing

When ESI is offered as evidence at a hearing on the merits, it is wise to make sparing objections, and those should be limited to challenging the credibility of the evidence, or its reliability or authenticity. Counsel should not make objections based on technical inadmissibility under judicial rules of evidence because these rules do not generally apply to arbitration. Instead, counsel could show the tribunal that the party offering the ESI selectively produced ESI helpful to its case, leaving out ESI that would help the other side's case, or produced ESI in an unhelpful or incomplete form, and at the hearing used the better or complete form for its own case.

To mount an authenticity challenge to ESI introduced into evidence, counsel will probably need to bring a forensic expert to the hearing to explain the technical aspects of how the alteration occurred. Many arbitration hearings conclude with counsel summarizing the facts developed at the hearing and legal arguments on the merits. If significant e-discovery issues arose during the hearing, counsel should be prepared to argue the legal significance of those issues and provide authorities on e-discovery law.[23] For example, if spoliation of evidence is claimed, counsel should ask the tribunal to infer from the spoliation that the missing ESI would have been harmful to the spoliator and provide the tribunal with cases supporting that relief.[24]

---

recalcitrant party. See generally Steven C. Bennett, "Who Is Responsible for Ethical Behavior by Counsel in Arbitration?" 63(2) *Dispute Res. J.* 38 (2008) (summarizing potential sanctions for improperties in arbitration).

[23] One very helpful place to commence any research on e-discovery issues is www.thesedonaconference.com. The Sedona Conference, composed of working groups of volunteers from law firms, e-discovery service vendors, judges and academics has spent considerable effort over the past few years in developing "best practice" recommendations in the e-discovery arena.

[24] *See* Irene C. Warshauer, "Electronic Discovery in Arbitration: Privilege Issues and Spoliation of Evidence," 61(4) *Disp. Resol. J.* 8 (2006).

XIII. Parting Thoughts

Electronic discovery is here to stay (in the United States, at least) and it is likely to play a role in arbitration in the coming years. Practitioners in arbitration will have to become familiar with e-discovery issues, such as ESI preservation and production. They also will have to carefully plan their client's approach to e-discovery in ADR and draft appropriate provisions to deal with it, depending on the client's business and the types of disputes it normally encounters. Practitioners also will need to be prepared to deal with e-discovery issues promptly and forthrightly once arbitration begins.

Because arbitration is flexible, e-discovery in arbitration will likely be more flexible than in conventional litigation. This more flexible approach could influence how e-discovery is handled in conventional litigation. For example, commentators have suggested that "special masters" be appointed to handle complicated e-discovery disputes in litigation.[25] Special masters are essentially court appointed experts, sometime serving as arbitrators or mediators. They may bring to e-discovery in arbitration some of the same values (flexibility and efficiency) that have been the hallmarks of arbitration in general.

---

[25] *See* generally, Steven C. Bennett & Cecelia Dickson, "E-discovery May Be a Job for Special Masters," *Nat'l L.J.,* July 17, 2006 at S5; Shira A. Scheindlin & Jonathan M. Redgrave, "Special Masters and E-Discovery: The Intersection of Two Recent Revisions to the Federal Rules of Civil Procedure," 30 *Cardozo L. Rev.* 347 (2008).

CHAPTER 27

ELECTRONIC DISCOVERY IN ARBITRATION: PRIVILEGE ISSUES AND SPOLIATION OF EVIDENCE

Irene C. Warshauer[*]

I. Introduction

"Electronic documents are no less subject to disclosure than paper records." So said the U.S. District Court for the Southern District of New York in *Rowe Entertainment v. William Morris Agency*.[1] Unlike paper records, which require most companies to rent storage space, electronic documents take up no additional space and the cost of storing them is negligible. Because there is little or no need to discard electronic files, a massive amount of electronic data, including email is now being retained. Much of the retained data is on backup tapes created for emergency uploading in case data is lost accidentally or otherwise.

Backup data is usually not easily searched. It tends to be stored on a daily or weekly basis, so it is not indexed by subject matter. The enormous amount of retained electronic data and the difficulty of searching it makes it very expensive and time-consuming to find documents sought to be produced for litigation or arbitration, and then review them to see if they can be withheld from production based on attorney-client and/or work-product protections. Using shortcuts to conduct a manual review of e-documents to meet discovery and hearing deadlines can lead to an inadvertent waiver of these protections. Spoliation of evidence may also occur through routine recycling of backup tapes, deletion of emails and changes in documents caused by

---

* Irene C. Warshauer is an active attorney, arbitrator and mediator in New York City. She serves on the American Arbitration Association's panel of arbitrators and mediators. Ms. Warshauer can be reached at icw@irenewarshauer.com

The views expressed herein are those of the author and not necessarily those of her clients or the AAA.

[1] 205 F.R.D. 421, 428 (S.D.N.Y. 2002).

automatic computer operations (metadata).[2] This can give rise to requests for the imposition of sanctions.

Arbitrators must deal with these issues while still preserving the speedier results, limited discovery and cost effectiveness of arbitration. This article will discuss recent court decisions on the discovery of electronic records (e-discovery) to help guide arbitrators and advocates on (1) inadvertent waivers of the protections afforded by the attorney-client privilege and the work-product doctrine, and (2) spoliation of evidence. It does not address the extent of e-discovery that might be appropriate to any particular arbitration.

II. Discovery Protections in Arbitration

The attorney-client privilege and the attorney work-product doctrine protect certain documents from discovery in litigation. These privileges are also generally recognized in arbitration. For example, Rule R-31 of the American Arbitration Association's Commercial Arbitration Rules, which governs the introduction of evidence at arbitral hearings, provides in subpart (c) that "[t]he arbitrator shall take into account applicable principles of legal privilege, such as those involving the confidentiality of communications between a lawyer and client."[3]

Accordingly, counsel may assert these privileges during discovery in arbitration and during the attempt to use privileged material as evidence at the arbitral hearing. In order to assert one of the legal privileges, the document at issue must be protected by the privilege and the privilege must not have been waived. A waiver can occur by producing the document to an adversary or another person not covered by the privilege. Waiver can occur from intentional disclosure or inadvertent production of a protected document.

A. Waiver of Legal Privileges

One standard used by courts to determine whether or not a legal privilege has been waived is set forth in *United States v. Rigas*.[4] In *Rigas*, the court evaluated:

---

[2] The term "metadata" is defined *infra* in section IV. Spoliation of Evidence and Metadata.

[3] The issues in this article are discussed under the Commercial Arbitration Rules of the American Arbitration Association. These rules are available on the AAA website at www.adr.org.

[4] 281 F. Supp. 2d 733, 735 (S.D.N.Y. 2003).

- the reasonableness of the precautions taken by the producing party to prevent inadvertent disclosure of privileged documents;
- the volume of discovery versus the extent of the specific disclosure issue;
- the length of time taken by the producing party to rectify the disclosure; and
- the overarching issue of fairness.

In *Atronic International GMBH v. SAI Semispecialists of America*,[5] the court applied the *Rigas* standard to two privileged emails between a party and its international counsel that were inadvertently produced because the attorney handling discovery for the producing party did not recognize the name of international counsel. The court found that the inadvertent production waived any privilege attached to the emails. The court said the precautions taken by the producing party were not reasonable because the emails, which went directly to the heart of the issues, did not state that they were "privileged" or "confidential."

The breadth of a waiver of a legal privilege varies by jurisdiction. Inadvertent production of a privileged document may waive the privilege only for that document or for all privileged documents on that subject or on all subjects. Arbitrators will look to the law designated by the parties in the arbitration agreement, but if the agreement is silent, they may look to the law of the jurisdiction in which they are sitting or to that jurisdiction's conflicts-of-law rules to determine the applicable law of waiver. The federal circuits have different controlling law on the effect of inadvertent production of privileged documents:

- The "strict accountability" rule holds that an inadvertent production waives the privilege. This rule is followed by the Federal and First Circuits.[6]
- The "to err is human" approach. This approach requires the waiver to be knowing and intentional. The Eighth Circuit follows this rule.
- The "balancing test." This approach is often used by district courts in the Second and Fourth Circuits.[7]

---

[5] 232 F.R.D. 160 (E.D.N.Y. 2005).

[6] EDNA SELAN EPSTEIN, THE ATTORNEY-CLIENT PRIVILEGE AND THE WORK-PRODUCT DOCTRINE 309 (4th ed. 2001).

[7] *Id.* at 310-11.

B. Development of "Claw-back" Agreements

As suggested above, the massive amount of electronic documents potentially subject to discovery greatly increases the number of documents that must be reviewed for privilege. It also makes the inadvertent production of a privileged document more likely. As a result, it has become increasingly common to see parties enter into agreements to disclose privileged materials provided the disclosure is not taken to entail a waiver as to all privileged matters. Because courts will give effect to such agreements, the parties by contract, so to speak, can avoid the general rule that partial disclosure on a given subject matter will bring in its wake total disclosure.[8]

Over the years, attorneys have also entered into agreements with opposing counsel to protect against waiver of the privilege. This agreement usually states that a party who inadvertently produces a privileged document may take it back once the inadvertent production is discovered. The time and cost involved in reviewing electronic documents for privilege has expanded the use of these "claw-back" agreements. An expansive version of these agreements permits a party to produce all of its relevant documents for review and selection by the requesting party without waiving the privilege. Once the requesting party selects the documents it wants, the producing party reviews those documents for privilege.

District courts in the Second Circuit have approved the use of claw-back agreements.[9] In the third of four "e-discovery" decisions in an employment discrimination suit captioned *Zubulake v. Warburg*, Judge Shira Scheindlin explained:

> [T]he producing party unilaterally decides on the review protocol. When reviewing electronic data, that review may range from reading every word of every single document to conducting a series of targeted key word searches. Indeed, many parties to document-intensive litigation enter into so-called "claw-back" agreements that allow the parties to forego privilege review altogether in favor of an agreement to return inadvertently produced privileged documents.

---

[8] Selan Epstein, *supra* n. 6, at 287-88.

[9] Zubulake v. Warburg, 216 F.R.D. 280, 290 (2003) [*Zubulake III*]. *See also* Eutectic Corp. v. Metco, 61 F.R.D. 35, 42 (E.D.NY. 1973).

Court approval of such agreements varies. One commentator noted that some district courts in New Jersey refused to enforce claw-back agreements.[10] In one case, a privileged memo was inadvertently disclosed "in the mistaken belief that the database from which it was produced contained only nonprivileged documents."[11] According to this commentator, "the court held that the privilege was waived, despite a claw-back agreement formalized by a trial court order." The court reasoned that "a claw-back order cannot preserve privilege when parties hand over documents without privilege review" and that, "even if disclosure is unintentional, waiver is avoided only if reasonable precautions are taken to avoid inadvertent production."[12]

1. Use of Claw-back Agreements in Arbitration

Parties to arbitration can avoid this problem by presenting the proposed claw-back agreement to the arbitrators at an early preliminary hearing, with a request for an order approving their use prior to relying upon them in the production of documents. Without advance approval, the panel may not recognize the legitimacy of a claw-back agreement and hold that the privilege has been waived. Should the question arise in a subsequent proceeding, the decision maker, whether another arbitration panel or a court, is much more likely to respect the privilege if the arbitration panel has entered an order approving a claw-back agreement.

C. Effect of Change in FRCP Rule 26(b)(5)

The Federal Rules of Civil Procedure (FRCP) have been amended to specifically address e-discovery. Although these rules do not apply to arbitration absent the parties' agreement to the contrary, the reasons for the amendment should be of interest to arbitrators and parties appearing before them.

The amendment to FRCP Rule 26(b)(5) (which with other amendments was approved without comment by the U.S. Supreme Court on April 12, 2006, and takes effect Dec. 1, 2006[13]) recognizes the exponential increase in problems of inadvertent production of privileged

---

[10] Andrew Rhys Davies, *"Claw-back" Agreements Lose Their Grip in Court*, NAT. L.J., July 24, 2006, *citing* Ciba-Geigy Corp. v. Sandoz Ltd., 916 F. Supp. 404 (D.N.J. 1995); Koch Materials Co. v. Shore Slurry Seal Inc., 208 F.R.D. 109, 118 (D.N.J. 2002).

[11] Ciba-Geigy Corp., *supra* n. 10.

[12] Rhys Davies, *supra* n. 10.

[13] U.S. Order No. 20, Court Rules, Administrative Office of the U.S. Courts, Federal Rules of Civil Procedure, Adoption and Amendments to Civil Rules.

material caused by e-discovery. The Report to the Standing Committee on Rules of Practice and Procedure, Judicial Conference of the United States by the Advisory Committee on the Federal Rules of Civil Procedure, September 2005, stated:

> The problems that can result from efforts to guard against privilege waiver often become more acute when discovery of electronically-stored information is sought. The volume of the information and the forms in which it is stored make privilege determinations more difficult and privilege review correspondingly more expensive and time-consuming yet less likely to detect all privileged information. Inadvertent production is increasingly likely to occur. Because the failure to screen out even one privileged item may result in an argument that there has been a waiver as to all other privileged materials related to the same subject matter, early attention to this problem is more important as electronic discovery becomes more common. Under the proposed amendments to Rules 26(f) and 16, if the parties are able to reach an agreement to adopt protocols for asserting privilege and work-product protection claims that will facilitate discovery that is faster and at lower cost, they may ask the court to include such arrangements in a case-management or other order.[14]

Rule 26(b)(5)[15] as amended permits a party claiming that privileged information has been inadvertently produced to notify the other party of the claim and the reason for it. After notification, the opposing party is

---

[14] For a general discussion of issues concerning electronic discovery, *see* THE SEDONA CONFERENCE, THE SEDONA PRINCIPLES: BEST PRACTICES RECOMMENDATIONS & PRINCIPLES FOR ADDRESSING ELECTRONIC DOCUMENT PRODUCTION (2003), available at www.thesedonaconference.org/publications_html.

[15] The amendment to FRCP 26(b)(5) that concerns us here would add new subparagraph B. This subparagraph states:

> Information Produced. If information is produced in discovery that is subject to a claim of privilege or of protection as trial-preparation material, the party making the claim may notify any party that received the information of the claim and the basis for it. After being notified, a party must promptly return, sequester, or destroy the specified information and any copies it has and may not use or disclose the information until the claim is resolved. A receiving party may promptly present the information to the court under seal for a determination of the claim. If the receiving party disclosed the information before being notified, it must take reasonable steps to retrieve it. The producing party must preserve the information until the claim is resolved.

required to return the document, or segregate and protect the document or destroy it; that party may not use the document in any way until the claim of privilege is resolved. In effect, the amendment recognizes claw-back agreements.

The amendment may not, however, protect against a waiver for inadvertently produced e-documents. *Hopson v. Mayor of Baltimore*, a 2005 decision by a district court in Maryland, though it recognized the reasons for claw-back agreements and the proposal to amend Rule 26, seriously questioned the effectiveness of such agreements in preserving attorney-client and work-product protections.[16]

Hopson involved a request "designed to discover the nature, extent and location of electronically stored records, the Defendants' IT capabilities, the nature of archived data, e-mail, and records retention policies."[17] In ruling on a motion to compel answers to interrogatories, the district court recognized that one major concern "was the cost and burden of pre-production privilege review of the records sought." It also noted the commentary that accompanied the proposal to amend FRCP Rule 26, which stated that the proposed amendment "does not address whether the privilege or protection that is asserted after production was waived by the production."[18]

Since amended Rule 26(b)(5) took effect in December 2006, parties have been able to raise the attorney-client privilege and the work-product doctrine after production of electronic records. But, as noted by the *Hopson* court and the commentary to the rule, the rule does not say that documents produced in accordance with its terms are protected from waiver of these privileges. For this reason, the *Hopson* court warned that "[a]though the use of 'non-waiver' agreements presently may be growing," their use is "certainly . . . not risk-free." The court pointed out that some commentators are "openly skeptical of the parties' ability to insulate themselves from waiver as against third-parties,[19] even if [nonwaiver agreements] are enforceable as between themselves."[20] The court

[16] Hopson v. Mayor of Baltimore, 232 F.R.D. 228 (D. Md. 2005).

[17] *Id.* at 230.

[18] The commentary states, "[T]he proposed amendment does not address the substantive questions whether privilege or work product protection has been waived or forfeited" by following the procedures set forth in the amended rule.

[19] Hopson, *supra* n. 16, 232 F.R.D. at 235.

[20] For this proposition the *Hopson* court cited Westinghouse Elec. Corp. v. Republic of the Philippines, 951 F.2d 1414, 1426-27 (3d Cir. 1991) (holding that an agreement between a litigant and the Department of Justice providing that documents produced in response to a DOJ investigation would not waive the privilege, does not preserve the privilege as against

concluded, "Absent a definitive ruling on the waiver issue, no prudent party would agree to follow the procedures recommended in the proposed rule."

III. Avoiding Waiver in Arbitration

Arbitration provides an advantage to parties concerned about waiver of privileges resulting from e-discovery, as arbitrators are particularly attuned to the concerns of the parties before them, and they are not required to analyze and conform to the latest court decision on the issue. Thus, it is vital for arbitrating parties to obtain an order from the arbitration panel (1) relieving them of the obligation to conduct a pre-production review of all e-documents for privilege, and (2) specifically ordering that the attorney-client and work-product privileges are not waived by the production of such documents. The fact that arbitrations are private proceedings is also beneficial.

Parties should still be concerned whenever privileged material is produced to an adversary. While the adversary may not be able to use the privileged documents, knowledge of what they contain may assist in the prosecution or defense of the adversary's case.

IV. Spoliation of Evidence and Metadata

"Spoliation is the destruction or significant alteration of evidence, or the failure to preserve property for another's use as evidence in pending or reasonably foreseeable litigation."[21] This generally means that parties have an obligation to preserve evidence that may be relevant to matters at issue in an arbitration as well as a litigation. Judge Scheindlin, in the fourth e-discovery decision in *Zubulake*, characterized this obligation as having to put a "litigation hold" in place to ensure the preservation of relevant documents.[22] In the fifth discovery decision in *Zubulake*, Judge Scheindlin held counsel to the same requirement, saying that counsel should "issue a 'litigation hold' at the outset of litigation or whenever

---

a different entity in an unrelated civil proceeding). It also cited Bowne v. AmBase Corp., 150 F.R.D. 465, 478-79 (S.D.N.Y. 1993) (nonwaiver agreement between producing party in one case not applicable to third party in another civil case).

[21] West v. Goodyear Tire & Rubber Co., 168 F.3d 776, 779 (2d Cir. 1999).

[22] Zubulake v. USB Warburg, 220 F.R.D. 212, 218 (S.D.N.Y. 2004) [*Zubulake IV*].

litigation is reasonably anticipated."[23] She also found that the litigation hold should be "periodically re-issued so that new employees are aware of it, and so that it is fresh in the minds of all employees." In addition, counsel must "communicate directly with 'key players' in the litigation" and periodically remind them of the preservation duty. In carrying out these duties, counsel should become familiar with the client's computer system, take affirmative steps to monitor and coordinate the client's discovery efforts, and monitor compliance.[24] According to Judge Scheindlin, "[c]ounsel must also make sure that all backup media which the party is required to retain is identified and stored in a safe place." For example, counsel could choose to take physical possession of relevant backup tapes or segregate them and place them in storage. Judge Scheindlin explained that "[b]y taking possession of, or otherwise safeguarding, all potentially relevant backup tapes, counsel eliminates the possibility that such tapes will be inadvertently recycled."

The spoliation rule has led to uncertainty about the obligation to preserve electronic data, given "electronic document retention policies that often include automatic deletion of certain data after a set period of time (particularly for email)."[25] But courts are addressing these issues. Judge Scheindlin discussed them in her e-discovery decisions. Based on her decisions, one commentator concluded that the litigation hold includes the duty to stop "any routine recycling of backup tapes as well as routine email deletion."[26]

Electronic documents also involve something called "metadata," which may not be accessible by the average computer user.[27] Metadata was defined in the *Sedona Guidelines: Best Practice Guidelines & Commentary for Managing Information & Records in an Electronic Age* as:

> [I]nformation about a document or file that is recorded by the computer to assist the computer and often the user in storing and

---

[23] Zubulake v. USB Warburg, 229 F.R.D. 422, 433-34 (S.D.N.Y. 2004) [*Zubulake V*] (motion for sanctions for failure to produce and tardy production of relevant evidence; decision addressed counsel's obligation to ensure that relevant information is preserved by giving clear instructions to the client to preserve such information and, perhaps more importantly, a client's obligation to heed those instructions). *See also* Steven A. Weiss, *Do Not Delete: Sanctions for Spoliation of Electronic Evidence*, 13(2) THE COMMITTEE ON PRETRIAL PRACTICE & DISCOVERY 6 (ABA Section of Litigation Spring 2005).

[24] Zubulake V, *supra* n. 23.

[25] Weiss, *supra* n. 23, at 6.

[26] *Id.*

[27] Sedona Conference, *supra* n. 14, at 5.

retrieving the document or file at a later date. The information may also be useful for system administration as it reflects data regarding the generation, handling, transfer, and storage of the data within the computer system.[28]

Metadata is further defined as: "all of the contextual, processing, and use of information needed to identify and certify the scope, authenticity, and integrity of active or archival electronic information or records."[29]

Metadata includes the computer system's automatic alteration of documents. Thus, information can be lost or changed. And when that happens in a litigation or arbitration, a claim for spoliation can result.[30] Deletion or changes to metadata, as well as scrubbing metadata to avoid disclosure of such information, can be deemed spoliation. Moreover, because of its hidden nature, "metadata . . . has the potential for inadvertent disclosure of confidential or privileged information."[31] This can result in a waiver of the attorney-client privilege or the work-product protection or both.

How courts have treated the discovery of metadata and its spoliation can provide guidance to arbitrators and parties. A federal court in California enforced an order to discover electronic data, including metadata. It did not deem the difficulty of redacting privileged information to be a reason not to sustain the order.[32] A federal court in Louisiana held that parties have an obligation to preserve metadata as part of their obligation to preserve evidence.[33]

The rules described above with regard to the identification, preservation and production of evidence and metadata should provide guidance in arbitration, even though arbitral discovery is more curtailed. Thus, parties to an arbitration (and their counsel) should have the same concern about preventing spoliation of evidence.

---

[28] *Id.* at 5. Thus, metadata could be the computer's automatic alteration of data, such as the insertion of the date of a revision of a letter, as opposed to its original date.

[29] Sedona Conference, *supra* n. 14, at Technical Appendix E.

[30] *See generally*, Marjorie A. Shields, Discoverability of Metadata, 2006 A.L.R. 6th at 6.

[31] *Id.*

[32] In re Verisign, Inc. Sec. Litigation, 2004 WL 2445243 (N.D. Cal. 2006).

[33] In re Vioxx Prods. Liability Litigation, 2005 WL 756743 (E.D. La. 2005).

V. Sanctions for Spoliation

A. Sanctions in Litigation

The case law on spoliation was largely developed prior to e-discovery. The usual sanction for spoliation was drawing "a negative inference concerning the content of the missing evidence against a party that has intentionally, and for an improper purpose, destroyed, mutilated, lost, altered, or concealed evidence."[34] That means inferring that the spoliated evidence was unfavorable to the interests of the party who destroyed it. This remedy punishes the spoliator by giving the party seeking discovery the benefit of the evidence had it not been destroyed.

Judge Scheindlin has commented on the *in terrorem* effect of an adverse inference: "When a jury is instructed that it may 'infer that the party who destroyed the potentially relevant evidence did so "out of a realization that the [evidence was] unfavorable," the party suffering this instruction will be hard-pressed to prevail on the merits.'"[35]

Judge Scheindlin has also set forth the burden of proof in order to obtain an adverse inference based on spoliation. The party seeking this sanction must establish:

> (1) that the party having control over the evidence had an obligation to preserve it at the time it was destroyed; (2) that the records were destroyed with a "culpable state of mind" and (3) that the destroyed evidence was "relevant" to the party's claim or defense such that a reasonable trier of fact could find that it would support that claim or defense.[36]

The Second Circuit has reasoned that "[t]he sanction of an adverse inference may be appropriate in some cases involving the negligent destruction of evidence because each party should bear the risk of its own negligence."[37]

Judge Scheindlin found that the plaintiff in *Zubulake* had not established that the content of the defendant's destroyed backup tapes was "relevant," something much harder to do with lost computer data than with physical evidence of an accident. Nevertheless, she granted

[34] Bronson v. Umphries, 138 S.W.3d 844, 854 (Tenn. Ct. App. 2003).

[35] Zubulake IV, *supra* n. 22, at 219-20.

[36] Zubulake V, *supra* n 23.

[37] Residential Funding Corp. v. DeGeorge Fin. Corp., 306 F.3d 99 (2d Cir. 2002).

plaintiff's motion to instruct the jury to draw an adverse inference as to emails deleted after a particular date and emails that were lost when defendant's "backup tapes were recycled."[38] In addition to finding that the defendant and its employees had been derelict in the duty to preserve e-documents, Judge Scheindlin also found that counsel (1) failed to communicate the direction not to destroy emails to employees with knowledge of the litigation, (2) failed to request files from a knowledgeable employee, and (3) failed to protect backup tapes.

Judge Scheindlin's quote above about the draconian effect of an adverse inference proved prophetic when the jury awarded the plaintiff in *Zubulake* $9.1 million dollars in compensatory damages and $20.1 million in punitive damages.

Other sanctions that courts have imposed for spoliation of evidence include an assessment of monetary damages and precluding the culpable party's witness from testifying. In *United States v. Philip Morris USA*,[39] the court precluded several corporate witnesses from testifying and imposed $2,750,000 in monetary sanctions against a company that deleted emails in violation of a preservation order. According to one commentator, one court went so far as to enter a default judgment against a defendant for its "destruction or failure to preserve electronically stored data, including metadata in violation of a discovery source."[40]

In another case, however, the Second Circuit vacated the dismissal of a complaint as a sanction against a personal injury plaintiff who destroyed physical evidence (a tire and a tire-changing machine), finding that the lower court abused its discretion.[41] The Second Circuit stated that "the applicable sanction should be molded to serve the prophylactic, punitive, and remedial rationales underlying the spoliation doctrine." It continued:

> The sanction should be designed to: (1) deter parties from engaging in spoliation; (2) place the risk of an erroneous judgment on the party who wrongfully created the risk; and (3) restore "the prejudiced party to the same position he would have been in absent the wrongful destruction of evidence by the opposing party."

---

[38] Zubulake V, *supra* n. 23, at 436.
[39] 327 F. Supp. 2d 21 (D.D.C. 2004).
[40] Weiss, *supra* n. 23 at 9.
[41] West, *supra* n. 21, 168 F.3d at 779.

Attorneys and parties have been sanctioned under the Federal Rules for dereliction of discovery duties. The court in *Qualcomm Inc. v. Broadcom Corp.*[42] sanctioned some particularly egregious discovery conduct. It involved the failure to produce tens of thousands of documents by Qualcomm. Magistrate Judge Barbara L. Major imposed sanctions on counsel for Qualcomm and the company, including over $8 million in attorneys' fees and reference of "the Sanctioned Attorneys to the State Bar of California for an appropriate investigation and possible imposition of sanctions."[43]

In a patent infringement case brought by Qualcomm, the defendant, Broadcom contended that any infringement claim had been waived, if Qualcomm participated in meetings concerning industry standards ("JVT"). Qualcomm's counsel denied its participation in the JVT communications and meetings both in pretrial proceedings and during the trial. Certain witnesses' testimony left the impression that a search or production of electronic data relating to Qualcomm's participation in the industry standards process had not occurred.

Post trial "Broadcom filed a written motion requesting that the Court sanction Qualcomm for its failure to produce tens of thousands of documents that Broadcom had requested in discovery."[44] Qualcomm's conduct was held to be unacceptable and in violation of the standard of good faith:

> Producing 1.2 million pages of marginally relevant documents while hiding 46,000 critically important ones does not constitute good faith and does not satisfy either the client's or attorney's discovery obligations. Similarly, agreeing to produce certain categories of documents and then not producing all of the documents that fit within such a category is unacceptable.[45]

During witness preparation, one of Qualcomm's attorneys discovered an email referencing the industry standard email list. The witness's laptop was searched several days later and had 21 emails relating to the JVT list.

The Qualcomm trial team decided not to produce these newly discovered emails to Broadcom, claiming they were not responsive to Broadcom's discovery requests. The attorneys ignored the fact that the

---

[42] 2008 WL 66932 (S.D. Cal. January 7, 2008).
[43] *Id.*
[44] *Id.*
[45] *Id.* at *18.

presence of the emails on Raveendran's computer undercut Qualcomm's premier argument that it had not participated in the JVT in 2002. The Qualcomm trial team failed to conduct any investigation to determine whether there were more emails that also had not been produced.[46]

Not only that, but several days after the discovery of these emails, the Qualcomm lawyers argued that the JVT email list should not be admitted into evidence, stating to the court "there are no emails…."[47]

Qualcomm's representatives testified on cross examination that no search of Qualcomm's computers had been made for emails relating to the JVT meetings and that Qualcomm had not produced 46,000 responsive documents. Magistrate Judge Major held that "Qualcomm's conduct warrants sanctions" as does the conduct of its counsel.

> The Court's review of Qualcomm's declarations, the attorneys' declarations, and Judge Brewster's orders leads this Court to the inevitable conclusion that Qualcomm intentionally withheld tens of thousands of decisive documents from its opponent in an effort to win this case and gain a strategic business advantage over Broadcom. Qualcomm could not have achieved this goal without some type of assistance or deliberate ignorance from its retained attorneys. Accordingly, the Court concludes it must sanction both Qualcomm and some of its retained attorneys.[48]

Magistrate Judge Major described the requirement that counsel and the parties to act "in good faith" in order for the discovery process to function:

> For the current "good faith" discovery system to function in the electronic age, attorneys and clients must work together to ensure that both understand how and where electronic documents, records and emails are maintained and to determine how best to locate, review, and produce responsive documents. Attorneys must take responsibility for ensuring that their clients conduct a comprehensive and appropriate document search.[49]

---

[46] *Id.* at*4-5.
[47] *Id.* at *5.
[48] *Id.* at *12.
[49] *Id.* at*17.

In other cases, sanctions have been imposed on parties and counsel for e-discovery abuses particularly when the Court finds they had a "culpable state of mind."[50]

B. Sanctions in Arbitration

Arbitration is clearly different from litigation. But an adverse inference can be drawn in arbitration for spoliation of evidence and it can be just as draconian because the arbitrators hearing the evidence of spoliation are the ones who will be deciding the merits of the case. In addition to drawing an adverse inference, arbitrators can shift to the spoliator the cost of additional discovery required because of the spoliation.

It is unlikely that arbitrators would sanction a party for spoliation by precluding testimony from witnesses. But arbitrators are the judges of the credibility of witness testimony and they decide the weight given to that testimony. It would also be highly unusual for arbitrators to issue a default judgment against a party who fails to produce e-documents or metadata.

What arbitrators can be expected to do and should do is apply appropriate sanctions for spoliation of evidence while still assuring that all parties receive a fair hearing.

C. Effect of Change to FRCP Rule 37(f)

The amendment to FRCP Rule 37(f), approved by the Supreme Court and effective Dec. 1, 2006, authorizes court-ordered sanctions for spoliation of electronic evidence as follows: "Absent exceptional circumstances, a court may not impose sanctions on a party under this rule for failing to provide electronically stored information that is lost as a result of the routine, good-faith operation of an electronic information system."[51]

The ability to issue sanctions under the amended rule does not apply to a failure to produce e-documents in good faith. The Committee Note states that "good faith in the routine operation of an information system may involve a party's intervention to modify or suspend certain features of that routine operation to prevent the loss of information, if that information is subject to a preservation obligation." Thus, putting a litigation hold on routine recycling or destruction may be required. Nonetheless, the *Sedona Guidelines* state that "it is unreasonable to

---

[50] *See e.g.*, In Re September 11th Liability Insurance Coverage Cases 243 F.R.D. 114 (S.D.N.Y. 2007).

[51] As noted above the Federal Rules of Civil Procedure do not apply in arbitration but can provide helpful guidance if issues covered by the rules or case law interpreting them arise.

expect parties to take every conceivable step to preserve all potentially relevant data."[52] While courts respect the *Sedona Guidelines*, they are not required to follow them.

VI. Conclusion

Extra care needs to be taken to preserve electronic data for anticipated or pending arbitration and to avoid spoliation of electronic evidence. The law concerning waiver of privileges in e-discovery and spoliation of evidence is developing. The best protection against a waiver of legal privileges in arbitration is for parties to agree to a claw-back agreement and have it approved by the arbitral panel with a specific statement that the privilege is not waived as to parties and nonparties to the arbitration. In the absence of a claw-back agreement, parties can ask the panel to enter an order providing for the same protection.

[52] Sedona Conference, *supra* n. 14, at 7.

CHAPTER 28

WAIVER OF PRIVILEGE UNDER FEDERAL EVIDENCE RULE 502 AND ARBITRATION PROCEEDINGS

Angela Foster[*]

I. Rule 502 of the Federal Rules of Evidence

Rule 502 of the Federal Rules of Evidence deals with the attorney-client privilege, the attorney work product rule, and the limitations on waiver of protections from disclosure. Rule 502(b) provides that a disclosure will not result in a subject matter waiver in a federal or state proceeding if:

(i) the disclosure is inadvertent;
(ii) the holder of the privilege or protection took "reasonable steps" to prevent disclosure; and
(iii) the holder "promptly" took "reasonable steps" to rectify the error.

Federal Rule of Evidence 502, which was amended in 2007 to develop a uniform treatment of intentional and inadvertent disclosure of privileged information in arbitration and court-related arbitration, provides guidance for practitioners on how to prevent a court from finding a subject matter waiver as a result of an inadvertent production of a privileged document. In addition to analyzing the amended rule, this chapter discusses recent case law suggesting that the amended rule applies to private arbitration as well.

Despite the best efforts of litigants to avoid disclosing privileged documents, mistakes may occur when a case involves an excessively large number of documents. The concern is that inadvertent disclosure of a

---

[*] Angela Foster, Ph.D., J.D. is a patent attorney of the Law Office of Angela Foster, in North Brunswick, NJ. The firm specializes in intellectual property matters and alternative dispute resolution.

privileged document can result in a waiver of all other privileged information dealing with the same subject matter. Prior to November 2007, when Federal Rule of Evidence 502 was amended, the rules in many jurisdictions provided that all disclosures of privileged information, including those that were inadvertent, resulted in a subject matter waiver. This rule led to complaints about the expense involved in protecting against disclosure of privileged information, the onerous results from accidental disclosures, and the fact that different jurisdictions took different approaches. Rule 502 was amended in late 2007 to address these circumstances.

First, Rule 502(a) makes clear that an intentional disclosure of privileged information in a federal court matter will result in a subject matter waiver in undisclosed documents dealing with the same subject matter "ought in fairness to be considered together" with the intentionally disclosed document. Dealing with the other side of the coin, Rule 502(b) provides that a disclosure will not result in a subject matter waiver in a federal or state proceeding if: (i) the disclosure is inadvertent; (ii) the holder of the privilege or protection took "reasonable steps" to prevent disclosure; and "promptly" took "reasonable steps" to rectify the error, "including if applicable, following Federal Rule of Civil Procedure 26(b)(5)(B)."

Rule 502(d) indicates that a party who makes an inadvertent disclosure can seek a protective order from the federal court stating that the privilege is not waived by disclosure connect with the litigation pending before the court. The same rule provides that if the court issues such an order, that order will be enforceable in federal and state court proceedings.[1] Rule 502(f) deals with arbitration, stating that it applies to court-ordered and court-mandated arbitration. There is no mention of private arbitration.

One year after the enactment of these changes to Rule 502,[2] the question of what constitutes "reasonable steps" to prevent disclosure (and therefore prove that the disclosure of privileged information was inadvertent) and prompt "reasonable steps" to remedy the disclosure still exists. Also unclear is how the rule applies to private arbitration procedures.

This chapter discusses Rule 502 arbitration-related cases involving unintentional disclosures in an attempt to fill in some of those gaps.

---

[1] An initial concern about Rule 502 was whether it provided state-to-state protection. The answer is no, since state separation prevents explicit language or guidance with this concern.

[2] Federal Rule of Evidence 502 was enacted into law on Sept. 19, 2008.

II. Recent Rule 502 Case Law

Over the past 5 years, courts have struggled to determine what constitutes a privilege or waiver, as well as the impact disclosure in arbitration proceedings could have on litigation. *Amobi v. District of Columbia Department of Corrections* raised all of these issues.[3]

The plaintiff, a corrections officer, was involved in an altercation with an inmate. One of the defendants, an official with the correction facility, called in the police, which led to the plaintiff's arrest. The defendant subsequently moved for plaintiff's removal from his position with the Department of Corrections.[4] At the removal hearing, the hearing officer determined that the plaintiff should be reinstated. On remand, the same hearing officer reversed that decision and suggested removal. The plaintiff appealed his removal to arbitration pursuant to the collective bargaining agreement and won reinstatement. During the arbitration proceedings, an attorney for one of the defendants inadvertently disclosed a memorandum created by an attorney advisor to the defendant District of Columbia. The defendants requested the return of the memorandum or its destruction. The plaintiff filed several motions for depositions regarding the memorandum while the defense motioned to quash the memorandum as confidential.

The plaintiff subsequently filed a lawsuit in federal court in the District of Columbia seeking damages for injuries suffered as a result of the defendant's actions. The issue before the court was whether the disclosure of the privileged memorandum during arbitration resulted in a waiver under Rule 502(b). The plaintiff argued that the disclosed memorandum was not privileged and even if it were, all privileges were waived. The defendants asserted that the disclosed memorandum was protected attorney work prepared for the arbitration proceeding, and that the disclosure to the plaintiff should not result in a waiver for the following reasons:

---

[3] *Amobi v. District of Columbia Dept. of Corrections,* 262 F.R.D. 45 (D.D.C. 2009).*Affirmed in Part, Reversed in Part and Remanded by Amobi v. District of Columbia Dept. of Corrections,* 755 F.3d 980, 410 U.S. App. D.C. 338, 38 IER Cases 1116 (D.C. Cir. Jun 27, 2014) (NO. 12-7090) (reversing the district court's summary judgment rulings in part that genuine issues of material fact persist concerning whether probable cause existed for the initiation and continuation of plaintiff's prosecution).

[4] Criminal charges were filed against the plaintiff in two separate state court cases, one of which was dismissed; the other resulted in an acquittal. *Id.*

(1) the disclosure was inadvertent
(2) the privilege was asserted during plaintiff's requests for the documents, and
(3) defense counsel took steps to recover the document immediately upon the discovery of the disclosure.

Addressing the issue of privilege, the court considered whether the attorney-client privilege or work product rule protected the memorandum. It concluded that the latter privilege (but not the former[5]) did apply because it was produced in anticipation of arbitration, a proceeding that is adversarial in nature and can be characterized as "litigation." Thus, the court held that work product prepared for an arbitration proceeding under a collective bargaining agreement for public employees should receive the same protection under the work product doctrine as materials processed in anticipation of a court proceeding.

Next, the court applied the three-part test in amended Rule 502(b) to determine whether a waiver should result from the disclosure of a document protected by a legal privilege. The court noted that prior to the amendment of Rule 502, most courts considered whether the party that produced the privileged document intended to do so or produced it by mistake. The court accepted the defendants' claim that the disclosure was inadvertent. Next it addressed whether the defendants took reasonable steps to prevent disclosure of, and then to recover, the privileged document. The court used the following five factors previously used by a majority of courts to make this determination:

(1) the reasonableness of the precautions taken,
(2) the time taken to rectify the error,
(3) the scope of discovery,
(4) the extent of disclosure, and
(5) the overriding issue of fairness.[6]

The court concluded that the defendants failed to show that they used any particular methodology to review documents for privilege. They also could not know how many total documents were produced. Therefore,

---

[5] However, the court held that the attorney client privilege did not apply because the memorandum was based on the defendants' review of a grievance packet for arbitration, the removal remand and the criminal trial transcript.

[6] *See* Fed. R. Evid. 502 Advisory Committee Note at Subdivision (b).

the court concluded that the defendants waived the attorney-client privilege by their inadvertent production of the attorney's memorandum.

In *Comrie v. Ipsco, Inc.*, a federal district court in Indiana also held that a disclosed privileged document resulted in a waiver.[7] The court held that a protective order designating a method for marking documents did not insulate a party from having to explain the procedures or methods it used to review documents for privilege.

In this case, the defendant produced more than 5,500 documents, one of which was allegedly a privileged document (it was marked "Exhibit 36," an email from defendant's general counsel to defendant's outside counsel). The defendant knew how many documents it produced but failed to tell the court about any document review procedures or methods it used to determine whether documents were privileged prior to producing them. Thus, it was unable to prove that it took reasonable steps to prevent disclosure (thereby failing to prove that the disclosure was inadvertent).

The court held that simply labeling documents as privileged or confidential was insufficient to establish that disclosure was inadvertent or to prove that precautions were taken to prevent disclosure. Therefore, the court concluded that defendant waived any claim of privilege to Exhibit 36.

Other courts have focused on the third inquiry of Rule 502(b): whether reasonable steps were taken to rectify the error. In *Coburn Group v. Whitecap Advisors, LLC*, the defendant had produced in discovery e-mails from its counsel and did not find out about it until plaintiff's counsel asked the defendant's witness about them at a deposition and defense counsel objected to their use.[8] The court held that the e-mails were protected attorney work product and that the privilege had not been waived, despite the fact that the defendant took more than four months to recover the e-mails. The court was satisfied that the defendant took reasonable steps to prevent disclosure because its paralegals reviewed the documents prior to production to determine if they were "prepared in anticipation of litigation."

The plaintiff argued that using paralegals to review documents for privilege was not reasonable since the defendant did not teach them what to look for. It also argued that documents not identified as confidential during the course of review meant that the review process was unreasonable. But the court rejected these arguments and held that amended Rule 502 does not

---

[7] 2009 U.S. Dist. Lexis 111965 (N.D. Ill. Nov. 30, 2009).

[8] 640 F. Supp. 2d 1032 (N.D. Ill. 2009).

require the producing party to engage in a post-production review to determine whether any protected communication or information has been produced by mistake.

Prior to the amendments of Rule 502, courts looked to the time between a party's disclosure of a privileged document and its taking action to remedy the disclosure to determine whether "prompt" action was taken, rather than the time that elapsed since the document was placed in the hands of the other party. However, the district court in *Coburn Group* concluded that under the amended rule, the relevant time is how long it took the producing party to act after it learned that the privileged document had been provided.

In *Fuller v. Interview, Inc.*,[9] a federal district court in New York also addressed whether privileged documents inadvertently disclosed in a parallel arbitration proceeding resulted in a waiver of the privilege. The court held that the privilege was not waived. Shortly after both parties produced documents, they agreed to engage in negotiations to settle the arbitration and litigation and, therefore, placed both proceedings on hold. In an effort to advance the settlement discussions, the defendant responded to interrogatories forwarded by the plaintiff. During this process the defendant discovered that it had inadvertently produced some privileged documents during its production.

Six months after realizing that it inadvertently produced privileged documents to the adversary, the defendant forwarded a letter to the plaintiff alerting him of the error and requested that the documents be destroyed or placed before the court for *in camera* review to test the claim of privilege. The defendant also forwarded to the plaintiff a set of redacted documents to replace those it had previously produced. The plaintiff did not respond to the defendant's letter or take any steps to return or destroy the documents. Rather, he held onto them for 10 months and later filed a motion to amend his pleading. According to the plaintiff, the documents demonstrated that the defense counsel was a party to the unlawful conduct alleged in the complaint and provided a basis for adding him as a named defendant in the action.

The defendant asserted that the documents in question were protected by the attorney-client privilege and were produced inadvertently in the course of a voluminous document production. The plaintiff argued that any privilege enjoyed by the documents should be considered waived by the defendant's production of them during arbitration. The defendant made

---

[9] 2009 U.S. Lexis 93157 (S.D.N.Y. Sept. 30, 2009).

several counter-arguments. First, it explained that it had taken precautions to screen 32,000 electronic documents and 2,000 hard copy documents for privilege. Second, the number of documents it inadvertently produced was small compared to the total number of documents produced. Third, the defendant stressed that it acted promptly to recover the documents, asserted the privilege, and sought the return of the documents upon realizing that an inadvertent disclosure had been made. The plaintiff, meanwhile, argued that the 10-month delay between defendant's initial disclosure of the documents and their efforts to remedy the error did not show prompt action.

As in *Coburn Group*, the district court in this case held that the relevant time frame for purposes of determining whether the disclosing party took prompt reasonable steps runs, not from the time the inadvertent disclosed is made, but from the time it is discovered. Accordingly, it concluded that the defendant was not unduly careless in producing the privileged documents or in seeking to rectify the error.

In Colorado, a federal district court held that a document given to the plaintiff during discovery, despite being listed on defendants' privilege log, was disclosed intentionally and that the disclosure resulted in a subject of matter waiver. In *Silverstein v. Federal Bureau of Prisons*,[10] the plaintiff, a prison inmate, received a document from the defendants written by one of their general counsels. The document discussed, among issues, whether there was a continued need for annual review of plaintiff's continued incarceration in solitary confinement. When the plaintiff requested an explanation regarding the document during a defendant's deposition, the defendant asserted that the document was privileged and refused to answer.

The court agreed that the document was entitled to the protection of the attorney-client privilege and the work product doctrine, but it questioned whether the defendants took reasonable steps either to prevent its disclosure or to promptly recover it after discovering the error. The court noted that the defendants had created a privilege log based upon the creator and recipient of the document, and even though this document was in the long, it produced it anyway based on the mistaken belief that the document had been previously distributed to third parties.

More important to the court's decision on waiver was the fact that after discovering the disclosure, the defendants never requested the document back or re-asserted the privilege. Therefore, the court concluded

[10] 2009 U.S. Dist. Lexis 121753 (D. Col. Dec. 14, 2009).

that the disclosure could not be considered "inadvertent" under Rule 502(b). Next, the court proceeded to determine whether the disclosure was intentional under Rule 502(a), in the sense that it gave the disclosing party an advantage in the litigation. The court found that the defendants' failure to seek recovery of the document provided support for an inference that the disclosure was intentional. Further, it determined that the substance of the document, combined with the fact that the plaintiff had no opportunity to challenge it, placed the plaintiff at a disadvantage. As a result, fairness required that other confidential documents with the same subject matter be considered together. Therefore, the court held that the disclosure resulted in a subject matter waiver.

In a federal district court case in Maine, the court determined that drafts of various legal forms involved in a patent infringement litigation were entitle to protection under the attorney-client privilege and that there was no waiver of that privilege.[11] The plaintiff in this case made a 540-page document production, but inadvertently produced 31 pages of privileged e-mails and correspondence from its counsel. Included in these pages were draft patent applications and related forms. The plaintiff sought to recover these documents 22 days later, notifying the defendant of the inadvertent disclosure and the defendant's use of privileged material in its proposed amended answer.[12] The defendant argued that the disclosed documents were not privileged attorney-client communications and that by disclosing the documents, the plaintiff waived any privilege attached to them. It also argued that the plaintiff's "attempt to reclaim these documents is not in the interests of fairness and justice" because they "directly support" defendant's defense that plaintiff's patent is unenforceable.

The court held that the 31 disclosed pages fell within the attorney-client privilege. The court accepted the emerging trend of applying the attorney-client privilege to drafts of patent applications. It also held that there is no legal requirement that an inadvertent disclosure must result in a waiver of the privilege whenever the documents at issue support the non-disclosing party's position because this would render almost every inadvertent disclosure an automatic waiver of any applicable privilege.

---

[11] *Ergo Licensing, LLC v. Carefusion303, Inc.*, 2009 U.S. Dist. Lexis117399 (D. Me. Dec. 14, 2009).

[12] On Nov. 23, 2009, defendant filed a motion to amend its answer and add two affirmative defenses— inequitable conduct and unclean hands; and a third count to its counterclaim that plaintiff 's patent is unenforceable. On Feb. 2, 2010, this motion was denied.

In a recent Massachusetts federal district court case, the court found that defendant's inadvertent disclosure to the arbitration panel that it had nominated the selected umpire did not provide grounds to enjoin the arbitration proceeding. The court based its findings that the inadvertent disclosure did not violate any provisions in the arbitration agreement and that the counter-party, plaintiff, would not suffer irreparable harm as a result of the disclosure.[13]

Plaintiff and defendant were parties to a series of reinsurance agreements, all of which contained a provision requiring the parties to arbitrate any disputes. After the umpire was selected by the party-appointed arbitrators, he requested statements of position from the parties. Defendant submitted its statement of position with an addendum that included its prior supplemental arbitration demand. The addendum contained information sufficient for the arbitrators and umpire to determine the method by which the umpire was to be selected and that defendant had proposed the selected umpire. Plaintiff advised the umpire of the defendant's erroneous submission and demanded that he withdraw because they believed knowledge of his selection would fundamentally corrupt the integrity of the process. *Id.* at *4. The umpire refused to withdraw. Plaintiff filed a motion to enjoin the arbitration and requested that the arbitration be stayed pending its motion but the arbitration panel refused to stay the arbitration.

Based on its motion to enjoin, plaintiff filed an emergency motion for temporary restraining order and preliminary injunction. To obtain a preliminary injunction, the moving party must establish that it is: (i) likely to succeed on the merits: (ii) likely to suffer irreparable harm in the absence of preliminary relief; (iii) that the balance of the equities tips in his favor: and (iv) an injunction is in the public interest. *Id.* at *5. Addressing whether plaintiff was likely to succeed on the merits, the court concluded that plaintiff's motion was an impermissible pre-award request to remove an arbitrator on the basis of bias. *Id.* at *10. The court next addressed whether plaintiff would suffer irreparable harm in the absence of preliminary relief. The court concluded that an adequate legal remedy existed in the form of a post-award challenge to the arbitration proceeding. *Id.* at *12-13. As for the remaining two elements, the court found that the balance of the equities did not tip in plaintiff's favor and the requested injunction was not in the public interest. *Id.* at *14-15.

---

[13] *Allstate Ins. Co. v. OneBeacon American Ins. Co.*, No. 13-12368-NMG, 2013 U.S. Dist. LEXIS 146826 (D. Mass., October 8, 2013).

III. Conclusion

Rule 502 as amended provides guidance and safeguards for handling disclosure of privileged information in federal court and in court-mandated proceedings. A few district courts have shed light on what are reasonable steps to prevent disclosure of privileged material and promptly rectify an inadvertent disclosure. In addition, some district courts are applying Rule 502 to inadvertent disclosure of privileged material in private arbitration. Thus, privileged documents inadvertently produced during arbitration proceedings are being treated similarly to those produced in court-mandated arbitration or in federal court under the amended Rule 502. Nevertheless, it remains the case that after 5years since the enactment of amended Evidence Rule 502, it may still be too soon to have a predictable uniform approach to inadvertent disclosure of materials protected by the attorney-client privilege or the work product doctrine.

CHAPTER 29

THE USE OF SUBPOENAS IN ARBITRATION

Leslie Trager[*]

I. Introduction

Documents in the possession or under the control of non-parties are sometimes vital to an arbitration. For this reason the ability to subpoena those documents is crucial. While subpoenas used in court litigation are enforceable nationwide, that is not the case for arbitral subpoenas issued in arbitration proceedings in the United States.[1]

The extent to which a subpoena may be enforced (and arbitrators should only issue them where they can be enforced) depends on both Federal and applicable state law. The Federal Arbitration Act (FAA) is usually held to limit enforcement of subpoenas to the state where the arbitration is being held, or, if the subpoena can be enforced in Federal court, to district court's boundaries. But there may be situations where, under the Revised Uniform Arbitration Act (RUAA), a subpoena may be enforced against a non-resident of the state in which the arbitration is held.

This article discusses these subpoena issues and how courts have dealt with them. Finally, it suggests that the problem of enforcing document subpoenas on non-parties who reside out of state could be overcome by having the arbitrators move the hearing location (for document production purposes only) to the state where the non-party resides.

II. FAA Section 7

The use of subpoenas in arbitration is governed by Section 7 of the FAA, which makes Section 45 of the Federal Rules of Civil Procedure

---

[*] Leslie Trager is a practicing attorney in New York City. He also serves on the American Arbitration Association's panel of commercial arbitrators.

[1] Parties in arbitral proceedings in foreign countries can obtain documents anywhere in the United States through a federal court proceeding under 28 U.S.C. 1782(a). *Intel Corp. v. Advanced Micro Data, Inc.*, 542 U.S. 241 (2004).

(Federal Rules or FRCP) applicable as well. If the subpoena is to be enforced in Federal court, the FAA will apply. Whether it also applies in state court is an open question, which will be discussed in part III.

If enforcement is contemplated for federal court, the court must have an independent basis for subject matter jurisdiction for the FAA does not provide a basis. *Vaden v. Discover Bank.*[2] This can be either diversity or Federal claim. For diversity, there must be complete diversity between the opposing parties. *Amgen, Inc. v. Kidney Center of Delaware County, Ltd.*.[3] Diversity between a party and the non-party subpoenaed is irrelevant. Federal claim jurisdiction exists where the arbitration statement of claim is based on a Federal statute or something similar so that the case could have been brought in Federal court, except for the arbitration agreement between the parties. *Vaden v. Discover Bank;*[4] *Cronin v. Citifinancial Services, Inc.*[5]

The FAA also requires subpoenas be signed by a majority of the arbitrators and made returnable at a hearing held before one or more of them.

Enforcement Against Out of State Persons

While some earlier cases held that there was nationwide service of process under Section 7 of the FAA, and that documents could be subpoenaed to a site without a hearing, there is little statutory support for that interpretation. The more recent cases have held that documents can only be subpoenaed to a hearing at which one or more of the arbitrators are present, even though this hearing does not need to be on the merits but only on the admissibility of the documents.

Thus, in *Security Life Insurance Co. of America v. Duncanson & Holt*[6] the Eighth Circuit held that arbitrators have implicit power to issue subpoenas for documents to allow a party's advance review of them without holding a hearing. It also held that there is nationwide jurisdiction to enforce this type of subpoena. The court found this power is implied from the arbitrator's authority to issue hearing subpoenas, stating, "[W]e do not believe an order for the production of documents requires compliance with Rule 45(b)(2)'s territorial limit."

---

[2] 556 U.S. 49,59 (2009).
[3] 95 F. 3d 562, 567 (7th Cir. 1996).
[4] Supra. At 62-63.
[5] 2009 U.S. Dist. Lexis 32389 (E.D. PA 2009), aff'd 352 Fed. Appx. 630 (3rd Cir. 2009).
[6] 228 F. 3d 865, 872 (8th Cir. 2000).

The Fourth Circuit has held that there is nationwide process in extraordinary circumstances—meaning that the party seeking the subpoena has shown special need or hardship.[7]

But in *Hay Group, Inc. v. E.B.S. Acquisition Corp.*,[8] the Third Circuit, in a majority opinion written by then-Circuit Court Judge Samuel Alito, held that the FAA does not authorize arbitrators to issue pre-hearing document subpoenas. The court expressly disagreed with *Security Life*'s ruling that the power to issue pre-hearing document subpoenas could be implied from the language of Section 7. However, it held that the arbitrators could subpoena non-parties to appear before them for a pre-merit hearing and bring the documents with them to this hearing. Judge Chertoff clarified this, in a concurring opinion, when he said:

> Under Section 7 of the Federal Arbitration Act, arbitrators have the power to compel a third-party witness to appear with documents before a single arbitrator, who can then adjourn the proceedings. This gives the arbitration panel the effective ability to require delivery of documents from a third party in advance, notwithstanding the limitations of Section 7 of the FAA.[9]

Judge Chertoff's concurrence is also useful for his statement that if there is a three-arbitrator panel, only a single arbitrator must attend the document production hearing.

The *Hay Group* case also discussed the territorial limitations of a court's subpoena power, holding that a document subpoena could be enforced only so long as the person being subpoenaed was subject to the district court's jurisdiction.

The Second Circuit followed the *Hays Group* case in *Life Receivables Trust v Syndicate 102 at Lloyd's*.[10] There the Court held that arbitrators could not compel a non party to the arbitration to produce documents without subpoenaing the documents to a hearing. But, following its earlier decisions in *Stolt-Nielsen SA v. Celanese AG*,[11] the

---

[7] *See Comsat Corp. v. Nat. Sci. Found.*, 190 F. 3d 269 (4th Cir. 1999). *See also Festos & Helen Stacey Found. v. Merrill Lynch Pierce Fenner & Smith*, 432 F. Supp. 2d 1375 (N.D. Ga. 2006) (holding that the district court had nationwide jurisdiction to enforce a document subpoena).

[8] 360 F.3d 404 (3d Cir. 2004).

[9] *Id.* at 413.

[10] 549 F. 3d 210 (2d Cir. 2008).

[11] 430 F.3d 567 (2d Cir. 2005).

Court held that that arbitral subpoenas do not have to be made returnable at a hearing on the merits but could be returnable at a preliminary, non-merits hearing. In *Stolt-Nielsen* the Court upheld a procedure whereby the arbitrators required a non-party to produce over 300 boxes of documents at a hearing that did not concern the merits of the case. When the documents were produced at the hearing, testimony was taken with respect to authenticity of the records and then the hearing was continued to give counsel the opportunity to review the documents contained in the boxes.

In *Guyden v. Aetna, Inc.*[12] the Second Circuit upheld a district court ruling that only one of the three arbitrators was required to be present for the document production hearing.

The *Hay Group*'s holding was also followed by the Second Circuit with respect to the territorial limits of a court in enforcing a subpoena. In *Dynegy Midstream Services L.P. v. Trammochem*,[13] the Second Circuit held that subpoenaed persons must be subject to the enforcing district court's jurisdiction. There the arbitration proceeding was located in New York City, but the person subpoenaed resided in Texas. The court held that the district court in New York did not have jurisdiction to enforce the subpoena. The court explained that under FRCP 45 (as it then existed), enforcement of a subpoena under Section 7 had to be in the district court covering the State of New York (or 100 miles from that court). However, under Section 7 of the FAA, a district court in Texas would not have jurisdiction to enforce the subpoena because that section requires enforcement in the "district in which such arbitrators … are sitting."

The recent amendment to FRCP 45 allows nationwide service for actions pending in Federal court, but enforcement of the subpoena must be done in the district court where "compliance is required." Rule 45(d)(3). Thus, under the new rule, arbitrators under Federal law would be limited to subpoenaing persons within the district in which they are sitting. There is also the possibility that the compliance district court could transfer any enforcement proceeding for the subpoena to the district court where the arbitration is being held if the arbitrator's subpoena is regarded as coming from the "issuing court" and the compliance court finds "exceptional circumstances." Rule 45(f). Since whether a district court might apply rule 45(f) cannot be known at the

---

12 544 F 3d 376(2d Cir. 2008).
13 451 F.3d 89 (2d Cir. 2006).

time the subpoena is issued, Rule 45(f) would not seem a good basis for arbitrators to issue jurisdictionally valid subpoenas.

III. State Law and Subpoenas

Because there must be an independent basis for jurisdiction other than the FAA to enforce a subpoena in Federal court, such as diversity or federal question jurisdiction, a party may have to enforce its subpoena in a state court. Some state courts have held that if a case involves interstate commerce, even if the parties' agreement contains a choice-of-law clause selecting the law of a particular state to apply to the proceedings, only the FAA governs.[14] This would not seem appropriate because the U.S. Supreme Court in *Volt Information Sciences Inc. v. Board of Trustees of Leland Stanford, Jr. University*,[15] held:

> There is no federal policy favoring arbitration under a certain set of procedural rules; the federal policy is simply to ensure enforceability according to terms, a private agreement to arbitrate. Interpreting a choice of law clause to make applicable state rules governing the conduct of arbitration—rules which are manifestly designed to encourage resort to the arbitral process—simply does not offend the liberal construction set forth in *Moses H. Cohen*, nor does it any other policy embodied in the FAA.

More recently in *Vaden v. Discover Bank* the Court held: "Given the substantive supremacy of the FAA but the Act's nonjurisdictional cast, state courts have a prominent role to play as enforcers of agreements to arbitrate."[16] Enforcement should include following state law procedures to the extent that they enhance the arbitration process, such as the enforcement of subpoenas.

Subpoenas would seem to be one of these procedural matters in which both state and federal law could apply without upsetting the federal arbitration scheme. The Revised Uniform Arbitration Act (RUAA) appears to give the arbitrators somewhat greater subpoena powers than the FAA. While RUAA § 17(a) provides that "an arbitrator

---

[14] *Suratt v. Merrill Lynch Pierce Fenner & Smith*, 2003 U.S. Dist. Lexis 26650 (S.D. Fl. 2003).

[15] 489 U.S. 468, 476 (1989).

[16] 556 U.S. 49, 58 (2009).

may issue a subpoena for attendance of a witness and for the production of records … at any hearing…," subsection (b) permits a deposition of a witness "who cannot be subpoenaed for or is unable to attend a hearing." This should also allow for documents to be subpoenaed to such deposition.

Section 17(g) of the RUAA provides that: "A subpoena or discovery-related order issued by an arbitrator in another State must be served in the manner provided by law for service of subpoenas in a civil action in this State … and enforced in the manner provided by law for enforcement of subpoenas in a civil action in this State." If all states passed the RUAA, there would be in effect the ability to serve a witness anywhere in the United States, presumably returnable at a hearing or deposition within the state where the witness is located. So far, 19 states have adopted the RUAA.

The RUAA will also be helpful in obtaining jurisdiction for a witness in a state which does not have the RUAA, but which does have the Uniform Interstate and Discovery Act. This Act, which has been adopted by 34 states, allows a clerk of the court or an attorney licensed within that state to issue a subpoena for a proceeding "in a court of record of a state other than this state."(See New York CPLR 3119). Section 17(f) of the RUAA provides: "All laws compelling a person under subpoena to testify … or a discovery proceeding as a witness apply to an arbitration proceeding as if the controversy were the subject of a civil action in this State." By this section, the RUAA makes arbitration the equivalent of court of record and, therefore, if the arbitration were being held in a state which had adopted the RUAA, a witness could be effectively served in a state which limits enforcement of out of state subpoenas to courts of record. Many states allow "an arbitrator and any attorney of record in the arbitration proceeding have the power to issue subpoenas."[17] But since the FAA limits the issuance of subpoenas to arbitrators, it is not clear that attorney issued subpoenas will be enforced. In addition, courts are more likely to enforce an arbitrator issued subpoena and leave relevancy to the arbitrators, while, with attorney issued subpoenas, courts are more likely to review if relevance is questioned. In *Platzer v. Merrill Lynch, Pierce, Fenner & Smith, Inc.*,[18] on an attorney issued subpoena, the court directed that the arbitrators determine, at least in the first instance, the relevancy of the subpoena

[17] N.Y.C.P.L.R. § 7505.

[18] 2003 N.Y. Misc. Lexis 2055 (N.Y. Co. 2003)

requests. *In Matter of Security Life Insurance Company of America*,[19] the court held it would not "second – guess the panel's judgment" as to relevancy.

IV. The Traveling Arbitrator

Given the gaps in enforcing subpoenas and the requirement that the enforcement is limited to those persons within the jurisdiction of the district or state court where the majority of the arbitrators "are sitting," the question is whether this gap can be closed by having an arbitrator on the return date of the subpoena sit in the same state or district where the witness is located.

Rule 11 of the AAA Commercial Arbitration Rules provides in the final paragraph:

> "The arbitrator, at the arbitrator's sole discretion, shall have the authority to conduct special hearings for document production purposes or otherwise at other locations if reasonably necessary and beneficial to the process."

Now, that the AAA has included this provision in its rules, it would seem that if the documents are important enough, an arbitrator can solve the problem of enforcement by holding the document hearing in the compliance district. The parties, having chosen the AAA to conduct the arbitration, should be held bound by the AAA's rules.

While the court in *Beck's Superior Hybrids, Inc. v. Monsanto Company* held that this procedure of the traveling arbitrator would violate section 7 of the FAA, the parties did not have the new AAA Rule 11 available to them, so this case should not be regarded as authority.[20]

V. Conclusion

Unless the arbitration is being held in a state where the RUAA allows depositions (at which the arbitrators would not be present), arbitrators should only sign document subpoenas returnable before one or more of the arbitrators at a hearing. Enforcing a document subpoena

---

[19] 228 228 F. 3d 865, 871 (8th Cir. 2000).
[20] 940 N.E, 2d 352 (2011).

against a person who resides outside the jurisdiction of a court where the arbitration hearing takes place may prove difficult. It is suggested that the best way to handle this is for the arbitrators to hold a separate hearing pursuant to AAA Commercial Rule 11 in the jurisdiction where the third party is located for the purpose of producing these documents. This procedure should only be exercised in the rare case where the arbitrators believe that the documents involved are very relevant and are likely to be critical to their decision.

CHAPTER 30

ENFORCING ARBITRAL SUBPOENAS: RECONSIDERING FEDERAL QUESTION JURISDICTION UNDER FAA SECTION 7

*Charles E. Harris II**

I. Introduction

This article examines three issues pertinent to the enforcement of arbitral subpoenas under FAA § 7:

(1) Does the nature and unique language of § 7 vest federal courts with federal question jurisdiction?
(2) Can a § 7 action commenced in state court be removed to federal court?
(3) (3) Can a state court dismiss a § 7 action on the ground that federal courts have exclusive jurisdiction?

The weight of federal judicial authority favors the view that the plain language of Section 7 of the Federal Arbitration Act (FAA) does not authorize arbitrators to issue third-party subpoenas for pre-hearing discovery. The rules of many alternative dispute resolution services, however, do not expressly prohibit such subpoenas. Thus, arbitrators regularly issue them, notwithstanding recent federal court decisions refusing to enforce them. Instead, parties are optimistically initiating enforcement proceedings in state courts, hoping to avoid this federal court precedent. But can these actions be removed to federal court on the ground that Section 7 confers original jurisdiction under the federal question statute, codified at Section 1331 of Title 28 of the United States

---

* Mr. Harris is a partner in the Litigation & Dispute Resolution Group at Mayer Brown LLP in Chicago. He has represented clients in domestic and international arbitrations and other forms of dispute resolution. He also has a varied litigation practice. Prior to joining the firm, he was a law clerk for the Hon. David D. Dowd Jr., U. S. District Court, Northern District of Ohio.

Code? Courts have generally held that other provisions of the FAA do not create a basis for so-called "federal question" jurisdiction under Section 1331.

Although some courts have applied this principle to Section 7, none have carefully considered whether the nature and unique language of Section 7 vest federal courts with this jurisdiction. This article addresses that topic as well as whether these actions can be removed to federal court under Section 1441 of Title 28, based on the text of Section 7 or the "substantial federal question doctrine." It also considers whether state actions may be dismissed because federal courts have exclusive jurisdiction to consider such actions.

II. FAA Enforcement of Arbitral Subpoenas

An arbitrator's authority to issue a third-party subpoena does not include the authority to enforce that subpoena against a third party. Only a court can compel a third party to comply with an arbitral subpoena. That authority resides in Section 7 of the FAA[1] (or a comparable state statute).[2] Section 7 reads in pertinent part:

> The arbitrators ... may summon in writing any person to attend before them or any of them as a witness and in a proper case to bring with him or them any book, record, document, or paper which may be deemed material as evidence in the case.... [I]f any person or persons so summoned to testify shall refuse or neglect to obey said summons, upon petition the United States district court for the district in which such arbitrators, or a majority of them, are sitting may compel the attendance of such person or persons before said arbitrator or arbitrators....[3]

---

[1] The FAA applies to all arbitrable transactions "involving commerce," 9 U.S.C. § 2, a term that the Supreme Court interprets broadly. *Citizens Bank v. Alafabco, Inc.*, 539 U.S. 52, 56 (2003).

[2] *Life Receivables Trust v. Syndicate 102 at Lloyd's of London*, 549 F.3d 210, 218 (2d Cir. 2008) ("the party seeking discovery is limited to § 7 as a vehicle to enforce the subpoena"); accord *Hay Group v. E.B.S. Acquisition Corp.*, 260 F.3d 404, 406 (3d Cir. 2004) ("An arbitrator's authority over parties that are not contractually bound by the arbitration agreement is strictly limited ... by the [FAA].").

[3] 9 U.S.C. § 7.

The federal circuits are split as to whether Section 7 authorizes arbitrators to issue subpoenas to third parties to the arbitration for prehearing discovery purposes.[4] That being said, recent federal court decisions have consistently held that the "straightforward and unambiguous" text of Section 7 does not authorize arbitrators to issue these subpoenas.[5]

III. Original Jurisdiction of Federal Courts

A federal court's original jurisdiction is determined by Section 1331, which provides that the district courts "have original jurisdiction of all civil actions arising under the Constitution, laws, or treaties of the United States.[6] A civil action "arises under" the federal law that creates the cause of action so federal question jurisdiction will generally exist if a federal statute creates a plaintiff's right to relief.[7] Thus, for example, a civil action under Section 1983[8] alleging a deprivation of rights by a person acting under color of law invokes a federal court's original jurisdiction.[9]

---

[4] *E.g.*, *Life Receivables Trust, supra* n. 2, 549 F.3d at 212 (acknowledging circuit split).

[5] *E.g.*, *id.* at 216-17 ("Section7 of the FAA does not authorize arbitrators to compel pre-hearing document discovery from entities not party to the arbitration proceedings."); accord *Hay Group, supra* n. 2, 260 F.3d at 411; *In re Proshares Trust Sec. Litig.*, No. 09 Civ. 6935, 2010 WL 4967988 (S.D.N.Y. Dec. 1, 2010); *Ware v. C.D. Peacock, Inc.*, No. 10 C 2587, 2010 WL 1856021 (N.D. Ill. May 7, 2010); *Empire Fin. Group v. Pension Fin. Servs., Inc.*, No. 3:09-CV-2155-D, 2010 WL 742579 (N.D. Tex. Mar. 3, 2010); *Kennedy v. American Express Travel Related Servs. Co.*, 646 F. Supp. 2d 1342, 1344 (S.D. Fla. 2009); see also *COMSAT Corp. v. National Sci. Found.*, 190 F.3d 269, 275-76 (4th Cir. 1999) (contemplating a "special need" exception under which a "party might, under unusual circumstances, petition the district court to compel pre-arbitration discovery upon a showing of special need or hardship").

[6] 28 U.S.C. § 1331. District courts also have jurisdiction in certain specified categories of cases, such as bankruptcy and maritime cases, 28 U.S.C. § 1333, as well as "all civil actions where the matter in controversy exceeds the sum or value of $75,000, exclusive of interest and costs, and there is diversity of citizenship between the parties. 28 U.S.C. § 1332. This article is not concerned with these bases of jurisdiction.

[7] *Murphey v. Lanier*, 204 F.3d 911, 912 (9th Cir. 2000) (quoting the district court as follows: "Because a suit generally 'arises under' the statute that creates the cause of action, 'if federal law creates a plaintiff's cause of action, [federal question] jurisdiction will generally be present."); *American Well Works Co. v. Layne & Bowler Co.*, 241 U.S. 257, 260 (1916) (Holmes, J.) ("A suit arises under the law that creates the cause of action.").

[8] In U.S. Code Title 42.

[9] *Grable & Sons Metal Prods. v. Darue Eng'g & Mfg.*, 545 U.S. 308, 314 (2006); see also *Ledford v. Sullivan*, 105 F.3d 354, 356 (7th Cir. 1997) (quoting *Livadas v. Bradshaw*, 512 U.S. 107, 132 (1994)) ("42 U.S.C. § 1983 creates a federal cause of

Case law has also established that, in limited circumstances, original jurisdiction can arise from a "well pleaded complaint" seeking relief that "necessarily depends on resolution of a substantial question of federal law."[10] This is sometimes referred to as the substantial-federal-question doctrine. As an example, in *Ayres v. General Motors Corp.*,[11] the 11th Circuit found that the district court had original jurisdiction to decide an action brought solely under Georgia's civil RICO statute,[12] because that statute "depends upon proving, as necessary predicate acts, a violation of the federal mail and wire fraud statutes." Hence, the resolution of that matter "depend[ed] entirely on interpretation of th[ose] federal" statutes.

IV. The FAA and Original Jurisdiction

Section 7 states, in relevant part, that "upon petition the United States district court ... may compel the attendance" of "any person ... summoned to testify" who refuses to voluntarily comply with an arbitral subpoena. This language seems to give federal courts original jurisdiction to hear Section 7 petitions. However, the general rule is that the FAA itself does not confer original jurisdiction on a district court and that another basis for federal court jurisdiction must exist, i.e., diversity of citizenship or a claim based on another federal statute. This rule has developed mainly from *dicta* in *Moses H. Cone Memorial Hospital v. Mercury Construction Corp.*, a 1983 Supreme Court decision delivered by Justice William Brennan.[13]

Footnote 32 of that decision states that the FAA "creates a body of federal substantive law[14] establishing and regulating the duty to honor an

---

action for 'the deprivation, under color of [state] law, of a citizen's rights, privileges, or immunities secured by the Constitution and laws of the United States.'").

[10] *Thornton v. Southwest Detroit Hosp.*, 895 F.2d 1131, 1133 (6th Cir. 1990); accord *Mikulski v. Centerior Energy Corp.*, 501 F.3d 555, 560 (6th Cir. 2007) (quoting *Franchise Tax Bd. v. Construction Laborers Vacation Trust*, 463 U.S. 1, 9 (1983): "the substantial-federal-question doctrine... applies 'where the vindication of a right under state law necessarily turn[s] on some construction of federal law'").

[11] 234 F.3d 514, 518-19 (11th Cir. 2000).

[12] Georgia Racketeer Influenced and Corrupt Organizations Act, Ga. Code Ann. § 16-14-1 et seq. (2011).

[13] 460 U.S. 1, 25 n. 32 (1983).

[14] Although known as a substantive statute that rests on the Commerce Clause, Justice Brennan characterized the FAA as "something of an anomaly in the field of federal court jurisdiction" in concluding that the FAA does not create original jurisdiction in the federal courts.

agreement to arbitrate, yet it does not create any independent federal question jurisdiction under 28 U.S.C. § 1331 or otherwise."[15] Justice Brennan seemed to base this conclusion on the language of Section 4, which, he noted, "provides for an order compelling arbitration only when the federal district court would have jurisdiction over a suit on the underlying dispute; hence, there must be diversity of citizenship or some other independent basis for federal jurisdiction before the order can issue."

Justice Warren E. Burger repeated Brennan's conclusion in footnote 9 of *Southland Corp. v. Keating.*[16] Burger wrote that the conclusion that the FAA does not create independent federal question jurisdiction under Section 1331 "seems implicit in the provisions in [Section] 3 for a stay by a 'court in which such suit is pending' and in [Section] 4 that enforcement may be ordered by 'any United States district court which ... would have jurisdiction under [T]itle 28, in a civil action or in admiralty of the subject matter of a suit arising out of the controversy between the parties.'" Thus, the language of Sections 3 and 4, unlike other sections of the FAA, literally necessitates that federal courts have an independent jurisdictional basis to entertain cases arising under those sections. This point is critical since Section 7 contains no such language, and neither Justice Brennan nor Justice Burger considered the language of Section 7.

Federal courts have consistently applied the *Moses H. Cone/Southland dicta* to other FAA provisions (including Section 7) that do not expressly require an independent basis for jurisdiction, even though they plainly read as if they confer federal question jurisdiction on the district court. An example is the 7th Circuit decision in *Amgen, Inc. v. Kidney Center of Delaware County, Ltd.*[17] The appeals court simply concluded that the "interpretation of the FAA" set forth in *Moses H. Cone* "establishes that the statute itself does not create subject matter jurisdiction for independent proceedings, whether they involve [Section] 4 or [Section] 7." The 2nd Circuit reached the same conclusion in *Stolt-Nielsen SA v. Celanese AG*, even while acknowledging that the language

---

[15] *See Southland Corp. v. Keating*, 465 U.S. 1, 15 n. 9 (1984); accord *Metro Indus. Painting Corp. v. Terminal Constr. Co.*, 287 F.2d 382, 384 (2d Cir. 1961); *Robert Lawrence Co. v. Devonshire Fabrics, Inc.*, 271 F.2d 402, 408 (2d Cir. 1959); *Krauss Bros. Lumber Co. v. Louis Bossert & Sons*, 62 F.2d 1004 (2d Cir. 1933).

[16] *Supra* n.15, 465 U.S. at 15 n. 9 (quoting FAA §§ 3 & 4).

[17] 95 F.3d 562, 567 (7th Cir. 1996); see also *In re Beck's Superior Hybrids, Inc.*, 940 N.E.2d 352, 359 (Ind. Ct. App. 2011) ("the weight of federal case law demonstrates that neither the Act generally nor Section 7 specifically confers on litigants independent federal subject matter jurisdiction").

of "Section 7 does explicitly permit an aggrieved party to bring a petition before a district court to enforce an arbitration subpoena."[18] It nevertheless concluded that "there is no reason to find that Section 7 does not require an independent basis for federal court jurisdiction when we already found that other provisions of the FAA containing similar language do."

Courts that have provided a reason for following the *dicta* in *Moses H. Cone* and *Southland* have mostly cited policy concerns as justification. For instance, several courts have said that finding federal question jurisdiction under some sections of the FAA and not others would be internally inconsistent, as well as inconsistent with the limited nature of federal jurisdiction.[19] For example, it might lead to a "drastic change in the scope of federal court activity."[20] In other words, it might lead to the filing of more cases. Parties wishing to enforce arbitral subpoenas for pre-hearing discovery served on third parties now readily seek enforcement in state courts. Even when there is an independent basis for federal jurisdiction, it would be prudent to do so because federal courts tend to hold that these subpoenas are unenforceable under Section 7.[21] In this situation, the party opposing enforcement would naturally like the state court to decline to enforce the subpoena. If that outcome is unlikely, could that party remove

---

[18] 430 F.3d 567, 572 (2d Cir. 2005).

[19] *E.g.*, *Harry Hoffman Printing v. Graphic Comm'ns Int'l Union, Local 261*, 912 F.2d 608, 611 n. 1 (2d Cir. 1990) ("Although the Court in both *Moses H. Cone Memorial Hospital* and *Keating* supported its conclusion by referring to the language of §§ 3 and 4 of the Act, rather than § 10, it would be anomalous to conclude, for example, that § 4 confers no jurisdiction to compel arbitration, but that § 10 confers jurisdiction to vacate an award once arbitration has taken place"); *General Atomic Co. v. United Nuclear Corp.*, 655 F.2d 968, 970 (9th Cir. 1981) ("to require independent jurisdictional grounds under other sections and not under § 9 renders the Act a patchwork of individual statutes bereft of any coherent plan") (internal quotation marks omitted).

[20] *Drexel Burnham Lambert v. Valenzuela Bock.* 696 F. Supp. 957, 961 (S.D.N.Y. 1988); *see also e.g.*, *Harry Hoffman Printing, supra* n. 19 ("to read § 10 as bestowing jurisdiction to vacate absolutely any arbitration award would open the federal courts to a host of arbitration disputes, an intent that we should not readily impute to Congress"); *Baltin v. Alaron Trading Corp.*, 128 F.3d 1466, 1471 (11th Cir. 1997) ("a narrow interpretation of section 10 is consistent with the limited nature of federal subject matter jurisdiction").

[21] *E.g.*, Petition for Letter Rogatory to Enforce Arbitration Subpoena, *Cleveland-Cliffs Iron Co. v. ArcelorMittal USA Inc.*, Case No. 011-CV-750387 (Cuyahoga County, Ohio Ct. C.P., filed March 7, 2011). In spite of recent authority holding otherwise, the petitioner in *Cleveland-Cliffs* argued that it is "well established" in the federal courts of Ohio "that arbitrators are authorized to issue third-party subpoenas for prehearing document discovery"; the "same logic [should] appl[y] to depositions." The court relied on *American Fed'n of Television v. WKBJ-TV (New World Commun'ns of Detroit, Inc.)* 164 F.3d 1004, 1009).

the case to federal court under Section 1441 where recent precedent is favorable on that point, or otherwise seek dismissal?

V. Grounds for Removal

Section 1441, the removal statute, permits a defendant to remove a state court action to federal court if the action would fall within the federal court's original jurisdiction under Section 1331, either because federal law creates the cause of action[22] or the plaintiff's right to relief necessarily depends on the resolution of a substantial federal question, i.e., the substantial-federal-question doctrine.[23] Courts generally apply three principles in deciding whether there is a "substantial" federal question sufficient to confer original jurisdiction on the district court: "(1) the state law claim must necessarily raise a disputed federal issue; (2) the federal interest in the issue must be substantial; and (3) the exercise of jurisdiction must not disturb any congressionally approved balance of federal and state judicial responsibilities."[24]

VI. Exclusive Jurisdiction of Federal Courts Under the FAA

In *Matter of Beck's Superior Hybrids*, a recent case in Indiana, an arbitration panel sitting in New York granted a pre-hearing petition by Monsanto to subpoena Beck's, an Indiana third party, to appear before a panel member in Indiana at a preliminary hearing, and bring with him certain business records related to its arbitration claim.[25] Because the subpoena called for Beck's to appear before a member of the arbitration panel, it did not suffer from the same defects as most discovery subpoenas. Recognizing that Monsanto and its adversary were both Delaware companies and that there was, thus, no independent basis for

---

[22] § 1441(a). See also *Davis v. North Carolina Dept. of Correction*, 48 F.3d 134, 138 (4th Cir. 1995).

[23] §§ 1331, 1441(b); See also *Eastman v. Marine Mech. Corp.*, 438 F.3d 544, 550 (6th Cir. 2006) (quoting *Thornton, supra* n. 10: "A claim falls within this court's original jurisdiction under § 1331 '[in] those cases in which a well-pleaded [c]omplaint establishes ... that the plaintiff[']s right to relief necessarily depends on resolution of a substantial question of federal law'"); *Mikulski supra* n. 10 (quoting *Franchise Tax Bd., supra* n. 10: "substantial-federal-question doctrine ... applies 'where the vindication of a right under state law necessarily turn[s] on some construction of federal law'").

[24] *E.g., Mikulski, supra* n. 10, 501 F.3d at 568 (citing cases).

[25] *In re Beck's Superior Hybrids, supra* n. 17, 940 N.E.2d at 354-55.

federal jurisdiction, Monsanto filed a petition to enforce the subpoena in an Indiana trial court, pursuant to Indiana Trial Rule 28(E). This rule permits the courts to assist foreign tribunals and litigants in pursuing discovery in Indiana's juris diction. The trial court agreed with Monsanto and ordered Beck's to comply with the subpoena.

On appeal, a divided court reversed and remanded, holding that federal district courts have exclusive authority to enforce arbitral subpoenas under Section 7. The court acknowledged that some courts have found that Section 7 requires an independent jurisdictional basis, but it held that under Section 7's "plain terms," Congress provided that the "United States district court for the district in which [the] arbitrators" are sitting is the exclusive forum to enforce an arbitration subpoena to a third party.[26] Thus, the court found that Section 7 preempted Indiana Trial Rule 28(E). It also distinguished Section 7 from other provisions of the FAA (such as Section 4) that, under Supreme Court rulings, require the application of state substantive law and therefore provide state and federal courts with concurrent jurisdiction.

VII. Applying These Principles to Section 7

A. Plain Language of Section 7

Courts considering whether Section 7 provides a basis for federal question jurisdiction have rarely, if ever, begun with the obvious question: Does Section 7 express an intent by Congress to grant federal courts original jurisdiction over actions to enforce third-party subpoenas issued by arbitrators?[27] As several courts have recognized, it arguably does.[28] Section 7's language seems unambiguous. It explicitly permits a party

[26] The dissenting judge said that the "exclusive" venue provisions of the Act apply only when a federal court would have subject matter jurisdiction over the action. Therefore, "[i]f there is no federal court jurisdiction, then this is simply an intrastate dispute," and in this circumstance Indiana Trial Rule 28(E) would apply. *Id.* at 368.

[27] *Chair King, Inc. v. Houston Cellular Corp.*, 131 F.3d 507, 510 (5th Cir. 1997) ("Inferior federal courts' 'federal question' jurisdiction ultimately depends on Congress's intent as manifested by the federal statute creating the cause of action.... The search for Congress's intent... must of course begin with the text of the statute itself."); *International Sci. & Tech. Inst., Inc. v. Inacom Communic'n*, 106 F.3d 1146, 1153-54 (4th Cir. 1997) ("Because federal-question jurisdiction ultimately depends on an act of Congress, the scope of the district courts' jurisdiction depends on that congressional intent manifested in statute.").

[28] *E.g., Stolt-Nielsen, supra* n. 18.

seeking to enforce such subpoenas to "petition the United States district court for the district in which such arbitrators, or a majority of them, are sitting to "compel the attendance of such person or persons before said arbitrator or arbitrators."[29] Thus, in terms of Section 1331, the right to enforce an arbitral subpoena certainly appears to "aris[e] under" one of the "laws ... of the United States"—Section 7 and only Section 7. Put differently, Section 7 creates the party's right to relief, which is enforcement of the arbitration subpoena. The exercise of jurisdiction in these circumstances is generally valid absent statutory direction to the contrary.[30] Restrictive language in Sections 3 and 4 provide contrary direction, but there is no such language in Section 7. There is also no language in the FAA that precludes federal question jurisdiction under its provisions as a whole. Furthermore, the FAA's legislative history expressly states that the Act is intended to "provide[ ] a procedure in the Federal courts" for the enforcement of arbitration agreements.[31]

B. Administrative and Labor Arbitration Subpoenas

Finding that Section 7 grants federal courts with jurisdiction to enforce arbitral subpoenas would seem consistent with court decisions that have found that similar language in other statutes constitutes a specific grant of federal question jurisdiction.[32] For example, the statute governing the judicial authority to enforce an administrative subpoena issued by the International Trade Commission under Section 333(b) of the Tariff Act, states:

---

[29] The original phrase was "United States court in and for the district." In 1951 it was changed to "United States district court for the district." S. Rep. No. 82-1020, at 2582 (1951). The legislative history provides no specific reason for this particular change, but the general purpose of the legislation that included this amendment was to "make a few improvements of a minor character in certain titles of the United States Code...." *Id.* at 2578.

[30] *United States v. Alisal Water Corp.*, 431 F.3d 643 (9th Cir. 2005) ("absent statutory direction to the contrary, a district court validly exercises its jurisdiction over actions 'arising under' federal laws").

[31] H.R. Rep. No. 68-96, at 2 (1924).

[32] E.g., *United States Int'l Trade Comm'n v. ASAT, Inc.*, 411 F.3d 245, 248, 250 (D.C. Cir. 2005) (holding that, under the text of ... 19 U.S.C. § 1333(b), the district court where an ITC inquiry is carried on "has subject matter jurisdiction to enforce the [c]ommission's subpoena"; expressly declining to find subject matter jurisdiction pursuant to the "general jurisdictional grants in 28 U.S.C. §§ 1331, 1337, 1345"); *F.T.C. v. Browning*, 435 F.2d 96, 99 (D.C. Cir. 1970) (§ 9 of the FTC Act "must be interpreted as a special grant of jurisdiction" to federal district courts to enforce subpoenas issued by the commission where an inquiry is conducted).

> [I]n case of disobedience to a subp[o]ena[,] the commission may invoke the aid of any district ... court of the United States in requiring the attendance and testimony of witnesses and the production of documentary evidence, and such court within the jurisdiction of which such inquiry is carried on may, in case of contumacy or refusal to obey a subp[o]ena issued to any corporation or other person, issue an order requiring such corporation or other person to appear before the commission....[33]

True, these are for the purpose of federal agency investigations, but these agencies, like private litigants, only have original jurisdiction to bring actions in federal court when that jurisdiction is conferred by Congress.[34] In addition to such administrative subpoenas, federal courts have original jurisdiction to enforce third-party subpoenas issued by labor arbitrators in arbitrations brought under the Labor Management Relations Act.[35]

Policy Concerns. The policy concerns that have made courts reluctant to deviate from the *dicta* in *Moses H. Cone* and *Southland* involving Sections 3 and 4 seem overstated and not supported by specific facts. First, as noted above, federal district courts already have federal question jurisdiction to enforce administrative subpoenas issued by government agencies and subpoenas by labor arbitrators.[36]

Second, finding that federal district courts have jurisdiction to enforce private arbitration subpoenas would likely not lead to a "drastic

---

[33] 19 U.S.C. § 1333(b).

[34] *See, e.g., Federal Nat'l. Mortg. Ass'n v. Hammond*, No. CV 11–00867, 2011 WL 2516498 (C.D. Cal. June 22, 2011) ("Certain federal agencies' charters provide that federal courts will have original jurisdiction over suits involving those agencies"; the Freddie Mac charter does but the Fannie Mae charter does not); *Mendrala v. Crown Mortg. Co.*, 955 F.2d 1132, 1135 (7th Cir. 1992) ("Congress specifically provided for the [Federal Home Loan Mortgage Corp.] to be an 'agency' for purposes of" having original jurisdiction for "bringing suit" in federal court and for "removal," but did not so provide for purposes of being a defendant (§ 1346) or for purposes of the [Federal Tort Claims Act] itself [§ 2671], it therefore intended the FHLMC not to be a federal agency for the latter purposes").

[35] *E.g., Teamsters Nat'l Auto. Transporters Indus. Negotiating Comm'n v. Troha*, 328 F.3d 325, 331 (7th Cir. 2003); accord *Walt Disney Co. v. National Ass'n of Broad. Employees & Technicians*, No. 10 Civ. 5982, 2010 WL 3563110, *slip op.* (S.D.N.Y. Sept. 10, 2010). The Labor Management Relations Act is at 29 U.S.C. § 185.

[36] *S.E.C. v. Lines Overseas Mgmt., Ltd.*, No. Civ. A. 04-302, 2005 WL 3627141 (D.D.C. Jan. 7, 2005) (SEC subpoena). See "Administrative and Labor Arbitration Subpoenas" at page 28 *supra*.

change" in federal court activity.[37] According to the Indiana appeals court in *Beck's Superior Hybrids*, in the 63 years since Section 7 was enacted, "there has not been a single reported appellate case where a state court has been involved in an enforcement action under that law." Thus, it could be that federal courts are already entertaining the majority, if not all, of these actions.

Furthermore, it is not unusual for Congress to confer jurisdiction on federal courts under certain provisions of a statute but not others. For example, in the Telephone Consumer Protection Act,[38] "Congress drew careful jurisdictional distinctions" between the various sections—mandating exclusive federal court jurisdiction over certain actions brought by states in one section, limiting private rights of action to state courts in another section and authorizing concurrent jurisdiction to federal and state courts in other sections.[39] Congress may have intended such a jurisdictional distinction between Section 7 and other sections of the FAA given the different language it used in drafting those provisions, the clear language of Section 7 and the logical rationale for encouraging matters under certain sections of the FAA, like Sections 3 and 4, to be heard in state courts.

As the court explained in *Beck's Superior Hybrids*, because Section 4 requires a court to interpret a contract to determine if arbitration is required, which is a substantive question of state law, "of course the states have jurisdiction over those issues" absent some underlying basis for federal question jurisdiction. Section 7, on the other hand, "requires no application of judicial power other than the mere enforcement of a subpoena" and "[i]n exercising that authority, there is no risk that the federal judiciary will misapply the law of the states."

C. Substantial-Federal-Question Doctrine

The factors courts use to determine whether there is a "substantial" federal question[40] arguably favor bestowing original jurisdiction on a federal court when an action seeking to enforce an arbitration subpoena to a third-party for pre-hearing discovery is filed in state court and the adversary seeks to remove it to federal court.[41]

---

[37] *See* n. 20 *supra*.

[38] 47 U.S.C. § 227.

[39] *ErieNet, Inc. v. Velocity Net, Inc.*, 156 F.3d 513, 516-17 (3d Cir. 1998).

[40] *See* "Grounds for Removal" on page 27, *supra*.

[41] When a party relies on both § 7 and a comparable state statute, only one statute needs to provide a basis for federal question jurisdiction for removal to be proper. See *Wisconsin Dept. of Corrections v. Schacht*, 524 U.S. 381, 387 (1998) (quoting 28 U.S.C. § 1441(c), and

First, a party's right to enforce such a subpoena under Section 7 (or a comparable state statute),[42] "necessarily raise[s] a disputed federal issue" as to whether the text of the statute authorizes arbitrators to issue this discovery.[43] Second, federal interest in this issue appears to be "substantial" for the following reasons:[44]

(1) The proper construction to be afforded Section 7's text is clearly an "important" issue as it concerns the scope of third-party discovery in arbitration.[45]
(2) This issue is not "anomalous or isolated" as evidenced by the multiple decisions addressing it.[46]
(3) A decision concerning the construction of Section 7 would not be "merely incidental," but dispositive of the outcome of an enforcement action.

Third, there is no evidence that the exercise of jurisdiction over these enforcement actions by the federal court would not disrupt the

---

noting that § 1441(c) "explicitly provid[es] discretionary removal jurisdiction over entire case where federal claim is accompanied by a 'separate and independent' state-law claim").

[42] *E.g.*, compare Ohio Rev. Code Ann. § 2711.06 ("The arbitrators ... may subpoena in writing any person to attend before any of them as a witness and in a proper case to bring with him any book, record, document, or paper which is deemed material as evidence in the case."), with the language in 9 U.S.C. § 7. It should also be noted that, to the extent a state statute allows broader discovery than § 7, it would arguably be unenforceable based on the conflict preemption doctrine. *Volt Info. Sci., Inc. v. Board of Trustees of Leland Stanford Jr. Univ.*, 489 U.S. 468, 477-78 (1989) (recognizing that a state arbitration act's procedural rule is preempted by the FAA if the effect of that state rule "would undermine the goals and policies of the FAA").

[43] *See* ns. 4 & 5, *supra.*

[44] *E.g.*, *Mikulski*, *supra,* n. 10, 501 F.3d at 570 (the following four factors are normally considered in addressing the substantiality of federal interest in a disputed issue: "(1) whether the case includes a federal agency... (2) whether the federal question is important (i.e., not trivial); (3) whether a decision on the federal question will resolve the case (i.e., the federal question is not merely incidental to the outcome); and (4) whether a decision as to the federal question will control numerous other cases (i.e., the issue is not anomalous or isolated)."

[45] Interpreting the relevant language of § 7 to allow full-blown third-party discovery in an arbitration could be contrary to the reasons that many parties agree to arbitrate as opposed to seeking relief in court. See, e.g., *COMSAT Corp., supra* n. 5 ("Parties to a private arbitration agreement forego certain procedural rights attendant to formal litigation in return for a more efficient and cost-effective resolution of their disputes... because [the parties] have elected to enter arbitration, neither may reasonably expect to obtain full-blown discovery from the other or from third parties.").

[46] *See* ns. 4 & 5, *supra.*

"congressionally approved balance of federal and state judicial responsibilities." As the Indiana appeals court noted in *Beck's Superior Hybrids*, there are no state court cases dealing with the enforcement of arbitral subpoenas.

D. Exclusive Jurisdiction

Beck's Superior Hybrids provides an argument for seeking dismissal of an action to enforce an arbitral subpoena filed in state court on the ground that federal courts have exclusive jurisdiction to consider these actions. An enlightened court may respond to the Indiana court's reasoning.

VIII. Conclusion

Convincing a federal or state court to consider whether the nature and unique language of Section 7 or the substantial-federal-question doctrine provides a basis for original jurisdiction in federal courts will be a challenge, given the wealth of authority to the contrary. The latter argument may be more acceptable to courts because it does not obviously contravene *Moses H. Cone's dicta*. Nevertheless, the decision in *Beck's Superior Hybrids* provides some hope that courts may be willing to seriously consider the argument that Section 7's text is a clear jurisdictional grant of exclusive jurisdiction to federal district courts.

If either argument above were accepted, an arbitrating party could decide to contest a state court action to enforce a subpoena seeking prehearing discovery from a third party by first removing that matter to federal court and then challenging the subpoena on the ground that the weight of authority has found that these subpoenas are unenforceable under Section 7. Another alternative is to move for dismissal in the state court based on the holding in *Beck's Superior Hybrids*. If these issues are properly briefed, there is a chance that the court could find that Section 7's language does, in fact, provide a basis for federal question, and maybe even exclusive, jurisdiction.

CHAPTER 31

USING EXPERTS IN ARBITRATION

George Ruttinger, Joe Meadows, and April Ham[*]

I. Introduction

In litigation, the basic routine for working with experts involves several steps. First, counsel selects a witness who can qualify as an expert under the evidentiary rules and can communicate well to a judge or jury. The expert must possess sufficient knowledge, skill, experience, training, or education in the subject matter of the dispute.[1] Next, counsel considers whether to also retain a consulting expert for assistance and to shield all work product.[2] Counsel then asks the testifying expert to analyze the facts and data and prepare a written report on the opinion. Afterwards, counsel will prepare the expert to be deposed and to testify at trial. Finally, at trial, counsel will "qualify" the expert under the applicable evidentiary rules and present the expert's opinion on either technical, scientific, or specialized matters to educate and persuade the trier-of-fact.

Arbitration differs from litigation.[3] The proceeding is more informal, the rules of evidence generally do not apply, and discovery is often

---

[*] George Ruttinger is a partner in the Government Contracts and International Dispute Resolution Groups of Crowell & Moring LLP. He is in Crowell's Washington, D.C. office and specializes in contract litigation and counseling. He has represented clients in state and federal courts, arbitration proceedings, mini-trials, mediations, and federal administrative agencies.

Joe Meadows is a litigation counsel in Crowell & Moring's Washington, D.C. office, where he-specializes in complex commercial litigation and arbitration matters, frequently working with and writing about experts.

April Ham is a litigation and antitrust associate in Crowell & Moring's San Francisco, California office.

[1] *See* Fed. R. Evid. 702.

[2] A fundamental difference between consulting and testifying experts is that the work product of the former, including facts and data shared with counsel, is generally non-discoverable. *See* Fed. R. Civ. P. 26(b)(4).

[3] This article assumes a commercial arbitration under the American Arbitration Association (AAA) Commercial Arbitration Rules without specialized orders or agreements governing expert discovery and/or the presentation of expert evidence. Where such orders

limited.[4] Furthermore, especially in complex commercial disputes, arbitrators usually possess knowledge or experience in the subject matter of the dispute. As such, arbitration can have advantages over litigation, including greater opportunities to use and present expert evidence. A number of these opportunities are addressed below.

II. Flexibility in Selecting Experts

Counsel has greater flexibility in selecting experts in arbitration because, unlike litigation, there is no requirement that a witness qualify as an expert under strict evidentiary rules before giving an opinion. So long as the expert can offer relevant and material testimony, the expert should be able to testify at the arbitration hearing. That testimony should be admitted and given as much weight as the arbitrator deems appropriate.[5]

Counsel also has more flexibility to select experts because the failure to admit relevant evidence may be a ground for reversal or modification of an arbitration award.[6] As a result, many arbitrators admit purported expert testimony into evidence and then give that testimony more or less weight as appropriate.[7] The testimony of a witness who can be shown to qualify as an expert under strict evidentiary rules, however, may well carry more weight.

The greater flexibility to select expert witnesses is an advantage when technically qualified witnesses are scarce, more than one witness is needed, the most desirable witness has a conflict of interest and therefore

---

or agreements exist, some of the opportunities discussed in this article are obviously unavailable. *See* AAA Commercial Rule R-1(a) (parties may agree to vary arbitration procedures) and R-32(a), (b) (arbitrator may exercise discretion to vary conduct of proceedings).

[4] *See* AAA Commercial Rule R-34(a) ("Conformity to legal rules of evidence shall not be necessary."). *See also* JAY E. GRENIG, 1 ALTERNATIVE DISPUTE RESOLUTION § 8:60 (3d ed. 2006) (same).

[5] *See* AAA Commercial Rule R-34(a) ("The parties may offer such evidence as is relevant and material to the dispute and shall produce such evidence as the arbitrator may deem necessary to an understanding and determination of the dispute.").

[6] *See* 9 U.S.C. § 10(a)(3) (reversal for "refusing to hear evidence pertinent and material to the controversy"). *See also Gulf Coast Indus. Workers Union v. Exxon Co., USA*, 70 F.3d 847, 850 (5th Cir. 1995) (affirming order vacating arbitrator's ruling where the arbitrator refused to consider material evidence and prevented a party from presenting additional evidence by misleading it into believing it need not present the evidence).

[7] *See* T.H. OEHMKE, 3 COMMERCIAL ARBITRATION § 93:7 Westlaw CMLARB (database updated May 2015) (fundamental fairness dictates that arbitrators hear purported expert evidence).

cannot participate in the arbitration, or the client's budget precludes high-end experts.

III. Other Considerations in Selecting Experts

An expert selected by counsel to testify in court must explain his or her opinion and analysis in simple, easy-to-understand terms with persuasive force. In arbitration, this is less necessary because arbitrators often have backgrounds in the subject matter of the dispute and do not require the same type of basic explanation. The expert can instead focus on more technical, and sometimes dry, matters because arbitrators can better understand them.

Arbitrators often question witnesses, including experts. More so than litigation, an expert should be able to "think on his feet" to respond to probing questions by arbitrators who have familiarity in the field in dispute. An expert only experienced in testifying on direct and cross-examination may not be comfortable with the idea of open questions from a knowledgeable arbitrator.

IV. Freedom in Preparing Experts and Their Reports

Counsel has more freedom in preparing an expert to testify in arbitration and fashioning the expert's written report. In litigation, anything a testifying expert witness considers in forming an opinion — facts, data, and sometimes communications with others — can be fair game for discovery.[8] For this reason, counsel may hesitate to share

---

[8] *See* Fed. R. Civ. P. 26(a)(2)(B) ("facts or data" considered by testifying expert is discoverable). Prior to the 2010 amendment to Rule 26, "data or other information considered" by a testifying expert was discoverable. The words "other information" were broadly interpreted to cover all information provided to testifying experts, including attorney work product, regardless of reliance by experts. The 2010 amendment extended protection to drafts of expert reports and communications between counsel and the expert, subject to the following three exceptions: (1) expert compensation, (2) facts or data provided by counsel that the expert considered in forming opinions, and (3) assumptions provided by counsel that the expert relied upon in forming an opinion. Fed. R. Civ. P. 26(b)(4)(C). Despite this change, the Advisory Committee noted that "facts or data" should be "interpreted broadly to require disclosure of any material considered by the expert, from whatever source, that contains factual ingredients," including facts or data not ultimately relied upon by the expert. Committee Note to 2010 Amendment to Rule 26. *See also In re Methyl Tertiary Butyl Ether (MTBE) Products Liab. Litig.*, 293

information or strategy with the testifying expert for fear of having to turn that over. Counsel may also hire a consulting expert as an extra measure of work-product security.[9]

Expert discovery is more limited in arbitration. Parties typically disclose the identity of their experts along with expert reports and related exhibits. Unless ordered by the arbitrator or agreed to by the parties, parties often do not depose experts.[10] Thus, counsel should feel more comfortable providing experts with all information, whether sensitive, relevant, or damaging, and exchanging thoughts and ideas with the expert. This approach can lead to a focused and powerful expert report, a well-prepared expert, and reduced costs for consulting experts or other mechanisms designed to protect otherwise discoverable work product.

Given these considerations, counsel should actually participate in drafting expert reports or detailed outlines. While such practice may not be advisable (or even allowed in some jurisdictions) in litigation, it can be a best practice in arbitration. Counsel can help make the final expert report more persuasive and less subject to attack on cross-examination. Counsel may even continue to refine the expert's opinions after the reports are exchanged. Facts or data may change or new information may surface. Since experts are less frequently deposed in arbitration, changes to final reports (if even allowed) may not be as damaging as they would be in litigation, where experts are typically deposed and any report changes are fully exposed on cross-examination.

F.R.D. 568, 577 (S.D.N.Y. 2013) ("Thus, even after the 2010 Amendment, the scope of expert discovery contemplated by Rule 26 is still expansive.").

[9] *See supra* n. 2.

[10] *See* AAA Commercial Rule R-22(a) (exchange of necessary information managed by the arbitrator to achieve "an efficient and economical resolution of the dispute, while at the same time promoting equality of treatment and safeguarding each party's opportunity to fairly present its claims and defenses) and Procedures for Large, Complex Commercial Disputes (LCC) rules L-3(f) (depositions may be ordered by arbitrators upon showing of good cause in "exceptional cases"). *See also Rintin Corp., S.A. v. Domar, Ltd.*, 374 F. Supp. 2d 1165, 1170 (S.D. Fla. 2005) *aff'd,* 476 F.3d 1254 (11th Cir. 2007) ("[D]iscovery is not guaranteed in arbitration and arbitrators have broad discretion as to grant or deny the ability to obtain discovery."); Stephen J. O'Neil, *Managing Depositions in Arbitration to Minimize Cost and Maximize Value*, 69 DIS. RES. J. 15, 17 (2014) (noting there is no express authorization for depositions in the AAA Commercial Rules and some arbitrators view depositions as the exception, not the rule).

V. Presenting the Expert

A. At the Hearing

Parties arbitrate disputes because of speed and cost factors. The hearing (or arbitration trial) happens within months of the initial demand and is often limited in duration. Counsel should gauge how much time will be spent on the expert.

Counsel might shorten the presentation to the ultimate opinion without factual basis or detail, or, in lieu of direct testimony, submit only the written expert report and/or an affidavit from the expert.

Counsel might prefer to submit only a written expert report or affidavit due to other concerns. The expert may not present well live, the opinion may cover a small issue, or the expert may have to travel to the hearing. The trade-off is that the arbitrators will likely give written expert reports less weight than live testimony, particularly when there has been no opportunity for cross-examination.[11]

Mode of questioning is another consideration. For example, should counsel use leading questions to focus the expert's testimony, save time, and/or control a talkative expert? Should counsel supplement the expert's testimony with the client's views of the factual and legal issues, either as an introduction to the hearing, as comments during it, or as part of concluding remarks? Arbitration rules do not prohibit leading questions or counsel providing the client's views of the issues, including expert issues, during the hearing. Some arbitrators may actually welcome these approaches to narrow the areas of disagreement and move the hearing along.[12] Another approach is to have the expert make a presentation with demonstrative aids, rather than a typical question and answer format.

---

[11] Note, however, that a party may request that the arbitrator order a witness, including an expert, whose testimony is represented by a party to be essential to appear in person for examination before the arbitrator. *See* AAA Commercial Rule R-35(a) ("If a witness whose testimony is represented by a party to be essential is unable or unwilling to testify at the hearing…either party may request that the arbitrator order the witness to appear in person for examination before the arbitrator at a time and location where the witness is willing and able to appear voluntarily or can legally be compelled to do so. Any such order may be conditioned upon payment by the requesting party of all reasonable costs associated with such examination.").

[12] *See* AAA Commercial Rule R-32(b) ("The arbitrator, exercising his or her discretion, shall conduct the proceedings with a view to expediting the resolution of the dispute and may direct the order of proof, bifurcate proceedings and direct the parties to focus their presentations on issues the decision of which could dispose of all or part of the case.").

Counsel who has confidence in the expert may invite the arbitrators to question the expert directly on controversial matters before cross-examination. Having arbitrators question the expert witness at this time may lessen the impact of a skillful cross and provide valuable insight into the direction the arbitrators are leaning. In addition, it provides counsel with an opportunity to make mid-course corrections if needed.

Counsel can also make choices concerning the form of the expert presentations. More than one expert may be presented at the same time using a panel of expert witnesses. This approach works well if more than one expert is necessary to address the same subject matter or if the individual experts would not make strong witnesses.

Parties may also agree to have the opposing sides' experts on, for example, damages, appear on a panel together in a practice referred to as expert witness conferencing or "hot-tubbing."[13] In this scenario, "dueling" experts present their opinions on a particular issue in a direct point-counterpoint manner. In this format, they may be questioned on their dueling opinions by both sides' counsel and the arbitrators. By agreement of the parties, they may even question each other, giving the arbitrators real-time insight into the competing views on the most contested issues. This format can narrow the issues in dispute between the parties, increase comprehension of the issues and reduce costs and time needed for a hearing. It can also provide additional benefits for the side with the stronger, more aggressive expert witnesses.[14]

B. After the Hearing

In litigation, a testifying expert has one opportunity to present the opinion: while on the stand. In arbitration, a testifying expert has additional opportunities.

---

[13] "Hot-tubbing," also known as the "Australian approach" to expert testimony, originated in Australia to reduce expert partisanship and has been implemented in other jurisdictions, including a few U.S. federal courts. *See* David Sonenshein, Charles Fitzpatrick, *The Problem of Partisan Experts and the Potential for Reform Through Concurrent Evidence*, 32 REV. LITIG. 1, 55, 56 (2013); Frances P. Kao et. al, *Into the Hot Tub…A Practical Guide to Alternative Expert Witness Procedures in International Arbitration*, 44 INT'L LAW. 1035, 1037 (2010).

[14] Although used less frequently, witness panels are also available in litigation. *See* Fed. R. Evid. 611. *See also* DAVID H. KAYE & DAVID A. FREEDMAN, REFERENCE MANUAL ON SCIENTIFIC EVIDENCE 89 (2d ed. 2000) (discussing witness panels and narrative testimony in litigation to "improve the judge's understanding and reduce the tensions associated with the expert's adversarial role").

For example, the expert may re-present his or her opinion as part of the post-hearing oral argument. This may help clarify issues or alleviate concerns that arose during the hearing. The expert might also testify again in bifurcated cases on damages or in post-hearing proceedings on the parties' proposed award of damages, such as in baseball arbitration. Often, the expert may be regarded as more knowledgeable on the subject of damages than counsel, especially in complex matters.

VI. Conclusion

More opportunities exist for using and presenting expert evidence in arbitration than in litigation. To best serve their clients, counsel should know the differences between the two forums and how they affect the presentation of expert evidence. For example, counsel in arbitration should know that:

- expanding or limiting expert discovery at the outset and within the arbitration agreement is possible;
- rules for qualifying experts in litigation are not mandatory in arbitration;
- use of consulting, non-testifying experts are unnecessary in arbitration;
- disclosing work product to an expert in arbitration is less problematic;
- counsel can play a more active role in drafting the expert report and focusing the expert opinion;
- counsel can choose alternative methods of presenting expert evidence, for example, offering an expert report or affidavit only, presenting a panel of experts, or agreeing to "dueling" expert panels; and
- expert testimony can be re-presented after the hearing.

The lesson here is that counsel in arbitration should think creatively about how best to use and present expert evidence. A lawyer who is still following litigation rules when working with experts in arbitration is probably leaving something valuable on the table.

CHAPTER 32

PRESENTING WITNESS TESTIMONY IN U.S. *DOMESTIC* ARBITRATION: SHOULD WRITTEN WITNESS STATEMENTS BECOME THE NORM?

*Raymond G. Bender**

I. Introduction

The direct testimony of fact witnesses in international arbitration is routinely presented in written rather than oral form. Written statements are intended to reflect the detailed testimony that a witness would offer if questioned orally at an arbitration hearing. The statements are typically signed by the witnesses, often under affidavit, and are exchanged with the other parties prior to the hearing. Each witness providing written direct testimony then will appear at the hearing for examination by the other side's counsel and the arbitrators.

This prevailing practice in international arbitration has not been embraced widely by advocates in U.S. domestic arbitration. There may be sound reasons for not wanting to use written witness statements in the context of any given dispute. But many arbitration advocates trained in U.S. court litigation appear to be unfamiliar with the use of written testimony, or they are unwilling to relinquish the common practice of presenting witness testimony live via the question-and-answer format.[1]

---

* Raymond G. Bender is an independent commercial Arbitrator serving in U.S. domestic and international disputes. He is a member of the American Arbitration Association's Roster of Commercial Arbitrators for Washington, D.C., Technology, and Large Complex Cases; the CPR Panel of Distinguished Neutral Arbitrators for Washington, D.C., Technology, and Cross-Border disputes; and the International Center for Dispute Resolution (ICDR) Panel of International Arbitrators. Mr. Bender has served in International Chamber of Commerce (ICC) and *ad hoc* arbitrations as well. He also is an Adjunct Professor at the Washington College of Law, American University, Washington DC, where he teaches Alternative Dispute Resolution Law.

[1] When used in arbitration (or other proceedings), written witness statements generally present the testimony of witnesses under the control of the sponsoring party, but not of witnesses who are hostile or require the issuance of a subpoena.

This article focuses on written witness statements in arbitration and highlights notable advantages that can be gained by their use. Among other things, presenting the direct testimony of fact witnesses in writing can streamline an arbitration hearing and afford significant efficiencies and cost savings. Countervailing factors may, of course, weigh against using written statements in some instances, but a new and searching look by U.S. counsel and arbitrators could instill a greater appreciation for written witness statements and a wider acceptance of their use in U.S. domestic arbitration.[2]

II. Written Witness Statements in International Arbitration

It is now common in international arbitration to exchange the written direct testimony of fact witnesses with opposing counsel and arbitrators in advance of the hearing. The use of witness statements is normally conditioned on the witness' appearance at hearing to be cross-examined by opposing counsel and questioned by the arbitrators. To some extent, this procedure reflects a convergence in international arbitration of different common law and civil law practices concerning the presentation of evidence generally.

In a common law system, such as in the United States, it is customary for advocates to present their witnesses live for questioning on direct examination, and then to offer those witnesses for cross-examination by opposing counsel. Civil law systems, in contrast, place greater emphasis on documentary evidence. Written witness statements might be used, and oral testimony may be permitted, but the questioning of witnesses in civil law jurisdictions ordinarily is pursued solely by the judge, although lawyers may suggest specific questions for a judge to pose. Cross-examination of witnesses by opposing counsel generally is not favored in civil law proceedings.[3]

---

[2] The usual practice regarding *expert witnesses* (as opposed to *fact witnesses*) in both domestic and international arbitration is for parties to exchange written expert witness reports in advance of an arbitration hearing, with the experts then appearing at the hearing for examination by the other side. A wider use of the same format for fact witnesses in U.S. domestic arbitration may serve the process and parties in meaningful ways.

[3] For discussions of the differences between common law and civil law legal systems regarding the presentation of evidence, *see* Siegfried H. Elsing and John M. Townsend, *Bridging the Common Law Civil Law Divide in Arbitration*, Arbitration International, Vol. 18, No. 1, LCIA (2002); and John Anthony Wolf and Kelly M. Preteroti, *Written*

Efforts to harmonize these practices in the context of international arbitration—which often includes parties, counsel and arbitrators from different legal cultures—led to an increasing use of written witness statements for direct testimony, followed by cross-examination of the witnesses by counsel for the other parties. A recent study on the views of in-house counsel, private practitioners and arbitrators involved in international arbitration reported that, over the prior five years, fact witness evidence was offered by exchange of written witness statements in a significant majority of arbitrations (87%), together with either direct examination at the hearing (48%) or limited or no direct examination at the hearing (39%).[4] In contrast, fact witness evidence was offered solely by oral testimony in only 13% of arbitrations.[5] Moreover, 59% of survey respondents believe that the use of written witness statements as a substitute for oral direct examination at the hearing is generally effective.[6]

Witness statements can be defined as "detailed presentations in writing of the testimony, including references to documents that are also presented, that a witness would give if questioned before the tribunal."[7] More specifically, the IBA Rules on the Taking of Evidence in International Arbitration delineate the items that should be included in each witness statement:

> (a) the full name and address of the witness, a statement regarding his or her present and past relationship (if any) with any of the Parties, and a description of his or her background, qualifications, training and experience, if such a description may be relevant to the dispute or to the contents of the statement;
>
> (b) a full and detailed description of the facts, and the source of the witness's information as to those facts, sufficient to serve as that witness's evidence in the matter in dispute. Documents on which the witness relies that have not already been submitted shall be provided;

Witness Statements—A Practical Bridge of the Cultural Divide, Dispute Resolution Journal (May-July 2007).

[4] *2012 International Arbitration Survey: Current and Preferred Practices in the Arbitral Process*, White & Case LLP and the School of International Arbitration, Queen Mary University of London, at 24 (2012).

[5] *Id.*

[6] *Id.* at 25.

[7] CPR Protocol on Disclosure of Documents and Presentation of Witnesses in Commercial Arbitration (2009), at 12.

(c) a statement as to the language in which the Witness Statement was originally prepared and the language in which the witness anticipates giving testimony at the Evidentiary Hearing;
(d) an affirmation of the truth of the Witness Statement; and
(e) the signature of the witness and its date and place.[8]

Today, most international arbitration rules envision the use of written statements to present direct testimony of fact witnesses, coupled with the witness's appearance at hearing for cross-examination and arbitrator questions. The rules of the AAA's International Center for Dispute Resolution (ICDR) provide, for example, that:

> Unless otherwise agreed by the parties or directed by the tribunal, evidence of witnesses may be presented in the form of written statements signed by them. In accordance with a schedule set by the tribunal, each party shall notify the tribunal and the other parties of the names of any witnesses who have presented a witness statement whom it requests to examine. The tribunal may require any witness to appear at a hearing. If a witness whose appearance has been requested fails to appear without valid excuse as determined by the tribunal, the tribunal may disregard any written statement by that witness.[9]

The London Court of International Arbitration (LCIA) rules provide that "[s]ubject to any order otherwise by the Arbitral Tribunal, the testimony of a witness may be presented by a party in written form, either as a signed statement or like document," and "[t]he Arbitral Tribunal and any party may request that a witness, on whose written testimony another party relies, should attend for oral questioning at a hearing before the Arbitral Tribunal."[10]

The International Chamber of Commerce (ICC) rules include references to written witness statements, and the ICC Commission Report on Controlling Time and Costs in Arbitration provides that

---

[8] Article 4.5 of the IBA Rules on the Taking of Evidence in International Arbitration (2010) (IBA Rules).
[9] Rule 23.4 of the ICDR International Arbitration Rules (2014).
[10] Articles 20.2 and 20.4 of the LCIA Arbitration Rules (effective October 1, 2014).

"[w]hen appropriate, witness statements can substitute for direct examination at a hearing."[11]

The Stockholm Chamber of Commerce arbitration rules state that "[t]he testimony of witnesses…may be submitted in the form of signed statements," and that "[a]ny witness …on whose testimony a party seeks to rely, shall attend the hearing for examination, unless otherwise agreed by the parties."[12]

The Singapore International Arbitration Center (SIAC) rules provide that "[t]he Tribunal may direct the testimony of witnesses to be presented in written form, either as signed statements or sworn affidavits or any other form of recording" and that, subject to the tribunal's discretion, "any party may request that such a witness should attend for oral examination."[13]

As reflected in these and other international rules, witnesses who submit written direct testimony generally are expected to appear at a hearing for cross-examination and tribunal inquiries. Indeed, knowledgeable commentators have observed that cross-examination is now the norm in international arbitration.[14] Parties can agree, of course, to waive cross-examination, which might occur in the case of secondary witnesses whose testimony is straightforward and non-controversial.

Some international arbitration rules authorize the tribunal to condition the use of written statements on the witness' appearance at hearing for cross-examination. For example, the rules of the World Intellectual Property Organization (WIPO) provide that the testimony of witnesses may be submitted in written form, "in which case the Tribunal may make the admissibility of the testimony conditional upon the witnesses being made available for oral testimony."[15] Similarly, JAMS international Rule 24.4 states that, in the discretion of the tribunal, "the presentation of witness testimony in the form of written statements may be made conditional upon the witnesses' appearance for the purpose of cross-examination."[16] The Stockholm Chamber rules state unequivocally that

---

[11] *See e.g.,* ICC Rules of Arbitration Article 24(1) and Appendix IV(e) (2012), and ICC Commission Report on Controlling Time and Costs in Arbitration at 14 (2012).

[12] Arbitration Rules of the Arbitration Institute of the Stockholm Chamber of Commerce (Stockholm Chamber), Article 28(2) and (3) (2010).

[13] Rule 22.4 of the SIAC Arbitration Rules (2013).

[14] *See e.g.*, William W. Park, *Arbitration's Protean Nature: The Value of Rules and the Risks of Discretion*, Mealey's Intl. Arb. Rep. (Vol. 19, Issue #5) 30 (2004), at 37.

[15] Article 56(d) of the WIPO Arbitration Rules (2014).

[16] Article 24.4 of the JAMS International Arbitration Rules (2011).

any witness on whose testimony a party seeks to rely "*shall attend a hearing for examination*, unless otherwise agreed by the parties."[17]

Other international rules permit the tribunal to consider written witness statements even in circumstances where a witness fails to appear for cross-examination, provided there is a valid reason or other exceptional circumstance. The ICDR Rules provide, for example, that "[i]f a witness whose appearance has been requested fails to appear *without a valid excuse* as determined by the tribunal, the tribunal may disregard any witness statement by that witness," inferring that the tribunal may still consider a written statement if the witness offers a legitimate reason for not appearing.[18] Similarly, the IBA Rules provide:

> If a witness whose appearance has been requested pursuant to Article 8.1 fails *without a valid reason* to appear for testimony at an Evidentiary Hearing, the Arbitral Tribunal shall disregard any Witness Statement related to that Evidentiary Hearing by that witness unless, *in exceptional circumstances,* the Arbitral Tribunal decides otherwise.[19]

Other rules state that if a witness fails to attend a hearing, the tribunal may disregard or exclude his or her written testimony altogether, or may discount the weight it places on such testimony.[20]

Civil law arbitrators possibly may be more inclined than common law arbitrators to admit a written witness statement into evidence if the witness, for a valid reason, were unable to appear at a hearing for cross-examination. This approach is consistent with the higher value civil law systems place on documentary evidence (over witness testimony), and on the relative dislike of cross-examination by civil law attorneys. In common law systems, on the other hand, especially in the United States, cross-examination of witnesses has become so engrained as a fundamental

---

[17] Article 28(3) of the Arbitration Rules of the Stockholm Chamber (2010) (emphasis added).

[18] Article 23.4 of the ICDR Rules (emphasis added).

[19] Article 4.7 of the IBA Rules (emphasis added).

[20] *See* Article 20.4 of the LCIA Rules ("If the Arbitral Tribunal orders that other party to secure the attendance of that witness and the witness refuses or fails to attend the oral hearing without good cause, the Arbitral Tribunal may place such weigh on the written testimony or exclude all or any part thereof altogether as it considers appropriate in the circumstances."); and Rule 22.4 of the SIAC Arbitration Rules ("If the witness fails to attend, the Tribunal may place such weight on the written testimony as it thinks fit, disregard it or exclude it altogether.").

due process right that many common law arbitrators would be reluctant to accept a written witness statement if the witness fails to appear at hearing.[21] In any event, most international arbitration rules afford arbitrators broad discretion to reject a witness statement entirely, or discount its weight, if a witness does not submit to an opposing party's cross-examination.

Although written witness statements are a mainstay of international arbitration, they still are not utilized widely in U.S. domestic arbitration.

III. Presenting Direct Testimony in Writing Is Common in Other U.S. Contexts

The use of written witness statements has long been used effectively in various federal and state administrative proceedings. For example, in the 1970's and 1980's, this author represented numerous parties in contested licensing proceedings before Administrative Law Judges of the Federal Communications Commission (FCC). It was standard practice in those cases to exchange the direct testimony of witnesses in writing in advance of the hearing, subject to cross-examination by opposing counsel at the hearing. This procedure was viewed generally by FCC litigators to be beneficial and effective in the context of contested, often high-stakes cases for the award of valuable broadcast and other communications-related licenses.

The adoption of written direct testimony as a civil trial convention also is gaining ground in U.S. courts.[22] For example, it was reported that at least eight of the sixteen U.S. District Court Judges for the Southern District of New York provide in their individual rules of practice that in civil non-jury trials the direct testimony of witnesses under the control of a party "shall be" by written witness statement, subject to cross examination

---

[21] *See* The College of Commercial Arbitrators Guide to Best Practices in Commercial Arbitration, at 438 (James M. Gaitis *et. al.* eds., 3rd ed. 2014) ("CCA Best Practices") which states: "If a witness fails to appear, arbitrators should invite counsel to give their views on the appropriate action to be taken. In the absence of a waiver of the right of cross-examination, a witness statement that has not been subjected to cross-examination should bear no weight," but which also provides that "[w]hen specific guidelines such as the IBA Rules have been adopted, those guidelines may determine how the tribunal should or must proceed."

[22] *See* Marc C. Goldstein, *Written Direct Testimony Gains Favor in US Courts: A Precursor for Domestic Arbitration Hearing Practice* (2011), available at http://arbblog.lexmarc.us/2011/05/written-direct-testimony-gains-favor-in-us-courts.

by the adverse party.[23] For example, the Rules of District Judge Ronnie Abrams provide that in non-jury cases the parties shall "submit to the Court and serve on opposing counsel…copies of affidavits constituting the direct testimony of each trial witness, except for the direct testimony of an adverse party, a person whose attendance is compelled by subpoena, or a person whom the Court has agreed to hear direct testimony live at the trial."[24] Within three business days after submission of such affidavits, "counsel for each party shall submit a list of affiants whom he or she intends to cross-examine at the trial" and "[o]nly those witnesses who will be cross-examined need to appear at trial."[25]

The rules or protocols of various U.S. domestic arbitration institutions permit the use of written witness statements in lieu of oral direct testimony. The AAA Commercial Rules provide, for example, that an arbitrator may "allow for the presentation of evidence by alternative means including…means other than an in-person presentation," and that such alternative means "must afford a full opportunity for all parties to present any evidence that the arbitrator deems material and relevant to the resolution of the dispute and, when involving witnesses, provides an opportunity for cross-examination."[26] The AAA Commercial rules also provide as follows:

> R-35. Evidence by Written Statements and Post-Hearing Filing of Documents or Other Evidence
>
> (a) At the date agreed upon by the parties or ordered by the arbitrator, the parties shall give written notice for any witness or expert witness who has provided a written witness statement to appear in person at the arbitration hearing for examination. If such notice is given, and the witness fails to appear, the arbitrator may disregard the written witness statement and/or expert report of the witness or

---

[23] *See Id.* at 1, noting that such rules can be viewed on the court's website at www.nysd.uscourts.gov/judges.

[24] Individual Rules & Practices in Civil Cases, Hon. Ronnie Abrams, United States District Judge, § 6.C.iv (Dec. 11, 2013), available at www.nysd.uscourts.gov/judge/Abrams. As a practical matter, written witness statements are utilized in arbitration or other proceedings to present the testimony of witnesses under the control of the sponsoring party, and not for witnesses who are hostile or who may require the issuance of a subpoena.

[25] *Id. See also* Individual Rules of Practice of Hon. Colleen McMahon. U.S. District Judge, at 12-13 (Nov. 26, 2013), available at www.nysd.uscourts.gov/judge/McMahon.

[26] Rule R-32(c) of the AAA Commercial Arbitration Rules (2013).

make such other order as the arbitrator may consider to be just and reasonable.[27]

The CPR Arbitration Rules (both administered and non-administered) state that the testimony of witnesses "may be presented in written and/or oral form as the Tribunal may determine is appropriate."[28] A related CPR protocol on the presentation of witnesses provides that each witness who has provided a written witness statement "*must* appear for examination at the evidentiary hearing by the opposing parties and the tribunal unless the parties and the tribunal agree otherwise," and that "[t]he tribunal may disregard the statement of any witness who fails to appear in support of it."[29]

The JAMS Comprehensive Arbitration Rules also appear to permit the use of written direct testimony under Rule 22 (e), which provides that an arbitrator may in his or her discretion "consider witness affidavits or other recorded testimony even if the other Parties have not had the opportunity to cross-examine, but will give that evidence only such weight as he or she deems appropriate."[30]

Despite this authority in U.S. arbitration rules, there appears to be a continuing reluctance to use written witness statements regularly in U.S. domestic arbitration. Perhaps this is understandable in the case of U.S. litigators who do not practice routinely in international arbitration and who therefore are more comfortable with the U.S. custom of presenting witnesses live.[31] As for arbitrators, those who serve in both international

---

[27] Rule R-35(a) of the AAA Commercial Arbitration Rules (2013).

[28] Rule 12.2 of the CPR Administered Arbitration Rules (2013) and Rule 12.2 of the CPR Non-Administered Arbitration Rules (2007).

[29] CPR Protocol on Disclosure of Documents and Presentation of Witnesses in Commercial Arbitration, Section 2(a)2 (2009) (emphasis added).

[30] Rule 22(e) of the JAMS Comprehensive Arbitration Rules (2014). Whether this JAMS rule encompasses written direct case witness statements is somewhat unclear, especially given the clarity of the JAMS *International* Arbitration Rules on the use of written witness statements (Article 24.4), as follows: "In the discretion of the Tribunal, evidence of witnesses may also be presented in the form of written statements signed by them. In the discretion of the Tribunal, the presentation of witness testimony in the form of written statements may be made conditional upon the witnesses' appearance for the purpose of cross-examination." Whatever may be the intent of JAMS Rule 22 (e), the JAMS domestic rules do not prohibit written witness statements to the extent the parties and the tribunal agree to use them.

[31] *See* David W. Rivkin, *21st Century Arbitration Worthy of Its Name*, Law of International Business and Dispute Settlement in the 21st Century, at 4 (2001) (asserting that counsel representing parties "frequently have less experience with international

and U.S. domestic arbitration will have had greater exposure to the use of witness statements in their international practice, and they may be more willing to broach the use of written direct testimony than arbitrators who serve solely in U.S. domestic disputes.[32] In any event, there are good reasons why all of the participants in U.S. domestic arbitration—parties, counsel and arbitrators alike—should be more open to the use of written witness statements.

IV. Benefits of Written Witness Statements

The advantages associated with written witness statements should persuade parties, counsel and arbitrators to consider using them more routinely in U.S. domestic arbitration.

First, presenting the direct testimony of witnesses in writing can save considerable hearing time and thereby achieve efficiencies and cost-savings, which are hallmarks of any arbitration. Depending on the complexity of the dispute, days or even weeks of oral hearings can be avoided by presenting direct witness testimony in writing in advance of the hearing.[33] Some costs are associated with the preparation of witness statements, but the time involved ordinarily is not much different than needed to prepare witnesses to testify orally.[34] Thus, limiting oral direct testimony where possible can reduce the duration and cost of a hearing to a significant extent.

---

arbitration than the arbitrators, so they seek to rely upon the procedures to which they are accustomed in their domestic litigation.")

[32] *See* Goldstein, *supra* note 22, at 2 ("Many U.S. arbitrators who sit in domestic as well as international cases prefer to have witness statements, but often encounter resistance from counsel unfamiliar with the practice.")

[33] *See* Thomas J. Tallerico and J. Adam Behrendt, *The Use of Bifurcation and Direct Testimony Witness Statements in International Commercial Arbitration*, 20 Journal of International Arbitration, Issue 3, p 295-305 (2003) ("Direct testimony written witness statements in commercial arbitration offer both speed and efficiency to the arbitral process, limiting the need for lengthy evidentiary hearings."); and Lawrence W. Newman and David Zaslowski, *International Arbitration: Witness Statements*, LAW.COM, available at http://www.law.com/jsp/article.jsp?id=1202421714165&slreturn=20140106173912 ("hearing time is dramatically reduced by compressing into written pages what would otherwise be hours of oral presentation.")

[34] *See* Rivkin, supra note 31, at 11. *See also* Daniel L. Small, *Preparing a Witness for Arbitration,* AAA Handbook on Commercial Arbitration, at 329 (2d ed. 2010), (noting that "communicating effectively in a question-and-answer format is an extraordinarily unnatural and difficult process, one that requires considerable preparation.").

The use of written witness statements is one of many techniques suggested by the College of Commercial Arbitrators (CCA) to achieve a fair and efficient arbitration hearing.[35] Specifically, the CCA notes that every day of hearing, which can require the attendance of lawyers, paralegals, client representatives and witnesses, typically can cost a party many thousands of dollars.[36] For this reason, the CCA urges arbitrators to discuss with counsel various steps geared toward achieving efficiency and cost-savings, including the use of written direct testimony for some or all witnesses appearing in the arbitration.

Second, the use of written statements permits everyone involved in an arbitration to be better prepared for the hearing, which also creates efficiencies. Each witness will have collected his or her thoughts to present testimony in a clear and cogent written narrative. Not everyone is an articulate speaker, and even with advance preparation, witnesses still can be confused and disorganized when testifying live. Indeed, testifying can be intimidating, even in the relatively informal setting of arbitration, and a poor performance by a witness can cause disruption and delay as counsel continues probing to clear up the record. As one attorney favoring witness statements observes: "arbitration should de-emphasize rhetorical skills and focus on the facts and law."[37]

Written witness statements also facilitate cross-examination by opposing counsel. Knowing what a witness' testimony will be in advance of the hearing obviously provides an opportunity to prepare effectively for cross-examination.[38] Witness statements avoid surprise at the hearing and eliminate requests for more time to prepare for cross-examination, or to review the transcript for that purpose, again creating efficiencies at the hearing.

Arbitrators also are more knowledgeable and prepared concerning the issues and evidence in a case when written witness statements are provided in advance. Parties should expect arbitrators to review the written testimony prior to hearing, which permits the tribunal to focus on

---

[35] *See* The College of Commercial Arbitrators Protocols for Expeditious, Cost-Effective Commercial Arbitration, at 75 (2010), available at www.thecca.net.

[36] *Id.*

[37] Gerry DeNotto, *International and U.S. Arbitration from a Business Perspective: The Importance of the Arbitration Clause*, at 2, Mediate.com (2013), available at http://www.mediate.com/articles/DeNottoG1.cfm.

[38] Tallerica & Behrendt, *supra* note 33, ("cross-examination can be more effectively prepared (especially in complex, technical disputes) with a consequent reduction in hearing time," quoting Robert Gorske, *An Arbitrator Looks at Expediting the Large Complex Case*, 5 Ohio St. J. Disp. Resol. 381 395 (1990)).

the key issues in the case, formulate relevant questions for the witness, and conduct the hearing more effectively and efficiently.

Even counsel who sponsor witnesses will be better prepared on the various claims and defenses involved in the arbitration. Written statements ordinarily are exchanged several weeks before the hearing, permitting counsel to focus well in advance on the elements of each claim and the proof needed to make their case.

Third, a written witness statement can be an important fact-finding tool which, to some extent, can serve as a substitute for a deposition if exchanged early enough in the proceedings.[39] Unlike the prevailing practice in international arbitration, where depositions generally are not permitted, U.S. arbitrators often allow some depositions based on need or good cause shown. Ordinarily, however, rather than sanction countless or unending depositions, U.S. arbitrators normally permit a reasonable number of depositions of limited duration. As a practical matter, this may mean that depositions in some cases will be limited to key witnesses. Having the testimony of secondary witnesses who may not be deposed in advance of the hearing can serve a fact-finding purpose which, while not equivalent to a deposition, should assist counsel to prepare effectively for cross-examination.

V. There Can Be Drawbacks Associated With Written Witness Statements

Not everyone favors the use of written witness statements and commenters have identified a number of concerns regarding this technique.

One criticism is that witness statements are drafted by lawyers and therefore the testimony is not as spontaneous and/or reflective of how a witness actually would present the facts if he or she were testifying live.[40] Relatedly, witness statements can deprive arbitrators of the ability to assess the witness' credibility on direct examination. It also has been suggested that because lawyers draft witness statements, a witness can place too

[39] *See e.g.*, New York State Bar Association Guidelines for the Arbitrator's Conduct of the Pre-Hearing Phase of Domestic Commercial Arbitrations ("N.Y. State Bar Assn Guidelines") at 17 ("From a discovery perspective, [written witness statements] can avoid or lessen the need for depositions since the cross-examining party has detailed advanced notice of the witness' direct testimony.").

[40] *See Id.*; and Rivkin, *supra* note 31, at 11.

much trust in the lawyer and might review the witness statement only cursorily.[41]

From the perspective of the party presenting the witness, one concern is that written statements lack the impact of live testimony and, accordingly, witness statements may not be the best means of persuading the tribunal concerning one's view of the case.[42] Also, when a witness does not present direct testimony live, the witness' first appearance is on cross-examination by opposing counsel. Lawyers decidedly do not want a tribunal's first impression of a witness to reflect his or her defensive reaction to hostile questioning on cross-examination.[43]

There are suitable responses to most, if not all of these concerns.

First, lawyers often do draft written testimony for their witnesses, but generally only after an interview of the witness concerning relevant facts and a discussion of specific details to include in the testimony. The process is not unlike preparing a witness for oral testimony, which itself can involve repetition or practice as to how the witness is going to testify at the hearing. In this author's experience, as both advocate and arbitrator, lawyers normally approach the preparation of written witness statements professionally and responsibly, and they understand that such statements need to be truthful and accurate. Witnesses also recognize the import of their written testimony, which they will need to sign or possibly submit under affidavit. As for a witness' undue reliance on a lawyer, or reviewing witness statements only cursorily, lawyers can and should admonish witnesses that they will need to defend their testimony under rigorous cross-examination (and arbitrator questioning), and that a witness can risk loss of credibility entirely if written testimony is approached in a careless or cavalier manner. Thus, the overall process, and particularly the role of the lawyers on both sides, is designed to ensure that written witness statements serve as a useful means for adducing evidence in arbitration.

Second, with respect to assessing witness credibility, arbitrators normally can gain sufficient insight as to credibility during cross-examination, as well as on re-direct, and also during questioning by the

---

[41] *See* N.Y. State Bar Assn Guidelines, *supra* note 39, at 17.

[42] Mark W. Danis, *Strategic Options with Foreign Witnesses in International Arbitration*, Association of Corporate Counsel Legal Resources, at 2 (2012), available at http://www.acc.com/legalresources/quickcounsel/sowfwiia.cfm.

[43] *See* John Wilkinson, *Streamlining Arbitration of the Complex Case,* 55 Dispute Resolution Journal 3, at 4 (Aug.-Oct. 2000).

tribunal itself after counsel have completed their examinations.[44] Moreover, as noted below, most U.S. arbitrators can be expected to permit some limited live questioning by counsel on direct examination so that the witness can become comfortable before being turned over to opposing counsel for cross-examination. This approach affords an arbitrator an additional opportunity to assess witness credibility during a shortened form of direct examination.

Third, the concern that a witness not be turned over for cross-examination before being at ease in the arbitral setting is a legitimate one, and it is therefore reasonable for counsel to request U.S. arbitrators to permit some brief direct examination (*e.g.*, 15 to 30 minutes) by counsel offering the witness. This approach "allows the witness to 'warm to the seat' and permits the tribunal to hear the witness testify in his/her own words."[45] Such questioning on direct might include brief background information about the witness, such as residence, age, education, professional and similar data. Counsel also may ask the witness to verify the truth or correctness of the written testimony and to make any appropriate corrections or updates. It also can be helpful for the witness to present a high-level summary of the key points of the testimony—which, as noted above, provides another window for the tribunal to assess credibility—although such live direct testimony should be abbreviated so as not to defeat a primary purpose of using written witness statements (*i.e.*, time savings and efficiency).[46]

Written witness statements may not be suitable in every case. For example, there may be arbitrations where the credibility of a key witness can be decisive in the outcome of the case. Arbitrators and counsel may wish to dispense with written testimony in that situation to permit a key witness or witnesses to testify live and thereby enable the tribunal to take the full measure of the witness.[47] Indeed, some commenters observe that

---

[44] *See* Rivkin, *supra* note 31, at 11 ("It is important for arbitrators to hear directly from witnesses and to be able to judge their credibility and the weight to be given to their evidence. This may be achieved, however, by requiring that any witness submitting direct testimony be available for cross-examination at the hearing.")

[45] CPR Protocol on Disclosure of Documents and Presentation of Witnesses in Commercial Arbitration, at 13 (2009).

[46] A witness should not be permitted to testify orally to matters not included in his or her written witness statement.

[47] *See* John Fellas, *A Fair and Efficient International Arbitration Process*, PLI Course Handbook on International Arbitration, at 13 (2007), available at http://www.google.com/url?sa=t&rct=j&q=&esrc=s&frm=1&source=web&cd=1&ved=0CB4QFjAA&url=http%

arbitrators may benefit by being able to assess the credibility of primary witnesses during direct testimony.[48] Another experienced practitioner notes that it might be important for a witness to speak directly to the tribunal where there are complicated facts or significant details that need to be communicated.[49] These and other circumstances might lead counsel and arbitrators in specific cases to conclude that, on balance, live direct examination of a key witness might be preferable to written testimony.

The foregoing suggests that attorneys and arbitrators in U.S. domestic arbitration should weigh the advantages and disadvantages of witness statements on a case-by-case basis. If such an analysis is objectively performed, this author believes that in most cases, and for most witnesses, the use of written witness statements could well become the norm in U.S. domestic arbitration (as it is in international arbitration). This conclusion assumes that certain practical measures are taken by arbitrators and counsel to realize the benefits of written witness statements and to ameliorate any potential drawbacks associated with their use.

VI. Practical Steps Relating to the Use of Written Witness Statements

Arbitration is a flexible process that permits participants to adopt procedures best suited to the needs of each particular dispute. In light of this flexibility, the participants in any U.S. domestic arbitration should consider the use of written witness statements as a routine matter when formulating procedures to govern the conduct of the proceedings. Indeed, arbitrators and counsel should, at a minimum, observe the following steps:

First, arbitrators should include the subject of witness statements as an item for discussion on the preliminary hearing conference agenda. Once an arbitrator or tribunal is appointed, the arbitration's first key event is the preliminary conference, at which the arbitrators and counsel make important decisions that shape the course of the proceedings to come. Proactive arbitrators typically circulate an agenda in advance of

---

3A%2F%2Fwww.pli.edu%2Femktg%2Fall_star%2Fintl_arb13.doc&ei=GZD3U6mAIMP9yQSd5oLoAw&usg=AFQjCNGmJbFnc2jvqdyMsg7-MEL5OwB98Q.

[48] *See e.g.*, Wilkinson, *supra* note 43, at 4 ("The arbitrators…can often benefit from hearing direct testimony from those primary witnesses, which they can use to assess credibility in a very different context from that of cross-examination."). *See also* New York Bar Association, at 17 ("oral direct testimony can be a good time for an arbitrator to assess credibility from a perspective other than cross-examination.").

[49] *See* Rivkin, *supra* note 31, at 12.

the preliminary conference and direct counsel to meet and confer—and to endeavor to reach agreement---on various procedures that will apply in the arbitration, including with respect to any motions, the nature and extent of discovery, the location and dates for the hearing, witness testimony, the presentation of documentary evidence, and a myriad of other preliminary issues.[50]

Most or all of these items are resolved by agreement of the parties or, if necessary, by ruling of the tribunal at or immediately after the preliminary conference. It is therefore essential that the topic of written witness statements appear as an item on the preliminary conference agenda to facilitate a candid discussion among counsel and arbitrators concerning their use.

Second, arbitrators should highlight the advantages of written witness statements, especially where there is resistance from counsel or where U.S. litigators are unfamiliar with the practice of presenting direct testimony in writing. Arbitrators surely have a duty in today's arbitration environment to identify efficiencies and cost-saving techniques which can inure to the benefit of the parties. Where there are countervailing factors that weigh against using witness statements, such as where witness credibility might be a decisive factor or, more precisely, where exposure to a witness' credibility solely or primarily on cross-examination may not be sufficient, then arbitrators should afford an opportunity at the preliminary conference for open and frank discussion of the subject. In other words, arbitrators in every case should provide a forum to consider the pros and cons of using written witness statements.

Third, as noted above, arbitrators should explore with counsel measures to create efficiencies and cost-savings in arbitration, and they may even use their power of persuasion to urge counsel to agree upon appropriate cost-effective techniques. However, arbitrators must approach the use of written witness statements guardedly and should never *require* the use of witness statements where counsel elect---based on witness credibility, complexity of facts, or any other reason---to present a witness' direct testimony live. Arbitration still is a creature of party agreement, and whatever the practice may be in the context of international arbitration, there is no warrant for arbitrators *to compel* the

[50] *See generally*, Raymond G. Bender, *Critical First Steps in Complex Commercial Arbitration—Appointing Qualified Arbitrators and Staging the Preliminary Conference,* Dispute Resolution Journal (Feb.-Apr. 2009), at 28 *et seq.*

use of witness statements in U.S. domestic arbitration in the absence of party agreement.

Indeed, experienced observers have noted that party agreement in this context is the preferred approach:

> The tribunal's power to order the witness statement procedure is derived from the parties' agreement to arbitrate, the rules the parties select to govern the arbitration, and acceptance of the panel. Accordingly, the parties' views and suggestions regarding the manner and use of witness statements should be given due regard by the tribunal. Thus, seeking the parties' agreement to the use of written statements is recommended as opposed to imposing the procedure on the parties in an order.[51]

The CCA Best Practices also advise: "[w]ith respect to critical lay witnesses, the use of written testimony probably should be approached with caution and ordered or permitted only if all parties consent and the arbitrators determine that the probative value of the testimony will not be unduly impaired."[52]

Fourth, the tribunal should condition the use of written statements on the witness' appearance at hearing for cross-examination by the other parties and questioning by the arbitrators, unless all parties and arbitrators agree that the witness need not appear. To put all parties on notice, this condition should appear in the scheduling order issued after the preliminary conference outlining the various procedures to govern the conduct of the arbitration.[53]

Fifth, upon request, arbitrators should permit sponsoring counsel to question a witness briefly on direct (*e.g.*, for 15 to 30 minutes) to provide a summary or overview of the testimony before the witness is turned over for cross-examination by opposing counsel. This procedure will permit the witness to become comfortable testifying before being

---

[51] Wolf and Preteroti, *supra* note 3, at 6.

[52] CCA Best Practices, *supra* note 21, at 190. *See also* Wilkinson, *supra* note 43, at 4 ("[using written statements] can save significant amounts of time, but arbitrators should exercise some restraint in imposing such a requirement.").

[53] As noted earlier, the right of cross-examination has become engrained in U.S. jurisprudence as a fundamental due process right. For arbitrators in U.S. domestic arbitration to accept a written statement where a requested witness fails to appear at hearing for cross-examination---even assuming a valid reason is offered---would be somewhat unusual (at least in this arbitrator's experience). In any event, should that issue arise, arbitrators have the power to address unusual or unique circumstances and rule accordingly.

subjected to potentially hostile cross-examination. It also will afford the arbitrators an opportunity to observe witness credibility during direct testimony, even if only briefly.

Sixth, the scheduling order issued by the tribunal following the preliminary conference should include the terms under which written witness statements will be used. Specifically, in addition to the condition that sponsoring witnesses must appear at the hearing for cross examination (and arbitrator questions), the order should identify any format requirements (*e.g.*, that the facts be stated in narrative, rather than question and answer form); provide that each statement shall be signed by the witness or submitted under affidavit; and note that upon taking the stand each witness will be expected to adopt the statement under oath as true and correct. The scheduling order also should set a date for witness statements to be exchanged and furnished to the arbitrators. Witness statements normally are prepared once discovery is complete—to facilitate reference by the witnesses to documentary or other evidence—and, depending on the complexity of the case, usually are exchanged from one to several weeks prior to the hearing.

Finally, arbitrators should fully embrace written witness statements and prepare to take every advantage presented by their use. Specifically, arbitrators should always review witness statements in advance of the hearing; be attentive during the cross–examination of each witness; and pursue arbitrator questioning independently where challenging facts or issues require greater understanding or clarification.

By taking the foregoing measures, U.S. arbitrators will signal to parties and counsel that they regard the use of written witness statements as a core feature of U.S. domestic arbitration in the same way international arbitrators value them in international arbitration. This kind of encouragement hopefully will inspire parties and counsel in U.S. arbitration to evaluate routinely the pros and cons of written witness statements; to consider in earnest (and with an open mind) the use of witness statements in each case; and to let go of old practices (*e.g.*, insisting on live testimony unnecessarily) which, while familiar and comfortable, may not be compatible with achieving efficiency and cost savings in arbitration.

VII. Conclusions

Written testimony by fact witnesses in international arbitration affords meaningful advantages for the process and the parties. Because written statements redirect the focus of an arbitration hearing from direct testimony to cross-examination, they reduce hearing time significantly and thereby promote arbitration's core values of efficiency and cost-savings. Witness statements also assist arbitration participants in preparing for hearing—witnesses can present relevant facts clearly and cogently in narrative form without fear of rhetorical shortcomings; surprise at the hearing is avoided and opposing counsel is better able to prepare for cross-examination; and arbitrators are able to focus on the key issues in dispute and manage the hearing more effectively and efficiently.

Perceived drawbacks associated with written witness statements can be surmounted or mitigated in most cases. The fact that lawyers often draft witness statements should not be a major concern. This form of lawyer assistance is not unlike the process of preparing a witness for live testimony. Witnesses also sign their written statements and/or attest to the truth and accuracy of their testimony, and witnesses risk not being taken seriously if they approach the process carelessly or cavalierly. As for witness credibility, arbitrators generally are able to assess witness credibility in most cases during cross-examination and on re-direct, as well as during any abbreviated direct examination that may be permitted. A witness' first appearance at a hearing should not be via hostile questioning on cross-examination. Accordingly, counsel should request the tribunal to permit each witness to offer limited direct testimony (*e.g.*, a high-level summary of the key points) to "warm to the seat" before being turned over for cross-examination.

U.S. arbitrators should implement practical steps to encourage U.S. counsel to consider using written witness statements in all or most domestic arbitrations. Listing witness statements on the preliminary hearing agenda and highlighting their benefits (and possible drawbacks) could result in an enhanced appreciation by counsel for this evidentiary tool. Arbitrators also should adopt appropriate procedural protections whenever witness statements are used—requiring each witness to appear at hearing for cross-examination and arbitrator inquiries, unless the parties and arbitrators agree otherwise; permitting an abbreviated direct examination before the witness is turned over for cross-examination; and specifying any precise arrangements regarding format, signatures, exchange dates, and other key requirements.

Ultimately, the decision in U.S. arbitration to present the direct testimony of fact witnesses either in writing or live should remain with the parties and their counsel, and arbitrators should never *require* counsel to use one method or the other. While written witness statements can offer decided advantages, notably significant efficiencies and cost-savings, there will be circumstances where the live testimony of some witnesses would be preferable. It is hoped, however, that elevating the discourse concerning witness statements might lead to a greater appreciation of their use by arbitrators and counsel alike. Indeed, it is not fanciful to suggest that, as they continue to gain favor in the U.S., written witness statements might well become the norm in domestic arbitration as they are in international arbitration.

CHAPTER 33

DISCOVERY IN COMMERCIAL ARBITRATION: HOW ARBITRATORS THINK

Charles J. Moxley, Jr. *

I. Introduction

When a case has been filed in federal or state court, litigators generally have a good idea of what discovery will be allowed. Federal and state rules of civil procedure set forth the standards for discovery in litigation, and a large body of case law elaborates on these standards.

Do we have anything similar in arbitration? Can counsel and the parties know with reasonable certainty how much discovery will be allowed in their commercial arbitration? What kind of discovery is typically permitted? Are the answers to these questions entirely within the discretion of the arbitrator? Is there a governing standard?

Given the confidentiality of arbitration, there are generally no published arbitral decisions on discovery questions in arbitration. So in this article I set forth some tentative answers to these questions in the context of domestic commercial arbitration based on my personal experience as an arbitrator in over 125 commercial cases, the varied experience of arbitrators with whom I have served. I also discuss the relevant rules of the American Arbitration Association (AAA) and other

---

* Charles J. Moxley, Jr., the principal in MoxleyADR LLC, has been an arbitrator on panels of the American Arbitration Association (AAA) for over 35 years, presiding over more than 250 cases, many of them large and complex involving multiple parties, substantial issues and high stakes. He trains arbitrators for the Dispute Resolution (DR) Section of the New York State Bar Association (NYSBA), teaches arbitration law at Fordham Law School, and serves as Distinguished ADR Practitioner in Residence at the Benjamin N. Cardozo School of law. He was recently selected by the AAA to provide training in effective arbitration practices in AAA training programs. This article is adapted from a presentation he made at the American Arbitration Association in New York in June 2005 on the process of selecting an arbitrator. Mr. Moxley welcomes comments from readers about their experiences with arbitrator selection. He may be reached at cmoxley@moxleyadr.com

arbitration institutions, as well as the treatment of discovery in the Revised Uniform Arbitration Act (RUAA).

II. Rationale for Discovery in Arbitration

Arbitrators generally have three primary objectives in deciding discovery disputes in a commercial case: (1) a speedier disposition than in litigation; (2) a less expensive process than litigation; and (3) a fair opportunity for both sides to prepare and try the case. Satisfying each of these objectives depends in large measure on the amount of discovery allowed in the arbitration. To obtain a speedier and less costly disposition, discovery, which consumes the bulk of time and attorney fees in litigation, needs to be more limited than in litigation. Yet the parties must have the discovery they need for a fair hearing.

As a result, the discovery that is automatic and often virtually unlimited in litigation is subject to close scrutiny in arbitration. The arbitration goals cited above cause arbitrators to require the parties to *justify* the discovery they seek. There is a bedrock amount of discovery in arbitration, particularly the reasonable disclosure of the parties' claims and defenses and the exchange of relevant documents. But beyond that, parties are generally only allowed to take depositions and serve interrogatories if they can demonstrate a real need for them. Of course, the parties' counsel may agree to more extensive discovery, although that can compromise the two main benefits of arbitration.

III. Discovery in Commercial Litigation

The discovery phase in a multi-million dollar commercial litigation typically takes years, not months. First counsel for the parties prepare and serve very broadly worded document discovery requests that ask to see all documents "in connection with or relating to" one subject or another. They also invariably prepare lengthy interrogatories and sometimes "requests to admit." They have to review and number their client's documents for document production purposes. Often, each side files objections to the other side's document requests, which could include claims of attorney-client privilege or attorney work product. The parties could end up in protracted motion practice fighting about these documents. Meanwhile, each side serves deposition notices on the other. It is not unusual to receive a dozen or even dozens of such notices.

Attorneys for the parties commonly seek to depose everyone who may have relevant information, even if the testimony is likely to be cumulative or redundant. They don't want to leave any stone unturned.

Litigators hate surprises and they generally find it unacceptable to wait until trial to take the testimony of important witnesses who are not under their control. They typically seek to depose every witness who could possibly show up at trial, even those who are fully on the record in documents and hence whose testimony is readily subject to cross-examination.

Although depositions are scheduled for months down the road, they rarely take place as scheduled because the attorneys or the witnesses are busy that day. It is common to defer depositions multiple times. A year could go by and they still have not been taken. Finally one party may get fed up and seek an order compelling the completion of discovery. If not, the judge may see that this case is not moving forward and will take matters into his or her own hands. The process initially developed to foster fair trials by avoiding unfair surprise at trial has taken on a life of its own, one that eats up years of time and incurs huge expenses for each side, often without telling counsel much that they did not already know from the documents and their own witnesses.

When depositions are taken, the lawyer taking them may make the session as long as possible in order to be sure to exhaust the deponent's knowledge. Sometimes, depositions result in disputes that have to go before a judge. This can occur when the deponent's counsel directs the witness not to answer or unilaterally cuts short the deposition.

Meanwhile, each side "responds" to the other's interrogatories and requests to admit, usually by giving the narrowest possible answer or no answer.

IV. Discovery in Arbitration

This is all very different in commercial arbitration. Arbitrators usually want the hearing to be scheduled within three to eight months. It would be a rare arbitration, and a particularly large or complex one at that, in which the arbitrators would be happy with an expanded hearing schedule that exceeds eight months. Arbitrators on the panel of the American Arbitration Association (on which I serve) are trained to believe it is their job to deliver the expedited proceeding that arbitration promises and the parties bargained for.

Thus, arbitrators generally have a different perspective on discovery. They do not want the parties to engage in a fishing expedition of the kind that is typical of discovery in litigation. They want to allow just enough discovery to permit each side to prepare and try its case, but no more. Arbitrators have a strong belief that witnesses should testify only once, and that is at the hearing. So there is no need to incur the expense of earlier (and generally protracted) depositions.

If a party reasonably needs to examine a person under the control of the adversary and asks the arbitrator to order this witness to be produced, the arbitrator will usually obtain the adversary's agreement to produce the witness at the hearing. Similarly, when the exigencies of a case require the testimony of a non-party witness who reside within subpoena-range of the hearing, the arbitrator will subpoena the witness but generally only for purposes of the hearing (i.e., not for a deposition).

When non-party witnesses reside beyond subpoena range, they could still agree to testify, and when they do agree, arbitrators prefer to have them testify live at the hearing. When it is difficult getting them there in person, video-conference technology makes it possible to have them virtually present at the hearing. Testimony by telephone, which involves little expense, is also possible and frequently used where it makes sense in the context of the particular case.

This does not mean that depositions are never allowed in arbitration. That is not the case. If the parties make a convincing case that a reasonable number of depositions of limited duration seem necessary, arbitrators will generally permit them.

Despite their penchant for deposing every witness, litigators who arbitrate have learned that they have the skills to capably cross-examine the other side's witnesses without depositions. To conduct the cross, they use the information they have learned from their informal investigation of the facts of the case, documents, witness lists and expert reports exchanged before the hearing. The huge number of depositions typically taken in litigation is not as important as litigators have come to believe.

V. What Is Reasonable?

The amount of discovery reasonably needed to arbitrate a particular case depends on the facts and circumstances. It is reasonable to need documents specifically related to the dispute. It is also reasonable to need to know the particulars of the other side's claims, defenses, purported damages and the like. If requested, arbitrators will generally direct that such information be provided.

Arbitrators typically establish the idea at the preliminary hearing that they expect counsel to work out any discovery issues that arise. When the parties' attorneys cannot resolve these issues by themselves, arbitrators are prepared to direct them if necessary.

VI. The Size of the Case

Parties are increasingly submitting huge commercial cases to arbitration. Cases in the tens and hundreds of millions of dollars and more are not uncommon. Some general counsel prefer to arbitrate cases of all sizes for the opportunity it gives them to pick a highly experienced arbitrator (or panel of arbitrators) with knowledge of the subject matter who can be selected with eyes open, rather than take a chance on the spin of the wheel in the court clerk's office.

Some general counsels at large corporations have stressed the importance of preserving the speed and economy in arbitration. Yet some cases have so much at stake that both parties may agree that they want the "no stone unturned" approach to discovery in arbitration. This is their right since arbitration is a process that belongs to the parties.

In large cases involving multiple issues, arbitrators will generally recognize the need for more substantial document exchanges, and possibly more than a couple of depositions and a limited number of targeted interrogatories. But they nonetheless try to keep the cases moving more expeditiously than would typically happen in court.

VII. The Easy Case

Discovery is easiest when the parties' arbitration clause specifies the scope of discovery. Occasionally the parties provide in their arbitration clause that the federal or state rules of procedure shall apply to discovery in arbitration, resulting essentially in pseudo-litigation before a private judge. In my experience, this is relatively rare (I would say anecdotally that it occurs in fewer than 5% of cases).

Arbitrators will apply the procedures specified in the parties' arbitration agreement. However, they are not prevented from trying to "jawbone" the parties' counsel into agreeing that what they actually need is more limited discovery, not more. ("Jawboning" is the term I use for the practice many arbitrators follow of probing for consensus on pre-hearing issues before ruling on them.) Arbitrators who educate themselves about the case can engage in a meaningful dialogue with the attorneys about what discovery is reasonably necessary (as distinguished from what they have stated is needed) and then build on that foundation to create consensus on a reasonable discovery plan.

To do this effectively, arbitrators try to develop an early understanding of the case. This is one of the reasons arbitrators invite counsel to discuss the case at the preliminary conference and at interim conferences throughout the discovery period. It is in counsels' interest to project their case as fully as possible whenever the opportunity arises.

VIII. The Most Typical Case

Although the parties could include the scope of discovery in their arbitration agreement, they rarely do. Usually the arbitration clause is silent as to the scope of discovery. However, if the agreement calls for arbitration by a particular arbitration institution or provides for arbitration under specific institutional rules, the institution's rules will be incorporated by reference, including the discovery provisions. (For example, an arbitration clause may provide for AAA arbitration or arbitration under the AAA Commercial Arbitration Rules.)

Discovery is normally one of the issues on the table at the first preliminary conference, which, in most instances, is conducted via a conference call. In a commercial case, counsel for the parties usually decide on the scope of discovery before the call is scheduled and advise the arbitrator of their agreement during the course of the conference call. The attorneys commonly agree to exchange relevant documents and to depose two or three of the adversary's witnesses.

Until a dispute arises, arbitrators generally will not get involved in document production issues. The attorneys know their case and if they can agree on document discovery, great.[1]

As to depositions, arbitrators will consider whether their use is really needed. Why depose a witness who lives within subpoena-range of the

[1] The subject of electronic discovery is beyond the scope of this article. Parties in arbitrations are often willing to limit electronic discovery in the interests of having an expeditious and economical proceeding, although there will increasingly be cases where it will be important. See, e.g., Irene C. Warshauer, "Electronic Discovery in Arbitration: Privilege Issues and Spoliation of Evidence," 61(4) *Disp. Res. J.* (Nov. 2006/Jan. 2007).

hearing or a witness under the control of the adversary? Counsel may need to be reminded that arbitration is different from litigation and has economy and efficiency as two of its goals. Often counsel will respond to this by agreeing that depositions are not necessary. Should this lead to concern that they are merely being deferential to the person who will resolve the dispute? Theoretically that is possible. But as a practical matter it should not be a concern if the attorneys understand that the arbitration process is supposed to be different from litigation, the arbitration involves a dispute between parties who are familiar with the matters in contention, and the relevant documents and witnesses will be available at the hearing.

IX. When Both Sides Want Depositions

When cajoling by the arbitrator does not work and both sides want to depose multiple witnesses, the arbitrator must step back and accept the idea that there will be more, rather than fewer, depositions in the case. But the arbitrator can continue to try to limit their number and duration.

In the unusual case where this does not work, arbitrators generally will respect counsels' agreement on the subject and allow the depositions to be taken, after warning them of the effect on the time and cost of the arbitration.

X. When One Side Does Not Want Depositions

What if one side wants depositions and other discovery and the other side objects? In that situation, there is a discovery dispute on which the arbitrator must rule. The arbitrator will generally decide based on what he or she thinks is fair, considering the need for an expeditious and economical process.

Some arbitrators will decide discovery disputes based on the parties' briefs. Others will hold a conference with the attorneys for both sides after the briefs are submitted, at which point the arbitrator will have a serious talk with counsel as they go through each disputed item one by one. I think this approach yields more enlightened rulings. Often, it is only necessary for the arbitrator to go through a few disputed items or types of items to establish guidelines, whereupon the attorneys work out the rest. Notwithstanding positions taken in party briefs, the attorneys tend to move towards consensus when the arbitrator suggests restraint on both sides in the service of figuring out what discovery would provide the requesting party with information it reasonably needs while protecting the objecting party's interests. When a sensible accommodation of each side's rights and interests is reached, the arbitrator will incorporate it in a ruling.

Where no consensus is reached, the arbitrator will have to go it alone, deciding the dispute based on the goals of arbitration and the interests and needs of both sides. The ruling will often bear a striking resemblance to the approaches the arbitrator suggested in the conference with the parties on the discovery dispute.

XI. AAA Rules

Decision making by arbitrators on discovery questions is not typically based on rules. This is because most arbitration rules give wide discretion to the arbitrator to determine the scope of discovery. Attorneys rarely argue for or against discovery based on an institution's arbitration rules. Yet it is interesting to see that the "expeditious/economical/fair" mantra that arbitrators generally use to decide discovery disputes reflects principles in the arbitration rules of leading arbitration organizations.

The AAA Commercial Arbitration Rules focus on information exchanges.[2] Rule 21(a) provides that the arbitrator, "consistent with the expedited nature of arbitration," may direct "the production of documents *and other information*." (Emphasis added) Rule 21(c) provides that the arbitrator "is authorized to resolve any disputes concerning the exchange of information." Thus, this rule places discovery issues in the discretion of the arbitrator, subject to the need for an expeditious proceeding.

The AAA Procedures for Large, Complex Commercial Disputes (which are included in the AAA Commercial Arbitration Rules) recognize the goals of having "a just, speedy and cost-effective resolution." Rule L-4(a) provides that "arbitrator(s) shall take such steps as they may deem necessary or desirable to avoid delay and to achieve a just, speedy and cost-effective resolution...." These rules also recognize the discretion of arbitrators in discovery matters. Rule L-4(c)–provides: "The parties may conduct such discovery as may be agreed to by all the parties provided, however, that the arbitrator(s) may place such limitations on the conduct of such discovery as the arbitrator(s) shall deem appropriate." The rule contemplates that if the parties cannot agree on discovery, "the arbitrator(s),

---

[2] The AAA rules are available at www.adr.org.

consistent with the expedited nature of arbitration, may establish the extent of the discovery."[3] Interestingly, Rule L-4(c) gives the arbitrator the discretion, in the interests of an expedited process, to override even the parties' agreement as to discovery.

Rule L-4(d) also explicitly addresses the issue of depositions and interrogatories. They may be permitted "in the discretion of the arbitration(s) and upon good cause shown …consistent with the expedited nature of arbitration" if the person to whom they are addressed has information "determined by the arbitrator to be necessary to determination of the matter."

Finally, Rule L-4(g) authorizes the arbitrator to resolve any discovery disputes.

The AAA's Employment Arbitration Rules use different language but are the same in principle. Rule 9 authorizes the arbitrator to order "discovery, by way of deposition, interrogatory, document production or otherwise" if the arbitrator "considers it necessary to a full and fair exploration of the issues in dispute, consistent with the expedited nature of arbitration."[4]

XII. Other Providers and the RUAA

Rule 17 of the JAMS Arbitration Rules is comparable to the AAA Rules, except that it contemplates one deposition per side, while leaving additional depositions to the discretion of the arbitrator based on "the reasonable need" for the information, the availability of other discovery options, and the burdensomeness of the request."[5]

Rule 11 of the Rules for Non-Administered Arbitration promulgated by the International Institute for Conflict Prevention and Resolution's provides that arbitrators may permit such discovery as they deem

---

[3] The extent of an arbitrator's power to order sanctions against parties for discovery abuse is addressed in Philip D. O'Neill, "The Power of Arbitrators to Award Monetary Sanctions for Discovery Abuse," 60(3) *Disp. Resol. J.* (Nov. 2005/Jan. 2006); Philip D. O'Neill, "Update: Mass. Allows Arbitrators to Award $$ Sanctions to Remedy Discovery Abuse," 60(2) *Disp. Resol. J.* (May-July 2006).

Section 17(d) of the RUAA provides, that the arbitrator may "take action against a noncomplying party to the extent a court could if the controversy were the subject of a civil action in this state." The RUAA is available at www.nccusl.org.

[4] The AAA Employment Arbitration Rules are available at www.adr.org.

[5] JAMS Comprehensive Arbitration Rules and Procedures are available at www. jamsadr.com.

appropriate, "taking into account the needs of the parties and the desirability of making discovery expeditious and cost-effective."[6]

The RUAA's[7] discovery provisions are similar to the provider rules above. The arbitrator's authority as to discovery is in Section 17(c). It provides: "An arbitrator may permit such discovery as the arbitrator decides is appropriate in the circumstances, taking into account the needs of the parties to the arbitration proceeding and other affected persons and the desirability of making the proceeding fair, expeditious, and cost effective." This provision covers discovery depositions.

Comment 3 to Section 17 states in the first paragraph that the approach to discovery in subsection (c) "follows the majority approach" under the case law involving the Federal Arbitration Act (FAA) and the 1955 Uniform Arbitration Act, which is that "unless the contract specifies to the contrary, discretion rests with the arbitrators whether to allow discovery." The second paragraph notes that, although Section 17(c) allows an arbitrator to permit discovery so that the parties can obtain necessary information, "the intent of the language is to limit that discovery by considerations of fairness, efficiency, and cost."

Depositions for purposes of the hearing are addressed in Section 17(b). This section states: "In order to make the proceedings fair, expeditious, and cost effective, upon request of a party to or a witness in an arbitration proceeding, an arbitrator may permit a deposition of any witness to be taken for use as evidence at the hearing, including a witness who cannot be subpoenaed for or is unable to attend a hearing." This provision goes on to say that "the arbitrator shall determine the conditions under which the deposition is taken."

XIII. Non-Party Witnesses

The above focuses on party discovery. Complex and largely unsettled issues arise when information is needed from non-party witnesses who are beyond subpoena-range of the site of the arbitration.[8] These issues include the extent to which, under the FAA[9] and other laws, a non-party witness may be compelled to produce documents or give

---

[6] CPR's rules are available at www.cpradr.org.

[7] *See* n. 5.

[8] *See, e.g.*, Leslie Trager, "The Use of Subpoenas in Arbitration," 62(4) *Disp. Resol. J.* (Nov. 2007/ Jan. 2008).

[9] 9 U.S.C. § 7.

testimony at a deposition or in a formal "hearing session" where he or she is located, and the related question of whether the arbitrators (or one member of a panel) may preside over the taking of this witness's testimony at that locale. These issues are beyond the scope of this article. However, it is worth noting again that non-party witnesses who are outside the jurisdiction of an arbitrator's subpoena are frequently willing to testify by teleconference or telephone conference at a time convenient to them in response to an informally transmitted subpoena, even though they could challenge the subpoena in court, or even ignore it and await enforcement proceedings. Some witnesses agree because of the potential time and expense of contesting the subpoena. Others do so out of a spirit of cooperation or respect for the arbitration process.

XIV. Conclusion

The principles for resolving discovery-related issues in arbitration are clear, sensible and workable. The vast majority of party discovery disputes in commercial cases are worked out among counsel. When counsel cannot agree, arbitrators will rule on the discovery issues by balancing the arbitration objectives of providing an expeditious and economical yet fair proceeding. Parties may provide for more expanded discovery in their arbitration agreements or they may subsequently agree to such discovery before the hearing.

CHAPTER 34

THE DEVELOPMENT OF REMEDIAL POWER: ARBITRATORS' ABILITY TO AWARD MONETARY SANCTIONS

Philip D. O'Neill, Jr.[*]

I. Introduction

Historically, American courts concluded that arbitrators do not inherently possess the full panoply of judicial powers to sanction abusive or otherwise noncomplying conduct during an arbitration,[1] with

---

[*] Philip D. O'Neill, Jr. is a domestic and international commercial arbitrator. Mr. O'Neill was the Nomura Lecturer in Law on International Arbitration at Harvard Law School in 2005. He has been an adjunct professor of international arbitration at Boston College Law School since 1989, and at Boston University Law School since 2011. Mr. O'Neill is a Fellow in the College of Commercial Arbitrators, and the Chartered Institute of Arbitrators. He is a chartered arbitrator as well.

[1] *See, e.g., InterChem Asia 2000 PTE. Ltd. v. Oceana Petroche, AG*, 373 F. Supp. 2d 340 (S.D.N.Y. 2005) ("[F]inding that the Arbitrator had inherent authority to sanction [an attorney] would directly contradict the principle that an arbitrator's authority is circumscribed by the agreement of the parties."); Seagate Technology, LLC v. Western Digital Corp. et als, 854 NW 2d 750, 761 (Minn. 2014)("…[A]rbitrators have no correlating inherent authority [to sanction] and receive their power from either the arbitration agreement or the Legislature.")(citation omitted). *Cf. Certain Underwriters at Lloyd's London v. Argonaut Ins.*, 264 F. Supp. 2d 926, 943 (N.D. Cal. 2003) (denying that arbitrator has inherent authority to impose a sanction analogous to civil contempt). *But cf. ReliaStar Life Insurance Company of New York v. EMC National Life Company*, 564 F3rd 81 (2nd Cir. 2009) (A broad arbitration clause "confers inherent authority on arbitrators to sanction a party that participates in the arbitration in bad faith such that a sanction may include an award of attorney's or arbitrator's fees"). *Compare, e.g., Grynberg v. BP Exploration Operating Co., Ltd.* 2010 WL 5137912 (NY Sup. Ct. Dec. 8, 2010)[Distinguishing a Federal Court's inherent right to sanction and also in a proceeding conducted under the Federal Arbitration Act "FAA"), with the statutory basis for courts in New York state, and the inability of arbitrators to award them in the absence of contractual authority] *aff'd* 92 A.D.3d 547 (First Dept. 2012)(as to vacatur of sanctions awarded by arbitrator as against public policy).

only rare exceptions.[2] Unless authorized by the parties in their agreement, in the applicable institutional arbitration rules incorporated by that agreement, or in the governing arbitration law, an arbitrator's remedial powers are limited. Typically, those limits are not a serious impediment to serving justice. But they can be in hard cases in which a key element of proof of a cause of action or the amount of damages resides, in whole or large part, in the control of a recalcitrant adversary who refuses to produce it. The harm from a party's misconduct can be substantial. For example, trade secret misappropriation claims often take their direction from the documentary trail. If the trail is false or materially incomplete due to non-production of critical documents, the work undertaken by the claimant's attorney and expert will be misdirected. The cost of this deflection can be staggering. With the stakes this high, it is reasonable to expect an arbitrator to be able to impose remedial sanctions that have meaningful *in terrorem* and/or economic effect.[3] However, that was not necessarily the case in most jurisdictions in the past, and there is only now an emerging trend finding such power in the interpretation of some arbitral institutional rules, and in applicable law, at least in those states that have adopted the Revised Uniform Arbitration Act of 2000. ("RUAA")(See discussion *infra*, on statutory empowerment).

Historically ADR providers typically trained their arbitrators to draw an "adverse inference"[4] from a party's refusal to produce documents in discovery. Suppose a party fails to produce documents leaving discrete

---

[2] *See, e.g., First Pres. Capital, Inc. v. Smith Barney, Harris Upham & Co., Inc.*, 939 F.Supp. 1559, 1565 (S.D. Fla. 1996)(Concluding arbitrators have authority to enforce their directives, including imposing punitive sanctions, such as dismissal of a claim). *See also Forsythe Int'l. S.A. v. Gibbs oil Co., 915 F. 2d 1017, 1023n.8 (5th Cir. 1990).*

[3] One court cautioned that if the amount of sanctions is more like a penalty than remedy, the right of appeal could be compromised. Thus, if parties provide monetary sanctioning power, its coercive exercise would need to be tested against federal appellate policy. *Lloyd's, supra* n, 1, 264 F. Supp. 2d at 944. The issue of whether an arbitrator has "authority to award attorney's fees in excess of the amount necessary to compensate for the losses and expenses" was expressly reserved by the Second Circuit Court of Appeals in circumstances where the fee award was compensatory and not challenged as punitive. *See ReliaStar, supra,* n.1, 564 F.3d at 89, n.3. In contrast, states take differing approaches. *Compare, e.g., Grynberg, supra* note 1, where an award of punitive damages was vacated for exceeding authority, *with Seagate, supra* note 1, which rejected any distinction between punitive and compensatory sanctions in concluding such an award was within the arbitrator's power to provide relief and/or a remedy under the applicable arbitral rules.

[4] *See, e.g.,* American Arbitration Association (AAA) Manual for International Arbitrators 69 (1999).

pieces in a chain of proof missing. In this instance, an arbitrator no doubt would be willing to fill in minor gaps with adverse inferences against the non-producing party. However, this remedy may not be acceptable to the arbitrator if the evidence that is withheld is the only evidence available to prove one or more elements of the claimant's causes of action or the amount of damages.[5] In a case like this, the arbitrator may be unwilling to make the necessary inferences. Yet, not all panels are deterred by the obstacle to quantifying damages created by the failure to produce documents. At least one panel awarded monetary sanctions in this situation, and was eventually upheld by the reviewing court.

In some cases, an arbitrator may preclude the introduction of evidence that has been abusively withheld during discovery.[6] This remedy has more potential *in terrorem* effect on the recalcitrant party than an "adverse inference;" indeed, it could be sufficient to persuade a party to fully comply with a direction to produce documents in a timely fashion. However, precluding the evidence would not necessarily help a party meet its burden of proving its claims, affirmative defenses, counterclaims or damages. Moreover, it would not eliminate the significant legal fees incurred in preparing the case without benefit of wrongly-withheld documents; that financial impact is not always fully satisfied either by inference or preclusion.

The issue of what remedial sanctioning power an arbitrator has or needs when confronted by a party who is stonewalling the document discovery process remains comparatively uncharted by the judiciary or legal scholars. Despite the relative paucity of precedent, sufficient principled guidance emerged from which to identify the means of creating or limiting sanctioning power through the exercise of party autonomy, even where it is not provided for in the choice of applicable rules or procedural law. This chapter extracts guidelines from existing precedent, seeking to help drafters of arbitration provisions understand how to fashion or limit sanctioning power by design, rather than by inadvertence. It also tells a cautionary tale for arbitrators who award

---

[5] *See,e.g., Superadio Ltd. Partnership v. Winstar Radio Productions, LLC,* 446 Mass 330 (2006) *reversing* 818 N.E. 589 (Mass App. Ct. 2004). (See discussion, *infra*); *Sealgate, supra* note 1.

[6] *Id.* at 594 ("It is clear that arbitrators have the power to enforce discovery orders by imposing some sanctions, such as not allowing the withheld documents in evidence."). *See, e.g., Seagate, supra* note 1, where an award of $400 million dollars was upheld that was grounded on evidence or defense preclusion as a sanction for fabricating evidence in the attempted defense of a particular trade secret misappropriation claim.

monetary sanctions and advocates who seek that remedy for their clients; the latter must be careful what they wish for; the former must be careful how they implement such sanctions. If they are not, the arbitral award may be vulnerable to challenge in a subsequent vacatur proceeding in many jurisdictions. This chapter suggests how best to meet these challenges.

Unfortunately, predictability in this area is compromised by the current disarray in judicial decisions. The confusion is largely driven by the application of different standards of review. Increasingly, though, by statute or institutional rule, the landscape in many jurisdictions is moving toward a structured approach that satisfies precedential demands that remedial sanctioning power be grounded in the agreement of the parties or by the legislature. Party autonomy is being served by those arbitral institutions that now expressly amend rules, at least in commercial cases, to provide generally or sanctioning power for rules violations.[7]. As one state court recently observed:

> "The arbitrator's ability to issue punitive sanctions is controlled by the arbitration agreement….Therefore, parties are able to include or exclude the use of punitive sanctions when constructing an arbitration agreement either through express provision or through incorporation of a particular set of arbitral rules."[8]

Decisions are thus left to the parties on whether to opt out of authorizing such remedial power, but the general trend is not to do so., for when parties entrust arbitrators to remedy problems, they include those relating to the process itself. As a cautionary note, however, the lack of uniformity still can impact cases for example where an institution has not amended its rules or only some of them; in ad hoc proceedings where no rules are chosen in the agreement to arbitrate; and in non RUAA states where the parties opt out of the FAA, such as in California through a general governing law clause.[9] This chapter helps chart both the historical landscape and current trends in the development of remedial sanctioning power, such as monetary awards, to aid drafters who would embrace or prefer to avoid them.

---

[7] *See*, e.g., AAA Commercial Rule 58(a); and CPR R16 (administered and unadministered domestic and international rules).

[8] Seagate, supra note 1, 854 NW 2d at 761.

[9] *Volt Info. Scis. V. Bd. of Trs.* 489 US.S. 468 (1989).

II. Informality of Arbitration

The informality and flexibility of arbitration has long been regarded as an attribute rather than a limitation of the process. Still, as Judge Learned Hand observed decades ago:

> [a]rbitration may or may not be a desirable substitute for trial and courts; as to that the parties must decide in each instance. But when they have adopted it, they must be content with its informalities; they may not hedge it about with those procedural limitations, which is precisely its purpose to avoid. They must content themselves with looser approximations to the enforcement of their rights, than those than the law accords them, when they resort to its machinery.[10]

The scope and nature of the arbitral process has matured over the years since Judge Hand's pronouncement. Today, private parties entrust highly complex disputes to the arbitration process. As the complexity of commercial disputes has grown, so too has the use of discovery to promote fair adjudication—sometimes at the expense of the traditional arbitral goals of economy and speed. But there was not concomitant growth in the arbitrator's ability to respond to abusive conduct during discovery until recently, albeit unevenly.

III. Document Discovery

A. Among Parties

The context in which sanctioning power arises is a function of the hearing preparatory process of information exchange. Document discovery is now a common preparatory step in domestic and international

---

[10] *American Almond Prods. Co. v. Consolidated Pecans Sales Co.*, 144 F.2d 448, 450 (2d Cir. 1944). *See Bowles Fin. Grp., Inc. v. Stifle, Nicholaus & Co.*, 22 f.3d 1010, 1011 (10th Cir. 1994)("Those who choose to resolve a dispute by arbitration can expect no more than they have agreed. One choosing arbitration should not expect the full panoply of procedural and substantive protection offered by a court of law."). *See also, Mitsubishi Motors Corp. v. Soler Chrysler Plymouth, Inc.*, 473 U.S. 614, 628 (1985)(By agreeing to arbitrate parties "trade[] the procedures and opportunities for review of the courtroom for the simplicity, informality, and expedition for arbitration.").

commercial arbitration.[11] Indeed, the pre-hearing conference usually focuses on the schedule for the parties' exchange of documents so that the parties can prepare for the hearing on the merits. Document production is not only a matter of custom and practice by American legal counsel, but it can also be a matter of entitlement[12]—at least in the absence of a provision in the arbitration clause expressly excluding or limiting discovery.[13]

The arbitrator's power to require document production by the parties during discovery is relatively clear. The source of that power can reside in: (i) the parties' agreement; (ii) the institutional arbitration rules governing the procedures, which either expressly authorize such discovery or place the scope of discovery in the discretion of the arbitrator; or (iii) applicable arbitration statutes, such as the Federal Arbitration Act (FAA).

The FAA has been construed to confer on arbitrators the power to compel the parties to exchange documents prior to the hearing. The Eighth Circuit approved this advance exchange procedure, finding that the arbitrator's power to order document production *by a party* prior to the hearing is "implicit" in the power to subpoena relevant documents for production at a hearing. It reasoned that "[a]lthough the efficient resolution of disputes through arbitration necessarily entails limited discovery process . . . this interest and efficiency is furthered by permitting a party to review and digest relevant documentary evidence prior to the arbitration hearing."[14]

In recent years arbitral institutions, like the AAA, have moved to narrow expansive discovery practice in which parties, usually as a result of counsel's preferences, were basically replicating the litigation discovery process. In response, systemic constraint on party autonomy evolved, first through institutional guidance to international arbitrators to adopt a

---

[11] *Compare, e.g.,* Rule L-4(c) of the AAA Large, Complex Cases Procedures (permitting arbitrators in absence of party agreement to establish extent of document exchange), *with* Article 19(3) of the AAA International Arbitration Rules. *See also* Rule 21(a) and (c) of the AAA Commercial Arbitration Rules.

[12] In the past Mass. Gen. Law ch. 251, § 7provided for document discovery in arbitration to be coextensive with that in Massachusetts Rules of Civil Procedure.

[13] Even if the agreement limited or prohibited document discovery, a tribunal that is convinced such discovery would expedite the hearing and dramatically reduce costs could instruct a resisting party that, unless it waived the limitation in the agreement, the tribunal will convene an evidentiary hearing so that the party seeking discovery could review the documents. While seldom acknowledged, this technique has been used successfully from time to time.

[14] *In re Security Life Ins. Co.*, 228 F. 3d 865, 870-71 (8th Cir. 2000).

different standard – that is, "material and relevant" instead of the court practice of "information reasonably calculated to lead to the discovery of admissible evidence." This practice subsequently was embraced as the default rule in domestic commercial cases.[15] It remains to be seen if such a narrowing, which remains subject to variance by party agreement, will serve to eliminate or reduce instances of production noncompliance that will invite sanctions requests. After all, a judgment call is now introduced into information exchange that did not exist before,. At the same time, those instances where abuse occurred often related to non-production of damages related records which would seem to readily fall within the ambit of the new standard.

B. Discovery from Third Parties

In contrast, the arbitrator's statutory authority to order pre-hearing document production in the hands of third parties was less than clear.[16] The Third Circuit concluded that Section 7 of the FAA did not extend to pre-hearing discovery from entities not parties to the arbitration proceeding. It narrowly construed Section 7, ruling that arbitrators could subpoena documents from third parties only for production at the hearing itself.[17] The Second Circuit agreed.[18] The Fourth Circuit, also noted that "[n]owhere does the FAA grant an arbitrator the authority to order non-parties to . . . provide the litigating party with documents during pre-hearing discovery." But then the Fourth Circuit partially opened the door to third-party discovery upon what it termed a showing of "special need or hardship."[19] The current trend seems to reject the "special needs" approach.[20] Thus, the forum may well impact the ability to obtain

---

[15] *See, e.g.,* AAA Rule 22(B)(iii) effective October, 2013).

[16] *Compare, e.g., In re Security Life and Meadows Indemnity Co. Ltd. v. Nutmeg Ins. Co.*, 157 F.R.D. 42, 45 (M.D. Tenn. 1994), *with Hay Group, Inc. v. E.B.S. Acquisition Corp.*, 360 F. 3d 404, 407 (3d Cir. 2004), *and Comcast Corp. v. National Sci. Found.*, 190 F. 3d 269, 275 (4th Cir. 1999). *See also Am. Fed'n of Television & Radio Artists v. WJBV-TV*, 164 F.3d 1004, 1009 (6th Cir. 1999); *Amgen, Inc. v. Kidney Ctr. of Del. Cty.*, 879 F. Supp. 878 (N.D. Ill. 1995); *Stanton v. Paine Webber Jackson & Curtis*, 685 F. Supp. 1241 (S.D. Fla. 1988). *Cf. Integrity Ins. Co. v. Am. Centennial Ins. Co.*, 885 F. Supp. 69 (S.D.N.Y. 1995).

[17] *See Hay Group, supra* n. 11.

[18] *Life Receivables Trust v. Syndicate 102 at Lloyd's of London*, 549 F.3d 210, 216-17 (2nd Cir. 2008).

[19] *Comcast, supra* n. 11. *See, e.g., In re Deiulemar Compagnia Di Navigazione S.p.A*, 198 F.3d 473 (4th Cir. 1999).

[20] *See, e.g., Life Receivables, supra* note 18, at 216-17 (collecting cases).

documents in the hands of third parties when sought as discovery, rather than as actual evidence for use in the arbitral hearing.

IV. The Scope of Arbitral Remedial Power

In U.S. litigation, it is common for parties to fight over discovery. The parties may seek relief from the court to compel compliance with discovery requests and/or sanctions for noncompliance. The sanctioning powers of a court are well known and need no explication here. It suffices to observe that the scope of the arbitrator's remedial powers when confronted with a party who fails to exchange documents is usually more limited than the power wielded by a judge or magistrate in most jurisdictions; this is particularly so with respect to monetary sanctions ordered against counsel[21] or a nonparty.[22]

The scope of the arbitrator's authority to award monetary sanctions for discovery abuse has not been explored by the courts with any frequency. When they have done so they have often ended up "divided not only on the proper result, but also on the method of analysis.[23] The division over punitive sanctions ranges from such remedial power being against public policy, to requiring sometimes specific authorizing language, while at other times not doing so. Still, as one federal district court observed: "[t]here is no categorical ban to an arbitrator's imposition of sanctions for noncompliance with his or her orders."[24] The rub, however, is what powers are affirmatively vested in the arbitrator through the exercise of party autonomy. Some clarity is now at least provided by statute in RUAA states, for Section 17(d) expressly provides that:

> "... the arbitrator may order a party to the arbitration proceeding to comply with the arbitrator's discovery-related orders ... and

---

[21] *Compare, e.g., InterChem, supra* n. 1, *with Polin v. Kellwood Co.*, 103 F. Supp. 2d 238, *on rehearing*, 138 F. Supp. 2d 126 (S.D.N.Y. 2000) (denying motion for reconsideration), *aff'd*, *Polin v. Wise-hart*, 34 Fed. Appx. 406 (2d Cir. 2002). In distinguishing the *Polin* case, the district court in *InterChem* relied on the difference in language between the AAA employment rules and the AAA commercial rules. Furthermore, since an attorney is not a party to the agreement to arbitrate, the arbitrator does not have a jurisdictional base from which to impose sanctions. *See, e.g., Millmaker v. Bruso and Sovereign Oil & Gas Co. II, LLC*, 2008 U.S. Dist. Lexis 79480 (S.D. Texas).

[22] *Compare*, *Berglund v. Arthosopic & Laser Surgery Center of San Diego, LP.*, 139 Cal. App. 4th 904, 914 (CA. Ct. Appls. 2006) (Exception to rule pursuant to California statute).

[23] Segate, supra note 1 at 760 (collecting example cases at n.7).

[24] *Lloyd's*, *supra* n. 1, at 933.

take action against a noncomplying party to the extent a court could if the controversy were the subject of a civil action in this State."

At the same time, the institutions addressing the subject have taken varied approaches in terms of which rules to address it in, which leaves it more open to courts to conclude there is a lack of such power when the set of rules does not address it. Similarly, where institutions like the AAA and CPR have amended their rules to expressly, albeit generally, provide for sanctioning power, there is a more express basis for the exercise of such power to include even monetary sanctions, where appropriate in cases of egregious behavior. However, where a case is proceeding ad hoc with no rules provided for in the agreement to arbitrate, or rules incorporated which do not have express general remedial power provided for, then the arbitrator is left with precedent to rely upon with reasoning that is now suspect in implying such power under the broad general remedial power that does not address noncomplying behavior, as with the evolving current rules of some institutions.

A. Role of Party Autonomy

In arbitration, the parties' agreement is the logical starting point to determine whether an arbitrator has remedial power that includes monetary sanctions. The agreement includes: (i) its express language; (ii) provisions incorporated by reference (e.g., institutional arbitral rules) or implication; and typically (iii) the procedural and substantive laws designated to govern the arbitration proceedings. Arbitration clauses today rarely, if ever, contain a provision that specifically authorizes arbitrators to sanction the parties for discovery abuse. More commonly, the parties' wishes concerning the arbitrator's powers are simply expressed by electing to arbitrate disputes under well-established institutional rules; only sometimes do the arbitrator's powers reside in other provisions of the contract, such as those deriving from authorizing legal fees to be shifted to the prevailing party. It is the rare court that finds the inherent power to order monetary sanctions for bad faith conduct in an arbitration to be grounded solely upon the general breath of an arbitration clause.[25]

---

[25] *See, e.g., ReliaStar, supra* n. 1. See also First Pres. Capital, supra note, at 939 F. Supp. At 1565; and David v. Abergel, 46 Cal. App. 4th, 1281, 54 Cal. Rptr. 2d 443, 445

B. Role of Institutional Rules

As noted above, when parties want institutional arbitration rules to apply to arbitration, they incorporate them by reference into their contract.[26] Parties expect these rules to be clear, or at least to be clarified by the courts. This allows drafters of arbitration agreements to make informed choices. However, the initial problem was that of inconsistent court decisions regarding the arbitrator's sanctioning power. Since the courts did not clarify this area with a consistent judicial gloss, adequate guidance to users became uneven and predictability problematic.[27] Although most institutional rules contain general provisions concerning the powers of the arbitrators, until relatively recently none said anything specifically about the power to sanction abusive conduct, when the AAA and CPR added general sanction provisions.[28] In other domestic cases and most international commercial disputes not governed by AAA or CPR rules, the institutional rules say nothing specifically about sanctioning power for nonconformance with the rules or arbitrator rulings. This is unfortunate since courts look to institutional rules selected by the parties where there is no express language on point in the contract. Thus, whether such power exists now depends on both the particular rules in question and how the courts in different jurisdictions interpret them.

For example, one court upheld an award of monetary sanctions in securities arbitration. In making the award, the panel relied on Section VIII of the National Association of Security Dealers "Notice to Members," which the reviewing court noted authorized "arbitrators to award attorneys' fees as a sanction for a failure of a party to properly

---

(1996)(Agreement granting "any remedy or relief to which a party is entitled under California law" grants powers of a court, including power to impose punitive sanctions.").

[26] The chosen rules apply unless otherwise agreed by the parties. Thus, the parties can vary the rules by agreeing on specific points. The nature of that agreement, such as the power to shift legal fees is subject to construction by the arbitrator. *See, e.g., Reliastar, supra* n.1. (Contractual provision requiring parties to bear their own fees and expeses does not preclude shifting). *See also Millmaker, supra* n.14.

[27] The confusion in judicial precedents is similar to that which private parties endured for years while courts grappled with arbitral power to award punitive damages. Ultimately the Supreme Court clarified that arbitrators have the power to award punitive damages, unless the parties exclude them. *Mastrobuono v. Shearson Lehman Hutton,* 514 U.S. 52 (1995). After this issue became settled, the AAA amended Article 28(5) of its international rules, but not the commercial rules. The difference in approach is probably due to concerns about enforcing punitive damage awards abroad.

[28] *See*, e.g. AAA Commercial Rule 58 and CPR International Rule 16.

make discovery unless they thought there was a substantial justification for the failure."[29] This rule is atypical though. Institutional arbitration rules typically do not address expressly monetary sanctioning power. Rather, they address an arbitrator's general procedural and remedial powers, or at most generally address the power to sanction noncomplying conduct without addressing the scope of such power. There are no illustrative powers referenced, such as monetary awards. The current AAA International Rules, while not specifically recognizing sanctioning power as do the Commercial Rules, do provide for noncompliance to be factored into cost shifting, which includes the possibility of attorney fees being awarded. At the same time, the rule creates the potential for confusion or inconsistency in assessing the scope of remedial power, for it specifically includes the power to draw an adverse inference, but not evidence preclusion.[30] Still, parties and arbitrators alike have looked at the broad grants of power in these rules in the past as possible inherent sources of authority for imposing monetary sanctions; the ability to continue to do so remains to be seen given the institutional track record of selective amendment to provide for remedial powers in the event of noncompliance. After all, why would an institution amend its existing general remedial provisions to add express powers for noncompliance if it thought that the existing general remedial powers sufficed?

Nevertheless, there are some leading precedents for the position that even the broad remedial powers conferred generally by the AAA's Commercial (and other) Rules include monetary sanctioning power – albeit in decisions that predate the amendment process. In one pertinent case, a party argued that the adversary should be sanctioned for not producing relevant documents, saying they were authorized by reading together the right to compel document exchanges with the remedial power of arbitrators in the AAA Commercial Arbitration Rules.[31] The panel accepted and relied on this argument in fashioning the award. The

---

[29] *McDaniel v. Bear Stearns & Co.*, 196 F. Supp. 2d 343, 364 (S.D.N.Y. 2002).

[30] Evidence preclusion was at the heart of the punitive sanctions in the Seagate case, supra note, yet that was a domestic case. The omission of evidence or claim/defense preclusive powers may be calculated to better serve the right to be heard, so central to award enforcement in the international context.

[31] *Superadio*, *supra* n. 4. The discovery dispute did not arise under the party's agreement; rather it arose from the proceedings themselves. *See also Todd Shipyards Corp. v. Cunard Line Ltd.* 943 F.2d 1056, 1064 (9th Cir. 1991) (Power of Arbitration Panel to award attorney fees under Rule 43 given the accepted 'bad faith conduct' exception to the "American Rule").

panel imposed sanctions to fill in the void in the proof of damages occasioned by the losing party's discovery abuse. However, reviewing the award *de novo*, the intermediate appellate court disapproved. First, it noted that the remedial rules did "not mention monetary sanctions and should not be construed as to sweep in matters not contemplated by the agreement, *i.e.*, to include matters beyond the issues submitted to arbitration." The court also observed that the rule authorizing arbitrators to resolve discovery disputes said nothing about the enforcement by monetary sanctions.[32] As such, that court did not consider the award a permissible exercise of inherent power under the AAA rules.

Subsequently, the highest court in Massachusetts reversed that intermediate appellate court and affirmed the arbitration award imposing monetary sanctions as damages for violation of a discovery order. In doing so, the court *deferred* to the arbitrators' interpretation of their remedial power under Rules 43(a) and 21(c) of the American Arbitration Association (AAA) Commercial Arbitration Rules. Rule 43(a) authorizes the arbitrator to award "any relief that the arbitrator deems just and equitable," while Rule 21(c) authorizes the arbitrator "to resolve any disputes concerning the exchange of information." Construing the rules together, the *Superadio* court reasoned that

> [t]o give arbitrators control over discovery and discovery disputes without the authority to impose mandatory sanctions for discovery violations and noncompliance with appropriate discovery orders, would impede the arbitrator's ability to adjudicate claims effectively in the manner contemplated by the arbitration process.

The court noted the absence of any language in the AAA rules limiting the means by which arbitrators may resolve discovery disputes or fashion relief in final awards. At the same time, it acknowledged the existence of contrary authority to its position. The deferential standard of review tipped the scale in this instance.

Although the *Superadio* decision seems to have accorded justice to the claimant (which was prevented from proving damages because the respondent failed to produce documents), the reasoning proved problematic for at least three reasons, particularly in comparison with carefully reasoned decisions of other courts. This could be a vulnerability going forward when other courts seek to gauge the decision's persuasive

---

[32] *Superadio*, *supra* n. 4, 818 N.E.2d at 593.

value in interpreting other institutional rules which do not have express provisions on sanctioning power.

To explain, first, the decision failed to state why a deferential standard of review should be applied when a tribunal is deciding its own remedial competence. Shouldn't a stricter standard be used, as was done in *First Options of Chicago, Inc. v. Kaplan*?[33] In that case, the Supreme Court applied a *de novo* review in considering the tribunal's competence to decide its own jurisdiction. *First Options* impliedly suggests that the deferential review given by the Massachusetts court in *Superadio* may be misplaced. By applying a deferential standard of review, the *Superadio* court licenses arbitrators to decide the scope of their own remedial power. As a result, arbitrators could, for example, decide that they have "inherent" power to shift attorney fees based on the "bad faith exception" to the longstanding "American rule" that parties typically bear their own legal fees.

This was precisely the reasoning employed by the Ninth Circuit in upholding an award of attorneys' fees as a sanction for a party's failure to arbitrate in good faith by unnecessarily extending the hearings.[34] That notion of bad faith conduct in hearings could logically be extended to the discovery context as well. Because not all courts adhere to that view (as explained *infra*), the result will be a lack of predictability and consistency in the interpretation of institutional rules dealing with remedies and discovery where deferential review is granted. This result suggests that the only way to curb such inconsistent interpretations of arbitral power would be for arbitral institutions to expressly modify their rules, or for legislatures to draft legislation on the point. There has been action on both fronts, with at least two institutions modifying some[35] or all of their rules to address general sanctioning power, while nearly half of the states have embraced the RUAA, with its express sanctioning empowerment.

Second, the reasoning in *Superadio* seems divorced from commercial reality. For years, the AAA educated arbitrators on its commercial panel that they could draw an adverse inference or preclude evidence as a sanction for discovery abuse. The AAA never took the official position that the commercial rules include the authority to issue monetary awards for noncompliance with discovery orders. As a result, experienced arbitrators and practitioners may have a similar reaction to *Superadio* as they had to the Supreme Court decision in *Volt Information Sciences v.*

[33] 514 U.S. 938 (1995).

[34] *See, e.g.*, *Todd Shipyards*, *supra*, note 21.

[35] The AAA modified its commercial and international rules, while the CPR modified its administered and un-administered domestic and international rules.

Board of Trustees. In *Volt*, the Supreme Court, applying a deferential standard of review, held that a contract provision making California law the governing law could be interpreted by a state court to include California's procedural law of arbitration. No one at the time thought that this result reflected the parties' real intent in framing a governing law clause. So *Volt* created a trap for the unwary. However, savvy drafters modified their arbitration agreements to include a provision making the Federal Arbitration Act (or if not applicable, a particular state law) expressly control the arbitration procedure. Today, institutions like the AAA are refining their arbitrator training to reflect the new rule and emerging empowerment.

Third, the *Superadio* court appears to have taken a result-oriented approach, believing it desirable to avoid resorting to the courts to referee discovery battles in arbitration. While judicial intervention would not be a desirable or particularly effective systemic means of dealing with arbitral discovery problems, the scope of arbitral power with respect to monetary or other punitive sanctions ought not to be left entirely to arbitral tribunals, whose decisions are likely to be less than consistent. Rather, the embryonic rule-making process evident here now and hopefully abroad going forward is far better equipped to incorporate systemic user input and to promote greater uniformity in experience, and hence serve predictability and planning in the exercise of party autonomy.

In another case, the arbitrator awarded legal fees as a sanction for late document production. The arbitrator relied on inherent powers in an AAA International Arbitration Rule providing authority to vary the procedures in the AAA rules. The arbitrator bolstered his conclusion that sanction awards were authorized with an anecdotal report that other AAA arbitrators had occasionally awarded sanctions under the rules.[36] On appeal, the sanctions award was upheld. However, in upholding the award, the reviewing court relied on AAA Commercial Arbitration Rule 43(d)(ii), which expressly authorizes "an award of attorney fees if all parties have requested such an award or it is authorized by law or their arbitration agreement." In this case, the parties both requested their attorney fees in their arbitral submissions. The court concluded that this sufficed to trigger Rule 43(d)(ii).[37]

It is important to understand that AAA Commercial Rule 43(d)(ii) alone was not construed to authorize legal fees to be shifted as a sanction

---

[36] *InterChem, supra* n. 1.

[37] *Id. See also, Certain Underwriters at Lloyd's v. Aronaut Insurance Co.*, 2009 U.S. Dist. Lexis 87827 (N.D. Ill. 2009).

or otherwise. The ability to shift legal fees under this rule depends on whether the parties agreed to this in their contract, or whether it is authorized by law, or whether they both asked for legal fees in their arbitration papers. Moreover, the broad authority granted elsewhere in Rule 43[38] is expressly tied to the "scope of the agreement of the parties."

The situation is different in employment cases heard under the AAA National Rules for the Resolution of Employment Disputes. Employment Rule 34, which deals with the award, provides in subsection (d) that arbitrators have the authority to "grant any remedy or relief they deem "just and equitable," as well as "any remedy or relief that would have been available to the parties had the matter been heard in court."[39] Rule 34(e) authorizes "reimbursement of representative's fees in whole or in part, as part of the remedy, in accordance with applicable law."[40] This means that attorney fees can be awarded in the specified circumstances. Despite this expansive language, courts have not consistently construed it when monetary sanctions were involved.

A different interpretive approach is illustrated in *Polin v. Kellwood*,[41] where a federal district court upheld an award of monetary sanctions under Rule 34. The court assumed the arbitrator had the inherent powers of a court:

> Since this case had started as an action in the court and was to come back to this court for review, the panel could grant any remedy that would have been available under a court's inherent power and explicitly, to protect the panel's integrity and the integrity of the arbitration process generally, which integrity the panel, headed by a lawyer, felt was being badly abused.[42]

The quoted language by the *Polin* court added a procedural condition precedent—the existence of prior litigation in the case. This additional requirement leads parties to the courts first. It thereby blurs the traditional separation between the courts and the arbitral forum—a divide that has long served the economy and efficiency of the arbitration process.

---

[38] Rule 43(a) of the AAA commercial rules provides in relevant part: "The arbitrator may grant any remedy or relief that the arbitrator deems just and equitable. . . ."

[39] Rule 34(d) in the AAA employment rules at that time; it is now Rule 39 under the current Employment Rules.

[40] Rule 34(e) in *id.*

[41] *Polin, supra* n. 14.

[42] *Id.*, 103 F. Supp. 2d at 264.

In contrast, a Maryland appeals court vacated an arbitration award under Rule 34 to the extent it included monetary sanctions for "unduly" prolonging discovery. In *MCR of America v. Greene*,[43] the court narrowly construed the phrase "applicable law" in Rule 34(e) to mean only the Maryland Arbitration Act. The court said it disfavored the recovery of counsel fees "[u]nless the arbitration agreement provides otherwise." Noting that Rule 34(e) dealt only with "legal fees," while other fees were addressed in Rule 34(d), it held that the parties had not agreed to shift attorney fees by incorporating the AAA rules.[44] The court concluded that the terms "remedy" and "relief" are too vague to include punitive sanctions. In stark contrast, most recently the Minnesota Supreme Court in *Seagate* drew the opposite conclusion (based on the plain and ordinary meaning),[45] and some years ago a court in California did so in the *David* decision.[46]

The court in *MCR* did not accept the arbitrator's position that Rule 11 of the Federal Rules of Civil Procedure (FRCP) supported the award of sanctions. Section 11 was inapplicable, the court found, because the offensive conduct occurred during the arbitration and was unrelated to the filing of any particular pleadings. The court also stressed that the arbitrator made no explicit findings of fact.[47] The court rejected the attempt to extend Maryland's counterpart to FRCP 11 to this case, even if the term "proceeding" were assumed to include an arbitration.[48] This result is similar to that reached in New York in the Grynberg case, although that decision was based on New York public policy considerations.[49]

---

[43] 811 A. 2d 331, 341 (Md. Ct. Spec. App. 2000).

[44] *Id.* at 344.

[45] 854 NW 2d at 762-635

[46] *David v. Abergel*, 46 Cal. App. 4th 1281, 54 Cal. Rptr. 2d 443, 445 (1996) (Concluding that an arbitration agreement granting "any remedy or relief to which a party is entitled under California law" grants all powers that a court would have, including the ability to impose punitive sanctions.).

[47] The AAA employment rules require arbitrators to give a reasoned award but not findings of fact and law. Rule 34 (c) provides, in relevant part: "The award shall . . . provide the written reasons for the award unless the parties agree otherwise. . . ." Traditionally, arbitrators in domestic commercial cases did not write reasoned awards, unless both parties request one. This practice is changing somewhat, at least in complex cases. *See* Rule 42(b) of the AAA commercial rules and compare with Article 27(2) of the AA International Rules.

[48] *MCR*, *supra* n. 32. State law authorized sanctions based on conduct committed "in bad faith and without substantial justification [in] maintaining or defending [a] proceeding." Because of its ruling, the court did not have to decide whether a "proceeding" actually included arbitration.

[49] *Grynberg* , *supra* note 1, 92 A.D. 3d at 548 ("The arbitrator's imposition of the $3 million award in sanctions against Jack Grynberg (Award 11) was punitive in nature,

Thus, even where institutional rules seem to make an remedial power coincide with judicial power, it will not ne construed that way when awards of monetary sanctions are Drafters who want arbitrators to have monetary sanctionin employment cases, for example, should not rely upo incorporating the AAA employment rules. This is particularl now since they have not been amended to add sanctioning noncompliance, in contrast to the current commercial and int rules. If employment contract drafters wish to eliminate inte risk from courts following the *MCR* decision and given institut changes in other contexts, then they would be better off inc provision in the arbitration clause expressly empowering the arb issue monetary sanctions for abuse of the discovery process. Whi so may needlessly highlight an issue that most parties never customizing the arbitration clause in this manner seems to be a necessa evil, at least for complex relationships that might require documentary proof should a dispute arise.

C. Shifting Attorney Fees

1. Reciprocal Requests in Pleadings

In commercial arbitration in the United States, parties often make reciprocal requests in their pleadings to recover their attorney fees. Some courts recognize that where there has been noncompliance with a document production directive, these mutual requests will support a sanctions award that shifts the prevailing party's legal fees.[50] These requests in the pleadings can be viewed as a *pro tanto* agreement by the parties to submit the issue of attorney fees to arbitration, thereby authorizing fee-shifting sanctions[51] under the AAA commercial rules.[52]

---

regardless of the label attached. Accordingly the award violated public policy and was properly vacated.)(Citations omitted).

[50] *See Interchem*, *supra* n. 1 (attorney fee award against losing party for evasive and dilatory document production was within the scope of arbitrator's authority.). *See also McDaniel*, *supra* n. 20, 196 F. Supp. 2d at 364-65. *Cf. MCR*, *supra* n. 33, 811 A. 2d at 338 ("The parties' agreement states only that '[t]he fees and expenses of any [arbitration] action shall be borne solely by the party against whom the decision is rendered. No mention is made of attorneys' fees, and, under such circumstances, the Court of Appeals has declared, the power to award attorney's fees will not be presumed.").

[51] *See, e.g.*, *InterChem*, *supra* n. 1. *See also*, *McDaniel*, *supra* n. 20, 196 F. Supp. 2d at 364-65 (acquiescence to award of attorney fees by failing to make a legal objection or by making its own demand).

ever, not all courts take this general view. The court in *MCR of* *a* is one example. There, the parties' contract provided for fee g. It stated that "[t]he fees and expenses of any [arbitration] action be borne solely by the party against whom the decision is ered." Additionally, the parties made attorney fee requests in both demand and the reply. Nevertheless, the court found no basis to shift gal fees as a remedy for discovery abuse. It ruled that the arbitration greement did not expressly authorize the shifting of attorney fees, and it distinguished the term "fees" from "legal fees."[53] The court denied any significance to the attorney fee requests in the arbitral pleadings, which it characterized as "routinely" made with "Pavlovian consistency."[54] The court also failed to recognize that in other jurisdictions, such as New York, attorney fee requests made in pleadings empower the arbitrator to make the shift.[55] The *MCR* decision seems plainly wrong in this respect and should be considered an "outlier' decision.

2. Contractual Provisions: Policy Considerations and Judicial Oversight

As discussed above, the power to award monetary or other punitive sanctions for abusive conduct, such as in discovery may be implied from an arbitration clause that provides for recovery of attorney fees. There is also a significant precedent for construing a broad arbitration clause alone as sufficient to confer equitable "inherent authority on arbitrators to sanction a party that participates in the arbitration in bad faith, and that such a sanction may include an award of attorneys' or arbitrators' fees."[56]

However, generally there was policy-based hostility to shifting attorney fees as a sanction power for discovery abuse based on these types of broad contract provisions alone, although some evolution in the view is

---

[52] AAA Commercial Rule 43(d)(ii) discussed in the prior case law provides, in relevant part: "The award of the arbitrator(s) may include: . . . (ii) an award of attorneys' fees if all parties have requested such an award or it is authorized by law or their arbitration agreement. . . ." That provision continued in the current rules and is now located at Rule 47. An issue that arises in circumstances where the parties each request attorney fees in their pleadings is whether one party may subsequently withdraw the request, and if so at what point in the process, to destroy party agreement in this regard. In practice, some arbitrators will require that the reciprocal requests be maintained through the closure of the hearings, which draws support in New York from existing precedent.

[53] *MCR*, *supra* n. 32, 811 A.2d at 338-39.

[54] *Id.* at 339.

[55] *See Polin*, *supra* n. 14, 132 F. Supp. 131.

[56] *See Relia Star*, *supra* n. 1, 544 F. 3rd at 86.

evident in certain more recent decisions that are grounded in party autonomy in the contractual process.[57] There are three concerns. First is the fear that it would "chill" resort to arbitration by consumers and employees.[58] However, that concern seems misplaced since litigation allows monetary sanctions as a remedy for discovery abuse. The worry is that inferring the authority to impose monetary sanctions from a general fee-shifting provision would be an economic deterrent to the use of arbitration to vindicate statutory rights. Since going to court would not result in shifting legal fees as a result of the American Rule (everyone pays his or her own legal fees) in the absence of bad faith, this seems to be a legitimate concern; but it is one that can be appropriately addressed by an express provision authorizing monetary sanctions or incorporating rules that recognize broad sanctioning power. Moreover, in an arbitral context as in litigation, at least in some instances, the fee shifting would be triggered by a finding of bad faith. Accordingly, the result would be the same regardless of forum in such circumstances.

The second reason for hostility to a fee-shifting sanction is that it might have a coercive effect and compromise a party's right to seek judicial review. That potential militates in favor of requiring that "any intent of the parties to afford contempt-like power on the arbitrator must be clearly evident."[59] (Whether such intent is evidenced would depend on the circumstances. If a clearly authorized monetary sanction "could pose a substantial impediment to judicial review and undermine the FAA policies . . ."[60] then it would be appropriate for the party against whom the sanctions have been imposed to seek a stay of implementation.[61] If the parties' agreement provides for the UAA 2000 to govern their arbitration under Section 17(d)[62] and does not otherwise authorize such sanctions, then the challenging party also could conceivably mount a preemption challenge. Finally, in some federal circuits, that party could be entitled to judicial review to see if the choice of state law was "clearly evidenced."[63]

---

[57] *See*, e.g., *Seagate, supra* note, 854 NW 2d at 765

[58] *See MCR, supra* n. 32, 811 A.2d at 342.

[59] *Lloyd's, supra* n. 1, 264 F. Supp. 2d at 944.

[60] *Id.*

[61] *See id.*

[62] *See* discussion under Statutory Empowerment, *infra.*

[63] *Id. Cf. Mastrobuno v. Shearson Lehman Hutton*, 514 U.S. 52 (1995); *and Sovak v. Chugai Pharm. Co.*, 280 F. 3d 1266 (9th Cir.), *cert. den.* 537 U.S. 825 (2002). *See also* discussion in text in Statutory Empowerment, *infra.*

A third related reason for hostility to fee shifting where there is discovery abuse in arbitration is that awards might be largely beyond review. The reasoning advanced is that when a judge sanctions a party, the reviewing court applies an "abuse of discretion" standard.[64] But when an arbitrator awards sanctions, the award is subject to review on more limited grounds. For example, the court in *Polin* (which actually upheld a monetary sanctions award in arbitration) stated: "[E]ven if the agreement had not endowed the panel with the power of a court, [a]rbitration awards are subject to very limited review in order to avoid undermining the twin goals of arbitration, namely, settling disputes efficiently and avoiding long and expensive litigation."[65]

However, this concern too is largely illusory. An arbitrator's awards of monetary sanctions could be scrutinized under statutory provisions permitting review for "exceeding powers."[66] True, some courts have said that they are constrained by precedent to construe this ground narrowly and so must give "considerable deference" to the arbitrator's judgment. However, others have applied a *de novo* standard of review in assessing the arbitrator's powers and whether they were exceeded.[67] Since there is a lack of uniformity in this area, the outcome is forum dependent at this time.[68] A court faced with this issue may well say, "[I]t is one thing to grant the arbitrator broader discretion than a court of law has to interpret a contract, even though it is less reviewable, but quite another to invest the arbitrator with the same discretion when it comes to defining their own powers."[69]

In short, because of this concern, courts should review *de novo* the jurisdictional aspect of a decision to award monetary sanctions under the "exceeding powers" prong of the vacatur statute.[70] The reason why a deferential standard of review should not be applied is that it "is appropriate where the parties indisputably agree to submit to arbitration, but if "the arbitrator's very authority to adjudicate the dispute is challenged, such obedience to the arbitrator's assertion of jurisdiction is inapt."[71] Last but not least, as noted above, the more rigorous scrutiny would be consistent with the U.S. Supreme Court decision in *First Options*.

---

64 *See, e.g., Mattoon v. City of Pittsfield*, 775 N.E.2d 770 (Mass. App. Ct. 2002).
65 *Polin, supra* n. 14, 132 F. Supp. 2d at 130.
66 *See* 9 U.S.C. § 10(a)(4).
67 *See, e.g., MCR, supra* n. 32, 811 A. 2d at 341.
68 *Compare ibid., with InterChem, supra* n. 1.
69 *MCR, supra* n. 32, 811 A.2d at 340.
70 *See, e.g., id.*
71 *Ibid.*, 811 A. 2d at 340.

As such, courts wishing to review *de novo* the existence of an arbitrator's sanctioning power would find ample precedent for doing so—despite the limited grounds for vacatur. Still, others may look first to whether the arbitrator places the power to sanction outside the contract itself.[72] In that situation a court might review the amount of the sanction *de novo* to ascertain if it is "arbitrary." On the other hand, where there is a source of sanctioning power, or an obstacle to raising the lack of power, that draws its "essence" from the contract itself (even if not expressly stated by the arbitrator), then the court may give deference to the arbitrator's determination.[73] This conclusion follows even in the face of a challenge to the award for "manifest disregard of the law,"[74] depending upon how the courts ultimately construe the viability of that doctrine in the aftermath of the U.S. Supreme Court decision in *Hill Street Associates, LLC v. Mattel, Inc.*[75] Historically courts just looked for "colorable" authority in support of the sanction power; if they found it, they gave deference to the arbitrator's judgment.[76] In any event, the drafter must be mindful that since courts have applied different standards of review, they leave parties subject to the vagaries of conflicting lower court approaches.

The conflicting cases construing the AAA employment rules highlight the potential significance of the standard of review to be applied. Where the court applied a deferential or highly limited standard of review, it upheld the sanctions award with no real scrutiny because the inherent powers of the court were also vested in the arbitrator. While the broad language of Rule 34(d) may support this result, the reasoning advanced in the *Polin* decision on reconsideration was troublesome, for it seems to needlessly invite the filing of lawsuits first so that the arbitral panel will have powers similar to that of a court. The approach of the court in *MCR*, which applied *de novo* review under Rule 34(d), is also problematic. That court focused on the lack of specific authority to issue monetary sanctions. It found that Rule 34(d) was "vague and ambiguous."[77] However, a court

[72] *See Lloyd's*, *supra* n. 1, 264 F. Supp. 2d at 938-39.

[73] *See id.*

[74] *Id. See also*, *McDaniel*, *supra* n. 20 196 F. Supp. 2d at 351, 364-65.

[75] *552* U.S. 576 (2008). There is a split among the Circuits as of 2015. The Fifth, Eighth and Eleventh circuits hold manifest disregard is no longer an applicable vacatur basis. The second, Fourth, Seventh, Ninth and Tenth circuits take the opposite view. In the middle are the First, Third and Sixth circuits which are in the middle and undecided.

[76] *See, e.g.*, *Polin*, *supra* n. 14.

[77] *MCR*, *supra* n. 32, 811 A. 2d at 344-45.

could take a less restrictive view since a plain reading of the language unconstrained by misplaced policy concerns could justify doing so.

In another instance, while the court said it was applying a deferential standard of review, that proved no impediment to substituting its own reasoning for that of the arbitrator. In *InterChem Asia*, driven by a need to apply a highly restrictive standard of review to the issue of the arbitrator's authority, the court found a "barely colorable" justification for the outcome—the fact that both parties had included requests for attorney fees in their arbitration pleadings. This allowed the court to conclude that the arbitrator had the parties' consent. It therefore applied Rule 43(d)(ii) of the AAA commercial rules. But the arbitrator had not relied on this source of sanctioning power, instead referencing only the AAA International Rules as an empowering source. The court also ignored the arbitrator's stated reason in the body of the award for the shift of legal fees as a sanction.[78] Yet, when the rationale for upholding an award is so divorced from the express reasoning that supported the very relief granted, it is hard to have confidence in the process, or in the restrictive standard of review.

At bottom, precedent is not promoting needed uniformity in construing institutional rules in this area of arbitration practice. Someone needs to clean up the mess courts have created so that drafters will have sufficient clarity from rule or precedent to rely on them. The fact that two leading arbitral institutions amended their rules to provide broadly for sanctioning power is a helpful start. How they will be implemented remains to be seen.

D. Suggestions for Drafters

Shifting responsibility for paying attorney fees as a sanction could make the difference between continuing to arbitrate or settling on unfavorable terms in cases where there has been significant document discovery abuse. Yet because of the American Rule, attorney fees can be shifted only if expressly authorized by statute or the parties' arbitration agreement,[79] which episodically is expansively construed, but not always, or in the event of a finding of bad faith.

---

[78] *See InterChem*, *supra* n. 1, and cases cited therein.

[79] *See Buckannon Bd. & Care Home, Inc. v. W. Va. Dep't of Health & Human Resources*, 532 U.S. 598, 602 (2001) ("[I]n the United States parties are ordinarily required to bear their own attorney fees—the prevailing party is not entitled to collect from the loser.").

Still, parties frequently decide for perfectly good commercial reasons not to put in their agreement a general clause shifting legal-fees. Similarly, they often decline to authorize the arbitrator to award reasonable attorney fees through mutual requests in the pleadings. But in failing to do so, they should recognize that they also are potentially restricting the arbitrator's remedial powers in a discovery abuse situation in many jurisdictions and under certain rules. This failing can compromise the integrity of the arbitration process.[80] Moreover, there is a risk that the federal policy of promoting arbitration could be frustrated once commercial parties become painfully aware through experience that arbitrators often have limited remedial power in this area. Thus, it would behoove drafters of dispute resolution clauses to embrace rules where possible that expressly authorize arbitrators to have remedial sanctioning power to address discovery abuses, or to consider doing so themselves in their drafting. In view of the conflicting judicial precedent and restrictive views of some courts, drafters should not rely on the grants of general arbitrator powers conferred by broad clauses or institutional arbitration rules. That is increasingly important with the emerging trend of some institutional rules selectively and expressly providing for sanctioning power, even after some courts have recognized it as inherent in the general remedial grants of powers to the arbitrator.

If there is no source of arbitral power to issue monetary sanctions, then a party who seeks them has little alternative but to resort to a court after non-compliance with a subpoena.[81] Yet, arbitration has long sought to minimize judicial intrusion to preserve both the speed and economy that are attributes of the process. The need for a judicial subpoena to deal with recalcitrant or abusive parties in arbitration opens the process to oversight by a judge who is far less conversant with the facts than the arbitrator in the case. Equally of concern, progress in the arbitral process may be held hostage and to litigation's typical plodding pace.

V. Statutory Empowerment

A final potential source of sanctioning power for arbitrators is in applicable statutes. It is well known that Section 7 of the FAA has been

---

[80] *See Polin*, *supra* n. 14, 132 F. Supp. 2d at 131 (quoting the panel's reasoning).

[81] *See Lloyd's*, *supra* n. 1, at 944 ("in light of the strong public policy favoring expeditious arbitration, the parties should not be banned from consensually conferring such power on the arbitrator; enforcement via sanctions by the arbitrator is likely to be more efficient than mandating judicial review and enforcement in every instance").

given different interpretations regarding the power to order document discovery from third parties. Restrictive interpretations are grounded in the plain language of the statute. Given the lack of "cover" afforded by existing federal statutory language, there seems little likelihood that courts will imply the power to impose monetary sanctions for abusive conduct during discovery from the power to compel production of documents. Indeed in one case specifically addressing this issue under the FAA, the court concluded there is no grant of inherent authority to impose monetary sanctions under Section 7.[82]

Until the UAA 2000 was adopted by the NCCUSL and approved and promoted by the American Bar Association House of Delegates, there was little reason for arbitrators to look at state arbitration laws as a source of sanctioning power. The authority in Section 7 of the 1955 UAA only provided for arbitral subpoenas and depositions for an arbitration hearing. This caused a number of courts to conclude that "pre-trial discovery is not available under our present statutes for arbitration."[83] This conclusion should change if or as more states enact the UAA 2000, which provides for pre-hearing discovery, particularly those in commercial centers. Moreover, Section 17(d) expressly provides that "[I]f an arbitrator permits discovery . . . the arbitrator may . . . take action against a noncompliant party to the extent a court could if a controversy were the subject of a civil action in this state."

As the comment to Section 17 observes, the UAA 2000 "establishes the authority of the arbitrator to oversee the pre-hearing process and enforce discovery-related orders in a same manner as would occur in a civil action, thereby minimizing the involvement of (and resort of the parties to) a court during the arbitral discovery process." This would be sufficient authority, unless state arbitration law does not apply. However, less than half the states have adopted the UAA 2000 to date.[84] None of

[82] *Lloyd's*, *supra* n. 1 at 944. The court likened the imposition of a fine for non-compliance with a civil contempt order issued by a court: the "contempt power derives solely a statutory grant of authority"; there is no such authority under the explicit FAA language. Compare the approach of California in Civ. Proc. Code Sections 1283.1 and 1283.05. *See generally*, *Berglund*, *supra* n. 15 (Power of arbitrators under those sections to enforce discovery subpoenas against nonparties in cases involving personal injury and death).

[83] *Rippe v. West Am. Ins. Co.*, 1993 WL 512547 (Conn. Dec. 2, 1993) (construing the 1955 UAA). *See, e.g.*, *Burton v. Bush*, 614 F. 2d 389 (4th Cir. 1980) (party to arbitration contract has no right to pre-hearing discovery).

[84] None of the adopting states have made changes to Article 17(d) that would impact a court's assessment of an arbitration panel's imposition of monetary sanctions for a failure to follow its discovery orders.

these jurisdictions hosts a major commercial arbitral center, with the exception of the District of Columbia. However, in light of decisions like *Superadio*, state legislatures may focus on the sanctions issue when deciding whether to enact the Uniform Arbitration Act as revised in 2000. Indeed, the Massachusetts legislature was contemplating that very issue when the Supreme Judicial Court decided *Superadio*. However, that did not deter the Court from judicially expanding arbitral remedies for discovery abuse (although the Court was deterred by legislative consideration in deciding a multijurisdictional practice issue of out-of-state lawyers representing parties in arbitrations in Massachusetts).

Still, it is unclear what would happen even if a state, including one that hosts a large arbitration center, does enact the UAA 2000. After the Supreme Court's decision in *Volt Information Sciences*,[85] which applied the California Arbitration Act based on a general choice of law provision in the parties' agreement, practitioners often expressly provided in the dispute resolution clause that the arbitration will be governed by the FAA. The Supreme Court decision in *Mastrobuono v. Shearson Lehman Hutton*,[86] which signaled to some courts a need for "clear evidence" of the intent to apply state arbitral law rather than the FAA,[87] did not change this drafting practice for many. Yet, that has not necessarily deterred state courts inclined to follow a state policy against punitive sanctions, as in New York.[88]

There are plenty of instances where commercial contracts contain only a general clause providing for state law to govern. When the interaction between the Volt and Mastrobuono decisions is unclear in the jurisdiction selected, the standard to be applied regarding the role of state arbitration law will likewise be unpredictable. The current state of law concerning generic choice of law clauses and their impact on arbitral procedure has been aptly described as a "morass of inconsistent principles."[89]

Thus, even in states that adopt the UAA 2000, there will be uncertain legal effect. This could lead to costly briefing of the issue of whether state arbitration law authorizes the imposition of arbitral monetary sanctions. There is no good reason to force parties and arbitrators to

---

[85] *Volt Info Sciences, Inc. v. Bd. of Trustees of Leland Stanford Jr. Univ.*, 489 U.S. 468 (1989).

[86] 514 U.S. 52 (1995).

[87] *See, e.g., Sovak v. Chungai Pharm. Co.*, 280 F. 2d 1266, 1269 (9th Cir. 2002); *Lloyd's, supra* n. 1.

[88] *See, e.g., Grynberg, supra* note one, 92 A.D. 3d at 548.

[89] Note, *An Unnecessary Choice of Law: Volt, Mastrobuono, and Federal Arbitration Act Preemption*, 115 HARV. L. REV. 2250, 2260 (2002).

wade into that morass, particularly when it can be easily clarified through appropriate drafting of the arbitration clause. To solve the problem, in most jurisdictions a drafter need only incorporate the language in Section 17(d) of the UAA 2000 in the contract. Better still, a more uniform and pervasive modification of institutional arbitration rules, here and abroad, would provide the requisite certainty, while eliminating traps for the unwary drafter.

VI. Conclusion

Given the significance of document discovery in today's complex commercial arbitration proceedings, it is vital to enhance the arbitrator's remedial ability to deal with abusive situations when they occur. Doing so would preserve the parties' confidence in arbitration, as well as the benefits of economy and efficiency. The varying approaches courts have taken to the arbitrator's ability to sanction abusive conduct under institutional arbitration rules have compromised predictability in this area. In these circumstances, arbitral institutions have now begun to take the lead by removing ambiguity from their rules, particularly for complex commercial cases. Still, even where such general empowerment changes have been made, implementation of them will benefit from institutional training. Where applicable rules have not yet been modified to provide expressly for such remedial powers, it could still be accomplished by drafters either expressly providing that arbitrators have the power to award sanctions for noncompliance, or by providing that they have the same remedial power as a judge would have if the matter were heard in court. Parties could always opt out by otherwise providing in their arbitration clause.[90] This would offer needed certainty without adversely affecting the attraction of arbitration. The alternative is the status quo, which goes "hand in hand" with the dictum of Justice Hand quoted at the outset of this article. The status quo works in most cases, but not all. It is time to address the potential ineffectiveness of arbitration in the hard cases by expressly providing adequate remedial power to arbitrators, ideally through institutional rules and predictable implementation of them.

---

[90] This is the situation with respect to punitive damages; in domestic arbitrations if parties do not want arbitrators to have the authority to award punitive damages, they should clearly say so in their arbitration clause.

Changing arbitration rules is not unprecedented. For example, the AAA changed its International Arbitration Rules to eliminate much of the arbitrator's power to award punitive damages following the Supreme Court decision in *Mastrobuono v. Shearson Lehman Hutton*. The risk with the broad judicial approach to arbitral sanctioning power in the *Superadio* case, and the few other decisions like it, is that they potentially invite a morass of inconsistent interpretations by arbitrators and courts alike to follow, particularly if a deferential rather than *de novo* standard of review is applied. Unfortunately, the reasoning of such decisions, while trying to promote a worthy result in the specific case, is not likely to serve the long-valued arbitral goals of predictability, efficiency and finality. An institutional solution through rule revision is the preferred course to assure consistency of interpretation and predictability. That process has begun and should be supported, both here and internationally.

PART VI:

ETHICS IN ARBITRATION PRACTICE

CHAPTER 35

2004 CODE OF ETHICS FOR COMMERCIAL ARBITRATORS EXPLAINED

*Bruce E. Meyerson and John M. Townsend**

I. Introduction

More than a quarter century ago, a small group of arbitrators and practitioners, representatives of the American Bar Association and American Arbitration Association, met over a long weekend, under the leadership of Judge Howard Holtzmann, to draft an important statement defining ethical duties for arbitrators in commercial disputes.[1] Their effort became the 1977 AAA-ABA Code of Ethics for Arbitrators in Commercial Disputes (the 1977 Ethics Code). It has proved to be an invaluable ethical framework for arbitrators and others involved in the dispute resolution field.

Many federal and state courts have cited the 1977 Ethics Code with approval as providing the preeminent definition of standards of conduct in the field.[2] The Seventh Circuit was careful to note, however, that the Code does not have the force of law: "Although we have great respect for the Commercial Arbitration Rules [of the AAA] and the Code of Ethics for Arbitrators, they are not the proper starting point for an inquiry

---

* Bruce E. Meyerson, a Mediator and Arbitrator in Phoenix, Arizona, is a former Judge of the Arizona Court of Appeals and a past chair of the ABA Section of Dispute Resolution. He participated as a member of the ABA delegation on the 2004 revision of the 1977 AAA-ABA Code of Ethics. He is an Adjunct Professor at the Arizona State University College of Law where he teaches ADR courses, including the course on Arbitration. He can be reached at brucemeyerson@msn.com.

John M. Townsend is a Washington, D.C., Partner of Hughes Hubbard & Reed LLP, where he chairs the Arbitration and ADR Group. He served as a member of the AAA delegation during the 2004 revision of the 1997 ABA-AAA Code of Ethics and was the Chairman of the AAA's Board of Directors from 2007 to 2010.

[1] Labor arbitration is generally conducted under the Code of Professional Responsibility for Arbitrators of Labor-Management Disputes.

[2] *E.g.*, Lifecare Int'l Inc. v. CD Med. Inc., 68 F.3d 429, 435 (11th Cir. 1995); Burlington Northern R.R. v. Tuco Inc., 960 S.W.2d 629, 636-37 (Tex. 1997).

into an award's validity.... The arbitration rules and code do not have the force of law."[3]

Because the practice of arbitration has developed significantly since 1977, committees of the ABA and representatives of the AAA began to review whether changes in the laws governing arbitration, the increasing globalization of commercial transactions, and changes in the public perception and expectations of arbitration required revisions to the 1977 Ethics Code. The ABA efforts were aided by representatives of the International Institute for Conflict Prevention and Resolution (CPR), the College of Commercial Arbitrators, and the National Arbitration Forum.

After several years of study and negotiations, agreement was reached by a joint ABA-AAA working group on a proposed revision (the 2004 Revision).[4] The Executive Committee of the AAA Board of Directors approved the 2004 Revision at its September 2003 meeting, and the ABA House of Delegates approved the revisions at the ABA Mid-Year Meeting in February 2004.[5] The 2004 Revision became effective March 1, 2004. The 2004 Revision preserves the style and format, and much of the language, of the 1977 Ethics Code. It is called a revision, rather than a new document, to signal its continuity with the many unchanged provisions of the 1977 Ethics Code and respect for the degree of judicial acceptance that it has achieved. All provisions of the 2004 Revision are subject to any contrary principles that may be found in governing law or applicable arbitration rules and also to the right of the parties to any arbitration to reach agreement on different rules and standards.

II. Presumption of Neutrality

A. In General

The most fundamental and far-reaching change contained in the 2004 Revision is the application of a presumption of neutrality to all

[3] Merit Ins. Co. v. Leatherby Ins. Co., 714 F.2d 673, 680 (7th Cir. 1983). *Accord* ANR Coal Co. v. Cogentrix of N.C., Inc., 173 F. 3d 493, 497n (4th Cir. 1999); Lifecare Int'l Inc., *supra* n. 2, 68 F. 3d at 435.

[4] The ABA members of the working group were Sara Adler, Carol Emory, Bruce Meyerson and Kenneth B. Reisenfeld. The AAA members were James H. Carter, Jr., John D. Feerick, Florence Peterson and John M. Townsend. Kathleen Scanlon of CPR participated in the working group meetings.

[5] The Report to the American Bar Association was prepared by Robert A. Holtzman, Benjamin H. Sheppard Jr. and Kenneth B. Reisenfeld. That report formed the basis of this chapter.

arbitrators, including party-appointed arbitrators. By contrast, the 1977 Ethics Code presumed that the party-appointed arbitrators to a three-person panel (tripartite arbitration) would not be neutral.[6] This meant that, in practice, they were not only free to act as advocates for the positions of the party that appointed them, they were expected to act that way. Under the 1977 Ethics Code, party-appointed arbitrators were to be considered "nonneutral unless both parties inform the arbitrators that all three arbitrators are to be neutral or unless the contract, the applicable arbitration rules, or any governing law requires that all three arbitrators be neutral."[7] Thus, absent contrary indications in the parties' agreement, the governing law or arbitral rules, the default rule was that all party-appointed arbitrators were considered nonneutral when no agreement for their neutrality had been made.

The 2004 Revision reverses the presumption of nonneutrality for party-appointed arbitrators. Instead, it establishes a presumption of neutrality for all arbitrators. Thus, they will all be held to the same standard. The presumption appears in the Introductory Note on Neutrality in the 2004 Revision, which states:

> This Code establishes a presumption of neutrality for all arbitrators, including party-appointed arbitrators, which applies unless the parties' agreement, the arbitral rules agreed to by the parties or applicable laws provide otherwise.

This presumption is reaffirmed in Canon IX.A of the 2004 Revision.

The concept of neutrality embodied in the 2004 Revision encompasses both independence and impartiality. This is codified in Canon I.B, which provides that an arbitrator should accept appointment only if fully satisfied that he or she can serve "impartially" and "independently" from the parties, potential witnesses, and the other arbitrators. The Comment to Canon I explains that arbitrators do not contravene the Canon if by virtue of experience or expertise they have views on certain general issues likely to arise in an arbitration, but emphasizes that "an arbitrator may not have prejudged any of the specific legal or factual determinations to be addressed during the arbitration."

As with the other provisions of the 2004 Revision, the presumption of neutrality is subject to contrary principles established by agreement of

[6] In this situation, the parties' agreement usually provides that each party will appoint one arbitrator and the third arbitrator will be appointed by the two party-appointed arbitrators.

[7] 1977 Ethics Code, Canon VII, Introductory Note.

the parties, the governing law or applicable arbitration rules.[8] For example, some parties in domestic arbitrations in the United States are likely to continue to prefer that their party-appointed arbitrators not be neutral.

In recognition of this preference, the 2004 Revision continues to permit party-appointed arbitrators to be partisan, but only when it is shown that "all parties" intended that they may be "predisposed" toward the party appointing them. This balance is struck by two provisions of new Canon IX. First, Canon IX.A provides: "In tripartite arbitrations to which this Code applies, all three arbitrators are presumed to be neutral and are expected to observe the same standards as the third arbitrator."

Then Canon IX.B states:

> Notwithstanding this presumption, there are certain types of tripartite arbitration in which it is expected by all parties that the two arbitrators appointed by the parties may be predisposed toward the party appointing them. Those arbitrators, referred to in this Code as "Canon X arbitrators," are not to be held to the standards of neutrality and independence applicable to other arbitrators.

The 2004 Revision refers to nonneutral arbitrators as "Canon X arbitrators" because that Canon establishes the special ethical obligations of party-appointed arbitrators who are not expected to meet the standards of neutrality.

The grouping of provisions applicable to non-neutral party-appointed arbitrators in Canon X represents an architectural solution designed to reconcile different points of view on the subject of non-neutral arbitrators. On one side, there were strong feelings that the endorsement of non-neutral party-appointed arbitrators in the 1977 Ethics Code had taken American domestic arbitration out of the mainstream of international arbitration, where the prevailing view is that all arbitrators, including party-appointed arbitrators, should be independent of the parties and impartial to the extent possible. Those sharing this position argued that a code of ethics could achieve international respect only if it

[8] The Introductory Note on Construction states: "All provisions of this Code should therefore be read as subject to contrary provisions of applicable law and arbitration rules. They should also be read as subject to contrary agreements of the parties. Nevertheless, this Code imposes no obligation on any arbitrator to act in a manner inconsistent with the arbitrator's fundamental duty to preserve the integrity and fairness of the arbitral process."

required all arbitrators to be neutral.[9] On the countervailing side was the view that use of nonneutral party-appointed arbitrators was an accepted, well established practice in many types of American domestic arbitration, and American courts have accepted the practice as consistent with legal standards established by the Federal Arbitration Act.[10] Those inclined toward this view did not necessarily think that the practice of allowing partisan party-appointed arbitrators was desirable—indeed, many have said that it has had regrettable effects on the arbitration process. But they nevertheless argued that a code of ethics should embrace (and provide guidance for) arbitrators serving in all legal and accepted forms of commercial arbitration.

The solution represented by the 2004 Revision demonstrates a firm preference for arbitrator neutrality, while providing a tent large enough to accommodate those who have specifically agreed otherwise. The 2004 Revision, therefore, provides that Canon X arbitrators are expected to observe all of the ethical obligations prescribed by the Code, except those from which they are expressly excused. However, these ethical obligations differ from those of neutral party-appointed arbitrators in several carefully defined respects. Canon X.A permits Canon X arbitrators to be "predisposed" toward the party who appointed them. Canon X.B provides that Canon X arbitrators are not obliged to withdraw because of alleged partiality when requested to do so by the non-appointing party. And Canon X.C allows Canon X arbitrators to generally engage in ex parte communications with their appointing party.

On the other hand, Canon X.A requires Canon X arbitrators to act in good faith and with integrity and fairness. These arbitrators may not, for example, engage in delaying tactics or harassment.[11] They are required to make the same disclosures of interests and relationships that were previously required by the 1977 Ethics Code only of neutral arbitrators.[12] And they are subject to specific limitations on the scope of their ex parte communications with the appointing parties and with the third arbitrator, although they are permitted far more freedom to engage in such communications than are neutral arbitrators.[13]

---

[9] They contended that an ethics code should deal with the ethical obligations of nonneutral party-appointed arbitrators in some sort of appendix, if it had to deal with them at all.

[10] *See, e.g.*, Delta Mine Holding v. AFC Coal Properties, 280 F.3d 815 (8th Cir. 2001).

[11] Canon X.A(1).

[12] Canon X.A, B.

[13] Canon X.C.

B. Effect on Drafting

Because the long-standing American practice has been to consider party-appointed arbitrators to be nonneutral, the change of this presumption in the ethics code will undoubtedly bring about a fundamental change in the drafting of tripartite arbitration agreements. From now on, attorneys who draft such agreements will be well advised to clarify in the arbitration provision the parties' understanding regarding the "status" of party-appointed arbitrators, particularly if they desire them to act as Canon X arbitrators (*i.e.*, to act as partisan arbitrators for the appointing parties).

III. Duties of Party-Appointed Arbitrators

A. Investigation and Disclosure of Status

One of the significant features of the 2004 Revision is contained in Canon IX, which imposes a duty on every party-appointed arbitrator to ascertain and disclose whether he or she will be acting as a neutral arbitrator or as a Canon X arbitrator. Canon IX.C(3) provides that, in the event of doubt or uncertainty, all party-appointed arbitrators should serve in a neutral capacity until such doubt or uncertainty is resolved. This ethical requirement is new.

Under Canon IX.C, each party-appointed arbitrator now has an obligation to (1) ascertain his or her status as early as possible (and not later than the first meeting of the arbitrators and the parties), and (2) provide a timely report on the subject to the parties and the other arbitrators.

Canon IX.C also imposes on each party-appointed arbitrator a duty to investigate in discharging their obligation to ascertain and disclose their status. Canon IX.C(1) calls for this investigation to include a review of the terms of the parties' written or oral agreement (or an agreement implied from an established course of dealings or well-recognized custom and usage in their trade or profession), the applicable arbitration rules, and the applicable law bearing upon arbitrator neutrality.

The status of the party-appointed arbitrator as neutral or non-neutral arbitrator is one subject that party-appointed arbitrators are expressly permitted to discuss ex parte with the appointing party.[14]

[14] Canon III.B(4).

Canon IX.C(2) provides that a party-appointed arbitrator's conclusion (following the required investigation) that the parties intended him or her to serve as a Canon X arbitrator may be overridden by the parties, the administering arbitral institution, or the arbitral panel. Until a party-appointed arbitrator reaches this conclusion (or is unable to reach a conclusion as to his or her status), he or she is required by Canon IX.C(3) to act as a neutral arbitrator (pending any contrary decision by the parties, the administering institution or the panel).

B. Disclosure of Interests and Relationships

The 2004 Revision subjects all arbitrators to the same obligations to disclose interests or relationships likely to affect impartiality or which might create an appearance of partiality. This is new. Under the 1977 Ethics Code, partisan party-appointed arbitrators were required to disclose information sufficient to describe the general nature and scope of any interest or relationship, but they were not required to provide the detail expected from neutral arbitrators.

Under the 2004 Revision, specifically, Canons II.A, X.B, all arbitrators, including Canon X arbitrators, are required to disclose any interest or relationship likely to affect their impartiality or which might create an appearance of partiality. This duty encompasses "any known ... financial or personal interest in the outcome of the arbitration" or existing or past relationships.[15]

The standard for disclosure of relationships in Canon II.A(2) of the 2004 Revision is new. It is whether known financial, business, professional or personal relationships "might reasonably affect impartiality or lack of independence in the eyes of any of the parties." Canon II.B requires prospective arbitrators to make a reasonable effort to inform themselves of relevant interests or relationships. And any doubt as to whether or not disclosure is to be made should be resolved in favor of disclosure.[16] The disclosure obligation defined by Canon II.A continues, as under the 1977 Ethics Code, throughout the arbitration.[17]

The 2004 Revision omits the Introductory Note that preceded Canon II of the 1977 Ethics Code. This Note adopted the approach to disclosure in the concurring opinion of Justice White in *Commonwealth Coatings Corp. v. Continental Casualty Co.*, the Supreme Court's only exploration

---

[15] Canon II.A(1) and (2).

[16] Canon II.D.

[17] Canon II.C.

of the subject of disclosure by arbitrators.[18] The 1977 Ethics Code's preference for Justice White's approach to disclosure and the closely related legal question of what constitutes "evident partiality," rather than the approach taken in Justice Black's plurality opinion, is now well established in the case law.[19] Thus, it appears that the 1977 Introductory Note is no longer needed.

An interesting new provision in the 2004 Revision, Canon II.H, deals with disclosure of confidential information. Under this provision, an arbitrator who believes that the Code's disclosure requirements call for privileged or confidential information to be divulged should either withdraw, or obtain consent to the disclosure from the person who provided the information.

Consistent with the principle of party autonomy, the 2004 Revision expressly states in Canon I.C that the existence of any relationship or interest "does not render it unethical for one to serve as an arbitrator where the parties have consented to the arbitrator's appointment or continued services following full disclosure of the relevant facts" in accordance with the Code. So long as the arbitrator makes a full disclosure of the interest or relationship, the parties are free to consent to continued service or appointment and the arbitrator may ethically accept the appointment or continue to serve.

IV. Communications with the Parties and the Other Arbitrators

The 2004 Revision clarifies the limits on permissible communications between arbitrators and the parties, and establishes new guidelines on communications between party-appointed arbitrators and the chair of the tribunal in tripartite arbitrations.

The 2004 Revision provides guidance, absent in the 1977 Ethics Code, on what a prospective arbitrator may discuss on an ex parte basis with the appointing party concerning the potential appointment. Canon III.B(1)

[18] 393 U.S. 145, 150 (1968), *reh'g den.*, 393 U.S. 1112 (1969). *See* Beebe Med. Ctr., Inc. v. InSight Health Serv. Corp., 751 A.2d 426, 441 (Del. Ch. 1999) ("the Code's pertinent provisions are drawn in large measure from the principles articulated in Justice White's concurrence"); Merit Ins. Co. v. Leatherby Ins. Co., 714 F.2d 673, 682 (7th Cir. 1983) ("the Code of Ethics for Arbitrators . . . treats Justice White's opinion as a surer guide to the view of the majority of the Supreme Court than Justice Black's").

[19] *See, e.g.*, *ANR Coal Co.*, *supra* n. 3, 173 F. 3d at 498-99; *Merit Ins.*, 714 F.2d at 682 ("Our court . . . treated Justice White's opinion as authoritative.").

limits the discussion to three general subjects: (1) the identities of the parties, counsel or witnesses, (2) the general nature of the case, and (3) the arbitrator's suitability or availability for the appointment. Discussion of the merits of the case is specifically prohibited, except to a limited extent for Canon X arbitrators.

In addition, Canon III.B allows a party-appointed arbitrator to consult with the appointing party concerning (a) the choice of the third arbitrator, (b) compensation, and (c) the status of the arbitrator as a neutral arbitrator or as a Canon X arbitrator.[20]

The 2004 Revision parallels recent changes to the AAA Commercial Rules that also address the subject of communication between the parties and a prospective arbitrator. New AAA commercial rule R-18(a) provides:

> No party and no one acting on behalf of any party shall communicate ex parte with an arbitrator or a candidate for arbitrator concerning the arbitration, except that a party, or someone acting on behalf of a party, may communicate ex parte with a candidate for direct appointment pursuant to Section R-12 in order to advise the candidate of the general nature of the controversy and of the anticipated proceedings and to discuss the candidate's qualifications, availability, or independence in relation to the parties or to discuss the suitability of candidates for selection as a third arbitrator where the parties or party-designated arbitrators are to participate in that selection.

The 2004 Revision provides more detailed guidance than does Rule R-18(a). For example, the 2004 Revision permits ex parte communications regarding arrangements for compensation, including the submission of routine requests for payment.[21] Canon III.B(3) and (4) allows both neutral and Canon X arbitrators to discuss with the party who appointed them the selection of the third arbitrator (as does AAA commercial rule R-18(a)). By contrast, the 1977 Ethics Code only allowed nonneutral party-appointed arbitrators to discuss selection of the third arbitrator with the party who appointed them.

---

[20] Canon III.B(2)(b), (3)(c), and (4).

[21] No similar provision is in the revised AAA commercial rules because these rules provide that all arrangements with regard to compensation should be made through the AAA. rule R-51(c).

Provided a Canon X arbitrator has disclosed the intention to engage in such communications, Canon X.C(2) permits this arbitrator to communicate with the appointing party concerning the merits or "any other aspect of the case," subject to certain enumerated exceptions. If these communications occurred prior to the arbitrator's appointment, or prior to the first hearing or the parties' first meeting with the arbitrators, a Canon X arbitrator is to disclose, at or before the first hearing or meeting, the fact that the communication took place. There is no obligation to disclose the content of the communication.[22] A single timely disclosure of the Canon X arbitrator's intention to participate in such communications in the future is sufficient. These provisions parallel those in the 1977 Ethics Code regarding nonneutral party-appointed arbitrators.

Canon X.C(4) of the 2004 Revision clarifies that Canon X arbitrators may not, at any time during the arbitration, communicate with the appointing party concerning the deliberations of the arbitrators or "any matter or issue taken under consideration by the panel after the record is closed or such matter or issue has been submitted for decision." It also carries forward the prohibitions contained in the 1977 Ethics Code against disclosure of the deliberations of the arbitrators or of any "final or interim decision" in advance of the time it is given to all parties.

Moreover, there are new restrictions on communications between Canon X arbitrators and the neutral arbitrator. The 2004 Revision prohibits these arbitrators from communicating orally with a neutral arbitrator concerning "any matter or issue" arising or expected to arise in the arbitration in the absence of the other Canon X arbitrator. Canon X.C(5) provides that if a Canon X arbitrator communicates in writing with the neutral arbitrator, that arbitrator must simultaneously provide a copy of the written communication to the other Canon X arbitrator. These provisions embody a fundamental reform designed to preserve the impartiality and independence of the neutral chair of the arbitral tribunal in tripartite arbitration proceedings when the two party-appointed arbitrators are acting as nonneutral arbitrators.

V. Arbitrator Suitability

In addition to imposing impartiality and independence standards that form the bedrock of the presumption of neutrality, the 2004 Revision also imposes an obligation on the arbitrator to determine his or her competence

[22] Canon X.C(3).

and availability to serve in the case. The 1977 Ethics Code only admonished prospective arbitrators not to accept an appointment if unavailable to conduct the proceeding promptly. Canon I.B of the 2004 Revision establishes new guidelines for a prospective arbitrator considering an appointment. An arbitrator may accept appointment only if fully satisfied that he or she: (1) can serve impartially; (2) can serve independently from the parties, potential witnesses, and the other arbitrators; (3) is competent to serve; and (4) can be available to commence the arbitration in accordance with its requirements and thereafter to devote appropriate time and attention to its completion. Canon X arbitrators are excused from items (1) and (2), but not from items (3) and (4), under Canon X.A(2).

VI. Advertising, Representation, and Compensation

The 1977 Ethics Code stated that solicitation of appointment as an arbitrator is inconsistent with the integrity of the arbitration process. The 2004 Revision eliminates this statement. Canon VIII provides that advertising and promotion of an individual's willingness or availability to serve as an arbitrator must be accurate and truthful, and must not imply any willingness to accept appointment other than in accordance with the Code. There is nothing in the 2004 Revision precluding an arbitrator from distributing advertisements in electronic or print medium, from making personal presentations to prospective users of arbitral services, or from responding to inquiries concerning the arbitrator's availability, qualifications, experience or fee arrangements.[23]

The 2004 Revision contains a provision that should interest those who follow developments in the rules governing the "practice of law." The 1977 Ethics Code forbade an arbitrator to deny to a party the opportunity to be represented by counsel; it also required the arbitrator to be courteous to parties and their lawyers. Canon IV.A and C in the 2004 Revision states that an arbitrator should not deny a party the opportunity to be represented by counsel "or by any other person chosen by the party." It also applies the duty of courtesy to the parties and their "representatives." These changes undoubtedly should be read in the context of recent efforts in some states to insist that arbitrating parties may only be represented by persons admitted to the bar at the place of arbitration. The Introductory Note on Construction cautions, however,

[23] Comment to Canon VIII.

that all provisions of the 2004 Revision are subject to contrary provisions of applicable law.

Finally, in order to bring together provisions relating to arbitrator compensation that had been separated in the 1977 Ethics Code, Canon VII of the 2004 Revision groups the ethical rules relating to the compensation of arbitrators in one place. These rules apply to all arbitrators. In a development that should be welcomed by parties and counsel, new Canon VII.B(3) includes a specific caution that "[a]rbitrators should not, absent extraordinary circumstances, request increases in the basis of their compensation during the course of a proceeding."

VII. Conclusion

The 1977 Ethics Code remains an historic document that greatly enhanced the integrity of and respect for arbitration process throughout the United States and the world. The 2004 Revision makes this Code even better and even more in tune with modern, contemporary practice. It also brings American standards closer to standards accepted in international commercial arbitration.

Postscript

Since this chapter was originally published in 2004, the 2004 Revision of the Code of Ethics has found widespread acceptance among users of commercial arbitration and the courts. While continuing to emphasize that the Code of Ethics does not have the force of law, courts have looked to the 2004 Revision as they did to the original Code of Ethics in formulating standards, especially for impartiality and disclosure.[24]

[24] *See, e.g. New Regency Prods., Inc. v. Nippon Herald Films, Inc.*, 501 F.3d 1101, 1109-10 (9th Cir. 2007)(citing 2004 Revision); *Positive Software Solutions, Inc. v. New Century Mortg. Corp.*, 436 F.3d 495, 503 (5th Cir. 2006), *rev'd en banc*, 476 F.3d 278 (5th Cir. 2007)(same; noting that Code of Ethics is not binding but is "highly significant"); *ALS & Assocs., Inc. v. AGM Marine Constructors, Inc.*, 557 F.Supp.2d 180, 184 (D. Mass. 2008); *Borst v. Allstate Ins. Co.*, 717 N.W.2d 42, 49-50 (Wis. 2006); *McGinity v. Pawtucket Mut. Ins. Co.*, 899 A.2d 504, 507-08 (R.I. 2006).

CHAPTER 36

MUST ARBITRATORS INVESTIGATE IN CONNECTION WITH THEIR DISCLOSURES? SOME COURTS OPEN THE DOOR TO EVIDENT PARTIALITY ATTACKS

Bethany L. Appleby[*]

I. Introduction

One of the selling points of arbitration under the Federal Arbitration Act (FAA) is the relative finality of an award.[1] Arbitration awards may be vacated only under limited circumstances, including if an arbitrator displays "evident partiality."[2] Although the FAA has not explicitly defined this standard, most federal courts agree that arbitrators are evidently partial if they have an "actual bias" towards a party or an "inferred bias" because they failed to disclose a conflict of interest.[3]

Arbitrators can minimize the risk of an "evident partiality" finding by making adequate disclosures to the parties. This chapter focuses on two federal circuits that have heightened their disclosure requirements by adding a "duty to investigate" in connection with arbitrator disclosures.[4] In other words, arbitrators may have an obligation to discover conflicts of which they may not even been fully aware.

---

[*] Bethany L. Appleby is a lawyer who represents franchisors in franchise litigation and is a partner in the New Haven, Connecticut, office of Wiggin and Dana LLP. She can be reached at bappleby@wiggin.com. The author would like to thank summer associate Timothy Wright for his help in updating this chapter.

[1] *See* 9 U.S.C. § 13 (2012) (providing that a judicially confirmed arbitration award has the same force and effect as a judgment).

[2] *Id.* at § 10(a).

[3] *See* Kathryn A. Windsor, *Defining Arbitrator Evident Partiality: The Catch-22 of Commercial Litigation Disputes*, 6.191 SETON HALL CIR. REV. 191, 192.

[4] A duty to investigate generally requires arbitrators to "make reasonable steps" to learn about potential conflicts of which they have actual or constructive knowledge. *See Schmitz v. Zilveti*, 20 F.3d 1043 (9th Cir. 1994).

In *Applied Industrial Materials Corp. v. Ovalar Makine Ticaret Ve Sanaya, A.S.*, the U.S. Court of Appeals for the Second Circuit imposed a duty on arbitrators to either investigate known conflicts of interest or inform parties that they did not investigate.[5] The Ninth Circuit in *Schmitz v. Zilveti* embraced a freestanding duty to investigate that is separate from the duty to disclose potential conflicts.[6] Although *Schmitz* limited its holding to arbitrations before the National Association of Securities Dealers, later Ninth Circuit opinions suggest an expansive, generalized duty to investigate. Arbitrators should consider their potential duty to investigate when preparing their disclosures to the parties.

II. The Second Circuit's Standard: Arbitrators Must "Investigate or Disclose"

In *Applied Industrial Materials*, the Second Circuit imposed a duty on arbitrators to either investigate known conflicts of interest or inform parties that they did not investigate.[7] In that case, Applied Industrial Materials Corp. (AIMCOR) commenced an arbitration against Ovalar Makine Ticaret Ve Sanayi, A.S. (Ovalar) under the FAA[8] alleging breach of a contract to deliver petroleum coke, a chemical created during oil refinery.

The parties selected Charles Fabrikant, president and CEO of Seacor Holdings, to serve as the chair of the arbitral tribunal. Before the hearings started, in September 2003, AIMCOR disclosed that it would be sold to Oxbow Industries and noted that the transaction might be "relevant to the disclosure issue." After receiving notice of this transaction, Fabrikant submitted a statement to the parties that he "ha[d] no personal or business relationship with any of the parties. . . . or their affiliates" and "reserve[d] the right to amend or add to this disclosure should future circumstances warrant it."

On April 16, 2005, after the parties agreed to bifurcate the liability and damages phases of the arbitration, Fabrikant e-mailed the parties,

---

[5] 492 F.3d 132, 137-38 (2d Cir. 2007).

[6] 20 F.3d at 1047-48.

[7] 492 F.3d at 137-38.

[8] The FAA applies to written provisions "in any maritime transaction or a contract evidencing a transaction involving [interstate] commerce to settle by arbitration a controversy thereafter arising out of such contract or transaction." 9 U.S.C. § 2. *See also* 9 U.S.C. § 1 (defining "commerce").

stating: "Gentlemen: it came to my attention yesterday, or day before yesterday, that my St. Louis office, which runs our barge operation under the name SCF, has recently been engaged [in conversation] with Ox-bow of Palm Beach. The subject of the conversation is a contract for the carriage of petroleum coke. He further stated that he "had no knowledge of such conversations taking place prior to the past week" and did "not participate in contract negotiations or get involved in day-to-day operations of SCF."

The email continued as follows: "I would like to amend my prior disclosures. At that time I did ask if there had been contacts between my group and these parties and there were none. I do not plan to become involved in discussions between SCF and Ox-Bow, should there be further conversations between them." He also wrote: "I do not feel my ability to decide this case on the merits is impaired." No party responded to this disclosure. On Sept. 22, 2005, the arbitral tribunal ruled against Ovalar on liability, with the third arbitrator casting the deciding vote.

Two months later, after retaining new counsel and learning that SCF had been transporting petroleum coke for Oxbow since 2004 (well before the liability award), Ovalar asked Fabrikant to withdraw from the tribunal. Fabrikant refused to withdraw, explaining to Ovalar that when he first learned that SCF was negotiating with Oxbow, he told SCF's president that he "wished to know nothing about SCF's conversations, or be a party to information about our activities with Oxbow or be consulted concerning any business with them."

Thereafter, Ovalar moved to vacate the award, and AIMCOR moved to confirm it. The U.S. District Court for the Southern District of New York granted the motion to vacate and denied the motion to confirm after concluding that Fabrikant, whose vote as chair of the tribunal was dispositive, acted with evident partiality by failing to investigate the potential conflict of interest of which he became aware during the arbitration. The court also found that Fabrikant should have earlier disclosed the Oxbow-SCF relationship and that his failure to investigate SCF's negotiations with Oxbow and resulting lack of knowledge did not excuse his lack of disclosure.

The Second Circuit affirmed, concluding that although there was no evidence of actual bias, there was evident partiality under the FAA. The court began its analysis by reaffirming its holding in *Morelite Construction Corp. v. New York City District Council Carpenter Benefit*

Funds.[9] Finding the "appearance of bias" standard to be "too low" and the "proof of actual bias" standard "too high," it held in *Morelite* that evident partiality will be found "where a reasonable person would have to conclude that an arbitrator was partial to one party to the arbitration."[10]

While acknowledging its commitment to "reasonable person" standard, the court observed that *Morelite* was not a disclosure case. Now faced with a disclosure issue, the court articulated a new "investigate or disclose" standard:

> [A]rbitrators must take steps to ensure that the parties are not misled into believing that no nontrivial conflict exists. It therefore follows that where an arbitrator has reason to believe that a nontrivial conflict of interest might exist, he must (1) investigate the conflict (which may reveal information that must be disclosed under Commonwealth Coatings) or (2) disclose his reasons for believing that there might be a conflict and his intention not to investigate.[11]

A. No Freestanding Duty to Investigate

The court emphasized that it was not creating a "freestanding duty to investigate." But it said that there is a duty to investigate "when an arbitrator *knows* of a potential conflict." In that situation, the court said, "a failure to either investigate or disclose an intention not to investigate is indicative of evident partiality."

Applying this principle, the court concluded that Fabrikant knew, at a minimum, that there was a potential conflict and, whatever he believed about its likelihood of influencing his decision, he was obligated to investigate the potential conflict and disclose its details. The court also found that because Fabrikant reserved the right to update his disclosure, he effectively "assured the parties" that he would update his disclosure when the need arose.

B. Second Circuit Decisions after Applied Industrial Materials

Since *Applied Industrial Materials* was decided, the Second Circuit revisited its "investigate or disclose" standard in *Scandinavian*

[9] 748 F.2d 79 (2d Cir. 1984).

[10] The court went on to hold that a father-son relationship between an arbitrator and an officer of one party to the arbitration rose to the level of evident partiality.

[11] *Applied Indus. Materials Corp.*, 492 F.3d at 137-38.

Reinsurance Co. Ltd. v. Paul Fire & Marine Insurance Co.[12] In *Scandinavian Reinsurance*, a reinsurance company successfully petitioned the U.S District Court for the Southern District of New York to vacate an award after discovering that two members of the arbitral panel were simultaneously serving as arbitrators in another, similar arbitration called Platinum.[13] Disagreeing with the lower court, the Second Circuit ruled that overlapping service does not necessarily indicate evident partiality.[14]

Writing for the Second Circuit's panel, Judge Sack clarified *Applied Industrial Materials* in two ways. First, he noted that the duty to investigate or disclose applies in circumstances where an "arbitrator thinks a nontrivial conflict may exist, *but is not sure*."[15] Although the court did not elaborate on the italicized phrase, the language suggests that the duty is enforced when an arbitrator has at least *notice* of a potential, nontrivial conflict. Second, Judge Sack modified the "reasonable person" test for nondisclosure: "[A]n arbitrator [who] fails to disclose a relationship or interest *that is strongly suggestive of bias* in favor of one of the parties" is evidently partial.[16] By framing nondisclosure in terms of bias, the court sent mixed signals. Does a potential conflict have to be "strongly suggestive of bias" before an arbitrator needs to investigate it? Was the court trying to define "nontrivial" conflicts? Although the court did not answer these questions, it did hold that "where an undisclosed matter is not suggestive of bias, vacatur . . . cannot be warranted under an evident-partiality theory."[17]

The court concluded that the arbitrators were not evidently partial for failing to disclose their service in the Platinum arbitration. Moreover, because they had actual knowledge of their previous involvement, the court did not need to "address any potential duty to investigate."[18]

---

[12] 668 F.3d 60, 72 (2d Cir. 2012).

[13] *Id.* at 63. Both arbitrations "overlapped in time, shared similar issues, involved related parties, [and] included . . . a common witness." *Scandinavian Reins. Co. v. St. Paul Fire & Marine Ins. Co.*, 732 F.Supp.2d 293, 307–08 (S.D.N.Y. 2010).

[14] *Scandinavian Reinsurance Co.*, 668 F.3d at 64.

[15] *See id.* at 73, n.17 (emphasis added).

[16] *Id.* at 72, 73 ("The evident-partiality standard is, at its core, directed to the question of bias . . . [It] was "[not] the purpose of Congress to authorize litigants to submit their cases and controversies" to arbitrators who are "biased against one litigant and favorable to another.") (citations omitted) (emphasis added).

[17] *Scandinavian Reinsurance Co.*, 668 F.3d at 73 (citations omitted).

[18] *Id.* at 74 n.19.

III. The Ninth Circuit's Standard: Qualified Duty to Investigate and Disclose

The Ninth Circuit has also cautiously embraced an affirmative duty to investigate potential conflicts in addition to its duty to disclose. In *Schmitz v. Zilveti*, an arbitrator, Conrad, failed to discover that his law firm previously represented the appellee's parent company, Prudential Insurance Co., in at least nineteen matters.[19] The appellees filed a dispute before the National Association of Securities Dealers ("NASD") alleging that the arbitrator was evidently partial. Under NASD's procedural rules, each arbitrator is required to disclose potential conflicts of interest, including financial interests and personal relationships to the parties.[20]

The district court refused to vacate the award, concluding that the arbitrator only had to disclose *known* conflicts.[21] On appeal, the Ninth Circuit disagreed, ruling that Conrad had a duty under the NASD Code to investigate his law firm's representation of Prudential Insurance. Arbitrators, the court held, have a duty under the NASD Code to investigate conflicts that is separate from, and in addition to, its *Commonwealth* duty to disclose.[22] If an arbitrator's failure to investigate or disclose creates a reasonable impression of partiality, then an award should be vacated.

Determining *when* an arbitrator evinces a "reasonable impression of partiality," however, is unclear. The court only gave one example: if an arbitrator has constructive knowledge of a conflict and an actual conflict exists, then a "reasonable impression of partiality can form."[23] *Schmitz* did not define "constructive knowledge," but the court observed that an arbitrator's suspicion (or notice) of a potential conflict can "create a

---

[19] *Schmitz*, 20 F.3d at 1044.

[20] *See* NATIONAL ASSOCIATION OF SECURITIES DEALERS, CODE OF ARBITRATION PROCEDURE, § 23(a).

[21] *Schmitz*, 20 F.3d at 1044.

[22] *Schmitz*, 20 F.3d at 1049 ("If the parties are to be judges of the arbitrators' partiality, duties to investigate and disclose conflicts must be enforced . . . ."). *Schmitz*'s duty to investigate is based both on (1) a party's expectation that an arbitrator will investigate conflicts and (2) the NASD's Code, which "require[s] arbitrators to make a reasonable effort to inform themselves of any existing or past financial, business, [or] professional . . . relationships that are likely to affect impartiality or might reasonably create an appearance of partiality or bias." *See id.* at 1049.

[23] *See Schmitz*, 20 F.3d at 1048.

reasonable impression of partiality if not investigated and disclosed."[24] This standard is similar to *Scandinavian Reinsurance* because, under either standard, arbitrators who have less than actual knowledge of a conflict owe a duty to investigate.

A. Ninth Circuit Decisions after Schmitz

Although *Schmitz*' precedential value is somewhat limited because it involved an arbitration conducted before the NASD that was subject to the NASD Code,[25] recent Ninth Circuit opinions suggest a similar relatively expansive duty to investigate. In *New Regency Productions, Inc. v. Nippon Herald Films*, the court held that any tribunal's procedures might trigger a duty to investigate as long as they require arbitrators to "make reasonable efforts to inform themselves of potential conflicts."[26] Going further, the court appeared to endorse a generalized duty to investigate, regardless of tribunal rules.[27]

In *New Regency Productions*, an arbitrator, William Immerman, failed to disclose that, during the arbitration, he accepted a job at a company that was negotiating a film project with one of the party's employees.[28] The arbitration was conducted before the American Film Marketing Association ("AFMA"). The court concluded that Immerman had a duty to investigate potential conflicts for two reasons: (1) the parties would have expected him to conduct a conflicts check when he accepted a high-level job at another company,[29] and (2) the AFMA's procedural rules require arbitrators to investigate conflicts[30]. In doing so, the court appeared essentially to impose a generalized duty to investigate. First, the court's reliance on any other reason to justify imposing an investigatory

---

[24] *Id.* at 1048. ("Also, an arbitrator may not know facts of which he may have been suspicious or of which he was on notice which, if true, would create a reasonable impression of partiality if not investigated and disclosed.").

[25] *See, e.g.*, *ANR Coal Co. v. Cogentrix of N. Carolina, Inc.*, 173 F.3d 493, 500 n.4 (4th Cir. 1999) (stating, in dicta, that *Schmitz* was decided "in the context of an arbitration conducted under [NASD] . . . which require[s] an arbitrator [to investigate]."); *Al–Harbi v. Citibank, N.A.*, 85 F.3d 680, 682 (D.C. Cir. 1996) (finding "no source for any such generalized duty").

[26] *New Regency Prods., Inc. v. Nippon Herald Films, Inc.*, 501 F.3d 1101, 1107-08 (9th Cir. 2007).

[27] *Id.* at 1111.

[28] *Id.* at 1103-04.

[29] *Id.* at 1009.

[30] *Id.*

requirement suggests that tribunal rules are not the only motivation.[31] Second, parties' expectations are an unwise rationale if the court was trying to narrow its duty to investigate.[32] Parties would likely always expect arbitrators to conduct a conflicts check and to disclose any connection to the parties.

Finally, the AFMA's procedural rules do not require arbitrators to investigate conflicts. The court cited Section 6.5, which provides that:

> A prospective *arbitrator shall disclose* to the Arbitral Agent and the parties in connection with such arbitrator's possible appointment as arbitrator *any circumstances likely to give rise to justifiable doubt* as to the arbitrator's impartiality or independence as to the parties or the matter in dispute in accordance with the procedural law of the jurisdiction of the place of the arbitration, or, if none is specified, then the laws of the State of California.[33]

Nothing in the provision states that arbitrators must *investigate* conflicts. If anything, it suggests that knowledge of a "circumstance" is required. Realizing that the language did not support a duty to investigate, the court proceeded referenced several additional guidelines, including the California Code of Civil Procedure ("CCCP")[34] and the American Bar Association's *Code of Ethics for Arbitrators in Commercial Disputes* ("AAA Code").[35] Only the latter requires arbitrators to "make a reasonable effort to inform themselves of any interests or relationships" subject to disclosure. By drawing on the AAA Code rather than the tribunal's AFMA Code, the court in *New Regency Productions* appears to have wanted to create a generalized duty to investigate while still conforming to *Schmitz*. Now, any court in the Ninth Circuit can invoke the AAA Code in deciding if an arbitrator owes a duty to investigate, regardless of the tribunal's rules.

---

31 *See id.* at 1108 (stating that *Schmitz* did not impose duty to investigate in *all* cases).

32 *Schmitz* also stated a similar proposition in justifying its "investigate or disclose" standard.

33 AMERICAN FILM MARKETING ASSOCIATION, RULES FOR INTERNATIONAL ARBITRATION § 6.5 (2002)(emphasis added).

34 CCCP requires arbitrators to "make a disclosure to the parties of any information which might cause their impartiality to be questioned."

35 AMERICAN ARBITRATION ASSOCIATION, CODE OF ETHICS FOR ARBITRATORS IN COMMERCIAL DISPUTES [AAA CODE] (2013).

IV. AAA Guidelines: When in Doubt, Disclose

Beyond the federal courts' decisions, a tribunal's arbitration rules are also important for determining obligations to disclose or investigate conflicts. As referenced in *New Regency Productions*, one popular framework is the AAA Code.[36] Although voluntary and non-binding, the Code recommends that arbitrators disclose interests or relationships that may affect their impartiality or even "*create* an appearance of partiality."[37] The duty is a continuing obligation throughout an arbitrator's service. More specifically, Cannon II(A) states that arbitrators shall disclose to the AAA the following:

> (1) any known direct or indirect financial or personal interest in the outcome of the arbitration;
> (2) any known existing or past financial, business, professional or personal relationships which might reasonably affect impartiality . . . in the eyes of any of the parties . . .[38]
> (3) the nature and extent of any prior knowledge they may have of the dispute; and
> (4) any other matters, relationships, or interests which they are obligated to disclose by the agreement of the parties, the rules or practices of an institution, or applicable law regulating arbitrator disclosure.[39]

Rule 17 of the AAA's *Commercial Arbitration Rules and Mediation Procedures* also states that: "[arbitrators] shall disclose to the AAA any circumstance likely to give rise to justifiable doubt as to the arbitrator's impartiality . . . including any bias or any financial or person interest in the result of the arbitration or any past or present relationship with the parties of their representatives."

AAA's disclosure requirements reflect a desire for arbitrators to take their responsibility as a neutral party seriously. If arbitrators have any doubt about a known conflict, they should disclose it.[40] Canon II(B) of the Code further requires that arbitrators make "a reasonable effort to

---

[36] *See id.*

[37] *See* AAA CODE, Canon II (emphasis added).

[38] Examples include relationships with co-arbitrators, parties, parties' lawyers, parties' companies, and witnesses.

[39] *See* AAA CODE, Canon II(A).

[40] *See id.* at Canon II(D).

inform themselves of any interests or relationships."[41] From a practical standpoint, arbitrators should treat Canon II(B) as an affirmative duty to investigate and should conduct (and update) conflicts checks to ensure adequate disclosures are made.

V. Conclusion

Claims of failure to investigate and disclose can provide a fresh opportunity for post-arbitration gamesmanship and could increase the number of attempts to vacate arbitration awards if arbitrators are not diligent in their disclosures. Best practices support performing a reasonable investigation in connection with disclosure. In any jurisdiction, arbitrators would be wise to follow the AAA Code, Canon II(B), which can serve as a helpful framework in instances where a federal circuit's standard is unclear.

[41] *See id.* at Canon II(B).

CHAPTER 37

DELAYING TACTICS IN ARBITRATION

*Alain Frécon**

I. Introduction

No one likes it when a party uses delaying tactics to stall the normal course of an arbitration, whether it is an *ad hoc* (*i.e.*, self-administered) or an administered proceeding.[1] It is generally assumed that the respondent is the most likely party to seek to delay the arbitration, arguably because it would benefit from a postponement of the outcome. However, experience teaches that this is not the exclusive privilege of respondents. Claimants have reasons of their own to instigate delay. Since arbitration is a voluntary process created by the parties for their own benefit, there is little doubt that one or both parties can exert enough control over the process to slow it down. A party may have a variety of reasons for doing so.

Fortunately, delaying tactics are rarely abused to the point of totally defeating the arbitration process. There are several reasons for this. First, parties generally do not want to increase the costs of arbitration. Second, their attorneys know that lengthy delays may cause confusion and prevent the arbitrator from focusing on the crucial issues and facts of the case. Third, arbitrators have the power to minimize delay through effective

* Alain Frécon has more than 30 years of experience with commercial and corporate transactions and international litigation. A member of the Minnesota State Bar and a qualified neutral under Rule 114, Minnesota General Rules of Practice, he has been serving as an arbitrator since 1976. He serves on the American Arbitration Association training faculty and is a mediator and arbitrator on the AAA panel for commercial, international and large, complex cases. He also serves on the panel of CPR and the ICC. He can be reached at Alain@freconlaw.com and at 612-338-6868. This article was prepared for a presentation on delaying tactics at the AAA Neutrals Conference held in San Antonio, Texas.

[1] In administered arbitration, an ADR provider acts as an intermediary between the parties and the arbitrator. The administering organization usually has promulgated arbitration rules under which the arbitration takes place.

management.[2] Well-trained, experienced arbitrators are more likely to have the skills necessary to curb a party's inclination to delay the process.

This chapter examines purposeful delaying tactics and when they are used. Then it addresses what arbitrators can do to minimize or eliminate these delays.

II. What Is a Delaying Tactic?

A delaying tactic[3] is any reason or excuse given to intentionally delay an arbitration from proceeding. The usual purpose of delaying tactics is to postpone the discussion of a particular topic or the resolution of a particular issue or to confuse the arbitrator about the merits of the case. Because delaying tactics are contrary to one of the goals of arbitration (an expeditious resolution of the case),[4] they tend to be perceived negatively. By lengthening the process, they increase costs and expenses and often antagonize the adversary. When delaying tactics are used, there is usually little doubt of their happening. Most of the time, a party who seeks a delay will file an unnecessary motion raising one or more legal or procedural issues, or fail to comply with a deadline. Either the arbitrator or a court, as the case may be, must rule on the motion or address the noncompliance before the process can continue.

Often, delaying tactics are triggered after a sudden event, such as an abruptly cancelled meeting, or the unexpected raising of a legal or procedural issue. For purposes of this article, the discussion of delaying tactics is divided into three broad categories: jurisdictional challenges, discovery-related motions, and other procedural challenges.

A. Jurisdictional Challenges

Jurisdictional challenges usually focus on one or more of the following: (1) the substantive law applicable to the dispute, (2) the law

---

[2] For a thoughtful article on management of the international case, *see* John Fellas, *A Fair and Efficient International Arbitration Process*, 59 (1) DISP. RESOL. J. 78 (Feb. April 2004).

[3] The term "tactic" is used to mean the knowledge or science of maneuvering. I do not mean to imply any pejorative connotation (such as connivance or artifice), even if the user of a delaying tactic was motivated by a desire to deceive.

[4] Tactics to delay the proceedings are not specifically addressed in arbitration rules, statutes and treaties, and they are rarely discussed in the arbitration literature. Commercial arbitration rules focus on procedures and efficient management of the process.

governing the arbitration procedure, (3) the arbitration rules of the administering organization,[5] (4) whether the arbitration clause covers this dispute and the parties, or (5) whether the contract containing the arbitration clause is valid. In all cases, it is important to distinguish legitimate legal challenges from delaying tactics. In the great majority of cases, delaying tactics are hidden behind what could be viewed, at first glance, as a legitimate challenge. A party who seeks a delay will usually see an ambiguity where there is none, file unnecessary motions, and generally be obstructive to the normal development of the arbitration. A legitimate jurisdictional challenge, such as to a truly ambiguous or pathological[6] arbitration clause, will trigger a lengthy delay, but that is not the purpose of the challenge.

Under the Commercial Arbitration Rules of the American Arbitration Association,[7] as well as those of other well-established ADR institutions, arbitrators have the authority to deal with these issues. If they decide these challenges promptly, all the while maintaining control over the arbitration process, delay can be minimized. However, a procedural challenge filed in court before the arbitrator is selected will probably cause a lengthy delay because of the time it takes to conduct court proceedings and because the challenger, if unsuccessful, could file an appeal with a higher court.

B. Discovery Challenges

Delaying tactics during discovery are quite common. Parties frequently claim that they are unable to schedule a site visit, or have a problem complying with the other side's discovery requests. For example, parties often fail to produce requested documents, or claim that the documents sought are missing or unavailable. They also may claim that certain witnesses are unavailable for extended periods of time.

---

[5] In *ad hoc* arbitration, the arbitrator takes care of administrative matters. In administered arbitration, the institution chosen by the parties handles such matters.

[6] The term was coined by Frederick Eisemann, a former Secretary General of the International Court of Arbitration of the ICC. A good example of a pathological clause states as follows: "In case of dispute, the parties agree to submit to arbitration, but in case of litigation, the Tribunal de la Seine shall have exclusive jurisdiction." This clause was cited in John Fellas, *supra* n. 2. For a concise, up-to-date review of recent decisions on the subject *see* John Fellas, *The Scope of Judicial Review of Arbitration Awards*, 230 (92) N.Y. LAW J. (November 7, 2003).

[7] *See* AAA commercial rules, R-8.

Discovery is one area in which arbitrators clearly have the authority and the duty to manage the arbitration so as to achieve efficiency.[8] In all instances, it is important for the arbitrator to pro-actively monitor the parties' progress in advancing the discovery process. Failing to do so often leads to last minute surprises. There are several management tools arbitrators can use to curb the inclination to delay discovery. For example, they can require the parties to demonstrate "good cause" for a postponement or a change in a response date. They can encourage the attorneys to bring all matters that could cause delay to the arbitrator's attention. Perhaps the most onerous action an arbitrator can take when a party persistently fails to comply with a discovery request is to draw a negative inference from that conduct. Thus, if a party failed to produce a document that would have contradicted the other party's position that performance was due by July 1, the arbitrator could infer, in reaching a decision on the merits, that the parties had agreed to a July 1 performance date. Typically, it suffices for an arbitrator to warn the parties of the consequences of dilatory tactics.

To encourage compliance, arbitrators can tactfully emphasize the importance of a particular discovery request and encourage the parties to voluntarily cooperate. Under most circumstances, this will bring about greater cooperation, at least for a time.

Under the AAA commercial rules, arbitrators are given express authority to deny the admission of cumulative or repetitive evidence, and to bifurcate proceedings, if appropriate for efficient management.[9] However, the goal of efficiency can collide with due process.[10] Arbitrators need not accord the same level of due process as is available in court. Had the parties wanted the full protection of judicial due process, they should not have agreed to arbitration. Due process in the context of arbitration arguably has a lower standard of protection—one that is satisfied by a fair procedure, equal treatment of the parties, and the opportunity for the parties to present their case.[11]

---

[8] *See id.*, R-32 (b). *See also* CPR Rule 9.2.

[9] AAA commercial rules,R-30(b), R-31(b), (c).

[10] The essential elements of "due process of law" are the right to notice and an opportunity to be heard and to defend oneself in orderly proceedings adapted to the nature of the case. The guarantee of due process requires that every person has a "day in court" and the benefit of "general law." *See* BLACK'S LAW DICTIONARY (revised 4th ed., 1968) (quoting *Dimke v. Finke*, 295 N.W. 75, 79 (Minn. 1940).

[11] Thus, a blunt refusal to hear, or denial of a request to discover, relevant documents could be enough to have the award set aside later on. *See* Rowe Entertainment v. William Morris Agency, 205 F.R.D. 421 (S.D.N.Y. 2002), *and* Zubulake v. USB Warburg, LLC,

When a party fails to comply with an allegedly abusive discovery request, the arbitrator must carefully balance the need for efficiency against the requesting party's need to obtain relevant information. Requests that are broadly worded "fishing expeditions"[12] probably can be denied without raising due process issues. A prudent approach that should satisfy the requirements of due process would have the arbitrator probe the relevance of each request by asking such questions as, "Why do you need these documents?" or "What is the relevance of that evidence?" These types of questions could help narrow the scope of the requests.

To deter a party from claiming that it was not afforded a full opportunity to present its case, arbitrators should explain all of their rulings to the parties. A party will rarely challenge an adverse ruling if the panel's reasons are clearly stated and not in total disregard of the law.

Some discovery requests are extremely burdensome, particularly those seeking numerous electronic files. The reason is that responding to such requests is a time consuming, costly and technologically complex project.[13] For this reason, arbitrators should not hesitate to question the relevance of such requests, taking into consideration the facts at issue and the size of each request.

For example, in a recent arbitration, the claimant asked the respondent (a Fortune 100 company with over 200 distributors worldwide) to produce "all internal e-mails and electronic data" pertaining to the product distributed under the contract. The claimant argued that the respondent had long planned to terminate the contract because it was restructuring its distribution network and wanted to grant that particular contract to another (presumably larger) distributor in a different country. The respondent claimed the production request was onerous and expensive. After a telephone conference with the arbitrator, the parties were able to agree to a more reasonable and focused discovery request at the claimant's expense.

Parties sometimes file mundane discovery motions, for example, asking for information or documents already known to them or even in

---

No. 02 Civ. 1243, 2003 WL 21087884 (S.D.N.Y. May 13, 2003) for a list of questions used by courts to determine if due process was hindered during the discovery process.

[12] Most judges despise so-called "fishing expeditions," which refer to broad and over-reaching discovery requests that may not seek the discovery of relevant information. Litigators use this tactic in the hope that "in the flow of documents produced" they will be able to find the "smoking gun," *i.e.*, the decisive document proving their case. Fishing expeditions are expensive, time-consuming and often inefficient. Therefore, they should be avoided in the context of arbitration.

[13] For an interesting article on the subject, *see* Sharon D. Nelson & John W. Simek, *Electronic Discovery*, 21 (4) GP SOLO 35 (June 2004).

their possession, solely to slow the arbitration. The parties' ingenuity in this respect is endless and arbitrators can be hard pressed to deny such motions outright. Each motion must be carefully evaluated. To prevent this type of motion practice from getting out of hand, the arbitrator can set time limits for filing motions, limit motion length, and set a short time frame for issuing a ruling.[14] To expedite rulings when there is a three-person panel, the arbitrators should first agree, and then obtain the parties' agreement, to having the chairperson decide all procedural and discovery motions without the input of the other two arbitrators.[15] However, a disgruntled party could later claim that the process was flawed because not all arbitrators were consulted on an "important" issue. Thus, the person serving as chair of the panel should be sensitive to each situation and decide which motions are important enough to be heard by the entire panel in order to avoid problems later on. If a party later complains about a decision by the chair alone, the party should be reminded of his or her agreement to that procedure.

Most institutional arbitration rules grant arbitrators fairly broad authority to decide what evidence is relevant to the case and, if relevant, whether the evidence is cumulative or repetitive, and thus should not be admitted.[16] They also give the arbitrators broad discretion as to how to conduct the proceedings. This discretion far exceeds what inexperienced arbitrators understand their authority to be and what experienced attorneys for the parties may lead them to believe. Most established arbitration rules authorize arbitrators to conduct an efficient arbitration. For example, the AAA commercial rules empower arbitrators to conduct the proceedings "with a view to expediting the resolution of the dispute" and give them discretion to "direct the order of proof, bifurcate proceedings and direct the parties to focus their presentations on issues the decision of which could dispose of all or part of the case."[17] Arbitrators should not hesitate to use the authority granted by such rules, since that is what they are retained to do.

It cannot be stressed enough that arbitrators must exercise their good judgment and not base their decisions on the fear of being reversed by a court. Many arbitrators make the mistake of liberally granting motions that an experienced arbitrator would deny with a reasoned explanation.

[14] *See* CPR Rule 9.2.

[15] *See* ICDR (AAA) International Arbitration Rules, art. 26.2; CPR Rule 9.1.

[16] *See* AAA Rules, R-32 (b); CPR Rule 9-3 (a).

[17] *See* AAA commercial rules, R-32; CPR Rule 9.2, 9.3(a), 12.1 & 12.4; UNCITRAL Rules, arts. 24 & 25.

Some arbitrators also fail to cut short unduly long examinations of witnesses whose testimony is largely repetitive, for fear that this could lead to the award being vacated. Instead, they could simply suggest that the party's counsel shorten the examination to avoid repetitive testimony.

When both parties engage in delaying behavior during the discovery phase, such as by postponing schedules and preparing extensive discovery requests, arbitrators can be rendered powerless to expedite the process. Institutional arbitration rules recognize the fact that the process belongs to the parties and suggest that the arbitrator should concur with the parties' requests for postponements in such circumstances.[18] Tactful pressures on both parties are the only recourse to minimize delays.

C. Other Delaying Tactics

Perceived procedural irregularities arising in connection with the selection of the arbitrator often are the basis for delaying tactics in arbitration. For example, a party may challenge an arbitrator for failing to disclose something that could raise questions about the arbitrator's impartiality. When these challenges are unsuccessful, as they usually are, the decisions are frequently appealed, giving rise to a steady flow of court decisions. Thus, arbitrators should take these challenges very seriously.[19]

Any challenge to the independence of an arbitrator needs to be dealt with swiftly. In *ad hoc* arbitration, the responsibility for hearing the claim falls to the very arbitrator whose independence is being challenged. In administered arbitration, the organization administering the proceeding typically will determine whether the challenge has validity.

Arbitrators are not judges and they must subrogate their personal views and perceptions to the greater integrity of the arbitration process. They must resign whenever a challenge to their impartiality or independence establishes cause at the level stated by the applicable rules.

Parties sometimes want their counsel to claim unfair treatment, bias or partiality in order to intimidate the arbitrator.[20] An arbitrator must promptly dispel unfounded complaints of unfairness, such as the claim that one side's requests are always denied while the other side's requests are always granted. One approach is to inform the parties that intimidation by

---

[18] *E.g.*, AAA commercial rules, R-30.

[19] *See* recent case law cited in *Arbitrator Update*, at 41-48 (AAA Department of Curriculum Development, 2004).

[20] Arbitrators should promptly respond to such accusations and demonstrate for the record that they are unfounded (assuming they are).

accusations of partiality will not work, and urge the parties to focus on the orderly presentation of their case.

From time to time, a party might refuse to make timely payments of the arbitrator's compensation or the arbitral organization's fee as a way of delaying the process. When an administered arbitration case is not "fully funded" (that is, one or more parties have defaulted in paying a required fee), the arbitral rules usually leave it to the discretion of the arbitrators to continue the proceedings or to put the case in "abeyance."[21] This unfairly fulfills the goal of the party seeking the delay. In *ad hoc* arbitration, putting a case in abeyance for nonpayment of the arbitrator's compensation creates a delicate ethical issue, since the arbitrator knows the identity of the defaulting party. In administered arbitration, arbitrators are admonished never to discuss compensation issues directly with the parties; the administering institution performs that role, thereby preserving the arbitrator's neutrality. But in *ad hoc* arbitration, there is no one to discuss compensation with the parties in place of the arbitrator. That said, I believe that arbitrators should not hesitate to put a case in abeyance if there is good reason to believe that they will not be compensated for their services. However, if the case is small and does not involve a lot of time, I suggest that an arbitrator consider serving pro bono before putting a case in abeyance.

Delays can be achieved by asking the arbitrator to retain an expert or requesting a site inspection. Such requests may not be intended to create delay but they do slow down the process, and increase the parties' costs and expenses.

In complex commercial or construction cases, experts can serve a useful function, clarifying or explaining certain aspects of the case. While commercial arbitration rules are usually silent on the subject, international arbitration rules typically grant arbitrators the right to appoint an expert for the sole purpose of advising them. Thus, arbitrators should use their best judgment when assessing a request for an expert. The arbitrator must consider the complexity of the case and whether having an expert would help narrow the issues and thus help expedite resolution. In most cases, appointing an expert for the sole purpose of advising the arbitrator is wasteful and inefficient. It probably would be more helpful to the arbitrator to have the parties' retain their own experts and then have these experts testify in each other's presence. This would give the arbitrator an opportunity to clarify issues or facts, or challenge

---

[21] *See* AAA commercial rules, R-54; CPR Rule 16.5.

particular aspects of the experts' testimony. In domestic arbitration, only in very rare instances would an arbitrator retain an expert.

If a party requests a site visit, the arbitrator must determine whether such a visit is likely to reveal relevant evidence. Many arbitrators believe that a site visit is extremely helpful. They do not think that photographs or videos make good substitutes.[22] However, if the site is far away or hard to access, the time and costs of transporting everyone there should be considered. Inconvenience to the arbitrator or panel, however, is not enough to deny a legitimate request for a site visit.

If the arbitrator orders a site visit, but one party refuses to participate, the arbitrator may proceed with the inspection in the absence of that party. But first, the arbitrator must advise all parties and then make sure that a detailed written report is given to them so that the absent party has an opportunity to comment. Failure to do so could constitute a sufficient ground to vacate the award.

Sometimes a party will request a change of counsel. This is rarely done just to cause delay but it could be used for that purpose. Besides disrupting the existing schedule, the appointment of new counsel means that the arbitrator will have to give the new attorney adequate time to learn the file. Unfortunately, arbitrators are powerless in this circumstance to keep the proceeding on track.

III. Additional Factors Contributing to Delay

A. Role of the Parties' Attorneys in Causing Delay

The actions of the parties' lawyers, rather than that of the parties themselves, are probably the most frequent perceived cause of delays in arbitration. The attorneys are doing what they believe is necessary to protect their clients' strategic interest or desires. In general, a lawyer will not slow the progress of arbitration unless he or she has determined that it is in the client's best interest or received instructions from the client to do so. This is consistent with the lawyer's duty of zealous representation. But when arbitration is the chosen process for resolving a dispute, lawyers also have an ethical duty to provide their clients with a process that is more expeditious and less expensive than litigation. This means avoiding unnecessary delays.

---

[22] Michael J. Altshuler, *Seeing Is Believing: The Importance of Site Visits in Arbitrating Construction Disputes*, 58 (3) DISP. RESOL. J. 36 (Aug.-Oct. 2003).

There is little doubt that the increased role of lawyers as counsel in arbitration (along with the fact that arbitrators are frequently lawyers or former judges) has complicated and, in general, lengthened the process. Arbitrators, commentators and scholars have expressed valid concerns about the increasing legalization (dare we say "lawyer control"?) of arbitration.[23]

However, it should be admitted that some legalization of the process has been rendered necessary as a result of the increased complexity of commercial transactions and the claims they generate. Moreover, when parties spend time and money to assert their contractual rights in arbitration, they can expect to be represented by counsel of their choosing. In addition, the influence of lawyers on the arbitration process has not been altogether bad because they have brought sophistication, clarity and focus to arbitration. No doubt the deliberation process that arbitrators must undertake has been greatly facilitated by the skills of lawyers in presenting facts and arguments. Thus, it would be shortsighted to view lawyers as having only a negative impact on the process. Given their positive contribution, delaying tactics by attorneys could be viewed as an incidental consequence of a process that arbitrators can learn to manage.

B. Motivation for Delays

Sometimes, a party seeks to delay arbitration in order to make it difficult for an adversary with less economic power or access to evidence to continue the process. When one party enjoys significantly larger financial resources, or controls most of the documentary evidence in the case, it can be tempting to extend or complicate the process as much as possible, in the hope that the other side will be forced to abandon the proceedings or agree to a settlement. More often, however, there are legal or business reasons for seeking to delay arbitration. A party may wish to delay the effect that an adverse award would have on its financial records, or desire to buy more time to allow another transaction to take place. Arbitrators are unlikely to know the real reasons for a party's delaying tactics. But that does not change their mission, which is to

---

[23] *See* Thomas J. Stipanowich & Peter H. Haskell, *Commercial Arbitration at Its Best*, CPR and the ABA Section of Business Law, Section of Dispute Resolution, 2001, quoting Louis Craco as follows: "Arbitration has become a legalistic method of adjudication." *See also* Gerald F. Phillips, *Is Creeping Legalism Infecting Arbitration?*, 58 (1) DISP. RESOL. J. 37 (Feb.-April 2003).

manage a process in an efficient way, without regard to a party's hidden motives or strategic need for delay.

C. Timing of Delays

One or both parties can use delaying tactics at any time—even before the demand is made. No particular phase of the arbitration process is more or less prone to delays. Each of the four phases of arbitration can be targeted for delaying tactics. Since parties usually want to contain their legal costs, they are more likely to choose a delaying tactic that produces a delay they can control.

1. The Demand Phase

Arbitrators have no ability to control delays that are triggered before they are selected. Most early delays are not that significant. The exception is a challenge to a poorly drafted or "pathological" arbitration clause. Delays result because such clauses raise legal issues pertaining to the validity or interpretation of the arbitration clause or the enforceability of an award. That's when the entire process gets off to a bad start. Take the case of an arbitration clause that fails to state with precision the place where the arbitration will take place. In that situation, a party could seize the opportunity to challenge the place where the other party brings the arbitration. If the clause provides that "the arbitration shall take place at a location mutually agreed to by the parties," the parties, who are already at odds, may not be able to perform the simple task of selecting a locale for the arbitration.

Another cause of early delay is when a party chooses not to respond to a notice from the administering organization stating that an arbitration demand has been filed. If no answer is filed, the rules generally presume that the respondent denies all claims.[24] This avoids further delay. But if the respondent never responds or communicates with the arbitral institution, the rules allow the arbitration to proceed without the respondent's participation, but only after notice to the non-responding party. Under some arbitration rules, after 14 days[25] a respondent can ask the institution for an extension of time to answer. Usually, arbitral organizations will grant an extension not exceeding 30 days. Following a late answer, a respondent can ask for further time to "amend" its answer before the

---

[24] *See* AAA commercial rules, R-4 (b), (c); CPR Rule 3.4.

[25] In compliance with the 15 days required by AAA commercial rules, R-4 (b), (c).

appointment of the arbitrator. This avoids the need to obtain the arbitrator's consent to the amendment.

Before the arbitrator or panel is selected, a party can ask the case administrator to hold one or more "administrative conferences" to discuss a broad range of issues, including arbitrator selection. Naturally, the scheduling of a conference (which can be held via telephone) is dependent on the availability of counsel and the parties. The combination of busy schedules and unforeseeable events can delay the conference by several weeks. It is important for the arbitrator to learn of delays before his or her selection since these delays can be a sign of future delaying behavior.

In *ad hoc* arbitration, if the arbitration clause is silent as to what happens when the respondent fails to answer, the demanding party will have to seek relief in a court having jurisdiction to compel arbitration. State arbitration laws must be consulted before submitting the controversy to the determination of a state court.[26] This, combined with a possible appeal of the court's decision, may generate lengthy delays.

Other delaying tactics include filing a complaint in a court in a different jurisdiction (or filing a new arbitration demand with an arbitration organization different from the one selected for the initial case),[27] and submitting an issue unrelated to the current arbitration. A party can also intentionally file a demand for arbitration with the wrong institution. Such tactics are rarely successful from a legal perspective but they can trigger several weeks or months of delays.

The process of selecting the arbitrator can also generate delays. Since there is no voir dire procedure in arbitration in which the attorneys can question the potential arbitrators, the selection process can seem to be an uncomfortable guessing game. As a result, an attorney may legitimately delay selecting the arbitrator while trying to seek reliable information about the candidates.

Another possible reason for delay early in the process may be a party's decision to challenge an arbitrator based on his or her disclosure statement (for example if it reveals a conflict of interest, bias, lack of independence, or inadequate qualifications or experience). Such legitimate challenges can take weeks, months, or longer.

---

[26] For example, *see* MINN. STAT. ANN. §§ 572.08-572.09.

[27] This is often referred to as "piecemeal" arbitration (or litigation) and its only purpose is to delay matters, increase costs and expenses and, confuse the issues. Unjustified court actions can be sanctioned (though such sanctions are extremely rare) if determined to be frivolous. No arbitration rule provides for sanctions for this type of behavior.

For example, in a recent arbitration administered by the AAA under the International Arbitration Rules of the United Nations Commission on International Trade Law, one party challenged a party-appointed arbitrator under Article 10, questioning his impartiality and independence, since he had chaired a panel in a different arbitration between the same parties. The AAA concurred with the challenging party and a new arbitrator was appointed. Several months later, the same party questioned the impartiality and independence of the second arbitrator due to his membership in the same law firm as the first arbitrator. Months later, after numerous exchanges of letters and requests for additional disclosure, the challenging party moved to remove the second arbitrator. With the parties' approval, the AAA appointed three independent, experienced arbitrators to a "special commission" for the sole purpose of considering this challenge. By the time the commission decided the issue (it took three months to reach a decision), it was almost the one-year anniversary date of the filing of the arbitration. This demonstrates how lengthy and expensive a challenge to an arbitrator can be.

In administered cases, arbitrators have no say in the outcome of a challenge to their appointment for it is the arbitral institution that will make the decision. A party could challenge the arbitrator's appointment in court, even though the court would probably rule that it has no authority to hear the case prior to issuance of the award.[28]

2. The Preliminary Hearing Phase

Once the arbitrator has been appointed, it is time to have the preliminary hearing (that is, a conference with the parties' attorneys). At this stage, the parties' ability to seek relief in court is greatly curtailed.[29]

The preliminary hearing is a critical part of the pre-hearing process. Scholars generally agree that arbitrators should demonstrate at the first preliminary hearing their case management skills and knowledge of the applicable arbitration rules.[30] The parties entrust the arbitrators with the responsibility for deciding the merits of the case and managing the process. Accordingly, they must deliver on that trust, making sure that

---

[28] Gulf Guaranty Life Ins. Co. v. Connecticut Gen. Life Ins. Co., 304 F.3d 476 (5th Cir. 2002) (held that a district court has no authority under the FAA to remove an arbitrator prior to issuance of the award).

[29] Except in the event of gross misconduct by the arbitrator or fraud, courts typically will refuse to interfere with the arbitration process.

[30] *See* James J. Myers, *Techniques for Managing Arbitration Hearings*, 51 (1) DISP. RESOL. J. (Jan.-March 1996).

the arbitration moves forward in an efficient manner, even while the parties' attorneys test the arbitrator's mettle by trying to control the process themselves. Just because the lawyers are more knowledgeable about the case at that particular time, there is no reason to relinquish control over the proceeding to them. Thus, arbitrators should establish their authority at the first preliminary hearing, using as much diplomacy as possible. At the same time, they should ask for the cooperation of the attorneys in adhering to the schedule established by mutual agreement.

By taking control at the preliminary hearing, the arbitrator can set the tone for the process to come. Of course, the arbitrator should be courteous.[31] Professional courtesy encourages cooperation and discourages erratic behavior. Being courteous, however, should not be interpreted as being weak. Indeed, the arbitrator should, when necessary, set the boundaries of acceptable behavior. This is critical to establishing credibility and authority in the eyes of the parties' attorneys. If a party can get away with delaying tactics early on, such uncooperative behavior is likely to continue. Delaying tactics are, in a way, a signal that the arbitrator has lost some control over the process.[32]

Taking charge of the agenda at the preliminary hearing, and deciding when and how issues like the scope and timing of discovery will be addressed, signals to the parties that they are dealing with an experienced arbitrator. When the parties have chosen a three-person panel, the chairperson will be the individual in charge. But first, all of the arbitrators should agree on the process for deciding procedural motions. It is vital for the panel to give the appearance of cohesiveness. Nothing is more harmful to the arbitration process than having a divisive panel whose members are openly at odds with each other. Deadlines are frequently set at the preliminary conference. Although some deadlines may need to be extended, in order to keep the arbitration on track, at least from a psychological point of view, the arbitrator should insist on their being timely met. This way the parties and their attorneys will consider the deadlines to be firm and seek postponements only for legitimate reasons.

---

[31] Canon IV of the "Revised Code of Ethics for Arbitrators in Commercial Disputes" guides arbitrators to be "patient and courteous to the parties, their representatives, and the witnesses and should encourage similar conduct by all participants."

[32] Regular training of arbitrators cannot be overemphasized. At training sessions, arbitrators also learn about the most recent techniques and arbitration-related court cases.

3. The Hearing Phase

It is at the hearing on the merits that the arbitrator's management skills, professional experience and knowledge of the case converge. So it is important for the arbitrator to maintain control over the proceeding and encourage the parties to stick to the schedule. If, instead, the arbitrator takes a *laissez faire* attitude toward any aspect of the arbitration, a party will have no qualms about asking for a postponement, or conducting unnecessarily long examinations of unimportant witnesses, or seeking cumulative or repetitive testimony from a series of witnesses.

To avoid delays based on the unavailability of witnesses or evidence, seasoned arbitrators often ask the parties for a list of witnesses, together with the order in which they will testify on direct and cross examination and the amount of time each examination will take. They may also ask for assurances from counsel that these witnesses will be available to testify at the hearing. In the event a witness is sick or called to an emergency meeting out of town, the arbitrator should consider whether the witness is crucial to the case. If so, perhaps the examination of this witness can be rescheduled at a later date. If not, perhaps the witness can submit a written statement or be questioned in a telephone or video conference. If the witness was deposed, it may not be necessary for the witness to testify on direct. Relevant portions of the deposition could be read into evidence as direct testimony. It is not always necessary for the arbitrator to hear a witness testify to his or her educational and professional background when that information is readily available in a deposition transcript. Arbitrators can be creative in finding ways for evidence to be admitted that need not comply with judicial standards of evidence.

An arbitrator should not hesitate to limit witnesses to those who are essential to the case. The parties' attorneys can be questioned as to the need for a particular witness, the scope of the proposed examination and its purpose. If the parties have agreed to use witness statements for less important witnesses, or if deposition testimony has been admitted, counsel should be allowed to cross-examine the witness only on the subject matter of the witness statement or deposition testimony. Of course, the arbitrator must obtain the parties' agreement to these ground rules earlier in the process at one of the preliminary hearings.

In addition to a postponement request, a party may file a garden-variety motion to interrupt the direct or cross-examination of a witness. Such motions are distracting to the arbitrator and obviously cause delay. Accordingly, before deciding whether to reject or entertain such a motion, the arbitrator should question the need for it and hear the comments of opposing counsel. If the arbitrator decides to hear the motion, opposing counsel should be asked to respond as quickly as practicable. Then the arbitrator can immediately rule on the motion or postpone the decision if warranted.

Unless they are vigilant, arbitrators can be manipulated by the parties and their attorneys into postponing the hearing or delaying its conclusion. Any delay invariably has a domino effect, leading to further delays because of the problem of re-scheduling new dates for the continued hearing. Accordingly, arbitrators should avoid granting postponements and limit tactics that cause delay but they must be prudent in exercising their managerial authority. If a party has shown sufficient cause for a postponement, the request should not be denied.

4. The Award Phase

After an arbitrator has heard all the evidence, the delicate phase of deliberations and drafting the award follows. Both can be subject to delays, but less so to delaying tactics by the parties or their attorneys.

Reaching a decision in an arbitration case is time-consuming, especially in a complex case involving a panel of arbitrators. Deliberations can be delayed by an uncooperative arbitrator. For example, non-neutral, party-appointed arbitrators may not cooperate in order to cater to the interest of the party that appointed them.[33] Unfortunately, little can be done to motivate an uncooperative arbitrator. One can complain to the administering organization, if any. But the only option is for the other two arbitrators to prepare a majority decision. This prevents having to delay the release of the award.

Arbitrators have different styles of deliberating. Most need a few days to review their notes and think about the entire case before reaching a decision, or, if there is a panel, agreeing to deliberate with other members of the panel. Usually, the arbitrators are willing to spend a few hours together immediately after the hearing to share common perceptions, exchange views and questions, and share responsibilities for the decision-making process. This is probably the most efficient approach, as it allows the arbitrators to promptly discuss the case after having just heard all the evidence.

Once a case has been decided, the award must be written. Arbitrators have an obligation to provide an award within the time stated by the

[33] Clearly a violation of the arbitrator's ethical duties (*see* Canon I, B of the Revised Code of Ethics, *supra* n. 31).

applicable arbitration rules. Traditionally, domestic arbitration awards were alarmingly brief—only a sentence or two to identify the winner and state how much the winner would get.[34] This made it easy for arbitrators to comply with the time requirements for issuing the award. However, not all parties were happy with this type of award. Anecdotal information indicates that parties in domestic arbitration, influenced by the common use of reasoned awards in international arbitration,[35] are now more often requesting a written explanation of the award. The reason is probably that parties simply want to know the factual and legal basis for the decision.

Drafting a reasoned award, however, can take more time than these rules allow for.[36] When all members of the panel are lawyers, egos, linguistic styles, standing in the community, age and professional celebrity can complicate the writing process. As a result, it may take longer than anticipated to generate a draft award. However, arbitrators have an obligation to provide a prompt award, which explains why some arbitral rules, such as those of the AAA, set a time limit for issuance of the award.

If a panel has been asked to write a reasoned award, the arbitrators must determine who will write it. Each arbitrator is usually given an opportunity to write part of the award and then review the sections written by the other arbitrators.[37] This process takes time, particularly if the arbitrators are working in different time zones and have busy schedules. There is little that can be done if an arbitrator fails to hold up his or her end in drafting or reviewing the award. There is also little to prevent an arbitrator from making significant editorial changes during the review process, although the chair of the panel can try to discourage this. When there are non-neutral, party-appointed arbitrators on a panel, drafting the award can become a last ditch effort to renegotiate fine points that were either overlooked or temporarily set aside during the arbitration.

---

[34] For example: "We found for Respondent and award…. "

[35] Canadian and most Western European arbitrators traditionally render full-fledged decisions containing a detailed description of the case, facts, legal issues, evidence presented, claims of the parties and reasoning.

[36] The award-rendering process is not considered "good cause" for an extension of time, (*see* AAA Commercial Rules, R-40) although parties do agree to such extension of time in most cases.

[37] *See* the Revised Code of Ethics, *supra* n. 31, which states in Canon IV.G, that "co-arbitrators should afford each other full opportunity to participate in all aspects of the proceedings."

Delays in preparing and finalizing the award can irritate other arbitrators on the panel, since they postpone the ultimate release of the award. The administering institution may provide some help in moving the award-writing process along.

D. Delays in Implementing the Award

Once the award has been issued, the parties can delay its implementation by requesting a modification or clarification of the award,[38] or by seeking to overturn the award. Such delays do not constitute delaying tactics per se, but they are worthy of mention.

Enforcement can be delayed when the losing party refuses to pay the amount awarded or continues to engage in an activity prohibited by the award. In these instances, the party seeking enforcement will have to obtain judicial assistance before it will be able to execute the award.

The losing party can seek to vacate the award in state or federal court.[39] But this is not an easy task. Vacating an award requires the moving party to establish significant failures in the arbitration process.[40] Moreover, there is a strong policy in favor of arbitration and the finality of awards. In other words, courts will hesitate to interfere with the decision of an arbitrator.

IV. Ethics and Efficiency

Arbitrators undertake to be fair and impartial and conduct an efficient arbitration proceeding. However, efficiency cannot substitute for fairness. Thus, arbitrators may not set a "break-neck" schedule if doing so could affect any party's ability to prepare and present its case. Arbitration should not be a race towards resolution. So, while efficiency must remain a priority of the arbitrator, it should not become an obsession. Some arbitration proceedings will take more time than others,

---

[38] Usually within 20-30 days from receipt of the award. *See* AAA Commercial Rules, R-48; CPR Rule 14.5.

[39] *See* § 10 of the Federal Arbitration Act.

[40] Each state has its own law governing arbitration, which contains specific time limits during which an award can be challenged. In Minnesota, an application to vacate an award must be made within 90 days after delivery of a copy of the award, *see* §572.19(2). The only exception to that time limit is the application predicated upon fraud, corruption or other undue means, which can be filed 90 days after such grounds are known or should have been known.

whether or not the parties engage in delaying tactics. Unless a party complains to the arbitrator that the process is too slow, or that the adversary is taking an inordinate amount of time to reply or execute certain tasks, the process is probably going at a fair pace.

On the other hand, if a party complains about delays, the arbitrator should immediately determine the true nature of the delay and whether it is justified and reasonable. Arbitrators must draw on their own personal experience and judgment in reaching a conclusion, as no arbitration rule will be of assistance. When one party complains about the adversary's conduct, the arbitrator may have to question (as diplomatically as possible) the party whose conduct is the subject of the complaint. This can put the arbitrator in a somewhat confrontational position. Some arbitrators feel uncomfortable in this role and will not step in when the process slows down. Whether this is due to inexperience, a dislike of confrontation, or a fear of giving offense, arbitrators must put aside their personal preferences and fears in order to provide the parties with an efficient, fair process.

A. Conflict of Interest

Since arbitrators are usually paid on an hourly or daily basis, they stand to make more money the more protracted the discovery, the more issues raised, the more cases relied on, and the longer the briefs. This conflict of interest with the parties seems to give arbitrators an incentive not to be too efficient. Were this conflict to guide the behavior of arbitrators, it could destabilize the integrity of the arbitration process.

However, I think it can be fairly said that most arbitrators are ethical and put their financial interests aside when they accept an appointment to a case. While arbitrators are not rewarded monetarily for their efficiency, they are rewarded with a reputation for efficiency. This makes them attractive candidates for appointment in other cases. Most arbitrators know this.

Of course, not all arbitrators are angels. One unethical arbitrator can taint the process. This is why it is so important for arbitral organizations to closely monitor arbitrators' billing practices and be outspoken about eliminating abuses. (The ICC has eliminated the problem by providing that arbitrators will receive compensation that is proportional to the size of the amount in dispute).[41] Arbitrators also should be self-policing on the issue of compensation and oppose clear cases of abuse. Most

[41] *See* ICC article 30.2 & app. III, art. 4.

arbitrators are willing to discuss these matters openly with their colleagues and make sure that they avoid even a shadow of impropriety.

The parties also need to recognize how their conduct reflects in the arbitrator's bill. If the parties cite extensive case law and other authorities in lengthy briefs, it will be partly their fault that the arbitrator's bill is high. Arbitrators should question the necessity for extensive citation of cases and reach an agreement with the parties about this at a preliminary hearing, well before the briefs are submitted.

Now that arbitration is so well accepted, we have "celebrity" arbitrators who have very busy professional calendars. It is no secret that some parties seek high-profile arbitrators, especially parties interested in delaying the ultimate resolution of the dispute. Even when the arbitrators are not celebrities, it is still difficult for arbitrators and the parties to find the time when everyone will be able to attend a single conference, let alone a block of hearing days.

When accepting cases, arbitrators, no matter how renowned, should never forget that they have an obligation to be available to serve.[42] The fact that arbitration is informal does not mean that it has to be out of control. I submit that an arbitrator who accepts a case should be reasonably confident that other professional commitments will not significantly interfere with the case just accepted. True, some schedule conflicts are unavoidable. But when the chairperson of an arbitral panel regularly experiences calendar conflicts, the other arbitrators should question the chair's ability to serve in that capacity and seek the assistance of the administering organization, in coordination with counsel.

V. Conclusion

A motivated and well-funded party may cause significant delays and even derail the arbitration process if the other party cannot afford the added expense. Because parties have the ability to fashion an arbitration clause best suited to their circumstances, it is advisable that they consider all these issues and adopt an ADR policy before they start negotiating their arbitration clause. Every effort they make toward simplifying the discovery process and establishing deadlines for the completion of the various phases of the arbitration process, including provisions regarding

---

[42] Canon X of the Revised Code of Ethics, *supra* n. 31.

challenges to the award and its later enforcement, will go a long way towards impeding the use of delaying tactics. To preserve the integrity and efficiency of the arbitration process, delaying tactics must be identified, carefully evaluated, limited and eliminated whenever possible.

Thus, arbitrators need to question the legitimacy of requests that would delay arbitration (without questioning the requester's good faith) and they should not hesitate to ask probing questions. Their task is to find a workable alternative that would avoid or limit the potential delay. Arbitrators need to learn how to be "diplomatically forceful" when necessary.

CHAPTER 38

WHO IS RESPONSIBLE FOR ETHICAL BEHAVIOR BY COUNSEL IN ARBITRATION?

*Steven C. Bennett**

I. Introduction

Arbitration is a significant (and growing) part of today's system of justice, albeit a largely private one. The ethical conduct of parties and attorneys in arbitration proceedings is essential to the legitimacy of the arbitration process. Arbitrators (at least in American Arbitration Association (AAA) proceedings) must follow the Code of Ethics for Arbitrators in Commercial Disputes (AAA/ABA Code).[1] This code stresses that arbitrators, as dispensers of justice, have a responsibility to the public as well as to the parties who request assistance in the resolution of disputes.[2]

---

* Steven C. Bennett is a partner in of Park Jensen Bennett LLP in New York City and the author of ARBITRATION: ESSENTIAL CONCEPTS (2002). The views expressed are solely those of the author, and should not be attributed to the author's firm or its clients.

[1] Available at www.adr.org. The Code of Ethics for Arbitrators in Commercial Disputes was promulgated in 1977 by a joint committee of the American Bar Association (ABA) and the American Arbitration Association (AAA).

[2] There are other ethics codes for arbitrators in the labor, maritime, and international fields. *See, e.g.*, FMCS Code of Professional Responsibility for Arbitrators of Labor-Management Disputes (1972), available at www.naarb.org; the International Bar Association's Code of Ethics for International Arbitrators (1987), available at www.iba.net; Society of Maritime Arbitrators, Code of Ethics, available at 6A BENEDICT ON ADMIRALTY §7-84.3 (1991). Ethics codes, however, do not necessarily have the force of law. *See* Merit Ins. Co. v. Leatherby Ins. Co., 714 F.2d 673, 680 (7th Cir. 1983) (the Code and AAA Rules "do not have the force of law"). Several states have legislated on specific ethical matters pertaining to arbitrators. *See* Carrie Menkel-Meadow, *Ethics Issues in Arbitration and Related Dispute Resolution Processes: What's Happening and What's Not*, 56 U. MIAMI L. REV. 949, 978-79 (2002) (citing examples and noting "absolute prohibition" of receipt of gifts or honoraria by arbitrators, adopted by California in the wake of "scandal" involving arbitrators who were given a cruise as a gift after their decision on behalf of a party).

There is no similar specific code of ethics for counsel in arbitration. Attorneys are subject to relevant state codes of lawyer conduct, generally modeled on the American Bar Association's Model Rules of Professional Conduct (ABA Model Rules). The prevailing view is that these codes apply to lawyers who serve as advocates in arbitration. But enforcing these ethical obligations in arbitration is another matter.

The questions addressed in this chapter are: Who is responsible for enforcing ethical conduct by attorneys in arbitration? What are the challenges involved? This chapter suggests ways that arbitrators may encourage ethical and deter unethical conduct by parties and counsel. In addition, it suggests that arbitration-sponsoring institutions should create ethics committees whose advice arbitrators may seek when they are unsure whether they have authority to address particular unethical conduct. Finally, this chapter concludes that arbitrators must take primary responsibility for policing ethical violations that affect the fairness of proceedings. Arbitrators must take reasonable steps to deter and, when appropriate, penalize such conduct, including imposition of appropriate sanctions.

II. Is Ethical Misconduct by Counsel a Serious Problem in Arbitration?

There is no documented, empirical answer to the question of the extent of unethical conduct in arbitration. Information on the scope of unethical behavior by attorneys in arbitration is largely anecdotal. For example, one commentator, reflecting on his 25 years' experience as a securities arbitrator, quickly recalled at least a dozen examples of unprofessional conduct by counsel.[3] If every arbitrator could so easily cite such instances of misconduct, a serious problem could appear.

The same commentator suggested that ethical violations could have serious consequences for parties and tribunals and threaten public confidence in arbitration as a viable dispute resolution system. For example, such violations could "result in unnecessary motions, longer hearings, duplication of effort and wasted time." Unethical behavior, moreover, could "slow the dispute resolution process and increase the cost of arbitration."[4]

---

[3] *See* J. Pat Sadler, *One Lawyer's Proposal for a Code of Professionalism in Securities Arbitration,* 1264 PLI/CORP 67, 77 (2001).

[4] *Id.* at 78.

The reputation of arbitration as a fair process certainly would suffer if attorneys felt free to engage in unethical conduct either because the arbitration process is flexible and for the most part private, or because attorneys in arbitration rarely see the same arbitrators more than once.

Arbitrators may conclude that enforcement of ethical standards upon counsel in arbitration is not part of an arbitrator's job. Arbitrators must decide only the specific issues submitted to them for resolution. They are generally appointed through a private process, and they are often subject to a duty of confidentiality. Also, reviewing courts generally defer to arbitrators and are reluctant to inquire into the conduct of arbitration proceedings. Thus, the temptation to ignore misconduct may be great. But it is clear that at least some minimal ethical standards should apply to attorneys in arbitration.

III. Do Ethics Rules Apply to Counsel in Arbitration?

There is some authority for the proposition that lawyer ethics codes do not apply in arbitration.[5] This is not the mainstream view. It makes sense that lawyer codes of professional conduct apply in arbitration because such codes broadly address lawyer conduct in society by requiring lawyers to adhere in all their professional acts to high standards of conduct.[6]

It is also logical that these codes apply to arbitration because arbitration is a well-accepted means of resolving legal issues. Thus, courts have recognized that arbitrators are quasi-judicial figures and enjoy the same immunity from civil liability as judges.[7] Similarly, at least one federal appellate court has held that witnesses who testify in arbitration are entitled to immunity from civil liability for such testimony.[8] There is little

---

[5] However, this authority may be limited to negotiations of a labor-management agreement. *See* Dunmore Police Ass'n v. Borough of Dunmore, 528 A.2d 299, 311 (Penn. Commw. Ct. 1987). The *Dunmore* arbitration involved proceedings to set the terms of a collective bargaining agreement. The union's counsel testified as the union's only witness. The court rejected the argument that the union's lawyer violated the "lawyer as witness" proscription of the Code of Professional Responsibility. It stated: "An arbitration panel is neither a court nor an administrative agency." It went on to say that arbitration in this context "represents an extension of the collective bargaining process."

[6] Robert M. Jarvis, *Arbitration Ethics*, *in* ALTERNATE DISPUTE RESOLUTION IN FLORIDA (2d ed. The Florida Bar, 1995).

[7] *See* Am. Eagle Fire Ins. Co. v. New Jersey Ins. Co., 148 N.E. 562, 564 (N.Y. 1925) (arbitrator "acts in a quasi-judicial capacity, and should possess the judicial qualifications of fairness to both parties").

[8] Rolon v. Henneman, 517 F.3d 140 (2d Cir. 2008).

reason to consider representation in arbitration as other than the practice of law.

The ABA Model Rules make clear that lawyers have ethical obligations in connection with the provision of non-legal services, saying, for the most part, that attorneys who provide both legal and non-legal services must comply with the ethics code in both regards.[9] Thus, state ethics codes should apply to attorneys serving as advocates in arbitration even if such work is somehow not the practice of law.

Courts have recognized that lawyers who breach certain ethical obligations in arbitration can be sanctioned. In a leading case, *People v. Bergmann*, the Colorado Supreme Court disbarred a Colorado lawyer for failing to file a client's demand for arbitration, despite repeated requests from his client.[10] The court held that the deliberate neglect of a legal matter (including arbitration) violated several disciplinary rules.

The informal nature of modern arbitration proceedings could suggest that ethical obligations, such as those governing the unlicensed practice of law, should be relaxed in arbitration. But there is no logical reason to believe this to be so. Legal representation remains legal representation, whether a lawyer wears a suit or a sports jacket. Furthermore, changes in the unauthorized practice of law rules are the result, not of a belief that ethics rules have no place in arbitration, but of the huge growth in commercial and international arbitration, requiring counsel to be able to engage in multi-jurisdictional practice of law.

The unauthorized practice of law cases have often involved fee disputes in which the client claims that it need not pay its attorney for representation in arbitration because the attorney was not licensed in the jurisdiction where the arbitration took place. In *Williamson v. John D. Quinn Construction Corp.*, the court rejected such a claim, holding that representing a party in arbitration does not amount to the practice of law and thus cannot constitute the unauthorized practice of law.[11] The court noted the "informal nature" of arbitration, and that its rules of evidence and procedures differ from litigation.[12]

---

[9] *See* Model Rules, R. 2.1 (duty to consider non-legal factors in providing advice), R. 5.7 (lawyer subject to Rules in provision of non-legal services).

[10] 807 P.2d 568 (Colo. 1991).

[11] 537 F. Supp. 613, 616 (S.D.N.Y. 1982). The court cited a New York ethics opinion—Committee Report, *Labor Arbitration and the Unauthorized Practice of Law*, 30 REC. ASS'N B. CITY N.Y. (No. 5/6, May/June 1975).

[12] The *Williamson* court also noted that the arbitration "fact finding process is not equivalent to judicial fact finding." *See* Prudential Equity Group, LLC v. Ajamie, 2008

However, this rationale is not accepted by all courts. The contrary view appears in *Birbrower Montalbano, Condon & Franc v. Superior Court.*[13] The California Supreme Court held in *Birbrower* that a New York law firm committed unauthorized practice of law (and thus was entitled to no fee) when its lawyers appeared in an arbitration proceeding in California. The court held that arbitration proceedings (despite their informal nature) "are important aspects of our judicial system." In response to this case, the California legislature changed the state Code of Civil Procedure, to permit a form of *pro hac vice* admission of foreign lawyers in California arbitrations. Similarly, the NASD Code of Arbitration for investor arbitration has recently been changed to allow out-of-state attorneys to represent parties in NASD proceedings, notwithstanding state law to the contrary.

In response to the need for more flexibility in multi-jurisdictional practice, the ABA formed a commission on multi-jurisdictional practice to explore the issue. The commission concluded that an exception to the rule against unauthorized practice of law is warranted for ADR proceedings, for several reasons. First, parties might have an interest in retaining counsel with particularized knowledge of the field in dispute. Second, parties might have developed relationships with lawyers who could assist in resolving the dispute through an ADR process. Third, the commission pointed out that, in many instances, knowledge of the laws of the jurisdiction in which an ADR proceeding takes place may not be particularly important. Thus, the commission proposed a new rule allowing out-of-state attorneys to represent clients temporarily in ADR proceedings in the state without violating rules on the unauthorized practice of law.

Connecticut has adopted a variant of this rule, but it conditions permission for out-of-state attorneys to practice arbitration in the state on the attorney's home state granting "reciprocity."[14] Connecticut's attorney ethics rules broadly define the practice of law as "ministering to the legal needs of another person and applying legal principles and judgment to the circumstances or objectives of that person." Included in this definition is

---

WL 510047 at *2 (S.D.N.Y. Feb. 27, 2008) (citing *Williamson*; noting "material differences between an arbitration and a judicial proceeding, with the former being far more informal and applying much less stringent rules of evidence and procedure").

[13] 949 P.2d 1 (Cal. 1998). *See* CAL. CIV. PROC. CODE § 1282.4; *see generally*, Samuel Estreicher & Steven C. Bennett, *Is Arbitration the Unauthorized Practice of Law?*, N.Y.L.J., Jan. 6, 2005, at 3.

[14] Conn. Rules of Professional Conduct, R. 5.5(c).

"[r]epresenting any person in a court, or formal administrative adjudicative proceeding or other formal dispute resolution process or in any administrative adjudicative proceeding in which legal pleadings are filed or a record is established as the basis for judicial review." The definition only excludes "[p]articipating in labor negotiations, arbitrations, or conciliations arising under collective bargaining rights or agreements."[15] Thus, representing parties in other forms of arbitration would be considered the practice of law in Connecticut.

While arbitration developed outside of litigation, the process recently adopted many of the trappings of modern litigation procedure. This development has been criticized. But until arbitration returns to its simpler roots, counsel must be prepared to respond when conventional litigation procedures are used in arbitration. This makes the case for requiring high standards of professionalism required by lawyer ethics codes to arbitration.

One aspect of that professionalism is the duty of lawyers to be as truthful and candid in all dealings with the arbitral tribunal as they would be with a court. This duty finds support in Rule 3.3(a) of the ABA Model Rules, which establishes the duty to avoid making false statements or failing to disclose legal authority to a "tribunal in the course of advocacy. Rule 1.0(m) defines that term as denoting, in relevant part, "a court, an arbitrator in a binding arbitration proceeding or a legislative body, administrative agency or other body acting in an adjudicative capacity." Moreover, Rule 4.1(a) of the ABA Model Code requires truthfulness in statements to persons other than clients, stating: "In the course of representing a client a lawyer shall not knowingly: (a) make a false statement of material fact or law to a third person."

Other ethical duties that advocates would have in arbitration include, for example, the duty to:

- provide competent representation to a client;[16]
- abide by a client's decisions concerning the objectives of representation;[17]
- consult with the client as to the means by which the client's objectives are to be pursued;[18]
- abide by a client's decision whether to settle a matter;[19]

[15] *Id.*
[16] ABA Model Rules of Professional Conduct, R. 1.2(a).
[17] *Id.* and R. 1.4(a)(2).
[18] *Id.*, R. 1.2(a).

- act with reasonable diligence and promptness in representing a client;[20] and
- explain matters to the extent reasonably necessary to permit the client to make informed decisions regarding the representation.[21]

There are surely other obligations in lawyer ethics codes that would govern advocates in arbitration.

IV. Do Arbitrators Have the Power to Sanction Unethical Attorney Conduct?

The ideal arbitration is efficient, cost-effective and imbued with fairness. To achieve these goals, the rules of institutional arbitration providers generally give arbitrators the power to control the proceedings and to award broad forms of relief.[22] Arbitrators generally are not limited to awarding relief allowed by law; they may "base their decision upon broad principles of justice and equity."[23] Since arbitrators manage the process, it falls to them to see that the arbitration process is fair and completed efficiently.[24] It follows from this essential fact that arbitrators

---

[19] *Id.*

[20] *Id.*, R. 1.3.

[21] *Id.*, R. 1.4(b).

[22] *See, e.g.*, Marshall & Co. v. Duke, 114 F.3d 188 (11th Cir. 1997) (arbitrators had power to award "damages and other relief" under NASD rules, including an award of attorney fees), *cert. denied*, 522 U.S. 1112 (1998); Mutual Serv. Corp. v. Spaulding, 972 F. Supp. 1126 (N.D. Ill. 1997) (same).

[23] Moncharsch v. Heily & Blase, 832 P.2d 899, 904 (1994). *See* James J. Marcellino, *Mediation and Arbitration—Ethical Considerations*, 32 BOSTON B.J. 5-6 (Sept./Oct. 1988) ("Rule 3.3's rationale is that it promotes the determination of truth, which is a fundamental objective of the adversarial system. Arbitration, adversarial in nature, is also fundamentally concerned with the determination of truth. Thus, the rationale for Rule 3.3 of promoting the determination of truth is equally applicable in the arbitration context."). The Restatement (Third) of the Law Governing Lawyers similarly treats both arbitration and litigation as matters subject to the ethical obligations of appearance before a "tribunal." *See* ch. 7, intro. cmt. (2000) (chapter governing representation before a "tribunal" would apply in contested arbitration and similar trial-type proceedings).

[24] *See* Jarvis, *supra* n. 6, at § 13.48 (1995) ("arbitrators have a duty to promote ethics, at all times"). Although most arbitrators are lawyers (and many are former judges), they are not necessarily familiar with all the rules of ethics (though they should be). Of course, some conduct (for example, lying, intimidating witnesses, attempting to bribe a decision maker) is so obviously malum in se that an arbitrator does not need an ethics code to recognize it.

have the authority to address abuses and disruption of the arbitration process.[25]

There is some case authority for this conclusion. For example, in *First Preservation Capital v. Smith-Barney*, an NASD panel of arbitrators granted a request to dismiss an arbitration as a sanction for discovery abuses.[26] On review, the court confirmed the award dismissing the case. The court expressly stated that arbitrators have the authority to halt proceedings where "abhorrent behavior" appears:

> The great discretion arbitrators have over the proceedings must include the ability to halt proceedings such as this one, where plaintiff's abhorrent behavior was so clearly disruptive to the proceedings. If arbitrators are not permitted to impose the ultimate sanction of dismissal on plaintiffs who flagrantly disregard rules and procedures put in place to control discovery, arbitrators will not be able to assert the power necessary to properly adjudicate claims. . . . Allowing parties . . . to abuse the process not only serves to undermine the principles of arbitration, it will ultimately diminish the integrity of any court in which information obtained through an abuse of arbitration is used.

Other types of sanctions that arbitrators could award include an allocation of the fees and costs of the proceedings, barring the assertion of claims or defenses, drawing adverse inferences, or precluding the submission of evidence or testimony.[27] Even monetary sanctions may be awarded in some cases.[28] The Supreme Judicial Court of Massachusetts upheld an arbitration award imposing monetary sanctions as damages for violation of a discovery order.[29] The arbitration was conducted under the AAA Commercial Arbitration Rules, which authorize arbitrators to resolve disputes involving information exchanges and to award "any relief that the arbitrator deems just and equitable."

---

[25] Canon I(G) of the AAA-ABA Code states: "An arbitrator should make all reasonable efforts to prevent delaying tactics, harassment of parties or other participants, or other abuse or disruption of the arbitration process."

[26] 939 F. Supp. 1559, 1565 (S.D. Fla. 1996).

[27] *See* Michele R. Fron & Kelly M. McIntyre, *Sanctions in Arbitration*, 1264 PLI/CORP 1143, 1145, 1151 (2001) (citing sanction examples).

[28] Phillip O'Neill, *Mass. Allows Arbitrators to Award $$ Sanctions to Remedy Discovery Abuse*, 61(2) DISP. RESOL. J. 8 (May-July 2006). The Massachusetts court acknowledged that there is contrary authority.

[29] Superadio Ltd. P'ship v. Winstar Radio Prods., 844 N.E.2d 246 (Mass. 2006).

Separately, the Fifth Circuit suggested in *dicta* that arbitrators may have the power to impose sanctions even when inappropriate conduct by counsel cannot be shown to have directly affected the outcome of the dispute. In *Forsythe International, S.A. v. Gibbs Oil Co. of Texas*, the court said in a footnote: "Misconduct, even when deemed irrelevant to the merits, may nevertheless subject offenders to other sanctions. Arbitrators may, for example, devise appropriate sanctions for abuse of the arbitration process"[30]

A. Do Arbitrators Have the Power to Sanction Counsel Directly for Their Misconduct?

Counsels' participation in arbitration on behalf of parties who are within the jurisdiction of the arbitral tribunal arguably constitutes consent of counsel (who are non-parties to the arbitration agreement) to be bound by the results of the arbitration.[31] In *Polin v. Kellwood Co.*, for example, the court confirmed an award that included sanctions against the claimant's counsel (half the cost of the arbitration, excluding attorney's fees).[32]

But there is contrary authority. In *Chem Asia 2000 Pte. Ltd. v. Oceana Petrochemical AG*, the court held that an arbitrator could impose sanctions on a party, but not on a party's attorney.[33] The court distinguished *Polin*, noting that it involved an NASD arbitration clause authorizing broad relief, including any relief "that would have been available to the parties had the matter been heard in court." But *Chem Asia* was a post-dispute submission to arbitration and the submission in that case permitted the arbitrator to award "any remedy or relief that the arbitrator deems just and equitable and within the scope of the agreement of the parties." The court found it significant that the submission agreement made no reference to the imposition of sanctions, or application of the Federal Rules of Civil Procedure (which do authorize sanctions on counsel in some circumstances). Absent an agreement on broad relief, the court questioned whether an arbitrator had inherent authority to award sanctions. The conflict between *Polin* and *Chem Asia* suggests that the arbitrator's ability

[30] 915 F.2d 1017, 1023 n. 8 (5th Cir. 1990) ("Arbitrators may, for example, devise appropriate sanctions for abuse of the arbitration process.") (*citing* Bigge Crane & Rigging Co. v. Docutel Corp., 371 F. Supp. 240, 246 (E.D.N.Y. 1973)).

[31] *See generally* Fredrick E. Sherman & Steven C. Bennett, *Binding Nonsignatories to Arbitrate: The Limits of the Federal Arbitration Act*, COM. L. ADVISOR 10 (1996).

[32] 103 F. Supp.2d 238 (S.D.N.Y. 2000). But *Polin* did not involve a pre-dispute arbitration agreement. The parties agreed to arbitrate after litigation had been commenced.

[33] 373 F.Supp.2d 340, 356-57 (S.D.N.Y. 2005).

to impose sanctions on counsel may depend on the terms of the arbitration agreement.

Fortunately, there are other tools arbitrators may use to deter unethical conduct by counsel. For example, in lieu of sanctions at the end of the process, arbitrators could bring up the issue of attorney ethics at an early preliminary conference and then ask counsel whether they will agree to be subject to sanctions if they behave unethically during the arbitration.[34]

Alternatively, on the authority of *Polin* and *Chem Asia*, arbitrators could announce, at the preliminary conference, or later in the event of misconduct by counsel, that they will hold the parties responsible for the misconduct of their counsel. Arbitrators also could make clear that unethical behavior will be viewed with skepticism (an indication, perhaps, that a party does not believe it has a credible position, sufficient to sustain without trickery).

B. Possible Objections to Arbitrators Sanctioning Attorney Misconduct

The scarce authority for arbitrator sanctioning of unethical conduct by counsel suggests, quite rightly, that there could be serious objections to arbitrator involvement in this area. One possible objection is the inability of counsel to obtain timely court review of an order sanctioning counsel. In general, review can be had only after the award is issued, for example for "corruption" of the process.[35] The distant threat of vacatur may have a less deterrent effect than other sanctions.[36]

---

[34] A standard form sanctions agreement could be drafted by the major arbitration-sponsoring organizations and bar associations. To avoid any risk of coercion, the form might be raised with the arbitrator by a case administrator before the first preliminary conference. The arbitrator could later be told whether both counsel had signed the sanctions agreement.

[35] *See* Gulf Guar. Life Ins. v. Conn. Gen. Life Ins., 304 F.3d 476, 490 (5th Cir. 2002) ("even where arbitrator bias is at issue, the FAA does not provide for removal of an arbitrator . . . prior to an award").

[36] A party seeking to vacate an award based on alleged attorney misconduct may be required to demonstrate that the misconduct had an effect on the award. *See* Chopra v. Investcape, Inc., 2003 WL 356325 at 3 (Mich. App. Feb. 18, 2003) (unpublished) (award upheld where party could not show counsel's misconduct "affect[ed] the validity of the arbitration award"); In Re Bankhead, 1985 WL 10399 at 2 (Ohio Ct. App. Mar. 18, 1985) (award upheld where attorney's unethical conduct was not one of the statutory grounds for vacatur).

Furthermore, courts afford arbitration awards a presumption of validity unless the fairness of the proceeding has been called into question.[37] Thus, deferential review may not effectively address the unethical conduct of counsel. The problem is exacerbated by the fact that some arbitration proceedings are not transcribed. And even when they are, the record may not reflect all of counsel's misconduct. Absent a reference to that misconduct in the award, it would be very difficult for a reviewing court to determine whether the misconduct occurred and whether it had an impact on the award. Moreover, the court's power to vacate an award for misconduct probably cannot be based on relatively minor ethical violations.

The objections to arbitrators sanctioning counsel for ethical breaches suggest the need for caution, but they are not an absolute barrier to sanctions.

C. Court Control of the Profession Remains Vital

Certain sanctions for attorney misbehavior, such as disqualification from representation for conflicts of interest and disbarment belong under the purview of the courts. For example, *Bidermann Industries Licensing, Inc. v. Avmar N.V.* involved a motion for a stay of arbitration of the issue of whether petitioner's counsel should be disqualified from representing the petitioner in arbitration proceedings. The trial court granted a stay and the Appellate Division affirmed, holding that only a court may rule on an attorney disqualification issue.[38] The court stated: "Issues of attorney disqualification . . . involve interpretation and application of the Code of Professional Responsibility and Disciplinary Rules, as well as the potential deprivation of counsel of the client's choosing."[39]

---

[37] *See* Andersons, Inc. v. Horton Farms, Inc., 166 F.3d 308, 328 (6th Cir. 1998) (FAA "expresses a presumption that arbitration awards will be confirmed"); 1 MARTIN DOMKE, COMMERCIAL ARBITRATION § 36:01 (2001) ("procedural fairness assumes even greater significance in light of the strict limits on judicial review of arbitration awards").

[38] 570 N.Y.S.2d 33 (1st Dept. 1991) (referring to disqualification as a matter of "overriding public policy considerations").

[39] *Id.* at 34. *See also* In re Erdheim & Selkowe, 51 A.D.2d 705, 705 (1st Dept. 1976) (arbitrators lacked the ability to censure attorneys this power "is reserved to the Appellate Division of the Supreme Court in each department"); (Munich Reins. Am. Inc. v. Ace Prop. & Cas. Ins., stating that the issue of attorney disqualification for an alleged conflict of interest is a substantive matter for the courts and not arbitrators). available at www.reinsurancefocus.com/uploads/MunichRe.pdf. By contrast, in Bell v. Seabury, 622 N.W.2d 347 (Mich. Ct. App. 2001), the arbitrators denied a motion to disqualify counsel. On review, the appeals court held that, because it could not be shown that the need for counsel's disqualification resulted in an adverse award, there was no ground to vacate the award.

Regulation of the legal profession presents a formidable problem for courts and bar association disciplinary bodies. Arbitrator regulation of attorneys in arbitral proceedings is not likely to intrude too far into the courts' domain because core regulations of the profession (such as bar admission, suspension, disbarment and the like) are so clearly beyond the purview of arbitrators. If arbitrators were to intrude too far into these areas, "public policy" concerns should allow for court review. Moreover, invoking these concerns, as in *Bidermann*, may permit immediate intervention by a court, to prevent such intrusions from going forward.[40]

If an arbitrator were to stray erroneously into areas exclusively regulated by the courts, an award based on such misplaced authority could be challenged on *de novo* review based on public policy concerns,[41] or "manifest disregard" of law.[42]

V. Confidentiality Concerns May Preclude Ethics Review

For many who choose arbitration over litigation, the preeminent advantage of the process is confidentiality. Canon VI(B) of the AAA-ABA Code of Ethics, states: "Unless otherwise agreed by the parties, or required by applicable rules or law, an arbitrator should keep confidential all matters relating to the arbitration proceedings and decision." On the other hand, attorneys have an obligation under the rules of professional conduct to report unethical conduct of other members of the bar. If this obligation applies to attorneys when they serve as arbitrators, the arbitrators would have conflicting ethical obligations—to maintain confidentiality and to report unethical conduct by counsel in arbitral proceedings.

There is relatively limited guidance on this conflict issue. In a 1977 Informal Opinion, the ABA Standing Committee on Ethics and Professional Responsibility declined to answer the question, at least in

[40] *See also* Larrison v. Scarola Reavis & Parent LLP, 812 N.Y.S.2d 243, 246-47 (N.Y. Sup. Ct. 2005) (whether law firm's one-sided arbitration agreement with client violated public policy was for court to determine).

[41] In Schoonmaker v. Cummings & Lockwood of Connecticut, P.C., 747 A.2d 1017 (Conn. 2000), the Connecticut Supreme Court applied a *de novo* standard of review of an arbitration award that the court said implicated issues of public policy. The court explained that heightened review is necessary to ensure that "public policy of this state is given the proper interpretation and application"). *Id.* at 1028 n. 10.

[42] *See* Yusuf Ahmed Alghanim & Sons v. Toys "R" Us, Inc., 126 F.3d 15, 24 (2d Cir. 1997).

the context of an attorney fee dispute.[43] But an ethics committee in Tennessee opined that fee arbitration committees were excused from their normal ethical obligations to report ethical misconduct.[44] At least one commentator has suggested that the answer may depend on whether the arbitration process is purely private or sponsored by a court.[45]

The concern for confidentiality in arbitration need not preclude arbitrators from taking steps to promote ethics and greater professionalism in arbitration. Arbitrators have authority to establish what will be deemed inappropriate or disruptive conduct in the arbitration and to advise counsel that such conduct could lead to sanctions, even if limited to the party whose counsel engaged in misconduct. The potential publication of an award imposing sanctions due to attorney misconduct (which would occur if proceedings were later brought to enforce or vacate the resulting award) could also encourage more ethical attorney behavior.

VI. Conclusion

The task of an arbitrator is hard enough already. Adding a duty to control ethical misconduct may complicate the main task, which is to decide the dispute. It may add to the cost of arbitration and delay dispute resolution. It also could deter qualified people from serving as arbitrators. Because parties in arbitration want a fair and impartial process, arbitrators must adopt fair procedures and see that they are followed.[46] This responsibility for a fair process inevitably puts policing attorney misconduct in arbitration under the arbitrators' control.

Institutional arbitration providers could help promote ethical attorney conduct in arbitration by offering education programs and developing specific sanctions for various kind of misconduct. One sanction that a provider's ethics committee might impose on an attorney who is a repeat

---

[43] *See* ABA Informal Ethics Op. No. 1393 (Aug. 9, 1977) (issue of confidentiality of arbitration of fee disputes presented "matter of law" not appropriate for ethics opinion).

[44] *See* Ethics Committee, Board of Professional Responsibility, Tenn., Formal Op. 89 (Aug. 8, 1989) (excuse from reporting obligation appropriate to "encourage greater participation and cooperation in the fee arbitration process").

[45] *See* Carrie Menkel-Meadow, *Ethics Issues in Arbitration and Related Dispute Resolution Processes: What's Happening and What's Not*, 56 U. MIAMI L. REV. 955 n. 32 (2002) (describing potential distinction as a "conundrum").

[46] *See* Canon I(F) of the AAA-ABA Code states: "When an arbitrator's authority is derived from an agreement of the parties, the arbitrator should neither exceed that authority nor do less than is required to exercise that authority completely."

offender is a suspension from appearing in future arbitrations that the provider administers.

Provider organizations could also help arbitrators carry out their responsibilities by establishing an ethics or grievance committee from which arbitrators could seek guidance when they have a problem with misconduct by counsel. Such committees could also hear complaints by the parties, not only about attorney misconduct, but also about arbitrator breaches of ethics.[47]

State bar disciplinary committees also could actively encourage more ethical conduct in arbitration. They could draft procedures for confidential proceedings to deal with ethical misconduct in arbitration. The result (the decision whether to impose discipline) could become public.[48]

Unless arbitration providers step in, arbitrators are the only actors in the process who can police ethics in arbitration. Courts cannot be primarily involved, since the whole purpose of arbitration is to eliminate burdens on the courts.[49] Bar association ethics committees can do nothing unless alerted to violations of professional ethics in the arbitration process, but such notification is unlikely to happen unless a party to the arbitration makes a complaint. Arbitrators probably cannot make such complaints due to their obligation of confidentiality.

If the arbitrator does not police ethics in arbitration, that leaves the "fox to guard the hen house."[50] Although most attorneys can be counted on to uphold their professional obligations, unfortunately, some do not. As our society becomes less civil, so may attorneys in their conduct in arbitration.

---

[47] *See* Menkel-Meadow, *supra* n. 45, at 970 ("the existence of a formal complaint and grievance procedure is likely to render that provider more acceptable to courts").

[48] In In re Ziman, 847 P.2d 106 (Ariz. 1993), a lawyer was disciplined for misconduct (including use of profanity in an arbitration). Although the lawyer was identified in the bar committee's decision, the parties and the details of the arbitration were not.

[49] *See* Commonwealth Coatings Corp. v. Continental Cas. Corp., 393 U.S. 145, 151 (1968) (judiciary should "minimize its role in arbitration" as judge of arbitrator impartiality"). In court-annexed arbitration, courts have imposed sanctions for attorney misconduct in arbitration. *See* Legair v. Circuit City Stores, Inc., 2006 WL 278405 (S.D. Ohio Feb. 3, 2006) (court held counsel in contempt and imposed sanctions for "dilatory tactics and unprofessional conduct" in arbitration). A court may admonish counsel for unprofessional conduct in arbitration, even where the conduct cannot be shown to have affected the award. *See* Barcume v. City of Flint, 132 F. Supp. 2d 549, 558 (E.D. Mich. 2001) (noting "years of unprofessional behavior" by counsel in arbitration, but denying motion to vacate award).

[50] Menkel-Meadow, *supra* n. 45, at 952.

Thus, even though ethics policing of counsel is not in the arbitrator's job description, and problems could arise while doing it,[51] the arbitrator's responsibility to control the process necessarily includes the obligation to promote ethical, professional conduct by parties and their counsel and, when appropriate, sanction ethical misconduct that would negatively affect the fairness of the process. The integrity of the arbitration process depends upon this remedy.

[51] One issue omitted from this discussion is how conflict-of-law principles apply to ethical obligations. In international arbitration, a transnational ethics code may need to be developed. The need for such a code has been proposed. Catherine A. Rogers, *Fit and Function in Legal Ethics: Developing a Code of Conduct for International Arbitration*, 23 MICH. INT'L L.J. 341 (2002); Catherine A. Rogers, *Context and Institutional Structure in Attorney Discipline: Developing an Enforcement Regime for Ethics in International Arbitration*, 39 STAN. J. INT'L L. 1 (2002).

CHAPTER 39

AN ARBITRATOR'S AUTHORITY TO AWARD ATTORNEY FEES FOR BAD-FAITH ARBITRATION

John W. Hinchey and Thomas V. Burch[*]

I. Introduction

During the classical period of Roman law, attorneys did not charge fees for legal advice or services.[1] Consequently, high legal fees were no deterrent to filing a lawsuit. To ensure that parties did not abuse these free services and initiate litigation in bad faith, Roman jurists adopted the principle of *lis crescens in duplum*, which allowed them to double the judgment against anyone who initiated litigation without good cause.[2] So began the long-standing tradition of penalizing parties for bad-faith litigation.[3]

Approximately 2000 years later, the U.S. Supreme Court adopted bad faith as an exception to the "American Rule" on shifting attorney

---

[*] John W. Hinchey is a former partner at King & Spalding LLP, and is now a full-time arbitrator and mediator with JAMS, who focuses his practice on domestic and international construction dispute resolution. He is a Past President of the American College of Construction Lawyers, former Chair of the ABA Forum on the Construction Industry He is co-author of a treatise, the International Construction Arbitration Handbook, published by ThomsonWest (2015 ed). He is a CIArb Chartered Arbitrator and currently arbitrates disputes for the American Arbitration Association, JAMS, the ICC, CPR, and the London Court of International Arbitration.

Thomas V. Burch joined the Georgia Law faculty in 2011 after starting his academic career as an assistant visiting professor at the Florida State University College of Law in 2009. He works closely with the law school's moot court program and Appellate Litigation Clinic. Before entering the legal academy in 2009, Burch was a litigation associate at King & Spalding in Atlanta, Ga.; Balch & Bingham in Birmingham, Ala.; and Hopping Green & Sams in Tallahassee, Fla.

[1] Werner Pfennigstorf, *The European Experience with Attorney Fee Shifting*, 47 LAW & CONTEMP. PROBS. 37, 40-41 (1984).

[2] *Id.* at 41. By the time of the Byzantine Empire, the practice of doubling judgments declined significantly because lawyers began charging fees. When lawyers began charging fees, a practice developed requiring the losing party to reimburse the winner for costs if the loser litigated in bad faith. *Id.* at 41-42.

[3] *See id.* at 40-44.

fees.[4] While the Court did not explain whether this exception applied in arbitration, it has since pushed a "national policy favoring arbitration,"[5] which has caused arbitration to become significantly more prevalent in the American adjudicatory process. As a result, courts have struggled to determine the extent, if any, that the principle of penalizing parties for bad faith applies in modern arbitration.

The answer depends on several factors. First, does the parties' contract grant the arbitrator authority to award attorney fees? If so, then the answer is clear. The arbitrator can make an award of attorney fees for bad-faith arbitration. If not, then one must look to the law that governs the arbitration agreement. That is the subject of this chapter.

We discuss an arbitrator's authority to award attorney fees for bad-faith arbitration under the Federal Arbitration Act (FAA), the Uniform Arbitration Act (UAA), the 2000 Revised Uniform Arbitration Act (RUAA), and the American Arbitration Association's (AAA) Commercial Arbitration Rules. We also examine the definition of bad faith, briefly address preemption under the FAA, and provide a short justification for allowing arbitrators to make bad-faith awards.

II. The Arbitrator's Power to Award Attorney Fees

Generally, arbitrators entertaining a claim for attorney fees must consider: (1) whether they have the authority to make such an award, (2) how to allocate the award between the parties, and (3) how much they should award.[6] As stated above, if the parties' agreement addresses these issues, then the arbitrator will decide the dispute in accordance with the agreement. The problem is that arbitration agreements frequently fail to address attorney fees. Accordingly, arbitrators often have to rely on case law interpretations of the arbitration rules that govern the proceeding. Unfortunately, the interpretations of rules concerning attorney fee awards based on a party's bad faith are inconsistent.

---

[4] *See* Alyeska Pipeline Serv. v. Wilderness Soc'y, 421 U.S. 240, 247, 257-60 (1975) ("[A] court may assess attorneys' fees . . . when the losing party has acted in bad faith."), *citing* F. D. Rich Co., v. United States ex rel. Indus. Lumber Co., 417 U.S. 116, 129 (1974).

[5] *See* Southland Corp. v. Keating, 465 U.S. 1, 10 (1984).

[6] *See* John Yukio Gotanda, *Awarding Costs and Attorneys' Fees in International Commercial Arbitrations*, 21 MICH. J. INT'L L. 1, 13 (1999).

A. *What Constitutes "Bad Faith" in Arbitration?*

"Bad faith" lacks a precise definition, as the ultimate meaning of the term depends on the facts and circumstances of the underlying controversy.[7] However, *Black's Law Dictionary* has characterized bad faith as a "dishonesty of belief or purpose,"[8] and courts generally tend to apply a similar definition.[9] Essentially, "bad faith" is a state of mind that is proved through conduct,[10] and it can include anything from needlessly delaying the arbitration proceeding,[11] to making unfounded allegations against the other party,[12] to unreasonable behavior before the commencement of the arbitration.[13]

B. *Bad-Faith Awards under the FAA*

The obstacle to making an award of attorney fees for bad-faith conduct lies in the laws that govern arbitration agreements, such as the FAA, which is silent on the arbitrator's authority to award such fees.[14] In view of this silence and the broad powers of arbitrators in general, several federal courts, including the Second, Ninth and Eleventh Circuits, have found that arbitrators may award attorney fees for bad-faith arbitration, and they declined, either implicitly or explicitly, to overturn such awards under Section 10 of the FAA.[15] For example, in *Todd*

---

[7] *See* Bundy v. Commercial Credit Co., 202 N.C. 604, 607 (1932).

[8] "[A] state of mind consisting in . . . observance of reasonable commercial standards of fair dealing in a given trade or business, or . . . absence of intent to defraud or to seek unconscionable advantage." BLACK'S LAW DICTIONARY 701 (7th ed. 1999).

[9] The Utah Supreme Court defined bad faith simply as the antithesis of good faith. Research-Planning, Inc. v. Bank of Utah, 690 P.2d 1130, 1132 (Utah 1984). The Ohio Supreme Court, in the context of an insurance dispute, defined bad faith as a lack of good faith that embraces more than mere bad judgment or negligence. "It imports a dishonest purpose, moral obliquity, conscious wrongdoing, breach of a known duty through some ulterior motive or ill will partaking of the nature of fraud." Spitler v. State Auto Mut., Ins., 61 Ohio St. 2d 242, 244 (1980).

[10] *See* Commercial Union Ins. Co. v. Liberty Mut. Ins. Co., 137 Mich. App. 381, 391 (1984).

[11] *See* Todd Shipyards Corp. v. Cunard Line, 943 F.2d 1056, 1064-65 (9th Cir. 1991).

[12] Marshall v. Duke, 114 F.3d 188, 189-90 (11th Cir. 1997).

[13] *See* Fond du Lac v. Fond du Lac, 158 Wis. 2d 729, 729 (Wis. Ct. App. 1990).

[14] *See* 2 MARTIN DOMKE, *ET AL.*, COMMERCIAL ARBITRATION § 48:1 (3d ed. 2003).

[15] *See* Reliastar Life Ins. Co. v. EMC Nat'l Life Co., 564 F.3d 81, 89 (2d Cir. 2009) (upholding the arbitrators' award of attorney fees for bad faith arbitration even though the parties' contract stated that each party would bear its own fees); *Marshall*, *supra* n. 12, 114 F.3d at 189-90; *Todd Shipyards*, *supra* n. 11, 943 F.2d at 1064-65. *See also* Bacardi Corp. v. Congreso de Uniones Industriales de Puerto Rico, 692 F.2d 210, 214 (1st Cir.

Shipyards Corp. v. Cunard Line, the arbitrators awarded attorney fees to Todd Shipyards as a consequence of Cunard unnecessarily extending the arbitration by a "considerable number of days."[16] The Ninth Circuit upheld the award, stating that "[i]n light of the broad power of arbitrators to fashion appropriate remedies and the accepted 'bad-faith conduct' exception to the American Rule, we hold that it was within the power of the arbitration panel in this case to award attorneys' fees."[17]

In *Marshall v. Duke*, the Eleventh Circuit similarly upheld an award of attorney fees, reasoning that "both parties sought an award of their fees without a jurisdictional objection from the other" and that "arbitrators have the power to award attorney's fees pursuant to the 'bad faith' exception to the American rule."[18] *Marshall* involved investor claims of improper conduct against securities brokers, including alleged conspiracies, fraud, abuse of the judicial process, and creation of a "sham" bankruptcy.[19] The arbitrators ruled that the investors' claims lacked merit and were asserted to extort a settlement from the brokers.[20] The District Court for the Northern District of Georgia upheld the award, including the bad-faith award of attorney fees, and the Eleventh Circuit agreed, citing the Supreme

---

1982) (implicitly recognizing that arbitrators may award attorney fees for bad faith); WMA Sec. v. Wynn, 105 F. Supp. 2d 833, 839 (S.D. Ohio 2000) ("Notwithstanding the panel's authority to award attorney fees, whether or not the statutes upon which the claims are formulated authorize the granting of fees, the statutes are supplemented by the common law exceptions of contract and bad faith."); Prudential-Bache Sec. v. Depew, 814 F. Supp. 1081, 1082-83 (M.D. Fla. 1993) (denying attorney fee award but implicitly recognizing that arbitrators may award attorney fees for bad faith); Household Mfg. v. Kowen Dev. Corp., 1993 U.S. Dist. Lexis 10987, at *5-10 (N.D. Ill. 1993) (arbitrator had authority under FAA to award attorney fees for bad faith), *modified on other grounds*, Eljer Mfg. v. Kowin Dev. Corp., 14 F.3d 1250 (7th Cir. 1994); Chase Bank USA, N.A. v. Hale, 859 N.Y.S.2d 342, 346 (N.Y. Sup. Ct. 2008) ("Under federal law, arbitrators have broad authority to decide disputes and to fashion remedies, especially where a commercial contract is governed by applicable rules of an arbitration forum authorizing the arbitrators to do so. Thus, where arbitrators find a claim to have been brought in bad faith, they may, in the exercise of their broad powers to fashion remedies, award attorneys' fees.").

[16] 943 F.2d at 1064.

[17] *See id.* The Ninth Circuit supported its decision by citing *Alyeska Pipeline*.

[18] *See Marshall*, *supra* n. 12, 114 F.3d at 190. According to the court, "[t]he arbitration panel did not explicitly say that the fee award was based on bad faith and submitted no findings in that regard." *Id.* However, the court stated: "[I]t is clear . . . that the decision was based on the claim of the broker appellees that they were entitled to fees based on the conduct of the claimant parties." *Id.* Accordingly, the court approved of the arbitrators ability to award attorney fees for bad faith.

[19] *See* Marshall & Co. v. Duke, 941 F. Supp. 1207, 1215 (N.D. Ga. 1995).

[20] *Id.* at 1215-16.

Court's opinion in *Alyeska Pipeline Services v. Wilderness Society*[21] to justify the award.[22]

In *Alyeska Pipeline*, the Supreme Court stated that "a court may assess attorneys' fees for the 'willful disobedience of a court order . . . as part of the fine to be levied on the defendant . . . or when the losing party has 'acted in bad faith, vexatiously, wantonly, or for oppressive reasons. . . .'"[23] While a literal reading of this opinion would only allow courts, not arbitrators, to award attorney fees for bad faith, federal courts have read the language more broadly because doing so aligns with the Supreme Court's "national policy favoring arbitration."[24]

C. Bad-Faith Awards under the UAA

Section 10 of the 1955 Uniform Arbitration Act provides that attorney fees are not recoverable in arbitration—unless authorized in the parties' agreement—and state arbitration laws based on the UAA generally reflect this principle.[25] Thus, state courts usually refrain from giving arbitrators the power to make bad-faith awards under state law.[26]

For example, in *Walton Acoustics v. Currahee Construction Co.*, the Georgia Court of Appeals held that arbitrators may not award attorney fees under Section 13-6-11 of the Georgia Code, which is Georgia's fee-shifting provision for bad-faith litigation.[27] The court reasoned that Section 9-9-17, which is modeled after Section 10 of the UAA, prohibits

---

[21] *Supra* n. 4.

[22] *See Marshall, supra* n. 12, 114 F.3d at 189-90 (adopting the arbitration panel's reliance on *Alyeska*); *Marshall & Co., supra* n. 19, 941 F. Supp at 1213 (same).

[23] *Alyeska Pipeline, supra* n. 4, 421 U.S. at 258-59, citing Toledo Scale Co. v. Computing Scale Co., 261 U.S. 399, 426-28 (1923); *F. D. Rich Co., supra* n. 4, 417 U.S. at 129.

[24] *See, e.g., Marshall & Co., supra* n. 19, 941 F. Supp at 1213 (upholding an arbitrators award of attorney fees for bad faith); Willoughby Roofing & Supply Co. v. Kajima Int'l, Inc., 776 F.2d 269, 270 (11th Cir. 1985) ("In light of the federal policy favoring arbitration at work here, our task is to resolve all doubt in favor of the arbitrator's authority to award a particular remedy."). *See also* 9 U.S.C. § 10 (2000); *Southland Corp., supra* n. 5, 465 U.S. at 10.

[25] Domke, *supra* n. 14, at § 48:1. Section 10 of the UAA states: "Unless otherwise provided in the agreement to arbitrate, the arbitrator's expenses and fees, together with other expenses, not including counsel fees, incurred in the conduct of the arbitration, shall be paid as provided in the award."

[26] *See id.*

[27] 399 S.E.2d 265, 266 (Ga. Ct. App. 1990).

arbitrators from making such awards.[28] So far, no Georgia court has reversed this part of the *Walton Acoustics* decision. However, the Court of Appeals decided *Walton Acoustics* nearly 20 years ago, and during those years the court has taken an increasingly progressive stance regarding an arbitrator's ability to award attorney fees.[29]

The Wisconsin Court of Appeals, similar to the Georgia Court of Appeals in *Walton Acoustics*, adopted a fairly conservative approach to attorney fees in *Milwaukee Teachers' Education Association v. Milwaukee Board of School Directors* when it stated: "To permit an arbitrator's essentially unreviewable finding that one party has acted in 'bad faith' to support an award of attorneys' fees when the parties have not agreed to that potential remedy would give the arbitrator powers beyond those delegated to him."[30] Since Wisconsin apparently had no code provision

---

[28] *Id.*; Ga. Code Ann. § 9-9-17 (2004). The court's reasoning was based on Section 9-9-17 being the most recent legislative pronouncement on attorney fees in arbitration.

[29] In 1989, the Georgia Court of Appeals stated that arbitrators could not award attorney fees under any circumstances. *See* Hughes & Peden v. Budd Contracting Co., 193 Ga. App. 656 (1989). Two years later, it followed the *Hughes & Peden* decision in *Walton Acoustics*, *supra* n. 27. In 1992, however, the Georgia Court of Appeals modified *Walton Acoustics* and *Hughes & Peden* to allow arbitrators to award attorney fees if the agreement granted arbitrators that power. *See* Hope & Assocs. v. Marvin M. Black Co., 422 S.E.2d 918, 919 (Ga. Ct. App. 1992). Six years after that, in Haddon v. Shaheen, 499 S.E.2d 693, 695 (Ga. Ct. App. 1998), the court stated that Section 9-9-13 of the Georgia Code provided the exclusive grounds for vacating an arbitration award and the court refused to overturn the arbitrator's award of attorney fees under any of those grounds—even though the arbitration agreement did not grant the arbitrator authority to award attorney fees. In 1999, the Georgia Court of Appeals upheld an arbitrator's award of attorney fees by stating that the parties implicitly agreed to arbitrate the attorney fees issue when they both submitted evidence on attorney fees at the arbitration hearing. Akintobi v. Phoenix Fire Restoration Co., 513 S.E.2d 507, 508 (Ga. Ct. App. 1999). In 2001, in Bush v. Northside Trucking, Inc., 556 S.E.2d 909, 911 (Ga. Ct. App. 2001), the Georgia Court of Appeals seemed to imply that arbitrators could make awards based on bad faith when it stated: "A defendant is not chargeable with the expenses of litigation unless he has acted in bad faith." Nevertheless, with the Georgia General Assembly's 2004 addition of "manifest disregard" as a ground for vacatur under the Georgia Arbitration Act, it is doubtful that Georgia courts will recognize the bad-faith exception in arbitration because Section 9-9-17 prohibits attorney fee awards in arbitration. *See* Ga. Code § 9-9-13 (2004); *see also* John W. Hinchey & Thomas V. Burch, *Georgia General Assembly Adopts "Manifest Disregard" as Ground for Vacating Arbitration Awards: How Will Georgia Courts Treat the New Standard?*, GA. B.J. (Feb. 2004).

[30] 147 Wis. 2d 791, 801 (Wis. Ct. App. 1988); *see also* Thompson v. Jespersen, 222 Cal. App. 3d 964, 968 (1990) ("To uphold an award of attorney's fees in the absence of an agreement to arbitrate the issue would result in gross unfairness which could only serve to frustrate the strong public policy favoring arbitration.").

similar to Section 10 of the UAA, the court said only that Wisconsin would follow the American Rule on fee-shifting —even citing *Alyeska Pipeline* to support that proposition.[31] Yet, despite this citation, the court refused to apply *Alyeska Pipeline*'s bad-faith exception in the context of arbitration.[32]

Two years later, however, in *Fond du Lac v. Fond du Lac*, the same court upheld an arbitrator's award of attorney fees for bad-faith conduct.[33] The court distinguished *Fond du Lac* from *Milwaukee Teachers' Education Association* by stating that the attorney fees in *Fond du Lac* were not related to the arbitration. Rather, the fees stemmed from the city's conduct prior to the arbitration, which resulted in increased costs to the parties.[34] This was an incredibly fine, and not entirely credible, distinction. Nevertheless, the Wisconsin Court of Appeals presumably still will not allow arbitrators to award attorney fees based on bad-faith conduct during arbitration.[35]

Rhode Island and Montana courts do not share Wisconsin's reservations about arbitrators making attorney fee awards based on the bad faith of one of the parties. They actually recognize the bad-faith exception in arbitration.[36] For example, in *Langmeier v. Kuehl*, Kuehl initiated a dispute over 900 square feet of property that he never owned, costing himself and the other parties tens of thousands of dollars in arbitration and litigation expenses.[37] Based on this conduct, the arbitrator awarded attorney fees to Langmeier, and the Montana Supreme Court upheld the award. The court simply stated: "[A]n arbitrator may, under limited circumstances, award attorney's fees through his equity powers where bad faith or malicious behavior is involved."[38] Similarly, in

---

[31] *Id.* at 795.

[32] *Id.* at 799-801.

[33] *See Fond du Lac, supra* n. 13, 158 Wis. 2d at 729.

[34] *Id.*

[35] This is true unless, of course, the parties' agreement authorizes such an award. *See Milwaukee Teachers' Educ. Ass'n, supra* n. 30, 147 Wis. 2d at 795; Winkelman v. Kraft Foods, Inc., 279 Wis. 2d 335, 351 (Wis. Ct. App. 2005).

[36] *See* Terrace Group v. Vermont Castings, Inc., 753 A.2d 350, 354 (R.I. 2000) (applying Vermont law, which the court said was similar to Rhode Island law); Langmeier v. Kuehl, 307 Mont. 499, 504 (2001).

[37] *Langmeier, supra* n. 36, 307 Mont. at 504.

[38] *Id.* Note that a *plaintiff* may not be able to recover bad-faith attorney fees in arbitration in Montana. *See* Harding v. Savoy, 323 Mont. 261, 278 (2004) ("[W]e have held where a party chooses to institute a suit against others, an award of attorney fees to the plaintiff will normally be precluded.").

Terrace Group v. Vermont Castings, the Rhode Island Supreme Court upheld a bad-faith award of attorney fees because Vermont Castings failed to show that the arbitrator manifestly disregarded the law.[39] Nevertheless, such decisions appear to be the exception rather than the rule, since most state laws forbid awards of attorney fees in arbitration.[40] This will begin to change, however, as more states adopt the 2000 RUAA because one of the revisions in this Act specifically allows arbitrators to award attorney fees where "authorized by law."[41]

D. Bad-Faith Awards under the RUAA

Section 21(b) of the RUAA takes a different approach to attorney fee awards than that of the UAA. Section 21(b) provides: "An arbitrator may award reasonable attorney's fees and other reasonable expenses of arbitration if such an award is authorized by law in a civil action involving the same claim or by the agreement of the parties to the arbitration proceeding."[42] Since the Supreme Court, in *Alyeska Pipeline*, "authorized" bad faith as an exception to the American Rule on fee shifting in civil claims, arbitrators in RUAA states arguably should be able to make bad-faith attorney-fee awards under Section 21(b) of the RUAA.[43] Yet, it may not be so simple. Some courts, even under the RUAA, may simply refuse to apply *Alyeska Pipeline*'s bad-faith exception in the context of arbitration.[44]

As an alternative, a court could decide whether the bad-faith award is "authorized" by some other state law. For example, as discussed in the following section, a court could look to its state's Prompt Pay Act to see if the arbitrator can make a bad-faith award under its provisions. Whether courts will do this under the RUAA, however, is unclear due to the lack of case law on the subject.

---

[39] *Vermont Castings*, *supra* n. 36, 753 A.2d at 354.

[40] *See Domke*, *supra* n. 14, at § 48:1.

[41] Revised Uniform Arbitration Act § 21(b) (2004).

[42] *Id.*

[43] *See Alyeska Pipeline*, *supra* n. 4, 421 U.S. at 240, 247, 257-60; *see also*, *Domke*, *supra* n. 14, at § 48:1.

[44] *See, e.g.*, *Milwaukee Teachers' Educ. Ass'n.*, *supra* n. 30, 147 Wis. 2d at 795. Although the Wisconsin Court of Appeals decided this case under the UAA, a court may similarly decide not to apply *Alyeska Pipeline*'s bad-faith exception under the RUAA. A technical reading of *Alyeska Pipeline* only makes the bad-faith exception applicable in court, not arbitration, and any court making its decision under the RUAA theoretically could decline to apply the bad-faith exception on this technicality.

E. Bad-Faith Awards under AAA Rules

Rule 47(a) of the AAA Commercial Arbitration Rules provides: "The arbitrator may grant any remedy or relief that the arbitrator deems just and equitable and within the scope of the agreement of the parties. . . ."[45] If the Rules stopped here, parties might not be able to recover attorney fees for bad-faith arbitration if the contract did not specifically authorize it.[46] Nevertheless, Rule 47(d)(ii), like the RUAA, permits arbitrators to award attorney fees if "authorized by law."[47]

For example, in *Rose Construction v. Raintree Development Co.*, the parties agreed to arbitrate all disputes arising under the contract in accordance with the then applicable AAA Construction Industry Arbitration Rules.[48] Rule L-6 of the AAA's Large, Complex Case Procedures for construction cases, which applied in this case, contained the same "authorized by law" language that is present in Rule 47(d)(ii) of the Commercial Rules.[49] Consequently, the Tennessee Court of Appeals looked to whether, under the then applicable Rule L-6, an award of attorney fees for bad faith was, in this case, "authorized" by Tennessee's Prompt Pay Act, which grants attorney fees to the prevailing party when the losing party acted in bad faith.[50]

Raintree insisted that Section 29-5-13 of the Tennessee Arbitration Code, which then prohibited arbitral awards of attorney fees, controlled the

---

[45] American Arbitration Association (AAA) Commercial Arbitration Rules, Rule 47(a) (2013). The AAA commercial rules are available at www.adr.org.

[46] *Compare* Thompson v. Jespersen, 222 Cal. App. 3d 964, 968 (1990) (overturning an award of attorney fees and stating that AAA Rule 43 required such an award to be within the scope of the parties' contract) *with Todd Shipyards*, *supra* n. 11, 943 F.2d at 1064-65 (upholding an award of attorney fees for bad faith under Rule 43 – prior to its amendment giving arbitrators the power to award attorney fees if authorized by law – absent a specific contractual grant of power).

[47] AAA Commercial Rules, *supra* n. 45, Rule 47(d)(ii). One difference between the "authorized by law" provision of RUAA Rule 21(b) and AAA Commercial Rule 47(d)(ii) is that even if the parties agree to abide by Rule 47(d)(ii), the reviewing court may still apply the state's equivalent of Section 10 of the UAA to prohibit an award of attorney fees. However, if a state has adopted the RUAA, then the state law would not prohibit attorney fee awards in arbitration because Rule 21(b) would replace the state's equivalent of UAA § 10.

[48] *See* Rose Constr. v. Raintree Dev. Co., 2001 Tenn. App. Lexis 961, at *14 (Dec. 31, 2001) (upholding an award of bad-faith attorney fees under the Tennessee Prompt Pay Act).

[49] AAA Construction Industry Arbitration Rules, Rule 48(d)(ii) (2015) has replaced and now contains the same "authorized by law" as in the previous L-6 (2004), available at www.adr.org.

[50] *Rose Constr.*, *supra* n. 48, 2001 Tenn. App. Lexis 961, at *14-15; *see also* Tenn. Code Ann. § 66-34-602(b) (2004) (Prompt Pay Act).

dispute, not the Prompt Pay Act, because the two statutes conflicted and Section 29-5-13 more clearly addressed the attorney-fees issue in arbitration proceedings.[51] The court disagreed with Raintree, finding that the statutes were "not inconsistent."[52] Section 29-5-13 allows attorney-fee awards where such awards are authorized by the parties' agreement. According to the court, the parties' contract incorporated AAA Rule L-6 by reference.[53] Therefore, since the contract incorporated Rule L-6, it allowed bad-faith awards where authorized by law. Accordingly the court held that Section 29-5-13 presented no obstacle, and it upheld the award under the Prompt Pay Act.[54]

III. Justification for Arbitral Awards of Attorney Fees for Bad Faith

Refusing to grant arbitrators the authority to make bad-faith awards unnecessarily limits the remedies available to parties who choose arbitration over litigation. As the Supreme Court stated in the oft-cited *United Steelworkers of America v. Enterprise Wheel & Car Corp.*:

> When an arbitrator is commissioned to interpret and apply the . . . agreement, he is to bring his informed judgment to bear in order to reach a fair solution of a problem. This is especially true when it comes to formulating remedies. There the need is for flexibility in meeting a wide variety of situations. The draftsmen may never have thought of what specific remedy should be awarded to meet a particular contingency.[55]

We also believe that courts should give arbitrators wide authority with respect to remedies, including the flexibility to make awards for bad

---

[51] *Rose Constr.*, *supra* n. 48, 2001 Tenn. App. Lexis 961, at *11-12; *see also* Tenn. Code Ann. § 29-5-13 (2004).

[52] *Rose Constr.*, *supra* n. 478 2001 Tenn. App. Lexis 961, at *12-13.

[53] *Id.* at *9-10.

[54] *Id.* at *14. The Tennessee Supreme Court denied Raintree's appeal. After the denial, the trial court confirmed the award in accordance with the Court of Appeals' decision. However, Raintree appealed the trial court's confirmation and the case once again returned to the Court of Appeals. When it did, the Court of Appeals held that the appeal was frivolous and awarded Rose Construction the costs of the appeal. *See* Rose Constr. Co. v. Raintree Dev. Co., 2004 Tenn. App. Lexis 758 (2004).

[55] 363 U.S. 593, 597 (U.S. 1960).

faith where necessary. Arbitrators are well equipped to make such decisions. For example, case law has already established that arbitrators have the authority to award punitive damages under the FAA and most state laws.[56] If arbitrators can award punitive damages, why not allow them to make awards of attorney fees for bad-faith arbitration? Doing so will produce the long-term benefit of deterring frivolous arbitration claims. Moreover, limited judicial review of arbitration awards is no reason to prohibit arbitrators from awarding attorney fees for bad faith. Even though courts grant wide deference to arbitrators' decisions, arbitrators still have an ethical and legal duty to follow the law.[57] Thus, arbitrators should have the ability to make bad-faith awards when necessary.

IV. Preemption Issues

If the parties' agreement calls for state arbitration law to apply but the agreement "involves" interstate commerce, would the FAA preempt the parties' choice of state law in determining whether arbitrators can award attorney fees for bad faith? The FAA applies to any "transaction involving commerce."[58] In *Allied-Bruce Terminix Companies v. Dobson,* the Supreme Court interpreted this language so that the FAA now applies to any transaction that "affects" interstate commerce, which significantly broadened the preemptive reach of the FAA.[59] Nevertheless, the FAA only preempts state laws that restrict the application of agreements to arbitrate.[60] It does not prevent agreements to arbitrate under state arbitration law.[61] Thus, in the situation posed above, federal law will determine the validity of the arbitration clause, while state law will

---

[56] *See* RUAA § 21, comment 1 (2004) ("[I]t is now well established that arbitrators have authority to award punitive damages under the FAA.... Federal authority is in accord with the preponderance of decisions applying the UAA and state arbitration statutes.").

[57] *See* Montes v. Shearson Lehman Bros., 128 F.3d 1456, 1459-60 (11th Cir. 1997).

[58] 9 U.S.C. § 2 (2000).

[59] 513 U.S. 265, 273-74 (1995).

[60] *Domke, supra* n. 14, at § 7.7.

[61] *Id.* In *Volt Information Sciences v. Leland Stanford Jr. University*, 489 U.S. 468, 477 (1989), the U.S. Supreme Court held: "The [Federal Arbitration Act] contains no express pre-emptive provision, nor does it reflect a congressional intent to occupy the entire field of arbitration." Accordingly, state law governing arbitration is preempted only "to the extent it actually conflicts with federal law—that is, to the extent that it 'stands as an obstacle to the accomplishment and execution of the full purposes and objectives of Congress.'" *Id.* (*quoting* Hines v. Davidowitz, 312 U.S. 52, 67 (1941)).

govern the rest of the contract,[62] including the rule on awards of attorney fees for bad-faith arbitration. If the state law chosen prohibits such awards, then the arbitrator probably will not be able to make an award of attorney fees for bad faith.[63]

V. Conclusion

In the cases we have analyzed, whether an arbitrator can make an award for bad faith generally depends on the controlling law and whether the award is being reviewed by a state or federal court. The FAA is silent on attorney fees and, therefore, does not preclude such awards. Thus, it is not surprising that federal courts usually refuse to overturn awards for bad faith, finding no ground to vacate under FAA Section 10.

However, if state law governs the arbitration proceeding, the arbitrator's authority to award attorney fees for bad-faith arbitration will depend on whether the state arbitration law is modeled on the RUAA, or whether the parties have incorporated the AAA rules, both of which allow such awards if "authorized by law." Nevertheless, parties who want their arbitrator to have authority to make bad-faith awards may want to consider expressly providing for such authority in the arbitration provision of their contract. This appears to be the simplest way to avoid all the confusion.

---

[62] *See* Domke, *supra* n.14, at § 7.7; *Allied-Bruce*, *supra* n. 59, 513 U.S. at 271-72.

[63] *See id.* If the parties' agreement is silent on controlling law, the answer simply depends on whether the underlying agreement "affects" interstate commerce. If it does, then the FAA controls and, despite the FAA's silence on attorney fees, the arbitrator should be able to award attorney fees for bad faith. *See* Ceco Concrete Const. v. J.T. Schrimsher Const., 792 F. Supp. 109 (N.D. Ga. 1992). If the parties have a choice-of-law clause designating state law as controlling the dispute, but another provision stating that the dispute will be heard according to the AAA Rules, then it may depend on whether the state has another statutory provision that allows bad-faith awards. *See Rose Constr.*, *supra* n. 48, 2001 Tenn. App. Lexis 961, at *14 (applying the Tennessee Prompt Pay Act, which authorized awards for bad faith, in an arbitration under the AAA Rules, even though Raintree argued that it conflicted with a state law that prohibited attorney-fee awards in arbitration).

PART VII:

Damages, Judicial Review and Enforcement of Arbitration Awards

CHAPTER 40

THE PUNITIVE DAMAGES REMEDY: LESSONS FOR DRAFTERS OF ARBITRATION AGREEMENTS

Michael D. Nolan and Andrew M. Leblanc[*]

I. Introduction

A principle well established in arbitration law is that, unless the parties expressly and unambiguously preclude an award of punitive damages in their arbitration clause, the arbitration tribunal will be able to award punitive damages. Federal courts applying this principle have recently expanded this doctrine to grant arbitration panels more freedom than trial courts to award punitive damages. Recently, the U.S. Court of Appeals for the Eighth Circuit re-affirmed this principle and ruled that it was not excessive for an arbitrator to award punitive damages that were 3,000 times the compensatory damages, even though these punitive damages would be excessive as a matter of law had they been awarded by a court.[1] This decision on punitive damages reinforces for attorneys the importance of employing direct and unambiguous language in crafting arbitration clauses. It also demonstrates the power of arbitrators to award damages that would not be permitted in traditional litigation.

II. Punitive Damages and Arbitration: Background

In 1995 the U.S. Supreme Court confirmed the power of arbitrators to award punitive damages in *Mastrobuono v. Shearson Lehman Hutton,*

---

[*] Michael D. Nolan is a partner in the Litigation and Arbitration Groups, and Andrew M. Leblanc is a partner in the Financial Restructuring and Litigation Groups, in the Washington D.C. office of Milbank, Tweed, Hadley & McCloy LLP.

[1] Stark v. Sandberg, Phoenix & Von Gontard, P.C., 381 F.3d 793, 803 (8th Cir. 2004), *cert. denied sub nom.* EMC Mortgage Corp. v. Stark, 125 S. Ct. 1943 (2005).

Inc.[2] In that decision, the Court upheld an arbitral award of punitive damages notwithstanding that the contract at issue was governed by New York law, which had legal precedent precluding punitive damage awards in arbitration. The arbitration clause incorporated the rules of the National Association of Securities Dealers, which specifically permitted punitive damages awards. The Supreme Court resolved the conflict between New York law and the party-selected arbitration rules by concluding that the choice-of-law provision applied only to substantive legal issues, and that the arbitration clause applied to non-substantive issues, including the award of damages. On this basis, the Court held that the application of New York law did not preclude an arbitral award of punitive damages.

Following *Mastrobuono*, lower courts have strictly construed contracts to determine whether there is a clear, express waiver of punitive damages awards in arbitration. For example, in *R. Allen Fox Ltd. v. Stratton Oakmont*, the court held that contract language stating that New York law would control the "rights and liabilities of the parties" was not broad enough to preclude an award of punitive damages in an arbitration and that only specific language could do so.[3] A California court considering the same contractual language arrived at the same conclusion, reasoning that an arbitration panel's award of punitive damages was not in "manifest disregard of the law" because there was no language specifically precluding punitive damages in the contract at issue.[4] The Eleventh Circuit upheld an award of punitive damages over an argument that the award violated due process rights.[5] The court held that *Mastrobuono*, which dealt with a "virtually identical" arbitration clause, confirmed that arbitrators have the right to award punitive damages and that there can be no due process violation when the dispute is between private parties.[6]

III. The *Stark* Case: Was the Right to Punitive Damages Waived?

The issue of the propriety of a punitive damages award surfaced again in *Stark v. Sandberg, Phoenix & von Gontard, P.C.*, in which the Eighth Circuit considered an appeal of a district court order vacating a $6

[2] 514 U.S. 52, 64 (1995).

[3] No. 93 C 2228, 1996 WL 288771, at *2-3 (N.D. Ill. May 29, 1996).

[4] *See* Greening v. Stratton Oakmont, No. C-95-4288, 1996 WL 61095, at *3 (N.D. Cal. Feb. 5, 1996).

[5] *See* Davis v. Prudential Sec., 59 F.3d 1186, 1189-90 (11th Cir. 1995).

[6] *Id.* at 1191-92.

million punitive award in arbitration and the companion award of $2,000 in compensatory damages.[7] The district court vacated the awards on two grounds: First, the contract precluded an award of punitive damages; second, the punitive award was excessive. The Eighth Circuit disagreed, reversing the district court's judgment and reinstating the award.

The case dealt with a lending agreement between the Starks and EMC Mortgage Corp. The arbitration clause in the parties' agreement stated that an arbitration award "shall in no event include consequential, punitive, exemplary or treble damages as to which borrower and lender expressly waive any right to claim to the fullest extent permitted by law."[8]

The parties ended up in arbitration as a result of a foreclosure dispute. The arbitrator found that the contract was ambiguous as to the availability of punitive damages because it stated that it was to be governed by both the Federal Arbitration Act (FAA), which allowed parties to waive punitive damages, and Missouri law, which did not. In light of the ambiguity, the arbitrator construed the contract against EMC, the drafting party. Accordingly, the arbitrator found that an award of punitive damages was not precluded by the parties' agreement and imposed punitive damages of $6 million against EMC. EMC moved to vacate the award and the district court granted the requested relief.

The Eighth Circuit agreed with the arbitrator's conclusion that punitive damages were not precluded, but it did not apply the arbitrator's reasoning. It ruled that the contract language unambiguously permitted a punitive damages award. The court interpreted the waiver language in the agreement as a "limited waiver" of punitive damages because it applied "only to the fullest extent permitted by law"—*i.e.*, only if the governing law permitted such a waiver.[9] Because Missouri law, the law governing the agreement, made waivers of punitive damages unenforceable under the facts of this case, the Eighth Circuit held that the contract unambiguously permitted an award of such damages. The court accepted that, under the FAA, parties can incorporate terms into their arbitration clause that are contrary to state law, but in its view, the parties had not done so in this contract. Accordingly, the court held that the award of punitive damages was proper.

The court also ruled "alternatively" that the arbitrator's finding of ambiguity in the contract was appropriate. It stated: "Words purporting

[7] *Supra* n.1.

[8] Appellant's Petition for Cert. at 1, *Stark, supra* n. 1.

[9] *Stark, supra* n. 1, 381 F.3d at 800.

to waive claims which cannot be waived 'demonstrate the ambiguity of the contractual language.'"[10] The court then concurred with the arbitrator's decision resolving the ambiguity against EMC.

A. The Amount of Punitive Damages Awarded

EMC also challenged the amount of the punitive award, claiming that $6 million, which was 3,000 times the actual damages awarded, was excessive and, therefore, in manifest disregard of the law. The mortgage company contended that the award was inappropriate under *State Farm Mutual Automobile Insurance. Co. v. Campbell*[11] and other recent Supreme Court decisions. In *State Farm*, the High Court reversed a punitive damage award that was 145 times actual damages, considering it to be excessive under the Due Process Clause. The Court said of its prior precedent on punitive damages that, although there is no bright-line rule, "[t]hey demonstrate what should be obvious: Single-digit multipliers are more likely to comport with due process, while still achieving the State's goals of deterrence and retribution, than awards with ratios in range of 500 to 1 or, in this case, of 145 to 1."[12] Because this limitation would obviously apply to a court considering a dispute, EMC contended that a similar limitation should apply to an arbitral award.

The Eighth Circuit found EMC's arguments unpersuasive. The federal appeals court explained that the "manifest disregard" standard requires the award to stand unless "the arbitrators clearly identif[ied] the applicable, governing law and then proceed[ed] to ignore it."[13] EMC had not, however, demonstrated that it had informed the arbitrator about limitations on punitive damages, notwithstanding that the arbitral award against EMC predated the *State Farm* decision. Thus, there was no evidence the arbitrators ignored the governing law. Accordingly, in the court's opinion, the arbitrator in *Stark* had not manifestly disregarded the law. The court recognized that the result may appear "draconian," but EMC "got exactly what it bargained for" in choosing "to resolve this dispute quickly and efficiently through arbitration."[14]

---

[10] *Id.* at 801-02.
[11] 38 U.S. 408 (2003).
[12] *Id.* at 425 (citations omitted).
[13] *Stark*, *supra* n. 1, 381 F.3d at 802 (citations and emphasis omitted).
[14] *Id.* at 803.

IV. Conclusion

An important lesson to be learned from the cases discussed above is that drafters of contract language must not fail to clearly express the intent to preclude punitive damages in an arbitral award. These cases also teach that courts appear to narrowly construe attempts to limit punitive damages in arbitration, making the drafter's task all the more important.

The provision excluding punitive damages awards in arbitration proceedings should be clear and unambiguous. It should state without qualification that such awards are not available to either party. A clause that purports to bar punitive damages without using the phrase "punitive damages" will likely fail in its goal. A clause that uses limiting language (such as "to the fullest extent of the law") in conjunction with denying the arbitrator the power to award punitive damages, could work against that intent. Because of the financial significance that a drafting error could have, drafters must consider carefully the choice of law governing the contract and the choice of arbitration rules, as these can play a part in the availability of punitive damages.

CHAPTER 41

NO PAY NO PLAY: HOW TO SOLVE THE NON-PAYING PARTY PROBLEM IN ARBITRATION

*Richard J. DeWitt and Richard J. DeWitt, III**

Preface

We first wrote about this issue in the February – April 2005 Dispute Resolution Journal. That article was subsequently updated, expanded and published as Chapter 28 of the 2010 American Arbitration Association Handbook on Arbitration Practice.

Our purpose in writing the Article and Chapter was to begin a discussion in the Arbitration community regarding what we believed and still believe is a serious issue of parties gaming the Arbitration Process.

Based on the articles[1] and cases citing our article and the chapter we were successful in initiating a discussion of the issue. However, though

* Richard J. DeWitt is a principal at DeWitt Law/ Resolve Disputes in Coral Gables, Florida. He has over 35 years' experience as a business and technology attorney and business executive. Mr. DeWitt serves as an arbitrator and mediator in domestic and international commercial, business, technology and employment disputes. He is a member of the American Arbitration Association's National Roster of Neutrals serving on its large, complex case panel, its commercial, employment and technology panels and its panel of Mediators the International Centre for Dispute Resolution Panel of Neutrals. He is also a Member of the CPR Institute panel of Neutrals and the CDRS Panel of Neutrals. He is a Florida Supreme Court Certificated Arbitrator and Florida Supreme Court Certified Circuit Civil Court Mediator. Mr. DeWitt is a member of the Florida Bar, a Fellow of the College of Commercial Arbitrators and Distinguished Fellow of International Academy of Mediators and a member of the National Academy of Distinguished Neutrals. He can be reached at 305-421-6400 or rdewitt@dewittlaw.net. His web sites are www.dewittlaw.net and www.resolvedisputes.net.

Richard J. DeWitt, III is an attorney at Arnstein & Lehr, LLP, in Ft. Lauderdale, Florida. He practices in the areas of land use, eminent domain, and government relations. He is a member of the Florida Bar, and can be reached at 954-713-7652 or rjdewitt@arnstein.com. The firm's websites are www.arnstein.com and www.eminentdomain.com.

[1] What to Do When A Party Fails To Pay Its Portion of Arbitration Fees, 59 No. 3 Prac. Law. 57; What To Do When A Party Fails To Pay Its Portion Of Arbitration Fees, Steve C.

there has been much discussion there has been little progress in resolving the non-paying party problem.

The solution we proposed, though not fully embraced by the Arbitration Community was partially, and we believe ineffectively incorporated in the AAA Rules.

The one area of the law recent court decisions seem to be clarifying is that the failure of a party to pay their share of the arbitrator's fees and costs constitutes a waiver of the right to arbitrate.

We have updated this chapter to reflect these developments with the goal of continuing the discussion of this issue.

I. Introduction

A continuing complaint of parties who put arbitration clauses in their commercial agreements is that they are not realizing the benefits of arbitration due to the nonpaying party problem. The problem arises when one party fails to pay its share of the required deposit for arbitrator compensation and administrative arbitration fees. This chapter discusses the practical implications and legal issues resulting from this problem and proposes a solution that should preclude parties from using nonpayment of deposits strategically as a means of "gaming" the arbitration process.

What happens when a party to arbitration fails to pay its share of a required deposit covering arbitrator compensation and arbitration fees? Generally, the other party is faced with the choice of:

(i) paying the nonpaying party's share of the deposit and then later seeking to be reimbursed the sums advanced as part of the final award; or
(ii) filing an action in court to obtain an order requiring the nonpaying party to advance the required deposit; or
(iii) discontinuing the arbitration and filing suit in court, claiming that the nonpaying party has waived the right to arbitrate.

These alternatives may not be available in some cases and, in some jurisdictions, courts are reviewing the alternatives. Where they are

---

Bennett, The Practical Lawyer; What to do When a Party Refuses to Pay Its Share of Arbitration Costs – Dispute Resolution Magazine Winter 2012; Stiffing The Arbitrators: The Problem Of Nonpayment In Commercial Arbitration Neal M. Eiseman1 & Brian Farkas, Harvard Negotiation Law Review; Costs, Costs, Costs: Managing Arbitration Costs and Dealing with the Non-Paying Party Eric Lindauer and Rob Shlachter, Portland, Oregon.

available, each alternative adds cost and delay to the resolution of the dispute and deprives the party who commenced arbitration of the main benefits of the process—that is, a faster, better, cheaper solution to resolving disputes. The ability of a party to stymie arbitration through nonpayment has the potential to discourage the use of arbitration to resolve commercial disputes, thus undermining the strong policy of encouraging arbitration that the courts have found to exist in the Federal Arbitration Act[2] (FAA) and state arbitration laws. Moreover, the options a party can use to resolve the nonpayment problem are not particularly advantageous.

II. The Alternatives

A. Advancing a Non-Paying Adversary's Deposit

Advancing the adversary's portion of a required deposit ends any hiatus in the arbitration due to nonpayment. This is probably the solution used in most cases and the one recommended by institutional arbitration providers like the American Arbitration Association (AAA). Under Rule R-54 of the AAA Commercial Arbitration Procedures, the expenses of arbitration "shall be borne equally" by the parties, unless they agree otherwise. AAA Rule R-57 allows for a suspension of proceedings in the event that all deposits are not advanced. It states:

> If arbitrator compensation or administrative charges have not been paid in full, the AAA may so inform the parties in order that one of them may advance the required payment.
>
> ....
>
> (e) Upon receipt of information from AAA that full payments have not been received, the arbitrator, on the arbitrator's own initiative or at the request of the AAA or a party, may order the suspension of the arbitration. If no arbitrator has yet been appointed, the AAA *may suspend* the proceedings (emphasis added).

However, having to advance a nonpaying adversary's deposit imposes an unfair burden. In a large, complex case, this can involve a significant

---

[2] 9 U.S.C. § 4.

financial expense that can deplete a party's resources and ability to prosecute its case. It also involves substantial risk that the nonpaying party will not be able to pay the amount advanced or any eventual award.

B. Order Enforcing Arbitration

The second option, filing an action in federal or state court to enforce the arbitration agreement and order the nonpaying party to advance its share of deposits, is expensive and time consuming. The law is well established that a party to a valid arbitration agreement may petition a court for an order directing the arbitration to proceed in the manner provided for in such an agreement.[3] However, this principle was not applied in a Ninth Circuit case involving the AAA rules.

In *Lifescan, Inc. v. Premier Diabetic Service,*[4] following the initial stages of arbitration but prior to the hearing, Premier informed the AAA it was unable to pay its pro-rata share of fees and costs. The arbitrators gave Lifescan the option of advancing Premier's share and recouping the amount advanced in a final award, but Lifescan declined to do so. Instead, Lifescan asked the arbitrators to continue the arbitration and bar Premier from presenting evidence. However, the AAA declined to proceed without Premier and suspended the proceedings.

Lifescan petitioned the district court to compel arbitration, order Premier to pay its pro-rata share of the deposit, and enter judgment against Premier on the underlying arbitration if it refused to pay. The district court granted Lifescan's petition, holding that Premier's failure to pay amounted to a "failure, neglect, or refusal" to arbitrate under Section 4 of the FAA and ordered Premiere to pay its pro-rata share of fees. Premier appealed. The Ninth Circuit reversed, holding that there was no "failure, neglect, or refusal" to arbitrate on Premier's part. The court reasoned that since the AAA Rules were incorporated into the parties' agreement, and these rules give the arbitrators discretion to apportion fees and expenses as appropriate, the arbitrators were authorized to decide whether the arbitration should proceed. Accordingly, the arbitrators acted within their discretion in deciding to allow the arbitration to continue, conditioned on Lifescan advancing the remaining fees. Thus, there was no basis for the district court to order Premier to pay the fees or to compel arbitration.

---

[3] Vanessa R. Elliot, *Arbitration Machination*, N.J.L.J. June 3, 2002.

[4] 363 F.3d 1010 (9th Cir. 2004).

Lifescan illustrates that, in addition to being costly and time consuming, requesting a court to enforce an arbitration agreement for nonpayment of fees may not be a solution.

C. Bring a Lawsuit in Court

The third option available to the party seeking to arbitrate is to abandon arbitration and sue in court. To defeat a defense based on the arbitration clause, the plaintiff can argue that the defendant waived its right to arbitrate through its failure to advance its share of the deposit for arbitration costs and fees.

There is a strong presumption in favor of arbitration and courts do not lightly infer a waiver of the right to arbitrate.[5] Inquiries into whether a party has waived this right tend to be fact-specific and are not governed by bright line rules.[6] The majority of federal court decisions consistently hold that the party asserting that a waiver has occurred bears a heavy burden of proof.

Courts generally consider three factors in conducting a waiver analysis: (1) the time that has elapsed from the commencement of litigation until the request for arbitration, (2) the amount of litigation activity to date, and (3) proof of prejudice.[7] But where litigation is commenced after an arbitration in which a respondent fails to pay its share of arbitration fees and costs, the first factor does not apply. However, the party seeking to litigate must show that the other party knew of its obligation to arbitrate but acted inconsistently therewith by failing to pay the arbitration fees. In addition, it must show the third factor—*i.e.*, that it suffered prejudice as a result of the alleged waiver.

Prejudice is the key inquiry.[8] Courts generally recognize two types of prejudice: substantive prejudice and prejudice caused by excessive cost and time delays. Substantive prejudice occurs when a party loses a motion on the merits and attempts to re-litigate the issue by initiating arbitration. Additionally, courts find prejudice when a party postpones initiating its contractual right to arbitrate and causes the other party to incur unnecessary delay or expense.[9] Refusal to pay half the filing fees

---

[5] Thyssen, Inc. v. Calypso Shipping Corp., S.A., 310 F.3d 102, 104-05 (2d. Cir. 2003).

[6] Cotton v. Slone, 4 F.3d 176, 179 (2d Cir. 1993).

[7] Louis Dreyfus Negoce S.A. v. Blystad Shipping & Trading, 252 F.3d 218, 229 (2d. Cir. 2001).

[8] *Thyssen*, *supra* n. 4, 310 F.3d at 105.

[9] *Id.*, *citing* Kramer v. Hammond, 943 F.2d 176, 179 (2d. Cir. 1991).

and costs has been found to constitute a waiver of the right to require arbitration.[10]

In *Sink v. Aden*,[11] the Ninth Circuit held that a party's prior default in arbitration precluded him from obtaining a stay of litigation pending arbitration under Section 3 of the FAA. In this case, Sink sued Aden in federal court for breach of an employment agreement. Pursuant to that agreement, which contained an arbitration clause, the court stayed the suit and referred the action to arbitration. Aden failed to pay or notify Sink of its inability to pay its pro-rata share of arbitration costs. Once the deadline for payment passed, the ADR provider informed the parties that it was suspending the arbitration due to nonpayment of fees. Sink filed a motion asking the arbitrator for an order of default, which the arbitrator granted. Sink then filed a motion with the district court to lift the stay of proceedings that had been entered pending arbitration. The district court granted the motion, finding that Aden was in default of the arbitration clause and had waived its right to arbitrate.[12]

Aden appealed to the Ninth Circuit, arguing that Section 4 of the FAA compelled the district court to return the parties to arbitration. The Ninth Circuit agreed with the district court, reasoning that Aden's failure to pay its pro-rata share of arbitration fees was a material breach of the arbitration agreement. Under these circumstances, it affirmed the order holding that Section 4 did not require the district court to send the parties back to arbitration.

In *Sink*, litigating was precisely what the parties agreed they would not do. Yet that is where they ended up. So neither party obtained the benefit of their bargain. Moreover, Sink had to incur additional costs and suffer additional delay trying to compel arbitration and later preparing papers for litigation in court.

The courts have taken a broader view of the waiver argument with one court holding that:

> "When the purpose of arbitration, to provide a cost-effective and efficient means of resolving a claim, is thwarted by a party's default in failing to pay the required fees, the paying party's right to have its dispute adjudicated and not to be unreasonably held at

---

[10] Sink v. Aden, 352 F.3d 1197 (9th Cir. 2003); Robert A. Harris, *When The Chickens Come Home To Roost*, CONN. L. TRIBUNE, Aug, 25, 2003.

[11] *Sink, supra* n. 9.

[12] *Id.*

the mercy of a nonpaying party outweighs the strong presumption in favor of arbitration, provided there is a factual basis for a finding of waiver."[13]

"Former employee was in default in proceeding with arbitration of employer's claims against him for misappropriation of trade secrets and breach of non-solicitation agreement, thus removing requirement for district court to stay proceedings in employer's action against employee, even though arbitrators did not make formal finding of default, where arbitration proceeding was terminated due to employee's failure to pay his share of arbitration fees."[14]

Thus, the three alternatives currently available to a party faced with a nonpaying adversary are far from satisfactory. They do not provide a better, faster, cheaper resolution of disputes. These solutions are flawed because they encourage and reward parties who "game" the arbitration process. They allow the nonpaying party to impose costs on its adversary, delay resolution of the matter and possibly avoid arbitration altogether. There should be a better way of solving this problem. We believe that there is.

III. Waiver: A Proposed Solution

Arbitration agreements generally require the claimant to pay the initial arbitration filing fee (if there is one) and for both parties to advance a deposit (in equal shares) sufficient to cover the arbitrator's fees and costs. When a party fails to pay its share of a required deposit, it is, in essence refusing to pay the arbitrator to hear its case.

We need a self-executing solution to prevent this from happening. The solution should encourage parties to pay for the process agreed to in their arbitration agreement. It should enhance the use and quality of arbitration. The solution we propose to address the nonpaying party problem is a waiver clause providing that the failure to pay a required deposit of arbitration costs and fees by either party constitutes a waiver

[13] Brandifino v. CryptoMetrics, Inc., 27 Misc.3d 513 (2010) 896 N.Y.S.2d 623, 2010 N.Y. Slip Op. 20062.

[14] Pre-Paid Legal Services, Inc. v. Cahill, 786 F.3d 1287 (2015).

by that party of the right to be heard, to present evidence, to cross-examine witnesses, and to assert counterclaims in the arbitration.[15]

We find an analogous concept in state corporation laws that bar a corporation from bringing or defending an action in court when it has failed to pay its annual corporate filing fees. Moreover, a written waiver is consistent with the contractual nature of arbitration and the allocation of part of the arbitrator's costs to the complainant as compensation for hearing its case, and part of the costs to the respondent as compensation for hearing its defenses and any counterclaim it may have.

A sample waiver clause to address the nonpaying party problem in commercial arbitration is:

> Proposed Waiver Clause to Solve the Nonpaying Party Problem
>
> Each party shall bear its own costs and expenses, an equal share of the arbitrators' compensation and administrative charges of the arbitration and shall make deposits with the [provider] of its share of the amounts requested by the [provider]. Failure or refusal by a party to pay its share of the deposits for arbitrators' compensation and administrative charges shall constitute a waiver by that party of its rights to be heard, present evidence, cross-examine witnesses and assert counterclaims. Informing the arbitrator(s) of a party's failure to pay its share of the deposits for arbitrators' compensation and administrative charges for the purpose of implementation this waiver provision shall not be deemed to affect the arbitrator(s) impartiality or ability to proceed with the arbitration.

The initial reaction to such a provision may be to question whether it violates due process and the concept of equal treatment of the parties required by arbitration laws. We believe that it does not. An explicit waiver should be consistent with the notion of party autonomy and we believe it is implicitly permitted under the FAA and most state arbitration laws.

---

[15] We discuss below why this proposed solution may not be appropriate in international, employment, or consumer agreements to arbitrate.

A. Contract and Waiver

Arbitration is a creature of contract[16] and the arbitration agreement itself constitutes a waiver of the right of access to the courts, the right to a jury trial, and the right to an appeal on most issues. Rights that are often waived include the right to jury trial,[17] the right to recover lost profits,[18] and consequential and punitive damages.[19]

Waivers are regularly used in all kinds of settings. There is no general doctrine of federal law preventing a waiver of constitutional or statutory rights in exchange for other things of value, such as lower prices or reduced litigation.[20] The courts have consistently held that, under the FAA, arbitration is strictly a matter of contract.[21] As such, parties generally are free to structure their arbitration agreements as they see fit and choose the terms under which they will arbitrate.[22] Moreover, as a general rule, parties are permitted to modify the provisions of federal and state arbitration laws by clear and explicit language unless such modification is specifically prohibited.

B. Federal Arbitration Act

The waiver clause we suggest is consistent with the FAA. The FAA requires arbitration agreements to be on the same footing as other contractual agreements and it provides that they are "valid, irrevocable and enforceable" absent factors that would "exist in law or equity for the revocation of any contract." Parties to arbitration agreements are free to customize the arbitration process as they see fit.[23] The FAA mandates that courts enforce these agreements according to their terms, and the courts have done so in arms-length, business-to-business agreements. Waivers of certain rights in arbitration agreements can raise issues of unconscionability in consumer and employment arbitration. However, we do not believe that this defense to enforcement would apply to this type of waiver in an arbitration agreement between sophisticated business parties.

---

[16] City of Alamo v. Garcia, 878 S.W.2d 664, 665 (Tex. App.-Corpus Christi 1994, no writ).
[17] Cole v. Burns Int'l Sec. Servs., 105 F.3d 1465, 1469 (D.C. Cir. 1997).
[18] Palmer v. Anderson, 603 P.2d 495 (Alaska 1979).
[19] Stark v. Sandberg, Phoenix & Von Gontard, P.C., 381 F.3d 793 (8th Cir. 2004).
[20] Carbajal v. H&R Block Tax Servs., 372 F.3d 903, 906-07 (7th Cir. 2004).
[21] Volt Info. Scis. v. Bd. of Tr. of Leland Stanford Jr. Univ., 489 U.S. 468, 472 (1989).
[22] *Id.*
[23] *Id.*

C. Uniform Arbitration Act (1955)

Out of the 49 states that have Arbitration statues, 35 states have adopted the 1955 Uniform Arbitration Act (UAA) and 14 states have adopted a modified version of the Act.[24] Section 5 of the 1955 UAA states: "*Unless otherwise provided* by the parties: . . . (b) the parties are entitled to be heard, to present evidence material to the controversy and to cross-examine witnesses appearing at the hearing (emphasis added). . ." From the italicized introductory language in Section 5, it is clear that the drafters of the 1955 UAA, and the legislators in states that adopted this Act in whole or in modified form, contemplated that the parties could modify the right to be heard, present material evidence and cross-examine witnesses at the hearing. Our proposed waiver clause simply and clearly indicates that the parties agree to waive the rights set out in Section 5(b) in the event either of them does not pay its share of any required deposit.

The drafters of the 1955 UAA knew how to restrict the use of waivers and they did so in Section 6, which states that a waiver of the parties' right to attorney representation prior to the proceeding or hearing is ineffective. It is significant that the states that enacted the 1955 UAA in its entirety did not consider it necessary to restrict waivers of the rights in Section 5(b).

As one of the states that adopted the 1955 UAA, Florida has similar provisions in its Arbitration Code. Section 682.06(2) provides that "[u]nless otherwise provided by the agreement or provision for arbitration: . . . (2) The parties are entitled to be heard, to present evidence material to the controversy and to cross- examine witnesses appearing at the hearing." Section 682.07 (2003) does not permit the parties to waive representation by an attorney prior to an arbitration proceeding. Thus, like the drafters of the 1955 UAA, the Florida legislature knew how to prevent a waiver, yet chose not to do so in Section 682.06(2).

D. The Revised Uniform Arbitration Act (2000)

The 2000 Revised Uniform Arbitration Act (RUAA) has so far been adopted in 13 states.[25] Section 15(d) of the RUAA is identical to Section 5(b) of the 1955 UAA. However, unlike the earlier UAA, the

---

[24] www.nccusi.org/update

[25] Hawaii, Nevada, New Jersey, New Mexico, North Carolina, North Dakota, Oregon Utah, Alaska, Colorado, District of Columbia, Oklahoma and Washington.

RUAA has detailed provisions in Section 4(b) and (c) stating which rights may not be waived. The rights in Section 15(d) are not among them. Section 4(a) addresses the rights that can be waived. It provides: "Except as otherwise provided in subsection (b) and (c), a party to an agreement to arbitrate or to an arbitration proceeding may waive or the parties may vary the effect of, the requirements of this [Act] to the extent permitted by law (emphasis added)."

Accordingly, in states that have adopted (and will adopt) the RUAA, Section 4(a) allows Section 15(d) rights (i.e., the right to be heard, present evidence, cross-examine witnesses, and present counterclaims) to be waived.

It should be noted that, absent an explicit waiver or other modification of Section 15(d), the parties are entitled to be heard, present evidence material to the controversy, and cross-examine witnesses appearing at the hearing. Thus, the denial of such rights by an arbitrator violates the right to a fundamentally fair hearing and due process.[26]

E. Oregon Statute

The "waiver approach" to the problem caused when one party fails to bear its share of arbitrator fees has already been accepted by the Oregon legislature and executive branch. In 1997, the Oregon legislature amended its arbitration statute to deal with this problem. It enacted Section 36.400(4), which states:

> The arbitrator shall not allow any party to appear or participate in the arbitration proceeding after the transfer unless the party pays the arbitrator fee established by court rule or the party *obtains a waiver or deferral of the fee from the court* and provides a copy of the waiver or deferral to the arbitrator (emphasis added).
>
> The failure of a party to appear or participate in the arbitration proceeding by reason of failing to pay the arbitrator fee or obtain a waiver or deferral of the fee does not affect the ability of the party to appeal the arbitrator's decision and award....

[26] Matter of Coty Inc. v Anchor Constr., No. 601499-02, 2003 WL 139551 (N.Y. Sup. Ct. Jan. 8, 2003), *aff'd*, 776 N.Y.S.2d 795 (N.Y. App. Div. 2004).

IV. Recommended Procedure and Limitations

The waiver clause we advocate should not lead to a default judgment against the nonpaying party. The claimant must still prove its case to the arbitrator at a hearing.[27] The nonpaying party may or may not show up, but because of the contractual waiver, should not participate. The arbitrator should proceed with the hearing, make a determination on the case presented by the claimant, and issue an award.

Our proposal to use a waiver clause to resolve the nonpaying party problem is limited to domestic commercial arbitration. We do not recommend it for international, employment and consumer arbitration.

In international arbitration conducted under the FAA or state arbitration laws, the issue is not the validity of the waiver, but the enforceability of the award in foreign jurisdictions under the New York Convention on the Recognition and Enforcement of Foreign Arbitral Awards (the New York Convention) and the Inter-American Convention on International Commercial Arbitration (the Panama Convention). The reason is the language in Article V, § 1(b) of the New York Convention stating that "recognition and enforcement of the award may be refused . . . [when it is proven] . . . (b) the party against whom the award is invoked . . . was otherwise unable to present his case." (Similar language appears in Article 5, § 1(b) of the Panama Convention.) Until courts recognize nonpayment as a legitimate ground to waive these rights, we caution against using the proposed waiver language where enforcement of an international award might be sought under the New York or Panama Conventions.

The waiver for nonpayment of arbitration fees and costs is best suited for domestic, business-to-business agreements. Employment and consumer arbitration agreements have a different character because they are often the product of unequal bargaining power between the parties. They create "the greatest tension between the function of law and the functionality of arbitration."[28] As a result, these agreements have been subject to strict review by the courts to determine whether they are procedurally and substantively unconscionable. Considering the importance of protecting consumers and employees from being taken advantage of by parties with greater bargaining power, the proposed

---

[27] American Arbitration Association, Commercial Arbitration Procedures, Rule R-57 (d), available at www.adr.org.

[28] THOMAS E. CHARBONNEAU, THE LAW AND PRACTICE OF ARBITRATION (2d ed. 2004).

waiver may not be upheld against a consumer or employee and we question whether it would be appropriate in that context.

The American Arbitration Association adopted Rule R- 57 which provides in part:

R-57 Remedies for Nonpayment

If arbitrator compensation or administrative charges have not been paid in full, the AAA may so inform the parties in order that one of them may advance the required payment.

(a) Upon receipt of the information from the AAA that payment for administrative charges or deposits for arbitrator compensation have not been paid in full, to the extent the law allows, a party may request that the arbitrator take specific measures relating to a party's non-payment.
(b) Such measures may include, but not limited to, limiting a party's ability to assert or pursue their claim. In no event, however, shall a party be precluded from defending a claim or counterclaim.
(c) The arbitrator must provide the party opposing a request for such measures with the opportunity to respond prior to making any ruling regarding the same.
(d) In the event that the arbitrator grants any request for relief which limits any party's participation in the arbitration, the arbitrator shall require the party who is making a claim and who has made appropriate payments to submit such evidence as the arbitrator may require for the making of an award.

Though this rule is a step in the right direction, it has little practical application since the vast majority of the non-paying parties are respondents, and if they are not paying the Arbitrators fees they are not likely to be asserting claims.

V. Conclusion

The nonpaying party is continues to be a growing problem in commercial arbitration. We believe that the use of a waiver clause such as we propose is a viable approach to solving this problem. It is one way to discourage nonpayment as a tactic in a process supported by strong legislative policy and federal and state court decisions as a faster, better, and cheaper solution to managing disputes.

CHAPTER 42

PREVAILING PARTIES AND ATTORNEYS' FEES

*Stephen P. Gilbert**

I. Introduction: The Arbitrator's Challenge

Arbitrators are often confronted with agreements allowing or requiring an award of attorneys' fees to the "prevailing party."[1] Even when arbitration agreements are silent about attorneys' fees, during the proceedings both sides often request them.

Statutes may allow arbitrators to award attorneys' fees even when not authorized by the parties' agreement or requested by the parties.[2]

Rules governing arbitrations usually expressly empower arbitrators to award attorneys' fees. For example, AAA Commercial Arbitration Rules, R-47(d)(ii) allows the arbitrator to award attorneys' fees "if all parties have requested such an award or it is authorized by law or their arbitration agreement."[3] UNCITRAL Arbitration Rules, Article 40 requires the arbitration tribunal to "fix the costs of arbitration in the final award" and defines "costs" to include "[t]he legal and other costs incurred by the parties in relation to the arbitration to the extent that the

---

* Stephen P. Gilbert (www.spgadr.com) is a patent, trademark, and copyright Attorney, an Arbitrator, and a Mediator and was a Partner at a major multinational law firm for over two decades, where he was co-leader of its IP practice group. He is a Fellow of the College of Commercial Arbitrators and a Fellow of the Chartered Institute of Arbitrators. Before becoming a lawyer, he worked as a chemical engineer and a computer programmer.

[1] Black's Law Dictionary, p. 1232 (9th ed. 2009) (emphasis in original), defines "*prevailing party*" as "[a] party in whose favor a judgment is rendered, regardless of the amount of damages awarded" and notes that "*prevailing party*" is "[a]lso termed *successful party*."

[2] *See, e.g.*, the revised Florida Arbitration Code (effective July 1, 2013), Section 682.11 ("Remedies; fees and expenses of arbitration proceeding"), Subsection 2: "An arbitrator may award reasonable attorney fees and other reasonable expenses of arbitration *if such an award is authorized by law in a civil action involving the same claim or* by the agreement of the parties to the arbitration proceeding" (emphasis added).

[3] American Arbitration Association, Commercial Arbitration Rules, effective October 1, 2013 (fee schedule amended and effective June 1, 2010).

arbitral tribunal determines that the amount of such costs is reasonable."[4] Some rules allow the arbitrator to award attorneys' fees even if not explicitly authorized by the parties' agreement or requested by the parties. For example, ICDR International Arbitration Rules, Article 31 requires the arbitration tribunal to "fix the costs of arbitration in its award" and specifies that "[s]uch costs may include ... the reasonable costs for legal representation of a successful party."[5]

Whether the arbitration agreement allows or requires an award of attorneys' fees, all the parties later request them, or the governing statutes or rules allow or mandate such an award, the arbitrator will likely have to decide who is the "prevailing party" because (at least in the U.S.) that seems to be the most common term used for denominating to whom attorneys' fees are to be awarded.

In court, "the general 'American rule' [is] that the prevailing party may not recover attorneys' fees as costs or otherwise."[6] Federal statutes that allow or require an award of attorneys' fees, and are thereby exceptions to the general rule, include antitrust, patent, and civil rights laws.[7] Even if attorneys' fees are not being awarded, it still may be

---

[4] United Nations Commission on International Trade Law, UNCITRAL Arbitration Rules, as revised in 2010.

[5] International Centre for Dispute Resolution, International Arbitration Rules, effective June 1, 2009 (fee schedule amended and effective June 1, 2010).

[6] Alyeska Pipeline Co. v. Wilderness Society, 421 U.S. 240, 245 (1975).

[7] Antitrust: "In any action under this section in which the plaintiff substantially prevails, the court shall award the cost of suit, including a reasonable attorney's fee, to such plaintiff." (15 U.S.C. § 26); patent: "The court in exceptional cases may award reasonable attorney fees to the prevailing party." (35 U.S.C. § 285); and civil rights: "In any action commenced pursuant to this subchapter, the court, in its discretion, may allow the prevailing party, other than the United States, a reasonable attorney's fee as part of the costs, and the United States shall be liable for costs the same as a private person." (42 U.S.C. § 2000a-3(b)). Not all U.S. fee-shifting statutes require "prevailing party" status for an award of attorneys' fees. *See, e.g.*, 29 U.S.C. § 1132(g)(1), which concerns protection of employee benefit rights: "In any action under this subchapter (other than an action described in paragraph (2)) by a participant, beneficiary, or fiduciary, the court in its discretion may allow a reasonable attorney's fee and costs of action to either party." In Hardt v. Reliance Standard Life Insurance Co., 560 U.S. 242, 130 S.Ct. 2149 (2010), the Supreme Court held that one did not have to be a "prevailing party" to be awarded attorneys' fees under § 1132(g)(1), 560 U.S. at ___, 130 S.Ct. at 2156, and that because plaintiff "achieved 'some success on the merits,' ... the District Court properly exercised its discretion" to award attorneys' fees to her, 560 U.S. at ___, 130 S.Ct. at 2159. Non-statutory "exceptions [to the general American rule against awarding attorneys' fees] are unquestionably assertions of inherent power in the courts to allow attorneys' fees in particular situations," for example, allowing the trustee of a fund or property, or a party preserving the fund or property, to

necessary to determine who is the "prevailing party," for example, to award costs other than attorneys' fees.[8]

What is often missing in the agreements, statutes, and rules allowing or requiring an award of attorneys' fees to the "prevailing party" is any touchstone to help tribunals readily determine who that party is. To be sure, there are some attempts in statutes to define "prevailing party," but the definitions often do not help because, for example, they are tautological.[9] Definitions of "prevailing party" in arbitration agreements are often no better, as shown by this sampling:

- the party in whose favor a final order or award is rendered;
- the party that is afforded greater relief;
- the party that prevails, whether affirmatively or by a successful defense, with respect to claims having the greatest value or importance as reasonably determined by the arbitrator; or
- the net winner of a dispute, taking into account the claims pursued, the claims on which the pursuing party was successful,

---

recover his or her attorneys' fees, assessing attorneys' fees for the willful disobedience of a court order, and assessing attorneys' fees if the losing party has acted in bad faith. Alyeska Pipeline, 421 U.S. at 257-260. "[T]the foundation for the historic practice of granting reimbursement for the costs of litigation other than the conventional taxable costs is part of the original authority of the chancellor to do equity in a particular situation." Sprague v. Ticonic National Bank, 307 U.S. 161, 166 (1939).

[8] Federal Rules of Civil Procedure, Rule 54(d)(1) reads in part as follows: "Unless a federal statute, these rules, or a court order provides otherwise, costs—other than attorney's fees—should be allowed to the prevailing party." Similarly, Idaho Rules of Civil Procedure, Rule 54(d)(1)(B) provides that "In determining which party to an action is a prevailing party and entitled to costs, the trial court shall in its sound discretion consider the final judgment or result of the action in relation to the relief sought by the respective parties. The trial court in its sound discretion may determine that a party to an action prevailed in part and did not prevail in part, and upon so finding may apportion the costs between and among the parties in a fair and equitable manner after considering all of the issues and claims involved in the action and the resultant judgment or judgments obtained." (Idaho Rules of Civil Procedure, Rule 54(e)(1), which concerns attorneys' fees, relies on that definition of "prevailing party": "In any civil action the court may award reasonable attorney fees … to the prevailing party or parties as defined in Rule 54(d)(1)(B), when provided for by any statute or contract.")

[9] For example, New York defines "prevailing party" in certain proceedings as "a plaintiff or petitioner in the civil action against the state who prevails in whole or in substantial part where such party and the state prevail upon separate issues." New York Civil Practice Law & Rules, Article 86, § 8602. Cal. Civ. Code § 1717(b)(1) defines a prevailing party in a contract dispute as "the party who recovered a greater relief in the action on the contract."

the amount of money sought, the amount of money awarded, and offsets or counterclaims pursued by the other party.

Consider having to determine who is the prevailing party and how much of its claimed attorneys' fees to award in the following situations. Assume there is a single claim for relief, for example, a demand for money damages, that claimant is awarded 100% of what it demanded, and that there is no counterclaim. Claimant is unquestionably the prevailing party and, barring unusual circumstances, should receive all of its reasonable claimed attorneys' fees. Now assume claimant receives only 10% of what it demanded. Is it still the prevailing party and, if so, how much of its reasonable attorneys' fees should it be awarded? Does it make any difference if that 10% recovery equals ten million dollars or if it equals one hundred dollars?

What if there are two claims for relief, one for monetary damages and the other for an injunction barring respondent from certain future activity. If claimant receives 100% of the damages requested and the injunction issues, it again is clearly the prevailing party and, barring unusual circumstances, should receive all of its reasonable claimed attorneys' fees. But what if it is awarded all of the damages but not the injunction? What if it is granted the injunction but not awarded any damages or only 10% of its requested damages? What if claimant asserts five claims, several for monetary damages and several for equitable relief, and claimant prevails on only some of them?

What if there are one or more counterclaims in each of the preceding cases and respondent prevails on none, one, or all of its counterclaims? What if the only claim on which claimant prevails is for monetary damages and the only counterclaim on which respondent prevails is for equitable relief? Does it make any difference if the set of claim(s) and the set of counterclaim(s) arise out of different situations (*e.g.*, a breach of contract by respondent and an unrelated breach of the same contract by claimant, a breach of one contract by respondent and a breach of a different contract by claimant)? Does litigation misconduct by either or both parties make any difference? What if some of the claims and/or counterclaims are frivolous?[10]

[10] "The determination of a 'prevailing party' becomes even more complicated in cases involving multiple claims and parties …; the granting of non-monetary relief to one or more parties …; and where the ultimate award of money damages does not adequately represent the actual success of the parties under the peculiar posture of the case. … These cases demonstrate the need for a flexible and reasoned approach to deciding in

There are numerous possibilities, many of which do not have an immediately clear-cut answer to the question "Who is the prevailing party?" let alone to the question "What portion of the prevailing party's reasonable attorneys' fees should be awarded?"

When dealing with attorneys' fees awards in commercial cases, most arbitrators will turn to the case law for guidance, and even though it is difficult to extract from it any widely applicable rules that can always help an arbitrator readily determine who is the prevailing party and what portion of its reasonable attorneys' fees should be awarded, the case law is still a good starting point.[11] Thus, this article first discusses several modern U.S. Supreme Court attorneys' fees cases that are often cited in commercial cases even though they themselves involved non-commercial disputes, then several federal and state court opinions that dealt with awards of attorneys' fees or costs in commercial disputes, and then a suggested approach for arbitrators who are considering awarding attorneys' fees.

II. U.S. Supreme Court Cases

In *Hensley v. Eckerhart*, 461 U.S. 424 (1983), a civil rights case, the issue was whether a partially prevailing plaintiff could recover attorneys' fees for legal services on unsuccessful claims. The Supreme Court said that a "typical formulation" for making the "threshold determination" of who is the prevailing party is whether that party "'succeed[s] on any

---

particular cases who actually is *the* 'prevailing party.'" Mountain States Broadcasting Company v. Neale, 783 P.2d 551, 556 n.7 (Utah Ct. App. 1989) (citations omitted; emphasis in original).

[11] The arbitrator must also consider other issues in connection with any award of attorneys' fees, including for which claims on which a party has prevailed may an award be made. For example, if the governing attorneys' fees clause provides for an award concerning *any dispute* between the parties, that would seem to be broad enough to cover contract claims as well as tort claims (*e.g.*, interference with contract, fraud in the inducement); however, awarding attorneys' fees for prevailing on tort claims would seem to be outside the scope of a clause that provides for an award of attorneys' fees for prevailing in *an action to enforce the contract*. *Cf.* Santisas v. Goodin, 17 Cal.4th 599, 607-08 (1998) ("In the event legal action is instituted by the Broker(s), or any party to this agreement, or arising out of the execution of this agreement or the sale, or to collect commissions, the prevailing party shall be entitled to receive from the other party a reasonable attorney fee to be determined by the court in which such action is brought" held to be broad enough to cover tort and contract claims: "If a contractual attorney fee provision is phrased broadly enough, as this one is, it may support an award of attorney fees to the prevailing party in an action alleging both contract and tort claims ….").

significant issue in litigation which achieves some of the benefit the part[y] sought in bringing suit.'"[12] The Court approvingly quoted a Fifth Circuit Court of Appeals case that said "the proper focus is whether the plaintiff has been successful on the central issue as exhibited by the fact that he has acquired the primary relief sought."[13]

The Court then considered how to quantify the attorneys' fees to be awarded.

> The most useful starting point for determining the amount of a reasonable fee is the number of hours reasonably expended on the litigation multiplied by a reasonable hourly rate. ...
>
> The district court also should exclude from this initial fee calculation hours that were not "reasonably expended." ....
>
> The product of reasonable hours times a reasonable rate does not end the inquiry. There remain other considerations that may lead the district court to adjust the fee upward or downward, including the important factor of the "results obtained." This factor is particularly crucial where a plaintiff is deemed "prevailing" even though he succeeded on only some of his claims for relief. In this situation two questions must be addressed. First, did the plaintiff fail to prevail on claims that were unrelated to the claims on which he succeeded? Second, did the plaintiff achieve a level of success that makes the hours reasonably expended a satisfactory basis for making a fee award?[14]

The Court answered the question it had posed (whether a partially prevailing plaintiff could recover attorneys' fees for legal services on unsuccessful claims) as follows:

> We hold that the extent of a plaintiff's success is a crucial factor in determining the proper amount of an award of attorney's fees under 42 U.S.C. § 1988. Where the plaintiff has failed to prevail on a claim that is distinct in all respects from his successful claims, the hours spent on the unsuccessful claim should be excluded in considering the amount of a reasonable fee. Where a

---

[12] 461 U.S. at 433 (*citing* Nadeau v. Helgemoe, 581 F.2d 275, 278-279 (1st Cir. 1978)).

[13] 461 U.S. at 433 n.8 (*citing* Taylor v. Sterrett, 640 F.2d 663, 669 (5th Cir. 1981)).

[14] 461 U.S. at 433-37 (footnote and citations omitted).

> lawsuit consists of related claims, a plaintiff who has won substantial relief should not have his attorney's fee reduced simply because the district court did not adopt each contention raised. But where the plaintiff achieved only limited success, the district court should award only that amount of fees that is reasonable in relation to the results obtained.[15]

Hewitt v. Helms, 482 U.S. 755 (1987), was a case under 42 U.S.C. § 1983 in which a prisoner claimed he had been denied due process and other rights. The Third Circuit Court of Appeals held his constitutional rights had been violated and said that holding was "'a form of judicial relief which serves to affirm the plaintiff's assertion that the defendants' actions were unconstitutional ....'"[16] The Supreme Court denied his request for attorneys' fees under 42 U.S.C. § 1988, saying that because Helms obtained no relief, he was not a prevailing party: he did not recover damages, no injunction or declaratory judgment was entered in his favor, and he did not obtain relief without benefit of a formal judgment, *e.g.*, through a consent decree or settlement. "Respect for ordinary language requires that a plaintiff receive at least some relief on the merits of his claim before he can be said to prevail."[17]

In *Rhodes v. Stewart*, 488 U.S. 1 (1988) (*per curiam*), the Supreme Court cited *Hewitt* and held that two prisoners were not "prevailing parties" under 42 U.S.C. § 1983 entitling them to an award of attorneys' fees because by the time the District Court issued its original order in their favor, neither was still in custody (one had died and the other had been released). The Court emphasized the importance of a judicial decree that changes the relationship of the parties: "'The real value of the judicial pronouncement—what makes it a proper judicial resolution of a "case or controversy" rather than an advisory opinion—is in the settling of some dispute *which affects the behavior of the defendant towards the plaintiff*.'"[18]

In *Texas State Teachers Association v. Garland Independent School District*, 489 U.S. 782 (1989), a civil rights case involving teachers, the Supreme Court said that if plaintiff "succeed[s] on 'any significant issue in litigation which achieve[s] some of the benefit ... sought in bringing suit,' the plaintiff has crossed the threshold to a fee award of some kind," that "to be considered a prevailing party within the meaning of § 1988, the

---

[15] 461 U.S. at 440.
[16] 482 U.S. at 759.
[17] 482 U.S. at 759-60.
[18] 488 U.S. at 4 (*citing Hewitt,* 482 U.S. at 761 (emphasis in original)).

plaintiff must be able to point to a resolution of the dispute which changes the legal relationship between itself and the defendant," and that "the degree of the plaintiff's overall success goes to the reasonableness of the award under *Hensley*, not to the availability of a fee award *vel non*."[19]

In *Farrar v. Hobby*, 506 U.S. 103 (1992), Supreme Court held that although the civil rights plaintiff was a "prevailing party" under 42 U.S.C. § 1988, it was not entitled to attorneys' fees because it recovered only nominal damages. The Court reaffirmed its views that "a plaintiff 'prevails' when actual relief on the merits of his claim materially alters the legal relationship between the parties by modifying the defendant's behavior in a way that directly benefits the plaintiff,"[20] that "the prevailing party inquiry does not turn on the magnitude of the relief obtained,"[21] and that "[i]n some circumstances, even a plaintiff who formally 'prevails' under § 1988 should receive no attorney's fees at all," for example, where plaintiff seeks compensatory damages but receives only nominal damages.[22]

Although the "catalyst theory" was less likely to be asserted by parties in commercial cases than in civil rights cases as a basis for being anointed prevailing parties, it is described for the sake of completeness. Under that theory, if plaintiff brought suit based on defendant's behavior and

---

[19] 489 U.S. at 791-93.

[20] 506 U.S. at 111-12. This principle was reiterated in Lefemine v. Wideman, 568 U.S. ___, 133 S.Ct. 9 (2012), where the Supreme Court held plaintiff was a prevailing party under 42 U.S.C. § 1988 because the District Court ruled that defendants had violated plaintiff's rights and enjoined them from engaging in similar conduct in the future, which "worked the requisite material alteration in the parties' relationship" under *Farrar* and *Rhodes*.

[21] 506 U.S. at 114.

[22] 506 U.S. at 115. But receiving only nominal damages does not necessarily disqualify a party from being the prevailing party and receiving its attorneys' fees. In Robinson v. City of Edmond, 160 F.3d 1275 (10th Cir. 1998), a First Amendment case, the Court of Appeals confronted the problem of awarding attorneys' fees to plaintiffs who had not prevailed on all of their claims (plaintiffs prevailed on their principal goal of removing the Latin cross from the city's official seal but not on their Free Exercise Clause claim, the claim for individual-capacity liability against city officials, or the claim for actual damages—they received only nominal damages). The appellate court said the trial court's holding that plaintiffs had achieved only partial success was "legally indefensible in light of the fact that all of the unsuccessful claims were intertwined with the successful claims through a common core of facts or related legal theories," that the cited Supreme Court cases "demonstrate that when a plaintiff achieves the principal goal of her lawsuit, lack of success on some of her interrelated claims may not be used as a basis for reducing the plaintiff's fee award," and that "'the most critical factor is the degree of success obtained.'" 160 F.3d at 1282-84.

defendant thereafter modified its behavior without a court ordering it to do so, plaintiff was considered the prevailing party. The Supreme Court put that theory to bed (at least for some Federal statutory claims) in *Buckhannon Board & Care Home, Inc. v. West Virginia Dept. of Health & Human Resources*, 532 U.S. 598 (2001). There, plaintiffs sought attorneys' fees under the Fair Housing Amendments Act and the Americans with Disabilities Act, both of which gave discretion to the courts to allow prevailing parties reasonable attorneys' fees. The Supreme Court noted that "enforceable judgments on the merits and court-ordered consent decrees create the 'material alteration of the legal relationship of the parties' necessary to permit an award of attorney's fees" but that "[a] defendant's voluntary change in conduct, although perhaps accomplishing what the plaintiff sought to achieve by the lawsuit, lacks the necessary judicial *imprimatur* on the change."[23] The Court said it could not "agree that the term 'prevailing party' authorizes federal courts to award attorney's fees to a plaintiff who, by simply filing a nonfrivolous but nonetheless potentially meritless lawsuit ..., has reached the 'sought-after destination' without obtaining any judicial relief."[24]

The question in *Sole v. Wyner*, 551 U.S. 74 (2007), was whether "a plaintiff who gains a preliminary injunction after an abbreviated hearing, but is denied a permanent injunction after a dispositive adjudication on the merits, qualifies as a 'prevailing party' within the compass of [42 U.S.C.] § 1988(b)?"[25] The Court held it did not. "We express no view on whether, in the absence of a final decision on the merits of a claim for permanent injunctive relief, success in gaining a preliminary injunction may sometimes warrant an award of counsel fees. We decide only that a plaintiff who gains a preliminary injunction does not qualify for an award of counsel fees under § 1988(b) if the merits of the case are ultimately decided against her."[26]

In *Fox v. Vice*, 563 U.S. 2, 131 S.Ct. 2205 (2011), the Supreme Court considered the award to defendant under 42 U.S.C. § 1988 of all of its attorneys' fees for all federal and state claims asserted against it by plaintiff. Defendant had prevailed on all federal claims, which the District

---

[23] 532 U.S. at 603-05 (emphasis in original).

[24] 532 U.S. at 606. *Buckhannon*'s elimination of the catalyst theory has been criticized on a number of grounds. *See, e.g.*, Loring, "The Catalyst Theory Meets The Supreme Court—Common Sense Takes a Vacation," *Boston College Law Review*, vol. 43, no. 4, pp. 973-1008 (2002).

[25] 551 U.S. at 77.

[26] 551 U.S. at 86.

Court had held were frivolous; plaintiff's state law claims, regarding which the District Court had not made any holding regarding frivolousness *vel non*, had been remanded. The Supreme Court elucidated a but-for test: "Section 1988 permits the defendant to receive only the portion of his fees that he would not have paid but for the frivolous claim. … So if a frivolous claim occasioned the attorney's fees at issue, a court may decide that the defendant should not have to pay them. But if the defendant would have incurred those fees anyway, to defend against *non*-frivolous claims, then a court has no basis for transferring the expense to the plaintiff."[27] Thus, the dispositive question is "not whether attorney costs at all relate to a non-frivolous claim, but whether the costs would have been incurred in the absence of the frivolous allegation."[28]

III. Federal and State Commercial Cases

The following sampling of federal and state commercial cases illustrates some of the different approaches used by courts for determining who is the prevailing party and how much to award.

When both parties prevail on their claims/counterclaims and the contract specifies that attorneys' fees are to be awarded to the prevailing party, some courts have employed the "net judgment" rule. *See, e.g., Mountain States Broadcasting Company v. Neale*, 783 P.2d 551 (Utah Ct. App. 1989):

> Our review of the relevant case law convinces us that under the provision at issue, there can be only one prevailing party even though both plaintiff and defendant are awarded money damages on claims arising from the same transaction.[8] … We hold that in the present circumstances the party in whose favor the "net" judgment is entered must be considered the "prevailing party" and is entitled to an award of its fees….
>
> [8] It appears that where both plaintiff and defendant recover in the same action but the counterclaim does not arise from the same transaction as the plaintiff's claim, both parties may be considered to have prevailed and, therefore, to be entitled to a portion of their fees. …[29]

[27] 563 U.S. at ___, 131 S.Ct. at 2215 (emphasis in original).
[28] 563 U.S. at ___, 131 S.Ct. at 2216.
[29] 783 P.2d at 556 (footnote and citations omitted).

Courts have noted the difficulty of applying the "net judgment" rule of *Mountain States* in cases having claims and counterclaims that are not all for money. *See, e.g., Stichting Mayflower Recreational Fonds v. Newpark Resources, Inc.*, 917 F.2d 1239 (10th Cir. 1990):

> We recognize the difficulty of applying a "net" rule in the context of multiple claims and actions for declaratory relief. Nevertheless, the *Mountain States* decision indicates a preference for such a rule, and we think the district court should attempt to weigh the relative success of the parties on the contract claims if it can find a reasoned basis for doing so. One possibility, for example, is to determine whether one party prevailed on the most significant issues underlying the dispute. The net judgment rule need not be mechanically applied, though, and *Mountain States* recognizes the need for a "flexible and reasoned approach" to deciding in particular cases who actually is the prevailing party. ... This flexible approach implies that the district court's assessment will be given due deference upon review.[30]

In *Schulz v. Hembree*, 975 F.2d 572 (9th Cir. 1992), the Court of Appeals considered how to determine the amount of attorneys' fees to award to defendants who had successfully defended against numerous claims, only two of which were subject to fee-shifting statutes.

> There are various allocation rules courts might apply when confronted with a multiple-claim lawsuit where a party is entitled to recover attorneys' fees under only some of the claims.
>
> One option is to focus on the marginal fees precipitated by the inclusion of [fee-]shifting claims.... The converse approach focuses on the total fees related to the [fee-]shifting claims. ...
>
> Both approaches are conceptually flawed. The marginal fees approach undercompensates the prevailing party, because some of the work done on ordinary claims will always benefit the litigation of the [fee-]shifting claims. Conversely, the total fees approach overcompensates: Some of the work benefiting both

[30] 917 F.2d at 1248 n.9 (citation omitted; emphasis in original).

> [fee-]shifting and ordinary claims might have been omitted had only the [fee-]shifting claims been brought.
>
> We therefore adopt an intermediate rule, one more closely tailored to the policies underlying fee-shifting statutes. We hold that the prevailing party may recover that amount in fees it would have incurred had the [fee-]shifting claims been litigated by themselves.[31]

In *Prosperi v. Code, Inc.*, 626 So.2d 1360 (Fla. 1993), the trial court entered a net money judgment for defendant-contractor (after offset) but also found that the attorneys' fees and costs incurred in the litigation flowed "directly, naturally, and proximately" from defendant-contractor's having filed certain false affidavits.[32] The trial court denied attorneys' fees to plaintiff-owner in view of the "net judgment" rule, and the intermediate appellate court affirmed. The Supreme Court of Florida reversed:

> The fact that the claimant obtains a net judgment is a significant factor but it need not always control the determination of who should be considered the prevailing party. We hold that in considering whether to apply the net judgment rule, the trial judge must have the discretion to consider the equities and determine which party has in fact prevailed on the significant issues.[33]

Because the trial judge had made it clear he believed plaintiff-owner was the innocent party (but felt constrained not to award him attorneys' fees under a strict application of the net judgment rule), the Supreme Court of Florida "quash[ed] the decision below and remand[ed] with directions that attorney's fees be awarded to the owner."[34]

Hsu v. Abbara, 9 Cal.4th 863 (1995), concerned California Civil Code Section 1717, which the Supreme Court of California said

> defines the phrase "party prevailing on the contract" as "the party who recovered a greater relief in the action on the contract," and it provides that a trial court "may also determine

[31] 975 F.2d at 576-77 (footnotes omitted).
[32] 626 So.2d at 1361-62.
[33] 626 So.2d at 1363.
[34] *Id.*

that there is no party prevailing on the contract for purposes of this section."[35]

The question to be answered was "whether a trial court may determine that there is no 'party prevailing on the contract' when the court renders a simple, unqualified decision in favor of the defendant on the only contract claim in the action."[36] The Court answered as follows:

> We agree that *in determining litigation success*, courts should respect substance rather than form, and to this extent should be guided by "equitable considerations." For example, a party who is denied direct relief on a claim may nonetheless be found to be a prevailing party if it is clear that the party has otherwise achieved its main litigation objective. ... But when one party obtains a "simple, unqualified win" on the single contract claim presented by the action, the trial court may not invoke equitable considerations unrelated to litigation success, such as the parties' behavior during settlement negotiations or discovery proceedings, except as expressly authorized by statute.[37]

In *Anderson v. Jensen Racing, Inc.*, 931 P.2d 763 (Ore. 1997), the Supreme Court of Oregon held that "prevailing party" for purposes of awarding attorneys' fees under the contract at issue meant "the party in whose favor final judgment is rendered" and that plaintiffs were the "prevailing party" because they were awarded contract damages even though they had failed to prevail on most of their claims, *e.g.*, for an accounting, for declaratory relief (all of the claims arose out of the contract).[38] In a concurring opinion, Justice Durham said comparing success by opposing parties on claims for different types of relief were "convoluted inquiries" that "bear the characteristics of a metaphysical attempt to compare the incomparable," "offer[ed] no particular solution to problems of this sort," and indicated he wanted to draw "attention to those complexities because contracting parties should realize the profound analytical problems that they can create for courts [or

[35] 9 Cal.4th at 865.
[36] 9 Cal.4th at 865-66.
[37] 9 Cal.4th at 877 (citations omitted; emphasis in original).
[38] 931 P.2d at 767 (footnote omitted).

arbitrators] when they agree only that, in the event of a contractual dispute, the 'prevailing party' shall recover attorney fees."[39]

In *Neal & Co., Inc. v. U.S.*, 121 F.3d 683 (Fed. Cir. 1997), the Court of Appeals for the Federal Circuit had occasion to consider Supreme Court "prevailing party" jurisprudence.

> [A] party may prevail without winning extensive damages. … In *Farrar*, the Court explained that "a plaintiff 'prevails' when actual relief on the merits of his claim materially alters the legal relationship between the parties by modifying the defendant's behavior in a way that directly benefits the plaintiff."
>
> . . .
>
> In this case, NCI qualifies as a prevailing party. Of its total original claim of $6,899,606, NCI received $792,143 in damages—11.5% of its claim. While the Government characterizes NCI's damage award as only minimal success, this court need not delve into the details of the award to determine whether it is "substantial" enough, or meets some undefined level of sufficiency. … Because NCI has obtained a sizable damage judgment, it qualifies as a prevailing party. Specifically, NCI prevailed on four of its nine claims, a sufficient realignment of the legal relationship between the parties to qualify NCI as the prevailing party ….[40]

In *Slane v. Mariah Boats, Inc.*, 164 F.3d 1065 (7th Cir. 1999), the Seventh Circuit Court of Appeals rejected a challenge to an award of costs to the "prevailing party" that had been made under Federal Rule of Civil Procedure 54(d)(1):

> Mariah argues that the court erred in awarding costs to Slane because Slane did not "prevail" in the suit; rather, Slane won two claims and Mariah won two. The district court correctly noted that when one party gets substantial relief it "prevails" even if it doesn't win on every claim. … Slane got $225,000 from the jury.

---

[39] 931 P.2d at 769.

[40] 121 F.3d at 685 (citations omitted).

By any definition, he won the battle. The court's conclusion that Slane prevailed was more than reasonable.[41]

In *Wilkes v. Zurlinden*, 984 P.2d 261 (Ore. 1999), plaintiff claimed it was owed about $19K (damages plus attorneys' fees) because of defendants' breach, and defendants claimed they were owed about $103K (damages plus attorneys' fees) because of plaintiff's breach and negligence. Both sides were denied affirmative relief on their respective claims, and the trial court designated defendants as prevailing party and awarded them attorneys' fees. The intermediate appellate court reversed and held neither side had prevailed; however, the Supreme Court of Oregon reversed, holding that because each side had defeated the other side's case, each side was a prevailing party and that the trial court had erred in designating only defendants as prevailing. The Supreme Court distinguished the *Wilkes* situation from the one in *Carlson v. Blumenstein*, 651 P.2d 710 (Ore. 1982), in which both sides had succeeded on their respective claims and been awarded damages. In *Carlson*, "the damages awards ... [were] 'netted' to determine the party in whose favor judgment was rendered," but the "netting" procedure was not possible in *Wilkes* because neither side was awarded any damages.[42]

In *Eighteen Mile Ranch, LLC v. Nord Excavating & Paving, Inc.*, 117 P.3d 130 (Idaho 2005), all of the defendants appealing a denial of attorneys' fees had successfully defended against plaintiffs' claim and one of the defendants (Nord Excavating) had recovered roughly one thousand dollars on its counterclaim, about 9% of what it had requested. The trial court held that neither side had prevailed, but the Supreme Court of Idaho reversed, saying the court below had "seemingly ignored the fact that ... [Nord Excavating] avoided all liability as a defendant," that "[a]voiding liability is a significant benefit to a defendant," and that "courts must not ignore the value of a successful defense."[43] The Supreme Court also held that the "individual Nords were also prevailing parties" because they had "achiev[ed] the most favorable outcome that could possibly be achieved."[44]

In *Trytek v. Gale Industries, Inc.*, 3 So.3d 1194 (Fla. 2009), the Supreme Court of Florida reaffirmed the "significant issues" test: "The reasoning supporting the decision in *Prosperi* to replace the 'net

---

[41] 164 F.3d at 1068 (citation omitted).
[42] 984 P.2d at 264 (citation omitted).
[43] 117 P.3d at 133.
[44] 117 P.3d at 133-34 (citation and footnote omitted).

judgment rule' with the 'significant issues' test conveys this Court's preference for a flexible rule that will achieve an equitable result with respect to the determination of the 'prevailing party,' irrespective of which party recovers a judgment on the lien claim."[45] The Court also noted that in some cases, there might be no prevailing party.[46]

In *Intercontinental Group Partnership v. KB Home Lone Star L.P.*, 295 S.W.3d 650 (Tex. 2009), the Texas Supreme Court framed the question to be answered as follows: "[W]hen a contract mandates attorney's fees to a 'prevailing party,' a term undefined in the contract, has a party 'prevailed' if the jury finds the other side violated the contract but awards no money damages?"[47] Because "prevailing party" was undefined in the contract, the Court "presume[d] the parties intended the term's ordinary meaning."[48] The Texas Supreme Court discussed *Hewitt* and *Farrar*, saying the U.S. Supreme Court's analysis was "helpful in this area,"[49] and then reversed the award of attorneys' fees to KB Homes, holding it was not a prevailing party because it "achieved no genuine success on its contract claim" ("KB Home sought over $1 million in damages, but instead left the courthouse empty-handed").[50]

In *Jorgensen v. Coppedge*, 224 P.3d 1125 (Idaho 2010), the trial court held neither side was the prevailing party for purposes of awarding attorneys' fees because it was "a split decision": defendants prevailed on the claim against them but did not prevail on their counterclaims. The Idaho Supreme affirmed, noting that "determination of prevailing party status is committed to the sound discretion of the district court" and that "when both parties are partially successful, it is within the district court's discretion to decline an award of attorney fees to either side."[51]

The appellate court in *Olsen v. Lund*, 246 P.3d 521 (Utah Ct. App. 2010), reversed the trial court's determination that neither side was the

---

[45] 3 So.3d at 1202 (emphasis in original).

[46] 3 So.3d at 1203-04.

[47] 295 S.W.3d at 652.

[48] 295 S.W.3d at 653 (footnote omitted).

[49] 295 S.W.3d at 653-54.

[50] 295 S.W.3d at 655. The Supreme Court of Texas in Epps. v. Fowler, 351 S.W.3d 862, 864 (Tex. 2011), favorably cited *Buckhannon* and *Intercontinental* and held that "a defendant [in a case in which plaintiff nonsuits a claim without prejudice] is not a prevailing party unless the court determines, on the defendant's motion, that the plaintiff took the nonsuit in order to avoid an unfavorable judgment" and that "because a nonsuit with prejudice immediately alters the legal relationship between the parties by its res judicata effect, a defendant prevails when the plaintiff nonsuits with prejudice."

[51] 224 P.3d at 1127 (citations omitted).

prevailing party and held defendant-sellers to be the "prevailing party" even though they had to pay damages to plaintiff-buyers. Plaintiffs had sued for fifteen alleged breaches of contract and recovered on two of them, for roughly 3% of what they had claimed. The Utah appellate court said:

> Our courts have developed a "flexible and reasoned approach" for determining which party has emerged the "comparative winner." ... It begins by identifying "the party in whose favor the 'net' judgment is entered." ... The "net judgment rule" will usually be "at least a good starting point," but it should not be "mechanically applied." ... "This approach requires not only consideration of the significance of the net judgment in the case, but also looking at the amounts actually sought and then balancing them proportionally with what was recovered." ... Consequently, "a party that makes an outrageous claim and then receives only a fraction of what it demanded"—though the net judgment winner—"will not likely be deemed the successful party." ...
>
> The focus should be on "which party had attained a 'comparative victory,' considering what a total victory would have meant for each party and what a true draw would look like." ... For example, where a plaintiff sued for $30,000 and the defendant claimed to owe nothing, "[a] 'draw' would have been a decision dividing the $30,000 equally," ... that is, a judgment in favor of plaintiff in the sum of $15,000. ... Where the defendant advances a counterclaim, the calculus changes. For example, in *A.K. & R. Whipple Plumbing & Heating v. Guy* ..., the plaintiff was claiming roughly $13,000, the defendants were claiming roughly $25,000, and the defendants reaped a net recovery of $527. ... The trial court properly declared a "draw" and awarded no attorney fees. ...[52]

The Court continued:

> Here, applying a flexible and reasoned approach, we conclude that Sellers [defendants] were the comparative winners at trial and thus the prevailing parties for purposes of the attorney fee provision of

[52] 246 P.3d at 523 (citations omitted).

> the … [contract]. We follow the approach of *A.K. & R. Whipple Plumbing & Heating v. Guy* …, considering "the amounts actually sought and then balancing them proportionally with what was recovered." … Here, the amount actually sought at trial was $23,866.98. Buyers recovered $754.77. This represents a success rate of slightly over 3% for Buyers [plaintiffs], whereas Sellers were almost 97% successful in defeating Buyers' claims at trial.
>
> This lopsided result was not a draw. … On the contrary, Sellers were without question the comparative winner. However pyrrhic in a larger sense, "comparative victory," … was theirs. Moreover, to the extent, if any, the larger costs of this case are relevant to the determination of the prevailing party, we note that Sellers made an offer of judgment for $5,000 before filing their answer. After twenty months of discovery and three and a half days of trial, Buyers recovered only 15% of this amount.[53]

In *Southern Wine & Spirit of Nevada v. Mountain Valley Spring Co., LLC*, 712 F.3d 397 (8th Cir. 2013), plaintiff obtained a judgment of $819,000 for breach of contract and $42,000 for account stated, and defendant obtained a judgment of $183,000 on its counterclaim for breach of an implied covenant of good faith and fair dealing. The contract required the non-prevailing party to pay the prevailing party its reasonable costs and attorneys' fees in any suit to enforce the agreement or collect monies owed thereunder.[54] The trial court held there was no "prevailing party" because "both parties won 'sizable jury awards by prevailing on significant issues'" and denied each side's fee request ($2.7 million requested by plaintiff and $1.3 million by defendant).[55] Plaintiff challenged the denial of its requested fees on several grounds, including that even if defendant's counterclaim was properly included in the analysis, the trial court had abused its discretion because plaintiff should have been designated the "prevailing party" since it had prevailed on three of its four claims and obtained a monetary award more than four times larger than that obtained by defendant.[56] However, the Court of Appeals affirmed, saying that applicable law did not require one party to

---

[53] 246 P.3d at 524 (citations omitted).
[54] 712 F.3d at 399.
[55] *Id.*
[56] 712 F.3d at 400-01 (citation omitted).

be designated as "prevailing" when both parties had been found to be at fault.[57]

IV. A Suggested Approach for Arbitrators

Before considering the specifics of the suggested procedure, it may be helpful to keep the following in mind: although the case law shows different approaches for determining who is the prevailing party, there is an overriding theme—the courts in all but the most clear-cut cases apply a varying combination of law and equity to the particulars of each case to make the determination.[58]

Turning now to the suggested procedure, first, confirm there is authority in the case at hand giving power to the arbitrator to award attorneys' fees to the prevailing party. The authority may stem from one or more of the following: the parties' agreement to arbitrate, later requests for attorneys' fees made by all parties, the governing rules, case law, and applicable statutes (each a "source of authority"). Resolve any inconsistencies in the power given by the different sources of authority.

Second, determine which categories of claims/counterclaims are eligible for an award of attorneys' fees. What do the sources of authority say? For example, does the arbitration clause specify that an award can be made of attorneys' fees incurred in "any proceedings to enforce the terms of this agreement," in "any proceedings arising out of or relating this agreement," or in "any proceedings relating to any dispute between the parties"?

Third, decide which claims/counterclaims, if any, are in the eligible categories.

---

[57] *Id.*

[58] Using combinations of law *and equity* when making legal determinations is obviously not unusual. For example, consider how legal determinations are made when assessing whether a defendant was negligent, whether a defendant's use of another's copyright-protected work of authorship was a "fair use," or whether the probative value of a piece of evidence outweighs its prejudicial effect. Many courts acknowledge and even mandate the strong role equity should play in making prevailing party determinations. *See, e.g., Prosperi* (trial judge must have discretion to consider equities and determine which party prevailed on significant issues), *Hsu* (in determining litigation success, courts should respect substance rather than form and be guided by equitable considerations), and *Trytek* (use of "significant issues" test reflects court's preference for flexible rule that achieves equitable result with respect to determination of "prevailing party").

Fourth, ascertain whether "prevailing party" is defined in the sources of authority or in any other applicable rule or statute. If it isn't (which seems to be the more common situation), consider what the *Intercontinental* court did: because "prevailing party" was not defined in the contract, the court "presume[d] the parties intended the term's ordinary meaning."[59] Such a presumption might give the arbitrator some additional leeway. Also bear in mind definitions in the literature of "prevailing party," *e.g.*, in Black's Law Dictionary: "[a] party in whose favor a judgment is rendered, regardless of the amount of damages awarded."[60] Of course, if there is governing law bearing on making the presumption used by the *Intercontinental* court, that law should be followed.

Fifth, consider whether any award is to be made to "a" or "the" prevailing party. "A" suggests more than one party may be entitled to an award, which may be helpful to the arbitrator if there are counterclaims; "the" suggests (but may not be dispositive as to whether) there can be only one prevailing party even if there are counterclaims.[61]

Sixth, assess the constraints or freedom the sources of authority place on or give the arbitrator in making the prevailing party determination. For example, does the arbitration agreement specify that the arbitrator can make the determination "in his/her sole discretion"?

Seventh, note whether the rules of decision for making the prevailing party determination have been pre-established. For example, do the sources of authority specify the rules of decision?[62] Does the arbitration clause specify the arbitrator is to make all decisions/awards in accordance with the law of a particular jurisdiction? If it doesn't but the arbitration clause is part of a larger agreement (*e.g.*, a license agreement), does that larger agreement contain a choice of law provision? If so, does that provision dictate the law applicable to the prevailing party determination? If the rules of decision are not preordained (*e.g.*, by

---

[59] 295 S.W.3d at 653 (footnote omitted).

[60] *See* n.1, above.

[61] "ORS 20.096(5) defines the prevailing party in an action as 'the party in whose favor final judgment or decree is rendered.' That subsection refers to 'the' party in the singular, which suggests that, under the statute, there can be only one prevailing party in an action. … [However,] [r]eference to 'the' prevailing party in ORS 20.096(1) and in ORS 20.096(5) does not exclude the possibility of more than one prevailing party when there is both a claim and a counterclaim on a contract and each party succeeds in defeating the other party's claim for relief." *Wilkes*, 984 P.2d at 264 (discussed above).

[62] The rules of decision may be just a definition of "prevailing party" or they may be more detailed (*e.g.*, instructions that only certain types of claims are to be considered in making the determination).

governing law, by the arbitration agreement, by subsequent agreement of the parties), the arbitrator may have a somewhat freer hand in making the determination.

Eighth, establish whether an award of attorneys' fees for each claim/counterclaim in the eligible categories is permissive or mandatory. Do the sources of authority specify that the arbitrator "may," "can," "shall," or "must" award attorneys' fees? If an award is mandatory ("the arbitrator must award reasonable attorneys' fees to the prevailing party"), does the arbitrator have the power to hold that neither party is the prevailing party or that both are prevailing? The arbitrator should consider as early in the proceedings as possible whether either holding is one the arbitrator might want to make and, if so and if it is not explicitly prohibited, the arbitrator should consider whether to ask the parties to agree on the record that the arbitrator has the power to make such a holding if it is not already clear that he/she can do so.[63]

Ninth, consider the following:

- the essence of the alleged wrong(s) for which each party seeks redress;
- the substantive outcome regarding each claim/counterclaim eligible for a fee award and how each outcome compares to what was requested;
- the relationship of the various claims/counterclaims to each other and to the essence of the alleged wrong(s) for which each party seeks redress, taking into account the significance/importance of each claim/counterclaim, whether each claim/counterclaim is eligible for a fee award, and whether or not the counterclaims arise out of or relate to the same transaction/contract/alleged wrong(s) as the claims;
- whether any of the claims/counterclaims were frivolous;
- the conduct of the parties (including their counsel) in the arbitration (*e.g.*, did either side unduly complicate or prolong the proceedings); and
- what the arbitrator's gut tells him/her about who won the case.

---

[63] Although it does not affect the prevailing party determination, the arbitrator should ascertain whether the source of authority specifies the award is to be of "reasonable" attorneys' fees (some attorneys' fees clauses do not so specify). If it doesn't, the arbitrator should consider having the parties agree on the record that any award of attorneys' fees will be of "reasonable" attorneys' fees.

An arbitrator possessing this information will be in a better position to: (i) follow or supplement the rules of decision that have been preordained (*e.g.*, by the arbitration agreement) or establish such rules, (ii) decide who, if anyone, is the prevailing party, and (iii) determine what attorneys' fees, if any, to award.

V. Making the Prevailing Party Determination

Pre-established rules of decision for making the determination should be followed, but if they have not been established or do not provide sufficient guidance in the situation at hand, the arbitrator must establish or supplement the rules and, as noted above, will likely turn to case law for guidance. Listed below are what courts have said about some of the more common situations/issues encountered when making prevailing party determinations.

- Who May Be A "Prevailing Party"?

A party who succeeds on any significant issue that achieves some of the benefit the party sought in bringing suit (*Hensley; Texas State Teachers Association*); a party who is successful on the central issue, as evidenced by obtaining the primary relief the party sought (*Hensley*); a party who receives at least some of relief the party sought (*Hewitt*); a party who prevails on the significant issues (*Prosperi*); a first party who receives relief that affects the behavior of the second party towards the first party (*Rhodes*); a first party who obtains relief that materially alters the legal relationship between the parties by modifying the second party's behavior towards the first party in a way that directly benefits the first party (*Farrar*).

- Tests/Approaches for Making "Prevailing Party" Determination

"Significant issues" test (*Hensley; Texas State Teachers Association; Prosperi; Trytek*); "net judgment" rule (*Mountain States Broadcasting; Stichting Mayflower; Prosperi*); "comparative winner" test: the party attaining comparative victory, considering what total victory would have meant for each party and what true draw would look like, in other words, prevailing party may be determined by considering amounts sought and then balancing them proportionally with what was recovered (*Olsen*); "flexible and reasoned approach" (*Stichting Mayflower; Olsen*); avoiding liability is of significant benefit and when determining who is prevailing party, courts should not ignore value of successful defense (*Eighteen Mile Ranch*); party is prevailing party because it "achiev[ed] the most favorable outcome that could possibly be achieved" (*id.*); courts should respect substance rather than form and be guided by equitable considerations (*Hsu*).

- A Party "Wins" but Does Not Recover Substantial Damages

Prevailing party inquiry does not turn on magnitude of relief obtained (*Farrar*); a party may prevail without winning extensive damages (*Neal & Co.*).

- A Party Succeeds on Some but Not All of Its Claims

If a party obtains substantial relief, it "prevails" even if it does not win on every claim (*Slane*); party is prevailing party even though it won only four of its nine claims because that resulted in "a sufficient realignment of the legal relationship between the parties" (*Neal & Co.*); party denied direct relief on claim may still be prevailing party if it is clear it has otherwise achieved main litigation objective (*Hsu*).

- A Party Obtains Some but Not All of the Relief It Requested on Its Claim

Party that received only 11.5% (about $790,000) of its $6.9 million claim still "qualifies as a prevailing party" because judgment was "sizable" (*Neal & Co.*); party that makes "outrageous claim" and receives only fraction of what it demanded (and although it is net judgment winner) will not likely be deemed prevailing party (*Olsen*); party winning only 3% (about $750) of amount sought was not prevailing party because other party was 97% successful in defeating claim (*id.*); party winning judgment that other side breached contract is not prevailing party where it sought over $1 million in damages but was awarded nothing (*Intercontinental*).

- Claimant and Counterclaimant Each Prevail on Some of Their Respective Claims/Counterclaims

Prevailing party is party who is comparative winner (*Olsen*); under "net judgment" rule, if claims and counterclaims arise from same transaction, there can be only one prevailing party, and party in whose favor the net judgment is entered is prevailing party (*Mountain States Broadcasting*); if first party prevails on claim, second party prevails on counterclaim, and claim and counterclaim do not arise from same transaction, both parties may be considered to have prevailed (*id.*); if one party wins one or more claims and another party wins one or more counterclaims and not all are monetary wins, determination of who is prevailing party may be made by determining which party "prevailed on the most significant issues underlying the dispute" (*Stichting Mayflower*); each side was a prevailing party because it defeated the other side's case (*Wilkes*).

- May There Be More Than One Prevailing Party?

If first party prevails on claim, second party prevails on counterclaim, and claim and counterclaim do not arise from same transaction, both parties may be considered to have prevailed (*Mountain States Broadcasting*); each side was a prevailing party because it defeated the other side's case (*Wilkes*).

- May Neither Party Be the Prevailing Party?

Within trial court's discretion to hold neither side was prevailing party because each party was partially successful (*Jorgensen*); law did not require one party to be designated as prevailing where both parties found to be at fault (*Southern Wine*); in some cases there may be no prevailing party (*Trytek*).

- May Party Be Prevailing Party Even if It "Loses"?

Party may be prevailing party because of the equities even if other party recovers net judgment (*Prosperi*); first party was prevailing party even though it had to pay damages to second party because second party prevailed on only two of fifteen claims for total of only 3% of damages claimed (*Olsen*).

VI. Quantifying the Award of Attorneys' Fees

Before making an award to the prevailing party, the arbitrator must know how much is being claimed as attorneys' fees and allowable other costs.[64] Unless the parties stipulate to those sums, the parties must submit evidence regarding the amounts requested. In arbitration, sometimes the substantive winner is announced and only that party makes a fee submission. Preferably, however, fee submissions in arbitration are made by both sides before any such announcement, *e.g.*, with or immediately after any final substantive briefing.

The parties may, of course, be asked to provide to the arbitrator the type of detailed fee submissions used in court proceedings, which typically contain extensive back-up documentation; however, there are alternatives that will save the parties time and money. For example, each party submits a declaration signed by its lead counsel containing only high-level detail and no back-up materials (the submission will likely be only two or three pages long). Each declaration shows the total hours and hourly rate for each fee earner (*e.g.*, attorney, paralegal), as well as the total for each disbursement/ expense category (photocopying, messenger/courier, fee for each expert witness, court reporter, travel, lodging, etc.).

A reasonable rule of thumb is that in most cases the number of fee-earner hours expended by the two sides will be within about one-third of one another, and the totals in many other categories will be equivalent.[65] Thus, each submission will act as a yardstick for the other, taking into account the relative simplicity/complexity of each claim/counterclaim/ defense and any inequalities between the two sides' cases dictated by the specifics of the situation. Arbitrators who themselves are/were practicing attorneys will have a feel for the reasonableness of the hours claimed by each side, which also acts as a check. In any case, the arbitrator can always ask questions and/or request detailed back-up. The suggested procedure will in the first instance save each side the time and expense required for preparing court-style detailed fee submissions and provide useful information to the arbitrator regarding the reasonableness of what is being requested.

---

[64] Attorneys' fees clauses or arbitration rules often specify that other arbitration costs (*i.e.*, other than attorneys' fees) are also to be awarded.

[65] Robinson v. City of Edmond, 160 F.3d 1275, 1284 (10th Cir. 1998) (evidence of hours expended by defense (opposing) counsel "is not, of course, an immutable yardstick of reasonableness, and it may be disregarded or discounted as a comparative factor if found to be unreasonable in its own right. However, here the effort expended by the defendants suggests at least that they viewed the case as sufficiently complex and serious to warrant the expenditure of large amounts of attorney time, and it highlights the tooth-and-nail litigating approach the city used in this case. In light of this tenacious effort by the city and its lawyers, the amount of attorney time expended by the plaintiffs begins to look more reasonable, not less").

- The "Lodestar"

As indicated by the U.S. Supreme Court in *Hensley*, "[t]he most useful starting point for determining the amount of a reasonable fee is the number of hours reasonably expended on the litigation multiplied by a reasonable hourly rate."[66] For a party, the total of each fee earner's reasonable hours multiplied by his/her reasonable hourly rate is often referred to as that party's "lodestar." Twenty-seven years after *Hensley*, the Supreme Court said the lodestar approach had "'achieved dominance in the federal courts ....'" *Perdue v. Kenny A. ex rel. Winn*, 559 U.S. 542, ___, 130 S.Ct. 1662, 1672 (2010) (citations omitted). Every federal circuit court of appeals has its own "lodestar" cases, many (if not most) of which cite *Hensley*.[67]

"[T]he Supreme Court has consistently upheld the lodestar calculation as the 'guiding light of [its] fee-shifting jurisprudence.'" *Bywaters v. U.S.*, 670 F.3d 1221, 1228-29 (Fed. Cir. 2012) (citations omitted), quoting *Perdue*. *Bywaters* further teaches as follows.

> In the years since *Hensley*, the Supreme Court's view on the degree of discretion afforded district courts in adjusting the lodestar figure has undergone change, *thus cabining the district court's ability to adjust the lodestar figure to only "rare" and "exceptional" cases*. ... Later cases have made clear that while the "amount involved and results obtained" remains a factor to be considered in determining a reasonable attorney fee, it cannot be a basis for reducing the lodestar figure where it could have been taken into account in calculating the lodestar figure in the first instance. In *Blum v. Stenson*, 465 U.S. 886 ... (1984), decided just one year after *Hensley*, the Court clarified that while "there may be circumstances in which the basic standard of

---

[66] 461 U.S. at 433.

[67] *See, e.g.*, Diaz v. Jiten Hotel Management, Inc., 704 F.3d 150 (1st Cir. 2012); Serin v. Northern Leasing Systems, Inc., ___ F.3d ___, Nos. 11-1778 & 11-2139 (2nd Cir. October 26, 2012); McKenna v. City of Philadelphia, 582 F.3d 447 (3rd Cir. 2009); Newport News Shipbuilding & Dry Dock Co. v. Holiday, 591 F.3d 219 (4th Cir. 2009); McClain v. Lufkin Industries, Inc., 649 F.3d 374 (5th Cir. 2011); Yellowbook Inc. v. Brandeberry, 708 F.3d 837 (6th Cir. 2013); Johnson v. GDF, Inc., 668 F.3d 927 (7th Cir. 2012); Al-Birekdar v. Chrysler Group, LLC, ___ F.3d ___, Nos. 08-3780 & 09-1091 (8th Cir. March 11, 2013); In re Bluetooth Headset Products Liability Litigation, 654 F.3d 935 (9th Cir. 2011); Zinna v. Congrove, 680 F.3d 1236 (10th Cir. 2012); Gray v. Bostic, 613 F.3d 1035 (11th Cir. 2010); New Jersey v. Environmental Protection Agency, 703 F.3d 110 (D.C. Cir. 2012); Bywaters v. U.S., 670 F.3d 1221 (Fed. Cir. 2012).

> reasonable rates multiplied by reasonably expended hours results in a fee that is either unreasonably low or unreasonably high," *the lodestar figure is "presumed" to be reasonable.* ... The Court also cautioned against "double counting" factors such as the "amount involved and results obtained" by adjusting the lodestar figure where those factors are fully reflected in the reasonable hourly rate of the attorneys and the reasonable number of hours expended. ... In particular, the Court noted that "[b]ecause acknowledgment of the 'results obtained' generally will be subsumed within other factors used to calculate a reasonable fee, it normally should not provide an independent basis for increasing the fee award."[68]

Because the lodestar (the sum of reasonable hours multiplied by reasonable hourly rates) is presumed to be reasonable, the major issues for the arbitrator before determining the lodestar (and, therefore, in most cases determining the attorneys' fees award) are the reasonableness of the requested hours and hourly rates.[69]

---

[68] 670 F.3d at 1229-30 (emphasis added; citations omitted).

[69] One leading attorneys' fee case pre-dating *Hensley* was Johnson v. Georgia Highway Express, Inc., 488 F.2d 714, 717-19 (5th Cir. 1974), a civil rights case in which the Fifth Circuit set forth twelve factors to be considered concerning the reasonableness of hours, hourly rates, and the fee: "(1) The time and labor required," "(2) The novelty and difficulty of the questions," "(3) The skill requisite to perform the legal services properly," "(4) The preclusion of other employment by the attorney due to acceptance of the case," "(5) The customary fee," "(6) Whether the fee is fixed or contingent," "(7) Time limitations imposed by the client or the circumstances," "(8) The amount involved and the results obtained," "(9) The experience, reputation, and ability of the attorneys," "(10) The 'undesirability' of the case .... [c]ivil rights attorneys face hardships in their communities because of their desire to help the civil rights litigant," "(11) The nature and length of the professional relationship with the client," and "(12) Awards in similar cases." Twenty-six years later, the Bankruptcy Appellate Panel of the Ninth Circuit Court of Appeals said there was a strong presumption that payment of the attorney's hourly rate constituted reasonable compensation, In re Meronk, 249 B.R. 208, 213 (BAP 9th Cir. 2000), and referred to the *Johnson* factors as an "obsolete laundry list," *id. Johnson* was also criticized by the Supreme Court. *See* Perdue v. Kenny A. ex rel. Winn, 559 U.S. 542, ___, 130 S.Ct. 1662, 1672 (2010) (citations omitted): "This [*Johnson*] method ... 'gave very little actual guidance to district courts. Setting attorney's fees by reference to a series of sometimes subjective factors placed unlimited discretion in trial judges and produced disparate results.' ... [T]he lodestar method is readily administrable ... and unlike the *Johnson* approach, the lodestar calculation is 'objective' ... and thus cabins the discretion of trial judges, permits meaningful judicial review, and produces reasonably predictable results."

- Hours

The arbitrator should consider what hours, if any, to exclude from the prevailing party's hours for claims: (i) for which an award of fees is not authorized (*i.e.*, claims not subject to fee-shifting), (ii) on which the prevailing party did not succeed, or (iii) that were frivolous. Following is a sampling of court pronouncements on some of the issues/situations likely to be encountered by an arbitrator when deciding what hours, if any, to exclude.

- o *Only Some Claims Subject to Fee-Shifting*

Party who prevailed on claims, not all of which were subject to fee-shifting, may recover attorneys' fees it would have incurred had fee-shifting claims been litigated by themselves (*Schulz*).

- o *All Claims Subject to Fee-Shifting, and Failure to Prevail on Claim Not Distinct from Successful Claims*

Party who obtains substantial relief should not have attorneys' fee reduced because it did not prevail on each contention, but if party achieves only limited success, award should be of only that amount reasonable in relation to results obtained (*Hensley*).

- o *All Claims Subject to Fee-Shifting, and Failure to Prevail on Claim Distinct from Successful Claims*

If party fails to prevail on claim distinct in all respects from successful claims, hours spent on unsuccessful claim should be excluded (*Hensley*).

- o *Frivolous Claims*

"But-for" test: if prevailing party's frivolous claim caused attorney's fees at issue, can decide losing party should not have to pay them, but if losing party would have incurred those fees anyway to defend against non-frivolous claim, losing party should pay them (*Fox*).

• Hourly Rates

Broadly speaking, the hourly rate is what is "appropriate in the relevant market"[70] or the "reasonable hourly rate for the region and for the experience of the lawyer."[71] "Courts calculate the reasonable hourly rate based on the 'prevailing market rate in the relevant community' for lawyers of comparable skill and experience; out-of-town lawyers thus may only recover the rate they would command in the local market."[72] "The Supreme Court has indicated that the reasonable hourly rates to be applied in determining the lodestar figure are the 'prevailing market rates in the relevant community.'"[73]

As discussed in *Johnson v. GDF, Inc.*, 668 F.3d 927, 933 (7th Cir. 2012) (citations omitted), a contingent fee arrangement presents additional problems for calculating a lodestar.

> The best evidence of an attorney's [hourly] market rate is his or her actual billing rate for similar work. … In this case, the district court concluded that Rossiello didn't establish his actual billing rate (which he claims is $600 per hour) because the evidence he presented didn't show how much he was actually

---

[70] *Al-Birekdar*, slip op. at Section III.B.i.

[71] In re Bluetooth Headset Products Liability Litigation, 654 F.3d at 941.

[72] *Yellowbook,* slip op. at Section IV.

[73] *Bywaters*, 670 F.3d at 1232 (citations omitted). "[T]he Supreme Court has been silent on how to determine the 'relevant community' under the URA [Uniform Relocation Assistance and Real Property Acquisition Policies Act of 1970] or any other fee-shifting statute. … As we have recognized, 'the courts of appeals have uniformly concluded that, in general, forum rates should be used to calculate attorneys' fee awards under other fee-shifting statutes.'" *Bywaters* 670 F.3d at 1232-33 (citation and footnote omitted). Arbitrators hearing cases in fora where hourly rates are comparatively high (*e.g.*, large cities on the East and West Coast) do not usually face the problem of whether to reduce the hourly rates of prevailing party's counsel. However, if a case is heard in a forum where hourly rates are comparatively low and the prevailing party has used counsel with comparatively high hourly rates, the Federal Circuit's observation in *Bywaters* 670 F.3d at 1233-34 (citations and footnote omitted), may be helpful to an arbitrator having to make a fee award: "[T]he forum rate applies absent some unusual justification for departing from it. While we [the Court of Appeals for the Federal Circuit] have not yet squarely addressed the issue, we recognize that several circuits have acknowledged an exception to the forum rule where local counsel is either unwilling or unable to take the case. We agree that such an exception is appropriate, but we also agree that it is applicable only in unusual situations. Such exceptions are permissible only where supported by specific evidence that no local attorneys possess the 'special expertise' necessary to take the case or that no local attorneys were willing to take the case."

> paid and for what kind of work. That was within the district court's discretion. The district court then properly turned to "the next best evidence" of the market rate for an attorney, like Rossiello, who maintains a contingent fee, namely, "evidence of rates similarly experienced attorneys in the community charge paying clients for similar work and evidence of fee awards the attorney has received in similar cases."... It is the fee applicant's burden to establish his or her market rate; if the applicant fails, the district court may make its own rate determination.

Armed with the reasonable number of hours and reasonable hourly rate for each fee earner, an arbitrator can calculate the lodestar. It will be a rare commercial case in which the lodestar is adjusted up or down, since most if not all of the factors that might otherwise cause such adjustment will have been taken into account in determining reasonable hours and rates (*see Bywaters*, above).[74]

VI. Conclusion

It seems appropriate to close with the following observation by the U.S. Supreme Court:

> [T]rial courts need not, and indeed should not, become green-eyeshade accountants. The essential goal in shifting fees (to either party) is to *do rough justice, not to achieve auditing perfection.* So *trial courts may take into account their overall sense of a suit, and may use estimates in calculating and allocating an attorney's time.* And appellate courts must give substantial deference to these determinations, in light of "the district court's superior understanding of the litigation." ... We can hardly think of a sphere of judicial decisionmaking in which appellate micromanagement has less to recommend it.[75]

[74] Years ago, courts considered many factors when determining whether the lodestar should be adjusted, *e.g.*, reputation of winning counsel, degree of difficulty of issues, quality of service rendered by winning counsel. However, under current jurisprudence, as suggested by *Bywaters*, all of those factors should already have been taken into account in determining the lodestar.

[75] *Fox*, 563 U.S. at ___, 131 S.Ct. at 2216 (emphasis added; citation omitted).

The arbitrator will be empowered as well as constrained by the parties' agreement, the governing rules, and any applicable statutes and decisional law. Within these confines, when considering whether to award attorneys' fees to a party and, if so, how much, the arbitrator must utilize his/her own good judgment, "tak[ing] into account … [his/her] overall sense of … [the arbitration]."[76]

[76] Paraphrasing *Fox*, 563 U.S. at ___, 131 S.Ct. at 2216.

CHAPTER 43

ENFORCEABILITY OF RELIGIOUS ARBITRATION AGREEMENTS AND AWARDS

Steven C. Bennett[*]

I. Introduction

While general principles of enforceability apply, novel First Amendment and public policy considerations can arise when religious forms of arbitration are used.

Arbitration is the process of settling disputes between parties by a private tribunal. Courts favor arbitration because it can provide a speedy, informal, and inexpensive alternative to litigation, and may reduce a court's docket.

The court's role with regard to review of the merits of an arbitration decision is limited by statute. A court generally may vacate an award only when fraud, corruption, or denial of due process has tainted the legitimacy of the award.[1] When review is allowed, it generally will be very deferential.

When parties agree to have their disputes settled by a religious tribunal, however, certain novel issues may arise. This article explores the enforceability of religious arbitration agreements and awards, as well as the First Amendment and public policy considerations that can arise when religious forms of arbitration are used. Before turning to these issues, it is helpful to discuss some basic principles of arbitration.

---

[*] The author is a partner at Park Jensen Bennett LLP in New York City. The views expressed are solely those of the author, and should not be attributed to the author's firm or its clients. Marie Aveni, a summer associate at Jones Day, assisted in the preparation of this article.

[1] *See* Federal Arbitration Act (FAA), 9 U.S.C. § 10; Revised Uniform Arbitration Act, § 23(a). See, e.g., *Abd Alla v. Mourssi*, 680 N.W.2d 569, 573 (Minn. Ct. App. 2004).

II. Enforceability of Arbitration Agreements

Arbitration is a voluntary process where parties agree to submit disputes to an arbitrator or a panel of arbitrators. In most circumstances, an agreement to arbitrate will be expressly stated in the contract between the parties.[2] Absent situations involving fraud, duress, or corruption, courts will generally uphold the terms of a freely negotiated arbitration agreement that explicitly and unambiguously reveals the intent of the parties to arbitrate. Parties enjoy great flexibility in that they can craft arbitration agreements that meet their needs.

Courts apply these general rules to arbitration provisions even when an arbitration proceeding is to be conducted by a religious tribunal. As New York courts have noted, "Arbitration in a religious forum has long been recognized as a valid approach to dispute resolution."[3]

III. Enforceability of Arbitration Awards

Under U.S. law, arbitration awards are generally binding and enforceable. Judicial review of arbitration decisions is considered to be "among the narrowest known to law."[4] A court may vacate an arbitration award only in limited circumstances, such as when there is fraud, corruption, arbitrator misconduct, or where arbitrators exceed their power. In addition, many courts recognize the power to vacate an award when an arbitrator acts in "manifest disregard" of the law. Generally to invoke this power, the record must show that an arbitrator knew the law and explicitly disregarded it.[5] Some courts will uphold the award as long as there is any "colorable justification" for the arbitrator's conclusion.[6]

---

[2] Parties may also agree to arbitrate after a dispute arises.

[3] *Tal Tours Inc. v. Goldstein*, 9 Misc. 3d 1117 (N.Y. Sup. Ct. 2005). See also *Mendel Schwimmer, UTA Satmar Boro Park v. Aron Welz, Keren Habinyan Hachudosh D'Rabeinu Yoel,* 2009 N.Y. Slip Op. 51230 (N.Y. Sup. Ct. Kings Cty. June 15, 2009) (unpublished), citing *Herzog v Oberlander*, 2008 N.Y. Slip Op. 50669, 19 Misc. 3d 1113, 2008 WL 880184 (N.Y. Sup. Ct., Kings Cty. 2008).

[4] *Dominion Video Satellite, Inc. v. Echostar Satellite L.L.C.*, 430 F.3d 1269 (10th Cir. 2005).

[5] *Id.*

[6] *Telenor Mobile Communications AS v. Altimo Holdings & Investments Ltd.*, 584 F.3d 396 (2d Cir. Oct. 8, 2009).

IV. Enforceability of Awards by Religious Tribunals

Various kinds of religious tribunals exist for some purposes in most religions.[7] There are, for example, Jewish tribunals known as the Beth Din, Islamic panels, and Christian panels associated with Peacemaker Ministries' Institute for Christian Conciliation (CC Institute).

Both federal and state courts have enforced religious tribunal decisions under the Federal Arbitration Act (FAA), state statutes modeled after the Uniform Arbitration Act (UAA) and the Revised UAA completed in the year 2000. Courts apply the same deferential standard of review to religious arbitration awards as they do to awards by non-religious arbitrators. As one court noted, "[C]ivil courts have only 'marginal review' power over the decisions of arbitral bodies, secular and religious."[8]

Thus, for example, in *Prescott v. Northlake Christian School*, a federal district court in Louisiana affirmed an award issued by a single arbitrator who applied biblical law and the Rules of Procedure for Christian Conciliation. Although the 5th Circuit vacated the award on grounds that the arbitration clause was ambiguous and remanded the case to the district court for further proceedings, on a second appeal, it upheld the district court's conclusion on remand that the award should be confirmed.[9]

The *Prescott* case arose out of an employment agreement between a private religious school and an elementary school teacher. The agreement provided that, "in conformity with the biblical injunctions of 1 Corinthians 6:1-8, Matthew 5:23,24, and Matthew 18:15-20 ... any claim or dispute arising out of, or related to, this agreement or to any aspect of the employment relationship" would be referred to "biblically-based mediation" and, if unsuccessful, binding arbitration. It also specified that arbitration be conducted under the procedure for Christian Conciliation. The agreement also stated, "This contract shall be interpreted under the laws of the state of Louisiana as if jointly authored by the parties."

The school informed the elementary school principal that her contract would not be renewed, that she should leave her position and would be paid her full salary and benefits through the contract term. Instead of

---

[7] *See* Note, Michael C. Grossman, "Is this Arbitration? Religious Tribunals, Judicial Review, and Due Process," 107 *Colum. L. Rev.* 169, 169-70 (2007), for a description of some of these religious arbitration systems.

[8] *Encore Productions v. Promise Keepers,* 53 F. Supp. 2d 1101 (D. Colo. 1999).

[9] *Prescott v. Northlake Christian School,* 244 F. Supp. 2d 659 (E.D. La. 2002), *vacated and remanded*, 369 F.3d 491 (5th Cir. 2004), *after remand, aff'd per curiam*, July 8, 2005) *cert den*, 2005 U.S. Lexis 9263 (Dec. 12, 2005) (Unpublished opinion)

complying with the dispute resolution provision in her employment agreement, the principal sued the school alleging gender discrimination, sexual harassment, retaliation, and breach of her employment contract.

Based on the dispute resolution provision, the school filed a motion to stay the court proceeding and compel mediation, which the district court granted, holding that it had no jurisdiction to decide the dispute because the parties had entered into a valid dispute resolution clause and had not waived it.

After mediation failed, the parties executed a form mediation/arbitration agreement furnished by the Christian Conciliation Institute. They agreed to be governed by the Christian Conciliation rules, which referenced the Montana Uniform Arbitration Act. The parties also made a few changes to the form mediation/arbitration agreement. They added a hand-written provision stating: "No party waives appeal rights, if any, by signing this agreement."

The parties submitted their dispute to a single arbitrator. After a hearing, the arbitrator issued an award in favor of the principal, holding that the school had breached its contractual obligation to resolve its conflict in accordance with the Bible. The arbitrator awarded the principal damages for injury to reputation and future loss of income. The principal moved to confirm the award while the school moved to vacate on numerous grounds. The district court confirmed the award and denied the school's motion to vacate. It rejected the argument that the award was the result of evident partiality, corruption, or arbitrator misconduct, finding that the school cited only "unsupported assertions that fail to rise to the required level of certainty and demonstrability." The court also rejected the argument that the arbitrator should have applied Louisiana law to interpret the parties' agreements, and thereby exceeded her powers by applying biblical law, stating that the award was rationally related to the parties' agreement. The court explained that the employment contract and Christian Conciliation Institute's arbitration agreement stressed the supreme authority of the Bible in the employment relationship, and thus the parties intended to be guided by the word of the Bible.

The court also rejected the school's argument that the scope of judicial review was extended beyond what the Montana Uniform Arbitration Act allowed by the handwritten addendum to the form arbitration agreement, which stated: "No party waives appeal rights, if any, by signing this agreement"). The court found from the face of the agreement that the phrase "if any" preserved whatever appeal rights were statutorily granted under the Montana statute.

The school appealed to the 5th Circuit, arguing that (1) the handwritten addendum expanded the arbitration agreement's scope of judicial review; (2) the arbitrator erred as a matter of law in ruling that the school breached its contract with the principal and that she was entitled to damages. It also reiterated the arguments made before the district court that the arbitrator exhibited evident partiality, engaged in misconduct and exceeded her authority under the state arbitration law.

The 5th Circuit first addressed the threshold issue of which state law governed interpretation of the handwritten addendum to the arbitration agreement. It held that Louisiana law governed the substance of the agreement, while Montana arbitration law controlled the arbitration procedures.

Next, it held that whether the parties' arbitration agreement contemplated expanded judicial review could not be determined because the agreement was ambiguous. Accordingly, the appeals court remanded the case to the district court with instructions to take evidence regarding the circumstances surrounding the formation of the contract and ascertain the parties' intentions with respect to judicial review.

On remand, the district court held an evidentiary hearing and again concluded that the parties had not contractually expanded the scope of review. It ordered enforcement of the arbitrator's award for the reasons given in its previous opinion. The school appealed again.

On the second appeal, the 5th Circuit affirmed.[10] It agreed that the arbitrator's award was rationally related to the employment agreement and not contrary to any express contractual provisions, either biblical or secular. In support of this conclusion the court noted: (1) The arbitrator had held that the contract did not require Louisiana law to apply to every aspect of the employment relationship; and (2) the employment contract stated the overarching principle that the parties' employment relationship and their arbitration and proceedings would be governed by biblical provisions.

Thus, the appeals court found that whether the contract was sustainable under Louisiana law was for a religious arbitrator, not for the court, because the parties "freely and knowingly contracted to have their relationship governed by specified provisions of the Bible, and the Rules of the Christian Conciliation Institute "indisputably contemplate that an arbitrator will have extremely broad discretion to fashion an appropriate

[10] *Id.* at 669.

remedy; and no language in the parties' contracts expresses their intent to depart from [those] Rules ...."

Much as in *Prescott*, state courts have also upheld the enforceability of arbitration awards rendered by religious tribunals. In *Abd Alla v. Mourssi*, a partner in a restaurant business filed a motion in a Minnesota state court to confirm an arbitration award against his partner rendered by an Islamic arbitration committee.[11] The court stated that the losing party was "not entitled to judicial consideration unless his application to vacate was predicated on fraud, corruption, or other undue means." In affirming the court's confirmation of the award, the Minnesota Court of Appeals stated: "Arbitration awards are strongly favored and a reviewing court must exercise 'every reasonable presumption' in favor of the arbitration award's finality and validity." The court stated that there was no clear proof of corruption, fraud, or any other undue means affected the award. The simple allegation that the arbitrator spoke to a "potential buyer" did not meet the requisite standard of "clear allegation of proof" to warrant vacatur of the award.

Both federal and state courts have held that they lack jurisdiction to resolve cases on the merits where a party has refused to comply with a written agreement to submit to arbitration before a religious tribunal. In *Encore Productions, Inc. v. Promise Keepers*, the district court in Colorado refused jurisdiction to settle a dispute before an arbitration proceeding took place.[12] The court held that a contract dispute between Encore, a provider of meeting organization services, and Promise Keepers, a religious association, had to be submitted to arbitration by a Christian conciliation program, consistent with the parties' agreement. The court dismissed all claims, stating, "A valid and unwaived arbitration clause deprives the court of subject matter jurisdiction until the dispute has been submitted to arbitration."

In *Meshel v. Ohev Sholom Talmud Torah*, another case on jurisdiction, members of a religious organization brought an action against a Jewish congregation seeking to enforce an agreement between the parties stipulating that a "Beth Din" should resolve disputes.[13] In holding that the Beth Din provision constituted an arbitration agreement, the court stated, "A written agreement to submit any existing controversy

---

[11] *Abd Alla, supra* n. 1, 680 N.W.2d at 571.

[12] *Encore Productions, supra* n. 8. 53 F. Supp. 2d at 1111.

[13] *Meshel v. Ohev Sholom Talmud Torah,* 869 A.2d 343 (D.C. 2005).

to arbitration or a provision in a written contract to submit to arbitration any controversy ... is valid, enforceable and irrevocable...."

V. Special Considerations in Religious Arbitration

When parties designate a religious tribunal to settle disputes certain special issues may develop.

First Amendment Issues. First Amendment problems could arise if the court interferes with religious doctrines through court review of an award. The First Amendment to the U.S. Constitution contains provisions commonly called the Establishment Clause and the Free Exercise Clause. It states: "Congress shall make no law respecting an establishment of religion or prohibiting the free exercise thereof." These 16 words circumscribe the role that civil courts may play in the resolution of disputes involving religious organizations. In the words of the *Meschel* court, "the Establishment Clause precludes civil courts from resolving disputes involving religious organizations when such disputes may affect religious doctrine or church administration," while "the Free Exercise Clause requires civil courts to defer to the decisions of the highest tribunals of hierarchical religious organizations on matters of religious doctrine, discipline, faith, and ecclesiastical rule, custom or law."[14] Thus, civil courts must decline jurisdiction in such cases and allow religious tribunals to decide these matters.

However the First Amendment does not place religious organizations above the law. Courts may resolve disputes involving religious organizations as long as they employ "neutral principles of law" and their decisions are not premised upon review of doctrinal matters, such as the rituals of worship or the tenets of faith. "Neutral principles of law" are secular legal rules the application of which does not entail theological or religious evaluations."[15]

When disputes arise as a result of an arbitration award rendered by a religious tribunal, some courts refuse to entertain the claims based on the First Amendment. In *El-Farra v. Sayyed*, an Islamic minister filed a wrongful termination suit against the Islamic center that fired him and the members of its executive committee, alleging defamation, tortious

---

[14] *Id.* The reason is that "judicial intrusion in religious disputes can advance religion or otherwise impermissibly entangle the civil courts in ecclesiastical matters."

[15] *Encore Productions*, *supra* n. 8, 53 F. Supp. 2d at 1112.

interference with contract, and breach of contract.[16] The claimant's contract provided that the Islamic center could terminate the contract through a unanimous vote of its executive committee and board of directors "on valid grounds according to Islamic jurisdiction (*Shari'a*)" upon 60-days notice to appellant. After an in-house arbitration over the minister's offensive behavior in his sermons and his interference in the center's administration, he received several warning letters, was subsequently placed on probation and then fired after an executive committee vote. The Supreme Court of Arkansas held that the trial court lacked subject matter jurisdiction to review this dispute, since "personnel decisions by church-affiliated institutions affecting clergy are *per se* religious matters and cannot be reviewed by civil courts."[17]

Similarly, in *Neiman Ginsburg & Mairanze v. Goldburd*, an attorney brought an action against another attorney with whom he had jointly represented a client, alleging that his reputation was injured when the defendant-attorney improperly obtained a *seruv* (a kind of contempt order) from a Jewish religious arbitration tribunal and published it to the Jewish community.[18] The Arkansas Supreme Court dismissed the action, stating: "this court has no power to review the Beth Din's determination that it was appropriate under Jewish law to issue the *seruv*." Further, the court noted, the "[p]laintiff's argument that he demanded and was entitled to a pure law determination and that a *seruv* should not have issued over his request is a purely ecclesiastical question...."

In contrast, other courts have accepted jurisdiction to hear cases either to confirm or vacate an award rendered by a religious tribunal, or to compel parties to submit to arbitration before a religious tribunal. In *Meshel*, the court stated that, even though the "underlying dispute between the parties goes to the heart of the governing structure of Ohev Sholom [a religious organization] and therefore may be beyond the jurisdiction of the court, the resolution of appellants' action to compel arbitration will not require the civil court to determine, or even address, any aspect of the parties' underlying dispute."[19] The court held that it needed only to decide whether the parties had an enforceable agreement to arbitrate and, if so, whether the underlying dispute fell within the scope of the arbitration clause. It accepted jurisdiction based on its view

---

[16] *El-Farra v. Sayyed*, 226 S.W.3d 792, 794 (Ark. 2006).

[17] *Id.* at 797 (citing *Kaufmann v. Shahan*, 707 F.2d 355 (8th Cir. 1983)).

[18] *Neiman Ginsburg & Mairanz, P.C. v. Goldburd*, 179 Misc. 2d 125, (N.Y. Sup. Ct. 1998).

[19] *Meshel, supra* n. 13, 869 A.2d at 354.

of the limited role a court plays when reviewing an award rendered by an arbitrator. According to the *Meshel* court, "neutral principles of law" can be used to determine whether any of the limited exceptions exist to render an award unenforceable; such review does not affect the religious aspects of the case.

Public Policy. Courts have recognized certain public policy limitations on what can be arbitrated. As stated by a New York court in *In re Meisels*, "Arbitration agreements are unenforceable where substantive rights, embodied by statute, express a strong public policy which must be judicially enforced."[20] Accordingly, arbitrations of matters involving child custody, estate distributions, and criminal violations have been found to contravene public policy. Such matters cannot be resolved by arbitration, whether secular or religious. A few courts have, however, suggested that public policy limitations could apply to other matters when a religious body is designated to arbitrate the dispute.

The *Meisels* case provides an example. In this case, the grandchildren of a rabbi sought to bring a guardianship proceeding before a Beth Din. The purpose of the proceeding was to appoint a guardian for an allegedly incapacitated person and his property. The court held that this type of proceeding was not a religious matter suitable for resolution by a Beth Din. The court also noted, "A finding of capacity or incapacity by an ecclesiastical court would not be binding or enforceable in a secular court." It suggested that, because a determination of a person's legal capacity could result in a restriction or even elimination of civil rights, public policy would bar an ecclesiastical court from determining the capacity issue.

Some courts have placed other public policy limitations on religious arbitration. For example, they have vacated awards where testimony has been categorically excluded based on gender, race, or religion.[21] Other courts have refused to confirm arbitration awards issued by a religious tribunal if flatly contrary to public policy. In *Hirsch v. Hirsch*, for example, a Beth Din court rendered an award giving joint custody of children to the parties, directed the husband to pay a certain sum of money in child support, and directed that marital property held in the

[20] *In re Meisels*, 10 Misc.3d 659 (N.Y. Sup. 2005).

[21] *See* Note, Grossman, *supra* n. 8, at 169, 195. See also *Joseph Kahan a/k/a Yosef Kahan v. Sarah Rosner a/k/a Sara Rosner et al.,* No. 2008-08484 (N.Y. App. Div. 2d Dep't Nov. 19, 2009), published in *N.Y.L.J.*, Nov. 23, 2009, p. 17, col. 3 (court denied enforcement to award in a Beth Din proceeding where a party to the award was prevented from having counsel of his choice and instead had to use counsel acceptable to the Beth Din; the court held that the waiver of the right to counsel is unwaivable).

wife's father's name be sold, with 50% allotted the husband.[22] On review, the court vacated the entire award on public policy grounds. The custody issue, as noted above, was not subject to arbitration; the child support award failed to comply with the Child Support Standards Act and was not in the best interests of the children. Finally, the portion of the award granting the husband proceeds from the sale of land was held to contravene public policy because it deprived the wife's father of his property without due process, since he was not a party to the arbitration.

More recently, in *Brisman v. Hebrew Academy of Five Towns and Rockaway*, a trial court vacated a Beth Din employment award granting back pay, reinstatement with tenure, and an annual salary of $100,000, because "strong and well defined policy consideration embodied in constitutional, statutory or common law prohibit ... certain relief from being granted by an arbitrator."[23] The court stated that the Beth Din ruling set a precedent that would limit the ability of private schools to hire and fire employees at will. Further, the court stated that the "the salary determination, which exceeded what co-workers earned, was "counterproductive to a harmonious and productive work environment."

VI. Conclusion

The hallmark of arbitration is flexibility. Parties are free to select arbitrators and procedures that will best serve their dispute resolution needs.[24] Arbitration before a religious tribunal may effectively address the values and concerns of some parties. In general, courts accept religious arbitration as just one more form that arbitration may take. In very limited circumstances, however, constitutional and public policy limitations must trump the freedom to arbitrate as the parties see fit.

---

[22] *Hirsch v. Hirsch*, 4 A.D.3d 451 (N.Y. App. Div. 4th Dept. 2004).

[23] *Brisman v. Hebrew Academy of Five Towns and Rockaway, No. 14160* (N.Y. Sup. Ct. Dec. 18, 2008), available at www.failedmessiah.typepad.com.

[24] *See* Steven C. Bennett, *Arbitration: Essential Concepts* 59 (2002).

CHAPTER 44

SUPREME COURT ADDRESSES *VOLT'S* CHOICE-OF-LAW TRAP: IS THE END OF THE PROBLEM IN SIGHT?

Archis A. Parasharami and Kevin Ranlett[*]

I. Introduction

Many contracts with arbitration provisions contain choice-of-law clauses specifying which state's law governs the contract. Attorneys drafting these clauses typically consider the chosen state's substantive law, not its arbitration procedures – which often differ from those of the Federal Arbitration Act (FAA), a statute enacted in 1925 to enforce arbitration agreements and preempt state laws that are hostile to arbitration. For example, state laws that single out arbitration agreements for special treatment or make certain disputes inarbitrable would ordinarily be preempted by the FAA. But during the last 25 years, some drafters of arbitration agreements have fallen into a trap for the unwary, as courts have interpreted choice-of-law clauses to choose state arbitration procedures as well as substantive law. More recently, in a largely overlooked portion of the decision in *Preston v. Ferrer,*[1] the U.S. Supreme Court took a welcome step toward eliminating this trap.

Moreover, as this article was going to press, the Supreme Court heard oral arguments in *DirecTV, Inc. v. Imburgia*, No. 14-462 (argued Oct. 6, 2015). At issue in *Imburgia* is whether an arbitration provision that specifies that it is inapplicable if its ban on class-wide procedures is unenforceable under "the law of [the customer's] state" is (a) governed by state law without reference to FAA preemption, or (b) by state law

---

[*] Archis A. Parasharami and Kevin Ranlett are partners in Mayer Brown LLP's Supreme Court & Appellate Practice and its Consumer Litigation & Class Actions Practice, of which Archis is co-chair.

[1] 552 U.S. 346 (2008).

taking into account the preemptive effect of the FAA. The decision may cast more light on the "choice-of-law" trap.[2]

In the meantime, this article describes the evolution of the trap and offers guidance to attorneys on how to avoid it.

II. The Choice-of-Law Trap

The choice-of-law trap emerged almost three decades ago out of a construction contract between Stanford University and Volt Information Sciences, an engineering firm. The parties had agreed to arbitrate disputes arising out of the contract, and to apply the law of the place where the project was located (California). Stanford later filed suit in California Supreme Court against Volt and two non-parties to the agreement. Volt moved to compel arbitration under the FAA,[3] and Stanford opposed the motion and requested a stay of arbitration. The trial court held that the choice-of-law clause incorporated California arbitration procedures, and therefore granted Stanford's request for a stay.[4] The California Court of Appeal affirmed, agreeing that the seemingly innocuous choice-of-law clause incorporated California arbitration rules in place of the FAA. The California Supreme Court denied Volt's petition for discretionary review.

The U.S. Supreme Court granted Volt's petition for review. It held that the FAA permitted state procedures to apply because the statute simply enforces arbitration agreements according to their terms. Although there was little evidence that the parties intended to abandon the FAA in favor of California arbitration law, the Court deferred to the state courts' interpretation of the choice-of-law clause, reasoning that "the interpretation of private contracts" "is ordinarily a question of state

---

[2] For more discussion of the issue presented in *Imburgia*, please see https://www.classdefenseblog.com/2015/03/supreme-court-grants-certiorari-to-address-interplay-of-federal-arbitration-act-and-state-law-savings-clause-in-arbitration-agreement/.

[3] Under the FAA, the motion to compel arbitration would have been granted, even if Standford's claims against the other defendants continued in litigation. See *Dean Witter Reynolds v. Byrd,* 470 U.S. 213, 221 (1985); *Moses H. Cone Memorial Hospital v. Mercury Const. Corp.*, 460 U.S. 1, 20 (1983).

[4] *See* Cal. Civ. Proc. Code § 1281.2(c) (permitting a court to deny a petition to compel arbitration when "[a] party to the arbitration agreement is also a party to a pending court action … with a third party, arising out of the same transaction or series of related transactions and there is a possibility of conflicting rulings on a common issue of law or fact").

law, which this Court does not sit to review."[5] Significantly, however, the Court noted that "whether application of" California's state arbitration rules in accordance with the terms of the arbitration agreement itself, would undermine the goals and policies of the FAA,"[6] and underscored that "due regard must be given to the federal policy favoring arbitration.[7]

Most drafters of arbitration agreements intend the FAA to apply because the FAA applies to all contracts "involving" interstate commerce. This concept has been understood to reach to the fullest extent of Congress's interstate commerce power.[8] Yet for many years after the Supreme Court's decision in *Volt Information Sciences Inc. v. Leland Stanford Jr. University*, in one arbitration-related case after another, the courts have misread *Volt* to hold that choice-of-law clauses waive the application of the FAA unless the arbitration agreement explicitly invokes the federal statute. As a result, parties who have relied on the FAA's protections became subject to the vagaries of often-hostile state laws that hindered, if not prohibited, arbitration of the parties' disputes.[9]

III. The Court Begins to Identify *Volt's* Limits

In *Mastrobuono v. Shearson Lehman Hutton,* decided six years after *Volt*, the Supreme Court began to fix the trap it had created. Here the Court construed a choice-of-law provision more narrowly, holding that it incorporated only the chosen state's substantive law, not its arbitration procedures.[10] The parties in *Mastrobuono* agreed to arbitrate disputes "in accordance with the rules of the National Association of Securities

---

[5] *Volt Info. Sciences. v. Board of Trustees of Leland Stanford Jr. Univ.,* 489 U.S. 468, 474 (1989).

[6] *Id.* at 477-78.

[7] *Id.* at 476.

[8] *See Citizens Bank v. Alafabco, Inc.,* 539 U.S. 52, 56 (2003); *Allied-Bruce Terminix Cos. v. Dobson,* 513 U.S. 265, 274-77 (1995).

[9] *See*, e.g., *Rhodes v. Consumers' Buyline,* 868 F. Supp. 368, 373 (D. Mass. 1993); *Armco Steel Co. v. CSX Corp.,* 790 F. Supp. 311, 319,20 (D.D.C. 1991); *Henry v. Alcove Inv.,* 284 Cal. Rptr. 255, 289 (Cal. Ct. App. 1991); *Hotz Corp. v. Carabetta Builders,* 1991 WL 321922 (Conn. Super. Ct. Nov. 29, 1991); *Yates v. Doctor's Assocs.,* 549 N.E.2d 1010, 1015-16 (Ill. App. Ct. 1990); *Albright v. Edward D. Jones & Co.,* 571 N.E.2d 1329, 1332-33 (Ind. Ct. App. 1991).

[10] 514 U.S. 52 (1995).

Dealers (NASD)" or other self-regulatory organizations, and also to apply "the laws of the State of New York."

During an NASD arbitration, the arbitrators awarded punitive and compensatory damages to Mastrobuono. Shearson Lehman moved to vacate the award because New York does not permit arbitrators to award punitive damages. The district court agreed and vacated the award, concluding that the choice-of-law clause incorporated New York arbitration law. The 7th Circuit affirmed. However, the Supreme Court granted review and reversed. It held that the *Mastrobuono* choice-of-law clause might "reasonably be read" to incorporate "only New York's substantive rights and obligations," without the state's "allocation of power" between courts and arbitrators. The Court added that choice-of-law provisions are generally designed to determine the relevant substantive law, while procedural rules of arbitration are decided separately. Accordingly, the choice-of-law clause was not "an unequivocal exclusion of punitive damages claim" under New York arbitration procedures. Considering the parties' selection of the NASD's arbitration rules, the Court held that the best way to "harmonize" the agreement was to read the choice-of-law clause "to encompass substantive principles" of New York law without any "special rules limiting the authority of arbitrators."

Mastrobuono's reasoning was persuasive – but arguably hard to square with *Volt*, as Justice Clarence Thomas contended in a spirited dissent.[11] The *Mastrobuono* majority reconciled the two decisions by noting that in *Volt*, the Court had deferred to a state court's construction of the contract, whereas in *Mastrobuono*, the Court had reviewed the judgment of a federal district court *de novo*, which freed it to adopt its own best reading of the contract.

Mastrobuono helped close the trap the Supreme Court had created in *Volt*, but it did not completely eliminate the problem. For the next decade, many lower courts found the holding in *Mastrobuono* to be confusing, perhaps because they did not perceive a difference between *Mastrobuono's* facts and those in *Volt*. Some courts read *Mastrobuono* as largely abrogating *Volt* and adopting a new rule for all courts as a matter of federal law.[12] Others pointed to the distinction between the plenary review in *Mastrobuono* and *Volt's* deference to state courts.[13]

---

[11] *Id.* at 64, 66-67 (Thomas, J., dissenting).

[12] *See Action Indus., Inc. v. U.S. Fid. & Guar. Co.,* 358 F.3d 337, 342 (5th Cir. 2004); *Sovak v. Chugai Pharm. Co.,* 280 F.3d 1266, 1269 (9th Cir. 2002); *Roadway Package Sys. v. Kayser,* 257 F.3d 287, 288-89 (3d Cir. 2001), superseded on other grounds, *Hall Street*

Meanwhile, a few state courts took pains to limit *Mastrobuono's* influence. In *Cronus Investments v. Concierge Services,* for example, a contract specified that California law would govern, but added that this designation "shall not be deemed an election to preclude application of the [FAA], if it would be applicable." The California Supreme Court nonetheless applied California arbitration law, holding that because the FAA did not fully preempt state procedural rules under *Volt*, the federal statute was not "applicable," and thus the "shall not be deemed" clause did not apply. The court also sought to limit *Mastrobuono* to its facts, stating that California arbitration law was not "a special rule limiting the authority of arbitrators."[14] Other state courts have also taken steps to apply their own state law, finding that parties who had not explicitly invoked the FAA could not expect to have its protections apply.[15]

IV. The *Preston* Decision

The confusion spawned by *Volt* and *Mastrobuono* has lasted for over a decade. In 2008, however, the Supreme Court signaled a different approach. In *Preston,* the Court protected parties' federal arbitration rights by applying a federal interpretation of choice-of-law provisions.

The contract in *Preston* contained a general choice-of-law clause selecting California law, and also provided for arbitration under American Arbitration Association (AAA) rules. After Preston initiated arbitration to recover management fees that he alleged were owed to him, Ferrer (better known as television's "Judge Alex") claimed that the contract was unenforceable because Preston was not licensed as a talent agent as required by state law. Relying on *Volt,* Ferrer further argued that the choice-of-law clause incorporated state arbitration procedures, which

---

Assocs. V. Mattel, Inc., 128 S. Ct. 1396 (2008); see also *1745 Wazee Ltd. v. Castle Builders Inc.*, 89 P.3d 422, 424-25 (Colo. Ct. App. 2003).

[13] *See*, e.g., *Wolsey, Ltd. v. Foodmaker, Inc.*, 144 F.3d 1205, 1212-13 (9th Cir. 1998); *Ferro Corp v. Garrison Indus.*, 142 F.3d 926, 935 (6th Cir. 1998); *Goff Group, Inc. v. Greenwich Ins. Co.*, 231 F. Supp. 2d 1147, 1151 (M.D. Ala. 2002).

[14] 107 P.3d 217 (Cal. 2005).

[15] *See*, e.g., *Glazer's Distribs. of Ill., Inc. v. NWS-III., LLC,* 876 N.E.2d 203, 212-13 (Ill. Ct. App. 2007); *Manson v. Dain Bosworth Inc.*, 623 N.W.2d 610, 614-16 (Minn. Ct. App. 1998); *Sterling Truck Corp. v. Sacramento Valley Ford Truck Sales, Inc.*, 751 N.E.2d 517, 519-20 (Ohio Ct. App. 2001); *Moscatiello v. J.J.B. Hilliard,* 939 A.2d 325, 329 (Pa. 2007); *Frizzell Construction Co. v. Gatlinburg, L.L.C.*, 9 S.W.3d 79, 85-86 (Tenn. 1999).

in this case called for the dispute to be decided by the state Labor Commissioner rather than an arbitrator.

The Court rejected Ferrer's choice-of-law argument by distinguishing *Volt*. First, the Court stated that state law had been used as a gap-filler in *Volt* because the arbitration agreement in that case had not addressed the particular proceedings at issue – *i.e.*, litigation involving third parties who were strangers to the arbitration agreement. By contrast, in *Preston,* the Court said there was "no other procedural void for the choice-of-law clause to fill."

Next, the Court pointed out that although the agreement in *Volt* had also chosen AAA rules, the petitioner there had never argued that this designation "trumped the choice-of-law clause contained in the contract." Thus, as in *Mastrobuono*, the Court limited *Preston's* choice-of-law clause to apply only to issues of substantive state law, leaving procedural issues to be resolved by the AAA's rules.

What is significant about this decision – something largely overlooked – is that *Preston* departs from the approach in *Volt*, which largely left the interpretation of choice-of-law clauses to the state courts to decide. To be sure, in *Preston* there was no state interpretation to accept, since the California Court of Appeal's error on the federal question had kept it from reaching the choice-of-law issue.[16] But once the Supreme Court corrected the error of federal law, it could have let a state court resolve any state-law issues on remand. It did not. Instead, the *Preston* Court construed the parties' contract on its own and determined that the "best way to harmonize" the adoption of the AAA rules with the selection of California law.[17] The Court saw no need to consult the state courts on what reading was best in light of the clear federal policy favoring arbitration.

Preston suggests that a general choice-of-law clause should not be read to trump the FAA, even if state law might read it otherwise, and especially when particular arbitral rules are chosen. By noting that *Volt* had not addressed the parties' selection of AAA rules, *Preston* implied that the result in *Volt* would have been different had the Court considered that fact. The *Preston* Court applied the interpretive principles that it found appropriate in light of the FAA, principles rooted in the federal

[16] *See* 489 U.S. at 474; *Ferrer v. Preston*, 51 Cal. Rptr. 3d 628, 633-34 (Cal. Ct. App. 2006).

[17] Quoting *Mastrobuono,* 514 U.S. at 63-64.

substantive law of arbitrability, and it arrived at a decision consistent with common sense as well as the federal policy favoring arbitration.

V. Conclusion

As *Preston's* choice-of-law holding is more broadly recognized by the lower courts, parties to arbitration agreements will no longer have to fear that a choice-of-law clause might frustrate their intent to arbitrate. For example, the 8th Circuit held that, under *Preston*, "an arbitration provision's incorporation of the AAA rules supersedes a choice-of-law provision contained in the same agreement."[18] The Fourth Circuit (and a number of district courts) have recognized that, under *Preston*, a "general choice-of-law provision" is "irrelevant to the decision whether the FAA applies" to the arbitration provision.[19] In addition, since *Preston* was decided, at least one state court has interpreted that case to demand clear evidence of the parties' intent – not just the existence of a choice-of-law clause designating state law – before finding a waiver of the FAA's protections.[20]

So far, however, *Preston's* implications for the choice-of-law trap has not been widely recognized – perhaps because *Preston* focused primarily on other issues. As a result, some courts have continued to invoke *Volt's* choice-of-law without so much as mentioning *Preston*.[21] A few courts have sought to limit *Preston* in the same way as *Mastrobuono,* interpreting *Preston* (like *Volt*) to treat state arbitration law as an acceptable gap filler whenever there is any arguable ambiguity for state law to fill.[22] And a few other courts have distinguished *Preston* and continued to apply *Volt*'s choice-of-law rule if the choice-of-law

---

[18] *Fallo v. High-Tech Inst.*, 559 F.3d 874, 879 (8th Cir. 2009).

[19] *Rota-McLarty v. Santander Consumer USA, Inc.*, 700 F.3d 690, 697 n.7 (4th Cir. 2012); *see also, e.g., BioMagic, Inc. v. Dutch Bros. Enters., LLC*, 729 F. Supp. 2d 1140, 1146 (C.D. Cal. 2010); *Protostorm, LLC v. Antonelli*, 2010 WL 2195679, at *7 (E.D.N.Y. May 28, 2010).

[20] *See Personnel Decisions, Inc. v. Bus. Planning Sys., Inc.*, 2008 WL 1932404, at *6 & n.37 (Del. Ch. May 5, 2008).

[21] *See*, e.g., *Best Interiors, Inc. v. Millie & Severson, Inc.*, 75 Cal. Rptr. 3d 1, 5-8 (Ct. App. 2008); *Duffens v. Valenti,* 74 Cal Rptr. 3d 311, 324 (Ct. App. 2008); *Hill v. NHC HealthCare/Nashville, LLC,* 2008 WL 1901198 (Tenn. Ct. App. April 30, 2008).

[22] *See Empire Film Prods., Inc. v. Arenas Entertainment,* 2008 WL 1799770, at *9 (Cal. Ct. App. Apr. 22, 2008).

clause specifically mentions the arbitration provision or the arbitration provision specifically mentions state arbitral rules.[23]

Preston's holding should be more widely recognized. Nonetheless, drafters of arbitration provisions should take care to specify precisely which procedures will govern the enforcement of arbitration agreements. A choice-of-law clause should not be read to select state arbitration procedures if the agreement explicitly provides that the interpretation and enforcement of the arbitration provision shall be governed by the FAA.[24]

So long as the choice-of-law trap exists, it is vital that drafters not leave the application of the FAA for future courts to decide. Additionally, litigants should consider removing cases to federal court when possible. Doing so will offer the parties a stronger chance of obtaining a sensible reading of their contracts and avoiding state-law hostility to arbitration.

---

[23] *See, e.g., Foulger-Pratt Residential Contracting, LLC v. Magrigal Condominiums, LLC*, 779 F. Supp. 2d 100, 109-11 (D.D.C. 2011); *Acquire II, Ltd. v. Colton Real Estate Group*, 153 Cal. Rptr. 3d 135, 144 (Ct. App. 2013).

[24] *See*, e.g., *Barrett v. Investment Mgmt. Consultants, Ltd.*, 190 P.3d 800, 801, 803 (Colo. Ct. App. 2008).

INDEX

[*References are to page numbers*]

F